문법·어휘

더 뉴텝스
실전연습 **500**

문법·어휘

더 뉴텝스
실전연습 500

지은이 NEW TEPS Research Team
펴낸이 정규도
펴낸곳 (주)다락원

초판 1쇄 발행 2018년 12월 6일
초판 3쇄 발행 2022년 11월 2일

편집 강화진, 유아름
디자인 김나경, 조화연, 토비트
영문 감수 Michael A. Putlack

다락원 경기도 파주시 문발로 211
내용문의 (02)736-2031 내선 533
구입문의 (02)736-2031 내선 250~252
Fax (02)732-2037
출판등록 1977년 9월 16일 제 406-2008-000007호

Copyright ⓒ 2018, 다락원

저자 및 출판사의 허락 없이 이 책의 일부 또는 전부를 무단 복제·전재·발췌할 수 없습니다. 구입 후 철회는 회사 내규에 부합하는 경우에 가능하므로 구입문의처에 문의하시기 바랍니다. 분실·파손 등에 따른 소비자 피해에 대해서는 공정거래위원회에서 고시한 소비자 분쟁 해결 기준에 따라 보상 가능합니다. 잘못된 책은 바꿔드립니다.

값 18,000원

ISBN 978-89-277-4129-9 14740
978-89-277-4127-5 14740(set)

http://www.darakwon.co.kr
다락원 홈페이지를 방문하시면 상세한 출판정보와 함께
동영상강좌, MP3자료 등 다양한 어학 정보를 얻으실 수 있습니다.

신유형 분석 반영!

뉴텝스 최강 실전대비서!

NEW TEPS Research Team

문법·어휘

더 뉴텝스 **실전연습**

500

다락원

문법 Contents

Contents

Q. NEW TEPS란 무엇인가요?

A. 최근의 영어사용 환경 변화와 영어교육 및 평가의 새로운 추세를 반영하고자 기존 TEPS 시험을 새롭게 개편한 영어 인증시험입니다.

Q. 그렇다면 어떻게 바뀌었으며, 가장 큰 변화는 뭔가요?

A. 각 영역의 문항 수(총 200문항 → 135문항)와 시험시간(약 140분 → 105분)이 축소되었습니다. 또한 청해와 독해 부분에 새로운 유형이 도입되었고 문법과 어휘 시험이 통합되었습니다.

구분	문제유형	문항수	제한 시간	점수 범위
청해 Listening Comprehension	**Part I** 한 문장을 듣고 이어질 대화로 가장 적절한 답 고르기 (문장 1회 청취 후 선택지 1회 청취)	10	40분	0 ~ 240점
	Part II 짧은 대화를 듣고 이어질 대화로 가장 적절한 답 고르기 (대화 1회 청취 후 선택지 1회 청취)	10		
	Part III 긴 대화를 듣고 질문에 가장 적절한 답 고르기 (대화 및 질문 1회 청취 후 선택지 1회 청취)	10		
	Part IV 담화를 듣고 질문에 가장 적절한 답 고르기 (1지문 1문항) (담화 및 질문 2회 청취 후 선택지 1회 청취)	6		
	신유형 **Part V** 담화를 듣고 질문에 가장 적절한 답 고르기 (1지문 2문항) (담화 및 질문 2회 청취 후 선택지 1회 청취)	4		
어휘 Vocabulary	**Part I** 대화문의 빈칸에 가장 적절한 어휘 고르기	10	통합 25분	0 ~ 60점
	Part II 단문의 빈칸에 가장 적절한 어휘 고르기	20		
문법 Grammar	**Part I** 대화문의 빈칸에 가장 적절한 답 고르기	10		0 ~ 60점
	Part II 단문의 빈칸에 가장 적절한 답 고르기	15		
	Part III 대화 및 문단에서 문법상 틀리거나 어색한 부분 고르기	5		
독해 Reading Comprehension	**Part I** 지문을 읽고 빈칸에 가장 적절한 답 고르기	10	40분	0 ~ 240점
	Part II 지문을 읽고 문맥상 어색한 내용 고르기	2		
	Part III 지문을 읽고 질문에 가장 적절한 답 고르기 (1지문 1문항)	13		
	신유형 **Part IV** 지문을 읽고 질문에 가장 적절한 답 고르기 (1지문 2문항)	10		
합계 14개 유형		135 문항	105분	0~600점

Q. 점수 체계에 변화가 있나요?

A. 기존의 200문항에서 135문항으로 문항수를 줄여 점수 체계를 변경하였습니다. 각 영역별 최고점수는 청해와 독해 각 240점이며, 어휘와 문법은 각 60점으로 총점 600점입니다.

Q. 기존 TEPS 점수와 NEW TEPS 점수의 환산은 가능한가요?

A. 기존 TEPS의 총점 990점과 NEW TEPS의 600점은 최고점수에 해당하며 동일한 능력으로 간주됩니다. 개정 전후 TEPS 점수 체계를 비교하는 환산표는 아래와 같습니다.

기존 TEPS	NEW TEPS
990~937	600~551
936~870	550~501
867~799	500~451
799~724	450~401
723~643	400~351
641~557	350~301
555~469	300~251
467~381	250~201
379~282	200~151
280~178	150~101

등급	점수	능력 검정 기준(Description)
1+급 (Level 1+)	526~600	**Native Level of English Proficiency** 외국인으로서 최상급 수준의 의사소통 능력. 교양 있는 원어민에 버금가는 정도로 의사소통이 가능하고 전문 분야 업무에 대처할 수 있음.
1급 (Level 1)	453~525	**Near-Native Level of Communicative Competence** 외국인으로서 최상급 수준에 근접한 의사소통 능력. 단기간 집중 교육을 받으면 대부분의 의사소통이 가능하고 전문 분야 업무에 별 무리 없이 대처할 수 있음.
2+급 (Level 2+)	387~452	**Advanced Level of Communicative Competence** 외국인으로서 상급 수준의 의사소통 능력. 단기간 집중 교육을 받으면 일반 분야 업무를 큰 어려움 없이 수행할 수 있음.
2급 (Level 2)	327~386	**High Intermediate Level of Communicative Competence** 외국인으로서 중상급 수준의 의사소통 능력. 중장기간 집중 교육을 받으면 일반 분야 업무를 큰 어려움 없이 수행할 수 있음.

등급	점수	능력 검정 기준(Description)
3+급 (Level 3+)	268~326	**Mid Intermediate Level of Communicative Competence** 외국인으로서 중급 수준의 의사소통 능력. 중장기간 집중 교육을 받으면 한정된 분야의 업무를 큰 어려움 없이 수행할 수 있음.
3급 (Level 3)	212~267	**Low Intermediate Level of Communicative Competence** 외국인으로서 중하급 수준의 의사소통 능력. 중장기간 집중 교육을 받으면 한정된 분야의 업무를 다소 미흡하지만 큰 지장 없이 수행할 수 있음.
4+급 (Level 4+)	163~211	**Novice Level of Communicative Competence** 외국인으로서 하급 수준의 의사소통 능력. 장기간의 집중 교육을 받으면 한정된 분야의 업무를 대체로 어렵게 수행할 수 있음.
4급 (Level 4)	111~162	
5+급 (Level 5+)	55~110	**Near-Zero Level of Communicative Competence** 외국인으로서 최하급 수준의 의사소통 능력. 단편적인 지식만을 갖추고 있어 의사소통이 거의 불가능함.
5급 (Level 5)	0~54	

문법

NEW TEPS 문법은 세 파트로 나뉘며 총 30문항이다. 어휘 30문항과 문법 30문항이 통합되어 총 60문항을 25분 동안 풀어야 하므로 시간 분배에 주의를 기울여야 한다.

PART I Choose the option that best completes each dialogue.

Part I은 두 사람의 대화문을 보고 빈칸을 채우는 문제이다. A와 B의 대화를 읽고 대화문의 빈칸에 들어갈 알맞은 문법을 고른다.

A: I wondered if _____ to think how I felt.

B: What? Did I do something wrong?

(a) you had stopped ever

(b) you had ever stopped

(c) you ever had stopped

(d) ever you had stopped

해석 A: 네가 한 번이라도 내가 어떻게 느꼈을지 생각해 본적이 있는지 모르겠어.
B: 뭐라고? 내가 뭐 잘못한 거라도 있니?

해설 ever는 조동사 had와 본동사 stopped 사이에 위치해야 자연스럽다.

정답 (b)

PART II Choose the option that best completes each sentence.

Part II는 문장의 빈칸에 알맞은 것을 찾는 문제이다. 서적, 신문, 잡지 등에 등장할 수 있는 문장이 출제되며, 문항당 한 문장으로 구성되어 있다. 비록 한 문장이기는 하지만 철저하게 논리를 따져봐야 하는 문장이 다수 출제되고 있다.

Many scientific discoveries could have been made way earlier _____ what we have today.

(a) if people in the past possessed

(b) if people in the past possess

(c) did people in the past possess

(d) had people in the past possessed

해석 과거의 사람들이 오늘날 우리가 가지고 있는 것을 지니고 있었다면 많은 과학적 발견들을 더 빨리 할 수 있었을 것이다.

해설 빈칸 뒤에 나온 what we have는 가정법 시제에는 영향을 미치지 않는다. 앞에서 could have p.p.가 나왔으므로 과거 사실의 반대를 가정하는 가정법 과거완료임을 알 수 있다. 여기서 if가 생략되고 주어 people과 had가 도치된 상황이다.

정답 (d)

Read each dialogue or passage carefully and identify the option that contains a grammatical error.

Part Ⅲ는 대화문 2문항, 지문 3문항을 읽고 어색하거나 틀린 문법을 찾는 문제이다. TEPS 문법 영역에서 가장 배점이 높고 어려운 파트이기도 하다.

(a) A: What a coincidence! Fancy meeting you here.

(b) B: Yeah, it's been long time. How have you been?

(c) A: I can't complain. How about you?

(d) B: Things couldn't be better.

해석 (a) A: 이런 우연의 일치가 있나! 당신을 여기서 만나다니.
(b) B: 그러게요. 오랜만이군요. 잘 지내셨나요?
(c) A: 아주 잘 지냈어요. 당신은 어때요?
(d) B: 이보다 더 좋을 수가 없어요.

해설 관사 문제이다. '오랜만이다.'라는 표현은 It's been a long time.으로 부정관사 a를 꼭 써야 한다. 따라서 (b)의 it's been long time을 it's been a long time으로 바꾸어야 한다.

정답 (b)

(a) Clinical tests are conducted on patients for two years after their operations took place. (b) During the follow-up period after their surgery, about 41% of the patients displayed dermatology diseases regardless of whether they were taking the active drug or the placebo. (c) The two groups were also similar with respect in the incidence of several types of skin troubles, including itches, rashes, and the need to be hospitalized or to undergo treatment for dermatological problems. (d) Those taking prescription pills were more likely to experience skin irritation.

해석 (a) 수술을 한 후, 환자들을 대상으로 임상실험이 2년간 실시된다. (b) 수술 후 후속 기간 동안 환자의 41퍼센트 정도가 실제 약을 복용했든 아니면 위약을 복용했든 상관없이 피부 질환을 보였다. (c) 임상실험에 참여한 두 그룹은 가려움, 발진과 같은 여러 종류의 피부 질환의 발병에 있어서나 피부 질환으로 인한 입원 혹은 치료를 받아야 하는 필요에 있어서도 비슷한 결과를 보였다. (d) 처방전 약을 복용하는 사람들은 피부 염증을 겪을 가능성이 더욱 컸다.

해설 전치사 문제이다. '무엇에 관해서'라는 표현은 with respect to이므로 (c)의 with respect in을 with respect to로 고쳐야 한다. Part Ⅲ에 나오는 전치사 문제는 with respect to처럼 외워서 쉽게 맞힐 수 있는 문제가 있기도 하고 내용 흐름을 따져서 맞혀야 하는 까다로운 유형도 있다.

정답 (c)

앞서 말했듯이 NEW TEPS 시험에서 어휘와 문법이 통합되었다. Part Ⅰ은 10문항이며 Part Ⅱ는 20문항이다. 통합된 25분 동안 60문항을 풀어야 하므로, 어휘 문제를 얼마나 빨리 푸는가가 고득점 달성에 중요한 요소가 되었다.

PART Ⅰ Choose the option that best completes each dialogue.

Part Ⅰ은 A, B 두 사람의 대화로 이루어져 있으며 구어체, 구동사, 이디엄 등 일상생활에서 나올법한 영어 표현을 묻는 영역이다. 구어체 표현 자체를 알아야 풀 수 있는 문제도 있지만 대화의 흐름을 파악하여 논리적으로 풀어야 하는 문제도 있다.

A: Please hand me the folder on the desk.

B: I beg your _____? I couldn't hear what you said.

(a) pardon

(b) question

(c) forgiveness

(d) permission

해석 A: 책상 위에 있는 서류철 좀 건네줄래요?
　　B: 뭐라고요? 당신이 하는 말을 못 들었어요.

해설 '다시 한 번 말해 줄래요?,' '뭐라고요?'는 "I beg your pardon?"으로 표현한다.

정답 (a)

PART Ⅱ Choose the option that best completes each sentence.

Part Ⅱ는 신문이나 저널에서 나올 법한 내용이 출제되는 문어체 영역으로 한 문장으로 구성되어있다. 동사, 명사, 형용사, 부사 같은 일반 문어체 어휘 및 이디엄이 출제된다.

The engineer was criticized for not correcting the _____ in the product.

(a) limitation

(b) flaw

(c) estimate

(d) feature

해석 그 기술자는 그 제품의 결함을 보완하지 않아서 비난을 받았다.

해설 어떤 행동을 하지 않은 것으로 인해 비난을 받았다고 했으므로 제품의 '결함'을 보완하지 않았다고 볼 수 있다.

정답 (b)

어휘 목표 달성을 위한 전략

기출어휘를 많이 익히자.

시험에 나왔던 것은 반드시 다시 나온다. 이번 달에 나온 어휘가 다음 달이나 그 다음 달에 바로 나오는 것은 아니지만 그리 멀지 않은 시간 내에 또 출제된다는 사실을 명심하자. 특히 다년치의 기출어휘를 외워두면 짧은 시간 안에 30문제를 해결하는 데 큰 도움이 될 것이다. 그렇다고 기출어휘만 암기해서는 안 된다. TEPS에는 매번 다양한 어휘가 출제되므로 꾸준히 어휘력을 늘려나가야 한다.

최대한 많은 문제를 풀어라.

익힌 어휘를 바탕으로 문제를 많이 풀어봐야 한다. 시간을 정해 놓고 문제를 풀어보는 연습도 필요하다. 특히 시험을 1주일 가량 앞둔 시점에서는 모의고사를 3회 정도 시간을 재면서 풀어 시간관리 연습을 하자.

독해를 많이 하자.

TEPS 어휘 문제 중에는 단순히 어휘 뜻만 알면 해결되는 문제보다는 제대로 문장의 의미를 파악해야 풀 수 있는 문제가 많다. 독해력 또한 어휘 영역에서 좋은 점수를 받을 수 있는 중요한 요소라는 점을 염두에 두자. 거기다 독해를 하면서 접하는 단어를 그때그때 외워두는 것도 TEPS 어휘 점수를 높이는 방법이 될 수 있다. 독해는 어휘 실력 향상의 발판이라는 사실을 명심해야 한다.

어휘에 목숨 걸지 마라.

TEPS 어휘 영역의 목표 점수를 만점보다는 40점대나 50점대로 잡자. 55점대 이상에 도전하는 것도 좋겠지만, 그 이상의 점수대까지 오르기 위해서는 적지 않은 시간과 정성을 들여야 한다. 따라서 일정 점수 이상이 목표라면 어휘는 이렇게 하는 것이 효과적이다.

초급자라면 고난도 문제에는 미련을 두지 말자.

200점대, 300점대 학습자라면 Part I과 Part II의 고난도 문제에는 미련을 두지 말자. 초보자 수준에서는 맞히기 힘든 상당히 어려운 어휘가 출제되기 때문이다. 고난도 문제를 모두 틀리더라도 문법에서 충분히 점수를 복구할 수 있다.

고득점을 원한다면 Part I과 Part II의 마지막 5문제를 노려라.

이미 고득점을 확보한 학습자들이 더 높은 점수를 받으려면 Part I과 Part II의 마지막 고난도 2~5문제를 맞혀야 한다. 여기에 더해 난이도가 높은 편인 이디엄 문제를 모두 맞히는 것도 고득점을 향한 길이다.

문법

68개의 Grammar Point

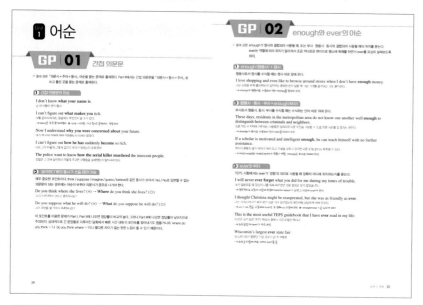

실제 NEW TEPS 시험에 출제되고 있는 총 68개의 문법 포인트를 정리했다. 목표 점수에 도달하기 위해 반드시 알아두어야 할 핵심 문법사항만을 담았다.

Check-up Test

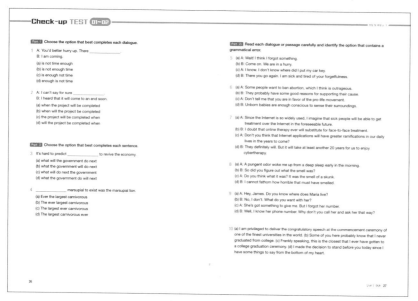

해당 문법 포인트에 관련된 NEW TEPS 유형 문제를 집중적으로 풀 수 있도록 구성했다. 실제 시험의 출제 데이터를 바탕으로 각 문법 포인트마다 자주 출제되는 Part에 맞춰 문제를 구성했다.

Actual Test

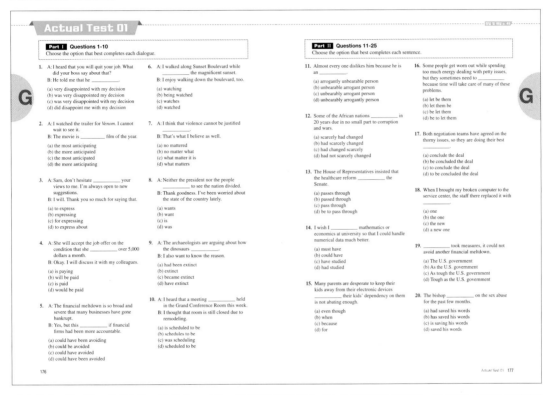

Actual Test 01

Part I Questions 1-10
Choose the option that best completes each dialogue.

1. A: I heard that you will quit your job. What did your boss say about that?
   B: He told me that he _____.

   (a) very disappointed with my decision
   (b) was very disappointed my decision
   (c) was very disappointed with my decision
   (d) did disappoint me with my decision

2. A: I watched the trailer for *Venom*. I cannot wait to see it.
   B: The movie is _____ film of the year.

   (a) the most anticipating
   (b) the more anticipated
   (c) the most anticipated
   (d) the more anticipating

3. A: Sam, don't hesitate _____ your views to me. I'm always open to new suggestions.
   B: I will. Thank you so much for saying that.

   (a) to express
   (b) expressing
   (c) for expressing
   (d) to express about

4. A: She will accept the job offer on the condition that she _____ over 5,000 dollars a month.
   B: Okay. I will discuss it with my colleagues.

   (a) is paying
   (b) will be paid
   (c) is paid
   (d) would be paid

5. A: The financial meltdown is so broad and severe that many businesses have gone bankrupt.
   B: Yes, but this _____ if financial firms had been more accountable.

   (a) could have been avoiding
   (b) could be avoided
   (c) could have avoided
   (d) could have been avoided

6. A: I walked along Sunset Boulevard while _____ the magnificent sunset.
   B: I enjoy walking down the boulevard, too.

   (a) watching
   (b) being watched
   (c) watches
   (d) watched

7. A: I think that violence cannot be justified _____.
   B: That's what I believe as well.

   (a) no mattered
   (b) no matter what
   (c) what matter it is
   (d) what matters

8. A: Neither the president nor the people _____ to see the nation divided.
   B: Thank goodness. I've been worried about the state of the country lately.

   (a) wants
   (b) want
   (c) is
   (d) was

9. A: The archaeologists are arguing about how the dinosaurs _____.
   B: I also want to know the reason.

   (a) had been extinct
   (b) extinct
   (c) became extinct
   (d) have extinct

10. A: I heard that a meeting _____ held in the Grand Conference Room this week.
    B: I thought that room is still closed due to remodeling.

    (a) is scheduled to be
    (b) schedules to be
    (c) was scheduling
    (d) scheduled to be

Part II Questions 11-25
Choose the option that best completes each sentence.

11. Almost every one dislikes him because he is an _____.

    (a) arrogantly unbearable person
    (b) unbearable arrogant person
    (c) unbearably arrogant person
    (d) unbearably arrogantly person

12. Some of the African nations _____ in 20 years due in no small part to corruption and wars.

    (a) scarcely had changed
    (b) had scarcely changed
    (c) had changed scarcely
    (d) had not scarcely changed

13. The House of Representatives insisted that the healthcare reform _____ the Senate.

    (a) passes through
    (b) passed through
    (c) pass through
    (d) be to pass through

14. I wish I _____ mathematics or economics at university so that I could handle numerical data much better.

    (a) must have
    (b) could have
    (c) have studied
    (d) had studied

15. Many parents are desperate to keep their kids away from their electronic devices _____ their kids' dependency on them is not abating enough.

    (a) even though
    (b) when
    (c) because
    (d) for

16. Some people get worn out while spending too much energy dealing with petty issues, but they sometimes need to _____ because time will take care of many of these problems.

    (a) let be them
    (b) let them be
    (c) let them
    (d) be to let them

17. Both negotiation teams have agreed on the thorny issues, so they are doing their best _____.

    (a) conclude the deal
    (b) be concluded the deal
    (c) to conclude the deal
    (d) to be concluded the deal

18. When I brought my broken computer to the service center, the staff there replaced it with _____.

    (a) one
    (b) the one
    (c) the new
    (d) a new one

19. _____ took measures, it could not avoid another financial meltdown.

    (a) The U.S. government
    (b) As the U.S. government
    (c) As tough the U.S. government
    (d) Tough as the U.S. government

20. The bishop _____ on the sex abuse for the past few months.

    (a) had saved his words
    (b) has saved his words
    (c) is saving his words
    (d) saved his words

해당 문법 포인트를 모두 학습하고 난 후 Actual Test를 풀어보면서 점수 상승의 극대화를 도모하는 코너이다. 시험에서 빈번히 출제되는 문법 포인트만 뽑아 문제로 만들었기 때문에 틀린 문제는 다시 복습하여 확실히 익혀두는 것이 좋다.

어휘

풀면서 익히는 Mini Test

우리말 문장을 보고 뜻이 맞는 영어 어휘를 찾아보는 간단한 형식의 퀴즈를 통해 자연스럽게 단어의 뜻을 익힐 수 있다.

Check-up Test

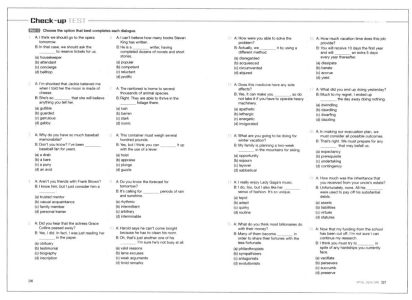

Mini Test에서 학습했던 어휘를 묻는 문제들로 구성되어 있다. 각 Voca Point에서 충분한 학습이 이루어졌는지 알 수 있다.

Voca Review

각 Voca Point를 끝마치기 전에 앞서 학습한 내용을 최종 점검하는 코너이다. Check-up Test에 나오지 않았던 어휘 위주로 구성하였다.

Actual Test

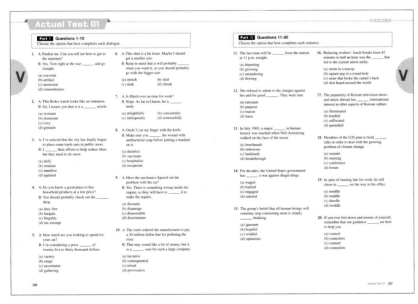

최신 출제 경향을 반영하여 실전 그대로의 분위기를 느낄 수 있는 Actual Test 6회분을 실었다. 최종적으로 문제를 풀며 실전에 대비할 수 있다.

문법

Grammar

Section
1

시험에 가장 자주 출제되는

Grammar Point

GP | 01 간접 의문문

□ 출제 경향 「의문사＋주어＋동사」 어순을 묻는 문제로 출제된다. Part Ⅲ에서는 간접 의문문을 「의문사＋동사＋주어」로
쓰고 틀린 곳을 묻는 문제로 출제된다.

❶ 간접 의문문의 어순

I don't know **what your name is**.
난 네 이름이 뭔지 몰라.

I can't figure out **what makes you** tick.
너를 움직이게 하는 원동력이 무엇인지 알 수가 없다.
→ what은 주격 관계대명사 ▶ tick ~(사람·기구 등이) 움직이다, 작동하다

Now I understand **why you were concerned about** your future.
네가 왜 너의 미래에 대해 걱정했는지 이제야 알겠다.

I can't figure out **how he has** suddenly **become** so rich.
나는 그가 어떻게 그렇게 갑자기 부자가 되었는지 모르겠어.

The police want to know **how the serial killer murdered** the innocent people.
경찰은 그 연쇄 살인범이 어떻게 무고한 사람들을 살해했는지 알아내려 한다.

❷ '생각하다'류의 동사가 쓰일 때의 어순

매우 중요한 포인트이다. think / suppose / imagine / guess / believe와 같은 동사가 쓰여서 Yes / No로 답변할 수 없는
의문문이 되는 경우에는 어순이 바뀌어 의문사가 문두로 나가야 한다.

Do you think where she lives? (✗) → **Where** do you think she lives? (○)
그녀가 어디에서 산다고 생각하나요?

Do you suppose what he will do? (✗) → **What** do you suppose he will do? (○)
그가 무엇을 할 거라고 추측하나요?

이 포인트를 이용한 문제가 Part I, Part II에 나오면 정답률이 비교적 높다. 그러나 Part Ⅲ에 나오면 정답률이 낮아지므로
주의하자. 상대적으로 긴 문장들로 이루어진 담화에서 빠른 시간 내에 이 포인트를 찾아내기도 힘들거니와 'where do
you think ~'나 'do you think where ~'이나 별다른 차이가 없는 듯한 느낌이 들 수 있기 때문이다.

GP | 02 enough와 ever의 어순

□ **출제 경향** enough가 명사와 결합되어 사용될 때, 또는 부사·형용사·동사와 결합되어 사용될 때의 위치를 묻는다.
ever는 역할에 따라 위치가 달라져서 조금 까다로운 편이므로 평소에 독해를 하면서 ever를 유심히 살펴보도록
하자.

❶ enough(형용사) + 명사

형용사로서 명사를 수식할 때는 명사 바로 앞에 온다.

I love shopping and even like to browse around stores when I don't have **enough** money.
나는 쇼핑을 무척 좋아하는데 심지어는 충분한 돈이 없을 때 그냥 가게를 둘러보는 것도 좋아한다.
→ enough가 형용사로 사용되어 명사 money를 앞에서 수식

❷ 형용사·동사·부사+enough(부사)

부사로서 형용사, 동사, 부사를 수식할 때는 수식하는 단어 바로 뒤에 온다.

These days, residents in the metropolitan area do not know one another well **enough** to
distinguish between criminals and neighbors.
요즘 대도시 지역에 거주하는 사람들은 범죄자와 이웃 주민을 구분할 수 있을 만큼 서로를 잘 알지는 못한다.
→ enough가 부사로 사용되어 부사 well을 뒤에서 수식

If a scholar is motivated and intelligent **enough**, he can teach himself with no further
assistance.
학자가 충분히 동기 부여가 되어 있고 지성을 갖추고 있다면 다른 도움 없이도 독학할 수 있다.
→ motivated와 intelligent가 형용사 역할, enough는 부사로 뒤에서 수식

❸ ever의 위치

TEPS 시험에서는 ever가 '경험'의 의미로 사용될 때 정확히 어디에 위치하는지를 묻는다.

I will never **ever forget** what you did for me during my times of trouble.
내가 힘들었을 때 당신이 나를 위해 해주었던 것을 절대로 잊지 않겠습니다.
→ 일반적으로 조동사 다음에 부정어 not이나 never가 오면 그 다음에 ever가 온다.

I thought Christina might be exasperated, but she was as friendly as **ever**.
나는 크리스티나가 매우 화가 났을 거라 생각했는데 예전처럼 상냥하게 대해 주었다.
→ as ~ as 원급 구문에서 ever는 두 번째 as 다음에 위치 ▶ exasperate ~을 노하게 하다

This is the most useful TEPS guidebook that I have **ever** read in my life.
이것은 내가 읽은 TEPS 학습서 중에서 가장 유용한 책이다.
→ 최상급일 때 ever가 자주 쓰임

Wisconsin's largest **ever** state fair
위스콘신에서 열렸던 가장 규모가 큰 주 박람회
→ 최상급 다음에 바로 이어서 ever를 씀

Part I Choose the option that best completes each dialogue.

1 A: You'd better hurry up. There _____.
   B: I am coming.

   (a) is not time enough
   (b) is not enough time
   (c) is enough not time
   (d) enough is not time

2 A: I can't say for sure _____.
   B: I heard that it will come to an end soon.

   (a) when the project will be completed
   (b) when will the project be completed
   (c) the project will be completed when
   (d) will the project be completed when

Part II Choose the option that best completes each sentence.

3 It's hard to predict _____ to revive the economy.

   (a) what will the government do next
   (b) what the government will do next
   (c) what will do next the government
   (d) what the government do will next

4 _____ marsupial to exist was the marsupial lion.

   (a) Ever the largest carnivorous
   (b) The ever largest carnivorous
   (c) The largest ever carnivorous
   (d) The largest carnivorous ever

Part III Read each dialogue or passage carefully and identify the option that contains a grammatical error.

5 (a) A: Wait! I think I forgot something.
   (b) B: Come on. We are in a hurry.
   (c) A: I know. I don't know where did I put my car key.
   (d) B: There you go again. I am sick and tired of your forgetfulness.

6 (a) A: Some people want to ban abortion, which I think is outrageous.
   (b) B: They probably have some good reasons for supporting their cause.
   (c) A: Don't tell me that you are in favor of the pro-life movement.
   (d) B: Unborn babies are enough conscious to sense their surroundings.

7 (a) A: Since the Internet is so widely used, I imagine that sick people will be able to get treatment over the Internet in the foreseeable future.
   (b) B: I doubt that online therapy ever will substitute for face-to-face treatment.
   (c) A: Don't you think that Internet applications will have greater ramifications in our daily lives in the years to come?
   (d) B: They definitely will. But it will take at least another 20 years for us to enjoy cybertherapy.

8 (a) A: A pungent odor woke me up from a deep sleep early in the morning.
   (b) B: So did you figure out what the smell was?
   (c) A: Do you think what it was? It was the smell of a skunk.
   (d) B: I cannot fathom how horrible that must have smelled.

9 (a) A: Hey, James. Do you know where does Maria live?
   (b) B: No, I don't. What do you want with her?
   (c) A: She's got something to give me. But I forgot her number.
   (d) B: Well, I know her phone number. Why don't you call her and ask her that way?

10 (a) I am privileged to deliver the congratulatory speech at the commencement ceremony of one of the finest universities in the world. (b) Some of you here probably know that I never graduated from college. (c) Frankly speaking, this is the closest that I ever have gotten to a college graduation ceremony. (d) I made the decision to stand before you today since I have some things to say from the bottom of my heart.

GP | 03 as ~ as / too ~ to / so ~ that

□ **출제 경향** as ~ as 원급이 사용되는 문장에서 as와 as 사이에 관사, 형용사, 명사를 어떻게 배치해야 하는지 묻는 문제가 특히 시험에 자주 출제되고 있다. as ~ as 원급이나 too ~ to, 또는 so ~ that 구문이 사용될 때, 그 사이에 들어가는 어구는 「형용사＋관사＋명사」 순서대로 쓴다는 점에 유의하자.

❶ 「형용사＋관사＋명사」 어순을 취하는 구문

■ as ~ as ... ...만큼이나 ~하다

You can be as **rich** as Bill Gates.
너는 빌 게이츠만큼이나 부자가 될 수 있다.

The new project is as **controversial an issue** as the pay hike that management attempted to tackle back in February.
그 새로운 프로젝트는 지난 2월에 경영진에서 해결하려고 시도했던 급여 인상 문제만큼이나 논란이 되는 사안이다.

▶ tackle (일 따위에) 달려들다

■ too ~ to ... 너무 ~해서 ...할 수 없다

This is an opportunity **too good to** be true.
이건 진짜라고 믿기에는 너무나도 좋은 기회야.

Going abroad to study is **too good an opportunity to** pass up.
유학 가는 것은 너무나도 좋은 기회라서 지나칠 수 없어.

▶ pass up (기회를) 놓치다; 퇴짜 놓다

■ so ~ that ... 너무 ~해서 ...하다

The book was so **interesting** that I couldn't put it down.
그 책은 너무 재미있어서 손에서 놓을 수가 없었다.

This computer is so **cutting-edge a device** that it is compatible with almost all of the devices.
이 컴퓨터는 너무나도 최첨단 기계이기 때문에 거의 모든 기계와 호환이 가능하다.

※ very는 so와 의미는 같지만 that절과 함께 쓸 수는 없다. 시험에는 「so＋형용사＋that＋주어＋동사」 구문의 so 자리에 very를 넣고 틀린 곳을 찾으라는 식의 문제가 출제된다.

The new CEO was *very* argumentative **that** it took time before decisions were made. (×)
→ The new CEO was **so** argumentative **that** it took time before decisions were made. (○)
새로 부임한 최고 경영자는 매우 논쟁적이어서 결정이 내려지기까지 시간이 걸렸다.

GP | 04 such / quite

□ **출제 경향** 앞서 학습한 문법 포인트와는 달리, such와 quite 뒤에는 「관사＋형용사＋명사」의 어순이 이어진다는 것에 주의해야 한다.

❶ 「관사＋형용사＋명사」 어순을 취하는 구문

■ such ~ that ... **매우[너무] ~해서 ...하다**

It was such **a terrible day** that we had no alternative but to call off the picnic.
날씨가 너무 나빠서 피크닉을 취소할 수밖에 없었다.

You are making me angry. Don't say such **silly things**.
넌 자꾸 나를 화나게 만드는구나. 그런 어리석은 말 하지 마.
→ 명사가 복수이므로 부정관사 a를 쓸 필요가 없다.

■ quite **매우 ~한**

We prepared for the event for months, and we expect quite **a good turnout**.
우리는 이 행사를 위해 수개월간 준비했고, 그래서 매우 많은 분들이 찾아줄 것이라 예상하고 있다.
▶ turnout (집회의) 출석자(수)

A: You had quite **a good result**.
　　넌 매우 훌륭한 결과를 냈어.

B: Thanks. I practiced a lot.
　　고마워. 연습 많이 했거든.

Check-up TEST 03~04

Part I Choose the option that best completes each dialogue.

1 A: What will the most important change to the curriculum be?

   B: Using search engines will be _____ reading and writing.

   (a) as essential as a skill
   (b) as a skill essential as
   (c) as a skill as essential
   (d) as essential a skill as

2 A: The court ruling was _____ that the parties concerned didn't know how to react.

   B: You're right. I did not expect any more surprises after the defendant's confession.

   (a) dramatic an ending so
   (b) so an ending dramatic
   (c) an ending dramatic so
   (d) so dramatic an ending

3 A: He has made a movie after publishing a novel three months earlier.

   B: Oh really? He had _____.

   (a) quite a year productive
   (b) quite productive a year
   (c) quite a productive year
   (d) quite year a productive

Part II Choose the option that best completes each sentence.

4 The government did not expect this statute to have _____ it would be applied to anything the attorney thinks when serving his client.

   (a) such a relevance broad that
   (b) such a broad relevance that
   (c) such broad relevance that
   (d) such broad a relevance that

5 The suspension of high-level military exchanges is _____ bypass.

   (a) too sensitive an issue to
   (b) too sensitive to an issue
   (c) too an issue sensitive to
   (d) too an issue to sensitive

6　The pharmacist opened a bottle of pills which have _____ that of ammonia.

    (a) a strong as smell as

    (b) a as strong smell as

    (c) as a strong smell as

    (d) as strong a smell as

Part III Read each dialogue or passage carefully and identify the option that contains a grammatical error.

7　(a) A: The ABC franchise has reopened after undergoing ten months of renovations.

    (b) B: Is it true that the franchise has added more product lines to its existing ones?

    (c) A: Yes, items offered by the ABC franchise have so a wide range that the company dominates the market.

    (d) B: That is why the banner on the front door of its headquarters says that it sells nearly everything that one needs.

8　(a) A: Alice saved her friend, who was thrown from a horse.

    (b) B: How could she take such heroic an action?

    (c) A: She did not waste any time putting her friend into the recovery position and calling for help.

    (d) B: It would be difficult for me to keep a cool head in a situation like that.

9　(a) Henry Carpenter is not the strongest performer, but he avenged the hideous injury suffered by his teammate Alison Hopeman by winning the game. (b) Hopeman was scoring 2.5 goals each game before breaking his arm during the match against Arsenal. (c) It was so an injury gruesome that the performance of Hopeman's team was noticeably unsteady throughout the rest of the game. (d) Henry Carpenter didn't waste the opportunity though and scored two goals for Hopeman.

10　(a) If there is one thing lasting about art, it is the fact that the use of recurring modes of expression leads to aesthetic fatigue. (b) A city inundated with a notionally bold modern art corridor like New York needs to separate itself from the contemporary style. (c) You might want to seek comfort at Oriental Gallery. (d) It is hosting the quite meticulous presentation of East Asian paintings.

GP | 05 사역동사가 쓰일 때의 어순

□ **출제 경향** TEPS 문법 시험에서는 어순 출제 비중이 꽤 높은데, 그 중 단골 메뉴가 사역 동사가 쓰일 때의 어순이다. 어순은 물론 목적어와 목적격 보어의 관계가 능동인지 수동인지도 잘 파악해야 한다.

❶ make / have / let

■ 「make / have / let + 목적어 + 동사원형」 **목적어로 하여금 ~하게 하다**

The owner **made the bouncers throw** the drunken men out of the club.
클럽 주인은 경비원들을 시켜 술 취한 남자들을 클럽에서 쫓아내도록 했다.
▶ bouncer 경비원, 기도(술집에서 술 취한 손님의 행패를 막는 사람)

The prison guards **let some of the prisoners smoke** and **drink** at night.
교도관이 일부 죄수에 한해서 밤에 담배와 술을 허용했다.

■ 「make / have / let + 목적어 + 과거분사」 **목적어가 ~되게 하다**

Where do you usually **have your hair done**?
너는 머리를 주로 어디서 하니?

You had better **have the tooth pulled** out.
너는 그 치아를 뽑는 게 낫겠다.

❷ get

■ 「get + 목적어 + to 동사원형」 **목적어로 하여금 ~하게 하다**

I don't think I can **get her to understand** what's going on here.
난 여기 현재 상황을 그녀에게 이해시킬 수 없을 것 같아.

■ 「get + 목적어 + 과거분사」 **목적어가 ~되게 하다**

A: How about going for a walk?
　산책 갈래?

B: I have to **get the job done** first.
　난 우선 이 일을 마무리해야 해.

GP | 06 빈도부사의 위치

□ **출제 경향** 동사의 빈도를 나타내는 빈도부사는 일반 동사 앞에 위치하거나 조동사 또는 be동사 뒤에 온다. 이것만 기억하면 빈도부사의 어순 문제를 푸는 데에는 어려움이 없을 것이다.

❶ 빈도부사의 종류와 쓰임

always 항상   **often** 종종   **usually** 보통   **sometimes** 때때로
never 결코 ～아니다   **hardly** / **rarely** / **seldom** / **scarcely** / **barely** 거의 ～하지 않다

You cannot **always** do what you want to do.
항상 네가 하고 싶은 것만 할 수는 없어.

The teacher **often** tries to help the poor children when they are in need of assistance.
그 선생님은 가난한 아이들이 도움을 필요로 할 때 종종 도우려고 한다.

It is **hardly** surprising that he got fired since he **never** worked properly.
그는 일을 제대로 한 적이 한 번도 없기 때문에 해고된 사실이 놀랍지 않다.

The drive **usually** takes 30 or 40 minutes when traffic is heavy.
교통 체증이 있을 때 차를 타고 가면 보통 대략 30분에서 40분가량 소요된다.

This equipment is **rarely** used in modern laboratories.
이 장비는 현대의 과학 실험실에서는 거의 사용되지 않는다.

I have **seldom** seen my father get angry.
나는 아버지께서 화내시는 모습을 거의 본 적이 없다.

※ hardly / scarcely / rarely / barely / seldom 등의 부사는 '거의 ～않다'라는 부정의 의미를 이미 담고 있기 때문에 not 이나 never와 같은 부정어와 함께 쓰일 수 없다.

My immediate supervisor has hardly *never* talked to me. (×)
나의 직속상관은 나에게 거의 말을 걸지 않는다.
→ hardly never가 아니라 hardly ever로 바꿔야 한다.

Check-up TEST 05~06

Part I Choose the option that best completes each dialogue.

1 A: Gabriel has served as the captain of the football team for the last three years.
   B: Right. He _____ meant for one of the most demanding positions in the game.
   (a) is always has seemed
   (b) has seemed always
   (c) always has seemed
   (d) has always seemed

2 A: Show me what the next procedure is.
   B: What you should do next is let the ice gradually _____ as the salt is added.
   (a) melted
   (b) melting
   (c) melt
   (d) to melt

3 A: How do you get consumers _____ recycled bags instead of plastic bags?
   B: We offer a huge discount for shoppers who bring eco-friendly bags.
   (a) use
   (b) to use
   (c) using
   (d) used

Part II Choose the option that best completes each sentence.

4 We _____ that an air marshal with a handgun is sitting next to us unless a terrorist shows his true colors.
   (a) would never realize
   (b) never would realize
   (c) would realize never
   (d) would be never realize

5 The Save Water Foundation says that in some countries, cutting subsidies for agricultural products, including corn, rice and wheat, is an effective way to get farms _____.
   (a) to waste less water
   (b) wasting water less
   (c) waste water less
   (d) wasted water less

Part Ⅲ Read each dialogue or passage carefully and identify the option that contains a grammatical error.

6 (a) A: How can I get my insurance premium assess?
   (b) B: If you have insurance with a large corporation, get a copy of your annual insurance report before you calculate your premium.
   (c) A: What if I want to figure out the right premium for my whole family?
   (d) B: You may want to call your state certification officer to get a list of certified accountants in your state.

7 (a) A: What happened here? Did you hit a streetlight with your car?
   (b) B: I managed barely to avoid the light but ran into a car which was parked next to the wall.
   (c) A: Are you okay? Let me help you go to the hospital.
   (d) B: I am okay. Could you call the police if you have a cellular phone?

8 (a) A: This is Jane McDonald from the ABC Medical Center. May I talk to Jonathan Carpenter?
   (b) B: He is not available at the moment. Would you like to leave a message?
   (c) A: I have his test results. Can you have him calling me as soon as he can?
   (d) B: You may want to let me know the results. I am his wife Lily.

9 (a) The 300-billion-dollar stimulus package hardly is worth anything compared with the true scale of the current financial crisis. (b) A greater financial crisis is looming. (c) Even the astronomical amount of the bailout money will hardly put a dent in it. (d) Indeed, economists have spotted a number of signs of a monstrous coming financial disaster in recent months.

10 (a) The AIDS incidence rate has remained nearly flat. (b) As the war on AIDS continues, new approaches are badly needed. (c) Attacking mutated genes has had limited results. (d) If one mutated gene is impaired, it lets others to take over.

GP | 07 도치가 일어나는 경우

□ **출제 경향** 부정의 의미를 담은 어구들이 강조를 위해 문두에 올 때가 있는데, 이때 주어와 동사의 위치가 바뀌는 도치가 일어난다. 이 도치된 부분이 어순 문제로 출제되므로 도치되는 순서를 잘 알아두도록 하자.

❶ 부정 의미어가 문두에 올 때

Hardly has the management seen such a passionate and confident recruit with a wide range of experience in the computer business.
경영진은 이처럼 열정적이고 자신감이 넘치면서도 컴퓨터 분야에 폭넓은 경험을 가지고 있는 신입사원을 이전에 본 적이 거의 없다.

Little did she know that she would be fired due to her lack of commitment.
그녀는 업무에 대한 헌신이 부족하다는 이유로 해고당할 거라고는 꿈에도 생각지 못했다.

Not until the wind began to let up did people come out of the building.
바람이 잠잠해지기 시작하자 사람들이 건물 밖으로 나왔다.

❷ 「no sooner ~ than...」 구문

다음 구문은 도치 어순 문제에 자주 출제되는 구문이므로 무조건 외우도록 한다.

No sooner + had + 주어 + p.p. + than + 주어 + 과거동사
　　　　　　　　　　(A)　　　　　　　　　　　　(B)

→ A하자마자 B했다.

No sooner had the cellist finished her performance **than** the audience **gave** her a standing ovation.
그 첼로 연주자가 연주를 끝내자마자 관객들이 기립 박수를 보냈다.

No sooner had the CEO sat down **than** the meeting **started**.
그 최고 경영자가 앉자마자 회의가 시작되었다.

GP | 08 양보구문

□ **출제 경향** 양보구문에도 종류가 많다. even though, although, though, despite, in spite of 등이 사용되는 구문 외에도, 실제로 TEPS 문법 어순 문제로 잘 출제되는 것으로는 no matter와 however가 사용된 구문, 형용사나 명사, 또는 동사가 문두에 나오는 구문 등이 있다.

❶ 주요 양보구문의 어순

■ 「no matter + 의문사 + 주어 + 동사」

No matter **where you may go**, I will always follow you.
네가 어디를 갈지라도 나는 항상 너와 함께 할 거야.
→ may는 생략 가능

No matter **how desperately you want** a gold medal, you will never get one unless you work your heart out.
네가 금메달을 아무리 절실히 원한다 하더라도 혼신의 힘을 다해서 훈련하지 않으면 절대로 가질 수 없을 것이다.
→ No matter how 다음에 형용사나 부사가 올 수도 있다.
▶ heart out 최선을 다하여

■ 「however + 형용사 / 부사 + 주어 + (조)동사」

However **rigorous the training might be**, the athletes must go through it in order to break their personal records.
훈련이 아무리 힘들다 할지라도 그 운동선수들은 개인 기록을 깨기 위해서 그 과정을 반드시 거쳐야 한다.

■ 「형용사 + as + 주어 + 동사」

Young as he is, he is a man of ability.
비록 어리긴 하지만, 그는 능력 있는 사람이다.

■ 「명사 + as + 주어 + 동사」

Coward as he was, he could not bear such an insult.
비록 그는 겁쟁이였지만 그러한 모욕은 참을 수 없었다.

■ 「동사 + as + 주어 + 조동사」

Try as you may, you can't get the job done in time.
네가 아무리 열심히 시도를 해 본들 그 일을 제 시간에 끝내진 못 할 거야.

Check-up TEST 07~08

Part I Choose the option that best completes each dialogue.

1 A: Seldom _____ to watch any figure skating competitions until Alison won the gold medal.

B: You're right. Isn't winning the gold medal what sports is all about?

(a) had anyone bothered
(b) anyone had bothered
(c) had bothered anyone
(d) anyone bothered had

2 A: Why don't the spectators look happy when their team is winning?

B: The spectators are hissing because, _____, the New York Yankees are on the way to yet another season of underperforming.

(a) no matter how ends this game up
(b) no matter how does this game end up
(c) no matter how this game ends up
(d) no matter this game how ends up

Part II Choose the option that best completes each sentence.

3 _____ to become the chairman of the legislative committee.

(a) Hardly Michelle Thomson was the best choice
(b) Hardly was Michelle Thomson the best choice
(c) Hardly was the best choice Michelle Thomson
(d) Hardly Michelle Thomson the best choice was

4 No sooner _____ of an aviation influenza outbreak than she received the results of the research from the scientists.

(a) she had raised the possibility
(b) she had the possibility raised
(c) had raised she the possibility
(d) had she raised the possibility

5 The biological systems of birds are wired to let them find their way home _____ on the Earth.

(a) no matter where they are
(b) no matter where are they
(c) no matter they are where
(d) no matter are they where

6 _____, the agenda prevented us from having in-depth discussions on the diplomatic situation in the war-torn African country.

(a) As broad it was
(b) Broad as it was
(c) Broad as was it
(d) As broad was it

Part III Read each dialogue or passage carefully and identify the option that contains a grammatical error.

7 (a) A: Scientists have discovered a new habitat for the Siberian tiger.
(b) B: Really? As far as I know, the species was first discovered in 1312 by English explorer Alexander Langston.
(c) A: Right. As hopeful Langston had been, the world's largest cat was never studied during the 14th century.
(d) B: People did not know whether the species still existed following the devastating Siberian wildfire.

8 (a) A: No sooner Daisy had finished her comeback concert than another scandal unfolded.
(b) B: How did she respond this time?
(c) A: She broke her silence to deny it.
(d) B: Poor girl. She has been thrown into the media spotlight again.

9 (a) A: I'm sad to be leaving behind all the trees and flowers I have been growing in my garden.
(b) B: Why don't you take some pictures? Hardly there is a better way to bring back old memories than by looking at pictures.
(c) A: I should do that. I can take out those photos and remember what a wonderful part of my life the garden has been.
(d) B: I am going to miss that maple tree that the kids used to climb.

10 (a) No matter how the ratio of loans to assets may be high, the risk management capacity of the bank ensures consumer protection. (b) Failure to maintain an adequate level of loan-to-asset ratio can lead to an unsafe and unsound financial status. (c) But our rate of lending will not have an adverse effect on our balance sheet management. (d) The board of directors, who is responsible for managing risks, has developed a new strategy to protect consumers.

GP | 09 so ~ that 구문과 도치

□ **출제 경향** 강조하기 위해 so ~ that 구문의 so 부분을 문장 맨 앞에 두면 도치가 일어난다. 「so + 형용사」를 문두에 위치
시킨 후 이어지는 어구의 어순을 묻는 문제가 주로 출제된다.

His daily schedule was **so** regularly timed that one could tell the hour of the day by what he
was doing.
그의 하루 일과는 너무나도 규칙적으로 시간이 짜여 있었기 때문에 그가 무엇을 하는지만 봐도 몇 시인지 알 수 있었다.

→ 주어는 his daily schedule, 동사를 포함한 서술부는 was so regularly timed이다. 전체적으로 보면 so ~ that 구문이 사용되었고, that
이하에 다시 주어와 동사가 나오고 있다. 이 문장이 도치되면 다음과 같다.

= **So** regularly timed **was his daily schedule** that one could tell the hour of the day by what
he was doing.

→ 결국은 so regularly timed를 문장 맨 앞으로 빼고 주어와 동사를 도치시킨 문장이다.

Her dance was **so** meticulously choreographed that everyone became mesmerized with it.
그녀의 춤은 매우 꼼꼼하게 안무를 맞추었기 때문에 모든 이들이 그 춤에 홀딱 빠졌다.

▶ meticulously 세심하게; 정확히   choreograph 안무하다

= So meticulously choreographed **was her dance** that everyone became mesmerized with it.

GP | 10 준동사의 부정

□ **출제 경향** to부정사·동명사·분사 등 준동사를 부정할 때는 부정어인 not이나 never를 이들의 바로 앞에 둔다. 아래 예문
들을 통해 각 경우를 세밀히 살펴보고 확실히 익혀두자.

The board of directors decided **not** to rush headlong into the new business.
이사회는 새로운 사업에 성급히 뛰어들지 않기로 결정했다.

▶ rush headlong into 성급하게 ~하다

Not to make a stupid decision, you have to make use of all the information.
어리석은 결정을 내리지 않기 위해서 모든 정보를 활용해야 한다.

I regret **not** having practiced a lot in preparation for the speech contest.
나는 웅변대회를 위해 충분히 연습하지 않았던 것이 후회가 돼.

Not having won a gold medal, he didn't show up at the press conference back home.
올림픽 대회에서 금메달을 따지 못한 그는 고국 기자회견장에 나타나지 않았다.

Never having been loved by anyone, the naive young man lost confidence in himself.
누구의 사랑도 받아보지 못했기 때문에, 그 순진한 젊은 청년은 자신에 대한 신뢰감을 잃었다.

GP | 11 구동사의 목적어

□ **출제 경향** pick up, take off, put on, talk about처럼 동사와 전치사 또는 동사와 부사의 조합으로 이루어진 어구를 구동
사라 한다. TEPS 문법 영역에서는 구동사를 얼마나 많이 알고 있는가 하는 부분보다는 구동사의 목적어가 대
명사로 나올 때 어순 배열을 잘 할 수 있는지를 묻는다.

1 구동사와 명사

명사는 구동사 사이, 또는 구동사 뒤에 놓일 수 있다.

Would you please turn down **the volume**?
볼륨 좀 낮춰 주시겠어요?

= Would you please turn **the volume** down?

Jennifer brought up **the subject** again.
제니퍼가 그 이야기를 또 꺼냈어.

= Jennifer brought **the subject** up again.

The company had to call off **the picnic** due to inclement weather.
악천후로 인해 회사는 피크닉을 취소해야 했다.

= The company had to call **the picnic** off due to inclement weather.

We crossed out **your name** from the list.
우리는 명단에서 당신의 이름을 지웠습니다.

= We crossed **your name** out from the list.

2 구동사와 대명사

명사와 달리, 대명사는 반드시 동사와 전치사 혹은 동사와 부사 사이에 와야 한다는 점을 꼭 기억하자.

I want you to pick **me** up at the airport. (○)

I want you to *pick up me* at the airport. (×)
네가 날 공항에 데리러 와줬으면 좋겠어.

Jason asked **me** out last night.
제이슨이 어제 나에게 데이트 신청을 했어.

Alex's encouragement really cheered **me** up.
알렉스의 격려로 나는 정말 힘이 났다.

Check-up TEST 09~11

Part I Choose the option that best completes each dialogue.

1 A: Harry urged us _____ the art exhibition where his work will be displayed.
   B: Let me see what I have on my schedule.

   (a) not skip
   (b) to skip not
   (c) to not skip
   (d) not to skip

2 A: Tommy told us that he was going to _____.
   B: I hope that she agrees to go on a date with him.

   (a) ask out she
   (b) ask out her
   (c) ask her to out
   (d) ask her out

Part II Choose the option that best completes each sentence.

3 Despite _____ in an election, I was actively campaigning to encourage people to turn out for the presidential election this Tuesday.

   (a) never voted
   (b) never having voted
   (c) having never voted
   (d) having voted never

4 So _____ when it gave students access to credit that it was left with unrecoverable loans and potentially insolvent customers.

   (a) was the Indian-based financial institution indiscriminate
   (b) indiscriminate was the Indian-based financial institution
   (c) indiscriminate the Indian-based financial institution was
   (d) was indiscriminate the Indian-based financial institution

5 _____ I still remember each and every word he said in it.

   (a) Incredible so was the president's speech that
   (b) The president's speech was incredible so that
   (c) The president's speech was that incredible so
   (d) So incredible was the president's speech that

6 _____, Tom needs more time to read textbooks than his classmates.

(a) Never having read many books before

(b) Having never read many books before

(c) Having read never many books before

(d) Having read many books never before

Part III **Read each dialogue or passage carefully and identify the option that contains a grammatical error.**

7 (a) A: What happened during today's episode after the war broke out between the vampires and the demons?

(b) B: Henry, the prince of the vampire kingdom, was sick of living in the darkness, so he abandoned his promise to wait for another million years and opened Pandora's Box.

(c) A: So did the freed demons kill Henry?

(d) B: Do you remember that Helena told Henry to not let the demons in if they entered the room of prayer?

8 (a) The new bus-only lane was more of an inconvenience than the car-free route for bus drivers. (b) The bus-only lane was filled with parked cars and street vendors. (c) In an attempt to address the issue, city officials crossed out it with black paint. (d) However, the situation got out of control following numerous complaints made by bus drivers and pedestrians.

9 (a) So commonplace these days pop songs are that are remade from foreign music that they barely seem worth noting. (b) But the pop version of the Korean song Arirang is a rather unusual remake of a Korean traditional song. (c) The album, which will be released next month, will be sold on the American continent. (d) Alex Kim heads a band comprised mostly of Korean-American musicians and singers, including Suzie Lee, Janet Park, and Anthony Kim.

10 (a) There was some turbulence in the convention hall. (b) Things have calmed down now, but people are still in a state of shock. (c) The public is waiting to hear a press briefing from a presidential spokesman. (d) It is said that so horrible the explosion was that no miners survived it.

□ **출제 경향** 원급, 비교급 어순 문제는 어렵지 않게 정답을 찾아낼 수 있지만, 여기에 배수사 문법 포인트가 추가되면 답을 찾는 데 시간이 다소 걸린다. 배수사는 일반적으로 목적어, 비교급, 원급 앞에 위치하므로 어순 문제에서 배수사가 목적어, 비교급, 원급 뒤에 왔다면 틀렸다고 보면 된다.

❶ 배수사 half / double / treble

In February, the lawyer earned **double** his usual monthly salary.
2월에 그 변호사는 평소에 받는 월 급여보다 두 배나 많이 벌었다.

The company paid me **half** the amount I had requested.
회사는 내가 요구했던 액수의 절반만을 지급했다.

The expense was **treble** the 2018 level.
지출이 2018년 대비 세 배였다.

❷ 「배수사＋as＋원급＋as」

The African continent is **four times** as large as the European one.
= The African continent is **four times** the size of the European one.
아프리카 대륙은 유럽 대륙보다 네 배나 넓다.

❸ 「배수사＋비교급＋than」

There were **four times** more books delivered than I had ordered.
내가 주문했던 것보다 책이 네 배나 더 많이 배달되었다.

The cars manufactured in Asia are **1.5 times** more efficient than the ones made in Europe.
아시아에서 제조된 차는 유럽에서 만들어진 차보다 연비가 1.5배 더 좋다.

GP | 13 특정 형용사의 어순

□ **출제 경향** 일반적으로 형용사는 명사 앞에서 수식하지만, something, anything, nothing처럼 –thing으로 끝나는 단어들은 형용사가 뒤에서 수식한다. 또한 명사를 직접 수식하지 못하고 서술적으로만 사용되는 형용사에 대해서도 확실히 알아두어야 한다.

❶ 「something / anything / nothing + 형용사」

something cold 뭔가 차가운 것   **anything elegant** 어떤 우아한 것
nothing serious 아무것도 아닌 일

A: Let's eat **something cold** for lunch. 점심으로 차가운 음식을 먹자.

B: As long as you pick up the tab. 네가 계산한다면야 문제없지.

→ cold something이라고 쓰면 틀린다.

▶ pick up the tab (식당이나 술집에서) 계산하다, 비용을 지불하다

Do you need **anything elegant** for the party?
파티를 위해 우아한 뭔가가 필요하신가요?

It's was **nothing serious**. Never mind. 별 것 아니었어. 신경 쓰지 마.

❷ 서술적으로만 사용되는 형용사

형용사 alive, awake, alone, afraid, alike는 명사 앞에서 수식할 수 없고, 서술적으로만 사용될 수 있으므로 특히 주의해야 한다.

I am **afraid** of making mistakes.
나는 실수하는 것이 두렵다.

A mountain climber who went missing during a blizzard has been found **alive** and well.
눈보라로 실종되었던 암벽 등반가가 무사히 생존한 채로 발견되었다.

The doctor stuck an endoscope down my throat, put a needle into my pancreas, and got a few *alive* cells from the tumor. (×)

→ The doctor stuck an endoscope down my throat, put a needle into my pancreas, and got a few **living** cells from the tumor. (○)

의사는 위내시경을 내 목안에 넣었고, 췌장에 바늘을 넣어 종양에 있는 살아있는 세포 몇 개를 뽑아냈다.

→ alive는 명사 앞에서 수식할 수 없는데, '살아있는 세포'라는 뜻이 되어야 하므로 alive cells를 living cells로 고쳐야 한다.

▶ endoscope 내시경 pancreas 췌장

Part I Choose the option that best completes each dialogue.

1 A: How about staying in a hotel that will make us feel comfortable?
  B: Staying in a hotel costs _____ renting a room in a youth hostel.

  (a) as much twice as
  (b) more twice than
  (c) as much as twice
  (d) twice as much as

2 A: Did you have a fruitful discussion at the international medical seminar held last Thursday?
  B: _____ that I learned.

  (a) There was useful nothing
  (b) There was nothing useful
  (c) There wasn't useful something
  (d) There wasn't something useful

3 A: A crowd of 70 people carrying cameras wandered by to see the _____ at midday.
  B: I guess the giant water mammal attracted so many people.

  (a) alive whale
  (b) dead whale
  (c) whale dead
  (d) awake whale

Part II Choose the option that best completes each sentence.

4 A grown chimpanzee consumes _____ a young one.
  (a) ten times as many as
  (b) so much so ten times
  (c) ten times as much as
  (d) as much so ten times

5 Most Asians eat only _____ recommended for good health.
  (a) half the amount of fruit and vegetables
  (b) the amount half of fruit and vegetables
  (c) the amount of fruit and vegetables half
  (d) the amount of fruit half and vegetables

6   It would be fair to say that TEPS is _____ any other English test.

(a) more difficult than two times
(b) difficult more than two times
(c) two times more than difficult
(d) two times more difficult than

Part III **Read each dialogue or passage carefully and identify the option that contains a grammatical error.**

7   (a) A: Have you ever seen anybody who spends money with no strings attached?
(b) B: You can contribute if you want a government whose policies are those you agree with.
(c) A: When he donated his hard-earned money to the political party, he was looking to get something in exchange for his donation.
(d) B: Maybe you are right. That's why everyone is saying that Amy Wilson must have done improper something when she donated $10,000 and then won the bid to construct the new park.

8   (a) A: Do you still want to sell your compact car?
(b) B: Yes. Do you think you might be interested?
(c) A: Maybe. Would you be willing to sell it for 30,000 dollars?
(d) B: I am willing to sell the car for the amount half you offered.

9   (a) A: The alone oil giant spent $50 million on the Republican campaign effort.
(b) B: Oil companies seem to take money from ordinary people like us and give it to political parties.
(c) A: In the coming month, the oil company will team up with a number of media corporations to raise $100 million to fund the election effort of the conservative party.
(d) B: When it is combined with donations made by other industries, it will be an enormous amount of money.

10   (a) If you're spending another sleepless night worrying about your business, you might want to see which lights are on in the houses on your street. (b) There is a high probability that you will see awake neighbors. (c) Millions of Americans are kept awake because of money troubles. (d) While the government seems to be confident that the outlook for the future is rosy, the public is not convinced.

Unit 2 동사

GP | 14 시제 일치와 예외

□ **출제 경향** 시제 일치 문제는 쉬운 듯하면서도 결코 쉽지만은 않다. 문법 지식은 물론 내용의 흐름까지 파악해야 풀 수 있는 문제가 나오기도 한다. 주절의 시제가 과거일 때 종속절에는 과거나 과거완료를 쓰는 문법 포인트를 묻는 문제가 가장 빈번히 출제된다.

❶ 시제 일치

I **ordered** the table that **was advertised** in the catalogue.
나는 카탈로그에 광고된 식탁을 주문했다.

He **stated** in court that he **had witnessed** the man kill an innocent woman.
그는 법정에서 그 남자가 아무 잘못도 없는 여성을 살해하는 장면을 목격했다고 진술했다.
→ 법정에서 증언한 것은 과거에 있었던 일이고 그 이전에 살해 장면을 목격한 것이므로 과거완료 'had + p.p.'를 사용했다.

The school principal **said** that he **would change** the curriculum in the years to come.
학교 교장은 앞으로 몇 년 사이에 교과 과정을 변경하겠다고 말했다.

❷ 시제 일치의 예외

■ 역사적 사실은 과거 시제로 쓴다.

The Korean War **broke out** on June 25, 1950, and an armistice was signed on July 27, 1953.
한국 전쟁은 1950년 6월 25일에 발발했고 휴전 협정이 1953년 7월 27일에 체결되었다.

■ 과학적 사실은 현재 시제로 쓴다.

Weightlessness **takes place** whenever all forces applied to an object are uniformly distributed across the object's mass.
무중력은 물체에 가해지는 모든 힘이 물체의 질량에 균일하게 분배될 때 발생한다.

■ 속담 · 금언 · 격언은 현재 시제로 쓴다.

Time **heals** all wounds. 시간이 약이다.

The walls **have** ears. 벽에도 귀가 있다.(낮말은 새가 듣고 밤말은 쥐가 듣는다.)

Everyone **has** a skeleton in the closet. 털어서 먼지 안 나는 사람 없다.

GP | 15 시간 부사절 / 조건 부사절

□ **출제 경향** 빈번하게 출제되는 문법 포인트이다. 파트 III에 나오면 정답을 찾아내기 쉽지 않으므로 시간 · 조건 부사절에
익숙해지도록 해야 한다.

❶ 시간 부사절을 이끄는 접속사

after   as soon as   before   by the time   while   until

A: Jerry, would you feed the dog? 제리, 개 밥 좀 줄래?

B: I will get around to it **as soon as I am done** with this. 이것만 끝내고 할게.
→ as soon as I am done with this는 '내가 이 일을 끝내자마자'라는 의미로, 아직 끝낸 것이 아니라 미래 시점에 끝낼 것을 염두에 두고 있다.
내용상으로는 미래의 일이지만 위의 접속사가 이끄는 시간 부사절에서는 이것을 미래 시제가 아닌 현재 시제로 쓴다는 점에 유의하자.

❷ 조건 부사절을 이끄는 접속사

as long as ~하기만 한다면   even if ~라 할지라도

only if ~하기만 하다면   unless ~하지 않는다면

in case ~일 경우에   provided that ~라고 가정하면

I will buy you a new smart phone **if you get** a perfect score on the math test.
네가 수학 시험에서 만점을 받으면 새 스마트폰을 한 대 사 주마.
→ 지금 수학 시험 만점을 받은 것이 아니다. 미래에 받을 것을 조건으로 걸고 있다. 조건 부사절에서는 내용은 미래라 하더라도 쓸 때는 현재 시제로
쓴다.

Part I Choose the option that best completes each dialogue.

1   A: Did you hear the news that a cyclone hit the southern region?
    B: Yes. When we _____ an incoming cyclone, we have to go inland to avoid
       the cyclone.

    (a) get a warning of
    (b) will get a warning of
    (c) got a warning of
    (d) will have gotten a warning of

2   A: What do you like to drink?
    B: Coffee is my favorite drink even though it _____.
    (a) kept me awake
    (b) keep me awake
    (c) keeps me awake
    (d) had kept me awake

Part II Choose the option that best completes each sentence.

3   The museum acquired a rock from a volcano that _____ more than five
    thousand years ago.

    (a) has erupted
    (b) erupted
    (c) had erupted
    (d) erupts

4   If a country _____ America with a missile, its protection system will keep the
    missile from doing any damage.

    (a) will try to hit
    (b) tried to hit
    (c) tries to hit
    (d) had tried to hit

Part III Read each dialogue or passage carefully and identify the option that contains a grammatical error.

5 (a) A: Why didn't you make it to the baseball game yesterday?
　(b) B: I was willing to go, but I have to take my son to the hospital.
　(c) A: What happened? Is he okay?
　(d) B: Yeah, he is fine now. The doctor said it was just an upset stomach.

6 (a) A: If you planned to do any sort of outdoor activities this weekend, you may want to think again.
　(b) B: How come? Is something bad going to happen this weekend?
　(c) A: The cold weather that has lasted for a few days is expected to continue over the weekend.
　(d) B: Oh no. That's disappointing news.

7 (a) A: Don't you think we should turn the pork chops over?
　(b) B: Not yet. I like them seared on the outside.
　(c) A: I didn't usually eat blackened meat because it causes cancer.
　(d) B: You're right. We shouldn't risk our health.

8 (a) The U.S. Commerce Department announced that America's GDP grows at an annual rate of 3.1 percent in the first quarter of the year. (b) This figure was below Wall Street's estimate of 3.6 percent and was the lowest in two years since the first quarter of 2016, when GDP rose 1.9 percent. (c) The main factor that put the brakes on economic growth was none other than high oil prices. (d) The hike in energy prices dampened consumer and business spending and worsened the trade deficit.

9 (a) This year marks the twenty-third anniversary of the founding of eBay. (b) In 1995, a software engineer named Pierre Omidyar wanted to establish a genuine online market culture in which buyers and sellers could agree on an ideal price. (c) Thus came the creation of eBay, which is an online auction service. (d) The founder, Omidyar, worked ceaselessly to make eBay a global giant, proving that hard work led to success.

10 (a) The government needs to build more public housing, including rental homes, until we have no more families without homes. (b) This will change people's perceptions of houses from being mere possessions to being objects of actual use. (c) The current lukewarm approach by the government will only increase the resistance of speculators. (d) Only when the government will combine the market principles of supply and demand with punitive taxes, will its policies prove effective.

GP | 16 현재완료 시제

□ **출제 경향** 동사 관련 문제 중에서도 현재완료 시제에 관한 문제는 매달 출제되고 있다. 현재완료가 쓰이는 상황과, 현재완료와 함께 쓰이는 어구를 파악해 두어야 한다.

① since가 사용되는 구문

■ '~이래로'의 뜻으로 쓰일 때

Since 2017, the company **has started** making a profit while its competitors **have lagged** behind.
2017년 이후로 그 회사는 수익을 내기 시작했는데, 반면 경쟁업체는 뒤쳐졌다.
→ 여기서 since는 전치사로 쓰였다. ▶ lag behind 뒤(쳐)지다

I **have studied** interpretation and translation **since** I attended an international conference.
국제회의에 참석한 이후로 나는 통번역을 공부하기 시작했다.
→ 여기서 since는 접속사로 쓰였다.

※ since가 '~이기 때문에'의 뜻일 때는 시제가 반드시 현재완료가 아니어도 된다는 점에 유의하자.

The government **decided** to allocate a huge amount of money for the IT sector **since** it believed the sector would make the world better than before.
정부는 IT 영역이 이 세상을 과거보다 더 낫게 만들 수 있을 거라 믿었기 때문에 매우 많은 액수의 돈을 IT 영역에 할당하기로 결정했다.

② 전치사 over / in / for가 사용되는 구문

아래 표현들은 '과거 특정 시점부터 지금까지'를 의미하기 때문에 현재완료 구문에 쓰는 것이 옳다.

over the years 지난 몇 년 사이에 걸쳐서   in the past decade 지난 10년 사이에
for the past 17 years 지난 17년 동안

Korea **has made** significant economic progress **over the past decade** to become one of the world's economic titans.
한국은 지난 수십 년 동안 괄목할 만한 경제 성장을 이루어 전 세계 경제 강대국 중 하나가 되었다.

③ 현재완료와 함께 쓰이는 부사

아래의 부사가 사용되었다고 해서 무조건 현재완료만을 써야 하는 것은 아니며, 일반적으로 현재완료 시제와 잘 어울려 쓰인다는 말이므로 기계적으로 적용하지 않도록 주의하자.

lately   until now   till now   before   so far   just   yet   already 등

A: I am bored to death. **Have you heard** any good stories **lately**?
정말 지루해 죽겠어. 요즘 뭐 재미있는 이야깃거리 없니?
B: Not many. 별로 없어.

Only a minor fraction of the oceans **has been explored until now**.
지금까지 해양의 단지 미미한 부분만이 탐험되었다.

I **have been** there many times **before**.
나는 거기에 여러 번 가봤다.

So far, nothing much **has been discussed** about the agenda.
지금까지 그 안건에 대해서 이야기된 바는 별로 없다.

No decision on the matter **has been made yet**.
그 문제에 관해서 아직까지 어떠한 결정도 내려진 바 없다.

A: Dinner? 저녁 먹을래?
B: Thanks for asking. But I**'ve already eaten**. 물어봐줘서 고맙지만, 이미 먹었어.

④ 내용의 흐름으로 시제를 파악해야 하는 구문

문장 속의 부사나 부사구를 힌트로 하여 시제를 파악할 수 있는 문제는 쉬운 편이지만 내용 흐름을 통해 논리적으로 현재 완료 시제임을 파악해야 하는 문제는 고난도에 속한다고 할 수 있다.

The program **has been** created to help academically challenged students learn better.
이 프로그램은 학습 장애가 있는 학생들이 보다 더 잘 배울 수 있도록 도움을 주고자 만들어졌다.

This is **one of the most interesting** books that I **have ever read**.
이것은 내가 읽었던 가장 재미있는 책 가운데 하나이다.
→ 최상급 + 현재완료

The new invention **has been** widely acclaimed and commended.
그 새로운 발명품은 널리 환호와 찬사를 받았다.
→ 발명품이 출시된 이후로 반응이 좋았다는 맥락이므로 현재완료 시제가 적절하다.
▶ acclaim 환호를 보내다 commend 칭찬하다

※명백한 과거 시제를 의미하는 yesterday, ago, last week / last month / last year 등은 현재완료 시제와 함께 사용하지 않는다.

I have been reading this book *a month ago*. (×)
→ I have been reading this book **for a month**. (○)
나는 한 달 전부터 이 책을 읽기 시작했다.
→ 한 달 동안 읽고 있다.

The movie has been running *last week*. (×)
→ The movie has been running **for the past week**. (○)
그 영화는 지난주부터 상영되었다.
→ 일주일 동안 상영 중이다.

Check-up TEST 16

Part I Choose the option that best completes each dialogue.

1 A: How come you are frowning?
   B: My back _____ since it began to rain.

   (a) had been aching
   (b) have been aching
   (c) has been aching
   (d) is aching

2 A: How is your brother adjusting to life overseas?
   B: He _____.

   (a) had been having a hard time
   (b) had a hard time
   (c) has having a hard time
   (d) has been having a hard time

Part II Choose the option that best completes each sentence.

3 My sister has been pursuing a career in nanotechnology _____ last June.

   (a) until she graduated
   (b) since she graduated
   (c) for she graduated
   (d) when she graduated

4 Learning a foreign language is especially difficult for those who _____ before.

   (a) had never learned one
   (b) have never learned one
   (c) never learned one
   (d) never learns one

Part III Read each dialogue or passage carefully and identify the option that contains a grammatical error.

5   (a) A: Hello. This is Susan. I stayed in your hotel three days ago.

    (b) B: Hello again, Susan. How may I help you?

    (c) A: I wonder if anyone on your staff happened to turn in a white purse.

    (d) B: No one mentioned finding one so far.

6   (a) A: I bought a new sweater at P&P. How do I look?

    (b) B: Fantastic! I had been seeing my boyfriend for a year now, and I think that might make a nice present for him.

    (c) A: Well, you'd better hurry up. There were only a few left when I was there.

    (d) B: I'd better leave now. Thanks.

7   (a) A: Look at her. She's been cutting out magazine articles all evening. Do you know what they are for?

    (b) B: Yeah, she's trying to find an effective weight loss program.

    (c) A: Did she ever tried cutting back on her caloric intake?

    (d) B: As far as I know, she has done that many times till now, but it has not worked.

8   (a) I recently witnessed a troubling scene when I took my grandchild out for a walk at a nearby park. (b) Several girls who looked like they were in junior high school were smoking under a tree. (c) I immediately have made them put out their cigarettes but felt unhappy all day long. (d) It is quite deplorable that our society is seeing minors smoking in wide-open public places.

9   (a) Few words can describe Korea's socioeconomic problems more adequately than the word "polarization." (b) If the widening gap of wealth between individuals is the root cause of social instability, then its economic origin can be found in the gap between big and small businesses. (c) The main reason is that big businesses had successfully undergone restructuring since the financial crisis — mostly at the expense of their subcontractors. (d) Large companies have more or less passed the burden of cost increases to their subcontractors by slashing supply prices.

10 (a) The four-man team led by world-renowned alpinist John Williams finally arrived at the North Pole. (b) William's team has been covering 2,000 kilometers in 54 days, with each member pulling a 100-kilogram sleigh full of supplies. (c) During the entire process, they had to battle temperatures as low as 55 degrees below zero and blizzards blowing snow at 14 meters per second. (d) The history of expeditions shows that an explorer's achievement often goes beyond the individual and boosts his or her nation's morale and self-esteem.

GP | 17 과거완료 시제/미래완료 시제

□ **출제 경향** 두세 달에 한 번씩 꼭 출제되는 문법 포인트로, 문맥 안에서 시제를 파악해야 하므로 쉽지 않은 유형이다. 하지만 문장 안에 시제를 파악할 수 있는 힌트들이 들어 있는 경우가 있으므로 잘 알아두면 문제를 푸는 데 훨씬 수월해질 수 있다.

❶ 과거완료 시제

과거완료는 기준이 되는 과거 시점이 있고, 그 시점보다 먼저 일어난 사건(대과거)을 나타낼 때 had p.p.로 쓰는 구문이다. 과거완료 시제가 문법 문제로 만들어지면 문장 안에 과거 시제를 일부러 배치해두어 대과거와의 구분을 확실히 해두므로, 이를 잘 파악해야 한다.

The much-hyped concert **had already started** when I finally arrived at the stadium.
대대적으로 광고되었던 콘서트는 내가 공연장에 도착했을 때 이미 시작되었다.
▶ hype 과대 선전하다; 선동하다

I **had played** baseball for two years when I had to stop playing it due to my knee injury.
무릎 부상 때문에 더 이상 야구를 할 수 없게 되었을 때 나는 야구를 2년 가량 해왔었다.

The rescue team stopped searching for the missing marines since the rescuers **had looked** almost everywhere.
구조대는 거의 모든 곳을 다 찾아봤었기 때문에 실종된 해병대원 수색작업을 중단했다.

When the party came to an end, half of the guests **had** already **left**.
파티가 끝났을 때 참석자 중 절반은 이미 파티장을 떠나고 없었다.

❷ 미래완료 시제

미래 시제는 '(미래에 무엇을) 할 것이다'라는 의미를 나타내고, 미래완료 시제는 '(특정 미래 시점에 행동을) 마무리하다'라는 뉘앙스이다. TEPS 문법에 출제되는 미래완료 시제 문제는 거의 정해져있는 편인데, 특히 전치사 by에 유의할 필요가 있다.

By 2100, about 20% of the exotic animals on Earth **will have become** extinct due to environmental degradation.
2100년이 끝날 때쯤이면 지구상의 희귀 동물 중에서 약 20퍼센트 가량이 환경 파괴로 인해 멸종될 것이다.
→ 2100년이 되면 그때부터 멸종되기 시작하는 것이 아니라 약 20퍼센트의 희귀 동물이 멸종되고 없는 상황이 되는 것이므로 미래완료 시제를 쓴 것이다. 일반적으로 미래완료 시제 구문에는 'by+시간 / 시점'이 잘 나온다는 점을 숙지하자.

I **will have read** about 10 comic books by the time James comes back from school.
제임스가 학교에서 돌아올 때쯤 되면 나는 약 10권의 만화책을 다 읽어버릴 것이다.

GP | 18 진행 시제

□ 출제 경향 TEPS 문법 영역에서 출제 빈도가 가장 높은 포인트는 과거 진행형이다. 종속절, 특히 when절의 주어가 특정 행동을 했을 당시에 주절의 주어가 '~을 하고 있는 중 이었다'는 내용인 경우, 주절의 동사 시제는 과거 진행형이 가장 자연스럽다. 오답 선택지로는 과거 시제 동사가 잘 나오는데, 과거 동사가 아니라 과거 진행형 동사를 선택할 수 있어야 한다.

❶ 과거 진행 시제

시험에 아래와 같은 문제가 나왔는데 선택지에 took a shower와 was taking a shower가 있다면 무엇을 정답으로 택하겠는가?

I _____ when the telephone rang.

전화벨이 울렸던 그 순간에 나는 '~을 하고 있던 중'이었기 때문에 과거 진행 시제를 써야 옳다. 따라서 옳은 문장은 다음과 같다.

I **was taking a shower** when the telephone rang.
전화벨이 울렸을 때 나는 샤워 중이었다.

❷ 현재 진행 시제

현재 진행 시제는 현재의 진행 상태뿐 아니라 가까운 미래를 의미하기도 한다.

The delegation **is coming** here in half an hour.
대표단이 30분 후에 도착할 예정이다.

❸ 미래 진행 시제

미래완료와 혼동할 수도 있으니 주의해야 한다. 미래완료는 특정 미래 시점에 행동이 마무리되는 것이고, 미래 진행은 미래 시점에 행동이 진행되고 있는 데에 초점을 둔 것이다.

I **will be playing** the piano in front of more than 1,000 people at this time tomorrow.
나는 내일 이 시간에 천 명이 넘는 관객들 앞에서 피아노를 치고 있을 것이다.

Part I Choose the option that best completes each dialogue.

1   A: What were you doing while we were talking on the phone?

    B: I _____ when we had a conversation.

    (a) was reading a newspaper

    (b) had been reading a newspaper

    (c) have been reading a newspaper

    (d) have read a newspaper

Part II Choose the option that best completes each sentence.

2   No one was more surprised than Susie to discover that Jane _____.

    (a) had gotten engaged

    (b) has gotten engaged

    (c) gotten engaged

    (d) gets engaged

3   When he retires, Professor Jackson _____ here for over 40 years, but his classes are never dull.

    (a) will have been teaching

    (b) will be teaching

    (c) will teach

    (d) has been teaching

4   His train _____ at the station right now.

    (a) was arriving

    (b) arrived

    (c) has arrived

    (d) is arriving

5   The lawyer _____ his plaintiff, but, unfortunately, he lost the prolonged legal battle yesterday.

    (a) was struggling to defend

    (b) struggled to defend

    (c) has struggled to defend

    (d) had struggled to defend

Part III Read each dialogue or passage carefully and identify the option that contains a grammatical error.

6   (a) A: What should we get your father for his birthday?
     (b) B: I had thought about getting him an electric razor.
     (c) A: But we got him an expensive razor last year, didn't we?
     (d) B: Yeah, I had forgotten about that.

7   (a) A: We are going on a picnic by the river.
     (b) B: You must be excited. Do you have everything you need?
     (c) A: Of course. I checked twice to see if I forgot anything.
     (d) B: I hope you have a good time.

8   (a) A: Why are you limping? Are you hurt?
     (b) B: I fell and hurt my knee yesterday, but it's not too serious.
     (c) A: What happened? I would imagine that you are the last person to fall and hurt yourself.
     (d) B: I tried to help an old lady who fall on a slippery floor.

9   (a) As the Dutch Senate passed a euthanasia bill by a vote of 46 to 28, around 10,000 people gathered outside Parliament to protest the decision. (b) The new law will have gone into effect 2 weeks after the Dutch king signs the bill. (c) The new law states that doctors involved in euthanasia must be convinced that the patient is terminally ill. (d) The legislation also states that a candidate must be Dutch and must submit a request for euthanasia in a written statement.

10 (a) I found myself wondering what device might have had a greater influence on human lives than the smart phone. (b) Almost every person has his or her own smart phone, and, in return, it exercises control over their lives. (c) According to a report released by the National Statistics Bureau, students use more smart phone than grownups. (d) That makes students increasingly exposed to violent or other harmful content.

GP | 19 특정 동사의 올바른 용법 1

□ 출제 경향 동사마다 그것이 취하는 목적어의 형태가 다르기 때문에 어떤 형태의 목적어를 취하는지 정확하게 알아야 한다.

① to부정사를 목적어로 취하는 동사

expect to V	~할 것을 예상하다	decide to V	~할 것을 결정하다
hope to V	~할 것을 희망하다	agree to V	~할 것을 동의하다
want to V	~할 것을 원하다	refuse to V	~할 것을 거절하다
plan to V	~할 것을 계획하다	fail to V	~하기를 실패하다
need to V	~할 것을 필요로 하다	afford to V	~할 여유가 있다
wish to V	~할 것을 바라다		

Sudan **expects to receive** more medical supplies and aid than ever before this year.
수단은 이전보다 올해에 더 많은 의료 용품과 원조를 받을 것을 예상하고 있다.

I **decided to drop** out of the accounting course.
나는 회계학 수업을 포기하기로 결정했다.

She applied to Harvard University but **failed to** get accepted.
그녀는 하버드 대학에 지원했지만 입학허가를 받지 못했다.

② 동명사를 목적어로 취하는 동사

admit V-ing	~하는 것을 인정하다	consider V-ing	~하는 것을 고려하다
enjoy V-ing	~하는 것을 좋아하다	quit V-ing	~하는 것을 그만두다
stop V-ing	~하는 것을 중단하다	mind V-ing	~하는 것을 꺼리다
avoid V-ing	~하는 것을 피하다	give up V-ing	~하는 것을 포기하다
discontinue V-ing	~하는 것을 중지하다	dislike V-ing	~하는 것을 싫어하다
appreciate V-ing	~하는 것에 감사하다	recommend V-ing	~하는 것을 권하다
risk V-ing	위험을 무릅쓰고 ~하다		

I am willing to **risk losing** everything.
나는 모든 것을 잃을 위험도 기꺼이 무릅쓰겠다.

I had no choice but to **discontinue paying** rent.
나는 집세 납부를 중단할 수밖에 없었다.

I **appreciate** your **helping** me out the other day.
일전에 저를 도와주셔서 감사합니다.

❸ 목적어로 to부정사와 동명사를 모두 취하는 동사

continue	계속하다	hate	싫어하다	intend	의도하다	love	좋아하다
begin	시작하다	start	시작하다	like	좋아하다	cease	중지하다

She **likes to be** the center of attention all the time.
= She **likes being** the center of attention all the time.
그녀는 항상 관심의 초점이 되기를 좋아한다.

The newly married couple **continued to scream** at each other.
= The newly married couple **continued screaming** at each other.
그 신혼부부는 계속해서 서로에게 소리를 질렀다.

❹ 「목적어+from V-ing」를 취하는 동사

다음 동사들에 관해서는 동사의 올바른 사용법과 어순이 통합되어 출제되므로 잘 알아두도록 하자. 목적어 뒤에 어떤 전치사나 동사형을 취하는지 등을 반드시 짚고 넘어가야 한다.

prevent+목적어+from V-ing	목적어가 ~하지 못하도록 막다
dissuade+목적어+from V-ing	목적어가 ~하지 못하도록 설득하다
discourage+목적어+from V-ing	목적어가 ~하지 못하도록 말리다

The government **prevented** its nationals **from going** abroad due to possible terrorist attacks.
정부는 테러리스트의 공격 가능성 때문에 자국민이 해외로 나가는 것을 막았다.

I **dissuaded** my wife **from smoking** so many times, but she declined to quit.
나는 아내에게 담배를 피우지 말라고 몇 번이나 설득했지만 그녀는 거절했다.

Over the years, civic groups have launched many programs to **discourage** teens **from smoking and drinking**.
많은 시민 단체들은 최근 몇 년 사이 십대 청소년들이 흡연과 음주를 못하도록 하는 프로그램을 시작했다.

Check-up TEST ⑲

Part I Choose the option that best completes each dialogue.

1   A: I really want to volunteer to help the Indonesians who have been suffering from the aftermath of the earthquake.
    B: I told you that is dangerous. But if you insist, I won't _____.
    (a) stop you to go
    (b) stop you to going
    (c) stop you going from
    (d) stop you from going

2   A: The school _____ a CCTV in a classroom to locate a stolen computer monitor.
    B: That is an unacceptable infringement of privacy rights.
    (a) admitted to install
    (b) admitted install
    (c) admitted installing
    (d) admitted for installing

3   A: I _____ from IP-TV.
    B: Me, too. We have to watch so many commercials between each program.
    (a) hate downloading TV programs
    (b) hate to download for TV programs
    (c) hate download TV programs
    (d) hate to downloading TV programs

Part II Choose the option that best completes each sentence.

4   The European Commission has _____ a plausible plan for sustained growth and liability reduction that can increase investors' confidence in the economy.
    (a) failed to lay down
    (b) failed laying down
    (c) failed lay down
    (d) failed of laying down

5   Auto analysts say that the massive recalls that affected all major carmakers have made it more difficult for car shoppers _____.
    (a) to avoid for buying faulty vehicles
    (b) to avoid to buy faulty vehicles
    (c) to avoid buy faulty vehicles
    (d) to avoid buying faulty vehicles

6 They sought a global audience through their effort to host the FIFA World Cup and fully
_____ their economic and democratic triumphs.

(a) expected showcasing
(b) expected to showcase
(c) expected of showcasing
(d) expected show case

Part III Read each dialogue or passage carefully and identify the option that contains a grammatical error.

7 (a) A: Are there any particular types you have in mind?
(b) B: I am considering to buy a clutch handbag.
(c) A: Then check out this adorable enamel clutch bag.
(d) B: Oh, it is very slick and pretty.

8 (a) A: We must not disappoint our viewers. They have waited for this drama for so long.
(b) B: I agree. But we should consider to delay the first release. The ratings competition these days is so intense.
(c) A: Since when have you cared about our competitors? You should have more confidence in our product.
(d) B: But we have spent a lot of money and energy since we started making this series. We should be more careful.

9 (a) The Alaska Resort Committee continues for approving the building of casinos. (b) A new law allows local casinos to set up and run poker games. (c) This month, it was reported that the committee had issued three licenses to casinos. (d) The committee's decision came after a public hearing on that issue had been held.

10 (a) During the Cold War, the balance of power dissuaded both the U.S. and the former Soviet Union from using nuclear weapons. (b) The heads of both countries knew that any nuclear attack would trigger a potentially destructive retaliation. (c) The decades-long standoff between the two powers came to an end. (d) An important challenge was how to discourage others possessing their own nuclear arsenals.

GP | 20 특정 동사의 올바른 용법 2

□ **출제 경향** 다음 동사들도 동사의 올바른 사용법과 어순이 통합되어 출제되므로 잘 알아두도록 하자.

❶ 전치사 to가 포함된 표현

> be committed[dedicated / devoted] to + 명사[V-ing] ~하는 데 혼신의 힘[최선]을 다하다
> be opposed to + 명사[V-ing] ~에 반대하다
> object to + 명사[V-ing] ~에 반대하다
> contribute + (목적어) + to + something ~에 (목적어를) 기부하다, ~하는 데에 기여하다
> look forward to + V-ing ~하는 것을 간절히 바라다

The Gracie family has been **devoted to spreading** the skills of jujitsu, the Brazilian marital art, for decades.
그레이시 가문은 수십 년 동안 브라질 무술인 주지츠(유술) 기술을 널리 퍼뜨리는 데 열정을 바쳐 왔다.

You might want to **devote** at least ten years **to** the work you are involved in if you want to be considered an expert.
전문가로 불리고 싶다면 적어도 십 년은 종사하는 분야에서 헌신적으로 일하는 것이 좋을 것입니다.

Not only students but also the professor **is opposed to** the tuition hike.
학생들뿐만 아니라 그 교수도 등록금 인상에 대해 반대한다.

The UN **contributed** $10 million **to** the earthquake fund.
유엔은 지진 성금으로 천만 달러를 기부했다.

This book **contributes** much **to** our **understanding** of the African continent.
이 책은 우리가 아프리카 대륙을 이해하는 데 크게 기여한다.

We are **looking forward to doing** business with you as soon as possible.
귀하와 가능한 한 빨리 거래를 시작하기를 고대합니다.

❷ 동사 take의 쓰임

> It takes + 시간 + for + 목적격 + to부정사
> = It takes + 목적어 + 시간 + to부정사
>
> ~을 하는 데 (얼마만큼의) 시간이 걸리다

It may **take** many years for the government **to crack** down on the corruption rampant in public office.
정부가 공직에 만연해 있는 부패를 척결하는 데 수년이 걸릴 수도 있다.

It **took** the company more than a year **to win** the bid.
회사가 입찰을 따내는 데 일 년이 넘게 걸렸다.

expect＋목적어＋to V 목적어가 ~하는 것을 예상하다

need＋목적어＋to V 목적어가 ~할 것을 필요로 하다

invite＋목적어＋to V 목적어가 ~하도록 초대하다

ask＋목적어＋to V 목적어가 ~할 것을 요청하다

encourage＋목적어＋to V 목적어가 ~하도록 장려하다

enable＋목적어＋to V 목적어가 ~하도록 가능케 하다

warn＋목적어＋to V 목적어가 ~하도록 경고하다

cause＋목적어＋to V 목적어가 ~하도록 야기하다

convince＋목적어＋to V 목적어가 ~하도록 납득시키다

remind＋목적어＋to V 목적어가 ~하도록 상기시키다

advise＋목적어＋to V 목적어가 ~하도록 조언하다

force＋목적어＋to V 목적어가 ~하도록 강요하다

allow＋목적어＋to V 목적어가 ~하도록 허용하다

persuade＋목적어＋to V 목적어가 ~하도록 설득하다

I **asked** one of my best friends **to lend** me some money.
나는 가장 친한 친구 중 한 명에게 돈을 빌려달라고 부탁했다.

Recent advances in computer technology have **allowed** the physically challenged **to choose** more options in the devices they use to communicate.
컴퓨터 기술이 최근 들어 발전하면서 장애인들이 의사소통하기 위해 사용하는 기계에 대한 선택의 폭이 더욱 넓어졌다.
▶ the physically challenged 신체장애가 있는

The police **warned** the suspect **to lay** down the weapon.
경찰은 용의자에게 무기를 내려놓으라고 경고했다.

The police finally succeeded in **persuading** the suspects **to give** themselves up.
경찰은 결국 용의자들이 자백하도록 설득하는 데 성공했다.
▶ give oneself up 자수하다; 항복하다

Slow music in department stores **encourages** shoppers **to spend** more money.
백화점에서 느린 음악이 나오면 구매자들은 돈을 더 많이 쓰게 된다.

The new technology is expected to **enable** doctors **to detect** cancer early.
그 신기술은 의사들로 하여금 암을 조기에 발견할 수 있게 해줄 것으로 기대된다.

Check-up TEST 20

Part I Choose the option that best completes each dialogue.

1 A: The manager counts the number of customers you _____ parts from IBM.
   B: Do I have to report the data on a daily basis?

   (a) convince to buy computer
   (b) convince buy computer
   (c) convince to buying computer
   (d) convince for buying computer

2 A: How do you like the video conference system your company purchased recently?
   B: It is great. The only downside is that _____ to master how to link up with all
      the attendees.

   (a) it took 40 minutes of me
   (b) I took 40 minutes
   (c) it took me 40 minutes
   (d) I took me 40 minutes

Part II Choose the option that best completes each sentence.

3 Our campaign is aimed at persuading as many people as possible _____ their
   right to vote.

   (a) to exercise
   (b) exercising
   (c) for exercising
   (d) exercise

4 We _____ our accomplishments this year since we have secured enough
   contracts to make profits for our shareholders and investors.

   (a) look forward to announce
   (b) look forward announcing
   (c) look forward announce
   (d) look forward to announcing

5 The board of directors couldn't _____ until the task force team came up with
   some solutions to address it.

   (a) continue the current impasse allow to
   (b) continue the current impasse to allow
   (c) allow the current impasse to continue
   (d) allow the current to continue impasse

Part III Read each dialogue or passage carefully and identify the option that contains a grammatical error.

6 (a) A: Alison is strongly opposed to admit Tony to the Anderson Church Committee.
(b) B: Alison is the only obstacle for Tony to overcome to become a member of the committee.
(c) A: The other people don't really have a reason to turn down Tony's application.
(d) B: You're right. Alison must be behind those who are against Tony joining the committee.

7 (a) A: How long do you think we have left before the world reaches the tipping point?
(b) B: Scientists say it will take only 20 years for the last glaciers on the Earth will disappear completely.
(c) A: That is a lot earlier than I had thought.
(d) B: Right. The reason is that melting glaciers expose the Earth's surface so that it absorbs more heat from the sun.

8 (a) A prenuptial agreement is a must-have for most couples planning to tie the knot. (b) The prenuptial enables for a couple to build trust and to increase their understanding of each other while eliminating the risk of mistakes and unpredictability. (c) According to a recent survey, almost half of all Canadian couples get divorced. (d) There are often legal battles over the assets that were accumulated during their marriages.

9 (a) The early years of my chairmanship at Texas University were littered with difficulties. (b) Thanks to the students, alumni, and faculty, who have been committed to realize a bright future for our university, I have been able to enhance the economic and social development of our university. (c) Our pursuit of academic prominence and research has contributed to the local community as well. (d) Texas University takes pride in meeting the academic needs of our citizens.

10 (a) The speed of digestion varies depending on people, and, for ordinary adults, it's usually between 24 and 72 hours. (b) After you eat, it takes about six to eight hours your stomach to process the food. (c) The food then goes to the colon, which digests the remaining food and absorbs water. (d) The removal of excess nutrition and food residue by the large intestine usually starts 24 hours after food has been eaten.

GP | 21 자동사로만 쓰이는 동사

□ **출제 경향** 자동사는 목적어를 취하지 않는다. 목적어를 취하려면 전치사를 먼저 동반해야 한다. 또한 자동사는 절대로 수동태로 사용될 수 없다. 이것이 TEPS의 문법 포인트이다.

❶ 시험에 빈출되는 자동사

appear 나타나다; ~처럼 보이다

happen[occur, take place] 발생하다

A result in B A로 인해 B라는 결과가 나오다

break out 발발하다, 발생하다

disappear 사라지다

exist 존재하다

A result from B B로 인해 A라는 결과가 나오다

remain ~인 상태이다

The supporters *were remained* unfazed and continued to pursue the plan to construct the landfill in the area. (×)

→ The supporters **remained** unfazed and continued to pursue their plan to construct the landfill in the area. (○)
지지자들은 꿈쩍하지 않고 그 지역에 쓰레기 매립지를 건설하는 계획을 계속해서 밀고 나갔다.

❷ 자동사와 전치사

특정 자동사의 경우 특정 전치사와 잘 어울려 쓰인다. 아래 목록은 다 외워야 한다.

account for ~을 설명하다; 차지하다

adjust to ~에 적응하다

agree with[to] ~에 동의하다

approve (of) ~을 승인하다

arrive at[in] ~에 도착하다

belong to ~에 속하다, 소속되다

complain of[about] ~에 대해 불평하다

comply with ~을 준수하다

consent to ~에 동의하다

consist of ~로 구성되다

converse with ~와 이야기를 나누다

deal with ~을 다루다

depend[rely/count] on ~을 의지하다, 기대다

experiment with ~에 관해 실험하다

graduate from ~을 졸업하다

happen to ~에게 발생하다

interfere with ~을 방해하다

look for ~을 찾다

look into ~을 조사하다

make up for ~을 보완하다, 메우다

refer to ~을 언급하다

reply to ~에 답변하다

respond to ~에 대응하다

rise to ~로 솟아오르다

sympathize with 상대방의 마음을 헤아리다

wait for ~을 기다리다

The scientists will **look into** a wide range of possible causes of the deaths of the amphibians.
과학자들은 양서류를 죽게 한 여러 있을 법한 원인에 대해 조사할 것이다.
▶ amphibian 양서류

Be careful when you **experiment with** chemical substances.
화학 물질에 관한 실험을 할 때는 조심해라.

I will **wait for** you until the end of my life.
나는 죽는 날까지 당신을 기다리겠습니다.

전치사를 취하지 않는 동사

□ **출제 경향** 타동사이지만 의미상 자동사처럼 보여서 전치사를 써야 할 것만 같은 동사가 있다. 그 때문에 실수를 하는 경우가 많으므로 다음의 혼동하기 쉬운 타동사 목록은 반드시 알아두어야 한다.

❶ 혼동하기 쉬운 타동사

alert people in the area (O) alert to people in the area (×)	지역 주민들에게 경고하다	explain the concept (O) explain about the concept (×)	그 개념을 설명하다
accompany friends (O) accompany with friends (×)	친구를 동반하다	greet the guest (O) greet to the guest (×)	손님을 환영하다
answer the question (O) answer with the question (×)	질문에 대답하다	jon the club (O) join in the club (×)	클럽에 가입하다
approach the station (O) approach to the station (×)	정류장에 접근하다	leave the house (O) leave from the house (×)	집을 떠나다
attend a conference (O) attend to a conference (×)	회의에 참석하다	marry a rich man (O) marry with a rich man (×)	부자와 결혼하다
await the delegation (O) await for the delegation (×)	임명을 기다리다	mention the report (O) mention about the report (×)	그 보도를 언급하다
contact the department (O) contact to the department (×)	부서에 연락하다	provide power (O) provide with the power (×)	전력을 공급하다
discuss the subject (O) discuss with the subject (×)	그 주제에 대해 토론하다	reach New York (O) reach to New York (×)	뉴욕에 도착하다
divorce her husband (O) divorce with her husband (×)	그녀의 남편과 이혼하다	resemble his father (O) resemble with his father (×)	그의 아버지와 닮다
enter the room (O) enter into the room (×)	그 방에 들어가다	sign the contract (O) sign in the contract (×)	계약서에 서명하다

It's time to **discuss** global warming, which is actually taking place around the world.
지금은 실제로 전 세계적으로 발생하고 있는 지구 온난화 문제에 대해서 이야기할 때이다.

Should you have any questions, **contact** the Customer Service Department.
문의 사항이 있으면 고객 서비스부로 연락 주십시오.

Would you **explain** the theory of relativity to me in an easy manner?
상대성 이론을 나에게 쉽게 설명해 줄래?
▶ relativity 상대성

The global population is expected to **reach** the 8 billion mark in 2080.
전 세계 인구가 2080년에 80억 명에 이를 것으로 예상된다.

Check-up TEST 21~22

Part I Choose the option that best completes each dialogue.

1 A: The Olympic torch will be _____ Rice Stadium at the University of Colorado tomorrow.

  B: Wow. Will we be able to watch the Olympic Games in a month?

  (a) reaching at
  (b) arriving at
  (c) arriving
  (d) reaching for

2 A: The global economy seems to be slipping into a deep recession.

  B: So economists _____ some ways to end the recession.

  (a) are discussing
  (b) are discussing about
  (c) are discussing on
  (d) are discussing with

3 A: Can you _____?

  B: Actually, I don't know either.

  (a) explain the concept to me
  (b) explain to me the concept
  (c) explain me to the concept
  (d) concept the explain to me

Part II Choose the option that best completes each sentence.

4 The question of what will be discussed at the meeting _____ the attitudes of the participants.

  (a) depends in
  (b) depends
  (c) depends for
  (d) depends on

5 Industrial goods often _____ material items, but they can also be services for people.

  (a) consist to
  (b) consist of
  (c) be consisted of
  (d) consist on

6   The mayor announced that the city accepted the green policy proposed by the governor, so the governor _____ him with a big hug after his speech.

(a) greeted
(b) greeted for
(c) greeted to
(d) has greeted

Part III Read each dialogue or passage carefully and identify the option that contains a grammatical error.

7   (a) A: Have you ever lost your baggage while traveling?
    (b) B: Yeah. It has happened to me three times.
    (c) A: That's terrible! Did you get it back?
    (d) B: Yes, but I had to await for my luggage.

8   (a) A: Are any more comfortable cabins available?
    (b) B: Sorry. This is our peak season.
    (c) A: I think we'll have to settle for the small cabin.
    (d) B: I'll contact to you if a large one is available tomorrow night.

9   (a) When a mountain range is seen from a distance, its peaks seem to rise the sky. (b) There seem to be no obstacles to hinder a person who would climb to the top. (c) But as you draw near, everything changes. (d) So is it with life.

10 (a) Cyber character assassination has reached at an alarming level. (b) Once an individual becomes a target online, a legion of netizens launches merciless attacks that leave the person hopeless and helpless. (c) Sadly, however, it has become commonplace in Korea, a country that prides itself on being a global IT powerhouse. (d) Recently, one high school girl ended her life after suffering from her schoolmates' false accusations.

Unit 3 분사

GP | 23 현재분사

□ **출제 경향** 분사는 매 회 시험에서 꼭 출제되고 있는데, Part I의 쉬운 문제에서부터 Part III의 어려운 문제에까지 다양한 난이도로 출제된다.

❶ 현재분사란?

(1) 동사에 –ing를 붙여 만든 형태이다.
(2) 명사와 분사의 관계가 능동의 성격을 띤다.
(3) '~하게 하는,' '~하는'으로 해석한다.
(4) 형용사 역할을 하고, 동사처럼 목적어 또는 보어를 취할 수 있다.

a taxi **carrying** four passengers 네 명의 승객을 태우고 있는 택시

soaring oil prices 치솟는 유가

due to **increasing** demand 증가하는 수요 때문에

a **challenging** task 힘든 과업

a **sleeping** baby 잠자는 아기

an **exciting** game 흥미진진한 경기

A **growing** number of people are learning English through the Internet.
점점 더 많은 사람들이 인터넷을 통해 영어를 배우고 있다.
→ 형용사 역할

The teacher saw Susie **cheating** on the test but let her continue to take the test.
선생님은 수지가 시험에서 부정행위하는 것을 보았지만 시험을 계속 보도록 했다.
→ 목적격 보어 역할

I was **taking** a shower when I heard a big noise.
큰 소음을 들었을 때 나는 샤워 중이었다.
→ 목적어 동반

GP | 24 과거분사

□ **출제 경향** 실제 시험에는 현재분사보다 과거분사의 출제 비율이 좀 더 높은 편이므로 잘 익혀두자.

❶ 과거분사란?

(1) 동사의 p.p. 형태이다.
(2) 명사와 분사의 관계가 수동의 성격을 띤다.
(3) '~되는,' '~된'으로 해석한다.
(4) 형용사 역할을 하고, 동사처럼 목적어 또는 보어를 취할 수 있다.

the **preferred** means 선호되는 수단

finished products 완제품(완성된 제품)

an **attached** document 첨부 문서(첨부된 문서)

an **excited** crowd 흥분한 군중

the books **ordered** online 온라인으로 주문된 책

a **broken** glass 깨진 유리

The Internet has become the **preferred** means when people learn English.
인터넷은 영어 학습 시에 선호되는 수단이 되었다.
→ 형용사 역할

The police had the terrorists **surrounded**.
그 테러리스트들은 경찰에 포위되었다.
→ 목적격 보어 역할

Many mountaineers have **lost** their lives when they tried to climb K2.
많은 산악인들이 K2를 등정하려다가 목숨을 잃었다.
→ 목적어 동반

The computer **delivered** two days ago turned out to be infected with viruses.
이틀 전에 배달된 컴퓨터가 바이러스에 걸려 있는 것으로 드러났다.
→ computer와 delivered 사이에 「관계대명사 + be동사」인 which was가 생략되었다.

Check-up TEST 23~24

Part I Choose the option that best completes each dialogue.

1 A: This printer does not work well.

   B: I can have it _____ right now.

   (a) fixing

   (b) fixed

   (c) fix

   (d) having fixed

2 A: Brad lost _____ that will be distributed to the executives at the yearly meeting.

   B: I think he is in trouble.

   (a) the attaching documents

   (b) the documents attaching

   (c) the attached documents

   (d) the documents attached

Part II Choose the option that best completes each sentence.

3 This novel is dedicated to the legacy of Admiral Lee, who was one of the greatest leaders _____ to the Korean people.

   (a) know

   (b) knowing

   (c) known

   (d) to know

4 The pianist, _____ in a better time, could get the best musical education in her country.

   (a) been born

   (b) having been

   (c) having born

   (d) born

5 Sandra _____ with the news that this year's bonus would be paid later due to the sudden economic slowdown.

   (a) became disappointing

   (b) became disappointed

   (c) became a disappointment

   (d) became to be disappointing

Part III Read each dialogue or passage carefully and identify the option that contains a grammatical error.

6   (a) A: Laura just gave me an invitation welcomed all of her friends to the wedding reception.
    (b) B: I wish I could go with you, but I have to watch my baby.
    (c) A: Can your mother babysit John just for a day?
    (d) B: In fact, I don't like Laura. She annoyed me all the time when we were in college.

7   (a) A: Can you believe the Lotte Giants lost again?
    (b) B: I don't know when the team will win again.
    (c) A: Yeah. I was hoping to see the team pulled off a win tonight.
    (d) B: They seemed like they were going to be invincible before the season started.

8   (a) A: Can you go to Miranda's housewarming party tonight?
    (b) B: I really want to go there, but I have to get my report doing first.
    (c) A: Okay. Next time, I hope you can go with us.
    (d) B: I really hope that I can do that.

9   (a) Although I once loved the teachings of my father, I confess I have never looked upon money as a form of enslavement. (b) I always feel rewarding when I make money for the services that I provide to my clients. (c) To be able to take a taxi instead of a bus is good for me. (d) Money is essential in my life, and I don't see it as useless.

10 (a) Autumn is my favorite season and many people like it, too. (b) Most of the trees change colors and shed their leaves, and falling leaves are everywhere on the streets. (c) Farmers are busy harvesting crops in the fields, and orchards are beautiful with ripe apples and persimmons. (d) Autumn is said to be a good season for reading.

GP | 25 분사구문

□ **출제 경향** 종속절과 주절에서 반복되는 부분을 없애기 위해 종속절을 분사로 시작하는 간단한 형태로 만드는데, 이를 분사구문이라고 한다. 분사구문의 개념을 이해하면 가장 기본적인 분사구문의 형태를 묻는 문제를 쉽게 풀 수 있다.

❶ 종속절의 주어와 주절의 주어가 같을 때

(1) 종속절의 접속사를 삭제한다.

(2) 종속절의 주어를 삭제한다.

(3) 종속절의 동사를 V-ing 형태로 쓴다. 분사의 형태가 being이면 생략할 수 있다.

If you turn left, you will find the police station on your left.

→ **Turning** left, you will find the police station on your left.

왼쪽으로 돌면 왼쪽 편에 경찰서가 있을 겁니다.

Because he was praised by his immediate supervisor, James felt very happy to work for him.

→ Being **praised** by his immediate supervisor, James felt very happy to work for him.

→ **Praised** by his immediate supervisor, James felt very happy to work for him.

직속상관에게서 칭찬을 들었기 때문에, 제임스는 그와 일하는 것이 매우 좋다고 느꼈다.

→ 현재분사의 형태가 being이면 생략할 수 있는데, 분사구문은 과거분사의 형태가 된다.

❷ 종속절의 주어와 주절의 주어가 같지 않을 때

(1) 종속절의 접속사를 삭제한다.

(2) 주절과 종속절의 주어가 다를 때는 종속절의 주어를 삭제하지 않고 남겨둔다.

(3) 종속절의 동사를 V-ing 형태로 쓴다. 분사의 형태가 being이면 생략할 수 있다.

As the book was written approximately 1,000 years ago, the historians were wrestling with the illegible letters.

→ **The book (being) written** approximately 1,000 years ago, the historians were wrestling with the illegible letters.

그 책은 약 천 년 전에 쓰여졌기 때문에 역사학자들은 읽기 힘든 글자를 파악하느라 고군분투했다.

→ 접속사가 있는 종속절의 주어가 the book이고 주절의 주어는 the historians로 서로 다르기 때문에 분사구문으로 만들 때 두 주어를 반드시 살려야 한다. being이 생략되어 과거분사의 형태가 되었다.

Since the party ended very late, the guests couldn't find any means of public transportation to get home.

→ **The party ending** very late, the guests couldn't find any means of public transportation to get home.

파티가 매우 늦게 끝나서 손님들은 집으로 갈 교통수단을 찾을 수가 없었다.

→ 접속사 since를 지운다. 종속절의 주어가 the party이고 주절의 주어는 the guests로 서로 다르므로 종속절의 주어를 살려야 한다. end는 '끝나다'라는 능동 개념으로 쓰인 자동사이므로 ending으로 표시해야 한다.

분사구문의 시제와 부정

□ **출제 경향** 분사구문의 시제와 태를 파악하여 종합적으로 묻는 문제가 출제된다. 또한 분사구문을 부정할 때는 부정어인 not이나 never를 분사 바로 앞에 두면 되는데, 이 포인트가 잘 출제되고 있다.

1 분사구문의 시제

분사구문을 만들 때 종속절의 시제가 주절의 동사보다 한 시제 앞설 경우에는 having p.p.(능동일 경우) 또는 having been p.p.(수동일 경우)로 표시한다.

Because Tom <u>felt</u> very proud of his accomplishments, Tom <u>decided</u> to ask for a raise.

= **Feeling** very proud of his accomplishments, Tom **decided** to ask for a raise.

탐은 자기가 이루어낸 업적이 매우 자랑스러웠으므로 급여 인상을 요청하기로 결심했다.

→ feeling의 시제와 decided의 시제가 과거로 같다.

Because the child <u>had been raised</u> in a family of Buddhists, the teacher couldn't force him to say a prayer before each meal at school.

= The child **having been raised** in a family of Buddhists, the teacher **couldn't force** him to say a prayer before each meal at school.

그 아이는 불교도 집안에서 성장했기 때문에 선생님은 그 아이에게 학교에서 매 식사 전에 기도하라고 강요할 수 없었다.

→ 학교에서 있었던 일보다 불교 집안에서 성장했던 것이 더 먼저 일어난 일이므로 시제 차이가 있다.

2 분사구문의 부정

분사구문을 부정하여 not이나 never가 문두에 위치하게 되면 일반적으로 '~않기 때문에'라는 '이유'의 의미로 해석되는 경우가 많다. 다음 예문들도 사실상 인과관계를 의미하고 있다고 할 수 있다.

Not knowing what to do when she approached, I just closed my eyes.

그녀가 다가왔을 때 무엇을 해야 될지 몰라서 나는 그냥 눈을 감아버렸다.

Never impressed by his artwork, the curator decided not to extend his contract.

그의 작품에서 깊은 인상을 전혀 받지 못한 큐레이터는 그와의 계약을 연장하지 않기로 결심했다.

Never having followed my inner voice before, I am now doing a job I don't like.

내면의 목소리를 따른 적이 없기 때문에, 지금 나는 좋아하지도 않는 일을 하고 있다.

Not having been persuaded to purchase a life insurance policy, I now regret not buying it.

생명 보험에 들라는 설득에 넘어가지 않았었는데, 지금은 보험을 가입하지 않은 것이 후회가 된다.

▶ life insurance policy 생명 보험 증서

Part I Choose the option that best completes each dialogue.

1 A: At last, Dr. Lee has found the key to analyzing the DNA sequence of the primate recently discovered in Africa.

   B: _____ a distinguished geneticist, he will win the Nobel Prize in the near future.

   (a) Having been
   (b) Is
   (c) Being
   (d) Was

2 A: John, do you have any plans for your summer vacation coming up next week?

   B: _____ a new project three days ago, I'm now considering whether to postpone my vacation or not.

   (a) Given
   (b) Having been given
   (c) Giving
   (d) Having given

3 A: _____, the country is now out of control.
   B: Other countries should hurry and offer assistance to the nation.

   (a) Done hit by a devastating earthquake
   (b) Hit by a devastating earthquake
   (c) Hitted by a devastating earthquake
   (d) Hitting by a devastating earthquake

Part II Choose the option that best completes each sentence.

4 _____ by her friends and family members, Tiffany felt relieved to know that she was not in danger anymore.

   (a) Surround
   (b) Surrounding
   (c) Surrounded
   (d) To surround

5 _____ the wages of his employees, the president of MF Technology is praised
 by his employees but criticized by the company's shareholders.

 (a) Never been cut
 (b) Never cut
 (c) Never cutting
 (d) Never having been cut

6 _____ so many times by unpleasant news such as assassinations, political
 wrangling, human trafficking, and war, I practically felt immune to any bad news.

 (a) shocking
 (b) shocked
 (c) Having shocked
 (d) Having been shocked

Part III Read each dialogue or passage carefully and identify the option that contains a grammatical error.

7 (a) A: As usual, Mr. Chun wasn't listening to what the others were saying.
 (b) B: But the thing is that he always comes up with creative solutions to our urgent
   concerns. Today was no exception.
 (c) A: Experienced cases like today's so many times, he's totally dependable.
 (d) B: Maybe that's why he doesn't get left out of any meetings.

8 (a) A: Hey, Joe. I heard your son got a job. Congratulations!
 (b) B: Thank you. I was very nervous when he had his job interview two days ago.
 (c) A: The market been so tight, it is very hard for job applicants to get decent jobs.
 (d) B: I think we adults should do something about this. We can't leave this to fate.

9 (a) A: How was the party last night? I heard it was fun.
 (b) B: Not so fun. I should have gone to the other party that was held in Springfield.
 (c) A: Why? The party was hosted by Miranda, the most celebrated socialite in our town.
 (d) B: Having not hosted a party before, she was slow to meet the needs of the partygoers.

10 (a) The Hubble Space Telescope is a telescope currently in orbit. (b) The first not space
 telescope, it may be one of the most versatile and famous telescopes in history. (c) It
 was launched into orbit in 1990 and has been operational since then. (d) The telescope is
 expected to function until 2018, and its successor — the James Webb Space Telescope —
 will take its place.

□ **출제 경향** 종속절의 주어가 일반인인 경우에는 주절의 주어와 다르더라도 생략한 후 관용표현처럼 쓰는데, 이러한 분사구문을 (비인칭) 독립분사구문이라고 한다. 이런 표현들은 그냥 외워두기만 해도 쉽게 해결되는 부분이다. TEPS 문법은 물론 청해, 독해 영역에 다 출제되니 확실히 알아두자.

❶ 시험에 자주 출제되는 독립분사구문

compared with　~을 비교하면, ~에 비해

all things considered　모든 것을 고려해 봤을 때

taking all things into consideration　모든 것을 고려하면

considering that + 주어 + 동사　~라는 점을 고려해봤을 때

given that + 주어 + 동사　~라는 점을 고려해봤을 때

generally speaking　일반적으로 말해서

frankly speaking　솔직히 말해서

granting that + 주어 + 동사　~라는 점을 인정한다 하더라도, 설사 ~라 할지라도

judging from　~으로 판단하건대

provided[providing] (that)　~라면

roughly speaking　대충 말해서

speaking of　~에 대해 말이 나온 김에, ~에 관해서 말한다면

speaking of which　(앞에서 말한 내용이) 나온 김에

strictly speaking　엄밀히 말해서

supposing + 주어 + 동사　만약 ~라면

weather permitting　날씨가 좋으면

Granting that he was drunk, I can't understand why he made such a stupid mistake.
술에 취했었다 하더라도 그가 왜 그런 멍청한 실수를 저질렀는지 이해할 수 없다.

Speaking of Susan, I haven't seen her lately.
수잔 얘기가 나왔으니 말인데, 난 최근에 그 애를 본 적이 없어.

Roughly speaking, I earn one million won a month.
난 한 달에 얼추 백만 원 벌어.

Taking all things into consideration, it seems that my health is worsening.
모든 것을 종합해 봤을 때 내 건강이 악화되고 있는 것 같아.

Part I Choose the option that best completes each dialogue.

1 A: Jane and Jason will get married soon.

   B: _____, Mark and Sophia will tie the knot, too.

   (a) Speaking
   (b) Speaking of
   (c) Speaking of which
   (d) To speak of which

2 A: _____ into consideration, I'll call her and say I'm not going to play her mind games anymore.

   B: Good for you. You have nothing to lose.

   (a) Taken all things
   (b) Taking all things
   (c) Being taking all things
   (d) Having been taken all things

Part II Choose the option that best completes each sentence.

3 _____ you didn't get this month's wages, you must pay your mortgage by tomorrow, or you'll lose your home.

   (a) Grant
   (b) Granting that
   (c) Have granted that
   (d) Having been granting that

Part III Read each dialogue or passage carefully and identify the option that contains a grammatical error.

4 (a) A: Why are you so aggressive now? You don't need to be so harsh toward her.
   (b) B: She didn't finish her daily assignment. That's all.
   (c) A: But she was crying.
   (d) B: Frankly spoken, that does not concern me at all.

5 (a) It was another Monday morning when two 17-year-old boys embarked on a shooting rampage at their high school. (b) 7 students and one teacher were killed, and 23 students were wounded. (c) Two years after that event, the school was doing fairly well, all things considering. (d) But the scars left by the disaster are still visible among the survivors.

관계사

GP | 28 관계대명사의 선행사

□ **출제 경향** 관계대명사 문제는 모든 영어 시험에 절대 빠지지 않고 등장한다. TEPS에서는 거의 평균 1~2문제 가량 출제되고 있다. 보통 기초만 확실히 잡으면 가뿐하게 맞출 수 있는 수준으로 나온다.

❶ 선행사가 사람일 때

■ **주격 역할을 할 때**

Charles is a self-taught and self-made artist **who** has been developing his artistic and photographic skills for close to 40 years.
찰스는 40년 가까이 자신의 미술 기교와 사진 기술을 발전시켜 온, 독학으로 자수성가한 예술가이다.

■ **소유격 역할을 할 때**

Is there any student **whose** name hasn't been called? 이름이 불리지 않은 학생이 있나요?

■ **목적격 역할을 할 때**

He is a world-class film director **whom** people around the world respect.
그는 전 세계인들이 존경하는 세계적인 영화감독이다.

■ **those who[that] ~하는 사람들**

Those who wish to go to the Amazon rainforest have to get vaccinated first.
아마존 열대우림에 가려는 사람들은 먼저 예방 접종부터 받아야 한다.

❷ 선행사가 사물일 때

■ **주격 역할을 할 때**

It's time for the government to implement the program to help the poor **which** has been around for decades. 지금은 정부가 빈민층을 돕기 위한 수십 년간 존속돼 왔던 프로그램을 시행할 때이다.

■ **소유격 역할을 할 때**

The poet is famous for his poems **whose** meanings are hard to understand.

= The poet is famous for his poems **the meanings of which** are hard to understand.
그 시인은 의미를 이해하기 힘든 시들로 유명하다.
→ 관계대명사 whose 앞에 사물인 선행사 poems가 있고, whose 뒤의 명사 meanings는 poems와 소유 관계이다. 이와 같이 선행사가 사물이고 소유격일 때 of which를 사용할 수도 있다.

■ **목적격 역할을 할 때**

The new technology **which** the research center is developing is expected to have a major impact on the industry.
연구 센터가 개발 중인 그 신기술은 그 업계에 큰 영향을 미칠 것으로 예상된다.

GP | 29 선행사와 동사의 수 일치

□ **출제 경향** 관계대명사가 사용될 때는 선행사와 관계대명사절에 속해 있는 동사의 수를 일치시켜야 한다. 따라서 관계대명사가 사용된 문장을 보면 기본적으로 선행사가 무엇인지, 관계대명사의 무슨 격 역할을 하는지, 선행사의 수는 단수인지 복수인지 등을 재빨리 파악해낼 수 있어야 한다.

다음 문장에서 틀린 부분을 찾아보자.

I have never seen such a good movie which were released just a week ago.
나는 일주일 전에 개봉된 그 영화만큼 훌륭한 영화를 본 적이 없다.
→ 위 문장에서 관계대명사 which의 선행사는 a good movie로 단수 명사인데 동사가 were, 즉 복수로 사용되었다. 따라서 were를 was로 바꿔야 한다.

The new changes may be unfortunate for some of the students who wishes to become a surgeon.
외과 의사가 되고 싶어 하는 일부 학생들에게 그 새로운 변화는 불운한 것일 수도 있다.
→ 위 문장에서는 관계대명사 who의 선행사가 some of the students로 복수인데 동사가 wishes, 즉 단수 형태로 사용되었으므로 틀린 문장이다. wish로 바꿔야 한다.

A Ferrari that are parked right next to St. Regis is surrounded by numerous passers-by.
세인트 레지스 레스토랑 바로 옆에 주차되어 있는 페라리 한 대가 많은 행인들에게 둘러싸여 있다.
→ that의 선행사가 '페라리 차 한 대(A Ferrari)'이므로 동사를 are parked가 아니라 is parked로 바꿔야 한다.

Part I Choose the option that best completes each dialogue.

1 A: To whom would you like to give these gift cards?

B: _____ pass my test will get them although I doubt anyone will do that.

(a) He that

(b) Those which

(c) Those who

(d) Those whom

2 A: Is there anybody _____ I haven't called on yet?

B: No. You called on everyone in this class.

(a) who

(b) whose

(c) that

(d) which

3 A: What do you think about the new CEO _____ a pay hike?

B: I doubt that he will keep his word.

(a) who promise

(b) who promises

(c) who were promising

(d) who promising

Part II Choose the option that best completes each sentence.

4 Michael Kim is a talented programmer _____ programming skills have been the subject of veneration among his coworkers.

(a) whose

(b) who

(c) which

(d) what

5 My professor told the students that they should buy some books _____ the Battle of Kursk.

(a) which describes

(b) which describe

(c) which were described

(d) which was described

6   The school is planning to provide the students _____ to study abroad with online study materials.

   (a) who wanted
   (b) who wants
   (c) who want
   (d) want

Part III **Read each dialogue or passage carefully and identify the option that contains a grammatical error.**

7   (a) A: My brother has changed jobs again.
   (b) B: Again? I heard he got a job just one month ago.
   (c) A: Yes. But he said there is another job which suit him best.
   (d) B: He doesn't seem able to hold down a job.

8   (a) A: Did you know that the band is having a concert next week?
   (b) B: Yes. I cannot wait to see the concert. I've already reserved a ticket.
   (c) A: I think the band has a great vocalist that voice is amazing.
   (d) B: You can say that again. I wish I had such a beautiful voice.

9   (a) Today, a government agency is planning to release the results of its most recent study into the psychological well-being of underprivileged children. (b) The study was conducted in order to determine how, if at all, children growing up in deprived conditions are affected psychologically. (c) The study was conducted over a period of three years. (d) In addition, more than 1,000 children whom ages varied from five to seventeen were the subjects of the study.

10 (a) Spam email is the practice of indiscriminately sending unsolicited and unwanted messages. (b) Spam emails, which sometimes carries worms and viruses, have been problematic since the Internet became popular in the mid 1990s. (c) Since sending spam emails costs virtually nothing, spammers are numerous, and it is estimated that about 85% of all email in the world is considered spam. (d) Internet service providers should be equipped with extra security functions to deal with the exponentially increasing amount of spam.

GP | 30 관계대명사와 전치사

□ **출제 경향** 관계대명사와 전치사 문제는 다소 까다로운 편으로, 실제 시험에 이 문제가 나오면 정답률이 매우 낮다. 관계대명사 뒤에 나오는 내용을 파악하여 숨어 있는 전치사까지 찾아내야 하기 때문에 문장을 면밀히 분석하는 것이 필요하다.

다음 문장에서 틀린 부분을 찾아보자.

Michael is the friend whom we stayed in the U.S. for three weeks.
마이클은 우리가 미국에서 3주간 함께 보낸 친구이다.

→ 관계대명사 whom 앞의 선행사 the friend는 사람이고 whom 뒤의 동사 stay는 목적어를 취할 수 없는 자동사이다. 문맥상 '미국에서 3주간 같이 보내다'라는 뜻이 되어야 하므로 '~와 함께, ~와 같이'라는 뜻을 지닌 전치사 with를 써야 한다.

Michael is the friend **with whom** we stayed in the U.S. for three weeks.

= Michael is the friend **whom** we stayed **with** in the U.S. for three weeks.

= Michael is the friend **that** we stayed **with** in the U.S. for three weeks.

GP | 31 관계대명사 삽입절

□ **출제 경향** 관계대명사절 내 삽입절의 역할을 묻는 문제가 종종 출제되므로 문법적 지식을 갖추고 있어야 함은 물론, 문장의 내용도 파악할 줄 알아야 한다.

다음 문장이 맞는 문장인지 그렇지 않은 문장인지 살펴보자.

I met Larry Page, one of the founders of Google, who I thought was a very extraordinary man.
나는 구글의 창업주 중 한 명인 래리 페이지를 만났는데, 내 생각에, 그는 매우 비범한 사람이었다.

→ 위 문장의 선행사는 Larry Page라는 사람이고, 주격 관계대명사인 who가 사용되었으며, 그 뒤로 동사 was가 나왔다. I thought은 단순한 삽입절로서, 있으나 없으나 전체 문장 구조에는 별 영향을 미치지 못한다.

다음 문장이 맞는 문장인지 그렇지 않은 문장인지 살펴보자.

I met Larry Page, one of the founders of Google, whom I thought to be extraordinary.
나는 내가 비범한 사람일 거라고 생각하는 구글의 창업주 중 한 명인 래리 페이지를 만났다.

→ 위 문장에서 I thought는 삽입절인가? 그렇지 않다. I thought Larry Page, one of the founders of Google, to be extraordinary에서 Larry Page, one of the founders of Google을 선행사로 빼버린 것이며, whom은 목적격 관계대명사이다.

GP | 32 관계대명사 what

□ **출제 경향** 관계대명사 what은 Part III에 잘 출제되는 문법 포인트이다. what을 써야 할 자리에 that을 쓰거나 that을 써야 할 자리에 what을 쓰고 틀린 부분을 찾으라고 하는 문제가 빈번히 출제된다.

1 관계대명사 what의 특징

(1) 선행사가 what 안에 포함되어 있다.
(2) '~하는[한] 것'으로 해석한다.
(3) 주격, 목적격 역할을 하며, 소유격은 없다.
(4) 보어의 역할도 한다.

관계대명사 what 안에는 선행사가 포함되어 있기 때문에 what 뒤에 불완전한 문장이 온다는 점을 생각하면 문제를 쉽게 풀 수 있다.

What the presidential candidate said during the election campaign turned out to be wrong.
선거 유세 기간 동안에 그 대선 후보자가 한 말은 거짓으로 드러났다.
→ 주격 역할

Don't put off till tomorrow **what** you can do today.
오늘 할 수 있는 일을 내일로 미루지 마라.
→ 목적격 역할

Not the company's reputation but its profits are **what** you have to take into consideration.
당신이 고려해야 하는 것은 회사의 명성이 아니라 수익이다.
→ 보어 역할

Part I Choose the option that best completes each dialogue.

1 A: Is the position _____ Mr. Seo applied still available? If so, I'll also apply for it.
   B: I'm sorry, but they announced yesterday that he would get the job.

   (a) which for
   (b) which
   (c) to which
   (d) for which

2 A: Bottoms up!
   B: Hey, don't let others do _____ you can't do.

   (a) that
   (b) what
   (c) which
   (d) whom

3 A: Stephanie is really arrogant. What do you think about her?
   B: She is the woman _____ lacking in respect for others.

   (a) who I believe is
   (b) whom I believe is
   (c) who I is believe
   (d) whom is I believe

Part II Choose the option that best completes each sentence.

4 When Mark finished the book _____ he had been working for almost a year, he felt like he was walking on air.

   (a) on which
   (b) which
   (c) for which
   (d) to which

5 Mr. Oh sends most of his salary to his wife and daughter in the U.S. except for _____ he needs to survive.

   (a) that
   (b) which
   (c) what
   (d) who

6 Sir Spencer Crystal, _____ as an extraordinary teacher, has passed away.

   (a) whom I remember

   (b) who I remember

   (c) I remember whom

   (d) I remember who

Part III **Read each dialogue or passage carefully and identify the option that contains a grammatical error.**

7 (a) A: Is your sister still playing video games?

   (b) B: Yes. She spends at least 10 hours a day on gaming and won't listen when I tell her to stop.

   (c) A: What is the name of the game which she is addicted?

   (d) B: It's *World of Wars*! Her gaming is getting out of hand, and I don't know what to do.

8 (a) A: Which I said yesterday wasn't my real opinion.

   (b) B: Really? I thought you had changed your mind yesterday.

   (c) A: Of course, I was somewhat swayed by her opinion. But that doesn't mean I agreed with her.

   (d) B: You shouldn't have made those foolish remarks yesterday. Now she is taking full advantage of your mistake.

9 (a) Joanna had planned to marry her fiancé — the man to who she was engaged — when he got home on Thursday. (b) Her future husband Brian boarded a plane to return home on Monday. (c) But, not long after the plane took off, it crashed due to mechanical malfunction and everyone in it was killed. (d) To her dismay, she had to wear a funeral dress instead of a wedding dress.

10 (a) Katherine and her husband Gilbert were accused of abusing their foster child. (b) The police found Jason, their two-year-old boy, had been brutally beaten, so they charged the couple with child abuse and battery. (c) They are blaming each other and claiming which the police say isn't true. (d) But the police say that they are guilty and that they should be punished.

□ **출제 경향** 관계대명사에는 바로 앞에 있는 명사를 수식하는 한정적 용법이 있고, 앞의 명사에 대해서 부가적으로 설명하는 계속적 용법이 있다. 시험에는 Part III에 관계대명사가 계속적 용법으로 사용된 문장에서, which가 쓰여야 할 자리에 that을 두고 틀린 부분을 찾으라고 하는 문제가 주로 출제된다. 관계대명사의 한정적 용법과 계속적 용법의 차이에 대해 명확하게 알아두자.

❶ 한정적 용법: 의미의 제한

Michael has two bestselling books **which** have sold more than one million copies.
마이클에겐 백만 부 이상 팔린 베스트셀러가 두 권 있다.
→ 마이클이 출판한 다른 책이 더 있을 수 있다.

❷ 계속적 용법: 선행사에 대한 부가 설명

Michael has two bestselling books, **which** have sold more than one million copies.
마이클에겐 두 권의 베스트셀러가 있는데, 그 책들은 백만 부 이상 팔렸다.
→ 마이클이 출판한 책은 두 권뿐이다.

※ 관계대명사가 계속적 용법으로 사용되면 that을 쓸 수 없고 which만 쓸 수 있다. 시험에 특히 빈출되는 포인트이니 꼭 기억해 두자.

Jason was so drunk and made such a stupid mistake at the party, *that* let down everyone. (×)

→ Jason was so drunk and made such a stupid mistake at the party, **which** let down everyone. (○)
제이슨은 너무 취한 나머지 파티에서 멍청한 실수를 했고, 모든 사람들을 실망시켰다.

GP 34 복합 관계대명사

□ **출제 경향** 복합관계대명사는 문장 내에서 부사 역할을 할 수 있고 주어나 목적어, 또는 보어 역할을 할 수도 있다. 세 가지 복합관계대명사 whatever / who(m)ever / whichever를 잘 알아두도록 하자. whichever와 whatever는 시험에 자주 출제되고 있는데, 오답률도 비교적 높은 편이다. 이 둘의 구분은 쉽지 않지만, whichever는 (주어진 범위 내에서) '선택'의 개념이고 whatever는 '내용'의 개념임을 생각하면 좀 더 수월하게 답을 찾을 수 있다.

❶ whatever: 무엇이든[무엇을] ~하든 상관없이

Whatever was discussed in the meeting, the two parties couldn't reach a compromise on the M&A.

회의에서 무엇이 논의되었건 간에 양측은 인수 합병에 대한 타협에 이를 수 없었다.

→ 부사 역할

At age 40, I regret not having followed **whatever** my heart says.

내 나이 40세에, 내 가슴이 하는 말이 무엇이든지 간에 따르지 않았던 것이 후회가 된다.

→ 목적격 역할

❷ who(m)ever: 누구든[누구를] ~하든 상관없이

Whoever runs for the presidency, the Democratic Party's candidate will surely fail to get elected.

누가 대통령직에 출마하든지 간에 민주당 후보자는 이번 선거에서 분명 낙선할 것이다.

→ 부사 역할

Whoever comes to the party is sincerely welcome.

파티에 오시는 분이 누구든 진심으로 환영하는 바입니다.

→ 주격 역할

Nowadays, you can marry **whomever** you want to.

오늘날, 사람들은 누구든 자기가 원하는 사람과 결혼할 수 있다.

→ 목적격 역할

❸ whichever: 어느 것이[어느 것을] ~하든 상관없이

Whichever mode of transportation you take, it will take you an hour to get there.

어떤 교통수단을 사용할지라도 목적지까지 한 시간은 걸릴 것이다.

→ 부사 역할

You can have **whichever** you like—the bestselling book or the unknown book.

그 베스트셀러든 저 유명하지 않은 책이든 네가 좋아하는 것으로 아무거나 가져도 돼.

→ 목적격 역할

Part I Choose the option that best completes each dialogue.

1 A: I've never been loved by _____ I've loved.
   B: Cheer up. You'll find your soulmate soon.

   (a) whatever
   (b) however
   (c) whoever
   (d) whomever

2 A: What a bunch of fruit on the table!
   B: Pick _____ you like.

   (a) whoever
   (b) whatever
   (c) whichever
   (d) whomever

Part II Choose the option that best completes each sentence.

3 _____ happens, he always gets up at six and takes a walk for 30 minutes.

   (a) Whoever
   (b) Whomever
   (c) Whichever
   (d) Whatever

4 The R&D center is issuing the visitors identification cards, _____ they have to wear the entire time that they are within the premises.

   (a) that
   (b) what
   (c) who
   (d) which

5 I was driving down the road, _____ ran parallel to the river.

   (a) which
   (b) that
   (c) what
   (d) who

Part III Read each dialogue or passage carefully and identify the option that contains a grammatical error.

6 (a) A: What is that tall building with the black banners on it?
   (b) B: Do you mean the 30-story building in front of us?
   (c) A: Yes. I didn't know that there was such a tall building in the city.
   (d) B: That's the Barrel Building, that was built a year ago when you were doing your military service.

7 (a) A: Ken, why are you tuning me out?
   (b) B: I'm not doing that. There must be some sort of a misunderstanding.
   (c) A: But you haven't answered my emails for the past two weeks.
   (d) B: No way. I always answer whichever email I receive.

8 (a) Curotian was a town located in the middle of the nation. (b) It was founded as a fortress, that was built in three weeks over two hundred years ago. (c) As soon as the fortress was established, the Russian army invaded the town and destroyed it. (d) Only documents remain that prove the town once existed.

9 (a) Convair was an American aircraft manufacturing company. (b) It was a pioneer of several aircraft, including delta-winged aircraft. (c) In addition to this, it developed large vacuum tubes, that were the precursors of CRT computer displays. (d) In the 1950s Convair shifted money and effort to its missile and rocket projects for the US Navy.

10 (a) An adulterer was brought into Jesus. (b) The people said she should be stoned and asked Jesus what he would do. (c) He told the crowd, "Let whomever is without sin cast the first stone." (d) Aware that they were not perfect, they went out one by one, and Jesus and the woman were left alone.

□ **출제 경향** 관계부사는 아주 자주는 아니지만 간간이 출제되고, 무엇보다 청해나 독해와도 연관이 있기 때문에 실제 예문들을 통해 쓰임을 잘 공부해두는 것이 좋다.

❶ 선행사에 따른 관계부사

관계부사는 앞, 뒤 문장을 연결시켜 주는 접속사적 성격을 띠는 동시에, 뒷문장에서 빠진 부사적 역할을 대신하기 때문에 부사적 성격도 띤다. 따라서 「접속사＋부사」의 성격이 강하다. 선행사가 무엇이냐에 따라 다음과 같은 관계부사를 사용할 수 있다.

선행사가 장소	선행사가 시간	선행사가 이유	선행사가 방법	선행사와 상관없이
where	when	why	how	that을 두루 사용

I still remember the bookstore **where** I first met Tom Cruise.
나는 톰 크루즈를 처음 만났던 서점을 아직도 기억한다.

= I still remember the place. + I first met Tom Cruise **at the bookstore**.

→ 관계부사도 부사이다. at the bookstore의 at이 맨 위 문장의 where에 들어가 있는 셈이다.

= I still remember the bookstore **that** I first met Tom Cruise **at**.

I miss the good old days **when** my best friend Minsu and I used to hang out together.
나는 가장 친한 친구인 민수랑 함께 어울려 다녔던 그 좋았던 옛 시절이 그립다.

= I miss the good old days. + My best friend Minsu and I used to hang out together **in the good old days**.

→ 시간 선행사 the good old days가 있고, 전치사 in은 관계부사 when 안에 포함돼 있는 셈이다.

= I miss the good old days **that** my best friend Minsu and I used to hang out together.

= I miss the good old days **during which** my best friend Minsu and I used to hang out together.

I don't know the reason **why** he didn't show up.
나는 그가 나타나지 않은 이유를 모르겠다.

= I don't know the reason. + He didn't show up **for the reason**.

→ 선행사 the reason이 '이유'를 나타내므로 관계부사 why로 받은 것이다.

= I don't know **the reason that** he didn't show up.

It's really difficult for me to understand **the way** the scoring system works.
점수 체계가 어떻게 돌아가는 것인지 나로서는 이해하기가 매우 힘들다.

= It's really difficult for me to understand the scoring system. + The scoring system works **in the way**.

= It's really difficult for me to understand **how** the scoring system works.

= It's really difficult for me to understand **the way that** the scoring system works.

≠ It's really difficult for me to understand *the way how* the scoring system works. (×)

→ 선행사가 '방법'일 때 선행사와 how를 같이 쓸 수 없다. 즉, the way how처럼 쓸 수는 없다.

Part I Choose the option that best completes each dialogue.

1   A: Do you still remember the day we first met?

B: Definitely. It was the day _____ my life completely changed.

(a) where
(b) which
(c) when
(d) why

Part II Choose the option that best completes each sentence.

2   The reason _____ she suddenly disappeared for a week and appeared again as if nothing had happened was a mystery to me.

(a) when
(b) why
(c) where
(d) which

3   It's hard to predict when the economy will grow again at a time _____ oil prices are soaring.

(a) what
(b) who
(c) how
(d) when

Part III Read each dialogue or passage carefully and identify the option that contains a grammatical error.

4   (a) A: Are you all right? You look pretty tired.
(b) B: I'm just not used to the new management program which our firm has adopted.
(c) A: May I give you some general information about what the program works?
(d) B: Thank you. That would be great.

5   (a) A 16-year-old boy was abducted by masked villains in front of the school. (b) When the police investigated this case, however, there was an ugly truth that shocked the entire country. (c) The boy had conspired with his friends to skip their classes and had staged the abduction. (d) Eventually, the police discovered the place which he and his friends, the coconspirators, were hiding from everyone.

Unit 5 능동과 수동

GP | 36 능동과 수동 파악하기

□ **출제 경향** TEPS 문법 Part III에서는 능동·수동의 의미를 묻는 문제가 반드시 출제된다. 그런데 흔히 알고 있는 crying baby와 같이 단순한 능동·수동의 의미를 묻는 문제가 아니라, 한 문장 혹은 한 단락 전체의 내용을 꿰뚫어야 능동인지 수동인지 파악할 수 있는 다소 어려운 문제가 출제되는 편이다. 즉, 문맥을 통해 파악할 수 있어야 한다.

다음 문장을 보고 무엇이 잘못되었는지 찾아보자.

Police have arrested Taliban operatives for smuggling chemical agents *using* for drug production in Afghanistan.
경찰은 아프가니스탄에서 마약 제조에 사용되는 화학 원료를 밀수한 혐의로 탈레반 첩보원을 체포했다.
→ 화학 원료는 마약 제조를 위해서 '사용되는 것'이지 화학 원료가 능동적으로 무엇을 어떻게 할 수 있는 것이 아니다. 즉 '마약 제조에 사용되는 화학 원료'라는 의미가 되어야 할 것이다. 따라서 using이 아니라 used로 바꿔야 다음과 같이 바른 문장이 된다.

Police have arrested Taliban operatives for smuggling chemical agents **used** for drug production in Afghanistan.

다른 예문들도 살펴보면서 능동, 수동의 의미를 구분해 보자.

I am *pleasing* to announce that all of the employees will get bonuses this month due largely to strong sales figures. (✕)
매출 호조로 모든 직원이 이번 달에 보너스를 받게 되었다고 발표하게 되어 기쁘게 생각합니다.

→ I am **pleased** to announce that all of the employees will get bonuses this month due largely to strong sales figures. (○)

The risks *associating* with taking drugs are greater. (✕)
마약 복용과 관련된 위험은 더 크다.

→ The risks **associated** with taking drugs are greater. (○)

GP | 37 수동태 관용 표현

□ **출제 경향** 능동·수동 문제는 기본적으로 의미를 따지면 풀 수 있는 문제들이다. 그런데 특정 표현을 외워두기만 하면 쉽게 풀 수 있는 문제들도 등장하므로, 그러한 표현들은 가능한 한 많이 외워두어야 한다.

❶ 자주 출제되는 수동태 표현

(be) advised to V	~하라고 충고를 받는	(be) asked to V	~하라고 요청받는
(be) expected to V	~할 것으로 예상되는	(be) excited to V	~해서 흥분되는
(be) forced to V	~하지 않을 수 없는	(be) honored to V	~해서 영광인
(be) inclined to V	~하는 경향이 있는	(be) pleased to V[with 명사]	~해서 기쁜
(be) reminded to V	~하라고 상기 받는	(be) required to V	~하라고 요청받는
(be) absorbed in	~에 열중하는	(be) associated with	~와 관련된
(be) committed to	~에 헌신하는	(be) concerned with	~와 관련 있는
(be) dedicated to	~에 헌신하는	(be) concerned about[over]	~을 걱정하는
(be) engaged in	~에 관여하는	(be) convinced of	~을 확신하는
(be) engaged to	~와 약혼한	(be) satisfied with	~에 만족해하는
(be) equipped with	~을 갖추고 있는	(be) dissatisfied with	~에 만족해하지 못하는
(be) known to	~에게 유명한	(be) fed up with	~에 싫증이 난
(be) known as	~로 유명한 〈자격〉	(be) opposed to	~에 반대하는
(be) known for	~해서 유명한 〈성질〉	(be) tied up at the moment	지금 바쁜

I **was absorbed in** deep thought.
나는 깊은 생각에 푹 빠져 있었다.

The religious community **is** largely **opposed to** stem cell research for the reason that it destroys embryos.
종교계는 배아를 파괴한다는 이유로 줄기 세포 연구에 대해 대체로 반대한다.

I **am honored to** deliver the congratulatory speech at your commencement from one of the prestigious universities.
명문 대학 중 한 곳인 이곳의 졸업식에서 축사를 하게 되어 영광으로 생각합니다.

His musical talent has **been** well **known to** the world.
그의 음악적 재능은 전 세계에 잘 알려져 있다.

Check-up TEST 36~37

Part I Choose the option that best completes each dialogue.

1 A: I _____ to deliver a speech as a valedictorian.
   B: You deserve it.

   (a) honor
   (b) am honoring
   (c) am honored
   (d) have honored

2 A: Can I speak to Mr. Brown now?
   B: I am afraid that _____ at the moment.

   (a) he ties up
   (b) he is tied up
   (c) he is tying up
   (d) he tying up

3 A: My daughter is so _____ in online shopping. What should I do?
   B: I think you should find something that can divert her interest from the computer.

   (a) absorbs
   (b) absorbing
   (c) absorbed
   (d) having absorbed

Part II Choose the option that best completes each sentence.

4 The prosecutors are _____ the truth of the evidence they presented in court.

   (a) convincing of
   (b) having convinced
   (c) convincing
   (d) convinced of

5 The police _____ criminal activities from taking root in the city.

   (a) has been committing to prevent
   (b) have been committing to preventing
   (c) has been committed to prevent
   (d) have been committed to preventing

Part III Read each dialogue or passage carefully and identify the option that contains a grammatical error.

6　(a) A: I'm fed with my boss. He is simply disgusting.
　　(b) B: What's the matter? I thought you got along well with him.
　　(c) A: Actually, I don't. He always gives me a hard time whenever I am working on a project.
　　(d) B: I think he just believes you are a pushover.

7　(a) A: Last night, some thugs started a fight with my younger brother.
　　(b) B: What happened? Is he all right?
　　(c) A: Of course. He knocked the living daylights out of them.
　　(d) B: They must be hospitalizing for treatment.

8　(a) Anwar El Sadat was the third president of Egypt. (b) He was hailed as a hero of the Arab world after launching the Yom Kippur War and achieving victories in its initial stage in 1973. (c) He also signed the Egyptian-Israeli Peace Treaty with Israeli Prime Minister Menachem Begin and received the Nobel Peace Prize, for which he was heavily criticized by Islamist extremists. (d) And, on October 6, 1981, he was killed by assassins during the annual victory parade commemorated the crossing of the Suez Canal during the 1973 war.

9　(a) Improvisation is what makes jazz different from other music genres. (b) It refers to performing without prior preparation or practice. (c) Jazz heavily relies on improvisation, calling the art of composing in the moment. (d) Jazz musicians are required to rise to a certain level of creativity to be able to improvise effectively.

10　(a) Former U.S. Vice President Dan Quayle was notorious for an intellectual lightweight. (b) During his vice presidency, he was widely ridiculed by the media as well as the public. (c) His most infamous blunder was correcting a contestant's correct spelling of "potatoes" to "potatos" during an elementary school spelling bee. (d) In fact, he was relying on cards provided by the school, included the misspelled card, and later he said he had trusted the materials provided by the school.

가정법

GP | 38 주요 가정법 구문

□ **출제 경향** 가정법 과거, 가정법 과거완료, 혼합가정법에 관한 문제는 거의 매달 출제된다. 가정법 문제는 해석해서 푼다기보다 형태를 보고 빨리 답을 찾아내는 것이 관건이므로 가장 기본적이고도 중요한 구문들을 확실히 알아두자.

❶ 가정법 과거

현재 사실의 반대, 혹은 현재 상황에서 실현 가능성이 희박한 일이나 상황을 가정한다.

> If + 주어 + 동사의 과거형 ~, 주어 + would / should / could / might + 동사원형 ~.
> └→ be동사는 무조건 were로 표현
>
> → 주어가 ~하면 주어가 ...할 텐데

If the CEO **had** a little more capital, he **would** surely **be** successful in the software business.
그 최고 경영자가 자본이 조금만 더 있다면, 소프트웨어 사업에서 분명 성공할 텐데.

❷ 가정법 과거완료

과거 사실과 반대되는 내용을 가정한다.

> If + 주어 + had p.p. ~, 주어 + would / should / could / might + have p.p. ~.
> → 주어가 ~했었더라면 주어가 ...했을 텐데

If I **had known** him earlier, I **could have asked** him for some advice on that matter.
내가 그를 더 일찍 알았더라면 그 문제에 관해서 조언을 구할 수 있었을 텐데.

❸ 혼합가정법

가정법 과거완료의 if절과 가정법 과거의 주절을 합친 형태이다. 주절에 today나 now와 같은 현재를 암시하는 힌트 단어가 반드시 등장한다.

> If + 주어 + had p.p. ~, 주어 + would / should / could / might + 동사원형 + ~now[today].
> → 주어가 ~했었더라면 주어가 지금 ...할 텐데

If he **had not been murdered** by the serial killer 10 years ago, he **would be attending college now**. 그가 10년 전 연쇄 살인범에게 살해되지 않았더라면 지금쯤 대학을 다니고 있을 텐데.

※ 가정법 문장에서 if를 생략하고 주어와 동사를 도치시킬 수 있다는 점도 기억해 두자.

If I had studied harder, I could have been accepted into the university.
내가 좀 더 열심히 공부했더라면 그 대학의 입학허가를 받을 수 있었을 텐데.

= **Had I studied** harder, I could have been accepted into the university.

GP | 39 가정법 미래 구문

□ **출제 경향** 가정법 미래는 매달 나오지는 않지만 잊혀질 만하면 출제되고 있다. 가정법 미래는 현재나 미래에 대한 강한 의심이나 있을 수 없는 일에 대한 가정을 나타낼 때 쓴다. TEPS에 출제되었던 포인트만 간략히 설명하겠다.

❶ 가정법 미래의 쓰임

■ **가정법 미래 1 강한 의심**

> If + 주어 + should + 동사원형 ~, 주어 + will / can / may / should + 동사원형 ~.
> → 주어가 ~한다면 주어가 ...할 것이다[할 텐데]

If rain **should** fall today, we will cancel the party.
= **Should rain** fall today, we will cancel the party.
혹시라도 오늘 비가 온다면 우리는 파티를 취소할 것이다.
→ 시험에는 if를 생략하고 Should rain fall로 도치시킨 상태에서 어순 문제가 출제되고 있다.

■ **가정법 미래 2 불가능한 일(= 절대 일어나지 않을 일)**

> If + 주어 + were to + 동사원형 ~, 주어 + would / should / could / might + 동사원형 ~.
> → 주어가 ~한다면(절대 일어나지 않을 일이 일어난다고 가정하면) 주어는 ...할 것이다.

If the sun **were to rise** in the west, I **would change** my mind.
행여나 태양이 서쪽에서 뜬다면 마음을 바꿀 것이다.

Even if the sun **were to rise** in the west, I **would not change** my mind.
태양이 서쪽에서 뜬다고 하더라도 마음을 바꾸지 않을 것이다.

시험에서는 if절의 동사 were to 부분을 문제로 만드는데, 예를 들면 다음과 같은 식이다.

I really hate him. Only if pigs _____, I would talk to him again.

(a) flew
(b) were to fly

→ 주절의 조동사로 would가 나왔다고 해서 가정법 과거라고 생각하면 안 된다. 절대로 그럴 일이 없을, 매우 불확실한 미래의 내용이므로 가정법 미래임을 알 수 있다. 따라서 동사는 were to fly가 적절하다. 해석해 보면 '나는 그가 정말 싫어. 혹시 돼지가 날아다닌다면(해가 서쪽에서 뜬다면) 그와 다시 이야기를 하겠지.'로, 무슨 일이 있어도 절대 그와 이야기를 하지 않겠다는 뜻이다.

Part I Choose the option that best completes each dialogue.

1 A: I am fed up with Jack's being late.
   B: You wouldn't say that if you _____ in his shoes.

   (a) am
   (b) be
   (c) were
   (d) will have been

2 A: If it _____ tomorrow, he would not leave.
   B: I don't know whether it will rain or not.

   (a) must rain
   (b) should rain
   (c) may rain
   (d) shall rain

3 A: I'm not ready to make a presentation on social problems.
   B: _____ anything, please call me.

   (a) If you would need
   (b) If you should need
   (c) If you were to need
   (d) If you have needed

4 A: I regret the mistake that I made in the contract negotiations.
   B: I _____ the same mistake if I had been in your situation.
   (a) will make
   (b) make
   (c) could have made
   (d) made

Part II Choose the option that best completes each sentence.

5 The employees at the company think that if the new CEO had not been hired two months
   ago, the company _____ different today.

   (a) would be
   (b) would have been
   (c) is
   (d) was

6   If I _____ be young again, I would marry him.

(a) were to
(b) had been to
(c) was to
(d) will be to

7   Many scientific discoveries could have been made much earlier _____ the knowledge that we have today.

(a) if people in the past possessed
(b) if people in the past possess
(c) did people in the past possess
(d) had people in the past possessed

8   Considering that she is a crafty person, it would be stupid _____ you accepted her request.

(a) as
(b) that
(c) when
(d) if

Part III Read each dialogue or passage carefully and identify the option that contains a grammatical error.

9   (a) A: I am now 32. Time flies!
(b) B: Don't worry about that since your're not really that old.
(c) A: What would you do if you were back in your 20s?
(d) B: I will play more and fret less.

10 (a) Dozens of coal miners have been hospitalized due to respiratory illnesses during the past decade. (b) The coal miners have clamored for better working conditions, which have been rejected by the management largely due to high expenses. (c) Labor unions are saying that if the mining company paid extra attention to the health of its workers, it would not be experiencing a labor shortage today. (d) Now is the time to come up with follow-up measures to revive the company in the region.

GP | 40 기타 가정법 구문

□ **출제 경향** 문장 내에 if가 없지만 if의 뜻이 포함되어 있는 가정법 구문들이 있다. 이러한 구문도 가정법에 속하므로 문형을 잘 익혀두어야 한다.

❶ '~이 있[었]다면'의 가정법 구문

■ with ~이 있다면(가정법 과거) / ~이 있었다면(가정법 과거완료)

With proper education programs, students these days **wouldn't have** to stay up late studying to get into good colleges.
적절한 교육 프로그램이 있다면 요즘 학생들이 밤을 새워가면서까지 좋은 대학에 들어가려고 공부할 필요가 없을 텐데.
→ 현재 적절한 교육 프로그램이 없어서 학생들이 밤을 새워가며 공부해야 한다는 의미로, 문두에 with를 사용한 가정법 과거 문장이다.

With enough funds to start a business, Jason **could have been** successful in the software industry.
사업을 시작할 충분한 자금이 있었더라면 제이슨은 소프트웨어 산업에서 성공할 수 있었을 텐데.
→ 과거에 사업을 시작할 충분한 자금이 없었기 때문에 성공하지 못했었다는 가정법 과거완료 문장이다.

❷ '~이 없[었]다면'의 가정법 구문

■ but for / without ~이 없다면(가정법 과거) / ~이 없었다면(가정법 과거완료)

But for the rain, we **would have** a nice vacation.
비만 아니라면 우리는 멋진 휴가를 보내고 있을 텐데.
→ 지금 비가 와서 멋진 휴가를 못 보내고 있다는 가정법 과거 문장이다. But for 자리에 without을 써도 된다.

Without the drought that hit the country, the stream here **might** not **have dried** up.
그 나라를 강타한 가뭄이 아니었다면 그 개울이 마르지 않았을 수도 있었다.
→ 가뭄이 그 지역을 강타했기 때문에 개울이 말랐다는 가정법 과거완료 문장이다.

■ If it were not for ~이 없다면(가정법 과거)

if를 지우면 it과 were의 자리가 도치된다는 점에 주의하자. 이 구문은 단어 하나하나 의미를 따지기보다는 통째로 외워버리는 것이 좋다.

> If it were not for + 명사(구)~, 주어 + would / could / might / should + 동사원형
> = Were it not for + 명사(구)~, 주어 + would / could / might / should + 동사원형

If it were not for water, no animals **could survive** on Earth.
= **Were it not for** water, no animals **could survive** on Earth.
물이 없다면 어떠한 동물도 지구에서 생존할 수 없을 것이다.

■ If it had not been for ~이 없었다면(가정법 과거완료)

'~이 없었다면'의 의미인 If it had not been for는 다음과 같이 if를 지우고 it과 had를 도치하여 Had it not been for로 바꿀 수 있다는 것을 알아두자.

> If it had not been for + 명사(구)~, 주어 + would / could / might / should + have p.p.
> = Had it not been for + 명사(구)~, 주어 + would / could / might / should + have p.p.

If it had not been for your help, my business **might have gone** bankrupt.
= Had it not been for your help, my business **might have gone** bankrupt.
당신의 도움이 없었더라면 아마 내 사업은 파산했었을지도 모릅니다.

❸ I wish 가정법 구문

■ 「I wish + 주어 + 가정법 과거 시제」 **~라면 좋을 텐데**

I wish I had a boyfriend now.
나도 지금 남자친구가 있다면 좋을 텐데.
→ 지금 남자친구가 없다는 의미의 가정법 과거 문장이다.

■ 「I wish + 주어 + 가정법 과거완료 시제」 **~였었다면 좋았을 텐데**

I wish I had had money then.
그때 돈이 있었다면 좋았을 텐데.
→ 그때 돈이 없었다는 의미의 가정법 과거완료 문장이다.

■ 「I wished + 주어 + 가정법 과거완료 시제」 **~였었다면 좋았을 텐데**

I wished I had worked out harder to make my body muscular last summer.
→ I was sorry (that) I had not worked out harder to make my body muscular last summer.
지난여름에 내 몸을 근육질로 만들기 위해 더욱 열심히 운동을 했었더라면 좋았을 걸 싶었다.

Part I Choose the option that best completes each dialogue.

1 A: Without proper care, the baby _____ the night.

B: And we all know that that was the moment when history changed.

(a) would not have survived

(b) would survive

(c) will not survived

(d) will not have survived

2 A: I envy you. I wish I _____ the entire mortgage on my home now.

B: Don't worry. I'm sure you'll also pay off your mortgage, but I admit that it takes time.

(a) could pay

(b) could have paid

(c) can pay

(d) can have paid

3 A: I had lunch with Sue yesterday. She is really sweet. Above all, she paid for lunch.

B: I wish _____ with you.

(a) I am

(b) I have been there

(c) I was there

(d) I had been there

4 A: Are you all right? I thought you were seriously injured.

B: _____ my bulletproof vest, I wouldn't be here now.

(a) Were it for

(b) Were not it for

(c) Had it not been for

(d) Had not been for

Part II Choose the option that best completes each sentence.

5 With the help of the employees at the mall, my 80-year-old mom _____ no trouble buying her first smart phone, but she returned empty handed.

(a) would have

(b) would had

(c) would have had

(d) would have not had

6   If it were not for his wife and kids, he _____ his job and follow his mentor's recommendation.

(a) will quit
(b) will have quitted
(c) would quit
(d) would have quitted

Part Ⅲ **Read each dialogue or passage carefully and identify the option that contains a grammatical error.**

7   (a) A: How did the shopping go? Did you get anything good?
(b) B: No. As luck would have it, there was a big demonstration in front of the department store.
(c) A: I doubt there's any good reason why the demonstrators were assembled there.
(d) B: They say that but for the mart, smaller stores will not be going bankrupt in such large numbers.

8   (a) A: You are not eating that much. Does the food taste awful?
(b) B: No. I always eat like a bird. I don't eat much no matter how tasty the food is.
(c) A: Well, I think that's the secret to your slim figure. Had been it not for your eating habits, you would have gained a lot of weight like me.
(d) B: I don't think there's any correlation between my eating habits and my weight.

9   (a) A: It's raining cats and dogs outside. What are you going to do?
(b) B: I'll drive home even though I'll be certain to get stuck in heavy traffic. Didn't you bring your car?
(c) A: No. I usually don't drive to the office due to the congested roads downtown. But I wish I driven it this morning.
(d) B: Don't worry. I'll take you to your home.

10   (a) A recently released report read that our nation spent $40 million promoting and advertising the potential risks of the H1N1 flu pandemic. (b) That figure was more than what was spent on vaccines, emergency responses, and risk management combined. (c) As a result, critics now argue that the government was irresponsible and reckless in spending the money. (d) They added that, with the proper intervention of independent outsiders, the government will act more responsibly.

Unit 7 조동사

GP | 41   의미로 맞히는 조동사

□ 출제 경향   조동사 문제는 Part I, II에 주로 출제되고 있는데, 정답을 찾기가 까다로운 편이다. 문법적 지식이 아니라 철저하게 내용 파악 위주로 접근해야만 정답을 찾아낼 수 있기 때문이다. 조동사 문제는 결국 정확한 독해 습관과 관련되어 있으므로 조동사의 정확한 의미를 사전에 숙지하고, 평소에 독해하면서도 조동사의 쓰임새를 주의 깊게 살펴보자.

❶ 기본 조동사 표현

■ should ～해야 한다 (의무), ～할 것이다 (예상, 추측)

National athletes **should** give up their personal interests for their country.
국가 대표 선수들은 조국을 위해 사적인 이익은 버려야 한다. → 의무

Traffic **should** be less congested today.
오늘 교통은 덜 복잡할 것이다. → 예상, 추측

■ must ～임에 틀림없다

You **must** have butterflies in your stomach since your voice is trembling.
네 목소리가 떨리는 것을 보니 긴장했음에 틀림없구나.
▶ have butterflies in one's stomach 안절부절 못하다

■ would ～하곤 했다

The soccer team **would** get up at 5 a.m. and practice until 8 p.m.
그 축구팀은 오전 5시에 기상해서 오후 8시까지 훈련을 하곤 했다.

❷ 「조동사 + have p.p.」 표현

■ must have p.p. ～했었음에 틀림없다

The serial killer **must have been** on the loose since innocent women continued to be murdered in the area.
그 지역에서 아무 죄 없는 여성들이 계속해서 죽어가고 있었기 때문에, 그 연쇄살인범이 잡히지 않고 계속 돌아다니고 있었음에 틀림없다.
▶ on the loose 범인이 잡히지 않고 돌아다니는

■ should have p.p. ～했어야 했는데 (하지 못해서 유감스럽다)

I **should have asked** for a raise last year.
작년에 급여 인상을 요청했어야 했는데 (못해서 아쉽다).

■ cannot have p.p. ～이었을 리가 없다

A: Richard **cannot have made** many mistakes on the test.
리차드가 그 시험에서 실수를 많이 했을 리가 없어.

B: Yeah. He studied a lot. 맞아. 그는 공부를 많이 했었지.

■ could have p.p. ～할 수 있었다 (그런데 하지 않았다)

The rescue team **could have saved** more people in the fire.
구조팀이 화재로부터 더 많은 사람을 구할 수 있었을지도 모른다 (그런데 그러지 못했다).

■ may[might] have p.p. ～이었을지도 모른다

He **might have lost** his way since he did not have a map.
그는 지도가 없기 때문에 길을 잃었을지도 모른다.

❸ 조동사의 관용표현

■ may[might] well + 동사원형 ～하는 것은 당연하다

You **may well comply** with the rules and regulations of the company.
당신은 당연히 회사 규칙과 규정을 준수해야 합니다.

■ may[might] as well A as B B할 바에 차라리 A하는 것이 더 낫다

You **may as well** study **as** play. 노느니 공부하는 것이 차라리 낫겠다.

You **may as well** mind your own business **as** worry about other people.
다른 사람들 걱정하느니 네 일이나 신경 쓰는 것이 낫겠다.

■ would rather A than B B하느니 A하는 편이 더 낫다

I **would rather** die **than** kneel. 무릎을 꿇느니 차라리 죽는 것이 더 나아.

■ cannot help V-ing ～하지 않을 수 없다

I **cannot help getting** bored during his rambling lectures.
그의 횡설수설하는 강의를 듣다 보면 싫증이 날 수밖에 없다.

■ had better ～하는 것이 낫다

You **had better** hire an experienced lawyer in order to win the case.
재판에서 이기려면 노련한 변호사를 선임하는 것이 좋을 거야.

■ ought to ～해야 한다

A: Taking a taxi in Seoul costs a lot.
서울에서 택시를 타면 비용이 너무 많이 나와.

B: You are right. We **ought to** have taken the subway.
네 말이 맞아. 우린 지하철을 탔어야 했어.

Check-up TEST 41

Part I Choose the option that best completes each dialogue.

1 A: I often have a heavy stomach when I wake up.
   B: You _____ eating ramen before you go to sleep.
   (a) would rather stop
   (b) may well stop
   (c) had better stop
   (d) cannot help stopping

2 A: It _____ not be as serious as you think.
   B: I hope so. But I still don't have any confidence in the situation.
   (a) must
   (b) may
   (c) can
   (d) will

3 A: My dog is definitely the outdoor type. How about your dogs?
   B: My younger dog likes running around in the park, but the older one _____ curl up at home and rest.
   (a) had better
   (b) rather
   (c) would rather
   (d) better

Part II Choose the option that best completes each sentence.

4 As we are all human beings, I'm pretty sure that you _____ predict what will happen even ten seconds from now.
   (a) cannot
   (b) should not
   (c) may not
   (d) would not

5 Given the enormous size of the crowd in the picture, there _____ have been a huge demonstration at that time.
   (a) must
   (b) can
   (c) cannot
   (d) will

6 The Tuskegee syphilis experiment, during which researchers didn't treat patients with effective cures for the disease, is a good example that some conspiracy theories _____ true.

(a) might well be
(b) would rather be
(c) cannot help being
(d) had better be

Part III Read each dialogue or passage carefully and identify the option that contains a grammatical error.

7 (a) A: My girlfriend bought me a Bluetooth speaker for my birthday.
(b) B: Wow. That's great. Could I take a look at it?
(c) A: Sure. Here it is. It's quite easy to handle.
(d) B: True. Even a two-year-old might use this.

8 (a) A: My account got hacked yesterday.
(b) B: Oh, gosh. How much damage did the hacker cause?
(c) A: First of all, I can't log in to my account since the hacker changed my password.
(d) B: You must have been more careful. Anyway, feel free to ask me if there is anything that you need for me to do.

9 (a) During the Civil War, the Confederates operated the first submarine, the *CSS Hunley*, to sink an enemy vessel in combat. (b) The submarine attacked and sank the *USS Housatonic* in Charleston Harbor on August 12, 1863. (c) But it also sank after the attack, claiming all crew members. (d) Researchers speculate that there will not have been enough oxygen in the submarine to have kept the crew alive for a long time underwater.

10 (a) Over the past year, Goldman Sachs has suffered from bad publicity. (b) Last week's fraud allegations from the Securities and Exchange Commission only made matters worse. (c) Most of us rather admit shoplifting than have anything to do with Goldman Sachs. (d) The firm is well on its way to becoming the world's most unloved bank.

Unit 8 접속사

GP 42 접속사의 기본 의미

□ **출제 경향** 접속사 문제는 주어진 문장에서 정확한 의미를 파악하는 문제로 출제된다. 쉬운 문제가 나올 때도 있지만 논리적인 상관관계는 물론, 시간 전후 관계도 따져야 답이 나오는 문제가 대부분이다. 가장 기본적인 접속사에 대한 설명은 생략하는 대신 뒤에 나오는 문제 풀이를 통해서 확인해보기로 하고, 여기서는 좀더 심도 있는 접속사에 대해서 살펴보도록 하자.

❶ 부정의 의미가 포함된 접속사

■ unless (= if not) **만약 ~이 아니라면, 만약 ~하지 않으면**

unless는 그 자체에 not의 의미를 포함하고 있다. 따라서 unless가 이끄는 절에 not을 쓰지 않도록 주의해야 한다.

Unless you hurry up, we won't make it to the airport in time.
네가 서두르지 않으면 우린 공항까지 제시간에 도착하지 못할 거야.

The president's approval rating will go down **unless** he cares about the most important issues.
대통령이 가장 중요한 현안을 돌보지 않으면 지지율이 하락할 것이다.

■ 「lest + 주어 + (should) + 동사원형」 **~하지 않기 위해서**

lest도 그 자체에 not의 의미를 포함하고 있으며 조동사 should와 함께 쓰인다. 여기서 should는 '~해야 한다'라는 의미라기보다는 '~하도록, ~이 가능하도록'의 뜻에 가까우며, 생략이 가능하다.

Hide the ring **lest** anyone else **should** see it.
다른 누구도 그 반지를 보지 못하도록 숨겨라.

The politician tried to buy the voters in his district **lest** he **be defeated** in the upcoming election.
그 정치인은 다가오는 선거에서 낙선하지 않기 위해 그 지역의 유권자들을 매수하려 했다.

❷ 양보의 의미를 나타내는 접속사

■ even if와 even though / though / although

even if는 가상의 일에 대해서 말하는 것이고, 의미는 whether or not에 가깝다. even though / though / although는 despite the fact의 뜻에 가깝고, 의미적으로 접근하면 '이미 일어난 일'에 대한 이야기를 하는 것이다.

Even if I pass the bar exam, I don't have any intention of becoming a lawyer.

설사 내가 변호사 자격시험을 통과한다 하더라도 나는 변호사가 될 생각은 없다.

▶ bar exam (미국) 변호사 자격시험

Even though I passed the bar exam, I didn't have any intention of becoming a lawyer.

비록 내가 변호사 자격시험을 통과했지만, 나는 변호사가 될 생각은 없었다.

■ albeit 비록 ~이기는 하지만

생소한 단어일 수 있겠지만 엄연한 접속사이고 문법 영역에서 접속사 문제로 출제된 바가 있으니 유의하도록 하자.

My work on the project was finished, **albeit** late.

비록 늦긴 했지만, 나는 그 프로젝트 일을 마무리했다.

The long, **albeit** unproductive, meeting finally came to an end.

그 긴 회의가 생산적이지는 못했지만 마침내 끝은 났다.

❸ 기타 접속사

■ or 〈부정문에서〉 ~도 ...도 (아니다) / 〈동격을 나타내어〉 즉, 다시 말해

The old man can't write **or** read.

그 노인은 쓸 줄도, 읽을 줄도 모른다.

biology, **or** the science which is concerned with the study of living things

생물학, 즉 살아 있는 것에 대한 연구와 관련 있는 학문

■ now that ~이기 때문에

이 표현은 TEPS 독해의 연결어 문제에 곧잘 등장한다. 접속사이기는 하지만 Now that he's gone.(그 사람이 가서 하는 말이야.)처럼 쓰기도 한다. 이렇게 말한 후에 그 사람에 대한 안 좋은 이야기를 하는 식이다.

The movie has been critically acclaimed **now that** it has an artistic value and is a commercial success.

이 영화는 예술적 가치를 지니고 있고 상업적 성공을 이루었기 때문에 영화 평론가로부터 좋은 평가를 받았다.

Choose the option that best completes each dialogue.

1   A: I was computer illiterate _____ I met my wife.
    B: Well, she is famous for her brilliant computer skills.

    (a) after
    (b) while
    (c) until
    (d) as

2   A: I think that the politicians in the opposition parties are bashing their opponent.
    B: I agree. They do that _____ the member win the coming mayoral election.

    (a) so that
    (b) lest
    (c) if
    (d) unless

3   A: Did you see Tom at work yesterday?
    B: _____ I am mistaken, he was not back at work yesterday.

    (a) If
    (b) Unless
    (c) Although
    (d) Lest

Part II   Choose the option that best completes each sentence.

4   The ACE team embarked on the project _____ the city approved the proposal
    of building a community center in the region.

    (a) if
    (b) while
    (c) as soon as
    (d) although

5   It will be difficult to salvage the sunken ship _____ the wind will be stronger
    and the rain will become heavier in the West Sea for the next few days.

    (a) now that
    (b) even though
    (c) and
    (d) now and then

6   He didn't feel good _____ he got promoted for doing what was expected of him.

(a) though
(b) if
(c) as soon as
(d) in spite of

Part III Read each dialogue or passage carefully and identify the option that contains a grammatical error.

7   (a) A: Where were you? You should have been here twenty minutes ago.
(b) B: I'm really sorry. I didn't mean to be late. I got on the wrong bus.
(c) A: Then you should have gotten off the bus before you realized that.
(d) B: I did. But traffic was heavy, and I had to wait another ten minutes for the right bus to come.

8   (a) A: Currently, some political bickering is going on because of the president's pet project.
(b) B: What are you talking about?
(c) A: The lawmakers from the ruling party are pressing ahead with an unnecessary construction project if doing so will please swing voters.
(d) B: What a shame!

9   (a) While there is a shortage of women studying the sciences, we have not given up hope that we can attract more. (b) Part of this has to start at the schools themselves, so we are encouraging science teachers to praise girls' work and to encourage them to become scientists. (c) Some teachers make a point of focusing on famous female scientists such as Marie Curie. (d) This way, girls will come to realize that women can succeed in the sciences.

10 (a) I am honored to be here at the graduation ceremony of one of the greatest universities in Korea. (b) I am here to tell you what kind of ambitions you should have to be successful in the future. (c) I would also like to tell you what you should do when you are faced with difficulties. (d) What I will tell you today will prove to be vital, unless difficult, to put into practice.

Unit 9 전치사

GP | 43 전치사의 기본 의미 1

□ **출제 경향** 전치사는 매달 한 두 문제 출제되고 있다. 보통 전치사의 기본 의미를 묻는 문제와 전치사의 관용표현을 묻는 문제가 출제된다.

1 in

■ **시간**

in the morning 아침에　　　　　　early **in** the morning 이른 아침에
this morning (○) 오늘 아침에　　　　*in* this morning (×)
next month (○) 다음 달에　　　　　*in* next month (×)
in three weeks 3주 후에　　　　　**in** December 12월에
in 2020 2020년에　　　　　　　　**in** summer 여름에
in the 21st century 21세기에　　　**in** the early 21st century 21세기 초반에
in the future 미래에　　　　　　　**in** the [near / foreseeable] future 가까운 미래에
in the past decade 지난 10년 사이에 → 현재완료 시제 문제로 매우 자주 출제된다.

■ **장소**

in the kitchen 부엌 (안)에서　　　　**in** South Korea / Seoul 한국 / 서울에서

■ **그 외**

언어	**in** Korean 한국어로　　**in** the Korean language 한국어로
색깔	**in** white 흰색으로　　**in** black 검정색으로
분야·대상	experience **in** a new field 새로운 분야에서의 경험 advance **in** technology 기술 발전
형태·크기	This computer model comes **in** a variety of colors and sizes. 이 컴퓨터 모델은 다양한 색깔과 크기로 출시되고 있다.

2 at

■ **시간**

at 12:30 12시 30분에　　　　**at** night 밤에　　　　　**at** present 현재
at the beginning of the month 월초에　　　　　　　**at** the end of the month 월말에

■ 장소

at the crossroads 교차로에서　　**at** the station / hotel / airport / post office 역 / 호텔 / 공항 / 우체국에서

※ **in** the station과 **at** the station의 차이

We met **in** the train station. 우리는 기차 역 안에서 만났다. → '내부'의 개념

We met **at** the train station. 우리는 (여러 곳이 있지만 다름 아닌) 기차역에서 만났다 → '위치'의 개념

3 on

■ 날짜(특정한 날)

on December 31　12월 31일에　　　　**on** Christmas day 크리스마스 날에

■ 장소

on the floor 바닥에서　　**on** the 12th floor 12층에서　　**on** the wall 벽면에

on the ceiling 천장에　　**on** the street 거리에서　　**on** a ship[a train / a plane] 배 [기차 / 비행기]에서

■ ～에 관하여

on Korean history 한국 역사에 관해서 → *about*도 '～에 관해서'라는 뜻이지만 *on*보다는 포괄적인 의미이다.

4 for

■ ～을 위한

This present is **for** you. 너를 위한 (너에게 줄) 선물이야.

This is a book **for** children. 이 책은 아이들 용이다.

■ ～로 향하는

I will leave Busan **for** Seoul. 나는 부산을 떠나 서울로 향할 것이다.

■ ～동안

for the past[last] three decades 지난 30년 동안
→ '30년 전부터 지금까지'의 의미이므로 현재완료 시제와 써야 한다. 동사 시제 문제와 관련해서 매우 자주 출제된다.

5 during

for의 용법과 혼동하지 않도록 한다. for 뒤에는 '기간(숫자)'이 오고, during 뒤에는 '때'를 의미하는 명사가 나온다.

during summer vacation 여름휴가 기간 동안 (O)　　*for* summer vacation (×)

during the training period 훈련 기간 동안 (O)　　*for* the training period (×)

He was taken to the remote island by some unknown people **during** the night.
그는 밤사이에 모르는 사람들에 의해 외딴 섬으로 실려갔다.

Check-up TEST 43

Part I Choose the option that best completes each dialogue.

1 A: Why are you looking at the tall, beautiful lady _____ black?

B: Because the lady wearing the black suit is my sister.

(a) on

(b) over

(c) in

(d) with

2 A: I was frantic when I found out that I was on the KTX train _____ Busan.

B: You were supposed to go to Gwangju to see your parents.

(a) in

(b) to

(c) at

(d) for

Part II Choose the option that best completes each sentence.

3 The demonstrators departed for Seoul _____ to beat the traffic and to be in front of the National Assembly to have their voices heard.

(a) on daybreak

(b) in daybreak

(c) after

(d) at daybreak

4 The Asian Foundation, which carries out research projects in Asian countries, was founded to shed light on the continent and to let the world know the great strides made by the Asian people _____ the continent's long history.

(a) since

(b) during

(c) depending on

(d) as well as

5 According to the news report, an underwater earthquake occurred in the Indian Ocean _____, and it caused huge tsunamis that swept ashore and killed people in many countries.

(a) in this morning

(b) this morning

(c) over the morning

(d) after in this morning

Part III Read each dialogue or passage carefully and identify the option that contains a grammatical error.

6 (a) A: What have you been doing lately?
   (b) B: I have been doing some research on Korean history on the 1910s.
   (c) A: It sounds like a lot of work.
   (d) B: It is. However, I really enjoyed studying it and even published a paper about the Japanese colonial rule in Korea.

7 (a) A: On early January, the prime minister will call an early election to gain the confidence of the public.
   (b) B: Do you think his party will win the election?
   (c) A: I can't say for sure, but he seems confident of victory.
   (d) B: I don't think calling an election is a good idea for him and his party. He stands a big chance of losing.

8 (a) Thanks to the increase on engine capacity, the performance of the car improved significantly. (b) The car, with its V6 5.0 liter engine, can reach 60 miles per hour in about 2.4 seconds. (c) It can perform so amazingly well thanks to a technological breakthrough. (d) However, the vehicle is not as fuel-efficient as its smaller brothers, with their 4.0 liter engines, are.

9 (a) The newspaper is written on the Korean language. (b) That's why it has a small circulation of 30,000. (c) Nowadays, senior officials at the newspaper company are considering publishing it in several languages in order to secure a larger number in readers. (d) However, what they need to do before that is hire translators.

10 (a) Ramadan is the ninth month of the Islamic calendar. (b) It is the month of fasting, during which Muslims refrain from eating, drinking alcoholic beverages, and smoking cigarettes from sunset to sunrise. (c) The point of fasting is to teach Muslims patience, modesty, and spirituality. (d) In the end of the ninth month, Muslims can enjoy the things that they did not do.

GP | 44 전치사의 기본 의미 2

□ **출제 경향** 시간과 장소를 나타내는 기본적인 전치사 이외에도, 여러 가지 전치사를 알아두면 쉽게 문제를 풀 수 있다.

❶ throughout과 since

■ throughout **~내내 (처음부터 끝까지의 기간) / 한 장소를 대상으로 모든 곳곳을 다**

throughout the year 1년 내내

He has been the best student **throughout** the school year. 그는 그 학년도 내내 최고의 학생이었다.

throughout the U.S. 미국 전역에서

BTS' new album has become popular **throughout** the world.
BTS의 새 앨범이 전 세계 방방곡곡에서 인기를 얻고 있다.

■ since **~한 이후로**

since가 전치사로 사용되면 무조건 '~한 이후로'라는 뜻이다. 이 때 문장의 동사는 완료 시제가 되어야 한다.

since 2018 2018년 이후로

The number of jobless people has increased dramatically **since** the economic recession.
경기 침체 이후로 실업자 수가 급격히 증가했다.

❷ until과 by의 구분

■ until **지속, 계속의 의미**

The riot continued **until** the police dispersed the disgruntled workers.
경찰이 불만에 쌓인 근로자들을 해산시킬 때까지 폭동은 계속되었다.

■ by **완료의 의미**

You must finish the report **by** noon.
넌 보고서를 정오까지 마무리해야 한다.
→ 정오 이전까지 보고서를 끝내기만 하면 되는 상황이다. 행동이 한 번만이라도 이루어지기만 하면 되는 '완료'의 의미

❸ between과 among의 구분

■ between **(둘) 사이에**

B comes **between** A and C in the English alphabet.
영어 알파벳에서 B는 A와 C 사이에 위치한다.

■ among **(셋 이상의) 사이에**

Pancreatic cancer has become common **among** Koreans due to their lifestyle changes.
췌장암은 생활양식의 변화로 인해 한국인들 사이에서 흔한 질병이 되었다.
▶ pancreatic cancer 췌장암

4 그 외의 전치사

■ beside ~옆에 (= next to / adjoining to / adjacent to)

Beside the pile of books are a pencil and an eraser.
책 더미 옆에 연필 한 자루와 지우개 하나가 있다.

■ under 아래에; ~중인; ~하에

A boat is cruising **under** a bridge.
보트 한 대가 다리 밑으로 지나가고 있다.

The building is **under** construction.
그 건물은 현재 건설 중에 있다.

Many changes have been made **under** the new management.
새로운 경영체제하에 많은 변화가 생겼다.

■ within (장소, 시간적으로) ~내에

You can discover some beautiful venues **within** two hours of Seoul.
서울에서 두 시간 내 거리에 있는 아름다운 장소들을 찾을 수 있을 것이다.
▶ venue 장소

■ prior to ~전에

Prior to leaving, make sure that you have everything you will need at the campsite.
출발하기 전에 야영지에서 필요한 모든 것들을 다 챙겼는지 확실해 해 두어라.

■ ahead of ~하기 전에; ~보다 앞서

The airport terminal construction is **ahead of** schedule.
공항 터미널 공사가 예정보다 빨리 진행되고 있다.

John is **ahead of** Mark in the competition.
존은 시합에서 마크보다 앞선다.

Check-up TEST 44

Part I Choose the option that best completes each dialogue.

1　A: If you marry me, I will always be there for you and will love you _____ the end of the world.

　B: I really want to believe you, but your actions make it hard for me to trust you.

　(a) until
　(b) by
　(c) at
　(d) in

2　A: The interstate _____ will cut the travel time between my hometown and Las Vegas by more than 30 minutes.

　B: Considering all the expenses and inconveniences borne by the citizens, the travel time should be reduced by another 30 minutes.

　(a) currently under construction
　(b) currently in construction
　(c) currently within construction
　(d) currently ahead of construction

3　A: Did the police catch the criminal who broke into the governor's residence?
　B: The case is still _____ investigation.

　(a) in
　(b) on
　(c) with
　(d) under

Part II Choose the option that best completes each sentence.

4　Cardiovascular diseases have become _____ Korean males over forty years of age.

　(a) some of the leading cause of the dead between
　(b) some of the leading causes of death among
　(c) some of the leading cause of the death among
　(d) some of the leading causes of death within

5   Equipped with state-of-the-art facilities, the movie theater _____ the concert hall was built in 2017 to attract young movie fans.

(a) besides
(b) adjacent to
(c) prior to
(d) ahead

6   The sales of the newly released book have increased rapidly _____ last month.

(a) on
(b) for
(c) since
(d) in

7   _____ the negotiations, all the executives from the two parties took deep breaths and thought about how to stay ahead of the game.

(a) Since
(b) Despite
(c) Prior to
(d) But for

Part III **Read each dialogue or passage carefully and identify the option that contains a grammatical error.**

8   (a) A: It looks like you are super busy.
(b) B: Please do not talk to me because my deadline is fast approaching, and I am running out of time.
(c) A: I think you can finish the job until midnight.
(d) B: I hope so.

9   (a) She was a leading actress in Russia for almost three decades. (b) She was considered something of a "national" actress by most critics. (c) However, she recently committed suicide, and, since then, she became a symbol of the problems that women still encounter in what is a very conservative society. (d) Sadly, it seems that she not only had problems in her personal life but was also bothered by people gossiping about her on the Internet.

10 (a) Now, the Thai economy pales in comparison with the Korean economy. (b) Per capita income in Korea is over $20,000 whereas in Thailand, it is just $1,000. (c) A member of the OECD, Korea currently has the 15th largest economy in the world. (d) However, in the 1960s, Thailand was well before Korea in terms of the sizes of their economies.

GP | 45 전치사의 관용표현 1

□ **출제 경향** 전치사의 관용표현은 외워두면 실제 시험에서 시간을 절약할 수 있게 해주므로 무조건 외우도록 한다.

❶ 결과의 전치사 to가 포함된 표현

be shot to death 저격당해 죽다	**be starved to death** 굶어 죽다
be stabbed to death 칼에 찔려 죽다	**be frozen to death** 동사하다
be burned to death 불에 타 죽다	

→ to와 death 사이에 관사를 쓰면 안 된다는 점에 유의하자.

The robber was **shot to death** when he refused to surrender.
그 강도는 투항하기를 거부하자 총에 맞아 사망했다.

Some of the penguins in the Antarctica were found **frozen to death** after the temperature went down significantly.
남극의 일부 펭귄은 기온이 급강한 후에 동사한 채로 발견되었다.

❷ ~의 비율[속도]로

at an alarming rate[pace] 놀라운 속도로	**at a snail's pace** (달팽이처럼) 느린 속도로
at a fast speed[pace] 빠른 속도로	

Aging population are growing **at an alarming pace** in some Asian countries.
일부 아시아 국가에서 인구 고령화는 놀라운 속도로 증가하고 있다.

The traffic was very heavy, and we were moving **at a snail's pace**.
교통 체증이 매우 심하여 우리는 느린 속도로 이동했다.

❸ 명사를 잘 동반하는 표현

access to ~에 대한 접근, 이용 권리[방법]	**approach to** ~에 대한 접근
advocate for ~을 지지하는 사람	**concern about[over]** ~에 대한 걱정
effect[impact] on ~에 대한 영향	**problem with** ~에 대한 문제
reason for ~에 대한 이유	**respect for** ~에 대한 존경
barring ~을 제외하고는, ~이외에; ~이 없으면	

Access to the Internet surely determines one's competitiveness.
인터넷을 이용할 수 있느냐로 한 사람의 경쟁력이 결정된다.

There are **concerns about** MERS, which is believed to be fatal to life.
생명에 치명적이라고 여겨지는 메르스에 관한 우려가 있다.

Respect for the elderly is considered important in Asian cultures.
아시아 문화권에서는 웃어른에 대한 공경을 중요하게 여긴다.

4 ~에도 불구하고

in spite of + 명사 (= despite + 명사) ~에도 불구하고
despite the fact[belief] that + 주어 + 동사 ~라는 사실[믿음]에도 불구하고

In spite of the blizzard, the mountaineers climbed Mountain Everest.
눈보라에도 불구하고 산악 등반가들은 에베레스트 산에 올랐다.

Despite the belief that men are born equal, the world doesn't treat them fairly.
사람은 평등하게 태어났다는 믿음에도 불구하고 세상은 사람을 공평하게 대하지 않는다.

5 기타 주요 전치사 관련 표현

as of ~(시간) 부로; ~현재로	**by means[virtue] of** ~에 의해서, ~의 도움으로
instead of ~대신에	**in lieu of** ~대신에
with regard to ~에 관해서	**regardless of** ~에 상관없이
from around the world 전 세계 곳곳에서	**in honor of** ~에게 경의를 표하여; ~을 기념하여

Regardless of sex and age, everyone was cordially invited to the party.
남녀노소 불문하고 모든 사람들은 이 파티에 정중하게 초대받았다.
▶ cordially 정중하게, 진심으로

The baseball fans held an event **in honor of** the deceased baseball player.
야구팬들은 작고한 그 야구 선수를 기리기 위해 행사를 열었다.

A computer has been a major boon to physically challenged people, who now have e-books **in lieu of** paper books.
이제는 종이로 된 책 대신 전자책을 보게 되어, 장애인들에게는 컴퓨터가 아주 요긴하게 되었다.
▶ boon 요긴한 것, 혜택

The intern could get the high-paying job **by virtue of** his wide range of experience.
그 인턴사원은 다양한 경험 덕택에 급여가 높은 일자리를 얻을 수 있었다.

Part I Choose the option that best completes each dialogue.

1 A: The earthquake that happened on Monday morning caused numerous problems in California.

B: I heard about that. The governor declared a state of emergency _____ midnight last night.

(a) until
(b) in
(c) as of
(d) on

2 A: Because of the recent financial crisis, the number of credit delinquencies is increasing _____ an alarming rate. It's a big problem.

B: If we do not solve this problem, people will be frustrated and disgruntled.

(a) at
(b) by
(c) on
(d) with

3 A: Did you say that you need the unpublished manuscript of *Harry Potter*? Then, monuments should be erected _____ me.

B: You must be kidding.

(a) instead of
(b) in lieu of
(c) in honor of
(d) by means of

4 A: Honey, will we make it to the airport in time?

B: We should arrive at 9 o'clock sharp _____ any unexpected delays.

(a) barring
(b) despite
(c) owing to
(d) instead of

Part II Choose the option that best completes each sentence.

5   The largest carmaker in Japan is considering giving its employees shares _____
    cash because of liquidity issues caused by a mechanical problem that led to a massive
    product recall.

    (a) for the sake of   (b) regardless of
    (c) in lieu of   (d) in the interest of

6   _____ many attempts to adopt universal health care, the effort has met with
    little success.

    (a) In spite of   (b) In spite in
    (c) In spite over   (d) Despite of

7   Respect _____ other people is highly valued as competition is escalating.

    (a) in   (b) of
    (c) for   (d) on

8   The global economic recession will especially have a major effect _____ the
    real estate market.

    (a) for   (b) on
    (c) with   (d) by

Part III Read each dialogue or passage carefully and identify the option that contains a
grammatical error.

9   (a) I am extremely pleased to have this opportunity to visit Korea for the first time since my
    appointment to the top position at my corporation. (b) I would like to note that, in the past
    fifty years, Korea has improved by leaps and bounds. (c) For instance, the country's per
    capita income has risen at astounding rate thanks to the hard work of the Korean people.
    (d) Additionally, the people in this country have worked tirelessly to develop the
    infrastructure, and the results are simply incredible.

10 (a) Only 30 years ago, access the Internet was spotty at best. (b) And, of course, the
    Internet was not yet available on mobile phones. (c) What is taken for granted today was
    difficult back then. (d) However, virtually every financial transaction is done in cyberspace
    at present.

GP | 46 전치사의 관용표현 2

□ 출제 경향 전치사의 관용표현은 외워두면 실제 시험에서 시간을 절약할 수 있게 해주므로 무조건 외우도록 한다.

1 형용사처럼 사용되는 표현

compared with ~에 비해

equivalent to ~와 동일한

similar to ~와 비슷한

consistent with ~와 일치하는

responsible for ~에 대해 책임이 있는

familiar with ~에 친숙한

How different is TEPS **compared with** TOEIC?
TEPS는 TOEIC과 비교해서 어떻게 다르지?

The company is **consistent with** new sets of rules and regulations with regard to climate change.
그 회사는 기후 변화와 관련된 새로운 규칙과 규정에 부합한다.

A mile is **equivalent to** approximately 1.6 kilometers.
1마일은 약 1.6킬로미터에 상당한다.

2 out of가 포함된 표현

out of curiosity 호기심에서

out of hand 손을 쓸 수 없는

out of work 실직 중인

out of order 고장 난

out of fun 재미로[장난으로]

out of date 구식의, 낡은

out of pity 불쌍히 여겨

out of place 제자리에 있지 않은

out of sight 안 보이는 곳에; 먼 곳에

run out of (~을) 다 써버리다, 바닥나다

Snap out of it. 기운 내.

I am just asking this question **out of curiosity**.
그냥 호기심에 물어보는 거예요.

Out of sight, out of mind.
눈에서 멀어지면 마음에서도 멀어진다.

The gas-guzzling SUV quickly **ran out of** fuel.
기름을 많이 먹는 그 SUV 차량은 연료가 금방 떨어졌다.
▶ gas-guzzling 연료 소비가 많은

Patrick has been **out of work** for almost a year since the economic recession began.
패트릭은 경기 침체가 시작된 후 거의 일 년간 실직 상태이다.

❸ for의 의미

■ 이유

Thank you **for** putting on such a wonderful party.

이렇게 멋진 파티를 열어주셔서 감사합니다.

I'd like to extend my gratitude to all of the guests **for** attending today's seminar.

오늘 세미나에 참석해 주신 모든 참석자 여러분들께 감사의 말씀을 전합니다.

▶ extend one's gratitude ~에게 감사를 전하다

■ ~에 비해서, ~치고는

You look young **for** your age.

나이에 비해서 훨씬 어려 보이시네요.

▶ for one's age 나이에 비해서

■ 선호

Most men showed a tendency of having a penchant **for** tall, blond, glamorous women when they are on blind dates.

대부분의 남자들은 소개팅 자리에서 키가 크고 금발이며 매혹적인 여성을 선호하는 경향을 보였다.

▶ have a penchant[preference] for ~을 매우 좋아하다

❹ 기타 전치사의 관용표현

■ for 찬성하는 / against 반대하는

A: I am going to vote **for** the Democratic Party in the upcoming election.

나는 다가오는 선거에서 민주당에 표를 던질 거야.

B: I am mostly **against** the policies of the Democratic Party.

난 민주당 정책에 대해서는 대체로 반대하는 편이야.

■ bring up 화제·문제 등을 꺼내다

A: Honey, you are spending too much on the lottery.

여보, 당신 복권에 돈을 너무 많이 쓰고 있어요.

B: I know. But I would be happy if you did not **bring up** that subject again.

나도 알고 있으니 그 얘긴 또 꺼내지 말아주었으면 좋겠어요.

■ in conjunction with ~와 함께, ~와 결합하여

The dinner is being held **in conjunction with** the company's awards ceremony.

회사의 시상식과 함께 저녁 만찬이 진행되고 있다.

Part I Choose the option that best completes each dialogue.

1   A: I am just asking this question _____ curiosity. What is the capital of
       Denmark?
     B: Beats me.

    (a) for
    (b) against
    (c) out of
    (d) with

2   A: I don't know what to take. There are too many pills that I should take.
     B: Don't take the blue pills in conjunction _____ the red ones.

    (a) with
    (b) against
    (c) for
    (d) instead

Part II Choose the option that best completes each sentence.

3   _____ Indonesia, South Korea is a small country with few natural resources
    but has an excellent pool of human resources.

    (a) Equivalent to
    (b) Consistent with
    (c) Comparing with
    (d) Compared with

4   These days, young adults have a penchant _____ online shopping in order to
    save on transportation costs.

    (a) in
    (b) on
    (c) with
    (d) for

5   One of the qualities that leaders should have is a sense of responsibility, which means that, at the end of the day, they are the ones who are responsible _____ anything that goes wrong.

(a) on
(b) with
(c) in
(d) for

6   Because he reneged on his election pledge, people who voted _____ him are feeling sorry for themselves.

(a) at
(b) for
(c) to
(d) against

Part III Read each dialogue or passage carefully and identify the option that contains a grammatical error.

7   (a) A: There are too many North Korean defectors flooding into the South.
(b) B: I fear that the situation is getting worse and might get out of the problem.
(c) A: I think it is time for the Seoul government to do something about it.
(d) B: What I am especially worried about is the internal collapse of the North Korean regime.

8   (a) A: How old are you? Minors are not allowed to enter.
(b) B: I came of age last month. People say that I look young to my age.
(c) A: Would you please take out your ID? I have to check it out.
(d) B: Here you are.

9   (a) A: Thank you so much with the support you gave me.
(b) B: I had hoped you would win the gold medal. But you did well.
(c) A: I am satisfied with all of your support and words of encouragement.
(d) B: Next time, you can do better than that.

10 (a) Fossil fuels are nonrenewable energy sources. (b) It takes millions of years for them to be formed. (c) And the reserves are being depleted much faster than new fossil fuels are being formed. (d) Now, humanity is getting out of them and might have to live without them in the future.

Unit 10 관사

GP 47 부정관사 a(n)와 관사 the

□ **출제 경향** 관사 관련 문제는 쉬운듯하면서도 까다로운 문제이다. 문장 내에서 알맞은 부정관사와 관사를 찾는 문제가 Part III에서 나오면 정답을 찾기가 어려우므로 평소에 관사 관련 문제를 많이 풀어서 익숙해져야 한다.

1 부정관사 a와 an의 구분

부정관사 a와 an은 발음으로 구분한다. 부정관사 뒤에 나오는 단어의 첫 시작 발음이 모음(a / e / i / o / u)일 경우 an을 쓰고 그 외에는 전부 a를 쓴다.

an orange, **an** office, **an** old tree, **an** umbrella → 부정관사 뒤의 발음이 모음이므로 an을 써야 한다.

an hour → hour의 자음 h는 묵음이 되어 [아우어]라고 발음된다. 발음이 모음으로 시작하므로 부정관사 an을 써야 한다.

a universe → 철자가 u로 시작하지만 발음은 [유]이므로 an이 아니라 a를 쓴다. [유]는 준자음이다.

an F clef (바 음자리표) → 철자는 자음 F로 시작하지만 첫 발음이 [에]이므로 부정관사 an을 써야 한다.

a European country → 철자가 모음 e로 시작하지만 발음은 [유]로 시작하기 때문에 an을 써야 한다.

2 Part III에 나오는 the 관련 문제

정관사 the는 다음과 같은 경우에 사용한다.

> (1) 앞에서 언급된 내용이 뒤에서 다시 언급될 때
> (2) 뒤에서 한정을 받을 때
> (3) 기타 특수한 경우

시험에는 (2)의 경우가 곧잘 나온다.

Success is completion of anything intended. (×)
Success is **the** completion of anything intended. (○)
성공은 의도한 어떤 것을 완결 짓는 것이다.
→ 위 문장에서 completion은 '의도한 것에 대한 완결'로, 뒤에서 의미의 한정과 제한을 받기 때문에 정관사 the를 붙여야 한다.

이제 다음 글에서 어색한 부분을 찾아서 고쳐보자. 답이 되는 부분은 실제 시험에 출제된 바 있는 문법 포인트이다.

(a) Tourism plays a big role in the economy of Hawaii. (b) Every month, thousands of the people visit Hawaii to relax. (c) The Hawaiian people live on the tourism industry. (d) Hawaii is never affected by any economic uncertainties.

(a) 관광산업은 하와이 경제에서 큰 역할을 수행한다. (b) 매달 수천 명의 사람들이 하와이에 방문하여 휴식을 취한다. (c) 하와이사람들은 관광산업에 의존하여 살아가고 있다. (d) 하와이는 경제적 불확실성에 전혀 타격을 받지 않는다.
→ (b)의 thousands of the people을 보면 the를 사용했으니 구체적인 특정인들로 한정지어져야 하는데, 위 단락에서는 문맥상 특정인들이 아니라 일반적인 사람들을 지칭하고 있다. 따라서 thousands of the people이 아니라 thousands of people로 쓰는 것이 바람직하다.

□ 출제 경향　breakfast, lunch, dinner와 같은 식사명 앞에는 기본적으로 관사를 사용하지 않는다. 그러나 형용사를 수반하게 되면 관사를 사용한다.

A: What do you want to have for **lunch**?
　　점심으로 뭐 먹고 싶어?

B: I'd like to eat something spicy.
　　뭔가 매운 걸 먹고 싶어.
→ for와 lunch 사이에 관사를 쓰면 안 된다.

A: Son, never skip **breakfast**. It's necessary for your studies.
　　얘야, 아침은 절대로 거르지 마라. 공부하려면 꼭 필요하단다.

B: I know, Dad. I read an article that said that eating **breakfast** helps brain activity.
　　저도 알아요, 아빠. 아침을 먹는 게 두뇌 활동에 도움이 된다는 기사를 읽었어요.
→ breakfast 앞에 관사를 쓰면 안 된다.

Having **a good breakfast** is important for students and workers since it sets the tone for the rest of the day.
아침 식사를 든든하게 하는 것은 그날의 나머지 시간이 어떠할지를 결정하기 때문에 학생과 직장인들에게 중요하다.
→ 관사 a를 쓴 이유는 breakfast 앞에 수식하는 형용사 good이 있기 때문이다.
▶ set the tone (습관·풍조를) 확립하다, 분위기를 형성하다[결정하다]

※ 때때로 앞에 형용사가 없어도 breakfast, lunch, dinner 앞에 관사 a가 오는 경우가 있다. have a lunch break나 make a dinner menu와 같은 것들인데, 여기서 관사 a는 lunch / dinner가 아니라 그 뒤에 나오는 break / menu와 호응한다.

Part I Choose the option that best completes each dialogue.

1   A: I know you are lying through your teeth. Your answer is as clear as mud. Tell me the truth.

B: I already did. I gave you _____.

(a) a honest answer
(b) a honest answers
(c) an honest answer
(d) an honest answers

2   A: What do you say to _____ with me tonight?
B: Let me check my schedule first.

(a) have dinner
(b) having a dinner
(c) have a dinner
(d) having dinner

Part II Choose the option that best completes each sentence.

3   In today's dog-eat-dog society, having _____ is a must, and earning an advanced degree will catapult you into a better position with better job security.

(a) an university degree
(b) a university degree
(c) university degree
(d) such a degrees

Part III Read each dialogue or passage carefully and identify the option that contains a grammatical error.

4   (a) A: I'm going to have nice dinner with Sue at a fancy restaurant tonight.
(b) B: That sounds like a good plan.
(c) A: Would you like to join us?
(d) B: If you are sure she won't mind, I'll go with you.

5 (a) A: How long does it take to go from Seoul to Busan by airplane?
   (b) B: I have never flown in an airplane, but I heard it takes a hour or so.
   (c) A: Really? That's a very short journey.
   (d) B: But I'll rather take a KTX train. It's cheaper and more convenient considering that you have to go to Kimpo Airport to fly and then arrive at Kimhae Airport before you can go to downtown Busan.

6 (a) The National Institute of Health will announce some new guidelines to improve the management of rheumatoid arthritis in adults. (b) Thousands of the people with rheumatoid arthritis are expected to benefit from the new guidelines. (c) The guidelines will be available on the Internet from March 1. (d) However, some medical professionals are saying that it is too premature to put the guidelines into practice.

7 (a) My daughter, who is in elementary school, recently came up to me and said that she was wealthier than I was as she showed me a 10-billion-won toy check. (b) She told me that most of her friends at school these days play with toy checkbooks while they are having the lunch. (c) The problem, however, is that these checks are marked with astronomical numbers ranging from a billion to a trillion won, so they are unrealistic in actual life. (d) As a result, these days, some youngsters who have no income recklessly use their credit cards and make their parents pay their bills.

8 (a) In front of a government house is a well. (b) Water in the well never goes dry even during severe droughts. (c) In the old days, many people depended on the well for water. (d) With the advent of modern-day lifestyles, the well has seen its status reduced from a source of life to a mere tourist spot.

9 (a) Rationale behind calling for the abolition of capital punishment is simple. (b) No one has the right to take another person's life. (c) Also, human judgment is not perfect. (d) Once someone is executed, there is no way to undo that in case the victim is later found to be innocent.

10 (a) Due to the economic recession, youth unemployment rate around the world is at record high levels these days. (b) In order to heighten the applicants' prospects of landing the job that they want, they try to become more competitive than others. (c) There are several crucial qualifications that personnel managers look for in their prospective employees. (d) Foreign language skills are highly valued among other things.

GP | 49 명사와 관사

□ **출제 경향** 특정 명사가 나올 때 관사를 빠뜨린 후 틀린 부분을 찾으라는 문제가 주로 출제된다.

❶ 셀 수 있는 명사와 관사

가산명사가 나올 때 그 명사가 단수형이면 앞에 부정관사 a[an] 또는 정관사 the가 와야 하고, 복수형이면 부정관사 없이 쓰거나 정관사 the를 쓴다.

다음 문장에서 틀린 부분을 찾아보자.

Because of their horrible experiences in the Iraq War, the soldiers have to see counselor on a monthly basis.
이라크 전에서 겪은 끔찍한 경험 때문에 병사들은 매달 상담사의 치료를 받아야 한다.
→ counselor는 셀 수 있는 명사이기 때문에 부정관사 a를 붙이거나 복수로 처리해야 한다. 간단한 문법이지만 실전에서는 의외로 답을 찾기 힘든 항목이므로 평소에 잘 익혀두어야 한다.

❷ the를 붙이는 국가 명

일반적으로 국가의 이름에는 the를 붙이지 않는다. 그러나 여러 주가 모여 이루어진 연방 국가나 군도로 이루어진 국가의 경우 the를 붙이는 경우가 있으니 알아두도록 하자.

the United States of America 미합중국   **the** Netherlands 네덜란드
the Philippines 필리핀   **the** Bahamas 바하마

❸ 호격과 관사

호격을 사용할 때, 즉 사람이나 사물을 부를 때는 명사 앞에 관사를 붙이지 않는다. 이런 문제는 Part III에 잘 나오는데, 단편적인 문법 지식을 가지고 접근하기보다는 문장의 전체 흐름을 조망하면서 호격이 사용되었는지 아닌지부터 신속하게 파악하는 것이 중요하다.

다음 예문들에서 틀린 부분을 찾아보자.

The boys, be ambitious.
소년들이여, 야망을 가져라.
→ '소년들이여'라고 부르는 것이므로 호격이다. 관사 없이 boys로 써야 한다.

A: I just finished reading this book. The good book.
이 책 이제 막 다 읽었어. 좋은 책이야.

B: What is it about?
무엇에 관한 내용인데?
→ A의 말에서 The good book.은 호격이다. 따라서 the를 빼야 한다.

GP | 50 주의할 관사의 쓰임

☐ **출제 경향** 수량이나 종류를 나타내는 단어 뒤에 한정사 및 관사가 쓰이는 용법을 묻는 문제가 종종 출제되므로 잘 익혀두도록 한다.

❶ 「most[any/some/all/none]+of+한정사」

most[any/some/all/none]+of의 경우, of 뒤에 한정사를 써야 한다. the, its, his, her, their 등의 한정사가 없으면 틀린 문장이다.

Most of the nations expressed deep concern over the spread of the epidemic that broke out in China.
중국에서 발생한 전염병의 확산에 대해 대부분의 국가가 깊은 우려를 표명했다.

It seems to me that **all of the** clothes on the table look attractive, but you only want the expensive ones.
내 눈에는 테이블에 놓여 있는 모든 옷이 좋아 보이는데 너는 비싼 옷들만 원하는구나.

Some of my credit cards in the purse on the table disappeared while I was answering the phone.
전화를 받는 동안 테이블 위에 놓여 있던 지갑 안에서 내 신용카드 몇 장이 사라졌다.

❷ 「kind[sort/type]+of+명사」

a/the/this 등의 「(단수) 한정사+kind[sort/type] of」 뒤에는 관사 없이 단수 명사가 오고, 「(복수) 한정사+kinds[sorts/types] of」 뒤에는 관사 없이 불가산 명사 또는 복수 명사가 온다.

This kind of food is called junk food.
이와 같은 음식을 정크 푸드라고 한다.
→ This kind of 뒤의 food 앞에 a나 the를 쓰면 틀린다.

What sort of bait do people usually use for salmon?
연어에는 주로 어떤 종류의 미끼를 씁니까?
→ bait 앞에 관사를 쓰면 틀린다.

There are various **types of flora and fauna** in the Amazon.
아마존에는 다양한 종류의 동식물군이 존재한다.
→ flora and fauna 앞에 관사를 쓰면 틀린다. ▶ flora and fauna 식물군과 동물군

❸ 「kind[sort]+of+형용사 또는 동사」: 다소, 약간

This box is **kind of** heavy for me to carry. 이 박스는 내가 들기에는 약간 무거운 편이다.
I **sort of** expected you to come late. 난 네가 늦게 올 거라고 얼마간 예상하고 있었다.

Part I Choose the option that best completes each dialogue.

1 A: Why do you look so disheartened? Did something serious happen to you?
   B: My doctor told me that I will lose _____ in 5 years.

   (a) most of all hair
   (b) most of my hair
   (c) most my hair
   (d) all almost of my hair

2 A: I'd like to sign up for yoga lessons next month.
   B: There are _____ that you can take.

   (a) several kinds of the yoga classes
   (b) the several kinds of yoga class
   (c) several kinds of yoga classes
   (d) several kind of yoga classes

3 A: _____ ! Can I have a full glass of water ASAP?
   B: No problem, sir. Just hold on a second, and I will bring it to you.

   (a) The waiter
   (b) A waiter
   (c) An waiter
   (d) Waiter

Part II Choose the option that best completes each sentence.

4 Jose Rizal was the most prominent advocate for reforms in _____ when it was colonized by Spain.

   (a) the Philippines
   (b) the Philippine
   (c) Philippines
   (d) Philippine

5 The lawmaker did little to make the people in his constituency happy, so it is no wonder that _____ in his district voted against him in the latest general elections.

   (a) most of the voters
   (b) most of voters
   (c) the most voters
   (d) all voters almost

Part III Read each dialogue or passage carefully and identify the option that contains a grammatical error.

6 (a) A: What do your clients do for a living?
   (b) B: Some of clients are irregular workers doing odd jobs that only pay minimum wage.
   (c) A: Do you charge them when they need your services badly but do not have enough money?
   (d) B: I usually give them a discount and only make them pay what they can. That way, I can give them a chance to save face.

7 (a) A: How did the interview go?
   (b) B: Pretty well. They offered me a position on the marketing team and said they would pay my tuition if I decided to get a marketing degree.
   (c) A: That's great. You've always wanted to do that kind of activity.
   (d) B: Yeah, so I will accept their offer.

8 (a) There was fire at a government complex in Seoul last night. (b) It is said that the fire was set by a disgruntled worker who was let go by his company a month ago. (c) The arsonist was, of course, arrested by the police for sabotaging public property. (d) He will face incarceration of up to 5 years or be fined as much as 50 million won.

9 (a) Vocative expressions are used in direct addresses when the identity of the party being addressed is expressly mentioned in a sentence. (b) One example is in the sentence, "I do not like a Kim." (c) Kim is a vocative expression pointing out the person being spoken to. (d) Grammatically, an article should not be used in front of a vocative expression.

10 (a) It is crucial that a leader communicate both a clear vision as well as a clear set of priorities to the people under his or her command. (b) This is true for any type of a leader, from multinational CEOs to four-star generals. (c) By making everyone from the highest ranking person to the lowest ranking one aware of what is going on, an individual will be able to lead more easily. (d) While this may seem obvious, surprisingly, there are many people in positions of leadership who fail to do this relatively simple task.

GP 51 관사의 관용표현

□ **출제 경향** 다음은 관사가 사용된 관용적인 표현들이다. 관사의 성격을 떠나 무조건 외워야 하는 필수 표현들이니 확실히 알아두도록 하자.

❶ 정관사의 관용표현

around **the** world 세계 곳곳에

in **the** future 미래에

in **the** distance 저 멀리, 먼 곳에

in **the** long run 긴 안목으로 보면, 결국은

in **the** short[long] term 단기적으로[장기적으로]

listen to **the** radio 라디오를 듣다

the tip of the iceberg 빙산의 일각

Where is **the** restroom? 화장실이 어디죠?

You have **the** wrong number. 전화 잘못 거셨습니다.

Do you have **the** time? 몇 시 입니까?

cf. Do you have time? 시간 있으세요?

on **the** go 끊임없이 활동하여, 바쁜

The intelligence agency collects information that comes from **around the world**.
그 정보기관은 전 세계에서 나오는 정보를 수집한다.

A: Can I speak to James? 제임스와 통화할 수 있을까요?

B: I am afraid that **you have the wrong number**. 전화를 잘못 거신 것 같군요.

Though it is going downhill, the economy will grow again **in the long term**.
지금은 경기가 하향세를 그리고 있지만 장기적으로 다시 성장할 것이다.

❷ 부정관사의 관용표현

a must 꼭 필요한 것

be at **a** standstill 답보[정체] 상태에 있다

as **a** result of ~의 결과로

reach **an** agreement 합의를 보다

It is **a** small world. 세상 참 좁구나.

Is it **a** he or **a** she? (아기나 동물이 태어났을 때) 아들[수컷]이니, 딸[암컷]이니?

as **a** whole 전반적으로, 대체적으로

all of **a** sudden 갑자기

come to **an** end 끝이 나다

Have **a** good time. 즐거운 시간 보내세요.

It is hard to **reach an agreement** when scientists debate global warming.
과학자들이 지구 온난화에 대해 토론하면 합의에 이르기가 어렵다.

Our relationship must **come to an end** since you cheated on me.
당신이 나를 속이고 바람을 피웠으니 우리 관계를 이제 끝내야겠어요.

As a whole, it takes about 10 years to become specialized in one field.
대체적으로 한 분야에서 전문가가 되기까지는 약 10년이 걸린다.

Part I Choose the option that best completes each dialogue.

1 A: When I first saw her, _____ , I didn't know what to say.
   B: I know what you mean. She is really gorgeous.

   (a) all of sudden
   (b) all of a sudden
   (c) all of the sudden
   (d) all of suddens

2 A: If you consume slow foods instead of fast foods, you will recover from your illness and
      become fit _____.
   B: Thank you, Doctor, for your words of encouragement. I will follow your advice.

   (a) in a long run
   (b) in the long run
   (c) on the short term
   (d) in a short term

Part II Choose the option that best completes each sentence.

3 *The Firm*, written by John Grisham, is _____ for those who want to learn legal jargon.

   (a) must-read
   (b) a must-read
   (c) the must-read
   (d) some must-read

4 More than 2,000 workers employed by the world's largest automaker were laid off at
   the beginning of this month, but industry insiders are saying that the layoffs are only
   _____ and that a significantly larger number of employees will lose their jobs
   in the months to come.

   (a) tips of an iceberg
   (b) a tip of the iceberg
   (c) the tip of the iceberg
   (d) the tip of an iceberg

Part III Read each dialogue or passage carefully and identify the option that contains a
grammatical error.

5 (a) There was a traffic accident on Highway 38 near the Singal exit ramp. (b) A passenger
   car and a pickup truck collided with each other. (c) Fortunately, no fatalities were reported.
   (d) However, the entire southbound lane from Singal to Daejeon is still at the standstill.

Unit 11 주어와 동사의 수 일치

GP 52 긴 주어가 나올 때

□ **출제 경향** 주어·동사 수의 일치 문제는 매달 빠짐없이 출제되며 Part III에 특히 잘 나온다. 주어가 긴 문장에서는 문장의 주어와 동사가 무엇인지 금방 파악하기가 쉽지 않으므로 이를 정확히 구분할 수 있어야 한다. 또한 그 주어가 단수인지 복수인지, 인칭은 어떠한지 등을 파악하는 훈련을 평소에 확실히 해두는 것이 좋다.

다음 각각의 문장에서 틀린 부분을 찾아보자.

One of the many aspects of a rare genetic condition called dermatopathia pigmentosa reticularis are that the person with it has no fingerprints.

망상 색소 피부병이라고 불리는 희귀 유전병의 여러 특징 중 하나는 이 병을 앓는 환자에게는 지문이 없다는 점입니다.

→ 위 문장의 주어는 One, 즉 여러 특징 중의 '하나'라는 뜻이다. 주어가 단수이므로 동사도 역시 단수가 되기 때문에 동사를 are가 아니라 is로 바꿔야 한다. 주어 부분이 매우 길어서 동사가 어디에 있는지 헷갈리는 이러한 유형이 잘 출제된다.

Former President Bill Clinton, who had an inappropriate relationship with Monica Lewinsky, then a White House intern, still get nagged by his political opponents for his misconduct.

빌 클린턴 전 대통령은 당시 백악관 인턴이었던 모니카 르윈스키와 부적절한 관계를 맺었었는데 아직까지도 정적들로부터 그 잘못된 행위에 대해 공격받고 있다.

→ 주어 부분이 길긴 하지만 문장 전체의 주어는 '빌 클린턴 전 대통령(Former President Bill Clinton)'으로, 관계대명사 who절은 이 주어를 수식하는 역할을 할 뿐이다. 주어가 3인칭이고 시제는 현재이므로 동사를 get이 아니라 gets로 바꿔야 한다.

Some civic group activists, having gone through many troubles during the 1980s and 1990s, is now leading the party.

일부 시민단체 운동가들은 1980년대와 1990년대에 온갖 고난을 다 겪고 난 후 이제는 당을 이끄는 주축이다.

→ 위 문장의 주어는 Some civic group activists로, some은 '일부, 여러 명'이라는 복수의 의미이고 activists가 복수형으로 쓰였으므로 동사는 is가 아니라 are가 되어야 한다. 삽입절은 주어·동사 수의 일치에 영향을 끼치지 않는다.

GP | 53　the number of / a number of / few

□ 출제 경향　the number of와 a number of의 의미와 문법적인 차이는 확연하다. 시험에 이 표현들이 나오면 일단 수 일치 문제가 아닌지 확인하자. 또한 few 자체에 복수의 의미가 있기 때문에 few만 보고도 바로 답을 찾아낼 수 있어야 한다.

❶ 「the number of 복수명사+단수동사」: ~의 수

In the European Union, **the number of women** who are graduating with degrees in science and engineering **is** on the rise.
유럽 연합에서 이공계 학위를 취득하고 졸업하는 여성의 수가 늘어나고 있는 추세이다.

❷ 「a number of 복수명사 + 복수동사」: 많은

A number of protesters are taking to the streets to fight corruption in officialdom.
수많은 시위자들이 공직사회의 부패와 싸우고자 거리로 나오고 있다.
▶ take to the streets 요구를 내걸고 가두 시위에 나서다

❸ 「few+복수명사+복수동사」

few에는 그 자체에 복수의 의미가 있으므로 다음과 같은 표현들이 주어로 나오면 그 뒤에는 무조건 복수 명사가 나와야 하고 동사도 복수 처리해야 한다.

few (수가) 거의 없는	a few (수가) 약간 있는
fewer (수가) 더 적은	fewest (수가) 가장 적은
only a few (수가) 몇 안 되는, 극히 소수만	quite a few 꽤 많은, 상당수의

Few people know how to cope with the crisis.
그 위기 상황에 어떻게 대처해야 하는지 아는 사람이 거의 없다.

Quite a few students are about to sign up for quantum mechanics.
상당수의 학생들이 양자 역학 수업을 막 신청하려는 참이다.

Check-up TEST 52~53

Part I Choose the option that best completes each dialogue.

1   A: How many years have passed since you came to Korea, John?
    B: It's 2018 now, so _____ have passed since I first set foot on Korean soil in 2000.

    (a) only a few years
    (b) the number of years
    (c) quite a few years
    (d) not a single year

Part II Choose the option that best completes each sentence.

2   The number of people residing in Seoul _____ one fifth of the entire population of South Korea, making Seoul the largest city in the country.

    (a) accounting for
    (b) accounts for
    (c) account for
    (d) is accounted for

3   Few _____ what caused the plane crash that killed more than 90 passengers.

    (a) survivors know
    (b) survivor knows
    (c) survivors knowing
    (d) survivors to know

4   As Steve has not saved money enough, there _____ that he can afford to buy.

    (a) is a few car
    (b) are a few cars
    (c) is few car
    (d) are few cars

Part Ⅲ Read each dialogue or passage carefully and identify the option that contains a grammatical error.

5 (a) A: Have you noticed any differences after the success of the TV drama in which you were the male protagonist?
   (b) B: When I walk down the street nowadays, few people recognize me and request my autograph.
   (c) A: You must be very happy and proud of yourself.
   (d) B: In the past, I was an obscure figure recognized by few people. Now, I feel like I have become a celebrity.

6 (a) One appealing aspect of living in cities are easy access to everything from shopping malls to movie theaters to urban parks. (b) One downside of urban life is breathing polluted air. (c) The main culprit of air pollution in cities is cars and motorcycles. (d) Vehicle exhausts are responsible for more than 50% of air contamination.

7 (a) For the longest time, health-conscious individuals have avoided eating chocolate despite its delicious taste. (b) In their view, chocolate is an unhealthy food for a number of different reason. (c) Included among these are its association with fat and refined sugar and its caffeine content. (d) Interestingly, recent research has proven that much of the bad reputation that chocolate has acquired is actually undeserved.

8 (a) Americans are usually very kind and friendly. (b) One American guy, whom I asked for directions, went out of his way to take me to the post office. (c) On the other hand, some Chinese people, including the old man who hit me on a crowded bus, is very rude.
   (d) People such as me tend to generalize certain things based on their experiences.

9 (a) A democracy movement took place in Korea in the 1980s. (b) Many of those protesters were young college students struggling to topple the military dictatorship. (c) When the demonstrations came to a head, martial law was proclaimed. (d) The number of civilians, including students, were shot and killed by heavily armed soldiers and police.

10 (a) A number of soldiers still unaccounted for in the maritime accident is more than 100.
   (b) They are feared to be dead because it has been almost 3 weeks since the accident occurred. (c) Their chances of survival are very slim given the facts that the temperature is very low and the weather is very windy. (d) However, the families of the missing soldiers are still hoping for their safe return.

□ **출제 경향** 상관 접속사는 함께 짝지어 쓰이는 접속사를 묻는 문제와 수 일치 문제로 출제된다.

❶ 함께 짝지어 쓰이는 접속사

both A and B A와 B 둘 다	**either A or B** A와 B 둘 중 하나
neither A nor B A와 B 둘 다 아닌	**not A but B** A가 아니라 B
not only A but also B A뿐만 아니라 B도	**A as well as B** B뿐만 아니라 A도

Both the religious community **and** the political community have voiced their concerns over the negative effects of stem cell research.
종교계와 정치계 양측 모두 줄기세포 연구의 부정적인 영향에 대해 우려를 표명해왔다.

Neither the management **nor** the workers try to reach an agreement on a pay hike.
노사 모두 임금 인상에 대한 합의에 도달하기 위해 최선을 다하지 않고 있다.

❷ 상관 접속사가 주어로 쓰일 때 동사의 수

both A and B	주어는 A, B 둘 다이므로 복수 동사를 쓴다.
either A or B neither A nor B not A but B not only A but also B	B에 맞춰 수를 일치시킨다.
A as well as B	A에 맞춰 수를 일치시킨다.

Either you or I **was** wrong on the question that was given by the math teacher.
너나 나 둘 중에 한 명은 수학 선생님께서 낸 문제를 틀렸다.

The professors as well as the dean of the department **are** willing to introduce a new scholarship program.
학과장뿐만 아니라 교수들도 새로운 장학금 프로그램을 도입하고자 한다.

GP | 55 either[neither/each]+of/작품 제목

□ **출제 경향** 다음 두 가지 경우, 많은 TEPS 수험자들이 동사를 단수형으로 써야 하는지 복수형으로 써야 하는지 혼동하곤 한다. 이번 기회에 확실히 알아두자.

❶ 「either[neither / each]+ of+복수명사+단수동사」

Either of the employees **is** able to handle the duties.
직원 두 사람 중 어느 누구나 그 업무를 처리할 수 있다.

Neither of the boxers **was** prepared to advance to the final round.
두 복싱 선수 모두 결승전에 진출할 만큼의 준비는 되지 않은 상태였다.

Each of the answers **is** worth 30 points.
정답은 각각 30점씩이다.

❷ 「책[작품] 제목+단수동사」

책 제목, 영화 제목, 강연 제목, 논문 제목 등을 표기할 때는 글씨 모양이 살짝 기울어진 이탤릭체를 사용한다. 제목이 복수형이라 하더라도 하나의 작품을 의미하기 때문에 당연히 단수취급을 한다. 이 문제는 Part III에서만 출제되고 있는데, 의외로 놓치기 쉬우므로 주의해야 한다.

Three Days to Kill, directed by McG is a must-see for those who are interested in crime thriller.
맥지가 연출한 〈3 Days to Kill〉은 범죄 스릴러에 관심이 있는 사람이라면 꼭 봐야 하는 영화이다.
→ 영화 제목이 'Three Days ~' 로 복수 형태이지만 단수 취급한다.

500 Spanish Verbs, published by ABC, a publishing company, is designed to help Spanish learners efficiently study the essential Spanish verbs.
ABC 출판사에서 펴낸 《스페인어 동사 500》은 스페인어 학습자가 필수 스페인어 동사를 효율적으로 학습하는 데 도움이 되도록 기획된 책이다.
→ 주어인 500 Spanish Verbs가 복수 형태로 표시되어 있지만 책 제목이기 때문에 단수 취급한다.

Part I Choose the option that best completes each dialogue.

1 A: Who got the answer right?

 B: Neither Susan _____ John got it right. They were ill-prepared for the
 contest because they had been sick for several days.

 (a) or

 (b) and

 (c) but

 (d) nor

2 A: Neither of the national football teams _____ beat the team from Brazil
 2 years ago.

 B: Brazil beat them both 5 to zero.

 (a) were able to

 (b) was able to

 (c) are able to

 (d) is able to

Part II Choose the option that best completes each sentence.

3 The company as well as its employees _____ persistently pursuing its goal of
 reaching $30 billion in exports and finally attained that number last year.

 (a) is

 (b) was

 (c) are

 (d) were

4 Neither of the 2 major foreign coffee shop chains _____ in the Korean market.

 (a) is doing well

 (b) are doing well

 (c) has well

 (d) have well

Part III Read each dialogue or passage carefully and identify the option that contains a grammatical error.

5 (a) A: Do you think Australia will come in first in this year's Asian Cup?
  (b) B: In my opinion, Japan will beat Australia.
  (c) A: Each of the nations have a chance to win, but I hope Australia prevails.
  (d) B: I hope otherwise.

6 (a) A: Not only I but also Jane work hard to pass the exam to become a judge.
  (b) B: How long have you been preparing for the bar exam?
  (c) A: I began studying law in 2016, so it has been 3 years.
  (d) B: I hope that you and Jane will be successful.

7 (a) Our nation is currently experiencing economic conditions that are unprecedented. (b) Last September was the forty-ninth consecutive month in which more jobs were created than were lost in the entire country. (c) This is the longest period of uninterrupted growth in the history of our country. (d) In addition, the number of exports, as well as the dollar value of these exports, have continued to rise for the past several months.

8 (a) North Korea is adept at brinkmanship and bluffing, as is often the case with Iran. (b) Neither of the 2 rogue states seem to care that much about the wellbeing or welfare of their citizens. (c) Poverty-stricken North Korea carried out some currency reforms only to experience some adverse side effects. (d) Many North Koreans are deserting their country for South Korea.

9 (a) The boat the president and his daughters was on capsized in the middle of the Pacific Ocean on Friday night. (b) Rumors have it that the boat was overturned as a result of an act of terrorism. (c) Several terrorist organizations claimed responsibility for the accident. (d) Fortunately, neither the president nor his daughters were hurt in the incident.

10 (a) *Cats*, written by English composer Andrew Lloyd Webber, is a musical. (b) The musical opened in the West End and on Broadway in 1981 and 1982, respectively. (c) In the West End, it ran for twenty-one years, and on Broadway, it ran for eighteen years. (d) *Cats* have been performed around the world many times and has been translated into more than 20 languages.

기타 문법 포인트

GP | 56 it과 one의 구분 / it과 them의 구분

□ 출제 경향 대명사는 주로 it과 one을 구분하는 문제로 종종 출제된다. 또한 긴 문장 내에서 앞서 언급한 명사를 단수인 it 으로 받아야 하는지 복수인 they[them]로 받아야 하는지를 구분하는 문제도 출제된다.

① it과 one의 구분

■ it 앞에 언급된 바로 그것

The board of directors unanimously agreed to **the proposal** to build another sports complex in the city even though minority shareholders voiced concerns over **it**.

이사회는 그 도시에 또 다른 스포츠 단지를 건설한다는 계획안에 만장일치로 찬성했지만 소액 주주들은 그 안에 대해 우려를 표명했다.

→ 앞에 언급된 단어 the proposal을 it으로 받았다. ▶ unanimously 만장일치로

■ one 앞에 나온 것과 비슷한 종류의 다른 것

The cars manufactured by the Saturn Company turned out to be defective, so Americans are buying other **ones**.

새턴 자동차 회사에서 생산된 차에 결함이 있는 것으로 판명되어 미국인들은 다른 차를 구입하고 있다.

→ ones는 앞에 나오는 The cars를 받지만 '새턴 사에서 제조되는 차'가 아니라 그것과 비슷한 종류의 차, 즉 일반적인 '자동차'를 의미한다.

② it과 them의 구분

앞서 언급된 명사가 단수인지 복수인지에 따라 it 또는 them으로 받는다. 문장이 길어지면 앞서 언급된 명사가 무엇이었 는지 찾기 어려워지므로, 대명사 문제가 나오면 무엇을 지칭하고 있는지 찾아내는 연습을 해야 한다.

다음 문장에서 틀린 부분을 찾아보자.

The government is looking for some ways to develop the country's infrastructure, and many businesses are coming up with it to do their part to improve society.

정부는 나라의 기간산업을 발전시키기 위한 몇 가지 방법을 모색하고 있고, 다수의 기업들은 그 방법들을 제안하며 사회 발전을 위한 자신들의 역할을 다하고 있다.

→ many businesses are coming up with it에서 it이 앞에 나오는 some ways를 받는 대명사로 쓰였는데, some ways는 복수이므로 it이 아니라 them으로 받아야 한다.

Part II Choose the option that best completes each sentence.

1   As a part of his home renovation project, he decided to replace his old chandelier with a sleek new _____.

(a) them

(b) the one

(c) one

(d) it

2   The company's first quarter profits rose 14%, but sales in North America continued to decrease as many customers stayed away from _____ flagship products.

(a) his

(b) many

(c) their

(d) its

Part III Read each dialogue or passage carefully and identify the option that contains a grammatical error.

3   (a) A: Did you hear the news that Mercury Finance filed for bankruptcy?

(b) B: I didn't hear that, but I knew it could happen.

(c) A: No way. The company collected a considerable amount of revenue last year, and analysts also said the company had a bright future.

(d) B: Information of real value comes from insiders. I'd like to introduce it to you if you want.

4   (a) A honeypot in a network refers to a trap to lure would-be attackers into one instead of having them disrupt servers. (b) A honeypot is an isolated system that is left unguarded while being constantly monitored by system administrators. (c) To be effective, a honeypot has to appear real enough to hackers, but the honeypot must not contain any data of real value. (d) Once an intruder breaks into the honeypot, the network administrator can examine the intruder and the method of intrusion.

5   (a) Many Koreans insist that few people know about Korean literature simply because so little has been translated into other languages and published in other countries. (b) However, this statement is false since over seventy books have been translated in English during the past decade. (c) Yet some people claim that many of these translations are in poor English, so people cannot fully understand it. (d) There is some truth in this, but the quality of many translations has been improving in recent years.

□ 출제 경향 TEPS 문법 시험에는 문법 문제라기보다는 어휘나 표현 관련 문제처럼 느껴지는 문제들도 다수 등장한다. 다음 표현은 확실히 외워두도록 하자.

1 주요 표현 (1)

leave something[a lot] to be desired 미진한 점이 있다[많다], 유감스러운 점이 있다[많다]

leave nothing to be desired 거의 흠잡을 데가 없다, 더 이상 바랄 것이 없다

have no choice[alternative] but to + 동사원형 ~하지 않을 수 없다, ~할 수밖에 없다

It is needless to say that~ ~라고 말할 필요도 없다

have yet to + 동사원형 아직 ~하지 못했다, 아직 ~하고 있지 않다

make it a rule to + 동사원형 ~하는 것을 규칙으로 하다, 늘 ~하기로 하고 있다

The speech by the president this morning **left something to be desired** because it was rambling and hard to follow.
오늘 아침에 있었던 대통령 연설은 산만하고 이해하기가 어려웠기 때문에 미진한 점이 있었다.
▶ rambling (말·글 등이) 산만한; 두서없는

This program **leaves a lot to be desired** even though it is very expensive.
이 프로그램은 매우 비싼데도 불구하고 부족한 점이 많다.

My new job teaching English **leaves nothing to be desired**. I have a high salary, friendly coworkers, and fringe benefits.
영어를 가르치는 내 새로운 일은 더할 나위 없을 정도로 좋다. 보수도 좋고 동료들도 친절하며 부가 수당도 있다.
▶ fringe benefit 부가 수당

North Korea **has no choice but to** abandon its nuclear program if it wants to receive international assistance.
북한이 국제사회의 지원을 받고자 한다면 핵 개발 계획을 포기하는 것 외에는 다른 선택의 여지가 없다.

It is needless to say that English is the lingua franca of the world.
영어가 세계 공통어임은 두말할 필요도 없다.
▶ lingua franca 국제어, 공통어

He **has yet to finish** the assignment due tomorrow.
그는 기한이 내일까지인 과제를 아직 끝내지 못했다.

I **make it a rule to** read more than three English books a month, which has helped dramatically increase my TEPS score.
나는 한 달에 영어책을 세 권 이상 읽는 것을 생활화하고 있는데, 그러다 보니 TEPS 점수가 급격히 오르는 데 도움이 되었다.

be worth V-ing ~할 가치가 있다

be busy V-ing ~하느라 바쁘다

end up V-ing 결국 ~하게 되다

cannot help V-ing ~할 수밖에 없다

have a hard time V-ing 힘들게 ~하다, ~하는 데 어려움을 겪다

spend [시간/노력] in[on] V-ing ~하는 데 시간[노력]을 들이다

have a good time 좋은 시간을 보내다

junior to ~보다 손아래인[나이가 어린]

senior to ~보다 손위인[나이가 많은]

too good to be true 너무 좋아서 사실이 아닌 것 같은

This weekly magazine **is worth reading** since it covers almost everything from economics to culture to sports.
이 주간지는 경제, 문화, 스포츠까지 거의 모든 영역을 다루고 있기 때문에 읽을 만한 가치가 있다.

I **was busy making** calls to potential customers who showed an interest in joining the club.
나는 클럽에 가입하는 데 관심을 보인 잠재 고객들에게 전화를 거느라 바빴다.

The military junta **ended up disintegrating** due to its lack of money.
그 군사 정권은 자금 부족으로 결국 붕괴되고 말았다.
▶ junta (쿠데타 이후) 권력을 장악하는 군사 정부 disintegrate 붕괴되다; 분해되다

The businessman **ended up** in jail due to embezzlement.
그 사업가는 횡령으로 결국 철창신세가 되었다.
▶ embezzlement 횡령

I **couldn't help laughing** at Fred when he said he was going to run in the upcoming election.
프레드가 곧 있을 선거에 출마할 거라고 말했을 때 나는 웃지 않을 수 없었다.

I have **had a hard time meeting** the deadline for the assignment.
나는 간신히 과제의 제출 기한을 맞추었다.

I **spent** a lot of time, money, and energy **working** on the book.
나는 그 책 작업을 하느라 많은 시간과 돈, 힘을 들였다.

I **had a good time** with many foreigners in the party.
나는 그 파티에서 여러 외국인들과 함께 좋은 시간을 보냈다.

I am **junior to** him by two years.
나는 그보다 두 살 어리다.

I am 7 years **senior to** him.
나는 그보다 일곱 살 많다.

You must be kidding. That is an opportunity **too good to be true**.
농담이지? 사실이라 믿기엔 너무 좋은 기회잖아.

Part I Choose the option that best completes each dialogue.

1 A: How was the inaugural speech the president gave yesterday?
   B: The speech _____.

   (a) left nothing to desire
   (b) left nothing to be desired
   (c) left nothing to be desiring
   (d) left nothing to have desired

2 A: _____ that computer skills are more important than ever in modern society.
   B: Yeah, I think computer illiterates cannot survive nowadays.

   (a) It's needless to say
   (b) It's needlessly to say
   (c) It's necessarily to say
   (d) It's necessary to be said

3 A: You look depressed these days.
   B: Yeah, I've been _____.

   (a) having a hard time to prepare for the final exam
   (b) having a hard time preparing for the final exam
   (c) having hard time to prepare for the final exam
   (d) having hard time preparing for the final exam

4 A: Could you give me a lift?
   B: Sorry. I can't. I am _____.

   (a) busy in cleaning my room
   (b) busy to clean my room
   (c) busy cleaning my room
   (d) busy for cleaning my room

Part II Choose the option that best completes each sentence.

5 The new edition of the book written by Thomas _____ because it has many mistakes.

   (a) leaves to be desired a lot
   (b) leaves desired to be a lot
   (c) leaves a lot to be desired
   (d) leaves a lot to be desiring

6   They _____ practice for more than 5 hours a day in order to be successful in their fields.

(a) make it a rule for
(b) make it a rule to
(c) make it rule for
(d) make it rule to

Part III   Read each dialogue or passage carefully and identify the option that contains a grammatical error.

7   (a) A: Did you hear that they're putting in a new strip mall in the city?
(b) B: Yeah, it's supposed to have some quality department stores.
(c) A: But some say it will have a negative impact on small businesses.
(d) B: Yeah, I think some small shops will end up to go out of business.

8   (a) A: Hey, Josie. It's time to go.
(b) B: Already? I really lost track of time watching this movie.
(c) A: Did you have good time?
(d) B: Yeah, everything was perfect.

9   (a) Once in the grip of poverty and underdevelopment, many Asians today end up to living in fear of fast-growing obesity. (b) From metropolitan areas to remote islands in the South Pacific, obesity has been emerging as a formidable health threat over the past decade. (c) The growing obesity epidemic can be attributed to higher living standards, rising fast-food consumption, and sedentary lifestyles. (d) In Japan, half of the adult population is overweight or obese.

10 (a) The popular cable television show *The Sopranos* has finally run its course and is coming to an end after eight years. (b) While the final episode has to air, this has not stopped people from speculating about it. (c) Many television commentators are curious as to how the show will end and, most importantly, who gets to live and who gets to die in the mafia-inspired program. (d) Viewers around the world will get to find out on June 10, which is when the final episode is scheduled to air.

GP | 58　당위성을 나타내는 that절

□ 출제 경향 주장·명령·요구·제안의 의미를 나타내는 동사, 명사, 형용사 뒤로 that절 이하의 내용이 '당위성'을 갖게 되면 「should+동사원형」을 쓰는데, 이때 should는 생략 가능하다. 이것이 TEPS 시험에 나오는 문법 포인트이다.

❶ 주장·명령·요구·제안의 동사

insist 주장하다　order 명령하다　demand 요구하다
suggest 제안하다　ask 요청하다　recommend 권고하다　　　＋that＋주어＋(should)＋동사원형
plead 탄원[애원]하다

The chief of the fire station demanded that those who survived the conflagration **should be** taken immediately to the hospital.

= The chief of the fire station demanded that those who survived the conflagration **be** taken immediately to the hospital.

소방서장은 대형 화재에서 생존한 사람들을 즉시 병원에 보내야 한다고 요구했다. ▶ conflagration 대형 화재

❷ 주장·명령·요구·제안의 명사

insistence 주장　order 명령　demand 요구
suggestion 제안　recommendation 권고　　　＋that＋주어＋(should)＋동사원형
plea 탄원[애원]

It was my father's suggestion that I **(should) save** money for a rainy day.
만일의 경우를 대비해 돈을 모아야 한다고 아버지께서 제안하셨다. ▶ for a rainy day 만일의 경우에 대비하여

The demand from the management that employees **(should) work** for more than 50 hours a week has been met with strong resistance.
직원들이 주당 50시간 이상 근무해야 한다는 경영진의 요구는 거센 반발을 받았다.

❸ 주장·명령·요구·제안의 형용사

It is + 　important 중요한　necessary 필요한
　　　　essential 필수적인
　　　　imperative 반드시 해야 하는　　　　　　　　＋that＋주어＋(should)＋동사원형
　　　　mandatory/obligatory/compulsory 의무적인

It is important that the government **(should) allocate** a large portion of the budget to education since it is for the future of our country.
교육은 우리나라의 미래이므로 교육에 상당 부분의 예산을 할당하는 것이 중요하다.

It is mandatory that poor children **(should) be** given equal education opportunities.
가난한 아이들에게 균등한 교육 기회를 제공해야 하는 것은 의무적이다.

Part II Choose the option that best completes each sentence.

1 It is imperative that the government _____ free lunches so that those children will not go hungry and can concentrate on their studies.

(a) gives children on welfare
(b) give children on welfare
(c) gives children in welfare
(d) give children in welfare

2 The Ministry of Patriots and Veterans Affairs recommended that those who fought and were killed in the Korean War from 1950 to 1953 _____ on the list of national honorees.

(a) be put
(b) should put
(c) puts
(d) will be put

Part III Read each dialogue or passage carefully and identify the option that contains a grammatical error.

3 (a) A: Why did all of the male students in our class join the military? Do they all love being soldiers?

(b) B: Of course not. Let me give you the answer. It is mandatory that all physically and mentally able men in Korea should have joined the army.

(c) A: Why is that? Isn't it a waste of time to force every man to serve in the armed forces?

(d) B: No, I don't think so. We are technically at war with North Korea. We have to be prepared.

4 (a) The Office of Government Ethics is an agency in the U.S. government. (b) It establishes the standards of conduct for the executive branch. (c) It issues rules and regulations governing criminal conflict of interest restrictions. (d) It also recommends that civil servants in the federal government abides by a code of ethics.

5 (a) Hypertension is a medical condition where the blood pressure is elevated. (b) It is also known as high blood pressure. (c) Usually, hypertension can be classified as either primary or secondary. (d) Patients with either type of hypertension are advised that they will stay away from eating salt or salty foods.

GP | 59 준동사의 의미상 주어 / 분사구문의 주어

□ **출제 경향** 준동사의 의미상의 주어를 단독적으로 묻거나 또는 의미상의 주어가 포함된 어구의 어순을 묻는 문제로 출제된다. 분사구문의 주어에 대한 문제로는 주절의 내용을 파악하여 분사구문의 주어가 올바르게 되어있는지 판별하는 문제가 잘 출제된다. 문법적으로만 접근하면 틀리기 쉬우므로 내용까지 파악해야 올바른 답을 찾을 수 있다.

❶ to부정사의 의미상 주어

■ 「for + 목적격 + to부정사」

It is time to wake up and smell the coffee.
이제 일어나서 정신 차려야 할 시간이다.
▶ smell the coffee 정신을 차리다

It is time **for the president** to wake up and smell the coffee.
이제 대통령이 일어나서 정신 차려야 할 시간이다.

■ 「of + 목적격 + to부정사」

to부정사의 의미상 주어의 성격 및 성품을 나타내는 형용사가 나올 경우, 전치사는 for가 아니라 of를 사용한다.

It is sweet **of** you to say that.
그렇게 말해주다니 넌 참 상냥하구나.

It is very kind **of** you to help me.
나를 도와주다니 당신은 참 친절하시군요.

❷ 동명사의 의미상 주어

■ 「목적격[소유격] + 동명사」

I object to saying yes to the plan.
나는 그 계획에 찬성하는 것을 반대한다.

I object to **his[him]** saying yes to the plan.
나는 그가 그 계획에 찬성하는 것을 반대한다.

❸ 분사구문의 주어

Giving his students something to read right after the lecture, *they asked* the professor how to do their assignment. (×)
→ Giving his students something to read right after the lecture, **the professor** was asked by his students how to do their assignment. (○)
수업이 끝나자 바로 학생들에게 읽을거리를 나누어 준 교수는 학생들에게 숙제를 어떻게 해야 하는지 질문을 받았다.
→ 위의 문장에서 giving의 주체, 즉 학생들에게 읽을거리를 주는 사람은 누구인가? 바로 교수이다. 그런데 연결된 문장의 주어는 they이고, 이 they는 his students(그의 학생들)를 받으므로 주어가 일치하지 않는 틀린 문장임을 알 수 있다. 따라서 올바른 주어인 the professor를 사용하여 수동태로 고쳐야 맞는 문장이 된다.

Part I Choose the option that best completes each dialogue.

1 A: Do you mind _____?
   B: Yes, I do. Smoking is allowed only in designated areas.

   (a) I smoke here
   (b) mine smoking here
   (c) my smoking here
   (d) smoking me here

2 A: Reaching out to shake hands, _____ on his face.
   B: It showed how much he had been waiting for that moment to invite you there.

   (a) a smile of welcome spread
   (b) he showed a smile of welcome
   (c) the expression of happiness spread
   (d) a smile of welcome was shown

Part II Choose the option that best completes each sentence.

3 For these reasons, it's absolutely critical _____ people who work without supervision to take seriously the issue of self-regulation.

   (a) for
   (b) of
   (c) to
   (d) in

Part III Read each dialogue or passage carefully and identify the option that contains a grammatical error.

4 (a) A: The man who inherited Mr. Wilson's chocolate factory donated his mansion and a million dollars to an orphanage.
   (b) B: It was so generous for him. He even registered himself as an organ donor.
   (c) A: I can't imagine spending my hard-earned money on others.
   (d) B: Me neither. A million dollars is a lot of money.

5 (a) Despite the anti-normalization atmosphere, many Palestinian journalists have continued their efforts to reach reconciliation with Israel. (b) Various reunions and encounters are the fastest ways to improve tolerance and acceptance between the two sides of the wall separating Jews and Arabs. (c) The private sector has acknowledged the need to counter those who are striving to foil the hope of reconciliation between Israel and Palestine. (d) By cutting off funding to their organizations, extremists can be pressured to cease their terrorism activities.

GP | 60 준동사의 시제

□ **출제 경향** 준동사는 단순 시제와 완료형 시제를 사용해야 하는 때의 구분, 의미의 차이, 어순 등 여러 문법 포인트를 묻는 문제로 출제될 수 있으므로 준동사의 특징을 확실히 짚고 넘어가야 한다.

① to부정사의 시제

■ **to부정사의 시제가 본동사와 같을 때**

It is nice **to talk** to you.
당신과 이야기를 나누게 되어 기쁩니다.
→ nice한 감정과 to talk의 행위가 거의 동일하게 일어난다.

■ **to부정사의 시제가 본동사보다 앞설 때**

It is nice **to have finished** the report.
이 일을 끝낸 것이 기쁘다.
→ nice한 감정보다 to have finished라는 행위가 먼저 일어났다.

② 동명사의 시제

■ **동명사의 시제가 본동사와 같을 때**

I don't like **being asked** to deliver a speech.
나는 연설해달라고 부탁받는 일을 좋아하지 않는다.
→ don't like의 시제와 being asked의 시제가 같다.

■ **동명사의 시제가 본동사보다 앞설 때**

The CEO didn't like **having been asked** to give a speech.
그 최고 경영자는 연설을 해달라고 요청 받았었는데 이를 별로 달가워하지 않았다.
→ 요청 받은 시점이 didn't like한 시점보다 앞선다.

③ 분사구문의 시제

■ **분사의 시제가 본동사와 같을 때**

Left alone, he felt hopeless and hapless.
혼자 남겨진 그는 절망적이고 불운하다고 느꼈다.
→ 혼자 남겨진 시점과 felt한 시점이 같다. ▶ hapless 불운한, 불행한

■ **분사의 시제가 본동사보다 앞설 때**

Having received no reply from headquarters, I called again.
나는 본사로부터 답변을 못 받았기 때문에 다시 전화를 했다.
→ 답변을 못 받은 시점이 전화를 다시 한 시점보다 앞선다.

Part I Choose the option that best completes each dialogue.

1 A: By the time you are 45 years old, you will have worked long enough _____
   enough money to pay back the student loan you took out.
   B: That's assuming that I will have worked without taking any time off.

   (a) have earned
   (b) to earn
   (c) to have earned
   (d) earned

2 A: I am ashamed of _____ in the past.
   B: Not everyone is born with a silver spoon in his or her mouth.

   (a) being poor
   (b) having poor
   (c) having been poor
   (d) poor

Part II Choose the option that best completes each sentence.

3 A 12-year-old swimmer shocked the world when he won the gold medal,
   _____ at a new world record of 48.21 seconds.

   (a) passing the finish line
   (b) having passed the finish line
   (c) to have passed the finish line
   (d) have passed the finish line

Part III Read each dialogue or passage carefully and identify the option that contains a grammatical error.

4 (a) A: Flying in from Canada for 13 hours yesterday, he has been working tirelessly to meet
       the deadline.
   (b) B: What is more surprising is that he will be 70 in two weeks.
   (c) A: It is not only his body that looks 50 but also his mind.
   (d) B: He is enthusiastic about challenging the limits of the human body.

5 (a) It is well known to many that the Chinese character that represents the word "crisis"
   is formed by two individual characters that have been placed next to one another. (b) The
   first represents "danger" while the second stands for "opportunity." (c) Today, I would like
   to speak to you about an ongoing crisis that offers us both danger and also opportunity.
   (d) I am speaking, of course, about the changes in the global climate that seem to be
   occurring for quite some time.

GP | 61 의미 차이에 유의해야 할 동사

□ **출제 경향** to부정사와 동명사를 모두 목적어로 취하는 동사 중에, 뒤에 to부정사를 쓰느냐 동명사를 쓰느냐에 따라 뜻이 완전히 달라지는 동사들이 있다. 의미 차이에 유의하여 다음에 나오는 경우들을 숙지해 두자.

❶ 목적어에 따라 의미가 달라지는 동사

■ forget + to부정사 **(미래에) ~할 것을 잊어버리다**

　forget + 동명사 **(과거에) ~했던 것을 잊어버리다**

My wife was angry at me because I **forgot to take** out the garbage this morning.
내가 오늘 아침에 쓰레기를 내놓는 것을 잊어버려서 아내가 나에게 화를 냈다.

I can never **forget hearing** the song for the first time.
나는 이 노래를 처음으로 들었던 때를 결코 잊지 못한다.

■ regret + to부정사 **(지금) ~하게 되어 유감이다**

　regret + 동명사 **(과거에) ~했던 것을 후회하다**

The board of directors **regrets to announce** that the company has to let a fifth of its employees go.
이사회는 직원의 5분의 1을 해고하기로 결정했다는 소식을 발표하게 되어 유감입니다.

I **regret** not **taking** the TEPS test this month.
나는 이번 달에 TEPS 시험을 치지 못한 것이 후회가 된다.

■ try + to부정사 **~하기 위해 노력하다**

　try + 동명사 **시험 삼아 ~하다**

I have **tried to wake up** early every morning and am accustomed to getting up early now.
나는 매일 아침 일찍 일어나려고 노력해왔으며, 이제는 일찍 일어나는 것에 익숙해졌다.

Have you ever **tried windsurfing**?
윈드서핑 해본 적 있니?

■ stop + to부정사 **~하기 위해 멈추다**

　stop + 동명사 **~하는 것을 멈추다**

"**Stop to smell** the roses" means to take the time to appreciate what is around you.
'장미향을 맡기 위해 가던 길을 멈춰라'라는 말은 당신 주변에 있는 것을 감상할 시간을 가지라는 뜻이다.

I **stopped investing** since the economic conditions were getting worse.
경제 상황이 점점 악화되고 있었기 때문에 나는 투자를 중단했다.

정답 및 해설 p. 45

Part I Choose the option that best completes each dialogue.

1 A: I _____ a cigarette. But I couldn't find a lighter.
   B: I am sorry to say that I have your lighter.

   (a) stopped light
   (b) stopped lighting
   (c) stopped to light
   (d) stopped lighter

2 A: I wish I lived in a house with a garden so that I could grow tomatoes and lettuce.
   B: If you don't have enough space for a garden, _____ some veggies in small
      cartons.

   (a) try to grew
   (b) try for growing
   (c) try to growing
   (d) try growing

Part II Choose the option that best completes each sentence.

3 I _____ the terms of the contract carefully before signing the agreement.
   (a) regret not to read
   (b) regret not reading
   (c) regret reading not
   (d) regret to read not

4 I wonder why the media _____ that he mistakenly admitted having an
   inappropriate relationship with his secretary.
   (a) forgot mentioning
   (b) forgot to mention
   (c) forget to mentioning
   (d) forgot to mentioning

Part III Read each dialogue or passage carefully and identify the option that contains a
grammatical error.

5 (a) A: Do you think the unemployment rate will stop rise in Greece this year?
   (b) B: Probably not. The increasing of jobs in the labor market will be delayed.
   (c) A: How long will we have to wait until we see the economy creating jobs in Greece?
   (d) B: In a few months, we will begin to see some healthy signs in the temporary labor
          market.

□ **출제 경향** 형태와 의미가 비슷하지만 각각 쓰이는 용법이 다르므로, 그 의미와 쓰임새를 알아두어야 한다.

❶ personal vs. personnel

■ personal **개인적인**

I was distracted by some **personal** matters when my life peaked.
내 인생이 정점에 달했을 때 나는 몇 가지 개인적인 문제로 혼란을 겪었다.

■ personnel **인사, 인원, 직원**

personnel은 단수와 복수의 형태가 같으므로 −s를 붙여서 쓰면 틀린 표현이 된다.

Personnel departments deal with the salaries, vacations, and promotions of employees.
인사과는 직원들의 급여, 휴가, 승진 문제를 다룬다.

Experienced **personnel** are key to making a company great rather than just good.
숙련된 직원은 단순히 좋은 회사가 아닌 훌륭한 회사를 만드는 데 꼭 필요한 요소이다.

❷ late vs. lately

■ late **형용사: 늦은 / 부사: 늦게**

He was **late** for the meeting that the CEO attended.
그는 CEO가 참석한 회의에 늦었다.

She married **late** because she was obsessed with advancing her career.
그녀는 직장 경력을 발전시키는 데 혈안이 되었기 때문에 결혼을 늦게 했다.

■ lately **부사: 최근에, 근래에**

Have you seen the professor **lately**?
최근에 교수님을 뵌 적 있니?

❸ thank vs. appreciate

동사 thank와 appreciate는 뜻은 같지만 사용법이 다르다.

■ thank 「thank + 사람 + for + 이유」

I **thanked** Mary **for** inviting me to the wonderful party.
나를 멋진 파티에 초대해준 데 대해 메리에게 감사를 전했다.

■ appreciate 「appreciate + 명사(구)」

사람이 아닌 행위에 초점이 있으므로, I appreciate you. 라고 하면 틀린 표현이 된다.

Thanks for coming to my daughter's wedding. I really **appreciate it**.
제 딸아이의 결혼식에 와주셔서 고마워요. 정말로 감사드립니다.

We **appreciate your support** in last year's election.
작년 선거 때 지지해 주셔서 감사합니다.

Part I Choose the option that best completes each dialogue.

1 A: You arrived _____ to our summer training session. What happened?

B: It took me longer than normal to obtain a visa to enter the U.S. this time.

(a) two weeks lately
(b) three weeks late
(c) a week lately
(d) a weeks late

Part II Choose the option that best completes each sentence.

2 The people living in this area know that we have the capability to handle most wildfires, especially since the members of the fire department underwent a _____ training program recently.

(a) personnel
(b) personal
(c) personnels
(d) personals

3 The players on the Indian team weren't themselves today, but they picked up the pace in the fourth quarter, which _____.

(a) was too lately
(b) wasn't too late
(c) wasn't too lateness
(d) wasn't too lately

Part III Read each dialogue or passage carefully and identify the option that contains a grammatical error.

4 (a) A: Can you tell the lady who is using the hula hoop to exercise away from the rest of the class?

(b) B: Why don't you tell her directly that you would appreciate if she were concerned about everyone else?

(c) A: You are an instructor who is responsible for our safety in this gym.

(d) B: Okay, I will talk to her, but I won't tell her to stay away from everyone else.

5 (a) The company plans to undergo restructuring to boost its productivity. (b) The company has taken a hard hit due to the economic recession. (c) According to its plan, the personal department has to reduce half of its workforce. (d) Fortunately, no employees at the company have said no to the restructuring plan.

GP | 63　It is (high) time that

□ 출제 경향 '~해야 할 시간이다'라는 뜻을 나타내는 표현들을 익혀보자. 특히 「it is time that + 주어 + 동사」 구문은 동사의 시제 문제로 잘 출제되고 있다.

❶ '~해야 할 시간이다' 표현

■ 「It is time that + 주어 + 동사(과거형/should + 동사원형)」 **~해야 할 시간이다**

It is time that the government **took** action to prevent criminals from roaming around this neighborhood.
범죄자들이 이 동네에서 배회하지 못하도록 정부가 조치를 취해야 할 때이다.
→ that 이하가 가정법 과거처럼 사용되어 과거시제인 took이 쓰였다. 즉 과거형이지만 해석은 현재로 한다는 점에 유의하자.

= **It is time that** the government **should take** action to prevent criminals from roaming around this neighborhood.

= **It is time for** the government **to take** action to prevent criminals from roaming around this neighborhood.

■ 「It is high[about] time that + 주어 + 동사(과거형/should + 동사원형)」 **~해야 할 적기이다**

It is high time that the rich **were made** to pay more taxes to help alleviate poverty.
빈곤을 해소하기 위해 부자들이 더 많은 세금을 내게 해야 할 적기이다.

= **It is high time that** the rich **should be made** to pay more taxes to help alleviate poverty.
→ '~해야 할 시간이다'라는 의미를 조금 더 강조하려면 time 앞에 high나 about을 쓴다.

= **It is about time for** the rich **to be** made to pay more taxes to help alleviate poverty.

GP | 64　「so + 주어 + 동사」와 「so + 동사 + 주어」

□ 출제 경향 「so + 주어 + 동사」는 '주어가 정말 그러하다'는 뜻으로 앞에 언급된 주어를 받는다. 「so + 동사 + 주어」는 '주어도 (또한) 그러하다'라는 뜻인데, 여기서 주어는 앞에서 언급된 주어가 아닌 다른 주어이다.

❶ 「so + 주어 + 동사」

A: Look at that. Here comes Anne Hathaway. She is so gorgeous, isn't she?
　　저기 봐. 앤 해서웨이가 오고 있어. 정말 매력적이야, 그렇지 않니?

B: Yeah, **so she is**. 그래, 그녀는 정말 매력적이야.

❷ 「so + 동사 + 주어」

A: Much has changed since we left high school. 고등학교를 졸업한 이후로 많은 것이 변했어.

B: **So have we**. 우리도 변했지.

정답 및 해설 p. 46

Part I Choose the option that best completes each dialogue.

1 A: I heard that you are going to study abroad next month.
   B: Yeah, I think it's time that I _____ to make my dream come true.

   (a) studied more
   (b) will study more
   (c) have studied more
   (d) had studied more

2 A: I really want to see the upcoming movie starring Brad Pitt.
   B: _____.
   (a) So do I
   (b) So I do
   (c) So am I
   (d) So I am

Part II Choose the option that best completes each sentence.

3 It's high time that countries around the world _____ to prevent nuclear proliferation.

   (a) should make ceaseless efforts
   (b) make ceaseless efforts
   (c) will make ceaseless efforts
   (d) have made ceaseless efforts

Part III Read each dialogue or passage carefully and identify the option that contains a grammatical error.

4 (a) A: Hello. May I speak to Mr. Castle?
   (b) B: I'm sorry. He is on the phone right now.
   (c) A: Well, can I talk to Mr. Kim on the marketing team instead?
   (d) B: Hold on a second. So did he.

5 (a) Electricity allows us to live our lives in ease. (b) A power disruption in our capital, however, will cause subways, elevators, and high-speed communication networks to come to a halt. (c) Keeping in mind that a reliable supply of electricity is a critical element to the well-being of the nation, related parties must actively engage in dialogue to reach a rational consensus. (d) And it is time that the government will make extensive efforts to adopt advanced technologies in electricity generation.

GP | 65 대부정사

□ 출제 경향 to부정사에서 언급되었던 똑같은 내용이 다시 반복될 경우에는 이를 생략하고 to까지만 쓰는데, 이를 대부정사라고 한다. 대부정사 문제는 거의 두세 달에 한 번씩 출제된다. 먼저 아래 대화 예문을 보자.

A: I am planning to sign up for a biology class this semester. Will you join me?
난 이번 학기에 생물학 수업을 신청할 계획이야. 같이 수업 들을래?

B: I'd love **to**, but I have to make sure I get into a literature class first.
그러고 싶지만 먼저 문학 수업을 반드시 들어야 해.
→ 위의 I'd love to 뒤에는 sign up for a biology class this semester가 생략되었다고 볼 수 있다. to까지만 쓰든지, 아니면 to sign up for a biology class this semester까지 다 써야 올바른 표현이 된다.

A: This is Michael. Can you make it to the destination on time?
나 마이클이야. 제시간에 목적지까지 도착할 수 있겠니?

B: I won't be able **to**. I am caught in traffic.
그렇게 못할 것 같아. 지금 차가 많이 막히거든.
→ B의 대답에서 대부정사를 다 풀어 써보면 I won't be able to make it to the destination on time.이다.

GP | 66 상호복수

□ 출제 경향 상호관계나 교환의 의미를 나타낼 때는 복수 명사를 사용하는데, 이를 상호복수라 한다. 상호복수 문법 문제는 숨은 그림 찾기와 같아서 해당 표현에 복수형 명사가 제대로 쓰였는지를 바로 확인할 수 있어야 한다. 다음의 표현들을 확실히 외우고, 시험에 이와 유사한 표현이 나오면 상호복수 문제임을 바로 파악하도록 하자.

make **friends** with ~와 친구가 되다
shake **hands** with ~와 악수를 하다
exchange **seats** with ~와 자리를 바꾸다
be on speaking **terms** with ~와 이야기를 나누는 사이이다

be on good **terms** with ~와 좋은 관계를 유지하다
take **turns** 교대하다
exchange **letters** with ~와 서신을 주고받다

The president of South Korea **shook hands with** his counterpart from the U.S.
한국 대통령은 미국 대통령과 악수했다.
→ shake a hand나 shake hand는 틀린 표현이다.

We had to **take turns** using the laptop computer since there was only one.
노트북 컴퓨터가 한 대밖에 없었기 때문에 우리는 번갈아가면서 사용해야 했다.
→ take a turn이나 take turn이라고 쓰면 틀린 표현이 된다.

Part I Choose the option that best completes each dialogue.

1　A: Sir, would you allow us to _____ with you?
　　B: Certainly. But could you wait for two minutes until I send this message?

　　(a) exchange for a seat
　　(b) exchange in seats
　　(c) exchange a seat
　　(d) exchange seats

2　A: Would you like to hear Dave Mathew's new album?
　　B: _____. When did you get it?

　　(a) I'd love to do
　　(b) I'd love to
　　(c) I'd love to do it
　　(d) I'd love to hear

Part III Read each dialogue or passage carefully and identify the option that contains a grammatical error.

3　(a) A: It's already been a few years since Mike moved to L.A.
　　(b) B: Yeah. Time really flies. I haven't seen him for two years though I am still exchanging email with him.
　　(c) A: How is he doing? Is he doing anything special?
　　(d) B: He is the same as always. He got a girlfriend, broke up with her, and then got another girl.

4　(a) A: Get a mask made of silicon that is mold-proof.
　　(b) B: I'd like to be, but I only have 20 dollars with me.
　　(c) A: The additional money you spend on selecting the right mask will pay off in the future.
　　(d) B: Why don't you lend me some money so that I can get the better one?

5　(a) Steven Tyler, the lead singer of Aerosmith, started abusing painkillers after nearly 20 years of continuous sobriety. (b) Since then, there have been rumors that Steve might leave the band and pursue a solo career. (c) And the rumors seemed to become reality when it was unveiled that the rest of the band members were barely on a speaking term with him. (d) But the singer assured everyone that he would never leave the band and resolved things with his fellow members.

□ **출제 경향** 비교급, 최상급에서 의미를 강조하기 위해 쓰이는 부사가 각각 다르다. 비교급에 쓰이는 부사를 최상급에서 사용하지 않았는지, 또는 최상급에 쓰이는 부사를 비교급에서 사용하지 않았는지 파악할 수 있어야 한다.

❶ 비교급을 강조하는 표현

비교급을 강조하는 표현으로는 a lot / by far / much / even / still / far가 있다. 해석은 '훨씬'으로 하며, 비교급 바로 앞에 이 단어들 가운데 하나를 쓰면 된다.

When I was a student, one of my friends was **much** older than the teacher.
학창 시절에 내 친구들 중 한 명은 선생님보다 나이가 훨씬 많았다.

Our department needs **even** more employees this year than the other departments do.
올해 우리 부서에는 다른 부서보다 훨씬 더 많은 직원이 필요하다.

It's **a lot** easier than I had expected.
그것은 내가 예상했던 것보다 훨씬 더 쉽다.

Korean is **far** more difficult than any other foreign language.
한국어는 다른 어떤 외국어보다도 훨씬 더 어렵다.

❷ 최상급을 강조하는 표현

■ 「by far + 최상급」 / 「최상급 + by far」

The captain of the soccer team was **by far the best** player.
= The captain of the soccer team was **the best** player **by far**.
그 축구팀의 주장은 단연코 가장 훌륭한 선수였다.

■ 「the best + 명사 + ever」

Pride and Prejudice, directed by Joe Wright, is **the best** movie **ever**.
조 라이트 감독이 만든 영화 〈오만과 편견〉은 단연코 최고의 영화이다.

■ 「the very best + 명사」

A: Who is **the very best** composer of all time?
역사상 단연코 최고인 작곡가가 누굴까?

B: Beats me.
모르겠는데.

Part I Choose the option that best completes each dialogue.

1 A: Did you decide to attend the program for new employees?
B: Of course. I heard that it's _____.

(a) the best program ever
(b) ever the best program
(c) the program best ever
(d) ever the program best

2 A: How was your trip to Singapore?
B: Fantastic. The museum that we visited there was _____ than we had imagined.

(a) very more interesting
(b) a lot more interesting
(c) very interesting
(d) a lot interesting

Part III Read each dialogue or passage carefully and identify the option that contains a grammatical error.

3 (a) A: I can't wait to read that article in Newsweek.
(b) B: Oh, it's hilarious. I picked up a copy the day before yesterday.
(c) A: Is the October issue already out?
(d) B: It hit the shelves last Thursday. I think the October issue is the best issue too far.

4 (a) A: I'm concerned that my dog isn't getting any better.
(b) B: Well, the veterinarian said the medication would take a few days to kick in.
(c) A: Yeah, but what if it doesn't work?
(d) B: I'm sure your dog will be very better in a few days.

5 (a) There is a rocky road ahead in implementing the nuclear deal reached in the North-South Korea talks, but the first step has been taken. (b) Most Koreans may have heaved sighs of relief, but one of even the happiest groups must have been economic officials and business leaders. (c) The agreement to end North Korea's nuclear program will ease long-term security risks. (d) It also upgrades the nation's sovereign credit rating.

the가 쓰이는 비교급 문장

□ **출제 경향** 「the+비교급, the+비교급」구문은 '~하면 할수록 더 ...하다'라는 뜻이다. 「the+비교급」 뒤에 나오는 어구의 어순을 배열하는 것이 출제 포인트이다. 또한 비교급 문장에서 「of the two+복수명사」를 사용하여 두 대상을 비교할 경우, 비교급 앞에 the를 사용한다.

❶ 「the+비교급, the+비교급」 표현

The more I think about you, **the more** I miss you.
당신을 생각하면 할수록 더욱 당신이 그리워져요.

The more people access the Internet, **the slower** its speed is.
사람들이 인터넷 접속을 많이 하면 할수록 인터넷 속도는 더욱 느려진다.

The more you know, **the more** you know you don't know.
많이 알면 알수록 자신이 모른다는 사실을 더 많이 알게 된다

❷ 「the+비교급, the+비교급」 관용 표현

The more, the better. 많을수록 좋다. (다다익선)
The sooner, the better. 빠를수록 더 좋다.
The more, the merrier. (손님 등이) 많으면 많을수록 더 즐겁다.

❸ 「the+비교급+of the two」

Of the two buildings in front of the church, the red one is **the** taller than the blue one.
교회 앞에 있는 두 채의 건물 중에서 빨간색 건물이 파란색 건물보다 더 높다.

Of the two CEOs from different backgrounds, the one from the poor family is **the** more popular with the staff.
출신 배경이 다른 두 CEO 중에서 가난한 가정 출신의 CEO가 직원들에게 인기가 더 많다.

A: Who do you like more, Jason or James?
제이슨과 제임스 중에서 누구를 더 좋아하니?

B: I like Jason more because he is **the** more intelligent **of the two**.
둘 중에서 제이슨이 더 지적이라 그가 더 좋아.

Part I Choose the option that best completes each dialogue.

1 A: Have you decided which car you are going to buy?
   B: Of those two cars, I want to buy the blue one, which is _____.

   (a) more style
   (b) most stylish
   (c) the most stylish
   (d) the more stylish

Part II Choose the option that best completes each sentence.

2 The longer you expose your skin to the sun, _____ of getting a sunburn you have.

   (a) the great chance
   (b) great the chance
   (c) the greater the chance
   (d) greater the chance

Part III Read each dialogue or passage carefully and identify the option that contains a grammatical error.

3 (a) A: Honey, haven't you replaced the frying pan yet?
   (b) B: No, I've been occupied doing some other things.
   (c) A: Hey, look at these pans on the Internet. Of these two frying pans, which one do you prefer to buy?
   (d) B: I think the floral pan is prettier of the two.

4 (a) The fact that Korea's suicide rate was ranked first among OECD countries last year should make us reflect seriously on our lives and society. (b) The National Statistical Office's 2018 mortality figures are especially embarrassing since suicide is rampant in all age groups. (c) The bigger our society becomes, more suicide occurs. (d) Most men in their 40s who committed suicide were those who faced growing burdens of supporting their families in the middle of a prolonged recession.

5 (a) Although I am an economics major in college, I find it difficult fully to understand many of the programs that financial institutions offer. (b) Recently, I received two offers for credit cards, and I took the one whose offer I thought was better of the two. (c) Still, I think I — and many other people — lack the opportunity properly to learn about financial matters. (d) It is my belief that a lack of knowledge is the cause of the emergence of credit card delinquents, negative attitudes toward wealthy people, and speculative investments.

Section

2

Actual Test 01~06

Grammar

Part I Questions 1-10

Choose the option that best completes each dialogue.

---

1. A: I heard that you will quit your job. What did your boss say about that?
   B: He told me that he _____.

   (a) very disappointed with my decision
   (b) was very disappointed my decision
   (c) was very disappointed with my decision
   (d) did disappoint me with my decision

2. A: I watched the trailer for *Venom*. I cannot wait to see it.
   B: The movie is _____ film of the year.

   (a) the most anticipating
   (b) the more anticipated
   (c) the most anticipated
   (d) the more anticipating

3. A: Sam, don't hesitate _____ your views to me. I'm always open to new suggestions.
   B: I will. Thank you so much for saying that.

   (a) to express
   (b) expressing
   (c) for expressing
   (d) to express about

4. A: She will accept the job offer on the condition that she _____ over 5,000 dollars a month.
   B: Okay. I will discuss it with my colleagues.

   (a) is paying
   (b) will be paid
   (c) is paid
   (d) would be paid

5. A: The financial meltdown is so broad and severe that many businesses have gone bankrupt.
   B: Yes, but this _____ if financial firms had been more accountable.

   (a) could have been avoiding
   (b) could be avoided
   (c) could have avoided
   (d) could have been avoided

6. A: I walked along Sunset Boulevard while _____ the magnificent sunset.
   B: I enjoy walking down the boulevard, too.

   (a) watching
   (b) being watched
   (c) watches
   (d) watched

7. A: I think that violence cannot be justified _____.
   B: That's what I believe as well.

   (a) no mattered
   (b) no matter what
   (c) what matter it is
   (d) what matters

8. A: Neither the president nor the people _____ to see the nation divided.
   B: Thank goodness. I've been worried about the state of the country lately.

   (a) wants
   (b) want
   (c) is
   (d) was

9. A: The archaeologists are arguing about how the dinosaurs _____.
   B: I also want to know the reason.

   (a) had been extinct
   (b) extinct
   (c) became extinct
   (d) have extinct

10. A: I heard that a meeting _____ held in the Grand Conference Room this week.
    B: I thought that room is still closed due to remodeling.

    (a) is scheduled to be
    (b) schedules to be
    (c) was scheduling
    (d) scheduled to be

Part II Questions 11-25

Choose the option that best completes each sentence.

11. Almost every one dislikes him because he is an _____.

(a) arrogantly unbearable person
(b) unbearable arrogant person
(c) unbearably arrogant person
(d) unbearably arrogantly person

12. Some of the African nations _____ in 20 years due in no small part to corruption and wars.

(a) scarcely had changed
(b) had scarcely changed
(c) had changed scarcely
(d) had not scarcely changed

13. The House of Representatives insisted that the healthcare reform _____ the Senate.

(a) passes through
(b) passed through
(c) pass through
(d) be to pass through

14. I wish I _____ mathematics or economics at university so that I could handle numerical data much better.

(a) must have
(b) could have
(c) have studied
(d) had studied

15. Many parents are desperate to keep their kids away from their electronic devices _____ their kids' dependency on them is not abating enough.

(a) even though
(b) when
(c) because
(d) for

16. Some people get worn out while spending too much energy dealing with petty issues, but they sometimes need to _____ because time will take care of many of these problems.

(a) let be them
(b) let them be
(c) be let them
(d) be to let them

17. Both negotiation teams have agreed on the thorny issues, so they are doing their best _____.

(a) conclude the deal
(b) be concluded the deal
(c) to conclude the deal
(d) to be concluded the deal

18. When I brought my broken computer to the service center, the staff there replaced it with _____.

(a) one
(b) the one
(c) the new
(d) a new one

19. _____ took measures, it could not avoid another financial meltdown.

(a) The U.S. government
(b) As the U.S. government
(c) As tough the U.S. government
(d) Tough as the U.S. government

20. The bishop _____ on the sex abuse for the past few months.

(a) had saved his words
(b) has saved his words
(c) is saving his words
(d) saved his words

G

21. As Jason didn't want to be late for his first date, he _____ since he left his house.

(a) had been running
(b) has been running
(c) has been run
(d) was running

22. _____ on stage than the audience greeted him with thundering applause.

(a) No sooner he appeared
(b) No sooner had he appeared
(c) No sooner he has appeared
(d) No sooner he had appeared

23. As the team took pains to _____ its losing streak, it finally managed its first victory last night.

(a) put an end to
(b) put end to
(c) put to an end
(d) put to end

24. The company _____ downsized, since it now shows improved flexibility and agility.

(a) could have been
(b) must have been
(c) could have
(d) has

25. You have to keep in mind that you may have to pay _____.

(a) extra charges your pension provider
(b) your pension provider to extra charges
(c) your pension provider of extra charges
(d) your pension provider extra charges

Read each dialogue or passage carefully and identify the option that contains a grammatical error.

26. (a) A: Can you help me out at the office?
    (b) B: I think you're pretty busy, right?
    (c) A: Yes. Lots of orders suddenly started coming in yesterday, so I need help.
    (d) B: Okay. Could you let me know the things what I should know before I start?

27. (a) A: Have you reserved the tickets for the benefit concert?
    (b) B: Not yet. I don't have time to reserve the tickets today.
    (c) A: How come? Are you occupied with work?
    (d) B: My sister is going to graduate high school this afternoon. I have to go to the ceremony.

28. (a) One thing that I have noticed is that liquids actually share some qualities that are connected to leadership. (b) One of these qualities is that some liquids can create solid connections without becoming rigid. (c) That is a challenge that many of our leaders face each and every days. (d) They need to avoid being too rigid when trying to implement strategies and other aspects of their jobs.

29. (a) Andrew Liveris, the chief executive of Dow, a chemical firm, claimed, "Water is the oil of the 21st century." (b) Like oil, water is an essential lubricant of the world economy. (c) And, as with oil, supplies of water – at least, the clean, easily accessible kind – are coming in enormous strain. (d) That's because of the growing global population and the emerging middle-lass in Asia.

30. (a) As airlines struggle to cope with rising fuel prices, they have been searching for new ways to generate "ancillary revenues." (b) This week, an American airline said it would start to be charged $7 for a pillow and blanket on some flights. (c) Other airlines are demanding extra for passengers to check in luggage. (d) In addition, airlines are considering making passengers pay $2.50 a minute to make calls and 50 cents for text messages.

You have reached the end of the (Vocabulary &) Grammar sections. DO NOT move on to the Reading Comprehension section until instructed to do so. You are NOT allowed to turn to any other section of the test.

Part I **Questions 1-10**

Choose the option that best completes each dialogue.

1. A: Have you _____ seen *Avengers: Infinity War*?
    B: Yes, I saw the blockbuster twice last month.

    (a) once
    (b) never
    (c) sometimes
    (d) ever

2. A: I was dumbstruck by the news that a euthanasia bill was passed in Congress.
    B: I feel _____ same way.

    (a) like
    (b) the
    (c) at
    (d) a

3. A: This is Asia Airlines. What can I do for you?
    B: I _____ to confirm my flight to New York from Incheon.

    (a) would like
    (b) have
    (c) like
    (d) will

4. A: How many guests _____ will come to the wedding reception tonight?
    B: Well, about 200 people were invited. Most of them will probably come.

    (a) you think
    (b) you do think
    (c) think
    (d) do you think

5. A: Did you remember _____ the money you borrowed yesterday?
    B: How could I have forgotten? I paid it all back.

    (a) paying back
    (b) to pay back
    (c) pay back
    (d) paid back

6. A: I don't remember what happened last night. I'm worried that I might have said something wrong.
    B: You _____ drunk so much.

    (a) shouldn't have   (b) could
    (c) wouldn't have   (d) should

7. A: Why didn't you go to Jay Z's concert with us yesterday? It was pretty awesome.
    B: I really _____, but I had to run some urgent errands for my mom.

    (a) would like to   (b) love to
    (c) want to   (d) wanted to

8. A: Wow, look at the enormous hotel over there.
    B: Yeah, they say it's _____ to accommodate over 1,000 guests at a time.

    (a) too large
    (b) enough large
    (c) large enough
    (d) large

9. A: People say the South Korean national soccer team could make the quarterfinals in this World Cup.
    B: I'm _____. The South Korean squad is mostly full of young, inexperienced athletes.

    (a) afraid not
    (b) don't think so
    (c) afraid so
    (d) not afraid

10. A: Did you see Roger Federer playing at the Masters this month?
    B: Yes, he _____ focused throughout the entire tournament.

    (a) will stay
    (b) stayed
    (c) has been staying
    (d) stays

Part II Questions 11-25

Choose the option that best completes each sentence.

11. The celebrities watched the performance from the seats which _____ to the stage.

(a) right were situated next
(b) were right situated next
(c) were situated right next
(d) were situated next right

12. After being almost completely destroyed during the Korean War, the country _____ dramatically over the past several decades.

(a) grew
(b) is growing
(c) grows
(d) has grown

13. If it had not been for my aerophobia, I _____ to France to become a chef.

(a) would go
(b) would have gone
(c) went
(d) will go

14. The prosecution _____ found any decisive evidence in the homicide case yet.

(a) hasn't
(b) is
(c) haven't
(d) has

15. I made a habit of going to the gym five days a week so as _____ any extra weight.

(a) to not put on
(b) not to put on
(c) to put not on
(d) never put on

16. I didn't do my homework again, so I'm afraid of _____ by my teacher.

(a) scolding
(b) be scolded
(c) having scolded
(d) being scolded

17. Being _____, Mark was promoted to the position of senior manager this year.

(a) such a competent employee
(b) so competent employee
(c) such competent an employee
(d) such competent employee

18. He, as well as his children, really _____ the chocolate cookies his wife bakes.

(a) is loved
(b) love
(c) loves
(d) is loving

19. _____ have any questions about the presentation I just gave, feel free to contact me at your convenience.

(a) You should
(b) Should you
(c) If should you
(d) Not should you

20. Harvard University has attracted the best and brightest students across the world since it _____ in 1636.

(a) established
(b) has established
(c) was established
(d) has been established

G

21. It was _____ science fiction movie that I look forward to watching it again in the future.

(a) such an impressive
(b) a such impressive
(c) so impressive
(d) such impressive a

22. Fossil fuels such as petroleum and coal are not inexhaustible resources, _____ renewable.

(a) nor they are
(b) neither are they
(c) nor are they
(d) neither they are

23. _____ Mike feels sorry for their loss, he thinks they brought it on themselves.

(a) Despite
(b) Since
(c) Because
(d) While

24. Soldiers for overseas missions should be dispatched, _____ in any circumstance.

(a) prepared to fight
(b) preparing for figh
(c) preparing to fight
(d) prepared for fight

25. Being involved in bribery scandal, the chairman found himself _____ in a catch-22 situation.

(a) catching
(b) catch
(c) has caught
(d) caught

Read each dialogue or passage carefully and identify the option that contains a grammatical error.

26. (a) A: Where did you go this summer?
    (b) B: I took a trip to Manchester, U.K.
    (c) A: Then you visited Old Trafford, the stadium of Manchester United, don't you?
    (d) B: Of course. How could I miss it?

27. (a) A: Where are you headed?
    (b) B: I'm on my way to Loli Department Store to buy some clothes.
    (c) A: I guess you must be fed up with clothes that are in your closet.
    (d) B: What do you mean? I just don't have something to wear this spring.

28. (a) Refrigerators are not devoid of moisture but in fact have a moisture level of around 11%. (b) However, each time that a person opens the refrigerator door, a certain amount of moisture manages to escape. (c) The result is that fruits, vegetables, and other foods can lose their freshness rapidly than they would if the door were not opened. (d) Fortunately, the development of plastic containers into which food can be placed allows people to preserve the moisture in the food and thus prevent it from quickly losing its freshness.

29. (a) Since North Korea's famine reached its peak in the 1990s, many North Koreans have crossed the border into China. (b) According to the U.S. State Department, an estimated 30,000-50,000 North Korean refugees currently stays in China. (c) They believe that their repatriation would lead to severe punishment, such as a few months of "labor correction" and even execution. (d) North Korea is generally known as one of the world's worst violators of human rights.

30. (a) Human rights refer to "the basic rights and freedom to which all humans are entitled." (b) However, there are still places where human rights are neglected or even abused. (c) In response, various NGOs and international organizations are working close with each government in order to protect people's human rights. (d) In 1948, the Universal Declaration of Human Rights was adopted by the United Nations General Assembly to facilitate the protection and promotion of human rights.

You have reached the end of the (Vocabulary &) Grammar sections. DO NOT move on to the Reading Comprehension section until instructed to do so. You are NOT allowed to turn to any other section of the test.

Part I **Questions 1-10**
Choose the option that best completes each dialogue.

1. A: Hello, Sara. What are you carrying? Maybe I can help you.
   B: It is very _____.

   (a) kind of saying that
   (b) kind of that to say
   (c) kind of you to say that
   (d) kind to you to say that

2. A: I am very excited to have a new teacher this semester. How is your teacher?
   B: I heard that mine is one of _____ teachers in our school.

   (a) the strictest
   (b) the most strict
   (c) the most strictest
   (d) the most stricting

3. A: I am anticipating dinner tomorrow at the Luxury Restaurant. Did you make a reservation there?
   B: Of course. I remembered _____ seats for us. Don't worry.

   (a) to reserve
   (b) reserving
   (c) reserve
   (d) to reserving

4. A: You know that we are not allowed to drive until we _____, don't we?
   B: Yes, you are right. I was wrong. Let's take driving lessons together next month.

   (a) will get our driver's licenses
   (b) would get our driver's licenses
   (c) get our driver's licenses
   (d) can get our driver's licenses

5. A: Did you see that the president lowered his head _____ to the sailors?
   B: I saw that. It was very touching moment.

   (a) by paying condolences
   (b) to paying condolences
   (c) to pay condolences
   (d) pay condolences

6. A: You know what? Simon _____ most of the 3-point shots during last night's game.
   B: You're right. But we know that his condition was not good.

   (a) must block
   (b) must have blocked
   (c) could have blocked
   (d) could block

7. A: I've known her for ten years, but it seems that she never puts on any pounds.
   B: Right. She never gains weight _____. She has a great metabolism.

   (a) no matter how much she eats
   (b) no matter how she eats
   (c) no matter how eating she is
   (d) no matter how she eats much

8. A: The snowfall yesterday was a record amount, so many drivers got stranded.
   B: As a result, neither those schools nor mine _____ now.

   (a) are opening   (b) are opened
   (c) is open   (d) is opening

9. A: It was North Korea that _____ the Korean War on June 25, 1950.
   B: Yes. That should not have happened. The war has divided our nation up to this day.

   (a) was started   (b) had started
   (c) has started   (d) started

10. A: The president is making a great effort to improve the economy these days.
    B: I think we cannot avoid another financial meltdown unless the financial industry itself _____ us to change to a better system.

    (a) leads
    (b) would lead
    (c) will lead
    (d) should lead

Part II **Questions 11-25**

Choose the option that best completes each sentence.

11. My mom made me a hamburger and I've
never seen _____ burger in my life.

  (a) such delicious-looking, giant
  (b) such giant, delicious-looking
  (c) such a delicious-looking, giant
  (d) such a giant, delicious-looking

12. Though Jim's performance last night
was beyond my expectation, he is not
_____ to stand shoulder to shoulder
with James.

  (a) enough of fast
  (b) fast enough
  (c) enough fast
  (d) of enough fast

13. The treasury secretary demanded that bankers
_____ for what they do.

  (a) should never be responsible
  (b) should respond
  (c) be more responsible
  (d) be more responsive

14. I wish I _____ more neutral during
the meeting where the participants thought
that I gave away my feelings.

  (a) had been
  (b) have been
  (c) must have been
  (d) were

15. The senator eagerly listened to the people's
opinions during the town hall meeting,
_____ there had been an increasing
amount of interest in his new bill.

  (a) even though
  (b) while
  (c) when
  (d) for

16. As he caused a disturbance by yelling at the
restaurant, two police officers _____
a nearby police station.

  (a) got out of him and took him to
  (b) got him out and took him to
  (c) got him out and took him
  (d) got out him and took him to

17. The majority of the people surveyed by the
magazine _____ Sam gave me said
yes to same-sex marriage.

  (a) which
  (b) of which
  (c) to which
  (d) what

18. The chairman was presumptuous enough
_____ comments concerning his
recent fraud case.

  (a) to make
  (b) to be made
  (c) making
  (d) of

19. As I try to find a good match for myself,
I realize that Jasmin is _____ for me.

  (a) one
  (b) her
  (c) the one
  (d) herself

20. _____, the rescue team never stopped
their search and rescue efforts since they
knew that the victims were still alive.

  (a) Wild were the wind and waves
  (b) Wild as the wind and waves were
  (c) As were the wind and waves
  (d) As if the wind and waves were

21. He _____ while running for the presidency over the past two years, and finally, he won the competitive election by a narrow margin.

(a) had made tireless efforts
(b) did make tireless efforts
(c) made tireless efforts
(d) has made tireless efforts

22. Seldom _____ considered by urban designers as a critical part of city construction.

(a) the importance of sewage treatment be
(b) the importance of sewage treatment is
(c) is the importance of sewage treatment
(d) be the importance of sewage treatment

23. By some miracle, Joe escaped death when he got in a huge car accident last night and his only injury _____ a scratch on his face.

(a) was none other than
(b) was nothing more than
(c) was no longer than
(d) was more than

24. My boss wants this project _____ by next Friday at the latest.

(a) to do
(b) doing
(c) done
(d) be done

25. Her colleagues thought that she _____ since she had not shown up for work for days.

(a) should have been let go
(b) must have been let go
(c) has been let go
(d) had been let go

Read each dialogue or passage carefully and identify the option that contains a grammatical error.

26. (a) A: The California Institute will announce it has made a significant finding that could pave the path to the new first drug for AIDS in almost 15 years.

(b) B: It is a very timely discovery because the currently used antiviral drugs are no longer effective at fighting AIDS.

(c) A: Scientists at the institute are studying the genetics of AIDS in an effort to solve the secret of reducing the impact of one of the most fatal diseases in the world.

(d) B: Hopefully, it will be a breakthrough in the war against AIDS, which has dragged on for too long.

27. (a) A: Creating incredible expectations, the movie is finally being released. I am so excited.

(b) B: I heard that the sequel will have weapons with upgraded firepower.

(c) A: Yes, the robot will blow up everything in its way.

(d) B: I have got to buy a ticket online before it's too late.

28. (a) The vice president of the bank stood before the hearing committee to testify about its failure to control its snowballing debt. (b) There, he was bombarded by a series of sharp attacks from several senators. (c) Those members claimed that if the firm has acted more responsibly, the ripple effect would have been weaker. (d) After the hearing, those who saw the questioning thought that the banker deserved to be retired.

29. (a) Leonardo da Vinci was a renowned inventor who lived during the Renaissance. (b) He drew sketches of airplanes approximately 400 years ago before the first plane took flight. (c) In addition to his inventions, da Vinci also created many pieces of art, included the Mona Lisa. (d) Da Vinci's inventions were way ahead of his time and his paintings are still loved by the whole world.

30. (a) The leaders of Britain's political parties did not touch on the country's energy policy since Britain has abundant natural resources. (b) North Sea oil and gas have given them three decades of plenty, allowing Britain happily to ignore the thorny issue of energy. (c) Yet the issue has haunted many other leaders of advanced, as well as developing countries for years. (d) However, as an unexpected change in public opinion in Britain was occurred recently, the country is clearly not free from the matter.

G

You have reached the end of the (Vocabulary &) Grammar sections. DO NOT move on to the Reading Comprehension section until instructed to do so. You are NOT allowed to turn to any other section of the test.

Part I **Questions 1-10**

Choose the option that best completes each dialogue.

1. A: Oh my gosh! I left my notebook on the bus.
   B: Really? _____ to do.

   (a) How foolish thing
   (b) What foolish a thing
   (c) How a stupid thing
   (d) What a foolish thing

2. A: I am really glad that your son finally got a job.
   B: Thanks a lot. I can't tell you _____.

   (a) how I am happy
   (b) how am I happy
   (c) how happy I am
   (d) how happy am I

3. A: What did you do last night? You look so tired.
   B: I sat up late all evening _____ to the rain falling on the roof.

   (a) listen
   (b) listened
   (c) listening
   (d) having listened

4. A: John seems to be a good guy. He works diligently.
   B: But he sometimes loses his temper, _____ is often the case with impatient young men.

   (a) that
   (b) whichever
   (c) what
   (d) as

5. A: A lot of people were killed in World War II.
   B: Perhaps the next war will be _____ we can even imagine.

   (a) crueler
   (b) more crueler than
   (c) as crueler than
   (d) crueler than

6. A: Kevin's life has a lot of ups and downs.
   B: _____ free of pain and worry lately?

   (a) Been he has
   (b) Has been he
   (c) He has been
   (d) Has he been

7. A: When did your company move to Tianjin?
   B: _____ we relocated there.

   (a) It's since fifteen years
   (b) Since fifteen years
   (c) It's been fifteen years since
   (d) Since it's fifteen years

8. A: Do you know that Korea hosted the Olympics?
   B: Of course! The Olympic Games _____ in Seoul in 1988.

   (a) were
   (b) has been
   (c) had been
   (d) was

9. A: Would you like to have lunch with me this Saturday?
   B: Sorry. I would like _____, but I have a previous engagement.

   (a) to
   (b) to do
   (c) to have it
   (d) to have

10. A: I will have an interview with HP's personnel director tomorrow.
    B: Wow. That is _____ to be lost.

    (a) so good a chance
    (b) such good a chance
    (c) too good a chance
    (d) quite good a chance

Part II Questions 11-25

Choose the option that best completes each sentence.

11. Hardly ever _____ for people entering college as there are today.

    (a) there have been so many choices
    (b) have there been so many choices
    (c) so many choices there have been
    (d) there so many choices have been

12. Over the hill and through the woods _____ his parents live.

    (a) where is the house
    (b) where the house is
    (c) is the house where
    (d) the house is where

13. If foreigners bring their passports to the bank, it will be easy for them to get their checks _____.

    (a) cashing
    (b) to cash
    (c) cash
    (d) cashed

14. _____ they are not perfect themselves, they are still able to create perfect institutions.

    (a) Though
    (b) Moreover
    (c) If
    (d) So

15. The overall warming trend of the last few years holds more significance _____ single year's trend.

    (a) than any does
    (b) does than
    (c) any does
    (d) than does any

16. I was put in the classroom with _____ who was notorious for his eccentricity.

    (a) other boy
    (b) another boy
    (c) other boys
    (d) another boys

17. This school, which was founded in 1954, has long been considered _____ in the country.

    (a) one of the led schools
    (b) one of the leading school
    (c) one of the leading schools
    (d) one of the led school

18. He _____ quit school until he finds a job.

    (a) had better not
    (b) had not better
    (c) not had better
    (d) never had better

19. Either her boyfriend's betrayal or her foster parents' criticism _____ her under a lot of stress.

    (a) have put
    (b) has put
    (c) putting
    (d) are putting

20. It is imperative that the city _____ more infrastructure for its citizens.

    (a) build
    (b) builds
    (c) has built
    (d) have built

G

21. It is necessary that they work _____ in order to achieve the desired results.

    (a) as fastly as possible
    (b) as fast as possible
    (c) fastly as possible
    (d) fast possible

22. A three-year-old child has a basic vocabulary of _____.

    (a) five thousands some words
    (b) some five thousands words
    (c) some five thousand words
    (d) five thousand some words

23. The attorney _____ that she wouldn't have to pay for the damages.

    (a) to his client assured
    (b) to his client had assured
    (c) had assured his client
    (d) had his client assured

24. The only way to keep your leather sofa clean is _____ using the proper cleanser, which will help prolong its life.

    (a) on
    (b) by
    (c) with
    (d) in

25. This is the organ _____ in the digestion of food and the regulation of the body's sugar level.

    (a) involving
    (b) having involved
    (c) involved
    (d) involve

Read each dialogue or passage carefully and identify the option that contains a grammatical error.

26. (a) A: Since its creation, our research lab focused on a number of diverse technologies.
   (b) B: What can we expect from the marriage of various technologies?
   (c) A: That's beyond our imagination. The possibilities are endless.
   (d) B: Do you mean that things that are impossible now will ultimately become possible?

27. (a) A: Is everything okay? You look perturbed.
   (b) B: Well, I'm facing some obstacles in trying to register for my courses.
   (c) A: Has you met with your advisor to discuss these problems?
   (d) B: Not yet. But I think that I ought to meet him pretty soon.

28. (a) I recently narrowly escaped an accident with an ambulance when I was passing through a yellow light at an intersection. (b) As I was halfway through the intersection, I saw an ambulance rushing in my direction disregard the red light. (c) Since I cannot make a sudden stop, I maintained my speed, only to see the ambulance heading straight toward me. (d) Both of us immediately stopped, but we came extremely close to colliding with each other.

29. (a) Most cities in the United States are not places that are easy for bicyclists to navigate through. (b) One of the main reasons for this is that the United States has a very well-developed car culture. (c) Because of the prevalence of cars, many people hesitate to ride their bikes to work. (d) So many city councils around the country are trying to create bicycle lanes and make their cities more bicycle-friendly places for cyclist.

30. (a) Many Koreans feel uneasy watching China and Russia conduct a massive joint military drill near their territory. (b) This apprehension grows further when they hear the United States, Japan, and Taiwan push for a counter-drill. (c) It is as if the major military powers are reviving the Cold War in Northeast Asia to gain global hegemony in the 21st century. (d) The arms race are making this region the most volatile part of the world.

G

You have reached the end of the (Vocabulary &) Grammar sections. DO NOT move on to the Reading Comprehension section until instructed to do so. You are NOT allowed to turn to any other section of the test.

Part I **Questions 1-10**

Choose the option that best completes each dialogue.

---

1. A: Hi, James. I haven't seen you in ages. Where have you been?

B: I was hospitalized because of a car accident. I have _____ gone outside for the past month.

(a) sometimes   (b) ever

(c) seldom   (d) not

2. A: The man I met in a bar was tall and handsome but dull.

B: Rarely _____ physically attractive.

(a) an intelligent individual does

(b) has an intelligent individual

(c) an intelligent individual is

(d) is an intelligent individual

3. A: You've recently put on a lot of weight, haven't you?

B: Yes, and it's really bothering me. I _____ work out again since summer is coming soon.

(a) need

(b) have

(c) should

(d) would like

4. A: Hey, where _____ this bus is headed?

B: I have no idea either. We'd better ask the driver.

(a) you do think

(b) you think

(c) do you think

(d) think you

5. A: What was the most impressive experience you had during your trip to the United States?

B: I will never forget _____ the Grand Canyon in Arizona.

(a) visited

(b) to visit

(c) visit

(d) visiting

6. A: I was caught in a shower on my way home. I got completely soaked by the rain.

B: Didn't you check the forecast? You _____ your umbrella before you went out.

(a) should have brought

(b) can bring

(c) should brought

(d) should bring

7. A: My boyfriend in the military sends me a letter once a week.

B: Really? What _____?

(a) he says

(b) did he say

(c) does he say

(d) has he said

8. A: Do you have _____ to buy such an expensive sports car?

B: No, I don't. But I'm going to pay for it in installments.

(a) many money

(b) enough money

(c) much money

(d) enough moneys

9. A: Why are you leaving so soon? It's still only nine o'clock.

B: _____ I have to go now. There's a TV show coming on soon that I don't want to miss.

(a) I should afraid

(b) I afraid

(c) I should

(d) I'm afraid

10. A: Do you know what's going on at the company you work for?

B: There _____ a lot of serious talk recently about having an initial public offering.

(a) was   (b) has been

(c) were   (d) have been

Part II **Questions 11-25**

Choose the option that best completes each sentence.

11. New York City, _____ the "Big Apple," is one of the most attractive tourist destinations in the United States.

    (a) calling
    (b) called
    (c) is called
    (d) having called

12. South Korea _____ great strides toward democracy since its military dictatorship ended in the 1980s.

    (a) made
    (b) makes
    (c) have made
    (d) has made

13. Because it was rush hour, Michelle took the subway; otherwise, she _____ to the airport on time.

    (a) would not have made it
    (b) will not make it
    (c) would not make it
    (d) made it

14. All my family _____ opposed to my marriage because my fiance is a divorced man.

    (a) is
    (b) have been
    (c) has
    (d) have

15. After lunch, she usually drinks strong coffee _____ doze at work.

    (a) so as not to
    (b) so as to
    (c) in order to not
    (d) not in order to

16. You should make it a habit to brush your teeth before _____ to bed.

    (a) be gone
    (b) go
    (c) to go
    (d) going

17. _____, the baseball coach reorganized the team after they lost the game.

    (a) Fluster
    (b) Flustering
    (c) Flustered
    (d) To fluster

18. According to UNICEF, currently, one out of every six children under the age of five in sub-Saharan Africa _____ from preventable diseases.

    (a) died
    (b) dies
    (c) die
    (d) dead

19. _____ see *Bohemian Rhapsody* tonight, please tell me if the movie is worth watching.

    (a) Should you
    (b) You should
    (c) If should you
    (d) Should

20. He has been searching for a job for more than a year even though he _____ a master's degree in engineering from a prestigious university.

    (a) has been
    (b) has
    (c) had
    (d) has had

21. I used to buy _____ to read on the subway on my way to work.

(a) a paper
(b) the paper
(c) paper
(d) papers

22. When it comes to the economy in the near future, I'm not an optimist, _____ a pessimist.

(a) nor am I
(b) and neither I am
(c) neither am I
(d) nor I am

23. _____ Bob opposed his boss's decision, he had no choice but to abide by it.

(a) Despite
(b) Since
(c) Because
(d) While

24. Cutthroat competition in the labor market has forced graduates to leave their universities _____ the workplace.

(a) much preparing for
(b) better prepared for
(c) better preparing for
(d) much prepared to

25. An expert in foreign relations said that North Korea sees its nuclear provocation as _____, not an end itself.

(a) a means to end
(b) means to an end
(c) a means to an end
(d) means to end

Read each dialogue or passage carefully and identify the option that contains a grammatical error.

26. (a) A: What are you up to this weekend?
    (b) B: Nothing special. What's up?
    (c) A: Let's go to the movies, don't we?
    (d) B: That sounds great to me.

27. (a) A: Do you know Mike won a many amount of money at the casino?
    (b) B: Wow. What do you think he is going to do with that money?
    (c) A: I bet he will buy a new luxury car.
    (d) B: So do I. By the way, why don't we go to Las Vegas?

28. (a) Countries around the world are turning to nuclear energy as the best option to meet their ever-growing energy needs while alleviating environmental concerns. (b) In order to promote the peaceful uses of nuclear energy while building more nuclear power plant, we must establish and maintain the relevant infrastructure to deal with nuclear-related issues. (c) In addition, we need to secure a stable supply of nuclear fuel and enhance our ability to dispose of nuclear waste in a more environment-friendly way. (d) That is why the role of the International Atomic Energy Agency has become more important than ever.

29. (a) Hydropower represents more than 15 percent of the world's electricity production. (b) And about 90 percent of the world's clean renewable energy comes from hydropower. (c) But other renewable forms of energy, such as wind and solar energy, will surpass hydropower in electricity generation short. (d) With greenhouse gases becoming a threat, renewable energy has the potential to meet the environmental, social, and economic demands of our time.

30. (a) The spread of information networks are become a new nervous system for the world. (b) When something happens in an area, the rest of us keep up with it in real time. (c) Therefore, we are able to respond in real time as well. (d) This is something that no one had even imagined just scores of years ago.

G

You have reached the end of the (Vocabulary &) Grammar sections. DO NOT move on to the Reading Comprehension section until instructed to do so. You are NOT allowed to turn to any other section of the test.

Part I **Questions 1-10**

Choose the option that best completes each dialogue.

---

1. A: Our country _____ having freedom of speech. That's the beauty of our nation.
   B: That's right. There should also be no segregation or discrimination.

   (a) prides on   (b) prides itself on
   (c) prides on itself   (d) prides itself

2. A: These days, I feel that I have a lot of problem. I want to get _____ from you.
   B: Don't worry. Everything is going to be fine soon. Just don't give up.

   (a) an advice
   (b) some advice
   (c) the advice
   (d) the advices

3. A: What do you think about Jessica?
   B: While _____ that Jessica is pretty, I still don't like her.

   (a) admit
   (b) admitted
   (c) admitting
   (d) admits

4. A: Why are you still hesitating to join the online shopping site?
   B: I am not going to join the site unless the company _____ to protect its customers.

   (a) should improve its security
   (b) will improve its security
   (c) would improve its security
   (d) improves its security

5. A: It's been almost seventy years since South Korea and North Korea were divided.
   B: This has cost a lot of time, energy, money, and lives while _____ more harm than good.

   (a) doing   (b) to do
   (c) done   (d) by doing

6. A: There was a huge oil spill in the U.S., and the environmental impact will be devastating.
   B: That's sad. The oil company _____ safety issues.

   (a) would have paid more attention to
   (b) should have paid more attention to
   (c) will have paid more attention to
   (d) has paid more attention to

7. A: My dad once tried really hard to quit smoking, but he failed.
   B: For his family, he should have quit smoking _____.

   (a) no matter how hard it was
   (b) no matter how hard it should be
   (c) no matter how hard was
   (d) no matter how it was

8. A: Neither the students nor the teacher _____ hurt while they were evacuating the school during the fire.
   B: Thank God. They are both safe.

   (a) is   (b) are
   (c) was   (d) were

9. A: What was the main point of the lecture today?
   B: North Korea _____ South Korea in 1950, and the two Koreas have been technically at war with each other since then.

   (a) has attacked   (b) had attacked
   (c) attacked   (d) attacking

10. A: _____ that I would win the lottery. But that was until today.
    B: You hit the jackpot, Jim! What are you going to do with all that money?

    (a) Never had I thought
    (b) Never have I thought
    (c) Never I had thought
    (d) Never I have thought

Part II Questions 11-25

Choose the option that best completes each sentence.

11. The company finally finished construction on the _____ building.

(a) tall, silver metallic
(b) silver, tall metallic
(c) tall, metallic silver
(d) silver, metallic tall

12. The majority of women and nonsmokers dislike those _____ smoke and spit on the street.

(a) to whom
(b) who
(c) whose
(d) whom

13. Since the huge oil spill incident, the president has insisted that the environmental damage _____.

(a) would minimized
(b) be minimized
(c) minimized
(d) be minimizing

14. I wish I _____ sing like that vocalist that completely mesmerized the audience at the concert last night.

(a) may
(b) should
(c) can
(d) could

15. _____ his dog barked to summon help, a search and rescue team could finally spot him.

(a) Even though
(b) Although
(c) While
(d) Since

16. To prevent further incidents, the manager instructed the workers to notify _____.

(a) him any unexpected events
(b) him of any unexpected events
(c) any unexpected events him
(d) any unexpected events of him

17. One study showed that the number of female smokers was decreasing, but the most recent study found that the figure _____ rising again.

(a) was
(b) were
(c) is
(d) are

18. Many of my friends bought that smart phone, which is the _____ I want.

(a) thing
(b) it
(c) one
(d) some

19. _____, he is very calculating and careful, which means you should not underestimate him or you will pay the price.

(a) As stupid he might look
(b) Stupid he might look
(c) Stupid as he might look
(d) As he might look stupid

20. The members of the House of Representatives and Senate _____ the issue of too-big-to-fail financial firms over the last year.

(a) have fiercely debated
(b) are fiercely debating
(c) fiercely debated
(d) were fiercely debated

G

G

21. By the time I arrived in the hotel lobby, she _____ for me for 30 minutes.

(a) had been waiting
(b) has been waiting
(c) has waited
(d) waiting

22. No sooner _____ than he was asked numerous questions by reporters.

(a) Madoff got out of court
(b) Madoff gets out of court
(c) had Madoff gotten out of court
(d) had Madoff get out of court

23. There is disagreement among IT firms _____ the reliability of cloud computing.

(a) when it come to
(b) when it comes to
(c) what it comes to
(d) what it come to

24. Apple's competitors thought that its new product sales _____ because consumers' reactions were not that positive.

(a) must have been sluggish
(b) should have been sluggish
(c) could have being sluggish
(d) can be sluggish

25. Both companies, having released long-awaited products, were shocked since _____.

(a) their designs looked strikingly alike
(b) their designs alike strikingly looked
(c) their designs alike looked striking
(d) their alike designs looked striking

26. (a) A: Our country's tourism industry still needs to be improved.
   (b) B: I agree. We have many great places and foods, but they are not introduced enough to foreign tourists.
   (c) A: Another problem is that Korean accommodation charges tourists a lot for their food and stays.
   (d) B: That's what I'm talking about. But the rest are almost perfect!

27. (a) A: What do you think the difference between people and animals is?
   (b) B: It is the fact that we get a warm feeling when we do good something for others.
   (c) A: Do you mean the volunteering and philanthropy that some people engage in?
   (d) B: Yes, most people attach a high value to working for others.

28. (a) In the past, several media pundits predicted that TV was slowly heading to its demise. (b) In the 1990s, a renowned American writer claimed that conventional television would be extinct by the end of the 20th century. (c) The reason behind his claim was that web-based media would displace TV since they can provide content on demand. (d) If he knew, however, the possibility of two-way communication between the Web and TV, he wouldn't had made such a claim.

29. (a) The climate in certain areas often determines which diseases may be found in these places. (b) For instance, many serious diseases are found only in places that are extremely warm. (c) Thus, areas such as Africa and Asia are sometimes home to some of the deadliest diseases known as man. (d) So the mortality rates in some areas with warm climates are often higher than they are for people residing in more frigid climates.

30. (a) Economists recently forecast that the American economy would undergo the biggest transformation in its history. (b) After years of research, based on economic indices and patterns, they are concluded that it is moving toward savings and exports and away from debt and consumption. (c) This macroeconomic transformation will also bring about a shift in lifestyles and working environments. (d) The problem is whether or not the U.S. economy is ready to embrace such a gigantic change amid the current chaos.

G

You have reached the end of the (Vocabulary &) Grammar sections. DO NOT move on to the Reading Comprehension section until instructed to do so. You are NOT allowed to turn to any other section of the test.

어휘

Vocabulary

Section

1

파트별
Voca
Point

Part I

중면서 익히는 Mini Test **다음 한글 뜻에 맞는 영어 표현을 고르시오.**

01 The project was a long time (ⓐ coming ⓑ going ⓒ getting).
그 프로젝트는 시간이 꽤 걸렸다.

02 I really (ⓐ thank ⓑ compliment ⓒ appreciate) your support for the product that our company is launching.
우리 회사가 런칭 중인 제품을 지지해주신 데 대해 감사의 말을 전합니다.

03 Don't be so (ⓐ modest ⓑ moderate ⓒ modified).
너무 겸손해하실 필요 없어요.

04 Let's (ⓐ separate ⓑ divide ⓒ split) the bill this time.
이번에는 비용을 나눠 냅시다.

05 I don't have any time to (ⓐ mess ⓑ spare ⓒ hold).
요즘에는 짬이 없어.

06 I am (ⓐ satisfied ⓑ nauseous ⓒ pleased) that I could help.
내가 도와줄 수 있어서 기쁘게 생각해.

07 I don't want to (ⓐ take up ⓑ take out ⓒ take off) your time.
당신의 시간을 빼앗고 싶지 않습니다.

08 Sorry for being late. I didn't (ⓐ recognize ⓑ relish ⓒ realize) what time it was.
늦어서 미안해. 몇 시였는지 몰랐어.

09 You have my (ⓐ word ⓑ trust ⓒ saying).
약속합니다.

10 What a (ⓐ rapid ⓑ pleasant ⓒ smiling) surprise.
깜짝 놀랐지만 그래도 기분은 좋아.

11 (ⓐ Keep ⓑ Remain ⓒ Hang) in there.
버티고 있어라.

12 I've had a (ⓐ short ⓑ mid ⓒ long) day.
오늘 하루는 참 힘들었어.

13 Your guess is as (ⓐ good ⓑ possible ⓒ bad) as mine.
모르기는 나도 마찬가지야.

14 Don't worry about it. It's (ⓐ in the building ⓑ on the house ⓒ in the store).
걱정 마세요. 그건 저희 가게에서 드리는 서비스입니다.

15 I wasn't (ⓐ born ⓑ taught ⓒ bred) yesterday.
난 세상 물정 모르는 바보가 아냐.

16 The (ⓐ dollar ⓑ buck ⓒ bill) stops here.
책임은 내가 질게.

정답 01 ⓐ 02 ⓒ 03 ⓐ 04 ⓒ 05 ⓑ 06 ⓒ 07 ⓐ 08 ⓒ 09 ⓐ 10 ⓑ 11 ⓒ 12 ⓒ 13 ⓐ 14 ⓑ 15 ⓐ 16 ⓑ

17 How shall I (ⓐ address ⓑ name ⓒ refer) you?
제가 당신을 어떻게 부를까요?

18 I saw it (ⓐ coming ⓑ going ⓒ predicting).
내 그럴 줄 알았지.

19 That (ⓐ keeps ⓑ makes ⓒ has) two of us.
나도 그렇게 생각해.

20 Don't take it (ⓐ up ⓑ off ⓒ out) on me simply because you are not happy about what's going on.
단순히 돌아가는 일이 마음에 들지 않는다고 나에게 화풀이하지 마.

21 I've got to get (ⓐ going ⓑ coming ⓒ moving).
난 이제 가 봐야겠어.

22 I will put you (ⓐ through ⓑ in ⓒ within) to the Personnel Department.
인사과로 연결해 드리겠습니다.

23 Tom is always (ⓐ punctual ⓑ lazy ⓒ tardy) for school since he goes to bed late.
톰은 잠을 늦게 자기 때문에 항상 학교에 지각한다.

24 The situation just got out of (ⓐ feet ⓑ hand ⓒ chest).
상황이 통제 불능 상태로 치달았다.

25 Why don't you come to your (ⓐ senses ⓑ feeling ⓒ wakeup)?
이제 정신 좀 차리는 것이 어때?

26 The administrative office is at the other (ⓐ site ⓑ end ⓒ limit) of the hall.
행정실은 홀 끝 맞은편에 있습니다.

27 I am (ⓐ awesomely ⓑ fabulously ⓒ awfully) sorry for the mistake.
그 실수에 대해 정말 미안해.

28 He made a (ⓐ fuss ⓑ feint ⓒ mass) about the service at the restaurant.
그는 레스토랑의 서비스에 대해 난리법석을 떨었다.

29 I am (ⓐ unsatisfied ⓑ unhappy ⓒ uncalled) about the salary.
나는 급여가 마음에 들지 않아.

30 You have to (ⓐ switch ⓑ transform ⓒ convert) to Line 2.
2호선으로 갈아타야 합니다.

31 It seemed that the teacher was (ⓐ under the climate ⓑ on the heels ⓒ under the weather) today.
선생님은 오늘 몸이 안 좋아 보였다.

32 I (ⓐ kicked ⓑ pulled ⓒ cut) some strings.
(어떤 상황에 영향력을 미쳤을 때) 내가 힘을 좀 썼지.

33 Wake up, everybody! It's time to (ⓐ hit ⓑ push ⓒ pass) the books.
모두들 일어나! 열심히 공부할 시간이야.

34 You will (ⓐ make or break ⓑ be in the middle of ⓒ get the hang of) it sooner or later.
당신은 조만간 요령을 터득할 것입니다.

35 Why don't you take a (ⓐ wild ⓑ tough ⓒ mixed) guess?
한 번 추측이라도 해보지 그래? / 느낌 오는 대로 찍어 보지 그래?

36 I was (ⓐ kept ⓑ moved ⓒ locked) out of the room.
방에 열쇠를 놔두고 문을 잠가 버렸어.

37 Jason is wayward. He should (ⓐ know ⓑ find ⓒ act) his age.
제이슨은 제멋대로야. 철 좀 들어야 해.

38 Christina is (ⓐ during vacation ⓑ on leave ⓒ on resting) due to her sudden illness.
크리스티나는 갑자기 몸이 아파서 휴가 중이다.

39 The chef (ⓐ fixed ⓑ ran ⓒ went) a delectable meal for the distinguished guests.
요리사는 내외 귀빈을 위해 맛있는 음식을 준비했다.

40 I couldn't exactly (ⓐ know ⓑ follow ⓒ move) the professor's rambling lecture.
나는 교수님의 두서없는 강의를 정확히 이해할 수 없었다.

41 You (ⓐ took out ⓑ took up ⓒ missed out) on a once-in-a-lifetime opportunity.
너는 일생에 한 번 찾아오는 기회를 놓쳤어.

42 I can't (ⓐ get out ⓑ make out ⓒ come out) the image in this photo.
나는 이 사진의 이미지가 무엇을 의미하는지 이해하지 못하겠어.

43 I will (ⓐ get by ⓑ show off ⓒ swing by) your house on my way home from work.
일 마치고 집에 가는 길에 너희 집에 잠깐 들를게.

44 She (ⓐ stood me up ⓑ stood me out ⓒ sorted me out) the other day.
일전에 그녀는 나를 바람 맞혔어.

45 James always (ⓐ takes care of ⓑ gets away with ⓒ runs away from) breaking the rules.
제임스는 항상 규칙을 어겨도 벌을 받지 않고 지나간다.

46 The driver (ⓐ dropped me off ⓑ set me off ⓒ came me off) at the airport.
운전사는 공항에서 나를 내려주었다.

47 The professor (ⓐ crushed ⓑ broke ⓒ destroyed) the concept down for the students.
교수님께서 그 개념을 학생들에게 자세히 설명하셨다.

48 I will get the job done by deadline, and this time I won't (ⓐ procrastinate ⓑ protect ⓒ proceed).
나는 마감기한까지 일을 마무리할 거고 이번에는 꾸물거리지 않을 거야.

49 I saw my grandfather (ⓐ sweeping ⓑ seeping ⓒ sipping) his coffee while sitting in a rocking chair.
나는 우리 할아버지가 흔들의자에 앉아서 커피를 홀짝이는 모습을 봤다.

50 I don't want Nick to (ⓐ boost ⓑ brass ⓒ brag) too much about himself.
닉이 자기 자랑을 너무 많이 안 했으면 좋겠어.

정답 34 ⓒ 35 ⓐ 36 ⓒ 37 ⓒ 38 ⓑ 39 ⓐ 40 ⓑ 41 ⓒ 42 ⓑ 43 ⓒ 44 ⓐ 45 ⓑ 46 ⓐ 47 ⓑ 48 ⓐ 49 ⓒ 50 ⓒ

51 (ⓐ Pump ⓑ Fill ⓒ Full) her up, please.
기름 가득 채워 주세요.

52 My mouth is (ⓐ watering ⓑ flooding ⓒ dampening).
입에서 군침이 도는데요.

53 (ⓐ Fancy ⓑ Coincidence ⓒ Chance) meeting you here!
너를 여기서 만나다니!

54 (ⓐ That's the spirit! ⓑ That's what I am talking about! ⓒ Way to go!)
(격려조) 바로 그거야!

55 What do you (ⓐ tell ⓑ say ⓒ mean)?
무슨 말을 하는 거야?

56 (ⓐ That's about it. ⓑ That's the way it goes. ⓒ That's the way to go.)
대충 그 정도입니다. / 그게 다입니다.

57 I am a (ⓐ normal ⓑ regular ⓒ frequent) here.
나는 여기 단골입니다.

58 There is no one here (ⓐ for ⓑ of ⓒ by) that name.
여기에 그런 이름을 가진 사람은 없습니다.

59 Who's on the (ⓐ call ⓑ line ⓒ receiver)?
(전화상에서) 누구시죠?

60 Who am I (ⓐ speaking ⓑ telling ⓒ referring) to?
(전화상에서) 누구시죠?

61 I'll have the (ⓐ usual ⓑ thing ⓒ food).
제가 늘 먹는 것으로 주세요.

62 The night is still (ⓐ young ⓑ premature ⓒ early).
아직 초저녁이야.

63 Don't (ⓐ kick ⓑ induce ⓒ force) yourself.
(술자리에서) 억지로 마시지 마세요.

64 That's a (ⓐ treat ⓑ case ⓒ steal)!
거저 주는 것이나 다름없습니다! / 공짜나 마찬가지입니다.

65 Could you (ⓐ vitiate ⓑ validate ⓒ claim) my parking ticket?
제 주차권을 확인해 주시겠어요?

66 My left leg is (ⓐ aching ⓑ asleep ⓒ painful).
내 왼쪽 다리가 저립니다.

67 What seems to be (ⓐ the trouble ⓑ a trouble ⓒ trouble)?
무엇이 문제입니까?

68 I don't have any (ⓐ right ⓑ say ⓒ talk) regarding this matter.
이 문제에 관해서 나는 발언권이 없어.

정답 51 ⓑ 52 ⓐ 53 ⓐ 54 ⓐ 55 ⓒ 56 ⓐ 57 ⓑ 58 ⓒ 59 ⓑ 60 ⓐ 61 ⓐ 62 ⓐ 63 ⓒ 64 ⓒ 65 ⓑ 66 ⓑ 67 ⓐ 68 ⓑ

69 I am not (ⓐ sacked out for ⓑ cut out for ⓒ made out for) this job.
나는 이 일에 안 맞아.

70 It's the thought that (ⓐ numbers ⓑ thanks ⓒ counts).
(선물을 받고) 마음만으로도 충분해요.

71 Money is not (ⓐ an issue ⓑ a trouble ⓒ a hassle).
돈이 문제가 아니다.

72 I (ⓐ forgot ⓑ missed ⓒ lost) track of time.
시간 가는 줄 몰랐어.

73 (ⓐ How do you find ⓑ What do you find ⓒ How do you think about) your new condo?
새로 마련한 아파트 어때요?

74 You (ⓐ asked in ⓑ asked for ⓒ asked with) it.
네가 자초한 일이야.

75 Tom acts as if he were (ⓐ anybody ⓑ nobody ⓒ somebody).
톰은 마치 자기가 뭐나 되는 듯이 으스대.

76 I am just (ⓐ exasperated ⓑ mortified ⓒ exacerbated).
몸 둘 바를 모르겠습니다.

77 Not that I (ⓐ believe in ⓑ know of ⓒ rely on).
내가 알기로는 아니다.

78 There's no way (ⓐ out ⓑ in ⓒ into).
빠져나갈 출구가 없어. / 진퇴양난이야.

79 I am running (ⓐ short ⓑ lacking ⓒ long) of money.
나는 돈이 다 떨어져 간다.

80 What do you (ⓐ watch ⓑ witness ⓒ see) in him?
그 사람 어디가 그렇게 좋은 거니?

81 It's first come, first (ⓐ served ⓑ saved ⓒ reserved).
선착순입니다.

82 I (ⓐ first ⓑ second ⓒ third) that.
저도 그렇게 생각합니다.

83 You have nothing to (ⓐ blow ⓑ draw ⓒ lose).
네가 손해 볼 건 없잖아.

84 The story (ⓐ relates to ⓑ makes out ⓒ falls for) me.
그 이야기 공감합니다.

85 That's the way it (ⓐ goes ⓑ moves ⓒ comes).
세상일이란 게 원래 그런 거야.

86 Don't make me a (ⓐ puppet ⓑ scapegoat ⓒ scavenger).
나를 희생양으로 만들지 마.

87 I am (ⓐ seeing ⓑ observing ⓒ watching) what I eat.
나는 먹는 것에 신경쓰고 있어.

88 I couldn't sleep (ⓐ a bat ⓑ a wink ⓒ an ink) last night.
어젯밤에 한숨도 못 잤어.

89 I am (ⓐ distinguishing ⓑ different ⓒ unlike) from what I used to be.
나는 예전의 내가 아니다.

90 What a grueling day at the office. I am completely (ⓐ assuaged ⓑ saved ⓒ spent).
회사에서 완전 녹초가 된 하루였어. 완전히 지친 상태야.

91 Jeffery had (ⓐ mixed ⓑ complicated ⓒ complex) emotions after he divorced his good-natured wife.
제프리는 성격 좋은 아내와 이혼한 후 만감이 교차했다.

92 He just (ⓐ messed around ⓑ hung around ⓒ tagged along).
그는 그냥 따라나섰다.

93 My friends and I are (ⓐ coming for ⓑ rooting for ⓒ flying for) Manchester United.
내 친구들과 나는 맨체스터 유나이티드를 응원하고 있어.

94 I will have to play it by (ⓐ ear ⓑ nose ⓒ eye).
즉흥적으로 대처할 수밖에 없지.

95 I don't have the (ⓐ guts ⓑ encouragement ⓒ conviction) to ask her out on a date.
나는 그녀에게 데이트 신청할 용기가 없다.

96 It takes a (ⓐ long ⓑ good ⓒ short) week to finish reading the book.
책을 다 읽는 데 족히 일주일은 걸린다.

97 I am not in the (ⓐ mood ⓑ feeling ⓒ state) for dancing.
나는 지금 춤출 기분이 아니야.

98 The doctor has an (ⓐ booking ⓑ opening ⓒ schedule) from 4:00 to 4:30 if you'd like to come by then.
의사 선생님께서 4시에서 4시 30분에 비는 시간이 있으니 그때 괜찮으시다면 들러 주세요.

99 The audience (ⓐ adorned ⓑ applauded ⓒ appraised) at the end of the violin performance.
청중은 바이올린 연주가 끝이 나자 박수갈채를 보냈다.

100 I used to (ⓐ babysit ⓑ housesit ⓒ moonlight) as an English instructor even though I worked as an interpreter.
나는 통역사로 일했지만 야간에는 부업으로 영어 강사로 일하곤 했었다.

Part I Choose the option that best completes each dialogue.

1. A: Nathan, it's 7:45! You slept through your alarm again.
   B: Oh, no! If I'm _____ for school one more time, I'm going to get detention.

   (a) absent
   (b) punctual
   (c) tardy
   (d) delayed

2. A: I study Spanish really diligently, so I guess you can say I'm somewhat good at it.
   B: Don't be so _____, Janice. Your Spanish is excellent.

   (a) modest
   (b) modern
   (c) moderate
   (d) meek

3. A: So the total comes to forty dollars. How do you want to pay?
   B: Why don't we _____ the bill? We can each pay twenty dollars.

   (a) cut
   (b) partition
   (c) divide
   (d) split

4. A: I hope you like your present. I picked it out especially for you.
   B: Don't worry. It's the thought that _____ most, right?

   (a) counts
   (b) means
   (c) registers
   (d) happens

5. A: My husband stayed up all night playing video games last night.
   B: It sounds to me like he needs to grow up and _____ his age.

   (a) resemble
   (b) act
   (c) understand
   (d) think

6. A: Brain, do you think you'll be adventurous and order something new tonight?
   B: As much as I'd like to, I think I'll just have the _____.

   (a) typical
   (b) usual
   (c) common
   (d) meal

7. A: Good afternoon. Could you please connect me to Nick Valencia?
   B: I'm afraid that there is no one here _____.

   (a) for that name
   (b) with that name
   (c) by that name
   (d) of that name

8. A: I heard that a new salsa club just opened downtown. Would you like to go?
   B: No, not tonight. I'm not really in the _____ for dancing.

   (a) state
   (b) attitude
   (c) condition
   (d) mood

9. A: Do you think the students understood the theorem you lectured about today?
   B: I think so. I _____ down all the information for them.

   (a) broke
   (b) tore
   (c) ran
   (d) dismantled

10. A: Where are you heading, ma'am?
    B: If you would, please _____ me off at the airport.

    (a) start
    (b) drop
    (c) place
    (d) meet

11 A: Which baseball team do you support?
B: Personally, I always _____ the home team.

(a) catch up
(b) muscle in
(c) root for
(d) pass out

12 A: George, I think you should just go up to Anna and tell her how you really feel.
B: Oh, I just don't have the _____ to do that.

(a) guts
(b) incentive
(c) ambition
(d) heart

13 A: Guys, it's getting late. I think we need to head home now.
B: What are you talking about? The night is still _____!

(a) immature
(b) early
(c) fresh
(d) young

14 A: I really need this job, Gary. Do you think you can help me out?
B: Let me _____ some strings and see what I can do.

(a) tug
(b) yank
(c) sever
(d) pull

15 A: Professor Martin's class is unbelievably difficult.
B: I hear you. He uses such advanced vocabulary that I can't _____ his lectures at all.

(a) announce
(b) follow
(c) presume
(d) track

16 A: I'm not so sure if I should bet on this race.
B: Why not? You have nothing to _____, except for a few dollars.

(a) earn
(b) provide
(c) lose
(d) realize

17 A: Honey, will you please set the table? Dinner's almost ready.
B: Oh, I can't wait to eat. My mouth is _____ already.

(a) harkening
(b) moisturizing
(c) salivating
(d) watering

18 A: Congratulations on catching the bank robbers.
B: Thank you. If we hadn't worked fast, they probably would have _____ with it.

(a) run up
(b) gotten away
(c) snuck off
(d) hidden out

19 A: Do we need to make reservations for the concert?
B: Nope. It's first come, first _____.

(a) served
(b) seated
(c) saved
(d) standing

20 A: How's your project coming along at work?
B: Terribly. I think I'm just not _____ the job.

(a) brought out for
(b) made out for
(c) worked out for
(d) cut out for

A 다음 영어 표현과 일치하는 한글 뜻을 고르시오.

01 You have my word.   ⓐ 약속할게. ⓑ 웃기지 마.

02 come to my senses   ⓐ 감동을 받다 ⓑ 정신을 차리다

03 Hang in there.   ⓐ 버티고 있어. ⓑ 열심히 해.

04 That makes two of us.   ⓐ 나도 잘 모르겠어. ⓑ 나도 그렇게 생각해.

05 You asked for it.   ⓐ 네가 자초한 일이야. ⓑ 네가 말했던 대로야.

06 It's on the house.   ⓐ 그건 무료입니다. ⓑ 그건 비밀입니다.

07 That's a steal.   ⓐ 거저 주는 것과 다름없다. ⓑ 못된 짓이다.

08 I saw it coming.   ⓐ 꽤 시간이 걸렸어. ⓑ 내 그럴 줄 알았지.

09 I second that.   ⓐ 동의합니다. ⓑ 반대합니다.

10 make a fuss   ⓐ 곤란하게 만들다 ⓑ 소란을 피우다

B 한글 뜻에 맞는 영어 표현을 완성하시오.

| ⓐ track | ⓑ asleep | ⓒ force | ⓓ regular | ⓔ spirit |
| ⓕ spare | ⓖ mortified | ⓗ buck | ⓘ line | ⓙ switch |

01 I don't have any time to _____. 요즘에 짬이 없어.

02 I lost _____ of time. 시간 가는 줄 몰랐어.

03 That's the _____! 바로 그거야!

04 My left leg is _____. 왼쪽 다리가 저려.

05 The _____ stops here. 책임은 내가 질게.

06 I am just _____. 몸 둘 바를 모르겠습니다.

07 I am a _____ here. 저는 여기 단골입니다.

08 _____ to Line 1 1호선으로 갈아타다

09 Don't _____ yourself. (술자리에서) 억지로 마시지 마세요.

10 Who's on the _____? (전화상에서) 누구시죠?

풀면서 익히는 **Mini Test** ▶ 다음 한글 뜻에 맞는 영어 표현을 고르시오.

기출 어휘

01 Let's sneak out for a smoke while the boss is (ⓐ dozing in ⓑ dozing off ⓒ dozing with).
사장님이 깜박 졸고 있는 동안 담배나 살짝 피러 나가자.

02 (ⓐ Back me up ⓑ Back me on ⓒ Back me off) at the meeting.
회의에서 나를 지지해 줘.

03 Don't (ⓐ pick in ⓑ pick on ⓒ pick up) the poor little girl, boys.
이 녀석들아, 불쌍한 그 어린 여자애를 괴롭히지 말거라.

04 What do you think (ⓐ brought about ⓑ brought with ⓒ brought up) new changes?
무엇이 새로운 변화를 가져다주었다고 생각합니까?

05 The labor union didn't (ⓐ give off ⓑ give for ⓒ give in) to the demands of the management.
노조는 경영진의 요구에 굴복하지 않았다.

06 Desperate times (ⓐ call for ⓑ call at ⓒ call off) desperate measures.
절박한 시기에는 절박한 조치를 필요로 한다.

07 The new style is rapidly (ⓐ catching in ⓑ catching on ⓒ catching up).
새로운 스타일이 급속히 인기를 끌고 있다.

08 The CEO (ⓐ gives in ⓑ gives off ⓒ gives on) an air of power.
그 최고 경영자는 힘이 넘쳐나 보인다.

09 Why don't you (ⓐ come into ⓑ come on to ⓒ come over to) New York and pay us a visit?
뉴욕에 들러서 우리를 방문하는 게 어떠니?

10 We can (ⓐ put you in ⓑ put you up ⓒ put you out) for the night.
당신을 하룻밤 우리 집에서 재워드릴 수 있습니다.

11 The computer is (ⓐ acting in ⓑ acting on ⓒ acting up) again.
컴퓨터가 또 말썽이네.

12 I have no choice but to (ⓐ drop by ⓑ drop off ⓒ drop out) of school.
나는 학교를 중퇴하는 수밖에 없었다.

13 I am going to (ⓐ turn in ⓑ turn off ⓒ turn out) for the day.
오늘은 이만 자러 가야겠어.

14 The senator (ⓐ ended on ⓑ ended off ⓒ ended up) in prison for embezzlement.
그 상원의원은 횡령죄로 결국 감옥에 투옥되었다.

15 The professor is not good at (ⓐ putting his ideas off ⓑ getting his ideas across ⓒ kicking his ideas off).
그 교수는 자기의 생각을 전달하는 데 있어 뛰어나지 못하다.

어휘 Check! 01 **doze off** 깜박 졸다 02 **back up** 지지하다; (주장 따위를) 뒷받침하다 03 **pick on** 괴롭히다 04 **bring about** 야기하다, 일으키다 05 **give in** 굴복하다 06 **call for** 요구하다, 필요로 하다 07 **catch on** 인기를 끌다 08 **give off** (냄새, 빛 등을) 발하다, 풍기다 09 **come over to** ~에 들르다 10 **put up** 재워주다, 숙박시키다 11 **act up** (기계가) 말썽이다 12 **drop out** 중도 하차하다, 중퇴하다 13 **turn in** 잠자러 가다 14 **end up** 결국 ~하게 되다 15 **get across** (취지, 생각 등을) 전달하다, 이해시키다

정답 01 ⓑ 02 ⓐ 03 ⓑ 04 ⓐ 05 ⓒ 06 ⓐ 07 ⓑ 08 ⓑ 09 ⓒ 10 ⓑ 11 ⓒ 12 ⓒ 13 ⓐ 14 ⓒ 15 ⓑ

16 These days, I am barely (ⓐ getting by ⓑ getting off ⓒ getting on).
요즘 나는 거우 입에 풀칠하고 산다.

17 I need more time to (ⓐ chew in ⓑ chew over ⓒ chew with) the proposal.
그 제안서에 대해 곰곰이 생각할 시간이 좀 더 필요해.

18 The baby just (ⓐ came off ⓑ started off ⓒ dropped off) to sleep.
아기는 막 잠이 들었다.

19 Don't come outside until the rain (ⓐ lets down ⓑ lets up ⓒ lets in).
비가 잦아들 때까지 밖으로 나오지 마라.

20 The old lady was (ⓐ taken aback ⓑ taken about ⓒ taken off) by the disobedient child.
그 나이 든 여성은 반항적인 아이 때문에 당황했다.

21 We rushed to the theater to (ⓐ make up for ⓑ put in for ⓒ sign up for) lost time.
우리는 손실된 시간을 만회하기 위해 극장으로 서둘러 달려갔다.

22 The incumbent mayor has decided to (ⓐ opt for ⓑ pick out ⓒ run for) governor.
현직 시장은 주지사에 출마하기로 결정했다.

23 The question is (ⓐ broken down ⓑ broken up ⓒ broken with) into three parts.
이 질문은 세 부분으로 나누어질 수 있다.

24 It is not that difficult to (ⓐ put out ⓑ put on ⓒ put with) some muscle and increase your weight.
근육을 붙이고 체중을 늘리는 것은 그리 어렵지 않다.

25 It later (ⓐ dawned on ⓑ dawned to ⓒ dawned with) me what Tiffany was trying to tell me earlier.
티파니가 일찍이 내게 말하려고 했던 것이 무엇인지 나중에서야 알게 되었다.

26 The serial killer was (ⓐ put in ⓑ put on ⓒ put away) for 30 years.
연쇄 살인범은 30년 형을 받고 감옥에 갇혔다.

27 I (ⓐ put up with ⓑ signed up for ⓒ made up for) Biology 101 again since I failed it last semester.
나는 지난 학기에 낙제했기 때문에 생물학 101 수업을 다시 신청했다.

28 I don't want to (ⓐ take out ⓑ take off ⓒ take up) too much of your time.
당신의 시간을 너무 많이 빼앗고 싶지 않습니다.

29 I want Rachael and Susan to (ⓐ make up ⓑ mark up ⓒ make for).
나는 레이첼과 수잔이 화해하기를 바란다.

30 Don't even (ⓐ bring in ⓑ bring on ⓒ bring up) the subject that we previously discussed during the meeting.
회의에서 우리가 전에 토론했던 주제를 꺼낼 생각도 하지 마라.

어휘 Check!

16 **get by** 하루하루 근근이 살아가다 17 **chew over** 곰곰이 생각하다 18 **drop off** 잠들다 19 **let up** (강도, 세기가) 약해지다 20 **take aback** 당황하게 하다 21 **make up for** 만회하다, 벌충하다 22 **run for** 출마하다 23 **break down** 분류하다; (수치를) 분석하다 24 **put on** 살이 찌다, 근육이 붙다 25 **dawn on** 알게 되다 26 **put away** (감옥, 병원에) 감금하다 27 **sign up for** ~에 등록하다, 신청하다 28 **take up** (시간, 장소를) 차지하다 29 **make up** 화해하다 30 **bring up** (주제, 이야기를) 꺼내다

정답 16 ⓐ 17 ⓑ 18 ⓒ 19 ⓑ 20 ⓐ 21 ⓐ 22 ⓒ 23 ⓐ 24 ⓑ 25 ⓐ 26 ⓒ 27 ⓑ 28 ⓒ 29 ⓐ 30 ⓒ

31 Never (ⓐ back down ⓑ back over ⓒ back up).
절대로 물러서지 마.

32 The project (ⓐ fell in ⓑ fell out ⓒ fell through) due to a lack of funding.
자금 부족으로 그 프로젝트는 성사되지 못했다.

33 I have to (ⓐ brush up ⓑ practice up ⓒ sign up) on my English before I go to Los Angeles.
나는 로스엔젤레스에 가기 전에 영어 공부를 다시 해야 한다.

34 You have to (ⓐ set in ⓑ set off ⓒ set with) early to avoid the traffic jam.
교통 혼잡을 피하려면 일찍 출발해야 할 거야.

35 If we (ⓐ chip in ⓑ chip on ⓒ chip out) some money, we can help Jeffery.
우리가 돈을 조금씩 내면 제프리를 도울 수 있을 거야.

36 Let's (ⓐ get down to ⓑ get off to ⓒ get along with) business.
그럼 본론으로 들어갑시다.

37 You did well today. Your presentation really (ⓐ stood off ⓑ stood out ⓒ stood with).
오늘 정말 잘했어. 네 발표는 정말 두각을 나타냈어.

38 Stop (ⓐ cutting at ⓑ cutting in ⓒ cutting out) on the conversation.
대화 중에 끼어들지 마라.

39 Let's (ⓐ cross down ⓑ cross at ⓒ cross out) all the unnecessary items on the list.
목록에서 불필요한 항목은 모두 지워버리자.

40 You are supposed to (ⓐ hand out ⓑ make out ⓒ run out) fliers to passers-by.
당신은 행인들에게 전단을 나누어줘야 합니다.

41 I heard that the murderer was planning to (ⓐ do himself at ⓑ do himself in ⓒ do himself out).
그 살인범이 자살하려 했다고 하네.

42 It took a few days for me to (ⓐ break in ⓑ break into ⓒ break out) my new shoes.
새로 산 신발을 길들이는 데 며칠이 걸렸다.

43 I (ⓐ took for ⓑ took out ⓒ took to) the new teacher immediately.
나는 새로 부임한 선생님을 보자마자 좋아하게 되었다.

44 You'd better (ⓐ grow down ⓑ grow off ⓒ grow up).
너 철 좀 들어야겠다.

45 Catherine just (ⓐ fell for ⓑ kicked for ⓒ ran for) the famous young actor the first time they met.
캐서린은 유명한 젊은 배우에게 첫눈에 사랑에 빠져버렸다.

46 I (ⓐ came across ⓑ came down ⓒ came for) many difficult words while reading *The Da Vinci Code*.
〈다빈치 코드〉를 읽는 동안 어려운 단어들을 많이 발견했다.

어휘 Check!

31 back down 물러서다, (주장을) 굽히다 **32 fall through** 실패하다, 실현되지 못하다 **33 brush up (on)** (공부를) 다시 하다; (기술을) 더욱 연마하다 **34 set off** 출발하다 **35 chip in** 비용을 여러 사람이 나누어서 내다 **36 get down to** 착수하다 **37 stand out** 두각을 나타내다, 눈에 띄다 **38 cut in on** 끼어들다, (말을) 자르다 **39 cross out** 줄을 그어 지워버리다 **40 hand out** 나누어주다, 분배하다 **41 do in** 죽이다 **42 break in** (구두, 차 따위의 물건을) 길들이다 **43 take to** ~을 좋아하게 되다 **44 grow up** 철들다; 성장하다 **45 fall for** 사랑에 빠지다; 속임을 당하다 **46 come across** (글을 읽다가 새로운 단어를) 만나다, 발견하다

정답 31 ⓐ 32 ⓒ 33 ⓐ 34 ⓑ 35 ⓐ 36 ⓐ 37 ⓑ 38 ⓑ 39 ⓒ 40 ⓐ 41 ⓑ 42 ⓐ 43 ⓒ 44 ⓒ 45 ⓐ 46 ⓐ

47 Jessica is (ⓐ getting out to ⓑ getting to ⓒ getting for) me these days.
요즘 제시카가 나를 화나게 하고 있어.

48 I just (ⓐ hit off ⓑ hit out ⓒ hit upon) an idea for borrowing money.
돈을 빌릴 수 있는 방법을 지금 막 생각해 냈어.

49 Let me (ⓐ jot at ⓑ jot down ⓒ jot up) the message for you.
내가 너에게 온 메시지를 적어둘게.

50 The soldiers (ⓐ zonked in ⓑ zonked out ⓒ zonked within) after their strenuous training exercise.
힘든 훈련 후에 병사들은 깊이 잠들었다.

51 I heard that Pat won the lottery. I was so shocked that I almost (ⓐ passed away ⓑ passed in ⓒ passed out).
패트가 복권에 당첨되었다고 들었다. 너무나도 충격을 받아서 기절할 뻔했다.

52 We just (ⓐ ran out of ⓑ ran for ⓒ ran away with) gas. And to make matters worse, we don't have money to buy more.
기름이 지금 막 다 떨어졌어. 그리고 설상가상으로 기름을 더 구입할 돈도 없어.

53 Can you give me some time? I would like to (ⓐ sleep at ⓑ sleep in ⓒ sleep on) the problem.
내게 시간을 좀 줄 수 있겠니? 이 문제에 대해 하룻밤 자면서 깊이 생각해 보고 싶어.

54 If you have a problem with the management, do not be afraid to (ⓐ speak off ⓑ speak out ⓒ speak over).
경영진에 불만이 있으면 솔직하게 터놓고 말하는 것을 두려워하지 마.

55 Stephanie is so hilarious. She (ⓐ cracks me off ⓑ cracks me up ⓒ cracks me on).
스테파니는 정말 재미있어. 나를 완전히 웃게 만든다니까.

56 Her voice (ⓐ took in ⓑ took off ⓒ took on) a more desperate tone.
그녀의 목소리는 좀더 절박한 어조를 띠었다.

57 The company my brother used to work for (ⓐ went under ⓑ went off ⓒ went up).
내 형이 일했던 회사가 파산했다.

58 I am really sorry to hear that your father got (ⓐ laid away ⓑ laid off ⓒ laid out).
너희 아버지가 해고되어서 유감이야.

59 I don't trust Jim anymore. He (ⓐ makes off ⓑ makes up ⓒ makes up for) stories all the time.
난 더 이상 짐을 믿지 않아. 그는 항상 이야기를 날조해내잖아.

60 The self-made man was (ⓐ brought down ⓑ brought off ⓒ brought up) by his grandmother.
그 자수성가한 사람은 할머니가 키웠다.

어휘 Check!
47 **get to** 괴롭히다, 짜증나게 하다 48 **hit upon** 생각해내다, 떠올리다 49 **jot down** 메모하다, 적다 50 **zonk out** 깊이 잠이 들다
51 **pass out** 기절하다 52 **run out of** (연료가) 떨어지다; ~을 다 써버리다 53 **sleep on** 하룻밤 자며 곰곰이 생각하다 54 **speak out**
할 말을 하다, 솔직한 의견을 말하다 55 **crack up** (사람을) 웃기다 56 **take on** (성질을) 띠다; 일을 떠맡다 57 **go under** 망하다, 파산하다
58 **lay off** 정리해고하다 59 **make up** (이야기를) 조작[날조]하다 60 **bring up** 양육하다

정답 47 ⓑ 48 ⓒ 49 ⓑ 50 ⓑ 51 ⓒ 52 ⓐ 53 ⓒ 54 ⓑ 55 ⓑ 56 ⓒ 57 ⓐ 58 ⓑ 59 ⓑ 60 ⓒ

Check-up TEST

Part I Choose the option that best completes each dialogue.

1. A: How have things been for you lately?
   B: After I got _____, I've had to live on unemployment.
   (a) laid off
   (b) eased up
   (c) struck together
   (d) worked out

2. A: I'm writing Rebecca a long letter of apology.
   B: That's a nice sentiment, but it won't _____ the fact that you forgot her birthday.
   (a) do away with
   (b) reach out to
   (c) make up for
   (d) get down to

3. A: Let me tell you the company's email address.
   B: Wait just a second. I want to _____ the information in my notebook.
   (a) wait about
   (b) fall through
   (c) screw up
   (d) jot down

4. A: Did you hear that Helen quit college?
   B: No, I didn't. She's too talented a student to _____ like that.
   (a) drop out
   (b) end up
   (c) reason with
   (d) jump in

5. A: We don't have any milk left.
   B: You should have let me know that we'd _____ it when I went grocery shopping.
   (a) run out of
   (b) fed up with
   (c) come over to
   (d) put down for

6. A: How's your work coming?
   B: Not well. I think I've _____ more than I can handle by accepting two assignments.
   (a) jumped at
   (b) emptied out
   (c) taken on
   (d) pulled apart

7. A: It looks like the president's popularity has plummeted lately.
   B: Yes, it has. Some have even _____ his resignation.
   (a) brushed up
   (b) called for
   (c) taken over
   (d) rung up

8. A: How has your financial situation been since you got laid off?
   B: Things have been tough, but I've been _____.
   (a) hanging out
   (b) staying put
   (c) getting by
   (d) laying down

9. A: When will the merger with the computer manufacturer be completed?
   B: It was expected to occur this month, but, unfortunately, negotiations _____.
   (a) got together
   (b) moved ahead
   (c) dropped off
   (d) fell through

10. A: Don't worry. We'll pay for your meal this evening.
    B: Allow me to _____ a twenty. It's the least I can do.
    (a) bend over
    (b) chip in
    (c) give up
    (d) turn in

11 A: I'm positive that I saw him at the party last week.

B: I can't trust you unless you _____ your claim with strong evidence.

(a) hand down
(b) give off
(c) back up
(d) call off

12 A: I can't believe that you stood up to that bully. You were amazing!

B: Well, I've never been one to _____ from a confrontation.

(a) back down
(b) buckle down
(c) bang out
(d) block off

13 A: How about if we try marketing our product on social websites?

B: That's a great idea. I think you just _____ the solution to our financial troubles.

(a) hit upon
(b) dug into
(c) tore down
(d) put towards

14 A: Why don't you keep the air conditioning running all summer?

B: We used to, but the company decided that it _____ too many resources.

(a) stood up
(b) freed up
(c) took up
(d) worked up

15 A: What is the itinerary for tomorrow?

B: We will _____ from the hotel at 8 a.m. before heading to the convention center.

(a) tap out
(b) run through
(c) fasten down
(d) set off

16 A: It seems as though there are no more announcements to make.

B: In that case, let's go ahead and _____ business.

(a) end up with
(b) get down to
(c) hold back from
(d) shut out of

17 A: Joe, I really think that Celine is the one.

B: You can't _____ every girl you meet, Andy.

(a) fall for
(b) kick back
(c) open up
(d) break away

18 A: Mom, I don't want to go to school. The girls are just too mean.

B: You should just tell your teacher the next time they _____ you.

(a) get around
(b) pick on
(c) grow upon
(d) come across

19 A: I regret reporting the robbery to the police.

B: You did the right thing. It is important to _____ when you see something wrong happening.

(a) speak up
(b) speak out
(c) move ahead
(d) move on

20 A: Do you find my lecture that uninteresting?

B: I'm sorry for _____, Professor, but I didn't get much sleep last night.

(a) getting about
(b) dozing off
(c) falling back
(d) waking up

Voca Review

A 다음 영어 표현과 일치하는 한글 뜻을 고르시오.

01 **brush up on** your math skills 수학 실력을 (ⓐ 연마하다 ⓑ 인정받다)

02 **bring about** inflation 물가인상을 (ⓐ 대비하다 ⓑ 일으키다)

03 **crack up** the audience 관객들을 (ⓐ 울리다 ⓑ 웃기다)

04 **bring up** the subject 주제를 (ⓐ 꺼내다 ⓑ 바꾸다)

05 **come across** a difficult word 어려운 단어를 (ⓐ 발견하다 ⓑ 이해하다)

06 **bring up** the children 아이들을 (ⓐ 혼내다 ⓑ 양육하다)

07 **break down** the requirements 필요한 것을 (ⓐ 분석하다 ⓑ 요청하다)

08 **break in** my new pants 내 새 바지를 (ⓐ 더럽히다 ⓑ 길들이다)

09 **make up** a story 이야기를 (ⓐ 날조하다 ⓑ 들려주다)

10 The rain **let up**. 비가 (ⓐ 내리기 시작했다. ⓑ 잦아들었다.)

B 한글 뜻에 맞는 영어 표현을 완성하시오.

ⓐ drop off　　ⓑ cut in on　　ⓒ get to　　ⓓ give off　　ⓔ put away
ⓕ pass out　　ⓖ put on　　ⓗ come over　　ⓘ sign up　　ⓙ stand out

01 _____ rudely 무례하게 말참견하다

02 _____ on the street 길거리에서 기절하다

03 _____ during the lecture 강의 시간에 잠들다

04 _____ the criminal 범죄자를 복역시키다

05 _____ to a friend's house 친구 집에 들르다

06 _____ during the interview 면접을 보는 동안 눈에 띄다

07 _____ a nice scent 좋은 향기를 내다

08 _____ for a class 수업을 신청하다

09 _____ weight 체중을 늘리다

10 They _____ me. 그들은 날 짜증나게 한다.

정답 **A** 01 ⓐ 2 ⓑ 3 ⓑ 4 ⓐ 5 ⓐ 6 ⓑ 7 ⓐ 8 ⓑ 9 ⓐ 10 ⓑ **B** 01 ⓑ 02 ⓕ 03 ⓐ 04 ⓔ 05 ⓗ 06 ⓘ 07 ⓓ 08 ⓘ 09 ⓖ 10 ⓒ

풀면서 익히는 Mini Test ▶ 다음 한글 뜻에 맞는 영어 표현을 고르시오.

01 Why don't you (ⓐ concede ⓑ concur ⓒ confide) your worries in me? Then you will feel better.
네 고민을 나에게 털어놓으면 어떻겠니? 그러면 기분이 나아질 거야.

02 We have been discussing the issue for more than 6 hours. Let's (ⓐ adjourn ⓑ admit ⓒ adjacent) the meeting until tomorrow morning.
이 문제를 여섯 시간 넘게 토의해 왔습니다. 내일 아침까지 회의를 중단합시다.

03 I can't trust Mike anymore. His acts (ⓐ befit ⓑ befriend ⓒ belie) his words.
마이크를 더 이상 믿지 못하겠어. 걔는 행동과 말이 일치하지 않아.

04 Even though this task is difficult, you have no choice but to (ⓐ protrude ⓑ persevere ⓒ pertain).
비록 이 일이 어렵지만 너는 꾸준히 하는 수밖에 없다.

05 Stop (ⓐ baking ⓑ dawdling ⓒ howling). We are running out of time.
그만 꾸물거려. 시간 없단 말이야.

06 Let's take a detour to (ⓐ circumnavigate ⓑ circumscribe ⓒ circumvent) the traffic congestion.
교통 혼잡을 피하기 위해서 우회하자.

07 One of your jobs is to (ⓐ tally ⓑ rally ⓒ inscribe) the number of defective products.
당신의 업무 중 하나는 불량 제품의 수를 집계하는 것입니다.

08 The (ⓐ background ⓑ cloud ⓒ shroud) of mystery has been lifted as the police have identified who killed the celebrity.
경찰이 누가 그 유명 인사를 죽였는지 파악함에 따라 수수께끼의 장막이 걷히게 되었다.

09 Did you read the (ⓐ advertisement ⓑ headline ⓒ obituary) of the pastor in today's newspaper?
오늘 신문에서 목사님의 부고 기사를 읽었니?

10 I don't follow what you are saying. What is the (ⓐ topic ⓑ gist ⓒ say) of your argument?
무슨 말을 하고 있는 건지 모르겠어. 네 주장의 요점이 뭐야?

11 James never likes to go out with us. He's kind of a (ⓐ betrayer ⓑ recluse ⓒ traitor).
제임스는 절대 우리와 함께 외출하는 것을 좋아하지 않는다. 그는 다소 은둔형의 사람이다.

12 Each month, I have to pay (ⓐ alimony ⓑ stipend ⓒ subsidy) to my former wife.
매달마다 나는 전 아내에게 위자료를 지불해야 한다.

13 We need more (ⓐ entomologist ⓑ pessimist ⓒ philanthropists) in this rapidly changing world to help people in need.
급격히 변화하는 세상에서 힘든 사람들을 돕기 위해 더 많은 자선가들이 있어야 한다.

어휘 Check! **01 confide** (비밀을) 털어놓다; 신뢰하다 **02 adjourn** (회의를) 중단하다 **03 belie** ~와 상반되다; 거짓임을 보여주다 **04 persevere** 꾸준히 하다, 인내심을 가지고 행하다 **05 dawdle** 빈둥거리다, 꾸물대다 **06 circumvent** 우회하다; (문제를) 교묘하게 회피하다 **07 tally** 집계하다; 일치하다 **08 shroud** 덮개, 장막 **09 obituary** (신문에 실리는) 부고 기사 **10 gist** 요점, 요지 **11 recluse** 은둔형 사람, 은둔자 **12 alimony** 이혼 수당, 위자료 **13 philanthropist** 자선가; 박애주의자

정답 01 ⓒ 02 ⓐ 03 ⓒ 04 ⓑ 05 ⓑ 06 ⓒ 07 ⓐ 08 ⓒ 09 ⓒ 10 ⓑ 11 ⓑ 12 ⓐ 13 ⓒ

14 The (ⓐ concierge ⓑ connoisseur ⓒ gourmet) at the hotel politely asked the drunken man to leave.

호텔 안내원이 만취한 고객에게 나가 달라고 정중히 요청했다.

15 Where is the (ⓐ autopsy ⓑ biopsy ⓒ obituary) report?

부검 보고서가 어디 있지?

16 Versatility is (ⓐ a liability ⓑ an asset ⓒ a maxim) in this global world.

다재다능은 세계화 시대에 자산이다.

17 It's such a (ⓐ hassle ⓑ deviation ⓒ jubilee) to go to the post office because the lines are so long.

줄이 너무 길기 때문에 우체국에 가는 것은 혼잡스러운 일이다.

18 How long have you been in love with Tony, the (ⓐ enigmatic ⓑ invidious ⓒ exasperating) chief designer?

네가 수수께끼 같은 수석 디자이너 토니와 사랑에 빠진 지 얼마나 되었지?

19 As an (ⓐ acid ⓑ acrid ⓒ avid) baseball fan, I always make sure to catch every game of the World Series.

열렬한 야구팬으로서 나는 항상 월드 시리즈의 모든 게임을 반드시 보려고 한다.

20 I have written more than 20 books in the past two years. I can say I am a (ⓐ persuasive ⓑ prolific ⓒ promiscuous) author.

나는 지난 2년 동안 20권 이상의 책을 썼다. 나도 이제 다작 작가라고 할 수 있겠다.

21 I don't like his (ⓐ affectionate ⓑ quirky ⓒ reticent) personality.

나는 그의 괴팍한 성격을 좋아하지 않아.

22 This cold medicine makes me (ⓐ lethargic ⓑ laborious ⓒ obnoxious).

이 감기약을 먹으면 나른해진다.

23 We have to make sure that the computer security system is (ⓐ unstable ⓑ obsolete ⓒ tamperproof).

컴퓨터 보안 시스템이 변조가 불가능하도록 확실히 해두어야 한다.

24 This pecan pie is (ⓐ off the beaten track ⓑ out of this world ⓒ up to date).

이 피칸 파이 맛이 정말 예술이다.

25 Don't worry too much about the making payments. You will get a two-month (ⓐ elegance period ⓑ grace period ⓒ time limit).

돈을 지불하는 것에 대해 너무 크게 걱정하지 않으셔도 됩니다. 2개월간의 지불 유예기간이 있으시거든요.

어휘 Check! 14 **concierge** 호텔 안내원 15 **autopsy** 부검 16 **asset** 자산; 유용한 것 17 **hassle** 혼잡스러움; 싸움 18 **enigmatic** 수수께끼 같은, 불가사의한 19 **avid** 열렬한, 열심인 20 **prolific** 다작의 21 **quirky** 괴팍한, 기벽이 있는 22 **lethargic** 나른한; 무기력한 23 **tamperproof** 변조가 불가능한 24 **out of this world** (이 세상 것 같지 않게) 정말 훌륭한 25 **grace period** (채무 등의) 지불 유예 기간

정답 14 ⓐ 15 ⓐ 16 ⓑ 17 ⓐ 18 ⓐ 19 ⓒ 20 ⓑ 21 ⓑ 22 ⓐ 23 ⓒ 24 ⓑ 25 ⓑ

26 (ⓐ Brace ⓑ Brake ⓒ Break) yourself. We're in for a bumpy ride!
마음 굳게 먹어. 차가 덜컹대기 시작할 거야!

27 I (ⓐ suppressed ⓑ coaxed ⓒ menaced) the baby into coming a little closer to me.
나는 아기를 구슬려 나에게 조금 더 가까이 오도록 했다.

28 I am much (ⓐ obligated ⓑ officiated ⓒ obliged) for your hospitality.
귀하의 환대에 매우 감사드립니다.

29 My office is around the corner and is (ⓐ adjacent to ⓑ adlib to ⓒ approximate to) the post office.
내 사무실은 모퉁이를 돈 곳에 있으며, 우체국 부근에 위치해 있다.

30 I take (ⓐ part ⓑ solace ⓒ pride) in reading books when I find myself in times of trouble.
나는 힘든 시기에 빠질 때 책을 읽으면서 위안을 삼는다.

기출 가능 어휘

31 The defeated soldiers (ⓐ hoisted ⓑ honed ⓒ hosted) the white flag.
패배한 군인들이 백기를 들어 올렸다.

32 Why don't we stop (ⓐ joking ⓑ quibbling ⓒ stigmatizing) over trivial things?
별것 아닌 것 가지고 그만 트집잡는 게 어때?

33 The driver smashed into the car in front of him because he was (ⓐ penalizing ⓑ persecuting ⓒ tailgating).
운전사가 앞차에 바짝 따라붙었기 때문에 바로 앞에 있던 차와 충돌했다.

34 My mother (ⓐ dissipated ⓑ berated ⓒ condoned) me for smoking and drinking.
담배 피우고 술 마신다고 어머니께서 날 심하게 혼내셨다.

35 You have to save a large sum to live off the (ⓐ admonished ⓑ accrued ⓒ accustomed) interest.
누적되는 이자만으로 생계를 이어나갈 수 있도록 많은 돈을 저축해야 한다.

36 I have a hard time (ⓐ acclimating ⓑ associating ⓒ ameliorating) myself to new environments.
나는 새로운 환경에 적응하는 데 어려움을 겪고 있다.

37 If you want to improve your reading ability, you have to (ⓐ persist ⓑ peruse ⓒ pursue) reading materials.
독해 능력을 향상시키고 싶다면 독해 자료를 정독해야 한다.

38 Did you hear that the serial killer was (ⓐ avowed ⓑ nabbed ⓒ raided)?
그 연쇄살인범이 잡혔다는 소식 들었니?

어휘 Check!
26 **brace oneself** 마음의[만반의] 준비를 하다 27 **coax ~ into ...** ~를 구슬려 ...하도록 시키다 28 **be obliged for** ~에 대해 감사해하다 29 **adjacent to** ~에 인접한, ~ 부근의 30 **take solace in** ~에서 위안을 삼다 31 **hoist** (돛, 기 등을) 올리다 32 **quibble** 트집 잡다, 옥신각신하다 33 **tailgate** 앞차에 바짝 따라붙다 34 **berate** 심하게 혼내다 35 **accrue** (이자가) 쌓이다; 축적하다 36 **acclimate** 적응하다, 순응하다 37 **peruse** 정독하다 38 **nab** 체포하다

정답 26 ⓐ 27 ⓑ 28 ⓒ 29 ⓐ 30 ⓑ 31 ⓐ 32 ⓑ 33 ⓒ 34 ⓑ 35 ⓑ 36 ⓐ 37 ⓑ 38 ⓑ

39 You have to follow the (ⓐ elasticity ⓑ inertia ⓒ specifications) outlined below.
아래에 명시되어 있는 구체적인 내용을 따라야 한다.

40 We are planning to have a brief (ⓐ salvage ⓑ sojourn ⓒ stability) in Hawaii.
우리는 하와이에서 단기간 체류할 계획이다.

41 This sofa (ⓐ coverage ⓑ covering ⓒ coverall) is waterproof.
이 소파 외피는 방수가 된다.

42 Do you still think (ⓐ aquarium ⓑ conservatory ⓒ acupuncture) is scientific?
아직도 침술이 과학적이라고 생각하니?

43 The megastore gives (ⓐ flaps ⓑ freebies ⓒ determents) to customers who spend more than ten dollars. Let's go!
그 대형 상점은 10달러 이상 돈을 쓴 손님들에게 경품을 준대. 가보자!

44 (ⓐ Dexterity ⓑ Disability ⓒ Discourse) is required to be a good craftsman.
훌륭한 공예가가 되려면 손재주가 필요하다.

45 We need to come up with (ⓐ casualty ⓑ contingency ⓒ continuity) plans to prepare for an economic crisis.
경제 위기에 대비하기 위한 긴급시 대책을 만들어 두어야 한다.

46 The store sells fake designer clothes to (ⓐ faint ⓑ versatile ⓒ gullible) people. I think you are one of them. You paid too much.
그 가게는 가짜 명품 옷을 잘 속는 사람들에게 팔아. 너도 그 중 한 명인 것 같구나. 돈을 너무 많이 지불했어.

47 The newcomer is really (ⓐ incorrigible ⓑ intangible ⓒ meticulous).
그 신참은 정말 구제 불능이야.

48 A (ⓐ neutral ⓑ shrieking ⓒ soothing) sound woke us up in the middle of the night.
한밤중에 날카로운 소리 때문에 잠에서 깨어났다.

49 The vegetation is (ⓐ lash ⓑ rush ⓒ lush) in this urban area.
이 도심지에는 초목이 우거져 있다.

50 Being a member of (ⓐ an exclusive ⓑ an inclusive ⓒ a recessive) club makes me feel tremendous pride.
아무나 가입할 수 없는 클럽의 회원이 되어 나는 굉장한 자부심을 느낀다.

어휘 Check!
39 **specifications** 구체적인 사항, 설명서 40 **sojourn** 체류; 체류하다 41 **covering** 외피, 덮개 42 **acupuncture** 침술 43 **freebie** 경품, 무료 상품 44 **dexterity** 손재주가 있음 45 **contingency** 뜻밖의 사고 46 **gullible** 잘 속는 47 **incorrigible** (사람 성격이) 구제할 수 없는; 제멋대로 구는 48 **shrieking** (소리가) 날카로운 49 **lush** (산, 나무가) 우거진 50 **exclusive** 배타적인; 회원을 엄선하는; 독점적인

정답 39 ⓒ 40 ⓑ 41 ⓑ 42 ⓒ 43 ⓑ 44 ⓐ 45 ⓑ 46 ⓒ 47 ⓐ 48 ⓑ 49 ⓒ 50 ⓐ

51 The rural area has only (ⓐ dense ⓑ intermittent ⓒ spurious) cell phone service.
시골 지역은 휴대전화 서비스 연결이 때때로 중단된다.

52 New recruits for the soccer team must first pass an (ⓐ exalted ⓑ exigent ⓒ exhaustive) physical test.
축구 팀의 새로운 선수들은 먼저 매우 철저한 신체 검사를 통과해야 한다.

53 He has very (ⓐ exorbitant ⓑ exquisite ⓒ extricated) taste in wine.
그는 매우 고급스러운 와인 취향을 갖고 있다.

54 My little sister is kind of (ⓐ passive ⓑ paltry ⓒ pouty).
내 여동생은 잘 토라진다.

55 When are you going to throw a (ⓐ housewarming ⓑ house-lifting ⓒ house-celebrating) party at your new home?
새로 옮긴 집에서 언제 집들이를 할 거야?

56 Tom is just a (ⓐ casual ⓑ natural ⓒ mythical) acquaintance.
톰과는 그냥 아는 사이에 불과하다.

57 Jeffery is such a (ⓐ sharp ⓑ specific ⓒ bright) dresser. He really knows what to wear to a party.
제프리는 옷을 세련되게 잘 입는 사람이다. 그는 파티에서 어떤 옷을 입어야 하는지 잘 안다.

58 That's such a (ⓐ jovial ⓑ lame ⓒ obtuse) excuse. Just make sure that won't happen again.
그건 구차한 변명에 불과해. 다시는 그런 일 없도록 해.

59 Boys, stop (ⓐ asking around ⓑ throwing out ⓒ thrashing around). This is a public place.
얘들아. 설치지 말거라. 여기는 공공장소란다.

60 Don't forget that you need to (ⓐ hang around ⓑ pull your weight ⓒ push ahead) if you want to get promoted.
승진하고 싶다면 맡은 일을 잘 해내야 함을 잊지 말아라.

51 **intermittent** 간헐적인; (접속 상태가) 때때로 끊기는　52 **exhaustive** 철저한　53 **exquisite** 고급스러운, 세련된　54 **pouty** 토라지기 잘하는　55 **housewarming party** 집들이　56 **casual acquaintance** 그냥 아는 사이　57 **sharp dresser** 옷을 잘 입는 사람　58 **lame excuse** 구차한 변명　59 **thrash around** 설치며 돌아다니다　60 **pull one's weight** 맡은 바 소임을 다하다

Check-up TEST

Part I Choose the option that best completes each dialogue.

1 A: I think we should go to the opera tomorrow.
   B: In that case, we should ask the _____ to reserve tickets for us.

   (a) housekeeper
   (b) attendant
   (c) concierge
   (d) bellhop

2 A: I'm shocked that Jackie believed me when I told her the moon is made of cheese.
   B: She's so _____ that she will believe anything you tell her.

   (a) gullible
   (b) guarded
   (c) garrulous
   (d) gabby

3 A: Why do you have so much baseball memorabilia?
   B: Don't you know? I've been _____ baseball fan for years.

   (a) a drab
   (b) a bare
   (c) a puny
   (d) an avid

4 A: Aren't you friends with Frank Brown?
   B: I know him, but I just consider him a _____ .

   (a) trusted mentor
   (b) casual acquaintance
   (c) family member
   (d) personal trainer

5 A: Did you hear that the actress Grace Collins passed away?
   B: Yes, I did. In fact, I was just reading her _____ in the paper.

   (a) obituary
   (b) testimonial
   (c) biography
   (d) inscription

6 A: I can't believe how many books Steven King has written.
   B: He is a _____ writer, having completed dozens of novels and short stories.

   (a) popular
   (b) competent
   (c) reluctant
   (d) prolific

7 A: The rainforest is home to several thousands of animal species.
   B: Right. They are able to thrive in the _____ foliage there.

   (a) lush
   (b) barren
   (c) stark
   (d) iconic

8 A: This container must weigh several hundred pounds.
   B: Yes, but I think you can _____ it up with the use of a lever.

   (a) hoist
   (b) appraise
   (c) plunge
   (d) guzzle

9 A: Do you know the forecast for tomorrow?
   B: It's calling for _____ periods of rain and sunshine.

   (a) rhythmic
   (b) intermittent
   (c) arbitrary
   (d) interminable

10 A: Harold says he can't come tonight because he has to clean his room.
    B: Oh, that's just another one of his _____. I'm sure he's not busy at all.

    (a) valid reasons
    (b) lame excuses
    (c) weak arguments
    (d) timid remarks

11 A: How were you able to solve the problem?
B: Actually, we _____ it by using a different method.

(a) disregarded
(b) acquiesced
(c) circumvented
(d) abjured

12 A: Does this medicine have any side effects?
B: Yes, it can make you _____, so do not take it if you have to operate heavy machinery.

(a) apathetic
(b) lethargic
(c) energetic
(d) invigorated

13 A: What are you going to be doing for winter vacation?
B: My family is planning a two-week _____ in the mountains for skiing.

(a) opportunity
(b) sojourn
(c) layover
(d) sabbatical

14 A: I really enjoy Lady Gaga's music.
B: I do, too, but I also like her _____ sense of fashion. It's so unique.

(a) tepid
(b) adept
(c) quirky
(d) routine

15 A: What do you think most billionaires do with their money?
B: Many of them become _____ in order to share their fortunes with the less fortunate.

(a) philanthropists
(b) sympathizers
(c) antagonists
(d) evolutionists

16 A: How much vacation time does this job provide?
B: You will receive 10 days the first year and will _____ an extra 5 days every year thereafter.

(a) dissipate
(b) berate
(c) accrue
(d) yield

17 A: What did you end up doing yesterday?
B: Much to my regret, I ended up _____ the day away doing nothing.

(a) dwindling
(b) dawdling
(c) dwarfing
(d) dazzling

18 A: In making our evacuation plan, we must consider all possible outcomes.
B: That's right. We must prepare for any _____ that may befall us.

(a) expectancy
(b) prerequisite
(c) undertaking
(d) contingency

19 A: How much was the inheritance that you received from your uncle's estate?
B: Unfortunately, none. All his _____ were used to pay off his substantial debts.

(a) assets
(b) liabilities
(c) virtues
(d) statutes

20 A: Now that my funding from the school has been cut off, I'm not sure I can continue my research.
B: I think you must try to _____ in spite of any hardships you currently face.

(a) vacillate
(b) persevere
(c) succumb
(d) preserve

Voca Review

A 다음 영어 표현과 일치하는 한글 뜻을 고르시오.

01 **adjourn** the meeting   회의를 (ⓐ 중단하다 ⓑ 주재하다)

02 **peruse** the newspaper   신문을 (ⓐ 정독하다 ⓑ 구독하다)

03 **nab** a bank robber   은행 강도를 (ⓐ 수배하다 ⓑ 체포하다)

04 an **exquisite** room   (ⓐ 커다란 ⓑ 세련된) 방

05 an **exhaustive** search   (ⓐ 철저한 ⓑ 민감한) 조사

06 an **enigmatic** comment   (ⓐ 중요한 ⓑ 불가사의한) 발언

07 **tally** the survey results   설문조사 결과를 (ⓐ 발표하다 ⓑ 집계하다)

08 **tailgate** the car   앞차에 (ⓐ 바짝 따라붙다 ⓑ 충돌하다)

09 pay **alimony** to him   그에게 (ⓐ 위자료 ⓑ 연체료)를 지불하다

10 a **shrieking** sound   (ⓐ 날카로운 ⓑ 부드러운) 소리

B 한글 뜻에 맞는 영어 표현을 완성하시오.

ⓐ sharp	ⓑ weight	ⓒ adjacent	ⓓ freebies	ⓔ acclimate
ⓕ berate	ⓖ gist	ⓗ grace	ⓘ housewarming	ⓙ solace

01 hold a _____ party   집들이를 하다

02 _____ to his office   그의 사무실에 인접한

03 _____ him for cheating   컨닝한 것에 대해 그를 심하게 혼내다

04 offer _____ to customers   고객에게 경품을 주다

05 during the _____ period   지불 유예기간 동안

06 the _____ her book   그녀의 책의 요점

07 pull my _____   맡은 바 내 소임을 다하다

08 take _____ in my friendship   우정을 통해 위안을 삼다

09 _____ dresser   옷을 잘 입는 사람

10 _____ to the change   변화에 적응하다

Part II

VP | 04 동사

01 The former president had little time to (ⓐ savor ⓑ scour ⓒ scrimp) his unbelievable victory.
전 대통령은 믿을 수 없는 그의 승리를 만끽할 시간이 없었다.

02 The celebrity was (ⓐ permeate ⓑ prosecuted ⓒ protested) for DUI.
그 유명인사는 음주 운전으로 기소되었다.

03 Corruption (ⓐ annihilates ⓑ perpetrates ⓒ pervades) government offices in our nation.
부패가 우리나라의 정부 기관에 널리 퍼져 있다.

04 The management called a meeting to (ⓐ evacuate ⓑ identify ⓒ isolate) the network's security leaks.
경영진은 네트워크 보안 누설 경로를 파악하기 위해 회의를 소집했다.

05 The bill (ⓐ perused ⓑ provoked ⓒ parsed) strong public opposition and caused demonstrators to protest in front of Capitol Hill.
그 법안은 대중들의 강한 반발을 불러 일으켰고 시위자들이 국회 의사당 앞에서 시위를 벌이는 원인이 되었다.

06 Global stock prices have (ⓐ plunged ⓑ soared ⓒ skyrocketed) across the board due to the subprime mortgage crisis.
서브프라임 모기지 위기 때문에 전 세계 주가가 일률적으로 폭락했다.

07 It's hard to (ⓐ elicit ⓑ incur ⓒ pinpoint) what has caused the global economic crisis.
세계적인 경제 위기의 원인이 무엇인지 정확히 꼬집어내기는 어렵다.

08 The civil servant was (ⓐ cast ⓑ cited ⓒ cracked) for embezzlement.
그 공무원은 횡령 혐의로 소환되었다.

09 Professor Langdon has a tendency to (ⓐ dash ⓑ detach ⓒ digress) from his main points of discussion.
랭던 교수는 자신의 토론 주제에서 벗어나는 이야기를 하는 경향이 있다.

10 At the end of the day, the police chief tried to (ⓐ shirk ⓑ shove ⓒ skid) his duties.
결국 경찰서장은 그의 의무를 회피하려 했다.

11 The senator has (ⓐ ameliorated ⓑ striven ⓒ tamed) to improve human rights in North Korea.
그 상원의원은 북한의 인권을 개선하기 위해 애써 왔다.

12 Her beauty and talent (ⓐ evaporate ⓑ exacerbate ⓒ exceed) those of the other contestants.
그녀의 미모와 재능은 다른 경쟁자들을 능가한다.

어휘 Check!

01 **savor** (냄새, 맛을) 음미하다; (경험, 시간을) 만끽하다 02 **prosecute** 기소[고소]하다; ~을 수행하다 03 **pervade** 만연하다, 널리 퍼지다 04 **identify** 정체를 밝히다, 파악하다 05 **provoke** 불러일으키다; 화나게 하다 06 **plunge** 폭락하다 07 **pinpoint** (문제점을) 정확히 파악하다, 꼬집어내다 08 **cite** 소환하다; 인용하다 09 **digress** (주제에서) 벗어나다 10 **shirk** (의무나 책임을) 회피하다 11 **strive** 노력하다, 애쓰다 12 **exceed** 능가하다, 뛰어나다

정답 01 ⓐ 02 ⓑ 03 ⓒ 04 ⓑ 05 ⓑ 06 ⓐ 07 ⓒ 08 ⓑ 09 ⓒ 10 ⓐ 11 ⓑ 12 ⓒ

13 Small companies usually (ⓐ castigate ⓑ crumble ⓒ court) job applicants by providing generous salaries.
규모가 작은 회사는 보통 두둑한 급여를 제공함으로써 구직자들을 유혹한다.

14 Adam (ⓐ splashed ⓑ splurged ⓒ sterilized) by spending his lottery winnings on a Ferrari and a Mercedes-Benz.
아담은 페라리나 메르세데스 벤츠에 복권 당첨금을 쓰며 돈을 흥청망청 썼다.

15 More and more companies are (ⓐ verifying ⓑ vanishing ⓒ vying) the credentials of their job applicants as a growing number of candidates forge their English competency certificates.
점점 더 많은 지원자들이 영어 능력 증명서를 위조하자 더욱 많은 회사들이 구직자들의 자격 증명서를 검증하고 있다.

16 The infantry officer was (ⓐ reprimanded ⓑ repudiated ⓒ retrieved) for mistreating war prisoners.
그 보병 장교는 전쟁 포로를 학대하여 질책을 받았다.

17 He was sentenced to death for (ⓐ instilling ⓑ instigating ⓒ investigating) a pro-democracy uprising.
그는 민주화 운동을 선동한 혐의로 사형 선고를 받았다.

18 AIDS patients were once (ⓐ savaged ⓑ stigmatized ⓒ vaporized), but civic groups are striving to prevent this.
에이즈 환자들은 한때 낙인 찍혔지만 시민 단체들은 이것을 막으려고 노력하고 있다.

19 Our beliefs can be (ⓐ shaped ⓑ saddled ⓒ spurred) by where we are born.
우리의 신념은 우리가 태어난 장소에 의해 만들어질 수 있다.

20 The doctor was (ⓐ allocated ⓑ suppressed ⓒ installed) as the chairman of the medical association.
그 의사는 의학 협회 의장으로 임명되었다.

21 It's hard to (ⓐ juggle ⓑ jumble ⓒ juxtapose) working and studying at the same time.
일과 공부를 동시에 병행하기란 어렵다.

22 North Korea has long been (ⓐ irrigated ⓑ isolated ⓒ revoked) despite the backing of the international community.
북한은 국제 사회의 도움에도 불구하고 오랜 기간 동안 고립되어 있었다.

23 The updated equipment is expected to (ⓐ deport ⓑ facilitate ⓒ groan) weapons development.
업데이트된 장비가 무기 개발을 용이하게 할 것으로 보인다.

24 The time has come for colleges to (ⓐ emaciate ⓑ epitomize ⓒ implement) distance learning programs.
이제 대학이 원격 교육 프로그램을 실행할 시간이 왔다.

25 The lack of a police presence (ⓐ stranded ⓑ triggered ⓒ waded) criminal activities in the area.
경찰의 부족이 그 지역에서 범죄 활동을 일으켰다.

어휘 Check!
13 **court** 유혹하다, 꾀다 14 **splurge** 돈을 흥청망청 쓰다 15 **verify** 입증하다, 검증하다 16 **reprimand** 꾸짖다, 질책하다 17 **instigate** 선동하다 18 **stigmatize** 낙인을 찍다 19 **shape** 만들다, 형성하다 20 **install** 취임시키다, 임명하다 21 **juggle** 병행하다; 저글링하다 22 **isolate** 고립시키다 23 **facilitate** 용이하게 하다; 촉진하다 24 **implement** 실행하다 25 **trigger** 유발하다, 일으키다

정답 13 ⓒ 14 ⓑ 15 ⓐ 16 ⓐ 17 ⓑ 18 ⓑ 19 ⓐ 20 ⓒ 21 ⓐ 22 ⓑ 23 ⓑ 24 ⓒ 25 ⓑ

26 It's hard to (ⓐ adapt ⓑ adept ⓒ adopt) to a new environment.
새로운 환경에 적응하기란 어렵다.

27 Pillows and blankets can (ⓐ ban ⓑ stimulate ⓒ obstruct) a baby's breathing.
베개와 담요는 아기의 호흡을 방해할 수 있다.

28 Some enterprises (ⓐ prohibit ⓑ protract ⓒ tarnish) their workers from smoking on the premises.
몇몇 기업체는 구내에서 직원들이 담배 피우는 것을 금지하고 있다.

29 The politician (ⓐ withdrew ⓑ withheld ⓒ withstood) from social activities as he was found to have had inappropriate relationships with some of his female staff members.
그 정치인은 여직원 몇 명과 부적절한 관계가 있었던 것이 드러나자 사회 활동에서 물러났다.

30 The parties concerned have to (ⓐ enact ⓑ fulfill ⓒ repeal) the terms of the contract.
계약 당사자들은 계약 조건을 이행해야 한다.

31 While people believe the renowned scientist is an innate genius, he (ⓐ devours ⓑ relishes ⓒ savors) books on everything whenever he has time.
사람들은 그 유명한 과학자가 타고난 천재라고 믿지만 사실 그는 시간이 있을 때마다 모든 분야에 관한 책을 탐독한다.

32 This history course is intended to help students (ⓐ broaden ⓑ deprive ⓒ perish) their understanding of the Renaissance.
이 역사 수업은 학생들이 르네상스에 대한 이해의 폭을 넓히는 것을 도와주려고 의도되었다.

33 David Simpson (ⓐ flabbergasted ⓑ pleaded ⓒ plowed) not guilty to 2 counts of murder, but everyone knew that he had committed the crimes.
데이빗 심슨은 두 건의 살인 사건에 대해 무죄를 주장했지만 모든 사람들은 그가 범행을 저질렀다는 것을 알았다.

34 The opposition party (ⓐ amended ⓑ assuaged ⓒ attempted) to introduce a bill that would cut taxes for poor people.
야당은 가난한 사람을 위해 세금을 감면하는 법안을 상정하려고 시도했다.

35 The airport (ⓐ surpasses ⓑ serves ⓒ transcends) as a gateway to Africa.
그 공항은 아프리카로 가는 통로 역할을 한다.

기출 가능 어휘

36 Smoking is strictly (ⓐ banished ⓑ banned ⓒ bemoaned) in public places.
공공장소에서의 흡연은 엄격히 금지된다.

37 The Internet (ⓐ represented ⓑ rekindled ⓒ rescinded) a window of opportunity for the underprivileged at the start of the 21st century.
21세기가 시작되면서 인터넷은 혜택을 덜 받고 있는 사람들에게 기회의 창을 의미했다.

 어휘 Check!

26 adapt 적응하다 [to] 27 obstruct 방해하다 28 prohibit 금지하다 29 withdraw 물러나다, 철수하다; (돈을) 인출하다 30 fulfill 이행 하다, 충족시키다 31 devour 탐독하다; 게걸스럽게 먹어대다 32 broaden (영역을) 넓히다 33 plead 주장하다, 변명하다 34 attempt 시 도하다 35 serve 역할을 하다 36 ban 금지하다 37 represent 의미하다; 대변하다

정답 26 ⓐ 27 ⓒ 28 ⓐ 29 ⓐ 30 ⓑ 31 ⓐ 32 ⓐ 33 ⓑ 34 ⓒ 35 ⓑ 36 ⓑ 37 ⓐ

38 The broadcasting committee (ⓐ enjoined ⓑ imposed ⓒ impoverished) restrictions on some TV programs to censor indecent content.

방송 위원회는 외설적인 콘텐츠를 검열하기 위해 몇몇 TV 프로그램에 제재를 가했다.

39 The rules and regulations must be strictly (ⓐ empowered ⓑ enchanted ⓒ enforced).

규칙과 규정은 엄격히 실행되어야 한다.

40 The U.S. (ⓐ elaborated ⓑ lifted ⓒ released) restrictions on North Korea as the reclusive country suffered from drought and famine.

그 은둔적인 나라가 가뭄과 기근으로 고통받게 되자 미국은 북한에 대한 제재를 해제시켰다.

41 I had no choice but to (ⓐ abolish ⓑ abstain ⓒ ascertain) from smoking and drinking as my health deteriorated.

내 건강이 나빠지면서 흡연과 음주를 절제할 수밖에 없었다.

42 The young and promising actor (ⓐ landed ⓑ lavished ⓒ rebutted) a leading role in the blockbuster film.

그 젊고 유망한 배우가 블록버스터 영화의 주연배우 역을 따냈다.

43 A group of beggars (ⓐ roamed ⓑ lubricated ⓒ snarled) through the metropolitan city before coming across a shelter.

한 무리의 거지들은 쉼터를 발견하기 전까지는 대도시 전역을 떠돌아다녔다.

44 Gullible customers were (ⓐ embellished ⓑ enrolled ⓒ enticed) into buying defective products by a savvy salesman.

순진한 고객들이 약삭빠른 영업사원에 의해 결함이 있는 제품을 구입하도록 유인당했다.

45 The troubleshooters (ⓐ enacted ⓑ mediated ⓒ repealed) disputes between two warring parties.

분쟁 조정인은 호전적인 두 당사자들 사이의 분쟁을 중재했다.

46 Demonstrators (ⓐ annulled ⓑ assembled ⓒ associated) to voice their concerns over a bill that was passed by the Senate.

상원에서 통과된 법안에 대해 우려를 표하고자 시위자들이 집결했다.

47 The health supplement is (ⓐ fortified ⓑ famished ⓒ reformed) with vitamins A and C.

그 건강 보조제는 비타민 A와 C가 강화되어 있다.

48 Violence can never be (ⓐ implored ⓑ legitimized ⓒ mitigated) under any circumstances.

폭력은 어떤 상황에서도 정당화될 수 없다.

49 At the shareholders' meeting, the CEO didn't (ⓐ deteriorate ⓑ disclose ⓒ disembark) any information about the merger.

주주 총회에서 최고 경영자는 합병에 관해 어떠한 정보도 밝히지 않았다.

어휘 Check! 38 **impose** (의무, 벌 등을) 부과하다 39 **enforce** 실행[시행]하다 40 **lift** (제재를) 해제하다 41 **abstain** 절제하다 42 **land** (계약을) 따내다; (노력으로) 획득하다 43 **roam** 떠돌아다니다 44 **entice** 유혹하다, 유인하다 45 **mediate** 중재하다, 화해시키다 46 **assemble** 집합하다; (기계를) 조립하다 47 **fortify** 강화시키다 48 **legitimize** 정당화하다 49 **disclose** 밝히다, 폭로하다

정답 38 ⓑ 39 ⓒ 40 ⓑ 41 ⓑ 42 ⓐ 43 ⓐ 44 ⓒ 45 ⓑ 46 ⓑ 47 ⓐ 48 ⓑ 49 ⓑ

50 Fear of an economic crisis (ⓐ delegated ⓑ elucidated ⓒ loomed) large in the minds of policy makers in the late 1990s.
1990년대 후반에 정책 입안자들의 마음에 경제 위기에 대한 공포감이 크게 다가왔다.

51 Neither the U.S. government nor the terrorist group was willing to (ⓐ compromise ⓑ intervene ⓒ mandate).
미국 정부와 테러 단체 모두 타협할 의사를 보이지 않았다.

52 To reduce swelling, it is advised to (ⓐ immerse ⓑ infuriate ⓒ negotiate) one's foot in cold water.
붓기를 가라앉히려면 발을 찬 물에 담가야 한다.

53 UN Secretary General (ⓐ imitated ⓑ implored ⓒ imposed) wealthy nations to provide assistance to Indonesia following the massive earthquake.
유엔 사무총장은 대규모 지진이 일어난 후에 인도네시아를 위해 도움을 제공해 달라고 부유한 국가들에게 간곡히 요청했다.

54 This swampland will be (ⓐ reckoned ⓑ refilled ⓒ reclaimed) for a housing development.
이 습지는 주택 개발지로 개간될 것이다.

55 The new filtration system is able to (ⓐ purify ⓑ quarantine ⓒ quell) all the air in the entire building.
새로운 여과 시스템은 전체 건물의 모든 공기를 정화할 수 있다.

56 Acquired Immunity Deficiency Syndrome is usually (ⓐ abbreviated ⓑ aggregated ⓒ annexed) as AIDS.
후천성 면역 결핍증은 보통 줄여서 에이즈(AIDS)라고 쓴다.

57 Making the same mistake again and again will (ⓐ optimize ⓑ specialize ⓒ spoil) your life.
같은 실수를 계속해서 반복하게 되면 당신의 인생을 망칠 것이다.

58 Dictatorships can be (ⓐ castigated ⓑ checked ⓒ chimed) by a political system that provides checks and balances.
견제와 균형을 제공하는 정치 시스템에 의해 독재정권은 견제받을 수 있다.

59 The glamorous actress was able to (ⓐ acknowledge ⓑ lessen ⓒ resurrect) the miniskirt in the 1970s.
그 관능적인 여배우는 1970년대에 미니스커트를 부활시킬 수 있었다.

60 The dean wanted to (ⓐ concoct ⓑ confer ⓒ compel) with some professors before making any decision about the tuition hike.
학장은 등록금 인상에 관한 결정을 내리기 전에 몇몇 교수들과 상의하기를 원했다.

61 The soccer team never (ⓐ altered ⓑ granted ⓒ meditated) its strategy, which led to its loss in the championship game.
축구팀은 결코 전략을 변경하지 않았고, 이로 인해 결국 결승전에서 패배하게 되었다.

62 In order to save money, you have to (ⓐ hassle ⓑ haggle ⓒ hustle) for discounts when you shop.
돈을 아끼기 위해서는 쇼핑할 때 할인을 위한 흥정을 할 수 있어야 한다.

어휘 Check!

50 **loom** (위험이나 불안이) 다가오다; 어렴풋이 나타나다 51 **compromise** 타협하다, 양보하다 52 **immerse** (물에) 담그다 53 **implore** 탄원하다, 간청하다 54 **reclaim** 개간하다 55 **purify** 정화하다 56 **abbreviate** 짧게 표기하다, 줄여 쓰다 57 **spoil** 망치다; (아이를 버릇없게) 키우다 58 **check** 견제하다 59 **resurrect** 부활시키다 60 **confer** 상의하다 61 **alter** 변경하다, 바꾸다 62 **haggle** (가격을) 흥정하다

정답 50 ⓒ 51 ⓐ 52 ⓐ 53 ⓑ 54 ⓒ 55 ⓐ 56 ⓐ 57 ⓒ 58 ⓑ 59 ⓒ 60 ⓑ 61 ⓐ 62 ⓑ

63　Their move to Wisconsin (ⓐ abolished ⓑ obviated ⓒ plundered) the need for summer clothes.
위스콘신으로 이사를 하자 여름옷은 필요 없게 되었다.

64　Under the scorching sun, a pride of lions is (ⓐ coaxing ⓑ enticing ⓒ foraging) for something to eat.
강렬한 햇볕 아래에서 한 무리의 사자들이 먹을 것을 찾아 돌아다니고 있다.

65　No one can (ⓐ constitute ⓑ institute ⓒ substitute) Jo Hyun woo as the number-one Korean goalkeeper.
한국 최고의 골키퍼로서 어느 누구도 조현우 선수를 대신할 수는 없다.

66　Herds of cows are serenely (ⓐ dozing ⓑ grappling ⓒ grazing) on the pasture.
소 떼가 목초지에서 평온하게 풀을 뜯고 있다.

67　This program is designed to (ⓐ assimilate ⓑ simulate ⓒ situate) the degree to which car passengers can suffer in a head-on collision.
이 프로그램은 차량 정면충돌 시에 탑승자가 차에 따라 타격을 입는 정도를 모의실험하기 위해 고안되었다.

68　According to a recent report, female scientists will (ⓐ bubble ⓑ constitute ⓒ infuriate) the majority by the year 2050.
최근의 한 보고에 따르면 2050년까지 여성 과학자들이 과학 관련 분야에서 과반수를 차지할 것이라고 한다.

69　The parents (ⓐ abandoned ⓑ accused ⓒ acquired) their son when they were chased by the police.
그 부모는 경찰에 쫓기자 자기 아들을 버렸다.

70　Many lower-income families in this area are living in houses that are (ⓐ appropriated ⓑ misappropriated ⓒ subsidized) by the government.
이 지역에 살고 있는 많은 저소득층 가구들이 정부가 보조금을 대는 주택에 살고 있다.

어휘 Check!　63 **obviate** (곤란, 필요성을) 제거하다　64 **forage** (먹이를 찾아) 돌아다니다, 이리저리 떠돌아다니다　65 **substitute** 대체시키다; 대체하다　66 **graze** 풀을 뜯다　67 **simulate** 모의실험[훈련]을 하다　68 **constitute** 구성하다　69 **abandon** 버리다　70 **subsidize** 보조금을 대다

정답　63 ⓑ　64 ⓒ　65 ⓒ　66 ⓒ　67 ⓑ　68 ⓑ　69 ⓐ　70 ⓒ

VP 04 동사　235

Check-up TEST

Part II Choose the option that best completes each sentence.

1 I'm out of cash, so I need to stop by the ATM and _____ some money.
(a) deposit
(b) select
(c) withdraw
(d) invest

2 The government has recently passed a law that _____ smoking in public places.
(a) enforces
(b) bans
(c) regrets
(d) situates

3 Human beings populate every corner of the globe because of their ability to _____ to virtually any environment.
(a) adopt
(b) invoke
(c) adapt
(d) revoke

4 If you want the best deals when shopping, you must be sure to _____ over prices.
(a) argue
(b) haggle
(c) quarrel
(d) contest

5 The car company is _____ to improve the quality of its products after receiving numerous customer complaints.
(a) meditating
(b) striving
(c) postponing
(d) ignoring

6 Bears are generally docile creates, but they can become dangerous when _____.
(a) provoked
(b) revoked
(c) invoked
(d) prohibited

7 When I was growing up, my mother had to _____ raising three children and holding two jobs.
(a) organize
(b) decipher
(c) fortify
(d) juggle

8 Unable to decide where to eat dinner, my wife and I _____ and ordered take-out.
(a) confused
(b) conserved
(c) collapsed
(d) compromised

9 Companies use flashy advertisements to _____ customers into purchasing their products.
(a) deceive
(b) repel
(c) entice
(d) tumble

10 Free-range cattle are allowed to _____ freely on pastures rather than be confined to pens.
(a) strut
(b) roam
(c) plunge
(d) assemble

11 To take notes quickly, it is important to
_____ common terms and phrases.
(a) promote
(b) implement
(c) abbreviate
(d) recite

12 Not having eaten in several days, the
survivors of the shipwreck _____ their
meals.
(a) devoured
(b) digested
(c) consumed
(d) swallowed

13 It is sunny now, but storm clouds are
_____ on the horizon.
(a) wandering
(b) looming
(c) receding
(d) implementing

14 The government _____ school lunches
to ensure that every student eats proper
meals.
(a) loans
(b) constitutes
(c) regulates
(d) subsidizes

15 The teacher _____ the students for
cheating on the test.
(a) congratulated
(b) reprimanded
(c) lauded
(d) elevated

16 After ignoring the law for several years,
the city has decided once again to
_____ a curfew for minors.
(a) repeal
(b) enforce
(c) detain
(d) obstruct

17 The political candidate _____ his
constituents for their support.
(a) implored
(b) regaled
(c) condemned
(d) voted

18 My doctor told me that I should _____
from alcohol if I want to live to old age.
(a) abstain
(b) indulge
(c) decline
(d) suspect

19 Playing social games is a great way to
break the ice and _____ conversation
among strangers.
(a) prohibit
(b) mediate
(c) facilitate
(d) discourage

20 Allegations of sexual misconduct among
a handful of religious leaders have
_____ the entire church.
(a) stigmatized
(b) emancipated
(c) personified
(d) invigorated

Voca Review

A 다음 영어 표현과 일치하는 한글 뜻을 고르시오.

01 **shirk** my responsibility 내 의무를 (ⓐ 깨닫다 ⓑ 저버리다)

02 **impose** a tax 세금을 (ⓐ 부과하다 ⓑ 내다)

03 **resurrect** an old system 낡은 제도를 (ⓐ 폐지하다 ⓑ 부활시키다)

04 **graze** on the hill 언덕에서 (ⓐ 풀을 뜯다 ⓑ 풀을 베다)

05 **obstruct** the passage 통행을 (ⓐ 방해하다 ⓑ 원활하게 하다)

06 **verify** the theory 이론을 (ⓐ 내세우다 ⓑ 검증하다)

07 **instigate** the crowd 군중을 (ⓐ 모으다 ⓑ 선동하다)

08 **confer** with my attorney 내 변호사와 (ⓐ 상의하다 ⓑ 다투다)

09 **alter** my mind 내 마음을 (ⓐ 바꾸다 ⓑ 결정하다)

10 **fulfill** his duties 그의 임무를 (ⓐ 포기하다 ⓑ 이행하다)

B 한글 뜻에 맞는 영어 표현을 완성하시오.

ⓐ disclose　　ⓑ prosecute　　ⓒ substitute　　ⓓ abandon　　ⓔ legitimize
ⓕ prohibit　　ⓖ reclaim　　ⓗ purify　　ⓘ broaden　　ⓙ pinpoint

01 _____ unwanted pets 원하지 않는 애완동물을 버리다

02 _____ the field 들판을 개간하다

03 _____ his secret 그의 비밀을 폭로하다

04 _____ the problem 문제를 정확히 짚어내다

05 _____ smoking in public places 공공장소에서 흡연을 금지시키다

06 _____ him for a felony 중죄로 그를 기소하다

07 _____ the air 공기를 정화하다

08 _____ ingredients 재료를 대체시키다

09 _____ his position 그의 입장을 정당화하다

10 _____ my knowledge 내 지식을 넓히다

정답 **A** 01 ⓑ 02 ⓐ 03 ⓑ 04 ⓐ 05 ⓐ 06 ⓑ 07 ⓑ 08 ⓐ 09 ⓐ 10 ⓑ **B** 01 ⓓ 02 ⓖ 03 ⓐ 04 ⓙ 05 ⓕ 06 ⓑ 07 ⓗ 08 ⓒ 09 ⓔ 10 ⓘ

풀면서 익히는 Mini Test ▶ 다음 한글 뜻에 맞는 영어 표현을 고르시오.

기출 어휘

명사

01 People say the singer has an ulterior (ⓐ motion ⓑ motivation ⓒ motive) for releasing her new album behind schedule.
그 가수가 예정보다 늦게 앨범을 출시한 데는 이면의 동기가 있다고 사람들은 말한다.

02 Once considered a (ⓐ novel ⓑ novelty ⓒ novice), the electronic dictionary now has become a thing of the past.
한때 새로운 물건으로 간주되었던 전자사전은 이제 과거의 유물이 되었다.

03 China has now become an economic (ⓐ tenure ⓑ titan ⓒ tumult) thanks to its huge contribution to the global economy.
현재 중국은 세계 경제에 크게 이바지한 덕분에 경제 대국이 되었다.

04 The newly introduced regulations are in (ⓐ compliance ⓑ completion ⓒ consideration) with international standards.
새로 도입된 규정은 국제 기준과 부합한다.

05 The economic (ⓐ amenity ⓑ crisis ⓒ territory) in Japan has caused a ripple effect around the world.
일본의 경제 위기는 전 세계에 파급 효과를 일으켰다.

06 The opposition party gained over 200 (ⓐ bills ⓑ mayors ⓒ seats) in the national election.
이번 전국단위 선거에서 야당이 200석 이상의 의석을 차지했다.

07 The boss thought he got along well with his (ⓐ novices ⓑ professionals ⓒ subordinates), which was not the case.
사장은 본인이 부하 직원들과 잘 지낸다고 생각했지만 그렇지 않았다.

08 No people can enter the (ⓐ premier ⓑ premises ⓒ premium) without proper identification cards.
적절한 신분증 없이는 어느 누구도 구내에 들어올 수 없다.

09 Some Asian doctors have recently made a major (ⓐ breakthrough ⓑ breakaway ⓒ breakup) in the treatment of AIDS.
몇몇 아시아 의사들이 최근 에이즈 치료에 있어 커다란 획기적인 성과를 만들어냈다.

10 You can find many examples of (ⓐ concoction ⓑ connotation ⓒ denotation) in literary works.
문학 작품에서 함축적 의미 사례를 많이 확인할 수 있다.

11 Perseverance is a key (ⓐ allegation ⓑ component ⓒ trial) for success.
인내심은 성공에 있어서 핵심적인 요소이다.

12 Some Asian countries were left in a financial (ⓐ pasture ⓑ predilection ⓒ predicament) due largely to soaring oil prices.
일부 아시아 국가가 주로 유가 상승으로 인해 재정적 곤경에 처하게 되었다.

어휘 Check!

01 **motive** 동기 02 **novelty** 새로운 물건, 신기한 물건 03 **titan** 대국, 거대한 것 04 **compliance** 부합; (기준의) 충족 05 **crisis** 위기
06 **seat** 의석; 좌석 07 **subordinate** 직원, 부하 08 **premises** 구내, 건물이 딸린 토지 09 **breakthrough** 획기적인 것
10 **connotation** 함축적 의미 11 **component** 요소 12 **predicament** 곤란, 곤경

정답 01 ⓒ 02 ⓑ 03 ⓑ 04 ⓐ 05 ⓑ 06 ⓒ 07 ⓒ 08 ⓑ 09 ⓐ 10 ⓑ 11 ⓑ 12 ⓒ

13 This time, it's hard to predict whether the president will grant (ⓐ amnesty ⓑ annuity ⓒ incentive) to political prisoners.

이번에 대통령이 정치범을 대상으로 사면을 할지 안 할지 예측하기 힘들다.

14 It is high time we come up with (ⓐ legitimacy ⓑ literacy ⓒ literature) programs for students who cannot read and write at grade level.

수준에 맞게 읽고 쓰는 데 어려움을 겪는 학생들을 위해 글을 읽고 쓰는 프로그램을 모색해야 하는 적기이다.

15 Europeans have (ⓐ a penchant ⓑ an adoption ⓒ a pervasion) for taking longer lunch breaks than Asians.

유럽인들은 아시아인들보다 좀 더 긴 점심시간을 선호한다.

부사

16 Asians are still (ⓐ aesthetically ⓑ genuinely ⓒ marginally) represented in the United States.

아시아인은 여전히 미국에서 아주 소수만 차지하고 있다.

17 The labor union (ⓐ strenuously ⓑ ironically ⓒ impartially) opposed the pay freeze.

노조는 급여 동결에 대해서 강력히 반대했다.

18 The speech by the leader of North Korea was reproduced (ⓐ consecutively ⓑ simultaneously ⓒ verbatim) in the state-run newspaper.

북한 지도자의 연설이 국영 신문에 말 그대로 다시 쓰여졌다.

형용사

19 Life is nothing but (ⓐ mediocre ⓑ petite ⓒ transient), so cherish each and every moment.

인생은 단지 일시적일 뿐이니 매 순간을 소중히 여겨라.

20 The professor is under criticism for having (ⓐ superlative ⓑ superficial ⓒ laborious) knowledge of quantum physics.

그 교수는 양자 물리학에 대해 피상적인 지식만을 갖고 있다고 하여 비난을 받고 있다.

21 As a judge, I find it (ⓐ forthcoming ⓑ imminent ⓒ incumbent) that the criminal see the inside of a prison cell.

판사로서 나는 그 범죄자가 감옥 생활을 하는 것이 필요하다고 봅니다.

22 The governor's (ⓐ licentious ⓑ brutal ⓒ relative) behavior involving his female secretary was disclosed by a veteran reporter.

여비서와 관련된 주지사의 음탕한 행동이 한 베테랑 기자에 의해 들통났다.

23 We have five sons who are all (ⓐ pliable ⓑ refractory ⓒ reliable). They never obey us and have their own way.

우리에게는 전부 다 말을 잘 듣지 않는 다섯 명의 아들이 있다. 그 애들은 절대 우리말에 복종하지 않으며 자기들 멋대로 한다.

---

13 amnesty 사면 **14** literacy 글을 읽고 쓸 줄 아는 능력 **15** penchant 선호, 좋아함 **16** marginally 아주 조금, 근소하게 **17** strenuously 강력히; 힘들게 **18** verbatim 말 그대로 **19** transient 일시적인; 덧없는 **20** superficial 피상적인 **21** incumbent (의무적으로) 꼭 해야 하는 **22** licentious 음탕한, 방탕한 **23** refractory 말을 잘 듣지 않는, (사람이) 다루기 힘든

정답 13 ⓐ 14 ⓑ 15 ⓐ 16 ⓒ 17 ⓐ 18 ⓒ 19 ⓒ 20 ⓑ 21 ⓒ 22 ⓐ 23 ⓑ

24 The project has been prepared with (ⓐ meticulous ⓑ captivating ⓒ palpable) care by the management.
그 프로젝트는 경영진에 의해 세심한 정성으로 준비되었다.

25 The murderer asked for a (ⓐ harsh ⓑ lenient ⓒ reciprocal) punishment, which the judge denied.
그 살인범은 관대한 처벌을 요청했지만 판사가 이를 거부했다.

명사

26 Her acting was dull and lacked (ⓐ finance ⓑ finesse ⓒ fiber).
그녀의 연기는 따분했으며 기교가 결여되어 있었다.

27 You don't have to spend a (ⓐ facade ⓑ forte ⓒ fortune) in order to make a good impression on your first date.
당신의 첫 번째 데이트 상대에게 좋은 인상을 남기기 위해서 거액의 돈을 쓸 필요는 없다.

28 Once considered an eyesore to the public, the Eiffel Tower is now one of the most highly regarded (ⓐ accolades ⓑ momentums ⓒ monuments) in the world.
한때 대중들에게 흉물스러운 건물로 간주되었던 에펠 탑은 이제 세계에서 가장 높이 평가되는 기념탑 중 하나이다.

29 Bed and breakfast (ⓐ accommodations ⓑ folks ⓒ fugitives) are popular among people in their 20s and 30s.
20대와 30대층 사람들에게는 숙박과 아침 식사를 제공하는 숙박 시설이 인기가 있다.

30 The central themes of many novels and television dramas these days revolve around personal (ⓐ vacancies ⓑ validities ⓒ vendettas).
요즘 들어 많은 소설과 TV 드라마의 주제는 개인적인 복수에 초점을 맞춘다.

31 This museum is the (ⓐ brainchild ⓑ theory ⓒ vandalism) of a young graduate who majored in anthropology.
이 박물관은 인류학을 전공한 한 젊은 대학원생의 두뇌의 산물이다.

32 This movie is an (ⓐ adaptation ⓑ adoption ⓒ appropriation) of a novel that resonated well with the public.
이 영화는 대중의 반향을 불러일으켰던 소설을 각색한 것이다.

33 Realizing he would be the (ⓐ guru ⓑ heir ⓒ terrain) to a large fortune, he lived a carefree life of debauchery.
거대한 재산을 상속받는 후계자임을 알고 그는 걱정 없는 방탕한 삶을 살았다.

---

24 **meticulous** 꼼꼼한, 세심한 25 **lenient** (처벌이) 관대한 26 **finesse** 기교, 수완 27 **fortune** 거액의 돈 28 **monument** 기념비[탑], 기념 건조물 29 **accommodations** 숙박 시설 30 **vendetta** 복수 31 **brainchild** 두뇌의 산물, 독창적인 계획[생각] 32 **adaptation** 각색; 적응 33 **heir** 후계자

34 It came as a surprise when the prime minister showed (ⓐ forbearance ⓑ intensity ⓒ offense) to the war criminals who had killed innocent people.
수상이 무고한 사람들을 죽인 전범들에게 관용을 보였는데 이는 놀라운 일이었다.

35 The board of directors rejected the (ⓐ throng ⓑ tenure ⓒ proposition) that a part of the company's profits should go to charities.
이사회는 회사 수익의 일부분을 자선 단체에 기부해야 한다는 제안을 거절했다.

36 The (ⓐ inauguration ⓑ inclusion ⓒ infringement) of the article in *The Washington Post* was welcomed by the Democratic Party.
민주당은 기사가 워싱턴 포스트에 포함된 것을 환영했다.

37 A salary (ⓐ cab ⓑ caprice ⓒ cap) was introduced to put a limit on the skyrocketing salaries of professional athletes.
스포츠 선수들의 치솟는 연봉에 제동을 걸기 위해 연봉 상한제가 도입되었다.

38 The security company was sued for a (ⓐ breach ⓑ prodigy ⓒ symbiosis) of contract as it sold its customers' information on the black market.
보안 회사가 고객의 정보를 암시장에 팔았기 때문에 계약 위반으로 고소당했다.

39 (ⓐ Fishes ⓑ Packs ⓒ Quarters) of dogs are chasing after a pickup truck carrying dog food.
개떼가 개 먹이를 싣고 있는 픽업 트럭을 뒤쫓고 있다.

40 Racks of designer clothes are on (ⓐ demand ⓑ display ⓒ offer) at the boutique.
옷걸이에 걸려 있는 명품 옷이 부티크에 진열되어 있다.

부사

41 (ⓐ Undoubtedly ⓑ Nefariously ⓒ Objectively), public interest in the case has declined.
의심의 여지없이, 그 사건에 대한 대중의 관심이 사그라들었다.

42 It was (ⓐ cordially ⓑ erroneously ⓒ intermittently) reported that the vice president's brother had been assassinated during the annual ceremony.
부통령의 동생이 연례행사에서 암살되었다고 잘못 보도되었다.

43 The businessman (ⓐ furtively ⓑ subjectively ⓒ transparently) handed an envelope full of 100-dollar bills to the politician.
그 사업가는 100달러 지폐로 가득 찬 봉투를 정치인에게 은밀히 건넸다.

어휘 Check! 34 **forbearance** 관용 35 **proposition** 제안; 진술, 주장 36 **inclusion** 포함 37 **salary cap** 연봉 상한제 38 **breach** (계약, 약속의) 위반 39 **pack** (개, 늑대 등의) 무리 40 **display** 전시 41 **undoubtedly** 의심의 여지없이 42 **erroneously** 잘못되게 43 **furtively** 은밀히

정답 34 ⓐ 35 ⓒ 36 ⓑ 37 ⓒ 38 ⓐ 39 ⓑ 40 ⓑ 41 ⓐ 42 ⓑ 43 ⓐ

형용사

44 If you want a more (ⓐ repellent ⓑ robotic ⓒ robust) flavor, add some extra spices to the recipe.
좀 더 강한 맛을 원한다면 요리법에 별도의 양념을 더 넣으세요.

45 Military service in Korea is (ⓐ compulsory ⓑ insatiable ⓒ rigorous). No one can avoid duty without just reason.
한국의 군 복무는 의무적이다. 합당한 이유 없이는 어느 누구도 의무를 피해갈 수 없다.

46 Jason, your homework is (ⓐ insouciant ⓑ sloppy ⓒ spendthrift). What's wrong with you these days? Even your math score is slipping.
제이슨, 네 숙제가 엉망이구나. 요즘에 무슨 일이라도 있는 거야? 수학 점수도 떨어지고 있잖아.

47 The death of the revered president was (ⓐ exacerbating ⓑ exasperating ⓒ excruciating) for many citizens in the country.
존경받던 대통령의 죽음은 그 국가의 많은 시민들에게 매우 큰 고통이었다.

48 The global economic slowdown is (ⓐ insurmountable ⓑ superstitious ⓒ synonymous) with corporate restructuring and layoff.
전 세계 경제 둔화는 기업의 구조조정과 정리해고를 의미한다.

49 (ⓐ Stark ⓑ Sturdy ⓒ Spacious) contrasts exist between TOEIC and TEPS, so don't think success on one will lead to success on the other.
토익과 텝스 시험 간에는 현격한 차이가 있으니 하나를 잘 봤다고 해서 다른 하나도 잘 볼 것이라고 생각하지 마라.

50 The Pope invited many (ⓐ perpendicular ⓑ prominent ⓒ promiscuous) politicians to promote sexual abstinence in order to halt the spread of AIDS.
교황은 에이즈가 퍼지는 것을 막기 위해 성적 금욕을 홍보하는 차원에서 많은 저명한 정치인들을 초대했다.

어휘 Check!
44 **robust** (향이나 맛이) 강한　45 **compulsory** 의무적인　46 **sloppy** 엉망인, 제대로 하지 않은　47 **excruciating** 고통이 매우 큰
48 **synonymous** 의미가 같은, 동일한　49 **stark** 현격한, 차이가 큰　50 **prominent** 저명한

정답 44 ⓒ　45 ⓐ　46 ⓑ　47 ⓒ　48 ⓒ　49 ⓐ　50 ⓑ

Check-up TEST

Part II Choose the option that best completes each sentence.

1 The airline provided overnight _____ for passengers whose flights had been cancelled.

(a) submissions
(b) consequences
(c) legislations
(d) accommodations

2 My father is a _____ lawyer in my hometown and is known by nearly everybody.

(a) distracting
(b) stubborn
(c) prominent
(d) temporary

3 Although hydrogen cars may become common in the future, for now they remain a _____.

(a) novelty
(b) portion
(c) grief
(d) designation

4 Many members of the older generation criticize today's youths as being overly _____ and materialistic.

(a) contradictory
(b) superficial
(c) infectious
(d) inept

5 The scientists made a tremendous _____ in the field of medicine by discovering a cure for the disease.

(a) breakthrough
(b) vaccination
(c) assignment
(d) privilege

6 The word "lazy" has negative _____ for most people.

(a) suggestions
(b) transmissions
(c) connotations
(d) denotations

7 For years, the painting was _____ attributed to Rembrandt when in reality it was painted by one of his students.

(a) absurdly
(b) implicitly
(c) erroneously
(d) methodically

8 The _____ for teachers in New York is 86,000 dollars per year.

(a) growth rate
(b) salary cap
(c) net income
(d) market share

9 The recent economic _____ exposed major deficiencies in the banking sector.

(a) crisis
(b) agreement
(c) tariff
(d) coalition

10 Tiffany was able to diffuse the tense situation through her _____ in dealing with people.

(a) canniness
(b) finesse
(c) deficiency
(d) aggressiveness

11 The price of consumer goods decreased _____ in November, down just 0.1 percent from the month before.

(a) undoubtedly
(b) marginally
(c) incrementally
(d) sufficiently

12 Our company is widely praised for the _____ detail we incorporate into our products.

(a) noxious
(b) inordinate
(c) predictable
(d) meticulous

13 The social networking website is the _____ of a Harvard University dropout.

(a) conception
(b) hierarchy
(c) brainchild
(d) facsimile

14 The contemporary design of the new city hall stands in _____ contrast to the Gothic architectural style of the original building.

(a) outlandish
(b) enchanting
(c) bleak
(d) stark

15 This unfortunate _____ could have been avoided with more careful planning.

(a) predicament
(b) pastime
(c) wreckage
(d) premonition

16 The government has decided to increase funding for reading programs with the aim of improving _____ among its citizens.

(a) discourse
(b) literacy
(c) acumen
(d) hyperbole

17 The main _____ of the application process is a face-to-face interview.

(a) component
(b) partition
(c) division
(d) segment

18 Not wanting to be noticed, the boy glanced _____ at the beautiful girl across the room.

(a) effusively
(b) vapidly
(c) furtively
(d) willingly

19 The theory rejects the _____ that living creatures are capable of evolving.

(a) paradigm
(b) proposition
(c) propagation
(d) pervasion

20 In South Korea, every eligible young man must complete a _____ two-year military enlistment.

(a) compulsory
(b) tactile
(c) persistent
(d) elective

Voca Review

A 다음 영어 표현과 일치하는 한글 뜻을 고르시오.

01 a personal **vendetta** 개인적인 (ⓐ 복수 ⓑ 사정)

02 an **heir** to the company 회사의 (ⓐ 재정 ⓑ 후계자)

03 grant **amnesty** (ⓐ 사면 ⓑ 상금)을 주다

04 **transient** symptoms (ⓐ 일시적인 ⓑ 충격적인) 증상

05 a **lenient** punishment (ⓐ 엄격한 ⓑ 관대한) 처벌

06 a **licentious** lifestyle (ⓐ 규칙적인 ⓑ 방탕한) 생활습관

07 **robust** flavor (ⓐ 강한 ⓑ 달콤한) 맛

08 a **breach** of contract 계약 (ⓐ 이행 ⓑ 위반)

09 an **incumbent** duty (ⓐ 불필요한 ⓑ 꼭 해야 하는) 임무

10 work **strenuously** (ⓐ 열심히 ⓑ 적당히) 일하다

B 한글 뜻에 맞는 영어 표현을 완성하시오.

ⓐ refractory ⓑ adaptation ⓒ pack ⓓ compliance ⓔ undoubtedly
ⓕ motive ⓖ synonymous ⓗ monument ⓘ excruciating ⓙ titan

01 _____ of wolves 늑대의 무리

02 a dishonest _____ 불순한 동기

03 a national _____ 국정 기념물

04 _____ true 의심할 여지없이 사실인

05 _____ words 동의어, 같은 뜻을 가진 단어

06 _____ to the environment 환경에 적응

07 en economic _____ 경제 대국

08 relieve _____ pain 매우 큰 고통을 가라앉히다

09 a _____ student 말을 안 듣는 학생

10 _____ with the criteria 기준을 충족하는

정답 **A** 01 ⓐ 2 ⓑ 3 ⓐ 4 ⓐ 5 ⓑ 6 ⓑ 7 ⓐ 8 ⓑ 9 ⓑ 10 ⓐ **B** 01 ⓒ 2 ⓕ 3 ⓗ 4 ⓔ 5 ⓖ 6 ⓑ 7 ⓙ 8 ⓘ 9 ⓐ 10 ⓓ

풀면서 익히는 **Mini Test** ▶ 다음 한글 뜻에 맞는 영어 표현을 고르시오.

기출 어휘

01 The board of directors unanimously voted to (ⓐ nationalize ⓑ liquidate ⓒ refute) the insolvent company.
이사회는 채무를 갚을 수 없는 회사를 매각한다는 데 만장일치로 투표했다.

02 The evidence seems to (ⓐ buttress ⓑ flee ⓒ squander) the argument that the actress was murdered.
그 여배우가 살해되었다는 주장을 증거가 뒷받침하는 것 같다.

03 The senator (ⓐ abrogated ⓑ abolished ⓒ eschewed) politics in favor of practicing law.
그 상원의원은 정치를 포기하고 변호사의 삶을 선택했다.

04 The time has come for the two Koreas to (ⓐ forge ⓑ elongate ⓒ ratify) a better relationship with each other.
남한과 북한이 서로 더 개선된 관계를 구축해야 할 시점이 왔다.

05 The church voted to allow women to be (ⓐ elected ⓑ ordained ⓒ swiveled) as priests.
그 교회는 여성이 목사로 임명될 수 있도록 투표했다.

06 Korean parents usually (ⓐ afflict ⓑ extricate ⓒ scrimp) and save money to provide a better education for their children.
일반적으로 한국 부모들은 매우 절약을 하고 돈을 모아 자녀에게 더 좋은 교육을 제공하려 한다.

07 The husband (ⓐ beseeched ⓑ castigated ⓒ reprimanded) his wife to take up aerobics without success.
남편은 아내에게 에어로빅을 시작하라고 간청했으나 소용없었다.

08 The heated debate on climate change finally descended into a (ⓐ repertoire ⓑ burlesque ⓒ schism).
기후 변화에 관한 열띤 토론은 결국 한 편의 촌극으로 끝났다.

09 The (ⓐ pertinacity ⓑ predisposition ⓒ ramification) of the athlete allowed her to win a gold medal at the Olympics.
운동선수의 끈기가 올림픽에서 금메달을 딸 수 있게 해주었다.

10 The planning team was dispatched to China, but none of the employees could speak the (ⓐ buoyancy ⓑ lingo ⓒ meteor).
기획팀은 중국에 파견되었지만 직원들 중 아무도 해당 언어를 말하지 못했다.

11 The poem was criticized for being laden with sexual (ⓐ euphemisms ⓑ innuendos ⓒ jargons).
그 시는 성적으로 빗대어 하는 말로 가득 차 있어 비판을 받았다.

12 Judging from the incongruity of its logic, it is apparent that the thesis has been written in (ⓐ an adherent ⓑ a coherent ⓒ a haphazard) way.
논리의 불일치성으로 봤을 때 이 논문은 무계획적으로 쓰여진 것이 확실하다.

어휘 Check! **01 liquidate** 매각하다, 청산하다 **02 buttress** 뒷받침하다, 지지하다 **03 eschew** 포기하다, 회피하다 **04 forge** (관계를) 구축하다; 위조하다 **05 ordain** 성직에 임명하다 **06 scrimp** 매우 절약하다 **07 beseech** 간청하다 **08 burlesque** 촌극, 희화 **09 pertinacity** 끈기 **10 lingo** 언어, 외국어 **11 innuendo** 빗대어 하는 말 **12 haphazard** 아무렇게나, 규칙 없이, 무계획적으로

정답 01 ⓑ 02 ⓐ 03 ⓒ 04 ⓐ 05 ⓑ 06 ⓒ 07 ⓐ 08 ⓑ 09 ⓐ 10 ⓑ 11 ⓑ 12 ⓒ

13 The secluded factory produces (ⓐ irrevocable ⓑ sparse ⓒ spurious) designer clothes.
외딴 곳에 있는 그 공장은 가짜 명품 옷을 만들어 낸다.

14 Although the professor is notorious for a highly (ⓐ idiosyncratic ⓑ ductile ⓒ bilateral) personality, his lectures are widely popular among students.
그 교수는 매우 특이한 성격으로 악명이 높지만 그의 강의는 학생들 사이에서 매우 인기가 있다.

15 After being elected governor, he became (ⓐ intricate ⓑ obsolete ⓒ teetotal).
주지사로 당선된 후 그는 술을 완전히 입에 대지 않게 되었다.

16 A black cat is (ⓐ an ominous ⓑ a poignant ⓒ a sanguine) animal in the West.
검은 고양이는 서양에서 불길한 동물이다.

17 Fame in the entertainment business is (ⓐ slipshod ⓑ ephemeral ⓒ peripheral). One day you're the talk of the town, and the next day you're forgotten.
연예계에서 명성이란 일시적인 것이다. 어떤 날은 당신이 장안의 화제겠지만 다음날이면 당신은 잊혀진다.

18 Greed is one of the (ⓐ elliptical ⓑ intractable ⓒ spatial) problems afflicting the financial community.
탐욕은 금융계를 괴롭히고 있는 해결하기 힘든 문제 중 하나이다.

19 Male superiority is deeply (ⓐ assimilated ⓑ biased ⓒ entrenched) in some Asian cultures.
남성 우월주의가 일부 아시아 문화에 뿌리 깊이 자리잡고 있다.

20 (ⓐ Amidst ⓑ Barring ⓒ Against) an unexpected traffic snarl, the bus carrying the national soccer squad will arrive ahead of schedule.
예상치 못한 교통 정체만 없다면 국가대표 축구팀을 태우고 있는 버스가 예정보다 빨리 도착할 것이다.

21 The bishop wasn't cowed into (ⓐ forsaking ⓑ grooming ⓒ insulating) his beliefs although the Secret Service did threaten him with a gun.
재무성 비밀 검찰국이 총으로 주교를 위협했음에도 불구하고 주교는 그의 신념을 버릴 정도로 겁을 먹지 않았다.

22 Some people in Scotland argue that Scotland should (ⓐ cement ⓑ lessen ⓒ secede) from the United Kingdom.
스코틀랜드의 몇몇 사람들은 스코틀랜드가 영국으로부터 분리되어야 한다고 주장한다.

23 The minister of defense was asked to (ⓐ abrogate ⓑ jitter ⓒ overhaul) the security agreement with Japan.
국방장관은 일본과의 안보 조약을 폐지해 달라고 요청받았다.

어휘 Check!

13 **spurious** 가짜의, 허위의 14 **idiosyncratic** 특이한 15 **teetotal** 술을 입에 대지 않는, 금주의 16 **ominous** 불길한 17 **ephemeral** 수명이 짧은, 덧없는 18 **intractable** (문제가) 해결하기 힘든; (사람이) 다루기 힘든 19 **entrenched** 자리 잡고 있는, 구축된 20 **barring** ~이 없다면, ~이 아니라면 21 **forsake** 저버리다, 버리다 22 **secede** 탈퇴하다, 분리하다 23 **abrogate** 폐지하다

정답 13 ⓒ 14 ⓐ 15 ⓒ 16 ⓐ 17 ⓑ 18 ⓑ 19 ⓒ 20 ⓑ 21 ⓐ 22 ⓒ 23 ⓐ

24 The governor was (ⓐ swayed ⓑ piqued ⓒ waned) by the government's decision not to provide additional funding for his state's education program.
주지사는 자기 주의 교육 프로그램에 재정 지원을 하지 않겠다는 정부의 결정에 분노를 표했다.

25 The police (ⓐ coerced ⓑ featured ⓒ groused) the witness into testifying during the murder trial.
경찰은 목격자에게 살인 재판에서 증언하라고 강요했다.

26 The old veteran (ⓐ harnessed ⓑ harped ⓒ hassled) on about his memories of the Korean War.
나이 든 참전 용사가 한국전쟁에서의 기억에 대해 되풀이해서 이야기했다.

27 The two warring nations didn't (ⓐ differ ⓑ resurrect ⓒ reconcile) their differences, which resulted in a series of wars.
사이가 좋지 않은 그 두 국가는 차이점을 조정하지 못했고, 이것으로 인해 연이은 전쟁이 발생했다.

28 Though the actor had hoped to (ⓐ sequester ⓑ slash ⓒ shirk) himself in the movie business, he could never get away from his other activities.
그 배우는 영화 업계에서 은퇴하길 원했지만 다른 활동에서 벗어날 수가 없었다.

29 (ⓐ Cronyism ⓑ Hypocrisy ⓒ Niche) is rampant in the political and religious communities.
위선이 정계와 종교계에 만연해 있다.

30 The vice president continued to deny being involved in the (ⓐ malfunction ⓑ malfeasance ⓒ malnutrition).
부통령은 부정행위에 연루되었음을 계속해서 부인했다.

31 Terrorists dressed in (ⓐ calamity ⓑ camouflage ⓒ cataclysm) stormed the embassy.
위장복을 입은 테러리스트들이 대사관에 쳐들어갔다.

32 The dictator's political (ⓐ dogma ⓑ downtime ⓒ duress) ruined many innocent people's lives.
독재자의 정치적 독단이 많은 무고한 사람들의 삶을 망쳤다.

33 The criminal asked for (ⓐ anarchy ⓑ clemency ⓒ inertia) though he did not receive it.
그 범인은 선처를 요구했으나 선처를 받지 못했다.

34 The (ⓐ guts ⓑ karma ⓒ niche) market is crucial for the survival of small-sized and mid-sized companies.
틈새시장은 소기업과 중소기업의 생존에 매우 중요하다.

35 Although the computer appears to be state of the art, it does not bear (ⓐ myth ⓑ scrutiny ⓒ scuttle).
그 컴퓨터는 최첨단처럼 보이지만 면밀한 검사에는 견디지 못할 것이다.

24 **pique** 화나게 하다; (호기심, 흥미를) 돋우다　25 **coerce** 강요하다, 강제로 시키다　26 **harp** 되풀이해서 이야기하다 [on]　27 **reconcile** (분쟁을) 조정하다; 화해시키다　28 **sequester** 격리하다, 은퇴시키다　29 **hypocrisy** 위선　30 **malfeasance** (공직자의) 부정행위　31 **camouflage** 위장　32 **dogma** 독단, 독단적 신조　33 **clemency** 선처, 관용　34 **niche** (시장의) 틈새; 적소, 꼭 맞는 일　35 **scrutiny** 면밀한 검사, 철저한 검토

정답 24 ⓑ　25 ⓐ　26 ⓑ　27 ⓒ　28 ⓐ　29 ⓑ　30 ⓑ　31 ⓑ　32 ⓐ　33 ⓑ　34 ⓒ　35 ⓑ

36 The old man has a (ⓐ penchant ⓑ proclivity ⓒ probation) for complaining about rising oil prices.
그 노인은 치솟는 유가에 대해서 불평하는 성향이 있다.

37 It is (ⓐ ill-fated ⓑ assiduous ⓒ remiss) of you not to call them back.
그들에게 다시 전화를 주지 않은 것은 태만한 행위이다.

38 The (ⓐ cardinal ⓑ imminent ⓒ reticent) rules of the World Trade Organization are specified in the charter.
세계 무역 기구의 주요한 규정들이 이 헌장에 명시되어 있다.

39 The wife felt ashamed of her husband's (ⓐ punitive ⓑ pusillanimous ⓒ putative) conduct during the dispute.
아내는 언쟁이 벌어지는 가운데 남편의 소심한 행동에 창피함을 느꼈다.

40 Globalization is a (ⓐ pungent ⓑ latent ⓒ perennial) issue of concern among both developed and developing countries.
세계화는 선진국과 개발도상국 모두에게 있어 여러 해 계속되는 쟁점 사항이다.

어휘 Check! 36 **proclivity** 성향, 기질 37 **remiss** 태만한 38 **cardinal** 주요한, 중요한 39 **pusillanimous** 겁이 많은, 소심한 40 **perennial** 여러 해 계속 이어지는; (식물이) 다년생의

정답 36 ⓑ 37 ⓒ 38 ⓐ 39 ⓑ 40 ⓒ

250

Part II Choose the option that best completes each sentence.

1 The U.S. Attorney General gave _____ warnings against illegal insider trading.
   (a) refractory
   (b) ominous
   (c) convulsive
   (d) ebullient

2 The teacher _____ traditional teaching methods on the grounds that they discourage learning.
   (a) eschews
   (b) flatters
   (c) plagiarizes
   (d) admonishes

3 In 1830, the kingdom of Belgium _____ from the Netherlands to become a separate nation.
   (a) seceded
   (b) ousted
   (c) beleaguered
   (d) perpetuated

4 After years of bitter discord, the two organizations were able to _____ their differences of political opinion.
   (a) abduct
   (b) epitomize
   (c) reconcile
   (d) vindicate

5 The U.S. Army issued a new _____ design that is able to blend into virtually any combat environment.
   (a) aberration
   (b) camouflage
   (c) disguise
   (d) specimen

6 As a teenager, I became aware of my parents' _____ when they told me to go to bed early but stayed up late themselves.
   (a) pretentiousness
   (b) deception
   (c) forthrightness
   (d) hypocrisy

7 It was the music of Dizzy Gillespie that _____ my interest in bebop and modern jazz.
   (a) sustained
   (b) piqued
   (c) fermented
   (d) placated

8 Following attempts at teaching and writing, Tony finally found his _____ working as a chef.
   (a) niche
   (b) acme
   (c) hiatus
   (d) coalition

9 Many parents today find their children _____ as they deliberately do the opposite of what they are told to do.
   (a) retractable
   (b) intractable
   (c) disagreeable
   (d) apprehensible

10 Parents _____ the school board not to close the local elementary school.
   (a) divulged
   (b) assuaged
   (c) beseeched
   (d) extenuated

11 Only the Vatican may _____ new bishops into the Catholic Church.

(a) consecrate
(b) admonish
(c) encounter
(d) ordain

12 I contend that taxes should not be levied in a _____ way but should be done systemically instead.

(a) foreboding
(b) meticulous
(c) haphazard
(d) deliberate

13 The _____ rule among medical practitioners is not to cause harm.

(a) cardinal
(b) pious
(c) staunch
(d) antithetical

14 The company was forced to _____ most of its assets when it became unable to repay its debts.

(a) expedite
(b) vie
(c) liquidate
(d) taper

15 Her _____ tendency to punctuate every sentence with "like" made her appear unintelligent to her peers.

(a) blatant
(b) repellent
(c) ornate
(d) idiosyncratic

16 Detractors claim the president's enthusiasm for education is _____ as he had vetoed several educational reforms throughout the year.

(a) disaffected
(b) spurious
(c) veracious
(d) premeditated

17 The British government _____ the unequal treaties it created with China at the conclusion of the Opium Wars.

(a) abrogated
(b) abridged
(c) admonished
(d) administered

18 Due to public outcry, the governor was impeached for _____ she committed during her time in office.

(a) multifariousness
(b) impropriety
(c) malfeasance
(d) delinquency

19 Though the film was marketed as being family friendly, it contained numerous racial _____, making it inappropriate for children.

(a) exculpations
(b) innuendos
(c) aberrations
(d) referendums

20 The _____ teacher attempted to appease her students by playing games rather than following the mandated curriculum.

(a) rabid
(b) pusillanimous
(c) gregarious
(d) obsequious

A 다음 영어 표현과 일치하는 한글 뜻을 고르시오.

01 **scrimp** on food　　　　음식을 (ⓐ 매우 낭비하다 ⓑ 매우 절약하다)

02 have the **pertinacity**　　(ⓐ 끈기 ⓑ 열의)를 갖다

03 grant **clemency**　　　　(ⓐ 관용 ⓑ 사면)을 베풀다

04 strictly **teetotal**　　　엄격하게 (ⓐ 금주하는 ⓑ 금연하는)

05 learn the **lingo**　　　　(ⓐ 악기 ⓑ 외국어)를 배우다

06 **forsake** his family　　　그의 가족을 (ⓐ 부양하다 ⓑ 저버리다)

07 **remiss** in his duty　　　그의 임무에 (ⓐ 열성적인 ⓑ 태만한)

08 **perennial** flower　　　(ⓐ 다년생의 ⓑ 화려한) 꽃

09 strict **scrutiny**　　　　엄격한 (ⓐ 정밀 조사 ⓑ 처벌)

10 **coerce** obedience　　　복종을 (ⓐ 거부하다 ⓑ 강요하다)

B 한글 뜻에 맞는 영어 표현을 완성하시오.

| ⓐ barring | ⓑ forge | ⓒ sequester | ⓓ harp | ⓔ buttress |
| ⓕ burlesque | ⓖ dogma | ⓗ entrenched | ⓘ ephemeral | ⓙ proclivity |

01 ＿＿＿＿＿＿ a relationship　관계를 구축하다

02 ＿＿＿＿＿＿ the theory　이론을 뒷받침하다

03 ＿＿＿＿＿＿ in our lives　우리 삶에 자리 잡은

04 ＿＿＿＿＿＿ my children　내 아이들을 제외하고는

05 a ＿＿＿＿＿＿ to wander　방랑하는 성향

06 ＿＿＿＿＿＿ on the story　이야기를 계속해서 반복하다

07 ＿＿＿＿＿＿ popularity　잠시뿐인 인기

08 political ＿＿＿＿＿＿　정치적인 독단

09 ＿＿＿＿＿＿ oneself from the world　세상으로부터 은둔하다

10 see a ＿＿＿＿＿＿　촌극을 보다

Section

2

500점대로 이끌어 주는

고마운 어휘

Part Ⅰ, Ⅱ

풀면서 익히는 Mini Test ▶ 다음 한글 뜻에 맞는 영어 표현을 고르시오.

필수 어휘

동사+명사

01 I am happy to (ⓐ bear ⓑ entertain ⓒ follow) your questions.
저는 여러분의 질문에 답해 드릴 수 있어서 기쁘게 생각합니다.

02 The child (ⓐ made ⓑ pushed ⓒ pulled) the trigger by accident and didn't know what the problem was.
아이는 실수로 방아쇠를 당겼고 무엇이 문제였는지 몰랐다.

03 As the time to (ⓐ address ⓑ bid ⓒ kick) farewell approached, we hugged each other.
작별 인사를 할 시간이 다가오자 우리는 서로 포옹했다.

04 The jury exited the deliberation room to (ⓐ deliver ⓑ hand ⓒ prepare) their verdict.
배심원단이 심의실에서 퇴장하며 평결을 내렸다.

05 The police couldn't (ⓐ assimilate ⓑ ease ⓒ identify) the cause of the fire which destroyed the whole building.
경찰은 건물 전체를 파괴한 화재의 원인을 파악할 수 없었다.

06 All citizens should (ⓐ enroll ⓑ exercise ⓒ push) their right to vote on election day.
모든 시민들은 선거일에 투표권을 행사해야 한다.

07 The country is (ⓐ making ⓑ striking ⓒ waging) a full-fledged war on terrorism.
그 나라는 테러와의 전면전을 펼치고 있다.

08 The time has come for the two Koreas to (ⓐ cast ⓑ forge ⓒ rush) cultural, economic, and sports ties.
남북한이 문화, 경제, 그리고 스포츠 관계를 구축해야 할 시간이 왔다.

09 The Department of Health reported that 50 people (ⓐ contracted ⓑ forged ⓒ imposed) the disease after eating contaminated meat.
보건부는 50명의 사람들이 오염된 고기를 먹고 그 병에 걸렸다고 보고했다.

10 During a recent military clash, the president (ⓐ abandoned ⓑ issued ⓒ launched) a statement denouncing what he called a provocation.
최근에 있었던 군사 충돌에서 대통령은 이번 사건을 도발이라고 비난하는 성명서를 발표했다.

11 The policy will (ⓐ bear ⓑ keep ⓒ make) fruit in the near future as long as they are financially supported on a regular basis.
규칙적으로 재정을 지원받는다면 그 정책은 가까운 미래에 성과를 거둘 수 있을 것이다.

어휘 Check! 01 **entertain questions** 질문에 응하다 02 **pull the trigger** 방아쇠를 당기다 03 **bid farewell** 작별인사를 하다 04 **deliver a verdict** 평결을 내리다 05 **identify the cause** 원인을 파악하다 06 **exercise the right** 권리를 행사하다 07 **wage a war** 전쟁을 일으키다 08 **forge ties** 관계를 맺다 09 **contract the disease** 병에 걸리다 10 **issue a statement** 성명서를 발표하다 11 **bear fruit** 열매를 맺다; 성과를 거두다

정답 01 ⓑ 02 ⓒ 03 ⓑ 04 ⓐ 05 ⓒ 06 ⓑ 07 ⓒ 08 ⓑ 09 ⓐ 10 ⓑ 11 ⓐ

12 The federal government announced that a disease called anthrax could (ⓐ pause ⓑ pose ⓒ post) a major threat to the public.
탄저병이라 불리는 질병은 일반인들에게 큰 위협을 가할 수 있다고 연방 정부는 발표했다.

13 When choosing a job, you should (ⓐ go ⓑ draw ⓒ follow) your heart and intuition.
직업을 선택할 때는 너의 마음과 직관을 따라야 한다.

14 The rising pop star refused to (ⓐ keep ⓑ obey ⓒ conclude) his contract with the major record company.
한창 뜨고 있는 팝스타가 대형 음반 업체와 계약을 체결하는 것을 거부했다.

15 The government formed a task force team to (ⓐ address ⓑ alter ⓒ emaciate) the problems rampant in its own organization.
정부는 조직 내의 만연한 문제를 해결하기 위해 전담반을 구성했다.

부사 +형용사

16 The leaders from both the ruling and opposition parties were (ⓐ blissfully ⓑ openly ⓒ preposterously) hostile to each other from the beginning.
여당과 야당의 대표들은 처음부터 서로에게 노골적으로 적대적이었다.

17 New York is one of the most (ⓐ densely ⓑ geopolitically ⓒ sparsely) populated cites in the world.
뉴욕은 세계에서 가장 인구 밀도가 높은 도시 중 하나이다.

형용사+명사

18 The senator had several (ⓐ daisy ⓑ rosy ⓒ thorny) issues that needed to be taken care of immediately, such as euthanasia, the death penalty, tax hikes, and education reform.
그 상원의원은 안락사, 사형제도, 세금 인상, 교육제도와 같은 즉시 처리해야 할 까다로운 문제가 있었다.

19 Teacher, I have a (ⓐ quick ⓑ rapid ⓒ short) question before you wrap up the class.
선생님, 수업이 끝나기 전에 간단한 질문이 있습니다.

20 The research is largely based on (ⓐ anecdotal ⓑ conspicuous ⓒ singular) evidence and thus has yet to gain recognition from the scientific community.
그 연구는 대체로 일화적인 증거에 기반을 두고 있기 때문에 아직 과학계로부터 인정을 받지 못하고 있다.

21 I have a feeling that I can score higher than 590 on the TEPS, but that might just be (ⓐ wished ⓑ wishful ⓒ wishing) thinking.
텝스 시험에서 590점 이상 받을 수 있을 거라는 느낌은 있는데, 어쩌면 희망사항에 불과할지도 몰라.

22 Did she say she is available? That's a (ⓐ stern ⓑ upright ⓒ downright) lie. She is married.
그녀가 애인이 없다고 하든? 그건 새빨간 거짓말이야. 그녀는 결혼했단 말이야.

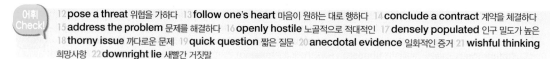

어휘 Check! 12 **pose a threat** 위협을 가하다 13 **follow one's heart** 마음이 원하는 대로 행하다 14 **conclude a contract** 계약을 체결하다 15 **address the problem** 문제를 해결하다 16 **openly hostile** 노골적으로 적대적인 17 **densely populated** 인구 밀도가 높은 18 **thorny issue** 까다로운 문제 19 **quick question** 짧은 질문 20 **anecdotal evidence** 일화적인 증거 21 **wishful thinking** 희망사항 22 **downright lie** 새빨간 거짓말

정답 12 ⓑ 13 ⓒ 14 ⓒ 15 ⓐ 16 ⓑ 17 ⓐ 18 ⓒ 19 ⓐ 20 ⓐ 21 ⓑ 22 ⓒ

23 You are in (ⓐ big ⓑ great ⓒ large) trouble.
너 정말 큰일 났다.

24 I had a (ⓐ gold ⓑ good ⓒ nice) reason to side with James and not you.
내가 네 편을 들지 않고 제임스 편을 들었던 데는 합당한 이유가 있었어.

25 The presidential election result was (ⓐ an ephemeral ⓑ a foregone ⓒ a nefarious) conclusion.
대통령 선거 결과는 이미 기정 사실화되었다.

26 The new basketball coach was given a (ⓐ black ⓑ blank ⓒ red) check for reorganizing his team.
신임 농구 감독은 팀을 재정비하는 데 있어 전면 권한을 부여 받았다.

27 When jurors can't reach a verdict, it is called a (ⓐ disabled ⓑ humble ⓒ hung) jury.
배심원들이 평결을 내리지 못할 때, 그것을 배심원 불일치라 일컫는다.

명사+명사

28 No matter how much the government tries to crack down on real estate (ⓐ suspicion ⓑ speculation ⓒ transformation), it seems that it never dies down.
정부가 부동산 투기를 잡으려고 아무리 노력해도 좀처럼 사그라질 기미가 보이지 않는다.

29 The politician has been on hunger (ⓐ hit ⓑ punch ⓒ strike) for one day and already seems emaciated.
그 정치인은 하루 동안 단식 투쟁을 했는데 벌써 매우 수척해 보인다.

30 The (ⓐ summit ⓑ best ⓒ top) talks are slated to be held in New York, where the police will tighten security.
정상 회담이 뉴욕에서 열릴 예정이며 경찰은 그곳의 보안을 강화할 것이다.

31 My young son is prone to (ⓐ shaking ⓑ motion ⓒ movement) sickness.
내 어린 아들은 멀미를 자주 한다.

32 The book is believed to bridge the generation (ⓐ difference ⓑ disparity ⓒ gap), one of the tricky issues that is easily found in advanced nations.
그 책은 선진국에서 쉽게 찾아볼 수 있는 까다로운 문제 중 하나인 세대 격차를 줄여 줄 것이라 생각된다.

33 The senator couldn't attend the reception because of jet (ⓐ lag ⓑ party ⓒ sickness).
상원의원은 시차로 인한 피로 때문에 환영회에 참석할 수 없었다.

34 Do you happen to know the average life (ⓐ cycle ⓑ length ⓒ span) of a dog?
혹시 개의 평균 수명을 아니?

35 The presidential candidate had an (ⓐ oblivion ⓑ inferiority ⓒ infringement) complex about his level of education.
그 대선 후보는 자신의 교육 수준에 대해 열등감을 가지고 있었다.

어휘 Check! 23 **big trouble** 큰 문젯거리 24 **good reason** 합당한 이유 25 **foregone conclusion** 기정 사실 26 **blank check** 백지 수표; 자유 재량, 마음대로 할 수 있는 권리 27 **hung jury** 배심원들이 의견 일치를 보지 못함 28 **real estate speculation** 부동산 투기 29 **hunger strike** 단식 투쟁 30 **summit talks** 정상회담 31 **motion sickness** 멀미 32 **generation gap** 세대차이 33 **jet lag** 시차로 인한 피로 34 **life span** 수명 35 **inferiority complex** 열등감

정답 23 ⓐ 24 ⓑ 25 ⓑ 26 ⓑ 27 ⓒ 28 ⓑ 29 ⓒ 30 ⓐ 31 ⓑ 32 ⓒ 33 ⓐ 34 ⓒ 35 ⓑ

Check-up TEST

Part I Choose the option that best completes each dialogue.

1 A: What type of trees are these?
   B: They are apple trees. They _____
      fruit every spring.

   (a) bear
   (b) show
   (c) possess
   (d) invade

2 A: Hey, Rachel. I have a _____
      question. Does the vending machine
      accept bills?
   B: No, I'm pretty sure that it only takes
      coins.

   (a) brief
   (b) fast
   (c) quick
   (d) drab

3 A: My cat will be 20 years old this month.
   B: Wow, that's quite impressive. The
      typical life _____ of a cat is 12 to
      15 years.

   (a) gap
   (b) span
   (c) period
   (d) distance

4 A: Listen, dear. I don't feel comfortable
      with you keeping a gun in the house.
   B: What do you mean? I'm just _____
      my right to bear arms.

   (a) recalling
   (b) promoting
   (c) considering
   (d) exercising

5 A: Can you describe for the court what
      you witnessed that night?
   B: Yes. I saw the woman yell at the man
      before finally _____ the trigger.

   (a) moving
   (b) pulling
   (c) grabbing
   (d) pressing

6 A: I noticed you always take medicine
      whenever we go on a road trip.
   B: Yeah, it's to help prevent motion
      _____ .

   (a) illness
   (b) condition
   (c) sickness
   (d) disease

7 A: How can Ellen afford so many clothes?
      I don't think I've seen her wear the
      same outfit twice.
   B: Her husband is well off, so each month
      she gets a _____ check to do
      whatever she wants with.

   (a) blank
   (b) empty
   (c) lost
   (d) vacant

8 A: Why don't you join the social
      networking site? Everyone is using it.
   B: I'm sorry, but I feel such technology
      poses a _____ to personal privacy.

   (a) warning
   (b) ritual
   (c) threat
   (d) grudge

9 A: I read in the paper that U.S. and North
      Korea are to resume their talks.
   B: Hopefully, this time they will be able to
      _____ closer ties with each other.

   (a) bolster
   (b) forage
   (c) furnish
   (d) forge

10 A: Do you know what the outcome of the
      trial was?
   B: It was a mistrial because of a _____
      jury.

   (a) hung
   (b) deliberate
   (c) taut
   (d) brazen

Part II Choose the option that best completes each sentence.

11 You are going to be in _____ trouble when your father gets home.
(a) quick
(b) large
(c) big
(d) high

12 A crowd of thousands turned out to _____ farewell to the late actor.
(a) bid
(b) mourn
(c) pay
(d) respect

13 In rapidly developing nations, the generation _____ is wider than in developed countries.
(a) space
(b) gap
(c) distance
(d) break

14 The White House issued a _____ condemning the attacks as an act of terrorism.
(a) speech
(b) testimonial
(c) statement
(d) response

15 Manila, the capital of the Philippines, is the most _____ populated city in the world.
(a) tightly
(b) densely
(c) rigidly
(d) closely

16 In spite of convincing evidence against the defendant, the judge _____ a verdict of not guilty.
(a) dispatched
(b) forwarded
(c) delivered
(d) sent

17 Following his speech, the diplomat _____ questions from news reporters.
(a) entertained
(b) considered
(c) appreciated
(d) intimidated

18 I suffered a severe case of jet _____ after traveling from London to Shanghai.
(a) fatigue
(b) lag
(c) weariness
(d) leg

19 Scientists have _____ a cause of Alzheimer's disease in a protein superstructure called amyloid beta.
(a) categorized
(b) identified
(c) exacerbated
(d) recuperated

20 Psychologists have ascertained that those suffering from an inferiority _____ tend to lash out at others to enhance their self-esteem.
(a) condition
(b) complication
(c) cognition
(d) complex

Voca Review

A 다음 영어 표현과 일치하는 한글 뜻을 고르시오.

01 address the problem   (ⓐ 문제를 분석하다 ⓑ 문제를 해결하다)

02 contract the disease   (ⓐ 병에 걸리다 ⓑ 병을 치료하다)

03 wage a war   (ⓐ 전쟁을 끝내다 ⓑ 전쟁을 일으키다)

04 a thorny issue   (ⓐ 주목을 끄는 문제 ⓑ 까다로운 문제)

05 a downright lie   (ⓐ 새빨간 거짓말 ⓑ 속기 쉬운 거짓말)

06 forge ties   (ⓐ 관계를 맺다 ⓑ 관계를 유지하다)

07 real estate speculation   (ⓐ 부동산 투기 ⓑ 부동산 폭락)

08 motion sickness   (ⓐ 고소 공포증 ⓑ 멀미)

09 a foregone conclusion   (ⓐ 기정 사실 ⓑ 불확실한 결론)

10 an inferiority complex   (ⓐ 우월감 ⓑ 열등감)

B 한글 뜻에 맞는 영어 표현을 완성하시오.

ⓐ issue	ⓑ summit	ⓒ conclude	ⓓ bid	ⓔ hostile
ⓕ wishful	ⓖ blank	ⓗ heart	ⓘ hunger	ⓙ trigger

01 _____ a statement   성명서를 발표하다

02 _____ thinking   희망사항

03 pull the _____   방아쇠를 당기다

04 _____ strike   단식투쟁

05 _____ talks   정상회담

06 openly _____   노골적으로 적대적인

07 a _____ check   자유재량

08 follow my _____   내 마음이 원하는 것을 행하다

09 _____ farewell   작별인사를 하다

10 _____ a contract   계약을 하다

풀면서 익히는 Mini Test ▶ 다음 한글 뜻에 맞는 영어 표현을 고르시오.

필수 어휘

ambience / ambiguous / ambivalent

01 The public reaction to the ruling was largely (ⓐ ambience ⓑ ambiguous ⓒ ambivalent).
이번 판결에 대한 대중들의 반응은 대체로 이중적이었다.

02 Some of the terms of the contract are (ⓐ ambience ⓑ ambiguous ⓒ ambivalent) and open to interpretation. 일부 계약 조건은 애매하며 해석의 여지가 있다.

03 The (ⓐ ambassador ⓑ ambience ⓒ embassy) of the restaurant goes well with its French cuisine. 그 식당의 분위기는 프랑스 음식과 잘 어울린다.

defer / detach / deter

04 The labor union and management decided to (ⓐ defer ⓑ detach ⓒ deter) negotiations involving the pay hike. 노동조합과 경영진은 급여 인상에 관한 협상을 연기하기로 결정했다.

05 Some countries implemented the death penalty in a bid to (ⓐ defer ⓑ detach ⓒ deter) violent crimes. 일부 국가는 폭력적인 범죄를 저지하고자 사형제도를 실행했다.

06 The millitary commander proposed (ⓐ deferring ⓑ detaching ⓒ deterring) a squadron to seize the island. 군 사령관은 그 섬을 장악하기 위해 중대를 파견할 것을 제안했다.

observation / observance

07 The scholar claimed that the (ⓐ observance ⓑ observation) of laws is strictly required in more advanced societies. 보다 선진화된 사회일수록 법의 준수가 엄중히 요구된다고 그 학자는 주장했다.

08 The scientists made some interesting (ⓐ observations ⓑ observances) about rare forms of life on the remote island. 과학자들은 그 외딴 섬에서 희귀한 종류의 생명체에 관한 몇 가지 흥미로운 관찰을 했다.

install / instigate / instill

09 The Conservative Party was under criticism for (ⓐ installing ⓑ instigating ⓒ instilling) nationalism in school children. 보수당은 학생들에게 민족주의 사상을 주입한다고 비난을 받았다.

10 The dissident was sentenced to life in prison for (ⓐ installing ⓑ instigating ⓒ instilling) an uprising. 그 반체제 인사는 반란을 선동했다는 이유로 종신형에 처해졌다.

11 I want you to (ⓐ install ⓑ instill ⓒ instigate) the air conditioner on the left wall.
에어컨을 왼쪽 벽면에 설치해주세요.

어휘 Check! 01 **ambivalent** 이중적인 감정을 가지는, 애증의 02 **ambiguous** 애매모호한 03 **ambience** 분위기 04 **defer** 연기하다 05 **deter** 저지하다, 막다 06 **detach** 파견하다 07 **observance** (법률이나 규칙의) 준수; (기념일의) 축하 08 **observation** 관찰 09 **instill** (사상을) 주입하다, 서서히 가르치다 10 **instigate** 선동하다 11 **install** 설치하다

정답 01 ⓒ 02 ⓑ 03 ⓑ 04 ⓐ 05 ⓒ 06 ⓑ 07 ⓐ 08 ⓐ 09 ⓒ 10 ⓑ 11 ⓐ

urban / urbane

12 Desperate measures are needed to curb (ⓐ urban ⓑ urbane) sprawl.
도시의 무질서한 확장을 억제하기 위해서 절박한 조치가 필요하다.

13 George Clooney is an (ⓐ urban ⓑ urbane) and charming actor loved worldwide.
조지 클루니는 전 세계적으로 사랑받는 세련되고 매력적인 배우이다.

rebuke / rebut / revoke

14 Now, are you ready to (ⓐ rebuke ⓑ rebut ⓒ revoke) your opponent's claim?
자, 이제 상대편의 주장을 반박하실 준비가 되었습니까?

15 The state can permanently (ⓐ rebuke ⓑ rebut ⓒ revoke) your driver's license for driving under the influence.
음주운전을 하면 주는 당신의 운전면허를 영원히 취소시킬 수 있다.

16 The manufacturing company was (ⓐ rebuked ⓑ rebutted ⓒ revoked) for not complying with safety regulations.
그 제조업체는 안전 규정을 지키지 않아서 비난을 받았다.

hangout / hangover / hanger-on / hang-up

17 I have a real (ⓐ hangout ⓑ hangover ⓒ hang-up) about my receding hairline.
나는 머리카락이 빠지는 것에 대한 큰 고민거리를 가지고 있다.

18 I drank too much last night. I need something to take care of my (ⓐ hangout ⓑ hangover ⓒ hanger-on).
어젯밤에 술을 너무 많이 마셨어. 숙취를 해소할 뭔가가 필요해.

19 The members of the club gather at their (ⓐ hangout ⓑ hangover ⓒ hang-up) on a monthly basis.
그 클럽의 회원들은 한 달 주기로 자신들의 거처에서 모임을 가진다.

20 The rich man is always surrounded by real friends as well as (ⓐ hangovers ⓑ hangers-on ⓒ hang-up).
그 부자는 콩고물이라도 떨어질까 기대하는 사람들뿐만 아니라 진정한 친구도 항상 있다.

어휘 Check! 12 urban 도시의 13 urbane 도시적인, 세련된 14 rebut 반박하다 15 revoke 취소시키다; 취소 16 rebuke 꾸짖다, 비난하다; 비난, 징계 17 hang-up 고민, 콤플렉스; 문제, 장애 18 hangover 숙취 19 hangout 거처, 자주 들르는 장소 20 hanger-on 무엇인가를 바라고 주위를 어슬렁거리는 사람

정답 12 ⓐ 13 ⓑ 14 ⓑ 15 ⓒ 16 ⓐ 17 ⓒ 18 ⓑ 19 ⓐ 20 ⓑ

outburst / outright / outward / outworn

21 You take that back! That's an (ⓐ outburst ⓑ outright ⓒ outward) lie!
그 말 철회해! 그것은 명백한 거짓말이야!

22 The defectors from North Korea showed signs of (ⓐ outburst ⓑ outright ⓒ outward) nonchalance.
탈북자들이 겉으로는 태연한 모습을 보였다.

23 The (ⓐ outburst ⓑ outright ⓒ outworn) ideas of the executives to overcome sluggish sales were rejected by the CEO.
부진한 매출을 극복하기 위한 임원들의 낡아빠진 생각은 최고 경영자에 의해 거부당했다.

24 I was alarmed by my girlfriend's violent (ⓐ outburst ⓑ outright ⓒ outworn).
나는 새로 사귄 여자 친구가 격한 감정을 터뜨리는 것을 보고 매우 놀랐다.

indolent / insolent / insolvent

25 After being (ⓐ indolent ⓑ insolent ⓒ insolvent) to his immediate supervisor, he is now without a job.
그는 직속상관에게 무례하게 굴고 난 뒤 현재 직장을 잃었다.

26 Many Korean companies were declared (ⓐ indolent ⓑ insolent ⓒ insolvent) during the financial crisis in 1998.
1998년 금융 위기 당시 많은 한국 기업들은 파산 선고를 할 수밖에 없었다.

27 Zack was punished for being (ⓐ indolent ⓑ insolent ⓒ insolvent) at school.
잭은 게을러서 학교에서 벌을 받았다.

anomie / anonymous / unanimous

28 Civic groups were (ⓐ anomie ⓑ anonymous ⓒ unanimous) in their opposition to the proposal.
시민 단체들은 그 제안에 대해 만장일치로 반대의 목소리를 냈다.

29 A huge sum of money was donated to an orphanage by an (ⓐ anomie ⓑ anonymous ⓒ unanimous) donor.
상당한 액수의 돈이 익명의 기부자에 의해 한 고아원에 기부되었다.

30 The financial crisis in 1998 caused a wave of (ⓐ anomie ⓑ anonymous ⓒ unanimous) in many parts of Asia.
1998년에 있었던 금융 위기는 많은 아시아 국가에 사회적 무질서 현상의 급증을 일으켰다.

 어휘 Check!
21 **outright** 명백한, 완전한 22 **outward** 외관의 23 **outworn** 낡은, 진부한 24 **outburst** 감정의 터짐 25 **insolent** 무례한 26 **insolvent** 파산한, 채무를 이행할 수 없는 27 **indolent** 게으른, 나태한 28 **unanimous** 만장일치의 29 **anonymous** 익명의 30 **anomie** 사회적 무질서, 아노미 현상

정답 21 ⓑ 22 ⓒ 23 ⓒ 24 ⓐ 25 ⓑ 26 ⓒ 27 ⓐ 28 ⓒ 29 ⓑ 30 ⓐ

Check-up TEST

Part I Choose the option that best completes each dialogue.

1 A: You don't look so good, Daniel. Have you caught the flu?
   B: No, I just had too much to drink last night, so now I have a terrible _____.

   (a) hangout   (b) hangover
   (c) hanger-on   (d) hang-up

2 A: Have you made a decision about the company's job offer?
   B: Not yet. I'm still _____ as to whether or not I should take the job.

   (a) ambulant   (b) ambience
   (c) ambiguous   (d) ambivalent

3 A: The city really needs to do something to curb the carjacking problem.
   B: Yes, and that is why it is going to _____ several hundred CCTV cameras throughout the city.

   (a) instill
   (b) install
   (c) instigate
   (d) instruct

4 A: What was the Supreme Court's ruling on the issue of corporate political spending?
   B: The court decided to outlaw it in a rare _____ decision.

   (a) unannounced
   (b) anonymous
   (c) unanimous
   (d) anomie

5 A: How are you going to make payments on your student loan now that you've lost your job?
   B: Fortunately, I am able to _____ the payments until my financial situation improves.

   (a) defer
   (b) deter
   (c) detach
   (d) detract

6 A: The state has made smoking in all public places illegal. I don't think it's such a good idea.
   B: Me neither. Instead of an _____ ban, they should make it illegal on a case-by-case basis.

   (a) outward   (b) outworn
   (c) outright   (d) outburst

7 A: Today, the city council is going to decide if they are going to create a green belt around the city.
   B: Well, I hope they vote in favor of it. Something needs to be done to stop the _____ sprawl from continuing.

   (a) urban   (b) urgent
   (c) urbane   (d) urging

8 A: My employer has gone out of business and hasn't paid my final paycheck. What can I do?
   B: I'm sorry to say that if your employer has become _____, then you have few options of recourse.

   (a) indolent   (b) inadvertent
   (c) insolent   (d) insolvent

9 A: It's ridiculous how much money the government has wasted building that new space telescope.
   B: Well, I believe that the _____ made with the telescope can give us a better understanding of our own planet.

   (a) observations   (b) observances
   (c) obsessions   (d) obscenities

10 A: I'm glad that you got rid of that harsh fluorescent lighting in favor of incandescent lighting.
   B: Thank you. I think changing the lights improved the overall _____ of the room.

   (a) ambivalence
   (b) ambiguous
   (c) ambience
   (d) ambition

Part II Choose the option that best completes each sentence.

11 All _____ appearances suggested that Ken and Heather were happy in their marriage.
(a) outworn
(b) outburst
(c) outright
(d) outward

12 The soldiers faced a strong _____ for intentionally disobeying orders.
(a) rebut
(b) rebuke
(c) revoke
(d) revolt

13 Everything about the project is solid save one _____: a severe lack of funding.
(a) hang-up
(b) hanger-on
(c) hangout
(d) hangover

14 Please refrain from _____ behavior as it will not be tolerated.
(a) indocile
(b) insolvent
(c) indolent
(d) insolent

15 Our store will be closed on December 25 in _____ of the Christmas holiday.
(a) obsession
(b) observance
(c) observation
(d) obscenity

16 Martin's suave and _____ character delighted his dinner guests immensely.
(a) urbane
(b) urban
(c) urgent
(d) urging

17 Many educators today complain that parents fail to _____ in their children a love for education.
(a) instate
(b) instill
(c) instigate
(d) install

18 The Department of Health _____ the restaurant's food license for violating several health codes.
(a) rebuked
(b) rebutted
(c) revoked
(d) revolted

19 The barbed wire fence _____ vandals from entering the factory grounds, but it does not stop them altogether.
(a) detaches
(b) defers
(c) deters
(d) detracts

20 By making the film's ending _____, I have allowed individuals to interpret it for themselves.
(a) ambitious
(b) ambience
(c) ambivalent
(d) ambiguous

Voca Review

A 다음 영어 표현과 일치하는 한글 뜻을 고르시오.

01 **outburst** of anger 분노의 (ⓐ 폭발 ⓑ 가라앉음)

02 an **outworn** custom (ⓐ 전통적인 ⓑ 낡은) 관습

03 an **indolent** worker (ⓐ 나태한 ⓑ 헌신적인) 직원

04 an **anonymous** informer (ⓐ 여러 명의 ⓑ 익명의) 제보자

05 comfortable **ambience** 편안한 (ⓐ 분위기 ⓑ 도구)

06 gangsters **hangout** 갱 단원들의 (ⓐ 범죄 ⓑ 은신처)

07 **instigate** rebellion 혁명을 (ⓐ 선동하다 ⓑ 박해하다)

08 **rebut** his argument 그의 주장을 (ⓐ 수용하다 ⓑ 반박하다)

09 **detach** the soldiers 군인을 (ⓐ 파병하다 ⓑ 모집하다)

10 **install** the program 프로그램을 (ⓐ 개발하다 ⓑ 설치하다)

B 한글 뜻에 맞는 영어 표현을 완성하시오.

| ⓐ defer | ⓑ outright | ⓒ deter | ⓓ unanimous | ⓔ rebuke |
| ⓕ observance | ⓖ urban | ⓗ anomie | ⓘ revoke | ⓙ outward |

01 _____ him from smoking 그가 담배 피우는 것을 저지하다

02 _____ appearance 외관적인 생김새

03 institutional _____ 제도적인 사회적 무질서

04 _____ the students 학생들을 꾸짖다

05 _____ development 도시 개발

06 _____ opposition 노골적인 반대

07 _____ her driver's license 그녀의 운전면허증을 취소하다

08 _____ of the rules 규칙의 준수

09 a _____ vote 만장일치의 투표

10 _____ the payments 상환을 연기하다

풀면서 익히는 Mini Test ▶ 다음 한글 뜻에 맞는 영어 표현을 고르시오.
필수어휘

select / appoint / elect

01 The president (ⓐ appointed ⓑ elected ⓒ selected) one of his friends as Secretary of State.
대통령은 자기 친구 중 한 명을 국무 장관으로 임명했다.

02 He was the first physically-challenged African American to be (ⓐ appointed ⓑ elected ⓒ selected) in the House of Representatives.
그는 하원에 최초로 당선된, 장애를 가진 아프리카계 미국인이다.

03 Participants are required to (ⓐ appoint ⓑ elect ⓒ select) the banner that is considered most fitted for their team.
참가자들은 자기 팀과 가장 어울리는 배너를 선택해야 한다.

wave / ripple / billow

04 The boat carrying 7 refugees sailed through the (ⓐ billows ⓑ ripples ⓒ waves) safely.
7명의 망명자를 태우고 있는 보트는 큰 파도를 뚫고 안전하게 항해했다.

05 The subprime mortgage crisis a decade ago had a (ⓐ billow ⓑ ripple ⓒ wave) effect on the global economy.
10년 전의 서브프라임 모기지 위기는 전 세계 경제에 파급효과를 미쳤다.

06 (ⓐ Billows ⓑ Ripples ⓒ Waves) of illegal Mexican immigrants are flooding the southern parts of the U.S.
파도처럼 밀려오는 멕시코 불법 이민자들이 미국 남부 지역에 몰려들고 있다.

collect / assemble / compile

07 It takes some time for a beginner to (ⓐ assemble ⓑ compile ⓒ collect) these parts correctly.
초보자가 이 부품을 정확하게 조립하는 데에는 시간이 제법 걸린다.

08 The detective (ⓐ assembled ⓑ collected ⓒ compiled) evidence that led to the capture of the murderer.
형사는 살인범의 체포를 이끈 증거를 수집했다.

09 This encyclopedia took 4 years to (ⓐ assemble ⓑ collect ⓒ compile).
이 백과사전은 편찬하는 데 4년이 걸렸다.

어휘 Check!

01 **appoint** 임명하다 02 **elect** (투표로) 선출하다 03 **select** 선택하다 04 **billow** (소용돌이 치는) 큰 파도; (불, 연기의) 기둥 05 **ripple** 잔물결; 파문; 영향 06 **wave** 파도; 파도처럼 밀려오는 사람 07 **assemble** (기계를) 조립하다; (사람을) 모으다 08 **collect** 수집하다, 모으다 09 **compile** 편찬하다

correlation / relationship

10 Linguists are studying the (ⓐ correlation ⓑ relationship) between early English education and fluency.
언어학자들은 영어 조기 교육과 유창함 사이의 상관관계를 연구 중이다.

11 The (ⓐ correlation ⓑ relationship) between the two neighboring nations has become strained due to recent military clashes.
그 두 이웃나라간의 관계는 최근의 군사적 충돌로 인해 경색되었다.

coalition / merger / union

12 The (ⓐ coalition ⓑ merger ⓒ union) forces are committed to preventing terrorist attacks on civilians.
연합군은 민간인을 대상으로 한 테러 공격을 막고자 혼신의 힘을 다했다.

13 One way for workers to join a traditional labor (ⓐ coalition ⓑ merger ⓒ union) is to be given voluntary recognition from their employer.
전통적인 노조에 가입하는 하나의 방법은 고용주로부터 자발적인 인정을 받는 것이다.

14 The (ⓐ coalition ⓑ merger ⓒ union) of the two companies will be announced later this week.
두 회사의 합병이 이번 주 말경에 발표될 것이다.

devour / munch / swallow

15 Don't (ⓐ devour ⓑ munch ⓒ swallow) this pill. Chew it for one minute.
이 알약을 삼켜서 먹지 마라. 1분 동안 씹어 먹어라.

16 The beggar (ⓐ devoured ⓑ munched ⓒ swallowed) on an apple.
그 거지는 사과 하나를 우적우적 먹었다.

17 The young and sturdy men (ⓐ devoured ⓑ munched ⓒ swallowed) everything on their plates.
그 젊고 건장한 청년들은 접시에 있는 모든 음식을 게걸스럽게 먹어치웠다.

parole / perjury / probation / ruling / sentence / verdict

18 Once a rising star in the company, Bernie was (ⓐ paroled ⓑ perjured ⓒ sentenced) to life in prison Monday for embezzlement.
한때 회사에서 촉망받는 스타였던 버니는 월요일에 횡령죄로 종신형을 선고받았다.

19 The convict will be eligible for (ⓐ parole ⓑ perjury ⓒ verdict) in 25 years.
그 죄수는 25년 후 가석방 자격이 주어질 것이다.

어휘 Check!

10 **correlation** 상관관계 11 **relationship** 관계 12 **coalition** 연합 13 **union** 통합; 노동조합 14 **merger** 합병 15 **swallow** 삼키다 16 **munch** (소리를 내며) 우적우적 먹다 17 **devour** (배가 몹시 고파서) 게걸스럽게 먹다 18 **sentence** 형을 선고하다; 형벌, 선고 19 **parole** 가석방

정답 10 ⓐ 11 ⓑ 12 ⓐ 13 ⓒ 14 ⓑ 15 ⓒ 16 ⓑ 17 ⓐ 18 ⓒ 19 ⓐ

20 The jury went into the deliberation room to reach a (ⓐ probation ⓑ verdict ⓒ ruling).
배심원단은 평결을 내기 위해 배심원실로 들어갔다.

21 Demonstrators took to the streets to protest a (ⓐ perjury ⓑ probation ⓒ ruling) made by
the federal court.
연방 법원에서 내린 판결에 항의하기 위해 시위자들이 거리를 점거했다.

22 If you commit (ⓐ perjury ⓑ sentencing ⓒ verdict) in court, you can be subject to criminal
prosecution.
법정에서 위증을 하면 형사 처벌 대상이 될 수 있다.

23 The former CEO of the company was put on (ⓐ perjury ⓑ parole ⓒ probation) for 2 years.
그 회사의 전 최고 경영자는 2년간 보호관찰을 받았다.

grant / stipend / subsidy

24 The Nobel Prize winner expected one million dollars in (ⓐ grants ⓑ stipends ⓒ subsidies)
but was given a much smaller amount.
노벨상 수상자는 백만 달러의 연구 보조금을 기대했지만 훨씬 적은 양만을 받았다.

25 These days, many farmers cannot survive without agricultural (ⓐ grants ⓑ stipends
ⓒ subsidies).
요즘에는 많은 농부들이 농업 보조금 없이는 살아남을 수 없다.

26 There is a nominal (ⓐ grant ⓑ stipend ⓒ subsidy) for the priest.
성직자에게는 명목상의 아주 적은 고정 월급이 있다.

detailed / immaculate / meticulous / specific

27 Can you be more (ⓐ immaculate ⓑ meticulous ⓒ specific) about what you just said?
방금 하신 말씀을 좀 더 구체적으로 말씀해 주시겠어요?

28 I want you to report the case to me in a more (ⓐ detailed ⓑ immaculate ⓒ meticulous)
manner.
이번 사건을 저에게 좀 더 세부적으로 보고해 주세요.

29 I try to be (ⓐ detailed ⓑ meticulous ⓒ specific) about everything, which makes me work
more slowly.
나는 매사 꼼꼼하게 일하려고 하는데 그러다 보니 더 천천히 일하게 된다.

30 The police officer's uniform looked (ⓐ immaculate ⓑ meticulous ⓒ specific).
그 경찰관의 제복은 티 하나 없이 깔끔해 보였다.

 어휘 Check! 20 **verdict** (배심원의) 평결 21 **ruling** 판결 22 **perjury** 위증 23 **probation** 보호관찰; 수습 기간 24 **grant** (연구 목적의) 보조금; (학교가 주는) 장학금 25 **subsidy** (정부가 기업이나 농업 분야에 제공하는) 보조금, 장려금 26 **stipend** (성직자가 받는) 고정 월급; (정기적인) 수당 27 **specific** 구체적인, 명확한 28 **detailed** 세부적인 29 **meticulous** 세심한, 꼼꼼한 30 **immaculate** 티 하나 없는, 깨끗한; 오류가 전혀 없는

정답 20 ⓑ 21 ⓒ 22 ⓐ 23 ⓒ 24 ⓐ 25 ⓒ 26 ⓑ 27 ⓒ 28 ⓐ 29 ⓑ 30 ⓐ

Check-up TEST

Part I Choose the option that best completes each dialogue.

1. A: The poor kitten must have been starving.
   B: I'll say. She _____ all the food we gave her in mere moments.

   (a) swallowed   (b) devoured
   (c) munched   (d) ingested

2. A: Do you know the procedure for running for public office?
   B: Actually, I do. You must simply raise 10,000 dollars and _____ 1,000 signatures from people in your community.

   (a) collect   (b) stockpile
   (c) assemble   (d) compile

3. A: It's great that you are going to do volunteer work, but how are you going to pay for your daily needs?
   B: Don't worry, Mom. The program will provide me with a small monthly _____ to cover the costs of food and such.

   (a) stipend
   (b) grant
   (c) subsidy
   (d) fund

4. A: This airport is amazing. Everything is so clean and in perfect working order.
   B: Yes, they have a large staff of cleaners and technicians to make sure everything remains _____.

   (a) meticulous
   (b) immaculate
   (c) specific
   (d) detailed

5. A: Were you able to go swimming today while you were at the beach?
   B: Actually, I wasn't because the _____ were dangerously large.

   (a) plumes
   (b) billows
   (c) ripples
   (d) waves

6. A: After several delays, peace talks between the two nations have finally resumed.
   B: That's good news. Maybe they will improve their _____ with each other after all.

   (a) correlation   (b) affiliation
   (c) connection   (d) relationship

7. A: So you finally secured a position at the company you've always dreamed of working for.
   B: Not necessarily. I'll be on _____ for the first three months and can be let go without notice at any time.

   (a) probation   (b) perjury
   (c) parole   (d) patrol

8. A: Your wife sure spends a lot of time getting ready before going out.
   B: Don't I know it. She's always been _____ about her appearance.

   (a) selective   (b) immaculate
   (c) detailed   (d) meticulous

9. A: The number-one cause of global warming is the automobile industry.
   B: Haven't you heard? The three largest automakers have formed a _____ that campaigns against global warming.

   (a) merger
   (b) coalition
   (c) union
   (d) fusion

10. A: Why are there so many police cars and fire trucks outside?
    B: A bomb went off in the Joyce Building this morning. You can easily see the huge _____ of smoke coming from the building.

    (a) waves
    (b) ripples
    (c) billows
    (d) swells

Part II Choose the option that best completes each sentence.

11 To prevent indigestion, be sure to chew your food at least 20 times before you _____ it.
(a) devour
(b) swallow
(c) munch
(d) taste

12 Following the _____, the two companies will become the largest telecom company in the world.
(a) merger
(b) union
(c) fusion
(d) coalition

13 Years of research suggests that there is a strong _____ between educational attainment and overall income as an adult.
(a) correlation
(b) relationship
(c) causation
(d) affiliation

14 For committing several heinous crimes, the serial killer received multiple life _____ in prison.
(a) sentences
(b) rulings
(c) verdicts
(d) judgments

15 The committee _____ Mr. Jeong chairman of the board by a narrow margin.
(a) appointed
(b) elected
(c) selected
(d) designated

16 This year, the university has awarded need-based _____ to nearly half of its students.
(a) funds
(b) capitals
(c) subsidies
(d) grants

17 Dr. Wagner was _____ dean of the Chemistry Department by the university.
(a) selected
(b) appointed
(c) elected
(d) opted

18 Masses of demonstrators turned out to protest the guilty _____ in the famous athlete's murder trial.
(a) decision
(b) verdict
(c) judgment
(d) sentence

19 My lawyer asked me to commit _____ in order to make our case more solid, but I refused to do so.
(a) patrol
(b) probation
(c) parole
(d) perjury

20 The magazine _____ the short stories it has published over the years into a hardcover book.
(a) collected
(b) assembled
(c) compiled
(d) gathered

Voca Review

A 다음 영어 표현과 일치하는 한글 뜻을 고르시오.

01 **assemble** the machine 　　　　　 기계를 (ⓐ 수리하다 ⓑ 조립하다)

02 make a **specific** plan 　　　　　 (ⓐ 구체적인 ⓑ 멋진) 계획을 세우다

03 **parole** of a prisoner 　　　　　 죄수의 (ⓐ 탈옥 ⓑ 가석방)

04 agricultural **subsidy** 　　　　　 농업 (ⓐ 연합 ⓑ 보조금)

05 **compile** the dictionary 　　　　　 사전을 (ⓐ 찾아보다 ⓑ 편찬하다)

06 identify their **correlation** 　　　　　 그들의 (ⓐ 상관관계 ⓑ 유착고리)를 밝혀내다

07 **merger** of two companies 　　　　　 두 회사의 (ⓐ 합병 ⓑ 연합)

08 be accused of **perjury** 　　　　　 (ⓐ 위증죄 ⓑ 사기죄)로 고발되다

09 a **detailed** information 　　　　　 (ⓐ 중요한 ⓑ 세부적인) 정보

10 an **immaculate** shirt 　　　　　 (ⓐ 티 없이 새하얀 ⓑ 유명 브랜드의) 셔츠

B 한글 뜻에 맞는 영어 표현을 완성하시오.

ⓐ grants	ⓑ ruling	ⓒ sentence	ⓓ select	ⓔ appoint
ⓕ munch	ⓖ ripple	ⓗ swallow	ⓘ union	ⓙ meticulous

01 _____ an applicant　지원자를 선택하다

02 _____ effects　파급 효과

03 research _____　연구 보조금

04 labor _____　노동 조합

05 _____ gums　껌을 삼키다

06 _____ him as the manager　그를 부장으로 임명하다

07 pay _____ attention to　~에 세심한 주의를 기울이다

08 unfair _____　불공평한 판결

09 _____ him to death　그에게 사형을 선고하다

10 _____ cookies　과자를 우적우적 씹어 먹다

VP 10 이디엄

풀면서 익히는 Mini Test ▶ 다음 한글 뜻에 맞는 영어 표현을 고르시오.

기출 어휘

01 Steve Austen is like a (ⓐ bull ⓑ dog ⓒ lion) in a china shop since he treats his friends in a violent way.
스티브 오스틴은 자기 친구들을 폭력적으로 대하기 때문에 거친 사람이라고 할 수 있다.

02 He is believed to be gallant, but fear of cockroaches is his Achilles (ⓐ elbow ⓑ heel ⓒ rib).
사람들은 그가 용맹하다고 생각하지만, 바퀴벌레를 무서워한다는 것이 그의 유일한 약점이다.

03 This report lacks coherence. That is a (ⓐ bug ⓑ fly ⓒ pest) in the ointment.
이 보고서는 일관성이 부족하다. 그것이 옥의 티다.

04 It's no use. You are (ⓐ switching ⓑ killing ⓒ beating) a dead horse.
소용없어. 헛수고할 뿐이야.

05 Paul has given me (ⓐ a wild goose chase ⓑ a lump in my throat ⓒ a shoulder to cry on) during my times of difficulty.
폴은 내가 힘들 때 의지가 되어 주었다.

06 The presidential candidate bent over (ⓐ backward ⓑ forward ⓒ side) to win the hearts of voters.
대선 후보는 유권자들의 마음을 잡기 위해 혼신의 힘을 다했다.

07 The new boss breathes down my (ⓐ cheek ⓑ nose ⓒ neck) all the time.
새로 온 사장님은 항상 나를 철저히 감시한다.

08 I have been unemployed for two years, so my wife has to bring home the (ⓐ apple ⓑ bacon ⓒ pie).
나는 2년 동안 실직한 상태여서 아내가 생활비를 벌어와야 한다.

09 The political wrangling between the ruling party and the opposition party eventually came to a (ⓐ head ⓑ forehead ⓒ nose).
여당과 야당 간의 정치 공방이 결국 정점에 이르렀다.

10 Racial discrimination has once again come to the (ⓐ facade ⓑ rear ⓒ fore) as several Asians have reported unfair treatment at their jobs.
몇몇 아시아 사람들이 일자리에서 불공평한 대우를 받은 것으로 보도되자 인종 차별 문제가 다시 한 번 주목을 받았다.

11 After a grueling training session, we were dead on our (ⓐ feet ⓑ legs ⓒ body).
혹독한 교육을 받고 나서 우리는 완전히 지쳐버렸다.

12 No matter how hard he tried, he dropped the (ⓐ money ⓑ button ⓒ ball) every time.
아무리 노력을 했어도 그는 매번 실패했다.

어휘 Check!

01 **a bull in a china shop** 거친 사람 02 **Achilles heel** 유일한 약점, 아킬레스건 03 **a fly in the ointment** 옥의 티 04 **beat a dead horse** 헛수고하다 05 **a shoulder to cry on** 어려울 때 의지가 되는 사람 06 **bend over backward** 혼신의 힘을 다하다 07 **breathe down one's neck** 철저히 감시하다 08 **bring home the bacon** 생활비를 벌다 09 **come to a head** 정점에 이르다, 절정에 달하다 10 **come to the fore** 주목을 받다; 중요한 역할을 하다 11 **dead on one's feet** 매우 지친 12 **drop the ball** 실패하다, 실수하다

정답 01 ⓐ 02 ⓑ 03 ⓑ 04 ⓒ 05 ⓒ 06 ⓐ 07 ⓒ 08 ⓑ 09 ⓐ 10 ⓒ 11 ⓐ 12 ⓒ

13 Why did you fly off the (ⓐ casket ⓑ handle ⓒ lid)?
왜 버럭 화를 냈던 거니?

14 Charlie foamed at the (ⓐ mouth ⓑ nose ⓒ tongue) after one of his best friends betrayed him.
찰리는 친한 친구 중 한 명이 자기를 배신한 후 매우 화를 냈다.

15 The proposal failed after the team leader got (ⓐ cold ⓑ cool ⓒ warm) feet.
팀장이 겁을 먹자 그 제안은 실패로 돌아갔다.

16 The CEO (ⓐ brought out ⓑ came out ⓒ went out) on a limb to revive the ailing company.
최고 경영자는 부실한 회사를 다시 살리기 위해 위험을 감수했다.

17 Trying hard is not enough. You have to go the extra (ⓐ mile ⓑ kilometer ⓒ yard).
열심히 하는 것만으로는 충분하지 않다. 그 이상으로 열심히 노력해야 한다.

18 Oil prices have gone through the (ⓐ desk ⓑ picture ⓒ roof) since the war in Iraq broke out.
이라크 전쟁이 터진 이후로 유가가 급등했다.

19 He looked agitated as my words hit (ⓐ family ⓑ home ⓒ house).
내가 한 말이 정곡을 찔렀기 때문에 그는 동요했다.

20 My mother hit the (ⓐ books ⓑ ceiling ⓒ road) when I failed the test.
내가 시험에서 낙제하자 어머니께서 노발대발하셨다

21 Budweiser, the King of Beers, is really hitting the (ⓐ jackpot ⓑ oasis ⓒ spot).
맥주의 왕, 버드와이저는 정말 맛있다.

22 Don't jump the (ⓐ fence ⓑ gun ⓒ cart). We don't know their intentions, yet.
너무 성급하게 굴지 마. 우리는 그들의 의도를 아직 몰라.

23 Don't jump on the (ⓐ bandwagon ⓑ top ⓒ platform). You should form your own opinions.
시류에 편승하지 마. 너 자신의 의견을 형성해야 해.

24 You have to keep your (ⓐ ear ⓑ eye ⓒ nose) to the ground.
여론을 잘 살펴야 한다.

25 Jessica bought a designer watch and handbag just to keep up with the (ⓐ Jason ⓑ Jasper ⓒ Joneses).
제시카는 단지 남에게 뒤지지 않으려고 명품 시계와 핸드백을 샀다.

26 Tom won the lottery, but he kicked the (ⓐ apron ⓑ bucket ⓒ can) two days later.
톰은 복권에 당첨되었지만 이틀 후 사망했다.

어휘 Check! ¹³ **fly off the handle** 버럭 화를 내다 ¹⁴ **foam at the mouth** 매우 화를 내다 ¹⁵ **get cold feet** 겁을 먹다; 주눅이 들다 ¹⁶ **go out on a limb** 위험을 감수하다 ¹⁷ **go the extra mile** 좀 더 열심히 하다 ¹⁸ **go through the roof** 급격히 치솟다 ¹⁹ **hit home** (말이나 행동이) 정곡을 찌르다 ²⁰ **hit the ceiling** 매우 크게 화를 내다 ²¹ **hit the spot** (음식의 맛이) 훌륭하다 ²² **jump the gun** 성급하게 굴다 ²³ **jump on the bandwagon** 시류에 편승하다 ²⁴ **keep one's ear to the ground** 여론을 살피다 ²⁵ **keep up with the Joneses** 남에게 뒤지지 않으려고 애쓰다 ²⁶ **kick the bucket** 죽다

정답 13 ⓑ 14 ⓐ 15 ⓐ 16 ⓒ 17 ⓐ 18 ⓒ 19 ⓑ 20 ⓑ 21 ⓒ 22 ⓑ 23 ⓐ 24 ⓐ 25 ⓒ 26 ⓑ

27 After the finals are over, we will be able to kick up our (ⓐ heels ⓑ palms ⓒ ribs).

기말고사가 끝나고 나면 우리는 한바탕 놀 수 있을 것이다.

28 I learned the (ⓐ different ⓑ hard ⓒ harsh) way not to confide everything to my coworkers.

나는 동료들에게 모든 것을 다 털어놓아서는 안 된다는 것을 절실히 배웠다.

29 Don't look a gift (ⓐ elephant ⓑ horse ⓒ zebra) in the mouth.

남이 주는 선물에 트집 잡지 마라.

30 Korea made (ⓐ defeat ⓑ destruction ⓒ mincemeat) of Greece in the soccer game, defeating them 2 to nil.

축구 경기에서 2대 0으로 이기며 한국은 그리스를 박살냈다.

31 There is more than meets the (ⓐ eye ⓑ visibility ⓒ vision).

보이는 것 그 이상의 무엇인가가 있다.

32 With no (ⓐ conditions ⓑ ropes ⓒ strings) attached, you will be given a bonus amounting 1,000 dollars every other month.

아무런 조건 없이, 당신은 두 달에 한 번씩 천 달러의 보너스를 지급받게 될 것입니다.

33 Tyson is an athlete who continuously (ⓐ drags ⓑ pulls ⓒ pushes) the envelope.

타이슨은 한계에 계속해서 도전하는 운동선수이다.

34 The novelist pushed up (ⓐ chrysanthemums ⓑ daisies ⓒ roses).

그 소설가는 죽었다.

35 I put my (ⓐ foot ⓑ hand ⓒ leg) in my mouth during a meeting with the CEO.

최고 경영자가 참가한 회의에서 나는 실언을 했다.

36 We paid back all the debt so we are (ⓐ going ⓑ sitting ⓒ walking) pretty.

우리는 모든 빚을 청산했기 때문에 상황이 좋다.

37 The time has come for you to spill the (ⓐ beans ⓑ corns ⓒ crops).

이제는 네가 비밀을 털어놓을 때가 되었다.

38 Her performance was outstanding. She (ⓐ brought ⓑ did ⓒ took) the cake.

그녀의 연주는 훌륭했어. 정말 잘하더라.

39 We need to think (ⓐ in ⓑ outside ⓒ within) the box to overcome this crisis.

이 위기를 극복하기 위해서는 창의적인 생각을 할 필요가 있다.

40 Steve has helped me for over a decade (ⓐ in ⓑ on ⓒ through) thick and thin.

스티브는 지난 십 년 넘게 좋을 때나 안 좋을 때나 나를 도와주었다.

어휘 Check! 27 **kick up one's heels** 한바탕 놀다 28 **learn the hard way** (호된 경험을 통해) 배우다 29 **look a gift horse in the mouth** 남이 주는 선물에 트집을 잡다 30 **make mincemeat of** 박살내다, 묵사발을 만들다 31 **more than meets the eye** 눈에 보이는 이상의 것, 숨겨진 것 32 **no strings attached** 아무런 조건 없이 33 **push the envelope** 한계를 넘어서다 34 **push up daisies** 죽다 35 **put one's foot in one's mouth** 실수[실언]하다 36 **sit pretty** 좋은 상태에 있다 37 **spill the beans** 비밀을 털어놓다 38 **take the cake** 훌륭하다; 상을 타다 39 **think outside the box** 창의적인 생각을 하다 40 **through thick and thin** 좋은 때나 안 좋은 때나

정답 27 ⓐ 28 ⓑ 29 ⓑ 30 ⓒ 31 ⓐ 32 ⓒ 33 ⓒ 34 ⓑ 35 ⓐ 36 ⓑ 37 ⓐ 38 ⓒ 39 ⓑ 40 ⓒ

41 Businesses must keep (ⓐ an ace ⓑ a diamond ⓒ a heart) in the hole to compete in today's market.
오늘날 시장에서 경쟁하려면 기업은 비장의 무기를 가져야 한다.

42 The car was nearly hit by the train. That was a (ⓐ close ⓑ dangerous ⓒ passing) call.
차가 거의 기차에 치일 뻔했다. 정말 위험한 순간이었다.

43 The newcomer is a pain in the (ⓐ knee ⓑ neck ⓒ temple).
그 신입 사원은 정말 골칫덩이다.

44 It turned out to be a (ⓐ hurricane ⓑ storm ⓒ tempest) in a teapot.
결국에는 별일 아닌 것으로 드러났다.

45 Don't worry about it. It's all in a (ⓐ month's ⓑ week's ⓒ day's) work.
너무 걱정하지 마. 늘 있는 일이야.

46 The decision was made at the (ⓐ tenth ⓑ eleventh ⓒ twelfth) hour.
막판에 결정이 내려졌다.

47 Because Thomas Huns had been defeated by the champion twice, he had no choice but to bite the (ⓐ bullet ⓑ knife ⓒ gun) and start training again.
토마스 헌즈는 두 번이나 챔피언에게 패배했기 때문에 이를 악물고 다시 훈련을 시작하는 수밖에 없었다.

48 Give me a (ⓐ globe park ⓑ ballroom ⓒ ballpark) figure.
대략적인 수치를 알려주세요.

49 Luna is a carbon (ⓐ copy ⓑ photo ⓒ paper) of her mother.
루나는 자기 어머니를 쏙 빼 닮았다.

50 I am surprised that you (ⓐ brought ⓑ came ⓒ made) such a long way.
네가 장족의 발전을 이루어서 놀랐어.

51 Bruce was completely (ⓐ down and out ⓑ plain and simple ⓒ up and running).
브루스는 완전히 빈털터리 신세가 되었다.

52 Trust me. If I am wrong about this, I will eat my (ⓐ hair ⓑ hat ⓒ nail).
내 말을 믿어. 만약 내가 틀리면 손에 장을 지질게.

53 My father is a self-made businessman. He started his business from (ⓐ dust ⓑ part ⓒ scratch).
나의 아버지는 자수성가한 사업가이다. 그는 밑바닥부터 사업을 시작했다.

어휘 Check!

41 an ace in the hole 비장의 무기 **42** a close call 위기의 순간 **43** a pain in the neck 거슬리는 사람[것], 골칫거리
44 a tempest in a teapot 별일 아닌 것 **45** all in a day's work 평범한 일, 늘 있는 일 **46** at the eleventh hour 마지막에, 막판에
47 bite the bullet 이를 악물고 버티다 **48** ballpark figure 대략의 수치 **49** carbon copy 꼭 빼닮은 사람[것] **50** come a long
way 장족의 발전을 이루다 **51** down and out 빈털터리인, 파산한 **52** eat one's hat (~하면) 손에 장을 지지다 **53** from scratch 아주
처음부터, 무(無)에서

정답 41 ⓐ 42 ⓐ 43 ⓑ 44 ⓒ 45 ⓒ 46 ⓑ 47 ⓐ 48 ⓒ 49 ⓐ 50 ⓑ 51 ⓐ 52 ⓑ 53 ⓒ

54 I got (ⓐ an aching ⓑ an inkling ⓒ a smashing) of what was going on when the police arrived at the scene.
경찰이 현장에 도착했을 때 나는 상황이 어떻게 돌아가는지 어렴풋이 알 수 있었다.

55 Rooney supposedly cheated on his wife again. Still, we have to give him the benefit of the (ⓐ question ⓑ correction ⓒ doubt).
루니가 이번에도 자기 아내를 놔두고 바람을 피운 것 같아. 그래도 일단은 그를 한 번 믿어봐야 해.

56 To be honest, I have (ⓐ an ax ⓑ a shovel ⓒ a hammer) to grind against the church.
솔직히 나는 교회 측에 불만이 있다.

57 You hit the nail on the (ⓐ head ⓑ forehead ⓒ heart). That's exactly what I am talking about.
네가 정확히 핵심을 찔렀구나. 내 말이 바로 그 말이야.

58 After working here for 7 years, I learned the (ⓐ dos and don'ts ⓑ ifs and buts ⓒ ins and outs) of the production process.
여기에서 7년간 일한 후에, 나는 생산 과정에 대해 속속들이 배웠다.

59 A big change is in (ⓐ store ⓑ rain ⓒ beach).
큰 변화가 있을 예정이다.

60 The price of the new laptop computer is in the (ⓐ neighbor ⓑ neighborhood ⓒ community) of 2 million won.
새로 출시된 노트북 컴퓨터의 가격은 약 2백만 원 정도이다.

61 You will find yourself at ease with this job once you (ⓐ know ⓑ learn ⓒ realize) the ropes.
일단 요령만 터득하면 이 일을 편하게 느낄 것이다.

62 The banker lost his (ⓐ shirt ⓑ pants ⓒ vest) on Wall Street.
그 은행원은 월가에서 빈털터리가 되었다.

63 Don't make a (ⓐ river ⓑ mountain ⓒ hill) out of a molehill.
과장하지 마.

64 You are advised not to make a (ⓐ clip ⓑ landscape ⓒ scene) in a public place.
공공장소에서 소란을 피워서는 안 된다.

65 Let's (ⓐ assemble ⓑ converge ⓒ meet) halfway.
서로 양보합시다.

66 The prison is located off the beaten (ⓐ road ⓑ track ⓒ off).
감옥은 사람의 발길이 닿지 않는 곳에 위치해 있다.

 어휘 Check! 54 **get an inkling of** ~을 어렴풋이 알다 55 **give ~ the benefit of the doubt** 일단 ~을 믿다 56 **have an ax to grind** 불만[원한]을 가지다 57 **hit the nail on the head** 핵심을 찌르다 58 **ins and outs** 세부적인 것, 자초지종 59 **in store** ~이 있을 예정인 60 **in the neighborhood of** 약, 대략 61 **learn the ropes** 요령을 터득하다; ~에 대해 배우다 62 **lose one's shirt** 망하다, 무일푼이 되다 63 **make a mountain out of a molehill** 하찮은 일을 과장해서 말하다 64 **make a scene** 소란을 피우다 65 **meet halfway** 타협하다, 양보하다 66 **off the beaten track** 사람의 발길이 닿지 않는

정답 54 ⓑ 55 ⓒ 56 ⓐ 57 ⓐ 58 ⓒ 59 ⓐ 60 ⓑ 61 ⓑ 62 ⓐ 63 ⓑ 64 ⓒ 65 ⓒ 66 ⓑ

67 We are (ⓐ in ⓑ on ⓒ off) the hook.
우리는 곤경에서 벗어났다.

68 I have only seen James once in a (ⓐ nick of time ⓑ blue moon ⓒ same page) since he started his new job.
제임스가 새로운 일을 시작한 뒤로 나는 그를 어쩌다 한 번씩만 만난다.

69 Quantum mechanics is (ⓐ in ⓑ on ⓒ over) my head no matter how hard I study.
아무리 열심히 공부해도 나는 양자 역학을 도저히 이해할 수 없다.

70 Hannah passed the TEPS with (ⓐ high ⓑ flying ⓒ low) colors by earning a perfect score.
한나는 만점을 받으며 텝스 시험을 성공적으로 치렀다.

71 I (ⓐ racked ⓑ crushed ⓒ rocked) my brain trying to solve this maddeningly difficult math problem.
나는 미치도록 어려운 수학 문제를 풀려고 노력하며 머리를 쥐어짰다.

72 Everyone has (ⓐ bones ⓑ a skeleton ⓒ a skull) in his or her closet.
누구나 숨기고 싶은 비밀이 있다.

73 I am sorry to offend you. It was a slip of the (ⓐ mouth ⓑ lips ⓒ tongue).
네 마음을 상하게 해서 미안해. 실언이었어.

74 He's the (ⓐ cutting ⓑ spitting ⓒ splashing) image of his father.
그는 자기 아버지를 꼭 빼닮았다.

75 When the boss is criticizing you, just take it with a grain of (ⓐ salt ⓑ sugar ⓒ wheat).
사장님이 당신을 비판할 때는 그냥 가감해서 들으세요.

76 I personally believe that Mercedes-Benz is the (ⓐ water ⓑ soup ⓒ cream) of the crop among luxury sedans.
개인적으로 값비싼 세단형 자동차 중에서 메르세데스 벤츠가 최상의 차라고 생각한다.

77 You always turn a (ⓐ deaf ear ⓑ blind eye ⓒ silent mouth) to my advice.
너는 항상 내 조언에 귀를 기울이지 않는구나.

78 It turned out that the CEO had secured a contract under the (ⓐ chair ⓐ desk ⓒ table).
최고 경영자가 뇌물로 계약을 따냈다는 것이 밝혀졌다.

79 It seems that you are still wet behind the (ⓐ eyes ⓑ ears ⓒ neck).
넌 아직 풋내기에 불과한 것 같구나.

80 I told you not to make fun of my weight again. That's the (ⓐ burden ⓑ straw ⓒ luggage) that broke the camel's back.
한 번만 더 몸무게를 갖고 날 놀리면 가만 두지 않겠어. 그건 내 인내심의 한계를 테스트하는 거야.

67 off the hook 곤경[처벌]을 면한 68 once in a blue moon 아주 드물게 69 over one's head 이해할 수 없는 70 pass with flying colors 성공하다 71 rack one's brains 머리를 쥐어짜다 72 a skeleton in the closet 숨기고 싶은 비밀 73 slip of the tongue 실언, 잘못 말함 74 the spitting image 빼닮은 것 75 take ~ with a grain of salt 가감해서 듣다 76 the cream of the crop 최고의 것 77 turn a deaf ear to ~에 귀를 기울이지 않다 78 under the table 뇌물로서, 불법으로 79 wet behind the ears 풋내기인 80 the straw that broke the camel's back 한계점

정답 67 ⓒ 68 ⓑ 69 ⓒ 70 ⓑ 71 ⓐ 72 ⓑ 73 ⓒ 74 ⓑ 75 ⓐ 76 ⓒ 77 ⓐ 78 ⓒ 79 ⓑ 80 ⓑ

Check-up TEST

Part I Choose the option that best completes each dialogue.

1 A: Good luck on your big day tomorrow!
   B: Thanks. I hope I don't _____ on the stage.

   (a) turn a blind eye
   (b) get cold feet
   (c) have a leg up
   (d) play it by ear

2 A: I'm sorry, officer. I didn't realize that I was going over the speed limit.
   B: All right. I'll let you _____ this time. But don't do it again.

   (a) around the clock
   (b) off the hook
   (c) down the tubes
   (d) on the rocks

3 A: Why don't we go ahead and move on to the product's advertising campaign?
   B: Hold on. Let's not _____. We still have to finalize the design.

   (a) call it quits
   (b) ring a bell
   (c) jump the gun
   (d) get the picture

4 A: Jerry's constant complaints are really getting on my nerves.
   B: I agree. He's a _____ to everybody in the office.

   (a) shot in the arm
   (b) pain in the neck
   (c) bundle of nerves
   (d) skeleton in the closet

5 A: This city seems to be much nicer than it was the last time I visited it.
   B: Yes, it really has _____ in the past few years.

   (a) bridged the gap
   (b) turned a blind eye
   (c) made out like a bandit
   (d) come a long way

6 A: Do you feel comfortable operating the cash register by yourself now?
   B: I'm still _____, but I think I'll get the hang of it soon.

   (a) making ends meet
   (b) learning the ropes
   (c) coming to a head
   (d) gathering steam

7 A: I heard the government is trying to crack down on illegal immigrant workers.
   B: That's right. It will impose strict fines on employers that hire workers _____.

   (a) under the radar
   (b) across the board
   (c) around the clock
   (d) under the table

8 A: You look exhausted. I think you should go home and get some rest.
   B: Even though I'm _____, I have to complete my shift.

   (a) bringing home the bacon
   (b) looking on the bright side
   (c) dead on my feet
   (d) running off my mouth

9 A: This painting is pristine except for the odd shape of the woman's mouth.
   B: Yes, that is a _____. I must go back and change it.

   (a) thorn in my side
   (b) fly in the ointment
   (c) house of cards
   (d) drop in the bucket

10 A: We have exactly thirty minutes to submit our proposal.
    B: Don't worry. I do my finest work _____.

    (a) at the eleventh hour
    (b) at the drop of a hat
    (c) in the hot seat
    (d) in the nick of time

Part II Choose the option that best completes each sentence.

11 The members of the All-Star Team represent _____ among NBA players.

(a) a close call
(b) the cream of the crop
(c) an open secret
(d) the bottom of the barrel

12 Senator Green was forced to step down from office after the press exposed

_____.

(a) an ace in the hole
(b) a nail in the coffin
(c) water under the bridge
(d) a skeleton in his closet

13 We are reluctant to report bad news to our manager out of fear that he will

_____.

(a) keep his cool
(b) fly off the handle
(c) beat a dead horse
(d) hit the floor

14 The philosopher's lecture went _____ in spite of my best efforts to follow along.

(a) across the board
(b) down and out
(c) under the table
(d) over my head

15 She may look naive, but there is more to her than _____.

(a) one string to her bow
(b) meets the eye
(c) one way to skin a cat
(d) you can shake a stick at

16 I encourage all citizens to _____ and help whenever they see someone in need of aid.

(a) play it by ear
(b) come to the fore
(c) kick the bucket
(d) come to a head

17 The potty-mouthed DJ rose to fame by _____ of what content was acceptable to put over the airwaves.

(a) pushing the envelope
(b) facing the music
(c) putting his foot in his mouth
(d) fighting an uphill battle

18 The singer really _____ when he made disparaging remarks about his record label on the talk show.

(a) put his foot in his mouth
(b) showed his hand
(c) opened the floodgates
(d) put the cart before the horse

19 _____ may increase your material possessions, but it will do little to promote your fiscal wellbeing.

(a) Bringing home the bacon
(b) Having an ax to grind
(c) Keeping up with the Joneses
(d) Thinking outside the box

20 The electronics company has _____ with its brilliant new cell phone design.

(a) a carrot on a stick
(b) an ace in the hole
(c) the best of both worlds
(d) nothing to show

A 다음 영어 표현과 일치하는 한글 뜻을 고르시오.

01 beat a dead horse   (ⓐ 한바탕 놀다 ⓑ 헛수고하다)

02 meet halfway   (ⓐ 타협하다 ⓑ 주장하다)

03 come to a head   (ⓐ 절정에 달하다 ⓑ 이성을 잃다)

04 kick the bucket   (ⓐ 망하다 ⓑ 죽다)

05 hit the ceiling   (ⓐ 급격히 치솟다 ⓑ 매우 화내다)

06 drop the ball   (ⓐ 실패하다 ⓑ 깜빡 잊다)

07 ins and outs   (ⓐ 세부적인 것 ⓑ 잊기 쉬운 것)

08 make a scene   (ⓐ 소란을 피우다 ⓑ 녹초가 되다)

09 a tempest in a teapot   (ⓐ 위기의 순간 ⓑ 별일 아닌 것)

10 spill the beans   (ⓐ 비밀을 털어놓다 ⓑ 험담을 하다)

B 한글 뜻에 맞는 영어 표현을 완성하시오.

ⓐ shirt   ⓑ limb   ⓒ rack   ⓓ bullet   ⓔ carbon
ⓕ slip   ⓖ strings   ⓗ scratch   ⓘ home   ⓙ mincemeat

01 from _____ 무(無)에서

02 lose one's _____ 망하다, 무일푼이 되다

03 no _____ attached 아무런 조건 없이

04 make _____ of 묵사발을 만들다

05 _____ one's brains 머리를 쥐어짜다

06 _____ of the tongue 실언, 잘못 말함

07 hit _____ (말이나 행동이) 정곡을 찌르다

08 _____ copy 꼭 빼닮은 사람

09 bite the _____ 이를 악물고 견뎌내다

10 go out on a _____ 위험을 감수하다

Section

3

Actual
Test 01~06
Vocabulary

Part I **Questions 1-10**
Choose the option that best completes each dialogue.

1. A: Pardon me. Can you tell me how to get to the museum?
   B: Yes. Turn right at the war _____ and go straight.

   (a) souvenir
   (b) artifact
   (c) memorial
   (d) remembrance

2. A: This Rolex watch looks like an imitation.
   B: Sir, I assure you that it is a _____ article.

   (a) resistant
   (b) dominant
   (c) cozy
   (d) genuine

3. A: I've noticed that the city has finally begun to place some trash cans in public areas.
   B: I _____ their efforts to help reduce litter, but they need to do more.

   (a) deify
   (b) retaliate
   (c) manifest
   (d) applaud

4. A: Do you know a good place to buy household products at a low price?
   B: You should probably check out the _____ shop.

   (a) duty-free
   (b) bargain
   (c) frugality
   (d) tax-exempt

5. A: How much are you looking to spend for your car?
   B: I'm considering a price _____ of twenty-five to thirty thousand dollars.

   (a) variety
   (b) range
   (c) assortment
   (d) gathering

6. A: This shirt is a bit loose. Maybe I should get a smaller size.
   B: Keep in mind that it will probably _____ when you wash it, so you should probably go with the bigger size.

   (a) stretch   (b) skid
   (c) stink   (d) shrink

7. A: Is Mitch ever on time for work?
   B: Nope. As far as I know, he is _____ tardy.

   (a) delightfully   (b) consistently
   (c) infrequently   (d) remorsefully

8. A: Ouch! I cut my finger with the knife.
   B: Make sure you _____ the wound with antibacterial soap before putting a bandaid on it.

   (a) disinfect
   (b) vaccinate
   (c) hospitalize
   (d) recuperate

9. A: Have the mechanics figured out the problem with the car?
   B: Yes. There is something wrong inside the engine, so they will have to _____ it to make the repairs.

   (a) dissuade
   (b) disparage
   (c) disassemble
   (d) discriminate

10. A: The court ordered the manufacturer to pay a 30 million dollar fine for polluting the river.
    B: That may sound like a lot of money, but it is a _____ sum for such a large company.

    (a) lucrative
    (b) consequential
    (c) trivial
    (d) provocative

Part II Questions 11-30

Choose the option that best completes each sentence.

11. The last train will be _____ from the station at 11 p.m. tonight.

(a) departing
(b) growing
(c) meandering
(d) fleeting

12. She refused to admit to the charges against her and for good _____: They were true.

(a) rationale
(b) purpose
(c) reason
(d) basis

13. In July 1969, a major _____ in human history was reached when Neil Armstrong walked on the face of the moon.

(a) benchmark
(b) milestone
(c) landmark
(d) breakthrough

14. For decades, the United States government has _____ a war against illegal drugs.

(a) waged
(b) battled
(c) engaged
(d) entered

15. The group's belief that all human beings will someday stop consuming meat is simply _____ thinking.

(a) ignorant
(b) hopeful
(c) wishful
(d) optimistic

16. Reducing workers' lunch breaks from 45 minutes to half an hour was the _____ that led to the current union strike.

(a) storm in a teacup
(b) square peg in a round hole
(c) straw that broke the camel's back
(d) shot heard around the world

17. The popularity of Korean television shows and music abroad has _____ international interest in other aspects of Korean culture.

(a) illuminated
(b) kindled
(c) suffocated
(d) quenched

18. Members of the G20 plan to hold _____ talks in order to deal with the growing problem of climate change.

(a) summit
(b) meeting
(c) conference
(d) forum

19. In spite of running late for work, he still chose to _____ on the way to his office.

(a) meddle
(b) waddle
(c) dawdle
(d) twiddle

20. If you ever feel down and unsure of yourself, remember that our guidance _____ are here to help you.

(a) council
(b) councilors
(c) counsel
(d) counselors

21. One of the easiest ways to _____ a nail-biting habit is to apply a bad-tasting substance to your fingernails.

(a) approach
(b) treat
(c) recover
(d) inhibit

22. An area man narrowly survived a _____ call during a recent white-water rafting trip.

(a) near
(b) second
(c) close
(d) tight

23. The small manufacturing company was successfully able to _____ a hostile takeover.

(a) repel
(b) repeal
(c) rectify
(d) remit

24. The development of rocket technology _____ a new age of space exploration.

(a) marshaled
(b) punctuated
(c) tolerated
(d) heralded

25. The accusation that I made unwanted advances toward my female staff is a _____ lie meant to ruin my reputation.

(a) discourteous
(b) downright
(c) hospitable
(d) probable

26. We required the assistance of _____ mediator to complete our negotiations.

(a) an interested
(b) a disinterested
(c) an uninterested
(d) an uninteresting

27. It seems that for every study claiming that drinking wine brings about health benefits, another one _____ it.

(a) espouses
(b) grooms
(c) bolsters
(d) refutes

28. The study suggests that self-esteem and feelings of depression are _____ related to one another.

(a) lucratively
(b) introspectively
(c) prospectively
(d) deceptively

29. I'm sorry, but Professor Hollings is away on _____ and will not return until next semester.

(a) colloquium
(b) edification
(c) tenure
(d) sabbatical

30. Drug enforcement agents are able to _____ only a small percentage of the narcotics entering the country.

(a) denigrate
(b) wrangle
(c) interdict
(d) flank

You have finished the Vocabulary questions. Please continue on to the Grammar questions.

Part I Questions 1-10

Choose the option that best completes each dialogue.

1. A: These flies keep buzzing around my head.
   B: Yeah, they are such a _____. Let me get my fly swatter and kill some of them.

   (a) fusion
   (b) retreat
   (c) nuisance
   (d) diploma

2. A: Here's a picture of my newborn son.
   B: I can definitely tell he's your child. He's _____ of you.

   (a) a broken record
   (b) the whole kit and caboodle
   (c) the moral fiber
   (d) the spitting image

3. A: How did you feel when you heard about the princess' death?
   B: I was completely _____ and broke down into tears right away.

   (a) devastated
   (b) elated
   (c) procrastinated
   (d) intrigued

4. A: The new manager has really turned this store around.
   B: I'll say. Our store went from a failing business to a _____ operation in no time at all.

   (a) lucrative
   (b) pricey
   (c) compelling
   (d) fabulous

5. A: Why did the coffee shop change its name?
   B: As far as I know, another shop claimed that the old name _____ their copyright.

   (a) obstructed
   (b) certified
   (c) infringed
   (d) aggravated

6. A: My heating bills in the winter are always so high.
   B: It sounds to me like your home needs more _____. That will help lower your heating costs.

   (a) insulation   (b) insurance
   (c) compliance   (d) complication

7. A: I still can't believe that the Heat won the championship game.
   B: Neither can I. Their opponents were _____ the better team, but the Heat lucked out in the end.

   (a) undoubtedly   (b) undeservingly
   (c) understandably (d) unabashedly

8. A: Sir, I feel that we have no chance of winning this battle.
   B: What makes you think that? We _____ the enemy forces 3 to 1.

   (a) simulate
   (b) fortify
   (c) outnumber
   (d) suppress

9. A: Clara's baby must be due pretty soon, right?
   B: Oh, I guess you didn't hear the news. She had a _____ and lost her baby.

   (a) miscarriage
   (b) mishap
   (c) miracle
   (d) mitigation

10. A: What aspect of your personality makes you a good fit for this job?
    B: I am _____ individual, so I will have no problems presenting my opinions to others.

    (a) a taciturn
    (b) a slothful
    (c) a resentful
    (d) an assertive

11. She refused to _____ and held to her principles in the argument.

    (a) concede
    (b) compromise
    (c) condone
    (d) constitute

12. Congress has just _____ a federal law legalizing same-sex marriages.

    (a) enacted
    (b) verified
    (c) pacified
    (d) enshrined

13. Many major world cities have reduced _____ by tightening emissions standards and converting public buses to hydrogen power.

    (a) preservation
    (b) pollution
    (c) recycling
    (d) anomaly

14. The two-way mirror is _____ on one side and opaque on the other.

    (a) transparent
    (b) lucid
    (c) fractured
    (d) dire

15. The city will _____ traffic from Main Street to Second Avenue during the construction work.

    (a) fulfill
    (b) initiate
    (c) divert
    (d) harness

16. You don't need to make reservations at the restaurant because it is _____.

    (a) better late than never
    (b) not my cup of tea
    (c) first come, first served
    (d) no strings attached

17. The forensic evidence _____ the eyewitness accounts of the events that night.

    (a) intimidates
    (b) corroborates
    (c) digresses
    (d) ascends

18. A nation's _____ department is usually responsible for setting national interest rates.

    (a) budget
    (b) treasury
    (c) profit
    (d) allocation

19. The military decided to _____ the defense plan, in spite of its astronomical costs.

    (a) implore
    (b) implement
    (c) intercept
    (d) interchange

20. Our _____ collection is housed on the first floor while temporary exhibitions are on the second.

    (a) permanent
    (b) preliminary
    (c) peripheral
    (d) prominent

21. Health inspectors closed down the restaurant due to its poor _____ conditions.

(a) prosaic
(b) sanitary
(c) lenient
(d) evocative

22. The night's television programs were _____ by the baseball game broadcast.

(a) pervaded
(b) preempted
(c) confiscated
(d) resumed

23. I decided to _____ to my fiance's religion shortly before our marriage.

(a) exchange
(b) change
(c) convert
(d) transfer

24. The sound of the ambulance sirens _____ throughout the city.

(a) resonates
(b) obliterates
(c) thrives
(d) resurrects

25. Police arrested the drug _____ for possession of narcotics with intent to distribute.

(a) merchant
(b) user
(c) hawker
(d) peddler

26. People in powerful positions are often surrounded by _____ underlings who provide only good news and offer words of encouragement.

(a) legitimate
(b) resilient
(c) obsequious
(d) proficient

27. The nation's economy was hit especially hard by the _____ and still has yet to recover.

(a) recruitment
(b) recuperation
(c) recession
(d) reception

28. I managed to transform this drab apartment into _____ decorated living space by making a few simple changes.

(a) a tantalizingly
(b) an urbanely
(c) a prudently
(d) a sordidly

29. We had to _____ most of our possessions when we evacuated from the hurricane.

(a) hospitalize
(b) render
(c) forsake
(d) augment

30. The income _____ between the upper and lower classes in the nation continues to widen.

(a) enmity
(b) plight
(c) influx
(d) disparity

You have finished the Vocabulary questions. Please continue on to the Grammar questions.

Part I Questions 1-10

Choose the option that best completes each dialogue.

---

1. A: Do you understand what Mr. Black wants us to do?

   B: Not really. He wasn't able to _____ his plan to me.

   (a) get across
   (b) enter into
   (c) knuckle under
   (d) open up

2. A: This _____ certainly is impressive.

   B: Yes. It was built to honor the veterans of the Vietnam War.

   (a) courtesy
   (b) editorial
   (c) reconciliation
   (d) monument

3. A: Can you show me your passport, please?

   B: I'm sorry. I don't have it. I didn't _____ I had to bring it.

   (a) organize
   (b) realize
   (c) recognize
   (d) appear

4. A: I thought you hired somebody to paint your room for you.

   B: I did, but he did a _____ job, so I'm doing it over myself.

   (a) sloppy
   (b) pristine
   (c) weighty
   (d) divine

5. A: So in order to start the car, I need to put the key in the ignition and crank the motor?

   B: That's exactly right. You _____.

   (a) speak with a silver tongue
   (b) hit the nail on the head
   (c) got in on the act
   (d) put the final nail in the coffin

6. A: The number of carjackings in this neighborhood has _____ increased lately.

   B: Right. The police should do something about it.

   (a) dully
   (b) luckily
   (c) sharply
   (d) readily

7. A: What did your manager think of your proposal?

   B: He told me _____ that it stinks.

   (a) bluntly
   (b) redundantly
   (c) crudely
   (d) vocally

8. A: Wow. Your hair is so _____ and shiny. What's your secret?

   B: I make sure to wash it every day using only organic shampoo.

   (a) polished
   (b) sleek
   (c) elegant
   (d) graceful

9. A: The president's new social security plan has not been very successful.

   B: Yes, and that is why the government is trying to _____ the old system.

   (a) establish
   (b) resurrect
   (c) invigorate
   (d) stabilize

10. A: The judge decided to sentence the murderer to only 5 years in prison.

    B: That punishment is much too _____ considering the seriousness of his crimes.

    (a) critical
    (b) complicit
    (c) lenient
    (d) licentious

Part II Questions 11-30

Choose the option that best completes each sentence.

11. In this cookie recipe, you can _____ apple sauce for eggs to reduce the calorie content.

(a) alternate
(b) nourish
(c) substitute
(d) invent

12. To maintain a healthy body weight, doctors recommend _____ between 2,000 and 3,000 calories each day.

(a) consuming
(b) prescribing
(c) swallowing
(d) breathing

13. The Korean restaurant opened its first international _____ in Beijing in 2010.

(a) division
(b) chain
(c) branch
(d) limb

14. After years of poor farming practices _____ the soil, crops could no longer be grown there.

(a) impoverished
(b) generated
(c) enriched
(d) evaporated

15. The millionaire had several _____ children with countless mistresses.

(a) scandalous
(b) illegitimate
(c) culpable
(d) imperative

16. Some police officers may occasionally bend the rules, but Officer Jones always _____.

(a) plays it by ear
(b) goes by the book
(c) keeps his eye on the ball
(d) has his hands full

17. The CEO will _____ the problems surrounding employee healthcare in his meeting today.

(a) tackle
(b) succeed
(c) address
(d) lecture

18. I must commend you on your _____ taste in clothing.

(a) full
(b) pliable
(c) impeccable
(d) whole

19. One renowned psychologist recently proclaimed that innate characteristics are _____ to environmental factors in regard to the development of one's personality.

(a) obstinate
(b) residual
(c) apathetic
(d) subordinate

20. My _____ about winning the lottery proved to be correct.

(a) promotion
(b) proposition
(c) premeditation
(d) premonition

21. Unlike most other farm animals, cattle need large tracts of land on which to _____.

(a) graze
(b) slaughter
(c) burrow
(d) lurk

22. After our team gained a twenty-point lead, it became clear that victory was a _____ conclusion.

(a) predetermined
(b) rudimentary
(c) surmountable
(d) foregone

23. Losing my job seemed to be a disaster at first, but it turned out to be a _____.

(a) blessing in disguise
(b) bolt from the blue
(c) diamond in the rough
(d) labor of love

24. A series of economic, military, and political ties still _____ the nation with its former colonies.

(a) bind
(b) unite
(c) resolve
(d) contemplate

25. A feeling of tremendous sadness _____ the novel.

(a) invades
(b) outstrips
(c) conveys
(d) pervades

26. The group criticizes many of today's television programs as being _____ and morally corrupt.

(a) staunch
(b) ethereal
(c) vacuous
(d) licentious

27. Due to contamination from nearby factories, the water in the river is no longer _____.

(a) pious
(b) prolific
(c) potable
(d) portable

28. Game companies have spent millions on advertising campaigns to _____ video games as an acceptable hobby for women.

(a) induce
(b) legitimize
(c) obliterate
(d) demean

29. Dubai has made efforts to curb the rampant real estate _____ that has plagued its housing market.

(a) speculation
(b) anticipation
(c) increment
(d) misappropriation

30. Every winter, my family _____ our home for Christmas with colorful lights and ornaments.

(a) bedecks
(b) heralds
(c) appeases
(d) rattles

You have finished the Vocabulary questions. Please continue on to the Grammar questions.

Part I **Questions 1-10**
Choose the option that best completes each dialogue.

1. A: I can't believe the director treated you so cruelly.
   B: Don't worry. She will _____ what she did to me someday.

   (a) pay for   (b) insist on
   (c) come by   (d) hear of

2. A: George quit his job and bought a mansion in the Caribbean. How could he afford to do that?
   B: Apparently he made a _____ in the real estate market.

   (a) shelter
   (b) fortune
   (c) venture
   (d) portion

3. A: I've been really stressed out lately because of work and taking care of the kids.
   B: It sounds to me like you need to _____ yourself with a day at the spa.

   (a) torture
   (b) embody
   (c) spoil
   (d) caution

4. A: I'm sorry to give you such late notice, but another friend is coming for dinner.
   B: That's no problem. We have a _____ amount of food for another person.

   (a) mobile
   (b) pathetic
   (c) serene
   (d) sufficient

5. A: Could you please _____ the television? I'm talking on the phone.
   B: Oh, I'm sorry. I'll do that.

   (a) distract
   (b) mute
   (c) fade
   (d) eliminate

6. A: I'm exhausted. How much longer will it be until we reach the top?
   B: Don't worry. The _____ is just up ahead.

   (a) peek
   (b) peel
   (c) peak
   (d) pear

7. A: Have you completed your itinerary for the vacation?
   B: I sure have. I've chosen spots off the beaten _____ to visit, such as Antarctica.

   (a) path
   (b) street
   (c) road
   (d) trek

8. A: Do the mechanics know what is wrong with the car?
   B: No, they weren't able to _____ the source of the problem.

   (a) overwhelm
   (b) identify
   (c) suppress
   (d) recruit

9. A: I'd like to go bowling this evening. Are you interested?
   B: Not really. I just _____ staying at home and watching television.

   (a) leave behind
   (b) come by
   (c) dispense with
   (d) feel like

10. A: I drove all the way across town to help you with your packing.
    B: Thank you very much, but you didn't have to _____ for me.

    (a) bend over backward
    (b) lose your temper
    (c) test the waters
    (d) go through the motions

Choose the option that best completes each sentence.

11. To help your skin look beautiful and radiant, be sure to _____ our exfoliating skin cream every night before going to bed.

    (a) cover
    (b) coat
    (c) apply
    (d) rub

12. People with bipolar disorder often experience feelings of _____ happiness and complete misery within moments of one another.

    (a) pitiful
    (b) sheer
    (c) inferior
    (d) assiduous

13. We were unable to deliver your package today, but we will make a second _____ tomorrow.

    (a) endurance
    (b) effort
    (c) allocation
    (d) attempt

14. The _____ of the interview will be posted on the website soon.

    (a) verse
    (b) conversion
    (c) transcript
    (d) transaction

15. My parents were very _____ and did not even allow me to have a boyfriend until college.

    (a) frugal
    (b) stern
    (c) tolerant
    (d) reclusive

16. When you receive a present you do not like, it is important to be considerate and not to _____.

    (a) stick out like a sore thumb
    (b) fly by the seat of your pants
    (c) look a gift horse in the mouth
    (d) make out like a bandit

17. Due to declining ridership, the city has been forced to increase its _____ for the public transportation system.

    (a) donations
    (b) grants
    (c) stipends
    (d) subsidies

18. In spite of protests from the international community, the rogue nation refused to _____ its nuclear weapon program.

    (a) betray
    (b) merit
    (c) abandon
    (d) enhance

19. Having never married, the king left no _____ to the throne.

    (a) representatives
    (b) beneficiaries
    (c) heirs
    (d) proteges

20. The _____ mayor lost to an upstart politician in her reelection campaign.

    (a) incumbent
    (b) elective
    (c) urgent
    (d) condescending

21. Much of the violence in the area has been _____ by the rival gangs.

(a) installed
(b) instilled
(c) instigated
(d) instructed

22. The man _____ in court that he had seen the defendant fleeing from the scene of the crime.

(a) verified
(b) vouched
(c) deposed
(d) testified

23. Not wanting to take sides, I decided to remain _____ in their argument.

(a) serene
(b) neutral
(c) upright
(d) deficient

24. At this restaurant, the meals take a _____ to the decor.

(a) deaf ear
(b) lesson
(c) backseat
(d) blue moon

25. You cannot copy the information from your sources _____ without citing them in your essay.

(a) inadvertently
(b) literally
(c) offhand
(d) verbatim

26. Increased hostilities between the two nations could _____ another war in the region.

(a) mediate
(b) trigger
(c) embark
(d) torture

27. Chameleons have the unusual _____ of being able to change their body color to match their surroundings.

(a) instinct
(b) adaptation
(c) motive
(d) phenomenon

28. The demand for the new video game console continues to _____ its supply, with millions of units flying off store shelves around the nation.

(a) overarch
(b) outstrip
(c) overturn
(d) outreach

29. This acid is able to _____ metal, so handle it with extreme caution.

(a) resolve
(b) absolve
(c) dissolve
(d) solve

30. Ever since I was a child, I enjoyed listening to my grandfather _____ on about stories from his childhood.

(a) grumble
(b) ramble
(c) scribble
(d) embellish

You have finished the Vocabulary questions. Please continue on to the Grammar questions.

Part I **Questions 1-10**

Choose the option that best completes each dialogue.

1. A: Andy claims that he is helping for my own sake.

   B: I doubt that. I'm sure he has other _____.

   (a) unions
   (b) suggestions
   (c) motives
   (d) adaptations

2. A: I'm glad that all our classes are finally over for the semester.

   B: For sure. Now, let's kick up our _____ and have some fun.

   (a) heels
   (b) socks
   (c) shoes
   (d) feet

3. A: Pardon me. Do I have to pay extra for the toiletries in my room?

   B: No, ma'am. They are _____.

   (a) extraordinary
   (b) complimentary
   (c) necessary
   (d) unrestrained

4. A: Honey, can you come here and help me _____ these groceries?

   B: No problem, dear.

   (a) make up
   (b) empty out
   (c) put away
   (d) look around

5. A: Where should I put these old magazines?

   B: Just _____ them up in the corner over there, please.

   (a) stock
   (b) alter
   (c) neglect
   (d) pile

6. A: Jacky, come here and look at this article. It's hilarious.

   B: Please don't _____ me. I'm trying to study.

   (a) scorn
   (b) distract
   (c) mourn
   (d) testify

7. A: Do we need any special equipment to see the comet, such as a telescope?

   B: I don't believe so. It should be _____ to the naked eye.

   (a) fluid
   (b) prominent
   (c) obscured
   (d) visible

8. A: This year's crop has been very poor.

   B: You're right, but that's the _____ outcome in a year with little rainfall.

   (a) enviable
   (b) inevitable
   (c) intangible
   (d) ineligible

9. A: How much farther is it to the next gas station?

   B: The sign said 30 miles, but I'm afraid that we'll _____ gas before then.

   (a) run out of
   (b) break out of
   (c) put up with
   (d) face up to

10. A: Whoa, be careful. If you step on a crack, you'll break your mother's back.

    B: Don't be silly. That's just a _____.

    (a) curiosity
    (b) fallacy
    (c) tongue twister
    (d) superstition

Part II Questions 11-30

Choose the option that best completes each sentence.

11. Due to the complex nature of the problem, a _____ solution is needed.

(a) ludicrous
(b) flagitious
(c) haphazard
(d) multifaceted

12. When frightened, a skunk _____ a powerful odor used to ward off predators.

(a) permits
(b) emits
(c) disposes
(d) contaminates

13. The _____ supermodel married the elderly billionaire in the hope of someday inheriting his vast estate.

(a) felicitous
(b) convivial
(c) morose
(d) avaricious

14. Our environmental group works to _____ sites that have been contaminated by industrial waste.

(a) ban
(b) navigate
(c) disinfect
(d) reclaim

15. Singapore is the pride of Southeast Asia with its glittering skyline and _____ economy.

(a) robust
(b) faultless
(c) misleading
(d) stark

16. Years of hostilities between the two groups _____ this morning as fighting broke out.

(a) turned a deaf ear
(b) jumped on the bandwagon
(c) came to a head
(d) bit the bullet

17. The stem cell research of the scientists has led to a _____ in AIDS treatment.

(a) breakthrough
(b) landmark
(c) milestone
(d) signpost

18. Hurricane Isabelle was _____ to a tropical storm after making landfall at dawn this morning.

(a) downgraded
(b) updated
(c) overturned
(d) renounced

19. Should you discover a _____ with our product, please return it to the following address for a complete refund.

(a) compliance
(b) component
(c) defect
(d) display

20. Prior to developing farms, our ancestors lived as hunter-gatherers who _____ for their meals.

(a) abandoned
(b) grazed
(c) scraped
(d) foraged

21. While sending text messages on her cell phone, Jenny became _____ to her surroundings.

(a) oblivious
(b) obsequious
(c) obsessive
(d) obvious

22. For years, the cigarette industry _____ consumers by having them believe that smoking is a harmless activity.

(a) misled
(b) facilitated
(c) prosecuted
(d) insulted

23. My brother was _____ child, preferring to play with dolls rather than toy cars.

(a) a bitter
(b) an odd
(c) a hyper
(d) a ripe

24. Visitors are _____ from taking photographs inside the exhibition.

(a) prohibited
(b) implored
(c) compelled
(d) tortured

25. For years, doctors have warned against _____ prescribing antibiotics as this allows viruses to become resistant to the drugs.

(a) rashly
(b) belatedly
(c) prudently
(d) frivolously

26. To open a bank account, you must be able to _____ your identity with a driver's license, birth certificate, or passport.

(a) testify
(b) verify
(c) nullify
(d) quantify

27. According to the most recent _____, the population of the city has decreased by nearly 10 percent.

(a) censure
(b) census
(c) consent
(d) consensus

28. I think I bit off more than I can _____ when I enrolled in 7 classes this semester.

(a) chew
(b) swallow
(c) taste
(d) handle

29. Today, I would like to _____ into a new topic of discussion: the Magna Carta.

(a) relinquish
(b) instigate
(c) scour
(d) delve

30. The health inspector was so _____ that she checked every possible nook and cranny for signs of contamination.

(a) meticulous
(b) repugnant
(c) hedonistic
(d) blunt

You have finished the Vocabulary questions. Please continue on to the Grammar questions.

Part I **Questions 1-10**
Choose the option that best completes each dialogue.

1. A: Do you still sell the double bacon
   cheeseburger? I don't see it on your menu.
   B: I'm sorry, sir, but we have _____ that
   item.

   (a) kept up with
   (b) come over to
   (c) given up on
   (d) done away with

2. A: That was a great Fourth of July
   celebration, wasn't it?
   B: It certainly was. I especially enjoyed the
   fireworks _____ at the end.

   (a) stain   (b) assault
   (c) display   (d) chaos

3. A: According to our most recent surveys,
   over half of our customers are male.
   B: Oh really? That _____ a major change in
   our market.

   (a) maximizes   (b) represents
   (c) incorporates   (d) downsizes

4. A: Doctor, I'm suffering from _____ back
   pain. Is there anything I can do to relive it?
   B: Have you tried wearing a back brace? That
   will help reduce the strain on your lower
   back.

   (a) extensive
   (b) habitual
   (c) routine
   (d) chronic

5. A: Excuse me. Could you please _____
   from smoking inside the restaurant?
   B: I'm sorry. I didn't know that smoking's
   not allowed.

   (a) compel
   (b) disassemble
   (c) refrain
   (d) hesitate

6. A: Why don't we play the board game you
   brought, Tim?
   B: I don't think we have enough people here.
   The game requires a _____ of 4 players.

   (a) minimum   (b) possession
   (c) riot   (d) novelty

7. A: It must have been difficult to get Drake's
   input on the project.
   B: Not at all. He _____ agreed to help us.

   (a) readily
   (b) painstakingly
   (c) begrudgingly
   (d) pointedly

8. A: How does the defense respond in light of
   these new allegations?
   B: Your honor, please allow me to _____
   with my client before making our plea.

   (a) retaliate
   (b) unearth
   (c) enlist
   (d) confer

9. A: I'm tempted by your proposal, but it
   sounds too good to be true.
   B: Ma'am, I guarantee you that my offer is
   genuine with no _____ attached.

   (a) ropes
   (b) knots
   (c) strings
   (d) lines

10. A: My wife and I have been thinking about
    getting a dog.
    B: Then why don't you get a collie? They are
    very friendly and _____ companions.

    (a) loyal
    (b) predictable
    (c) aggressive
    (d) lenient

Choose the option that best completes each sentence.

11. All students must _____ the general education requirements in order to graduate from the university.

    (a) unveil
    (b) uphold
    (c) kindle
    (d) fulfill

12. Whenever I visit a foreign country, I like to _____ myself in the nation's culture.

    (a) detain
    (b) immerse
    (c) encourage
    (d) recall

13. Feminists object to the media's _____ of women as helpless and subservient to men.

    (a) graduation
    (b) confirmation
    (c) portrayal
    (d) skepticism

14. The World Weightlifting Federation has _____ bench shirts because they give their wearers an unfair advantage.

    (a) excluded
    (b) omitted
    (c) precluded
    (d) banned

15. Kelly's enthusiasm is _____ and causes everybody to share her intensity.

    (a) overwhelming
    (b) contagious
    (c) sentimental
    (d) impeccable

16. When Jim comes over for dinner, we never have any leftovers because he _____.

    (a) eats like a horse
    (b) has his cake and eats it too
    (c) bite the dust
    (d) clears the table

17. Living abroad is an excellent way to see more of the world and _____ your horizons.

    (a) restrict
    (b) naturalize
    (c) uphold
    (d) broaden

18. The _____ of married men and women have changed in recent years, with an increasing number of husbands staying at home to raise the children.

    (a) sections
    (b) roles
    (c) tasks
    (d) ranks

19. My driver's license _____ in a month, so I'll have to go to the DMV soon to renew it.

    (a) expires
    (b) concludes
    (c) perishes
    (d) dies off

20. We will use this computer model to _____ the effects of the drug on the human body.

    (a) relish
    (b) restore
    (c) simulate
    (d) expel

21. Hybrid cars are an _____ means of transportation as they use up to 70 percent less fuel than traditional automobiles.

   (a) economic
   (b) absolute
   (c) economical
   (d) obsolete

22. Please note that the front entrance will be locked after 8 a.m., so it is essential that you are _____ for class.

   (a) immediate
   (b) punctual
   (c) delinquent
   (d) seasonable

23. The company has decided to _____ a new employee training program to ensure that all personnel keep abreast of the latest industry developments.

   (a) activate
   (b) enforce
   (c) implement
   (d) operate

24. A section of the Bay Bridge _____ into the water during rush hour traffic this morning and seriously injured dozens of commuters.

   (a) ascended
   (b) disturbed
   (c) subsided
   (d) collapsed

25. The government has _____ restrictions on the amount of money private companies are allowed to donate to political campaigns.

   (a) threatened
   (b) penalized
   (c) imposed
   (d) gouged

26. Just a scant few generations ago, it was not considered _____ for young couples to hold hands in public.

   (a) lucid
   (b) typical
   (c) proper
   (d) habitual

27. Health officials are urged to _____ citizens against the flu in order to prevent another outbreak.

   (a) inoculate
   (b) innovate
   (c) innocuous
   (d) inculpate

28. To correct a child's misbehavior, punishment must be _____ immediately after the negative behavior has occurred.

   (a) diagnosed
   (b) prescribed
   (c) sanctioned
   (d) administered

29. Here at Global Dynamics, we value employees who do not just follow the herd but can _____.

   (a) go by the book
   (b) think outside the box
   (c) step out of line
   (d) take a shot in the dark

30. Some simple ways for your family to help protect the environment include taking public transportation and _____ using water and electricity.

   (a) nocturnally
   (b) judiciously
   (c) vicariously
   (d) heedlessly

You have finished the Vocabulary questions. Please continue on to the Grammar questions.

신유형 분석 반영!

뉴텝스 최강 실전대비서!

NEW TEPS Research Team

문법·어휘

정답 및 해설

더 뉴텝스 **실전연습**
500

다락원

문법
Grammar

Section 1

시험에 가장 자주 출제되는
Grammar Point

Unit 1 어순

Check-up TEST 01~02

1	(b)	2	(a)	3	(b)	4	(c)	5	(c)
6	(d)	7	(b)	8	(c)	9	(a)	10	(c)

1 (b)

해석 A: 서두르는 게 좋을걸. 시간이 별로 없어.
　　B: 가고 있어.

해설 enough가 형용사로 사용되어 명사를 수식하면 명사 바로 앞에 위치한다. '충분한 시간'을 의미하므로 enough time이 옳으며 부정어 not은 be동사 뒤에 온다.

어구 **had better** ~하는 것이 낫다

2 (a)

해석 A: 이 프로젝트가 언제 마무리가 될지 확실히 말씀 못 드리겠어요.
　　B: 제가 듣기로는 조만간 끝날 거라던데요.

해설 간접 의문문이므로 「의문사＋주어＋동사」 형식을 취하면 된다.

어구 **for sure** 확실히　　**complete** 완성시키다, 마무리하다
come to an end 끝나다, 마무리되다

3 (b)

해석 정부가 경제를 다시 살리기 위해 다음에 무엇을 할지 예측하기 어렵다.

해설 간접 의문문이므로 「의문사＋주어＋동사」 어순을 취하면 된다.

어구 **predict** 예측하다　　**revive** 회생시키다, 다시 살리다

4 (c)

해석 지금까지 존재해 왔던 가장 큰 육식성 유대류 동물은 유대류 사자였을 것이다.

해설 ever는 최상급 바로 다음에 붙어서 '그 동안 가장 ~해온'의 의미를 나타낸다. carnivorous나 marsupial이 다소 어려운 단어이긴 하지만 어순 문제이기 때문에 ever의 위치만 정확히 안다면 답을 쉽게 찾을 수 있다.

어구 **carnivorous** 육식성의　　**marsupial** 유대류 동물(코알라, 캥거루처럼 배에 주머니를 가지고 있는 동물), 유대류 동물의

5 (c)

해석 (a) A: 잠깐 뭔가를 깜박한 것 같아.
　　(b) B: 빨리 해. 서둘러야 해.
　　(c) A: 알아. 내가 자동차 키를 어디에 뒀는지 모르겠단 말이야.

(d) B: 또 시작이다. 네 건망증에는 정말 진절머리가 나.

해설 (c)의 간접 의문문을 보면 동사 know가 사용되었기 때문에 「의문사＋주어＋동사」 어순을 지켜야 한다. I don't know where did I put을 I don't know where I put으로 바꿔야 한다.

어구 **in a hurry** 서둘러서　　**There you go again.** 또 저런다. 또 시작이야.　　**be sick and tired of** 진절머리 나다
forgetfulness 건망증

6 (d)

해석 (a) A: 어떤 사람들은 낙태를 금지하길 원하는데 이것은 터무니없는 일이라고 생각해.
　　(b) B: 아마도 그와 같은 명분을 지지하는 나름의 합당한 이유가 있겠지.
　　(c) A: 네가 낙태 반대 운동을 지지한다고 말하는 것은 아니겠지.
　　(d) B: 아직 태어나지 않은 아기라 하더라도 주위를 감지할 의식이 충분히 있어.

해설 enough가 부사로 사용되어 형용사를 수식할 때는 형용사 바로 뒤에 위치한다. (d)에서 enough conscious가 아니라 conscious enough로 바꿔야 한다.

어구 **ban** 금지하다　　**abortion** 낙태　　**outrageous** 터무니없는
cause 대의명분; 원인　　**Don't tell me that** 설마 ~라고 말하려는 것은 아니겠지　　**in favor of** ~에 찬성하는
pro-life 낙태를 반대하는　　**conscious** 의식이 있는
sense 감지하다　　**surroundings** 주위, 환경

7 (b)

해석 (a) A: 인터넷이 아주 광범위하게 사용되고 있기 때문에 몸이 아픈 사람도 가까운 미래에 인터넷을 통해서 치료를 받을 수 있을 것 같아.
　　(b) B: 온라인 치료가 직접 대면해서 하는 치료를 대신할 수 있을 것 같지는 않아.
　　(c) A: 앞으로 몇 년 안에 인터넷 애플리케이션이 우리 일상생활에 더 큰 영향을 미칠 거라고 생각하지 않니?
　　(d) B: 분명히 그렇긴 하겠지. 하지만 우리가 사이버 치료를 누리려면 적어도 20년은 더 걸릴 거라고 생각해.

해설 ever의 위치는 조동사와 본동사 사이에 위치할 때 가장 자연스럽다. (b)의 ever will substitute를 will ever substitute로 바꿔야 한다.

어구 **in the foreseeable future** 가까운 미래에　　**therapy** 치료, 요법　　**substitute** 대체하다　　**face-to-face** 얼굴을 마주 대하는, 정면의　　**ramification** 영향, 여파　　**in the years to come** 향후 몇 년 내에　　**definitely** 명백히, 확실히

8 (c)

해석 (a) A: 오늘 아침 일찍 시큼한 냄새 때문에 깊은 잠에서 깨어났어.
　　(b) B: 그래서 그게 무슨 냄새인지 알아냈니?
　　(c) A: 무슨 냄새였을 것 같아? 스컹크 냄새였어.
　　(d) B: 냄새가 얼마나 고약했을지 추측도 못하겠구나.

해설 간접 의문문에 동사 think가 사용되었다. think / suppose / believe / guess / imagine이 사용되면 간접 의문문의 의문사가 문장 맨 앞으로 이동해야 한다. (c)는 Do you think what it was?가 아니라 What do you think it was?로 바꿔야 한다.

어구 **pungent** (냄새가) 시큼한, (냄새가) 탁 쏘는　**odor** 냄새　**figure out** 이해하다, 알아내다　**skunk** 스컹크　**fathom** 헤아리다, (깊이를) 측정하다

9 (a)

해석 (a) A: 이봐 제임스. 마리아가 어디 사는지 아니?
　　(b) B: 아니. 마리아한테 무슨 볼 일이 있는데?
　　(c) A: 마리아가 나한테 줄 게 있거든. 그런데 내가 그 애 전화번호를 잊어버렸어.
　　(d) B: 내가 전화번호를 알아. 네가 직접 전화해서 물어보는 게 좋겠다.

해설 간접 의문문의 어순을 묻는 문제이다. Do you know와 Where does Maria live?가 합쳐지면 「의문사 + 주어 + 동사」의 어순이 적절하다. 따라서 Where does Maria live?를 Where Maria lives?로 고쳐야 한다.

10 (c)

해석 (a) 세계에서 가장 우수한 대학 중 한 곳에서 졸업식 축사를 하게 되어 영광으로 생각합니다. (b) 여러분 중 일부는 아마도 내가 대학을 졸업하지 못했다는 사실을 알고 있을 겁니다. (c) 솔직히 말해서 지금이 제가 대학 졸업식장에 가장 가까이 온 순간이지요. (d) 저는 오늘 진심으로 드릴 말씀이 있기 때문에 여러분 앞에 서기로 결심했습니다.

해설 ever는 조동사 have와 본동사 gotten 사이에 위치하는 것이 자연스럽다. 따라서 (c)에서 ever have gotten보다는 have ever gotten이 되어야 옳다.

어구 **be privileged to V** ~하는 것을 특혜로 생각하다　**congratulatory speech** 축사　**commencement** 졸업식; 시작　**fine** 우수한, 훌륭한　**from the bottom of my heart** 내 가슴 깊은 곳에서, 진실로

══ Check-up TEST 03~04 ══

1	(d)	2	(d)	3	(c)	4	(b)	5	(a)
6	(d)	7	(c)	8	(b)	9	(c)	10	(d)

1 (d)

해석 A: 교과과정에서 가장 중요한 변화는 무엇이 될까요?
　　B: 검색 엔진을 사용하는 것이 읽기와 글쓰기만큼이나 필수적인 기술이 될 거예요.

해설 관사, 형용사, 명사가 as ~ as 사이에 위치할 때 어순은 「as + 형용사 + 관사 + 명사 + as」가 되어야 한다. 따라서 as essential a skill as가 적절하다.

어구 **curriculum** 교과과정　**search engine** (컴퓨터의) 검색 엔진　**essential** 필수적인

2 (d)

해석 A: 법원 판결이 너무나도 극적으로 끝나서 관련 당사자들이 어떻게 대응할지를 몰랐어요.
　　B: 당신 말이 맞아요. 난 피고의 자백 이후 더 이상의 놀라운

일은 예상하지 못했지요.

해설 so ~ that 사이에 관사, 형용사, 명사를 어떻게 배치해야 하는가를 묻는 문제이다. 「so + 형용사 + 관사 + 명사 + that」 어순으로 쓰면 된다.

어구 **ruling** 판결　**dramatic** 극적인　**ending** 종결, 결말; 대단원　**the parties concerned** 관련 당사자들　**defendant** 피고　**confession** 자백

3 (c)

해석 A: 그는 소설책을 3개월 일찍 출간한 후에 영화 한 편을 찍었어.
　　B: 그래? 그는 상당히 생산적인 한 해를 보냈구나.

해설 quite 뒤에 나오는 어순은 「관사 + 형용사 + 명사」이다. 따라서 quite a productive year가 옳은 표현이다.

어구 **publish** 출간하다　**productive** 생산적인

4 (b)

해석 정부는 이 법령이 변호사가 고객을 위해서 일할 때 어떤 것에나 적용시킬 만큼 광범위한 관련성을 가지고 있을 것이라고는 생각지 못했다.

해설 such ~ that 사이에 「관사 + 형용사 + 명사」 어순을 묻는 문제이다. such a broad relevance that이 맞다.

어구 **statute** 법령　**broad** 광범위한　**relevance** 관련성　**apply** 적용하다　**attorney** 변호사　**serve** 서비스를 제공하다

5 (a)

해석 고위급 군사 교류 중단은 너무나도 민감한 사안이어서 그냥 지나칠 수가 없다.

해설 too ~ to 용법에서 관사, 형용사, 명사를 배치할 경우 어순은 어떻게 되는지를 묻고 있다. 「too + 형용사 + 관사 + 명사 + to」 어순을 지키면 된다.

어구 **suspension** 중단　**high-level** 고위급의　**military exchange** 군사 교류　**sensitive** 민감한　**bypass** 우회하다, 지나치다

6 (d)

해석 그 약사는 암모니아 냄새만큼이나 강력한 냄새를 풍기는 알약병의 마개를 열었다.

해설 as ~ as 원급 비교에서 as와 as 사이에 관사, 형용사, 명사를 넣을 때 어순은 「as + 형용사 + 관사 + 명사 + as」 순이다. 따라서 as strong a smell as가 옳다.

7 (c)

해석 (a) A: ABC 프랜차이즈가 10개월간의 수리 끝에 재개장을 했어.
　　(b) B: 그 프랜차이즈 회사가 기존의 상품에다 더 많은 상품을 추가했다는 게 사실이니?
　　(c) A: 맞아. ABC 프랜차이즈에서 제공하는 상품은 범위가 아주 넓어서 이 회사가 시장을 장악하고 있어.
　　(d) B: 그래서 본사 정문에 사람들이 필요한 거의 모든 것을 다 판다는 현수막을 붙인 거구나.

해설 so ~ that 사이에 관사, 형용사, 명사가 오게 되면 그 어순을 「형용사 + 관사 + 명사」 순으로 맞춰야 한다. (c)에서 so a

4

wide range는 so wide a range that이 정확한 표현이다.

어구 **franchise** 프랜차이즈, 가맹 사업 **reopen** 재개장하다 **renovation** 수리; 개혁, 혁신 **product line** 상품군, 제품 라인 **existing** 기존의 **dominate** 장악하다 **headquarters** 본사

8 (b)
해석 (a) A: 앨리스가 말에서 떨어진 친구를 구했어.
(b) B: 어떻게 앨리스가 그렇게 영웅적인 행동을 취할 수 있었니?
(c) A: 앨리스는 한시도 지체하지 않고 친구가 회복 자세를 취하게 했고 도움을 요청했어.
(d) B: 나라면 그런 상황에서 냉정을 유지하기가 어려울 거야.

해설 (b)에서 such 다음에 취하는 어순은 「관사 + 형용사 + 명사」이다. 따라서 such a heroic action으로 고쳐야 한다.

어구 **heroic** 영웅의 **recovery** 회복 **call for help** 도움을 요청하다 **keep a cool head** 냉정을 유지하다

9 (c)
해석 (a) 헨리 카펜터는 가장 강력한 선수는 아니지만 경기에 이김으로써 그의 동료 앨리슨 호프만이 겪고 있던 끔찍한 부상에 대한 복수를 한 셈이다. (b) 호프만은 아스날과의 경기에서 팔이 부러지기 전까지는 게임당 2.5골을 기록하고 있었다. (c) 너무나도 끔찍한 부상이어서 호프만의 팀은 남은 경기 내내 현저하게 불안한 모습을 보였다. (d) 하지만 헨리 카펜터는 이 기회를 놓치지 않았고 호프만을 위해 2골을 기록했다.

해설 so ~ that 구문은 「형용사 + 관사 + 명사」 어순을 취해야 한다. (c)의 so an injury gruesome that을 so gruesome an injury that으로 바꿔야 한다.

어구 **avenge** 복수하다 **hideous** 끔찍한 **score** 득점을 기록하다 **gruesome** 으스스한, 무서운; 고된, 고통스러운 **noticeably** 현저하게 **unsteady** 불안정한

10 (d)
해석 (a) 예술에 관해서 변하지 않는 것이 한 가지 있다면, 되풀이되는 표현 양식의 사용은 미적 피로감에 이르게 한다는 사실이다. (b) 뉴욕과 같이 관념적으로 과감한 현대 예술 회랑으로 가득한 도시는 현대적 스타일과 거리를 두어야 한다. (c) 당신은 어쩌면 오리엔탈 갤러리에서 편안함을 찾길 원할 수도 있겠다. (d) 이곳에서는 매우 섬세한 동아시아 그림전을 열고 있다.

해설 quite 뒤에는 「관사 + 형용사 + 명사」 어순이 와야 하며, 관사가 quite 앞에 놓일 수 없다. 따라서 (d)의 the quite meticulous presentation을 quite a meticulous presentation으로 바꿔야 한다.

어구 **recurring** 되풀이되는 **mode** 방법, 방식, 양식 **aesthetic** 심미적인, 미적인 **fatigue** 피로 **inundated with** ~로 넘쳐나는 **notionally** 관념적으로 **bold** 과감한 **corridor** 복도, 회랑 **separate** 분리하다 **contemporary** 동시대의 **host** 주최하다, (행사를) 열다 **meticulous** 세심한, 완벽한

▬ Check-up TEST 05~06 ▬

1	(d)	2	(c)	3	(b)	4	(a)	5	(a)
6	(a)	7	(b)	8	(c)	9	(a)	10	(d)

1 (d)
해석 A: 가브리엘은 지난 3년간 축구팀 주장으로 활약해 왔어.
B: 그렇지. 그는 항상 경기에서 가장 힘든 포지션 중 하나를 맡을 운명인 것 같았어.

해설 빈도부사 always는 조동사 has와 본동사 seemed 사이에 위치한다. has always seemed가 올바른 표현이다.

어구 **serve** 역할을 다하다; ~에 봉사하다 **captain** 주장 **be meant for** ~이 되도록 예정하다, ~이 될 운명이다 **demanding** 힘든, 지치게 하는

2 (c)
해석 A: 다음 절차가 뭔지 알려주세요.
B: 다음으로 해야 할 일은 소금을 첨가하면서 얼음이 천천히 녹게 하는 거야.

해설 동사 let 뒤에 목적어를 쓰고 이어서 동사원형을 써야 한다. let the ice gradually melt가 올바른 표현이다.

어구 **procedure** 절차 **gradually** 점차적으로 **add** 추가하다, 첨가하다 **melt** 녹다

3 (b)
해석 A: 어떻게 소비자로 하여금 비닐 봉투가 아닌 재활용 봉투를 사용하게 하시나요?
B: 우리는 친환경 봉투를 가져 오시는 쇼핑객들에게 할인을 아주 많이 해드리지요.

해설 사역동사 get은 목적어와 동사의 관계가 능동일 때 「get + 목적어 + to동사원형」 형태를 취해서 '목적어로 하여금 ~하게 하다'의 뜻을 나타낸다.

어구 **recycled** 재활용된 **plastic bag** 비닐 봉투 **eco-friendly** 친환경적인

4 (a)
해석 테러리스트가 자기의 본성을 나타내지 않는 한, 우리는 권총을 소지한 여객기 보안요원이 옆에 앉아 있는지 결코 알 수 없을 것이다.

해설 never는 빈도부사로 조동사 would와 본동사 realize 사이에 위치해야 한다.

어구 **air marshal** 여객기 보안 요원 **handgun** 권총 **show one's true colors** 본성을 드러내다; 의도한 바를 보이다

5 (a)
해석 세이브 워터 재단에 따르면 일부 국가의 경우 옥수수, 쌀, 밀을 비롯하여 농산물에 대한 보조금을 삭감하는 것이 농가로 하여금 물을 덜 낭비하게 하는 효과적인 방법이라고 말한다.

해설 동사 get이 사역동사로 사용되었고 농가가 물을 덜 쓰도록 하는 것이므로 「get + 목적어 + to동사원형」 형태를 취해야 한다. 따라서 get farms to waste less water가 적절하다. 여기서 목적어인 farms는 농장이 아니라 농업에 종사하는 농가

로 보는 것이 의미상 자연스럽다.

어구 **foundation** 재단 **subsidy** 보조금 **agricultural** 농업의 **corn** 옥수수 **wheat** 밀

6 (a)

해석 (a) A: 제 보험료를 어떻게 산정하나요?
(b) B: 대형 보험회사의 보험을 가지고 계시다면 보험료 산정 이전에 연간보험의 고지서 사본을 준비해두세요.
(c) A: 가족 전체의 적정 보험료를 계산하고 싶으면 어떻게 하면 되죠?
(d) B: 주 공인 담당관에게 연락해서 거주하시는 주의 공인 회계사 리스트를 받으시면 됩니다.

해설 (a)에서 get이 사역동사로 사용되었고 목적어인 my insurance premium이 보험료 산정을 '당하는' 수동적인 입장이다. 그러므로 get my insurance premium assess가 아니라 get my insurance premium assessed로 표현해야 한다.

어구 **insurance** 보험 **premium** 보험료 **assess** 평가하다, 산정하다 **corporation** 기업 **copy** 사본 **calculate** 계산하다 **figure out** 계산하다; 알아내다 **state** 주 (미국의 행정 단위) **certification** 공인 **certified accountant** 공인 회계사

7 (b)

해석 (a) A: 여기서 무슨 일이 일어났나요? 차로 가로등을 박은 거예요?
(b) B: 가로등은 가까스로 피했지만 벽 옆에 주차되어 있던 차를 들이받았어요.
(c) A: 괜찮으세요? 병원에 가시도록 도와드릴게요.
(d) B: 전 괜찮아요. 휴대폰 가지고 계시면 경찰에 전화 좀 해주실 수 있을까요?

해설 (b)에서 빈도부사 barely는 본동사 managed 앞에 위치해야 한다. managed barely가 아니라 barely managed로 바꿔야 한다.

어구 **streetlight** 가로등 **manage to V** (그럭저럭) ~하게 되다 **run into** (차가) ~와 충돌하다

8 (c)

해석 (a) A: ABC 메디컬 센터의 제인 맥도날드입니다. 조나단 카펜터 씨와 통화할 수 있을까요?
(b) B: 지금 안 계시는데요. 메시지를 남기시겠습니까?
(c) A: 테스트 결과가 나왔습니다. 가능한 한 빨리 저에게 전화해 달라고 해 주시겠어요?
(d) B: 저에게 결과를 알려주셔도 되는데요. 저는 그 사람 아내인 릴리라고 합니다.

해설 (c)의 have him calling에서 have는 사역동사로 사용되었다. 즉, 그에게 전화를 하라고 시키는 것이고 전화를 하는 행위는 능동이다. 따라서 「have + 목적어 + 동사원형」 형태로 써야 한다.

어구 **at the moment** 지금 현재로는 **leave a message** 메시지를 남기다

9 (a)

해석 (a) 현 금융 위기의 실제 규모를 고려해 본다면 3,000억 달러 규모의 경기 부양책은 어떠한 가치도 없는 셈이다. (b) 더 큰

금융 위기가 닥쳐오고 있다. (c) 심지어 천문학적인 규모의 구제 자금도 현 위기 상황에 영향을 거의 미치지 못할 것이다. (d) 실제로 경제학자들은 최근 몇 달 사이에 끔찍한 금융 재난이 닥쳐오고 있다는 많은 징후를 포착했다.

해설 빈도부사 hardly는 be동사 다음에 위치해야 한다. 따라서 (a)의 hardly is worth anything을 is hardly worth anything으로 바꿔야 한다.

어구 **stimulus package** 경기 부양책 **compared with** ~와 비교해 봤을 때 **financial crisis** 금융 위기 **loom** 어렴풋이 나타나다; 거대한 모습을 나타내다 **astronomical** 천문학적인 **bailout money** 구제자금 **put a dent** 손상을 가하다 **spot** 포착하다 **monstrous** 끔찍한 **coming** 곧 있을, 다가오는

10 (d)

해석 (a) 에이즈 발병률이 제자리를 유지하고 있다. (b) 에이즈와의 전쟁이 계속되는 가운데 새로운 치료법이 절실히 요구되고 있다. (c) 돌연변이 유전자를 공격하는 방법은 제한된 결과만을 보였다. (d) 돌연변이 유전자는 손상을 입으면 다른 유전자가 그 자리를 대신하게 한다.

해설 사역동사 let은 「let + 목적어 + 동사원형」 어순을 취한다. lets others to take over를 lets others take over로 고쳐야 한다.

어구 **incidence** (사건·질병 따위의) 발생 비율; 출현 **flat** 평평한; (상태가) 제자리인 **approach** 접근법, 치료법 **mutated** 돌연변이가 된 **gene** 유전자 **limited** 제한된, 한정된 **impair** 손상시키다 **take over** (~의 자리를) 차지하다, 점령하다

▬ Check-up TEST 07~08

1	(a)	2	(c)	3	(b)	4	(d)	5	(a)
6	(b)	7	(c)	8	(a)	9	(b)	10	(a)

1 (a)

해석 A: 앨리슨이 금메달을 따기 전까진 굳이 피겨 스케이팅 경기를 보려는 사람이 거의 없었어.
B: 맞아. 금메달을 따는 것이 스포츠의 전부일까?

해설 부정 의미의 부사 seldom이 문두에 위치하면 주어와 조동사는 도치된다. 따라서 Seldom had anyone bothered가 올바른 표현이다.

어구 **seldom** 좀처럼 ~않는; 드물게 **competition** 경기, 경쟁 **bother to V** 일부러 ~하다, ~하려고 애쓰다

2 (c)

해석 A: 자기네 팀이 이기고 있는데 왜 관중들이 별로 안 좋아하는 것처럼 보이지?
B: 이 경기가 어떻게 끝이 나든지 간에 뉴욕 양키스 팀은 또한 차례 부진한 시즌을 맞게 되는 셈이라서 관중들이 야유를 하고 있는 거야.

해설 「no matter + 의문사 + 주어 + 동사」 양보구문이다. no matter how this game ends up으로 표현해야 한다.

어구 **spectator** 관중 **hiss** 야유하다 **on the way to** ~으로 향하고 있는 **yet another** 또 한 차례 **underperforming**

저조한 경기력

3 (b)

해석 미셀 톰슨은 입법 위원회의 위원장으로는 최적임자가 아니었다.

해설 본래 문장은 Michelle Thomson was hardly the best choice ~지만 hardly를 문두로 빼면 주어와 be동사는 도치된다. 따라서 Hardly was Michelle Thomson ~이 올바른 표현이다.

어구 **chairman** 위원장　**legislation** 입법　**the best choice** 최적임자; 최고의 선택

4 (d)

해석 그녀는 조류독감 발생 가능성을 상향 조정하자마자 과학자들로부터 연구 결과를 받았다.

해설 「No sooner had + 주어 + p.p. ~ than + 주어 + 과거동사」구문을 확실히 외우도록 하자. 시험에 어순 문제로 곧잘 출제된다.

어구 **aviation influenza** 조류독감　**outbreak** 발발, 발생

5 (a)

해석 새의 생체 시스템은 새가 지구상 어디에 있다 하더라도 집으로 가는 길을 찾아올 수 있도록 설계되어 있다.

해설 「no matter + 의문사 + 주어 + 동사」양보구문 문제이다. 앞에 언급된 birds를 대명사 they로 받아 no matter where they are로 표현하면 된다.

어구 **biological** 생체의, 생물의　**be wired to V** ~하도록 설계되다

6 (b)

해석 포괄적인 안건이기는 했지만, 그 안건 때문에 전쟁으로 폐허가 된 아프리카 국가의 외교적 상황에 대해 심도 있는 토론을 할 수 없었다.

해설 「형용사 + as + 주어 + 동사」양보구문이다. 따라서 Broad as it was가 맞다.

어구 **broad** 광범위한, (범위가) 넓은　**agenda** 안건　**prevent + A + from + V-ing** A가 ~하는 것을 못하게 하다　**in-depth** 심층적인　**diplomatic** 외교의, 외교적인　**war-torn** 전쟁으로 폐허가 된

7 (c)

해석 (a) A: 과학자들이 시베리아 호랑이의 새로운 서식지를 발견했어.
　　(b) B: 정말? 내가 알기론 시베리아 호랑이 종은 영국의 탐험가 알렉산더 랭스턴에 의해 1312년에 최초로 발견되었어.
　　(c) A: 맞아. 랭스턴은 기대에 부풀었지만 전 세계에서 가장 큰 그 고양잇과 동물은 14세기 동안에는 연구된 적이 없었어.
　　(d) B: 사람들은 이 종이 파괴적인 시베리아 산불 후에도 여전히 생존했는지 아닌지 몰랐어.

해설 「형용사 + as + 주어 + 동사」양보구문을 묻는 문제이다. (c)의 의미를 보면 '~이긴 했지만'이라는 양보의 의미이므로 Hopeful as Langston had been으로 써야 한다.

어구 **habit** 서식지　**species** (동식물의) 종　**explorer** 탐험가　**devastating** 파괴적인　**wildfire** 산불

8 (a)

해석 (a) A: 데이지의 컴백 콘서트가 끝나자마자 또 다른 스캔들이 터졌어.
　　(b) B: 이번에는 데이지가 어떻게 대응했니?
　　(c) A: 침묵을 깨고 사실을 부인했어.
　　(d) B: 불쌍하게 됐어. 또 언론의 도마 위에 올랐군.

해설 No sooner가 문두에 위치하게 되면 주어와 had는 도치되어야 한다. (a)의 No sooner Daisy had finished를 No sooner had Daisy finished로 고쳐야 한다.

어구 **unfold** 사건이 터지다, 사건이 전개되다　**break one's silence** 침묵을 깨다　**deny** 부인하다　**spotlight** 조명, 스포트라이트

9 (b)

해석 (a) A: 그동안 정원에서 키웠던 나무와 꽃을 모두 다 남겨두고 떠나려니 슬퍼.
　　(b) B: 사진이라도 찍어두지 그래? 과거의 추억을 떠올리는 데는 사진을 보는 것 만한 게 없잖아.
　　(c) A: 그래야겠어. 사진들을 꺼내 보면서 이 정원이 내 인생에서 얼마나 멋진 부분을 차지하고 있었는지 떠올릴 수 있을 거야.
　　(d) B: 아이들이 타고 놀던 저 단풍나무가 그리워지겠지.

해설 (b)의 두 번째 문장에서 부정 부사 hardly가 문두에 쓰였기 때문에 주어 there와 동사 is의 위치가 바뀌어야 한다. 따라서 Hardly there is를 Hardly is there로 고쳐야 한다. 또는 도치구문이 아니라 원래의 일반적인 어순으로 써서 There is hardly a better way ~ 라고 해도 된다.

어구 **leave behind** 남겨두고 떠나다　**bring back a memory** 기억을 되살리다, 추억을 일깨우다　**maple tree** 단풍나무　**climb** 타다, 오르다

10 (a)

해석 (a) 자산 대비 부채 비율이 아무리 높다 할지라도 은행의 위기관리 능력은 소비자 보호를 보장한다. (b) 적정 수준의 자산 대비 부채 비율을 유지하지 못할 경우 위험하고 불안정한 재무 상태에 이를 수도 있다. (c) 그러나 우리의 대출 비율은 대차대조표 관리에 부정적인 영향을 미치지 않을 것이다. (d) 위기관리를 책임지고 있는 이사진은 소비자를 보호하기 위해 새로운 전략을 마련했다.

해설 「No matter + 의문사 + 주어 + 동사」양보구문에서 약간 변형된 유형이다. No matter how로 사용될 경우 형용사와 부사는 주어, 동사 뒤에 위치하지 않고 의문사 how 뒤에 온다. 그래서 「No matter how + 부사 / 형용사 + 주어 + 동사」형태가 된다.

어구 **ratio** 비율　**loan** 부채　**asset** 자산　**risk management** 위기관리　**capacity** 능력　**ensure** 확실하게 하다, 보장하다　**unsound** 건전하지 못한; (경제적·재정적으로) 견실하지 못한　**financial status** 재무 상태　**lending** 대출　**adverse effect** 역효과, 부정적인 영향　**balance sheet** 대차대조표　**board of directors** 이사회　**strategy** 전략

1	(d)	2	(d)	3	(b)	4	(b)	5	(d)
6	(a)	7	(d)	8	(c)	9	(a)	10	(d)

1 (d)

해석 A: 해리는 그의 작품이 전시될 미술 전람회를 놓치지 말라고 우리에게 당부했어.
B: 내 스케줄이 어떤지 좀 살펴볼게.

해설 「urge + 목적어 + to부정사」 형태로 쓰며, to부정사를 부정하려면 to 바로 앞에 not을 쓴다.

어구 art exhibition 미술 전람회　display 전시하다

2 (d)

해석 A: 토미가 그녀에게 데이트 신청을 할 거라고 우리에게 말했어.
B: 난 그녀가 그와 데이트를 하길 바라.

해설 대명사 her는 구동사 ask out 사이에 위치해야 한다. 대명사는 반드시 「동사 + 전치사」, 「동사 + 부사」 사이에 위치해야 한다.

어구 ask ~ out ~에게 데이트를 신청하다　go on a date 데이트하다

3 (b)

해석 나는 한 번도 선거에서 투표를 해본 적이 없었음에도 불구하고 이번 화요일에 있을 대통령 선거에 참여하라고 적극적으로 캠페인을 벌이고 있었다.

해설 Despite는 전치사이므로 뒤에 명사나 동명사가 와야 한다. 동명사를 부정하려면 바로 앞에 부정어인 not이나 never를 쓰면 된다.

어구 actively 적극적으로　campaign (선거) 운동하다, 캠페인을 벌이다　turn out 나타나다　presidential election 대통령 선거

4 (b)

해석 인도에 본사를 두고 있는 그 금융 기관은 학생들에게 돈을 빌려줄 때 너무나도 무차별적이어서 회수할 수 없는 대출금과 잠재적으로 채무 불이행 소지가 있는 고객들을 떠안게 되었다.

해설 원래 문장은 The Indian-based financial institution was so indiscriminate that~이다. So ~ that 부분을 도치하여 내용상 indiscriminate를 더욱 강조하는 문장이므로 So indiscriminate was the Indian-based financial institution that~으로 쓰는 것이 옳다.

어구 indiscriminate 무차별적인　-based (본사가) ~에 위치한　financial institution 금융기관　credit 신용 대출[판매], 외상; 대출 금액; 예금(액)　unrecoverable 회수할 수 없는　loan 대출　potentially 잠재적으로　insolvent 채무 불이행의

5 (d)

해석 대통령의 연설이 너무나도 대단했기 때문에 나는 아직도 연설에서 그가 한 모든 말을 다 기억한다.

해설 원래 문장은 the president's speech was so incredible that I still remember each and every word he said in it.이다. 이 문장에서 so incredible의 의미를 강조하기 위해 문두에 두면 주어, 동사가 도치되어야 하므로 So incredible was the president's speech that ~이 되어야 옳다.

어구 incredible 대단한

6 (a)

해석 톰은 이전에 책을 많이 읽지 않았기 때문에 교과서를 읽을 때 그의 급우들보다 시간이 더 많이 필요하다.

해설 선택지에 공통적으로 들어가 있는 having read many books는 완료분사구문이다. 분사구문에서 부정 처리를 하려면 not이나 never를 분사구문 앞에 붙이면 된다.

어구 classmate 급우

7 (d)

해석 (a) A: 뱀파이어와 악마와의 전쟁이 일어난 후에 방영된 오늘 이야기는 어떻게 됐니?
(b) B: 뱀파이어 왕국의 왕자인 헨리가 어둠 속에 사는 것이 지겨워서 백만 년을 더 기다리겠다는 약속을 저버리고 판도라의 상자를 열어버렸어.
(c) A: 그러면 풀려난 악마들이 헨리를 죽였니?
(d) B: 악마가 기도의 방으로 들어오려고 하면 안으로 들여보내지 말라고 헬레나가 헨리에게 말했던 거 기억나?

해설 to부정사를 부정하려면 not이나 never를 to부정사 바로 앞에 둔다. 따라서 (d)의 to not let을 not to let으로 바꿔야 한다.

어구 break out 발발하다, 발생하다　vampire 뱀파이어　demon 악마　abandon (계획·목적 따위를) 단념하다, 포기하다　open Pandora's Box 판도라의 상자를 열다, 문제를 야기시키다　free ~을 (…에서) 자유롭게 하다, 해방[석방]하다　prayer 기도

8 (c)

해석 (a) 새로운 버스 전용차선은 버스 기사들에게 자동차 통행금지 노선보다 더 많은 불편을 주었다. (b) 버스 전용 차선은 주차된 차와 길거리 노점상들로 가득 메워졌다. (c) 이 문제를 해결하기 위한 시도로 시 당국은 검은색 페인트로 버스 전용 차선을 지워버렸다. (d) 그러나 버스 기사들과 보행자들이 수없이 불평을 제기함에 따라 상황을 걷잡을 수 없어졌다.

해설 (c)에서 cross out은 구동사이고 목적어로 it(= bus-only lane)이 사용되었다. 목적어가 대명사이면 구동사 사이에 들어가야 하므로 crossed out it이 아니라 crossed it out으로 바꿔야 한다.

어구 bus-only lane 버스 전용차선　inconvenience 불편함　car-free route 자동차가 없는[자동차 통행금지의] 노선　street vendor 노점상　attempt 시도　address (문제를) 해결하다　city official 시 공무원　cross out 줄로 그어 지워버리다　numerous 수많은　pedestrian 보행자

9 (a)

해석 (a) 오늘날에는 외국 음악을 리메이크한 팝송이 너무 많아서 그다지 주목할 만한 가치가 없어 보인다. (b) 그러나 한국 노래 〈아리랑〉의 팝 버전은 한국 전통 노래를 독특하게 리메이크했다. (c) 다음 달 출시될 예정인 이 앨범은 아메리카 대륙에서 판매될 것이다. (d) 알렉스 김이 수지 리, 재닛 박, 앤소니 김을 포함해 대부분 한국계 미국인 음악가와 가수들로 구성된 밴드를 이끈다.

해설 (a)는 so ~ that 구문을 도치시킨 것이므로 주어와 동사의 위치도 바꾸어야 한다. 따라서 So commonplace these days pop songs are를 So commonplace these days are pop songs로 고쳐야 한다.

어구 commonplace 아주 흔한　remake 리메이크하다; 리메이크 작품　note ~에 주의하다, 주목하다　release 출시하다, 개봉하다　comprised of ~로 구성된

10 (d)

해설 (a) 컨벤션 홀에서 약간 소란이 있었다. (b) 지금은 상황이 진정되었지만 아직도 사람들은 충격을 받은 상태이다. (c) 대중들은 대통령 대변인의 기자 회견을 기다리고 있다. (d) 너무나도 끔찍한 폭발 사고였기 때문에 살아남은 광부가 없다고 한다.

해설 (d)에서 강조를 위해 So horrible이 문두로 왔기 때문에 주어와 동사가 도치되어야 한다. So horrible the explosion was를 So horrible was the explosion으로 고쳐야 옳다.

어구 turbulence 소란, 혼란　convention 집회, 대표자 회의　calm down 진정하다　a state of shock 충격 상태　press briefing 기자 회견　presidential spokesman 대통령 대변인　explosion 폭발　miner 광부

Check-up TEST 12~13

| 1 | (d) | 2 | (b) | 3 | (b) | 4 | (c) | 5 | (a) |
| 6 | (d) | 7 | (d) | 8 | (d) | 9 | (a) | 10 | (b) |

1 (d)

해석 A: 편안하게 지낼 수 있는 호텔에 묵는 것이 어떨까?
B: 호텔에 묵으면 유스호스텔에서 방 빌리는 것보다 비용이 두 배나 더 들잖아.

해설 'as 형용사 as' 원급 비교 표현에서 '몇 배'를 의미하는 배수사는 바로 앞에 위치해야 한다. 그리고 호텔 비용은 돈, 즉 셀 수 없는 명사 개념이므로 as much as로 표현해야 한다.

어구 rent a room 방을 빌리다　youth hostel 유스호스텔

2 (b)

해석 A: 지난주 목요일에 열린 국제 의학 세미나에서 유익한 이야기를 나눴니?
B: 유익한 내용이 아무것도 없었어.

해설 형용사가 nothing을 수식할 때는 nothing 앞이 아니라 뒤에서 수식하므로 nothing useful로 표현해야 한다. 선택지 (d)는 부정문에서 something을 쓰지 않기 때문에 틀린 표현이다.

어구 fruitful 유익한　medical seminar 의학 세미나

3 (b)

해석 A: 카메라를 든 70명의 사람들이 한낮에 죽은 고래를 보려고 돌아다녔어.
B: 그 거대한 수중 포유동물이 아주 많은 사람들의 이목을 끌었나보네.

해설 alive와 awake는 명사 앞에서 한정적 용법으로 수식할 수 없

고 서술적으로만 쓰이는 형용사이므로 (a)와 (d)는 오답이다. '죽은 고래'를 표현할 때 형용사 dead는 명사 앞에 위치해야 하므로 (b)가 옳다.

어구 wander 이곳저곳 돌아다니다　midday 정오, 한낮　mammal 포유동물　attract (주의, 흥미를) 끌다

4 (c)

해석 다 자란 침팬지는 어린 침팬지보다 음식을 열 배 더 먹는다.

해설 '~보다 (몇) 배 더 …한'이라는 뜻의 「배수사 + as + 원급 + as」 구문으로, 음식 섭취량은 불가산명사 개념이기 때문에 as much as로 써야 한다. 따라서 (c) ten times as much as가 답이다.

어구 consume 먹다

5 (a)

해석 대부분의 아시아인들은 과일과 채소를 건강 권장량의 반 정도만 먹는다.

해설 배수사 half나 double은 수[분량]를 언급하고자 하는 대상 바로 앞에 사용되어 '절반의,' '두 배의' 의미를 나타낸다. 따라서 the amount of fruit and vegetables 바로 앞에 half가 위치해야 한다.

어구 recommend 권장하다

6 (d)

해석 TEPS 시험은 다른 영어 시험보다 두 배는 더 어렵다고 말해도 크게 무리가 없다.

해설 배수사 비교급의 어순 문제이다. 「배수사 + 비교급 + than」의 어순을 취하므로 two times more difficult than이 올바른 어순이다.

어구 it could be fair to say~ ~라고 말하는 데 크게 무리가 없다

7 (d)

해석 (a) A: 아무런 조건 없이 돈을 쓰는 사람을 본 적이 있니?
(b) B: 네가 동의하는 정책을 펴는 정부를 원한다면 돈을 기부할 수도 있지.
(c) A: 힘들게 번 돈을 정당에 기부할 때는 기부금을 대가로 무엇인가 바라는 것이 있기 때문일 거야.
(d) B: 네 말이 맞을 수도 있어. 그래서 사람들이 에이미 윌슨이 10,000달러의 기부금을 내고 새로운 공원 건설 입찰을 따내자 부적절한 행동을 했다고들 말하는 것이지.

해설 문장의 호흡은 길지만 답은 간단하게 나오는 문제이다. (d)에서 형용사 improper는 something 앞이 아니라 뒤에서 수식해야 한다.

어구 with no strings attached 아무런 조건 없이　contribute 기부하다　donate 기부하다　hard-earned 어렵게 번　political party 정당　in exchange for ~의 대가로　improper 부적절한　win the bid 입찰을 따내다　construct 건설하다

8 (d)

해석 (a) A: 아직도 선생님의 소형차를 팔 생각이 있으신가요?
(b) B: 그렇다네. 관심 있나?
(c) A: 어쩌면요. 3만 달러에 파실 의향이 있으세요?

(d) B: 자네가 제시한 액수의 절반 가격에 팔 용의가 있지.

해설 (d)에서 the amount you offered(자네가 제시한 액수)의 '절반'에 팔 용의가 있다는 것이므로 half를 the amount you offered 앞에 써야 한다.

어구 compact car 소형차 be willing to 흔쾌히 ~하다

9 (a)

해석 (a) A: 그 거대 정유 업체 한 곳에서만 공화당 선거 운동에 5,000만 달러를 썼어.
(b) B: 정유 업체들은 우리처럼 평범한 사람들에게서 돈을 빼앗아가서 그 돈을 정당에게 주는 것 같아.
(c) A: 앞으로 한 달 뒤에 그 정유 업체가 다수의 언론 기업과 힘을 합쳐서 1억 달러를 조성할 거고 그 보수당의 선거 운동 자금을 대출 거야.
(d) B: 그 돈이 다른 산업체의 기부금과 합쳐지면 엄청난 액수가 되겠네.

해설 서술적 형용사 alone은 명사 앞에서 쓰일 수 없다. 대신 명사 바로 뒤에 와서 그것이 유일함을 나타내어 '~혼자'라는 뜻으로 쓰인다. '그 거대 석유 회사 혼자서'라는 말이므로 alone을 the oil giant 뒤에 두어 the oil giant alone으로 써야 한다.

어구 giant 거대 기업 Republican 공화당(의) effort 운동, 노력 political party 정당 team up with ~와 힘을 합치다 corporation 기업 fund 자금을 대다 conservative 보수적인 combine 합치다

10 (b)

해석 (a) 사업을 걱정하면서 또 하룻밤을 지새우고 있다면 이웃의 어느 집에 불이 켜져 있는지 확인하고 싶어질지도 모른다. (b) 이웃 주민들이 깨어있는 것을 볼 가능성이 아주 높다. (c) 수백만에 달하는 미국인들이 돈 문제 때문에 잠을 이루지 못하고 있다. (d) 정부는 미래 전망이 밝다고 자신하는 듯하지만 대중은 이를 신뢰하지 못하고 있다.

해설 awake는 서술적 형용사이므로 명사 앞에서 한정적 용법으로 사용될 수 없다. 따라서 you see neighbors are awake로 바꿔야 한다. 혹은 '잠에서 깨다'라는 뜻의 동사로도 사용되는데, 「지각동사 + 목적어 + 원형동사」의 형태로 쓰므로 see neighbors awake라고 쓸 수도 있다.

어구 sleepless 잠 못 이루는 probability 가능성 confident 자신감에 가득 찬 outlook 전망, 예상; 광경; 견해 rosy 밝은, 장밋빛의, 낙관적인 the public 대중, 국민 convince 납득시키다

Unit 2 동사

Check-up TEST 14~15

1	(a)	2	(c)	3	(c)	4	(c)	5	(b)
6	(a)	7	(c)	8	(a)	9	(d)	10	(d)

1 (a)

해석 A: 사이클론이 남부 지역을 강타했다는 소식 들었니?
B: 그래. 사이클론이 접근한다는 경고를 듣게 되면 내륙 쪽으로 가서 피해야 해.

해설 사이클론 경보를 듣는 것은 미래에 있을 일이지만, 시간 부사절에서는 미래의 내용을 현재 시제로 표현한다.

어구 incoming 들어오는; (수익 등이) 생기는 inland 내륙; 내륙으로

2 (c)

해석 A: 마실 거리는 무엇을 좋아하세요?
B: 각성 효과를 주기는 하지만, 커피를 가장 좋아합니다.

해설 B의 말은 화자의 현재 습관과 사실을 언급하므로 현재 시제로 일치시키는 것이 옳다. 따라서 keeps me awake로 써야 한다.

3 (c)

해석 그 박물관은 5,000년도 더 전에 폭발한 화산에서 나온 바위를 입수했다.

해설 박물관 측에서 바위를 입수한 것은 과거이고 화산이 폭발한 것은 그 이전이므로 과거보다 앞선 과거완료 시제를 사용해야 한다. 따라서 had erupted로 쓰는 것이 적절하다.

어구 acquire 얻다, 입수하다 volcano 화산 erupt (화산 등이) 폭발하다, 분화하다

4 (c)

해석 만일 어떤 나라가 미국에 미사일 공격을 감행한다면, 미국의 방어 시스템이 그 미사일로 하여금 어떠한 피해도 입히지 못하게 할 것이다.

해설 지금 현재 일을 언급하는 것이 아니라 미래의 일에 대해서 설명하는 것이다. 시간이나 조건의 부사절에서는 내용이 미래라 하더라도 현재 시제로 쓴다. 따라서 If a country tries to hit America가 정확한 표현이다.

어구 missile 미사일 protection 보호

5 (b)

해석 (a) A: 어제 왜 야구 경기 보러 오지 않았어?
(b) B: 가려고 했었는데 아들을 병원에 데리고 가야 했어.
(c) A: 무슨 일이야? 아이는 괜찮고?
(d) B: 응, 지금은 괜찮아. 의사 말로는 그냥 복통이라더군.

해설 (b)에서 아이를 병원에 데리고 간 것은 과거의 일이므로 I have to take를 I had to take로 바꿔야 한다.

어구 make it to (장소에) 나타나다 upset stomach (갑작스러운) 복통

6 (a)

해석 (a) A: 이번 주말에 야외 활동을 계획할 거라면 다시 생각해보는 게 좋을 거야.
(b) B: 왜? 이번 주말에 안 좋은 일이라도 있다니?
(c) A: 며칠 동안 지속되었던 추운 날씨가 주말 동안 계속될 것 같대.
(d) B: 이럴 수가. 듣고 싶지 않은 소식이야.

해설 (a)는 '이번 주말에 ~할 예정이라면'이라는 미래의 의미를 담

고 있다. 조건의 부사절 안에서는 내용이 미래라 하더라도 쓸 때는 현재로 써야 하므로 If you planned to do를 If you plan to do로 고쳐야 한다.

어구 **any sort of** 어떤 종류의 **outdoor activity** 야외 활동 **How come?** 왜? **last** 지속되다

7 (c)

해석 (a) A: 돼지고기를 뒤집어야 하지 않을까?
(b) B: 아직. 난 겉이 지글지글 익은 것을 좋아해.
(c) A: 암을 유발할 수 있기 때문에, 난 보통 탄 고기는 먹지 않아.
(d) B: 네 말이 맞아. 건강을 위험에 빠드리진 말아야지.

해설 탄 고기를 먹지 않는다는 내용은 화자의 성향이나 습관을 말하는 것이기 때문에 시제를 현재로 처리해야 한다. 따라서 (c)의 I didn't usually eat을 I don't usually eat으로 바꿔야 한다.

어구 **turn over** 뒤집다 **pork chop** 돼지고기 토막(갈비가 붙은 것) **sear** 지글지글 태우다 **blacken** 검게 하다 **risk** 위험에 빠드리다

8 (a)

해석 (a) 미국의 GDP가 올해 1분기에 연 3.1퍼센트 성장했다고 미국 상무부가 발표했다. (b) 이 수치는 월가에서 예측한 3.6 퍼센트보다는 밑돌았고, 2016년 1분기 당시 GDP가 1.9 퍼센트 성장했을 때 이후로 2년 만에 가장 낮은 수치이기도 하다. (c) 경제 성장이 주춤한 주된 이유는 다름 아닌 높은 유가 때문이다. (d) 에너지 비용의 상승으로 인해 소비자 및 기업 지출이 주춤하게 되었고 무역 적자도 악화되었다.

해설 올해 1분기 3.1퍼센트 성장을 기록한 사실은 명백한 과거 내용이므로 America's GDP grows를 America's GDP grew로 바꿔야 한다.

어구 **Commerce Department** 미국 상무부 **annual rate** 연 이율; 연 사용료[요금] **quarter** 분기 **figure** 수치 **estimate** 추산치 **put the brakes on** ~에 브레이크를 밟다, 주춤하게 하다 **none other than** 다름 아닌 **oil prices** 유가 **hike** 인상 **dampen** 주춤하게 하다 **worsen** 악화시키다 **deficit** 부족액, 적자

9 (d)

해석 (a) 올해는 e베이 창립 23주년을 맞이하는 해이다. (b) 1995년 피에르 오미디아르라는 소프트웨어 엔지니어가 구매자와 판매자가 이상적인 가격에 대해 동의할 수 있는 진정한 온라인 시장 문화를 만들고자 했다. (c) 그래서 온라인 경매 서비스를 제공하는 e베이가 탄생하게 되었다. (d) 창립자 오미디아르는 끊임없이 노력하여 e베이를 글로벌 기업으로 만들어놓음으로써 열심히 일하면 성공할 수 있음을 입증했다.

해설 '열심히 일하면 성공한다'는 말은 격언이나 금언에 가깝다. 즉, 이 격언이 사실임을 몸소 입증했다는 의미이다. 격언이나 금언은 동사 시제를 현재로 처리하므로 hard work led to success를 hard work leads to success로 써야 한다.

어구 **mark** (몇 주년을) 맞이하다 **anniversary** 기념일 **genuine** 진정한 **auction** 경매 **founder** 창립자 **ceaselessly** 끊임없이 **giant** 거대 기업

10 (d)

해석 (a) 정부는 집 없는 가정이 없어질 때까지 임대 주택을 포함하여 더 많은 공영 주택을 지어야 한다. (b) 이렇게 되면 사람들이 집을 바라보는 시각이 단지 소유의 개념에서 실사용의 대상 개념으로 바뀔 것이다. (c) 현재 정부의 미온적인 접근법은 투기 세력의 저항만 더욱 증가시킬 것이다. (d) 정부가 수요와 공급의 시장 원칙을 징계적 차원의 세금과 함께 조합할 때에만 정부의 정책이 실효를 거둘 것이다.

해설 '정부가 정책을 조합할 때'라는 말은 아직까지 정책을 조합하지 않았다는 뜻이다. 즉 미래의 이야기이다. 시간 부사절에서는 미래의 내용을 현재 시제로 쓴다. 따라서 (d)의 Only when the government will combine을 Only when the government combines로 바꿔야 한다.

어구 **public housing** (저소득층을 위한) 공영 주택 **rental homes** 임대주택 **perception** 시각, 견해, 개념 **mere** 단순한 **possession** 소유 **actual use** 실사용 **lukewarm** 미온적인, 미지근한 **approach** 접근법 **resistance** 저항 **speculator** 투기꾼 **combine A with B** A와 B를 조합하다 **supply and demand** 수요와 공급 **punitive** 징계의

Check-up TEST ⑯

1	(c)	2	(d)	3	(b)	4	(b)	5	(d)
6	(b)	7	(c)	8	(c)	9	(c)	10	(b)

1 (c)

해석 A: 왜 얼굴을 찌푸리고 있는 거야?
B: 비가 내린 이후로 허리가 아파.

해설 since가 '~한 이후로'의 의미로 사용되면 주절의 동사는 현재완료 시제로 쓴다. 따라서 has been aching이 적절하다.

어구 **frown** 얼굴을 찌푸리다 **ache** 아프다, 쑤시다

2 (d)

해석 A: 네 형은 해외 생활에 어떻게 적응하고 있니?
B: 힘든 시간을 보내고 있나 봐.

해설 같이 사용된 어구상의 힌트는 딱히 보이지 않으므로 내용의 흐름을 통해 시제를 찾아야 한다. 해외로 간 시점 이후로 힘든 시간을 보내고 있다는 문맥이므로 현재완료 시제로 쓰는 것이 가장 적절하다.

어구 **adjust** 적응하다 **have a hard time** 힘든 시간을 보내다

3 (b)

해석 내 여동생은 지난 6월에 졸업한 이후로 나노 기술 분야에서 직업을 찾으려고 노력해왔다.

해설 since(~한 이후로)가 접속사로 사용되었다. 주절의 동사 시제는 현재완료로 처리하고 since절의 동사는 과거로 써야 한다. 따라서 since she graduated가 올바른 표현이다.

어구 **pursue** ~을 얻으려고 애쓰다; 뒤쫓다 **graduate** 졸업하다

4 (b)

해석 외국어를 학습하는 것은 이전에 한 번도 외국어를 배워본 적

이 없는 이들에게는 특히나 어렵다.

해설 과거 특정 시점부터 지금까지도 외국어를 배워본 적이 없다고 판단해야 한다. 이는 현재완료를 의미하므로 have never learned one이 가장 적절하다.

어구 **foreign language** 외국어

5 (d)

해석 (a) A: 안녕하세요. 저는 수잔입니다. 3일 전에 이 호텔에 투숙했었어요.
(b) B: 안녕하세요, 수잔 씨. 어떻게 도와드릴까요?
(c) A: 혹시나 거기 직원분 중 하얀색 지갑을 보신 분이 계신가 해서요.
(d) B: 아직까지 하얀색 지갑을 찾았다는 직원은 없었는데요.

해설 so far(지금까지)가 나오면 동사 시제는 현재완료가 알맞다. 따라서 (d)의 No on mentioned를 No one has mentioned로 고쳐야 한다.

어구 **staff** 직원 **happen** 우연히 ~하다 **turn in** 제출하다 **so far** 아직까지

6 (b)

해석 (a) A: P&P에서 새 스웨터를 샀어. 어때 보여?
(b) B: 멋진데! 내가 일년 정도 남자친구를 만나고 있는데 그 스웨터가 그에게 좋은 선물이 될 것 같아.
(c) A: 서두르는 게 좋을 거야. 내가 갔을 때 몇 개 남지 않았었어.
(d) B: 지금 바로 가야겠네. 고마워.

해설 여자는 과거인 1년 전부터 지금까지 남자친구를 만나고 있으므로 과거완료가 아닌 현재완료 시제가 적절하다. 따라서 (b)의 I had been seeing을 I have been seeing으로 바꿔야 한다.

7 (c)

해석 (a) A: 쟤 좀 봐. 오늘 저녁 내내 잡지 기사만 오리고 있군. 저걸 다 뭐에 쓰려고 그러는지 알아?
(b) B: 응, 효과적인 체중 감량 프로그램을 찾고 있는 거야.
(c) A: 칼로리 섭취량을 줄이려고 한 적은 있기라도 한 거야?
(d) B: 내가 알기로는 지금까지 여러 번 시도해왔지만 효과가 없었나 봐.

해설 내용상 특정 과거시점에서 지금까지 어떠한 방법을 사용해 본 적이 있는지를 묻고 있으므로 (c)의 Did she ever tried를 Has she ever tried로 바꿔야 한다.

어구 **cut out** 오려내다, 가위질하다 **weight loss** 체중 감량 **cut back on** ~을 줄이다 **caloric intake** 칼로리 섭취

8 (c)

해석 (a) 최근에 손주를 데리고 근처 공원에 산책을 나갔다가 걱정스러운 장면을 목격했다. (b) 중학생으로 보이는 몇몇 여학생들이 나무 아래에서 담배를 피우고 있었다. (c) 나는 즉시 담배를 끄게 했지만 하루 종일 기분이 좋지 않았다. (d) 미성년자가 개방된 공공장소에서 담배 피우는 모습을 볼 수 있는 사회라니, 매우 한탄스럽다.

해설 과거 사건에 대해서 이야기를 풀어가고 있는 글이다. 미성년자가 담배를 피운 것과 글쓴이가 담배를 끄라고 한 일은 현재

까지 이어지지 않는 명백한 과거 사건이다. 따라서 (c) 문장은 현재완료 시제가 아니라 단순 과거 시제로 써야 한다.

어구 **witness** 목격하다 **trouble** (정신적으로) ~을 괴롭히다, 걱정시키다; 짜증나게 하다 **put out a cigarette** 담배를 끄다 **deplorable** 한탄스러운 **minor** 미성년자 **wide-open** 공간이 넓은 **public place** 공공장소

9 (c)

해석 (a) 한국의 사회경제적 문제를 '양극화'라는 말보다 더 적절하게 묘사할 수 있는 말은 드물다. (b) 커지는 개인 재산 격차가 사회 불안정성의 근본 원인이라고 한다면, 경제적 원인은 대기업과 중소기업의 격차에서 찾을 수 있을 것이다. (c) 주된 이유는 대기업이 주로 하청업체의 희생으로 금융 위기 이후 구조조정을 성공적으로 거쳐왔다는 것이다. (d) 대기업은 공급 가격을 삭감함으로써 비용 인상분의 부담을 어느 정도는 하청업체에 전가했다.

해설 (c)에 since가 사용되었으므로 주절에는 현재완료를 써야 한다. 따라서 big businesses had successfully undergone을 big businesses have successfully undergone으로 바꿔야 한다.

어구 **socioeconomic** 사회경제적인 **adequately** 적절하게 **polarization** 양극화 **widening** (격차가) 벌어지는 **gap** 격차, 간극 **root cause** 근본적인 이유 **instability** 불안정성 **origin** 기원 **undergo** 경험하다, 겪다 **restructuring** 구조조정 **financial crisis** 금융위기 **at the expense of** ~의 희생을 대가로 **subcontractor** 하청업체 **more or less** 다소 **pass the burden** 부담을 전가하다 **slash** 삭감하다

10 (b)

해석 (a) 세계적으로 유명한 등산가 존 윌리엄이 이끄는 4명으로 구성된 팀이 마침내 북극에 도착했다. (b) 윌리엄 팀은 54일만에 2,000킬로미터를 이동했는데, 각 구성원은 보급품으로 가득 찬 100킬로그램의 썰매를 끌었다. (c) 전 이동 과정 동안 영하 55도까지 떨어지는 기온과 초속 14미터에 달하는 폭설을 일으키는 눈보라와도 싸워야 했다. (d) 탐험 역사를 보면 한 탐험가의 성취는 개인을 넘어서 그 나라의 사기나 자긍심을 고취시킨다는 것을 알 수 있다.

해설 윌리엄 팀이 북극 탐험을 한 것은 명백한 과거의 일이므로 현재완료를 쓸 수 없다. (b)의 has been covering을 covered로 바꿔야 한다.

어구 **lead** 이끌다 **world-renowned** 세계적으로 유명한 **alpinist** (알프스) 등산가 **the North Pole** 북극 **cover** (특정 지점에서 다른 지점까지) 이르다, 커버하다 **sleigh** 썰매 **blizzard** 눈보라 **expedition** 탐험 **achievement** 성취, 성과 **boost** 고양시키다 **morale** 사기 **self-esteem** 자존; 자부심, 자만

▬ Check-up TEST 17~18 ▬

1 (a)	2 (a)	3 (a)	4 (d)	5 (d)
6 (b)	7 (c)	8 (d)	9 (b)	10 (a)

1 (a)

해석 A: 너 우리 통화하는 동안 뭘 하고 있었니?
　　B: 통화하면서 신문을 읽고 있었어.

해설 오답률이 비교적 높은 문제이다. '통화하고 있었을 때 무엇을 하고 있는 중 이었다'는 내용이 되어야 자연스럽다. 따라서 과거 진행형인 was reading a newspaper로 표현하는 것이 적절하다.

어구 conversation 대화

2 (a)

해석 제인이 약혼했음을 알고 가장 놀란 사람은 수지였다.

해설 소식을 듣고 놀란 것은 과거 시점이고 제인이 약혼을 한 것은 그 이전이다. 기준 시점의 과거보다 더 먼저 일어난 일은 과거 완료인 had p.p.로 표현해야 한다.

어구 discover ~을 깨닫다; 발견하다　get engaged 약혼하다

3 (a)

해석 잭슨 교수가 은퇴하면 40년 이상 교단에서 가르치게 되는 셈이지만 그의 수업은 결코 지루하지 않다.

해설 잭슨 교수가 은퇴하는 시점은 미래이다. 그 시점이 되면 40년이 넘게 계속 가르치고 있는 셈이 되므로, 선택지 가운데 미래 완료 진행형이 가장 자연스럽다.

어구 retire 은퇴하다　dull 지루한

4 (d)

해석 그가 타야 할 기차가 지금 역에 도착하고 있다.

해설 문장 속에 right now라는 힌트가 있다. 지금 현재 일어나고 있는 동작을 의미하므로 현재진행형 is arriving으로 표현하는 것이 적절하다.

5 (d)

해석 그 변호사는 원고를 변호하느라 고생했으나 아쉽게도 어제 장기간의 법적 공방에서 패소했다.

해설 시제를 묻는 문제이다. 어제 이전의 과거부터 어제 패소할 때까지 계속 노력을 한 것이므로 과거완료 시제가 적절하다.

어구 struggle to V ~하느라 애쓰다, 고군분투하다　defend 변호하다, 옹호하다　plaintiff 원고, 고소인　prolonged 장기적인　legal battle 법적 싸움, 법적 공방

6 (b)

해석 (a) A: 당신 아버님 생신 선물로 무엇을 준비할까?
　　(b) B: 전기면도기를 사 드릴까 하고 생각하고 있던 참이었어.
　　(c) A: 그런데 우리 작년에 비싼 면도기 사드렸잖아, 안 그래?
　　(d) B: 그렇군. 내가 그 사실을 잊고 있었네.

해설 과거완료 문제가 출제될 때는 주로 과거 사실을 미리 언급해 두고 그 과거 시점에 대비되는 그 이전의 과거완료 시제 내용을 언급하는 경우가 많다. 즉, 단독적으로 과거완료 시제만 나오는 경우는 드물다는 것이다. 선택지 (b)에서 갑자기 I had thought~라고 과거완료 시제로 말할 이유가 없다. 그보다는 막연히 '나는 생각하고 있었다' 라고 과거진행형으로 표현하는 것이 자연스럽다. 따라서 I had thought about을 I was

thinking about으로 써야 한다.

어구 electric razor 전기면도기

7 (c)

해석 (a) A: 우린 강가로 피크닉을 갈 거야.
　　(b) B: 기대되겠다. 필요한 것은 다 챙겼고?
　　(c) A: 물론이지. 잊어버린 것은 없는지 두 번이나 확인했어.
　　(d) B: 즐거운 시간 보내길 바라.

해설 (c)의 두 번째 문장은 무언가를 챙기는 것을 잊어버렸을지도 (대과거) 몰라서 확인했다(과거)는 말이므로 forgot을 had forgotten으로 고쳐야 한다.

어구 go on a picnic 피크닉 가다　see if ~인지 확인하다

8 (d)

해석 (a) A: 다리는 왜 절뚝거리니? 다친 거야?
　　(b) B: 어제 넘어져서 무릎을 다쳤어. 근데 그렇게 심각하진 않아.
　　(c) A: 어떻게 된 거니? 내가 아는 넌 넘어져서 다칠 사람이 결코 아닌데 말이야.
　　(d) B: 미끄러운 바닥에 넘어진 노부인을 도우려고 했었지.

해설 (d)에서 노부인이 넘어진 것이 노부인을 도우려고 했던 일보다 더 먼저 일어난 일이므로 fall을 과거완료 시제인 had fallen으로 고쳐야 한다.

어구 limp 다리를 절다　be the last person to V ~할 사람이 절대 아닌　slippery 미끄러운

9 (b)

해석 (a) 네덜란드 상원이 안락사 법안을 46대 28로 통과시키면서 약 만 명의 사람들이 의회 밖에 모여 이번 결정에 항의했다. (b) 이 법안은 네덜란드 국왕이 서명을 하면 2주 후에 법적 효력을 가지게 된다. (c) 이 법안에 따르면 안락사 시술을 하는 의사는 환자가 말기 상태임을 확신해야만 한다. (d) 또한 이 법안에 따르면 안락사를 희망하는 이는 네덜란드인이어야만 하고 안락사 요청을 문서로 제출해야 한다.

해설 법안은 네덜란드 국왕이 서명한 이후 법적 효력을 가지게 될 것이다. (b)는 법적 효력을 가지게 된다는 단순한 미래 내용을 나타내는 것이므로 미래완료 시제가 아니라 단순미래 시제로 나타내는 것이 적절하다. 따라서 will have gone into effect를 will go into effect로 고쳐야 한다.

어구 Senate 상원　euthanasia 안락사　bill 법안　Parliament 의회　protest 저항하다　go into effect 효력을 발휘하다　state 명시하다, 진술하다　legislation 법안　convince 확신시키다　terminally 말단으로, 종점으로　candidate 지원자; 후보자　submit 제출하다　statement 성명서

10 (a)

해석 (a) 인간의 삶에 스마트폰보다 더 큰 영향을 미칠 수 있는 기기가 무엇이 있을까 하고 생각한 적이 있었다. (b) 거의 모든 사람들이 각자의 스마트폰을 가지고 있고, 그래서 그들의 삶을 지배한다. (c) 통계청이 발표한 보고서에 따르면 학생들이 성인보다 스마트폰을 더 많이 사용한다. (d) 그로 인해 학생들이 폭력적이거나 다른 유해한 컨텐츠에 점점 더 많이 노출되고 있다.

해설 (a)에서 I가 '우리 삶에 큰 영향을 미치는 것이 무엇인가'라고 생각하는(wondering) 상황에서는 그 시점이 기준이고 현재가 되는 것이므로 might have had를 might have로 바꿔야 한다.

어구 **device** 기기, 장비 **have a great influence on** 지대한 영향을 미치다 **in return** 그 대신에; 답례로; 회답으로 **exercise** (권력·권리를) 행사하다, 휘두르다 **control** 지배(력), 통제(력), 단속, 감독 **the National Statistics Bureau** 통계청 **grownup** 성인 **expose** 노출시키다 **violent** 폭력적인 **harmful** 유해한

Check-up TEST ⑲

1	(d)	2	(c)	3	(a)	4	(a)	5	(d)
6	(b)	7	(b)	8	(b)	9	(a)	10	(d)

1 (d)
해석 A: 지진의 여파로 고통 받고 있는 인도네시아인들을 돕기 위해 봉사에 꼭 참여하고 싶어요.
B: 그건 위험하다고 했잖니. 하지만 정 그렇다면 가는 걸 말리진 않을게.

해설 '목적어가 ~하지 못하게 하다'는 「stop + 목적어 + from + V-ing」의 형태로 쓴다. 따라서 (d)의 stop you from going이 알맞다.

어구 **volunteer** 자원하다, 자원봉사를 하다 **aftermath** 여파, 영향 **earthquake** 지진 **insist** 주장하다, 고집하다

2 (c)
해석 A: 학교측에서 도둑맞은 컴퓨터 모니터를 찾으려고 교실에 CCTV를 설치한 것을 시인했어.
B: 그건 도저히 용납할 수 없는 사생활 침해야.

해설 동사 admit는 동명사를 목적어 취하는 동사이므로 admitted installing으로 써야 한다.

어구 **admit** 시인하다, 인정하다 **install** 설치하다 **unacceptable** 받아들일 수 없는 **infringement** 침해

3 (a)
해석 A: 난 IP-TV에서 프로그램을 다운받는 게 싫어.
B: 나도 마찬가지야. 프로그램 중간에 광고를 너무 많이 봐야 하잖아.

해설 동사 hate는 목적어로 to부정사와 동명사를 둘 다 취할 수 있다. (b)는 download 뒤에 for가 있어서 답이 될 수 없다. download는 목적어를 바로 동반하는 타동사이기 때문이다. (c)는 hate와 download라는 두 개의 동사가 연결 장치 없이 바로 이어져 있으므로 틀린다. (d)는 hate to download라고 고치면 답이 될 수 있다.

어구 **commercial** 광고 **download** 다운로드하다

4 (a)
해석 유럽 위원회는 경제에서 투자자의 신뢰감을 향상시킬 수 있는, 지속 가능한 성장과 부채 감소를 위한 타당한 계획을 마련하지 못했다.

해설 동사 fail은 to부정사를 목적어로 취할 수 있다. failed to lay down이 정확한 표현이다.

어구 **European Commission** 유럽 위원회(EU의 사무국 격인 집행 기구) **plausible** 타당한, 그럴듯한 **sustained** 지속된 **liability** 부채 **reduction** 감소 **investor** 투자자 **confidence** 자신감; 신뢰 **lay down** 정하다, 마련하다

5 (d)
해석 자동차 전문가의 말에 따르면 모든 주요 자동차 제조업체에 영향을 미쳤던 대량 리콜 사태로 인해 자동차 구매객은 불량 차량 구입을 피하기 어려워지고 있다.

해설 동사 avoid는 동명사를 목적어로 취한다. 따라서 to avoid buying faulty vehicles가 올바른 표현이다.

어구 **analyst** 분석가, 전문가 **massive** 대규모의 **recall** 리콜 **affect** 영향을 미치다 **faulty** 결함이 있는

6 (b)
해석 그들은 FIFA 월드컵을 개최하려는 노력을 통해 전 세계 관중을 찾아가려 했고, 그들의 경제적·민주적인 업적을 선보이기를 전적으로 기대했다.

해설 동사 expect는 to부정사를 목적어로 취할 수 있다. 따라서 expected to showcase로 쓰는 것이 적절하다.

어구 **seek** ~을 찾다, 찾으러 가다 **host** 개최하다 **showcase** 선보이다 **democratic** 민주주의의 **triumph** 성과, 위업

7 (b)
해석 (a) A: 특별히 마음에 두신 유형이 있습니까?
(b) B: 클러치 핸드백을 구입할까 해요.
(c) A: 그렇다면 이 예쁜 에나멜 클러치 백을 보세요.
(d) B: 오, 아주 매끈하고 예쁜데요.

해설 동사 consider는 동명사를 목적어로 취하며, to부정사는 목적어로 취할 수 없다. (b)에서 I am considering to buy를 I am considering buying으로 바꿔야 한다.

어구 **clutch (handbag)** 클러치 핸드백 (끈·손잡이가 없는 여성용 소형 핸드백) **adorable** 예쁜 **enamel** 에나멜 **slick** (모양이) 매끈한; 멋진 **check out** ~을 확인하다, 조회하다

8 (b)
해석 (a) A: 우리의 시청자들을 실망시켜선 안 됩니다. 시청자들은 너무 오랫동안 이 드라마를 기다려 왔어요.
(b) B: 동의합니다. 하지만 첫 편 방영 연기를 고려해 봐야 해요. 요즘 시청률 경쟁이 너무 치열하잖아요.
(c) A: 언제부터 경쟁자들을 신경 쓰는 거죠? 우리의 제작물에 좀 더 자신감을 가지셔야 합니다.
(d) B: 하지만 이번 시리즈 제작을 시작한 이래 많은 비용과 에너지를 투입했어요. 우린 좀 더 신중해야 한다고요.

해설 consider는 목적어로 동명사를 취하는 동사이다. 따라서 (b)의 consider to delay를 consider delaying으로 고쳐야 한다.

어구 **disappoint** ~을 실망시키다 **rating** 시청률, 청취율 **intense** 격렬한 **care about** 신경 쓰다 **competitor** 경쟁자 **confidence** 자신감, 신뢰 **careful** 주의 깊은, 조심성 있는

9 (a)

해석 (a) 알래스카 리조트 위원회는 카지노 건설을 계속해서 승인 한다. (b) 새로운 법은 현지 카지노 업체를 설립하여 포커게임 영업을 할 수 있도록 허용한다. (c) 이번 달에 위원회가 세 건 의 면허를 카지노에 발행했다고 보도되었다. (d) 위원회의 결 정은 이 문제에 대해 공청회가 열린 이후 나왔다.

해설 continue는 to부정사와 동명사를 목적어로 취할 수 있 다. (a)에서 '카지노 건설 승인을 위해서 위원회가 계속된다 (continue for approving)'라고 하면 문맥이 통하지 않는다. 글 전체적으로 볼 때 '카지노 승인을 계속한다'는 말이 논리적 으로 맞다. 따라서 continues for approving을 continues approving 또는 continues to approve로 바꿔야 한다.

어구 approve 승인하다 set up 설립[설치]하다 run 영업하다 issue 발행하다 license 면허(증) public hearing 공청회

10 (d)

해석 (a) 냉전 기간 동안, 권력의 균형으로 인해 미국과 구(舊) 소비 에트 연방은 핵무기를 사용할 수 없었다. (b) 양국 수반은 어떤 핵 공격이든 잠재적으로 파괴적인 보복을 일으킬 수 있음을 알고 있었다. (c) 두 강대국 사이의 수십 년 간의 대치 상황은 끝이 나게 되었다. (d) 남아있는 중요한 과제는 어떻게 다른 국 가들이 자체 핵무기를 소유하지 못하도록 단념시키는가 하는 것이었다.

해설 동사 discourage는 「discourage + 목적어 + from + V-ing」 로 쓴다. discourage others from possessing으로 표현 해야 한다.

어구 the Cold War 냉전 the balance of power 권력의 균형 nuclear weapon 핵무기 head 정상, 수반, 대통령 trigger 야기시키다, 촉발하다 potentially 잠재적으로 destructive 파괴적인 retaliation 보복 decades-long 수십 년 간의 standoff 대치 상황 powers 강대국 come to an end 종결되다 challenge 과제, 도전 discourage ~을 못하게 하다, 단념시키다 possess 소유하다 arsenal 병기고, 무기

■ Check-up TEST ②⓪ ■

1	(a)	2	(c)	3	(a)	4	(d)	5	(c)
6	(a)	7	(b)	8	(b)	9	(b)	10	(b)

1 (a)

해석 A: 매니저는 당신이 IBM의 컴퓨터 부품을 구입하도록 설득 한 고객의 수를 계산합니다.
B: 제가 매일 마다 그 데이터를 보고해야 합니까?

해설 동사 convince는 「convince + 목적어 + to동사원형」 형태 로 사용될 수 있다. you 앞에는 목적격 관계대명사 which가 생략된 것이므로 convince to buy computer가 맞다.

어구 count 계산하다, 세다 convince 확신시키다, 설득시키다 report 보고하다 on a daily basis 매일 마다

2 (c)

해석 A: 최근에 귀사에서 구입한 비디오 회의 시스템은 어떻던가

요?
B: 정말 훌륭해요. 유일한 단점이 있다면 제가 모든 참석자와 연결하는 방법을 배우는 데만 40분이 걸렸다는 거예요.

해설 '시간이 걸리다'를 표현하는 동사 take는 「take + 사람목적어 + 시간」 형태로 쓴다. 따라서 it took me 40 minutes로 쓸 수 있다. 주어를 it으로 써야지 사람으로 쓰면 안 된다.

어구 downside 단점 link up 연결시키다 attendee 참석자

3 (a)

해석 우리의 캠페인은 가능한 한 많은 사람들이 투표권을 행사하도 록 설득하는 데 목적이 있습니다.

해설 동사 persuade는 「persuade + 목적어 + to동사원형」의 어 순을 취한다. as many people as possible이 목적어이므 로 뒤에는 to exercise가 오면 된다.

어구 campaign 캠페인, 운동 be aimed at ~을 목표로 하다 persuade 설득하다 exercise ones' right 권리를 행사하다

4 (d)

해석 주주와 투자자들에게 이익을 남겨줄 수 있을 만큼 계약을 충 분히 따냈기 때문에, 올해는 우리의 성과를 발표할 수 있기를 고대합니다.

해설 look forward to(~을 고대하다) 뒤에는 동사원형이 아니 라 동명사나 명사가 와야 한다. 따라서 look forward to announcing이 올바른 표현이다.

어구 accomplishment 성과, 업적 secure 얻다, 확보하다 contract 계약 make a profit 이익을 내다 shareholder 주주 investor 투자자

5 (c)

해석 이사회는 대책 위원회가 그에 대처할 해결책을 제시할 때까지 당시의 난관이 지속되는 것을 허용할 수 없었다.

해설 continue는 뒤에는 to부정사가 오므로 (a)와 (b)는 일단 답에 서 제외한다. 동사 allow는 「allow + 목적어 + to동사원형」의 어순을 취하므로, 이 형태를 가장 잘 맞춘 것은 선택지 (c)이 다. the current impasse가 목적어에 해당한다.

어구 board of directors 이사회 current 현재의 impasse 난관 task force 특별조사단, 대책 위원회 come up with (해결책을) 제시하다 address (문제 따위에) 본격적으로 착수하 다, 대처하다

6 (a)

해석 (a) A: 앨리슨은 토니를 앤더슨 교회 위원회에 받아들이는 것 에 관해서 강력하게 반대해.
(b) B: 위원회의 임원이 되기 위해서 토니가 극복해야 할 유일 한 난관이 바로 앨리슨이야.
(c) A: 다른 구성원들은 토니의 지원을 거절할 이유가 없어.
(d) B: 네 말이 맞아. 앨리슨은 토니의 위원회 입회를 반대하 는 이들을 지지하고 있음에 틀림없어.

해설 be opposed to(~에 반대하다) 뒤에는 동사원형이 아니 라 명사나 동명사가 와야 한다. 따라서 (a)의 opposed to admit을 opposed to admitting으로 바꿔야 한다.

어구 admit ~에 입장[입회, 입학]을 허가하다; 인정하다 obstacle 난관, 장애 overcome 극복하다 turn down 거절하다

application 지원, 신청   be behind (사람을) 지지하다, 합세하다

7 (b)

해석 (a) A: 이 세상이 한계점에 이르기까지 얼마나 남았다고 보세요?
(b) B: 과학자들은 지구에 있는 마지막 빙하가 완전히 사라지기까지 20년밖에 안 걸릴 거라고 주장하고 있어요.
(c) A: 내가 생각했던 것보다 훨씬 더 이르네요.
(d) B: 맞아요. 빙하가 녹아서 지구 표면을 더욱 노출시켜 태양으로부터 더 많은 열을 흡수하기 때문이죠.

해설 '시간이 걸리다'를 나타내는 동사 take는 「it takes + 목적어 + 시간 + to부정사」 혹은 「it takes for + 목적격 + to부정사」 형태로 쓸 수 있다. (b)에서 「for + 목적격」으로 for the last glaciers on the Earth가 나왔으므로 will disappear를 to disappear로 바꿔야 한다.

어구 tipping point 전환점, 한계점   glacier 빙하   expose 노출시키다   absorb 흡수하다

8 (b)

해석 (a) 혼전계약서는 결혼하려는 대부분의 커플들에게 꼭 필요한 것이다. (b) 혼전계약서는 실수와 불확실성이라는 위험을 제거하는 한편, 신뢰를 구축하고 서로에 대한 이해를 높여 줄 수 있다. (c) 최근 설문 조사에 따르면 캐나다 부부의 절반에 육박하는 수가 이혼을 한다. (d) 결혼 기간 동안 축적된 자산에 관한 법적 투쟁도 종종 발생한다.

해설 동사 enable은 「enable + 목적어 + to부정사」의 어순을 취한다. (b)에서 전치사 for는 불필요하므로 enables for a couple을 enables a couple로 바꾼다.

어구 prenuptial agreement 혼전 계약서   tie the knot 결혼하다   build trust 신뢰를 구축하다   unpredictability 불확실성   get divorced 이혼하다   legal battle 법적 투쟁   asset 자산   accumulate 축적하다

9 (b)

해석 (a) 내가 텍사스 대학교에서 위원장을 맡았던 초기에는 어려운 일들이 너무 많았다. (b) 우리 대학이 보다 밝은 미래를 실현하도록 힘써준 학생, 동문, 교수진 덕택에 우리 대학의 경제적이고 사회적인 발전을 이룰 수 있었다. (c) 학문적 우수성의 추구와 연구는 지역 사회에도 기여했다. (d) 텍사스 대학교는 우리 시민의 학문적 요구를 충족시켜 주는 데 자부심을 가진다.

해설 commit가 '~하는 데에 힘쓰다'의 뜻으로 쓰이려면 「be committed to + 명사」의 형태가 되어야 한다. 따라서 (b)의 committed to realize를 committed to realizing으로 바꿔야 한다.

어구 chairmanship 의장[회장]직   be littered with ~로 점철되다   alumni 동문   faculty 교수진   realize 실현시키다   enhance 발전시키다   pursuit 추구   prominence 우수성   contribute 기여하다   community 지역사회   take pride in ~에 자부심을 가지다   meet the needs 필요를 충족시키다

10 (b)

해석 (a) 소화의 속도는 사람마다 다른데, 일반 성인은 보통 24시간

에서 72시간 사이이다. (b) 식사한 후 위가 음식을 처리하는 데는 6시간에서 8시간이 걸린다. (c) 그 다음에 음식물이 대장으로 가면 대장이 남은 음식을 소화하고 수분을 흡수한다. (d) 대장에 의한 초과 영양분과 음식찌꺼기 제거는 일반적으로 음식물을 섭취한지 24시간 후에 시작된다.

해설 「take + 시간 + for 목적어 + to부정사」 형태를 취해야 하므로 (b)에서 takes about six to eight hours your stomach를 takes about six to eight hours for your stomach로 바꿔야 한다.

어구 digestion 소화   depending on ~에 따라   colon 결장, 대장 전체   residue 나머지, 잔여   large intestine 대장

▌Check-up TEST 21~22

| 1 | (b) | 2 | (a) | 3 | (a) | 4 | (d) | 5 | (b) |
| 6 | (a) | 7 | (d) | 8 | (d) | 9 | (a) | 10 | (a) |

1 (b)

해석 A: 올림픽 성화가 내일 콜로라도 대학 라이스 스타디움에 도착한다.
B: 우와. 한 달 후면 올림픽 대회를 볼 수 있단 말이지?

해설 선택지 중 reach는 타동사이기 때문에 전치사를 동반할 수 없고, arrive는 자동사이므로 다음에 전치사를 쓸 수 있다. Rice Stadium에 알맞은 전치사는 장소를 나타내는 at이므로 빈칸에는 arriving at이 적절하다.

어구 torch 횃불, (성화) 봉송   Olympic Games 올림픽 대회

2 (a)

해석 A: 세계 경제가 깊은 침체기에 빠져들고 있는 것 같아.
B: 그래서 경제학자들이 경기 침체를 끝내는 방법에 관해서 토론하고 있어.

해설 '~에 관하여 토론하다'라는 뜻으로 사용되는 discuss는 타동사이므로 뒤에 전치사 about이 필요 없다. discuss 다음에 바로 목적어가 나와야 한다.

어구 slip into ~속으로 미끄러지다   recession 경기 침체

3 (a)

해석 A: 이 개념을 나에게 설명해 줄래?
B: 사실 나도 잘 몰라.

해설 동사 explain은 바로 뒤에 목적어가 온다. 「explain + 목적어 + to + 사람」으로 쓰므로 explain the concept to me가 올바른 표현이다.

어구 concept 개념

4 (d)

해석 회의에서 무엇을 논의하느냐는 참석자들의 태도에 달려있다.

해설 '~에 달려있다'는 동사 depend에 전치사 on을 사용하여 표현한다.

어구 attitude 자세, 태도   participant 참석자

5 (b)

해석 산업 제품은 종종 물질적인 제품으로 구성되어 있지만, 사람을 위한 서비스도 될 수 있다.

해설 동사 consist(~로 구성되다)는 전치사 of를 동반한다.

어구 **industrial** 산업의　**goods** 제품, 상품, 물건　**material** 물질의, 물질적인　**item** 제품

6 (a)

해석 그 시장은 주지사가 제안한 녹색 정책을 받아들이겠다고 발표했기 때문에, 주지사는 그의 연설 후 그를 크게 포옹하면서 맞이해 주었다.

해설 '상대방을 맞이하다, 환영하다'라는 의미의 타동사 greet는 뒤에 사람목적어를 바로 취한다. 단순 과거 사실이므로 현재완료 시제인 (d)는 올 수 없다.

어구 **mayor** 시장　**green policy** 녹색 정책, 친환경 정책　**propose** 제안하다　**governor** 주지사　**hug** 포옹

7 (d)

해석 (a) A: 여행하다가 짐을 잃어버린 적 있니?
(b) B: 어, 그런 일이 세 번이나 있었어.
(c) A: 안됐다! 짐을 다시 찾기는 했니?
(d) B: 응, 하지만 내 짐을 기다려야 했어.

해설 '~을 기다리다'라고 할 때 wait for는 맞지만 await for라고 쓸 수는 없다. await는 타동사이므로 바로 뒤에 목적어를 취한다. 따라서 (d)의 await for는 wait for가 되어야 한다.

어구 **baggage** 짐　**get back** 회수하다

8 (d)

해석 (a) A: 좀 더 아늑한 객실 있습니까?
(b) B: 죄송합니다만 지금은 성수기여서요.
(c) A: 그러면 작은 방으로 만족해야겠군요.
(d) B: 내일 밤에 큰 방이 나오면 연락드리겠습니다.

해설 (d)에서 contact는 타동사이므로 전치사 to 없이 바로 목적어인 you가 나와야 한다.

어구 **cabin** 객실　**peak season** 성수기　**settle for** 불만스럽지만 받아들이다, 참다

9 (a)

해석 (a) 멀리서 산맥을 바라보면 산봉우리가 하늘을 배경으로 솟아있는 것 같다. (b) 산 정상에 오르려는 사람을 막을 것이 아무것도 없어 보인다. (c) 그러나 근처로 가까이 다가갈수록 모든 것이 변한다. (d) 인생도 마찬가지다.

해설 (a)에서 rise는 자동사이므로 바로 이어서 명사가 올 수 없다. 뒤에 전치사 to나 against를 쓴 다음에 명사가 올 수 있다.

어구 **mountain range** 산맥, 산악지대　**peak** 산봉우리　**obstacle** 장애물　**hinder** 막다, 방해하다　**climb to the top** 산 정상을 오르다　**draw** 가까이 가다

10 (a)

해석 (a) 사이버상에서의 인신공격은 놀라운 수준까지 이르렀다. (b) 한 개인이 온라인상에서 타깃이 되면 수많은 네티즌들이 가차 없이 공격을 가하여 당사자를 절망과 무력감에 빠뜨린다. (c) 그러나 애석하게도 세계적인 IT 강국이라는 사실에 자

부심을 가지고 있는 한국에서 이와 같은 일이 비일비재해지고 있다. (d) 최근 한 고등학교 여학생은 급우들의 허위 비방으로 괴로워하다가 자살했다.

해설 (a)문장을 해석하다 보면 '놀라운 수준에까지 이르렀다'는 뜻이라 전치사 at이나 to를 쓰기 쉽겠지만 reach가 '어떤 결과·상태에 이르다'라는 뜻으로 쓰일 때는 타동사이므로 전치사가 필요 없다.

어구 **character assassination** (공인(公人) 등에 대한) 중상, 비방, 인신공격　**alarming** 놀라운　**legion** (수많은) 무리　**launch attacks** 공격을 가하다　**merciless** 가차 없는　**hopeless** 희망이 없는　**helpless** 무력한　**commonplace** 흔한　**pride oneself on** ~에 대해 자부심을 가지다　**powerhouse** 최강자, 최강팀; 발전소, 동력실　**false** 거짓의, 허위의　**accusation** 비난; 고소, 고발; 죄

Unit 3 분사

=== **Check-up** TEST 23~24 ===

1 (b)	2 (c)	3 (c)	4 (d)	5 (b)
6 (a)	7 (c)	8 (b)	9 (b)	10 (b)

1 (b)

해석 A: 이 프린터가 제대로 작동하지 않아.
B: 내가 지금 바로 고칠 수 있어.

해설 여기서 have는 사역동사로 사용되었다. 목적어 it(프린터)이 '수리되는' 것이므로 과거분사를 써서 「have + 목적어 + p.p.」 형태로 써야 한다. 따라서 (b) fixed가 정답이다.

2 (c)

해석 A: 브래드가 연간 회의에서 임원들에게 배포될 첨부 문서를 분실했대.
B: 그 사람 이제 큰일 났네.

해설 첨부 문서, 즉 '첨부된' 문서라는 의미이므로 수동 개념이다. 따라서 attached document라고 해야 한다. (d) the documents attached는 '~에 첨부된 문서'라는 뜻이므로 뒤에는 어디에 첨부된 것인지 그 대상이 나와야 한다. 예를 들면 the document attached to the monthly report(월간 보고서에 첨부된 문서)처럼 써야 자연스럽다.

어구 **distribute** 배포하다　**executive** 임원, 간부　**yearly** 연간의　**be in trouble** 곤경에 빠지다

3 (c)

해석 한국인들에게 알려진 가장 훌륭한 지도자 중 한 명이었던 이순신 장군의 업적에 이 소설을 바칩니다.

해설 수동의 의미로 '~에게 알려진'이라는 뜻이 되어야 하므로 과거분사 known이 와야 한다.

어구 **be dedicated to** ~에게 바치다, 헌정하다　**legacy** (과거의) 유산, 유물　**admiral** 해군장성

4 (d)

해석 더 좋은 시대에 태어난 그 피아니스트는 조국에서 최상의 음악 교육을 받을 수 있었다.

해설 The pianist와 could get~ 사이에 The pianist를 부연 설명하는 관계대명사절이 삽입된 문장이다. 관계대명사절은 '더 나은 시대에 태어난'이라는 의미가 되어야 하는데, 태어나는 것은 본인의 의지와 상관없이 '태어나게 되는' 것이므로 수동형인 born으로 표시하여 who was born in a better time이 된다. 여기서 주격 관계대명사인 who와 be동사인 was는 생략 가능하므로, The pianist, born in a better time, could get~이 올바른 문장이 된다

5 (b)

해석 산드라는 올해 보너스 지급이 갑작스러운 경기 하락으로 인해 연기될 것이란 소식을 듣고 실망했다.

해설 disappoint는 '실망시키다'라는 뜻의 동사이다. 소식을 듣고 Sandra가 '실망하게 된' 것이므로 능동의 뜻을 갖는 disappointing이 아니라 수동의 성격을 띤 disappointed를 써야 한다.

어구 disappoint 실망시키다　due to ~ 때문에　economic slowdown 경기 침체

6 (a)

해석 (a) A: 로라가 방금 나한테 자기의 모든 친구들이 결혼식 피로연에 오는 것을 환영한다는 초대장을 줬어.
(b) B: 나도 같이 가고 싶지만 아이를 봐야 해.
(c) A: 너희 어머니가 존을 하루만 봐주시면 안 되니?
(d) B: 사실은, 난 로라를 좋아하지 않아. 대학 다닐 때 늘 나를 괴롭혔거든.

해설 (a)는 '그녀의 친구 모두가 오는 것을 환영하는 초대장'이라는 뜻이므로 능동의 의미를 가진 현재분사를 쓰는 것이 알맞다. 따라서 welcomed가 아니라 welcoming이라고 표현해야 한다.

어구 invitation 초대장　wedding reception 결혼식 피로연　watch[babysit] a baby 아기를 돌보다　annoy 짜증나게 하다, 괴롭히다

7 (c)

해석 (a) A: 롯데 자이언츠가 또 졌다니 믿어져?
(b) B: 그 팀이 언제 다시 이기게 될지 모르겠어.
(c) A: 그러게. 오늘 밤 경기에서 롯데가 이기길 바라고 있었는데.
(d) B: 시즌이 시작하기 전에는 마치 무적의 팀일 것 같았지.

해설 (c)에서 롯데 팀이 경기에서 '이기기를' 바란 것이므로 능동의 의미이다. 능동의 의미를 가질 때 지각동사 see는 「see + 목적어 + 동사원형/현재분사」의 형태로 쓰므로, 과거분사 pulled 대신 pull이나 현재분사 pulling이 와야 한다.

어구 pull off a win 경기에서 이기다　invincible 최강의, 무적의　season (스포츠 경기에서) 시즌

8 (b)

해석 (a) A: 오늘 밤 미란다네 집들이에 갈 수 있어요?
(b) B: 정말 가고 싶은데 제 보고서를 먼저 마무리해야 해요.
(c) A: 알았어요. 다음번에는 우리와 같이 갈 수 있으면 좋겠군요.
(d) B: 나도 정말 그렇게 하고 싶어요.

해설 (b)의 I have to get the report doing first.에서 get은 '~하게 하다'라는 사역동사이다. 보고서는 사람에 의해서 '마무리되는' 것이므로 능동을 나타내는 현재분사 doing이 아니라 수동을 나타내는 과거분사 done으로 쓰는 것이 적절하다.

어구 housewarming party 집들이　get the report done 보고서를 마무리하다

9 (b)

해석 (a) 한때 나는 아버지의 가르침을 매우 좋아하긴 했지만, 돈이 나를 노예로 만든다고 생각한 적은 한 번도 없음을 고백한다. (b) 나는 고객들에게 제공하는 서비스에 대한 대가로 돈을 벌 때면 늘 보람을 느낀다. (c) 버스 대신 택시를 탈 수 있는 것도 나는 좋다. (d) 내 인생에서 돈은 꼭 필요하며, 나는 돈이 쓸모없다고 생각하지 않는다.

해설 rewarding은 '보람 있는, 보람을 느끼게 하는 것'(능동)이고, rewarded는 보람찬 일을 하여 '보람을 느끼는'(수동) 것이다. (b)에서는 일을 하고 돈을 받으면 '보람을 느낀다'는 의미이므로 rewarding을 rewarded로 바꿔야 한다. 참고로 rewarding은 Helping the poor is such a rewarding experience.(가난한 사람을 돕는 것은 매우 보람찬 경험이다.)처럼 내가 보람을 느끼는 것이 아니라 그 경험 자체가 보람을 느끼게 하는 일일 때 쓴다.

어구 teaching 가르침　confess 고백하다　look upon A as B A를 B로 간주하다　enslavement 노예화; 노예 상태　make money (많은) 돈을 벌다　client 고객　essential 필수적인　see A as B A를 B로 간주하다　useless 쓸모없는

10 (b)

해석 (a) 가을은 내가 가장 좋아하는 계절이고, 많은 이들 역시 가을을 좋아한다. (b) 대부분의 나무에 단풍이 들기 시작하고 나뭇잎이 떨어져 낙엽은 거리 어디에나 있다. (c) 농부들은 밭에서 농작물을 수확하느라 바쁘고 과수원은 잘 익은 사과와 감으로 아름답다. (d) 가을은 책 읽기에도 좋은 계절이라고 사람들은 말한다.

해설 (b)에서 falling leaves라고 하면 '떨어지고 있는 나뭇잎들'이란 뜻이다. 나뭇잎이 ~are everywhere on streets(거리 어디에나 있다)라고 했으므로 '떨어진' 나뭇잎, 즉 '낙엽'에 관한 이야기임을 알 수 있다. 낙엽은 falling leaves가 아니라 fallen leaves라고 해야 한다.

어구 shed (잎을) 떨어뜨리다; (눈물을) 흘리다　harvest 수확하다　crop (농)작물　orchard 과수원　ripe 익은　persimmon 감

■■ Check-up TEST 25~26 ■■■

1 (c)	2 (b)	3 (b)	4 (c)	5 (c)
6 (d)	7 (c)	8 (c)	9 (d)	10 (b)

1 (c)

해석 A: 이 박사가 마침내 아프리카에서 최근 발견된 영장류의

DNA 염기서열을 분석할 실마리를 찾았다고 해.

B: 이 박사는 워낙 저명한 유전학자여서 조만간 노벨상을 받을 거야.

해설 주절은 콤마 이하의 he will win~이고 빈칸이 있는 부분은 분사구문에 해당하므로 현재분사 구문을 써서 Being을 쓰면 된다. (b)와 (d)는 문법적으로 틀리며, (a)의 경우, 종속절의 내용이 주절보다 한 시제 앞선 것이 아니므로 답이 될 수 없다.

어구 at last 마침내   analyze 분석하다   key 비결, 실마리   the DNA sequence DNA 염기서열   primate 영장류   distinguished 저명한   geneticist 유전학자

2 (b)

해석 A: 존, 다음 주부터 여름휴가인데, 무슨 계획 있어요?

B: 3일 전에 새로운 프로젝트를 받아서 휴가를 연기할까 말까 생각 중이에요.

해설 대화의 전체 시점은 현재이다. 그런데 three days ago라는 것은 과거로, 현재의 대화 이전에 프로젝트를 받은 것이므로 한 시제 앞선 일이다. 또한 주어 I에게 프로젝트가 '주어진' 것이기 때문에 수동 완료분사구문인 (b)가 정답이다.

어구 coming up 다가오는   postpone 연기하다

3 (b)

해석 A: 파괴적인 지진에 타격을 입어서 그 국가는 현재 통제불능 상태야.

B: 다른 국가들은 서둘러서 그 나라에 원조를 제공해야 해.

해설 분사구문 문제이다. 그 나라가 지진에 타격을 '입은' 것이므로 수동형이 와야 하는데, hit는 과거분사도 hit이다.

어구 hit (병, 재해 등이) 급습하다, 타격을 주다; 때리다   devastating 파괴적인, (막심한) 피해를 주는   earthquake 지진   out of control 통제 불능인   offer assistance to ~에게 원조를 제공하다

4 (c)

해석 친구들과 가족에게 둘러싸여 티파니는 자신이 더 이상 위험에 처해 있지 않음을 알고는 안도했다.

해설 주절의 주어인 Tiffany의 입장에서 보면 친구들과 가족에 의해 '둘러싸인' 것이므로 수동의 뜻을 갖는 과거분사 Surrounded로 표현해야 한다.

어구 surround 둘러싸다   relieved 안도감을 느끼는   be in danger 위험에 처한

5 (c)

해석 직원 급여를 결코 삭감하지 않는 MF 테크놀로지의 사장은 직원들에게는 찬사를 받지만 회사 주주들로부터는 비판을 듣는다.

해설 직원들의 급여를 삭감하는 행위는 the president의 능동적 행위이므로 cutting으로 써야 하고 부정어 never는 분사 바로 앞에 두면 된다.

어구 cut 삭감하다   wage 급여, 임금   praise 칭찬하다   criticize 비판하다   shareholder 주주

6 (d)

해석 암살, 정치적 논쟁, 인신매매, 그리고 전쟁과 같은 불쾌한 소식에 너무나 많은 충격을 받았었기 때문에 사실상 나는 어떤 나쁜 소식을 들어도 무감각했다.

해설 주절을 보면 주어가 나쁜 뉴스를 들어도 무감각하다고 말하고 있다. 그 이유는 이미 그 이전에 나쁜 소식에 충격을 많이 받았기 때문이다. 따라서 주절보다 종속절의 시제가 한 시제 앞서므로 완료분사구문으로 써야 한다. 또한 '충격을 받다'라는 수동의 의미이기 때문에 Having been shocked로 쓰는 것이 가장 적절하다.

어구 unpleasant 불쾌한   assassination 암살   wrangling 언쟁, 다툼   human trafficking 인신매매   immune 면역이 생긴

7 (c)

해석 (a) A: 늘 그렇듯이 전 씨는 다른 사람들의 말을 듣지 않더군.

(b) B: 하지만 중요한 것은 그 사람이 우리에게 닥친 시급한 문제에 대해 항상 창의적인 해결책을 제시해준다는 거지. 오늘도 예외가 아니었잖아.

(c) A: 그가 오늘과 같은 일들을 여러 차례 겪었기 때문에 그는 전적으로 신뢰할 만해.

(d) B: 아마도 그것 때문에 어떤 회의에도 그를 절대 빼놓지 않나봐.

해설 (c)를 보면 현재시제인 주절보다 분사구문의 내용(그가 그와 같은 일을 여러 번 겪었던 것)이 한 시제 앞선다. 따라서 Experienced가 아니라 완료분사구문인 Having experienced로 표현해야 한다.

어구 as usual 늘 그렇듯, 평소와 다름없이   the thing is that 요는, 실은, 문제는   come up with (해답을) 내놓다, 생각해내다   creative 창의적인   urgent 시급한   exception 예외   dependable 믿을 만한   leave out 빼다, 배제시키다

8 (c)

해석 (a) A: 이봐, 조. 아들이 직장을 잡았다면서. 축하하네!

(b) B: 고마워. 아들이 이틀 전에 면접 보러 갔을 때 내가 아주 긴장이 되더라고.

(c) A: 시장 상황이 너무 좋지 않아서 구직자들이 괜찮은 일자리를 구하기 어렵지.

(d) B: 우리 어른들이 뭔가를 해야 한다고 생각해. 단지 운에 맡겨둘 수는 없어.

해설 (c)를 보면 주절의 주어와 종속절의 주어가 다르므로, 종속절의 주어는 남겨두고 분사구문을 만들었다. 종속절의 원래 문장은 'Because the market is so tight'이므로 be동사 is를 been이 아니라 현재분사인 being의 형태로 써야 한다. being은 일반적으로 생략 가능하므로 The market so tight라고 해도 된다.

어구 applicant 지원자   decent 괜찮은, 좋은   fate 운명

9 (d)

해석 (a) A: 어젯밤 파티는 어땠니? 재미있었다고 들었는데.

(b) B: 그렇게 재미있지는 않았어. 스프링필드에서 열린 다른 파티에 갔어야 했어.

(c) A: 아니 왜? 그 파티는 이 지역에서 가장 유명한 사교계의 명사 미란다가 주최한 거였잖아.

(d) B: 이전에 파티를 열어본 적이 없어서인지 파티 참석자의 요구에 좀처럼 부합하지 못하더라고.

해설 분사구문을 부정하려면 not이나 never를 분사 바로 앞에 위치시켜야 한다. 따라서 (d)의 Having not hosted를 Not having hosted로 바꿔준다.

어구 **should have p.p.** ~했어야 했다   **host** (파티를) 주최하다   **celebrated** 저명한   **socialite** 사교계의 명사   **slow to** ~하는 데에 느린   **meet the needs of** 필요한 점[요구]을 충족시키다   **partygoer** 파티에 잘 다니는 사람

10 (b)

해석 (a) 허블 우주 망원경은 현재 지구 궤도를 돌고 있는 망원경이다. (b) 최초의 우주 망원경은 아니지만 역사상 가장 다방면으로 쓸모 있고 유명한 망원경 가운데 하나일 것이다. (c) 1990년 발사되어 궤도에 진입하였으며 그 이후로 계속 가동되고 있다. (d) 허블 우주 망원경은 2014년 혹은 그 이후까지 작동할 것으로 보이며, 뒤를 이어 제임스 웹 스페이스 망원경이 허블 우주 망원경의 역할을 대신하게 될 것이다.

해설 분사구문을 부정하려면 분사 바로 앞에 부정어를 써야 하므로 (b)에서 The first not space telescope가 아니라 Not the first space telescope가 되어야 한다. 원래는 Not being the first space telescope인데 being은 생략 가능하다.

어구 **telescope** 망원경   **in orbit** 궤도에 있는, 궤도를 도는   **versatile** 다재다능한; 여러모로 쓸모 있는   **launch** (어뢰·유도탄 따위를) 발사하다, 쏘아 올리다   **operational** 작동[사용] 중인   **function** 작동하다, 기능을 하다   **successor** 후임자, 후계자   **take one's place** 자리를 차지하다; ~을 대신하다

━━**Check-up TEST 27**━━

1 (c)   2 (b)   3 (b)   4 (d)   5 (c)

1 (c)

해석 A: 제인과 제이슨이 곧 결혼한대.
B: 말이 나와서 하는 말인데, 마크와 소피아도 결혼할 거래.

해설 '말이 나와서 하는 말인데'라는 표현은 speaking of which이다.

어구 **tie the knot** 결혼하다

2 (b)

해석 A: 모든 것을 고려해 봤는데, 그녀에게 전화해서 더 이상 그녀의 심리전에 휘둘리지 않겠다고 말하겠어.
B: 잘 결정했어. 넌 잃을 게 아무 것도 없잖아.

해설 '모든 것을 고려해 봤을 때'라는 표현은 taking all things into consideration이다.

어구 **mind games** 심리 조작[전술], 심리전

3 (b)

해석 이번 달 급여를 못 받았다 하더라도 내일까지 주택 담보 대출금을 지불하셔야 합니다. 그렇지 않으면 집을 잃게 될 겁니다.

해설 '설사 ~라 할지라도, ~라는 점을 인정한다 하더라도'라는 뜻의 독립분사구문은 「granting that+주어+동사」이다.

어구 **mortgage** 주택 담보 대출

4 (d)

해석 (a) A: 너 지금 왜 그렇게 공격적이니? 그녀에게 그렇게까지 거칠게 할 필요는 없잖아.
(b) B: 그녀가 매일 나가는 과제를 끝마치지 않았거든. 그게 다야.
(c) A: 그래도 그녀가 울었잖아.
(d) B: 솔직히 말해서, 그녀가 울든 말든 상관없어.

해설 '솔직히 말해서'는 frankly spoken이 아니라 frankly speaking이다.

어구 **aggressive** 공격적인   **harsh** 엄격한, 거친   **assignment** 숙제   **concern** 걱정시키다, 걱정하다

5 (c)

해석 (a) 여느 때와 다름없던 어느 월요일 아침, 두 명의 17세 소년들이 그들이 다니던 고등학교에서 총기 난사를 벌였다. (b) 7명의 학생과 교사 한 명이 사망했고 학생 23명이 부상을 당했다. (c) 그 사건으로부터 2년이 흐른 후, 모든 것을 고려해 보면, 학교는 매우 잘 운영되고 있었다. (d) 그러나 생존자들에게는 그 참사가 남긴 상처가 아직 남아 있다.

해설 (c)에 나오는 '모든 것을 고려해 봤을 때'라는 표현은 all things considered이다.

어구 **embark** (행동으로) 옮기다, 착수하다   **shooting rampage** 총기 난사   **wound** 부상을 입히다   **fairly** 매우, 꽤   **scar** 상처   **disaster** 참사, 재난   **visible** 눈에 보이는   **survivor** 생존자

Unit 4 관계사

━━**Check-up TEST 28~29**━━

1 (c)   2 (c)   3 (b)   4 (a)   5 (b)
6 (c)   7 (c)   8 (c)   9 (d)   10 (b)

1 (c)

해석 A: 누구에게 이 상품권을 주실 거예요?
B: 그럴 수 있는 사람이 있을지 모르겠지만 내 시험을 통과하는 사람이 이걸 받게 될 거야.

해설 will get의 주어가 되는 관계대명사절을 만들어야 한다. '사람들'이라는 뜻의 대명사 those를 선행사로 내세우면 which는 적절하지 않다. 또한 pass 앞에는 주격 관계대명사가 필요하므로 (c) Those who(~하는 사람들)가 정답이다.

어구 **gift card** 상품권, 기프트 카드   **doubt** 확신하지 못하다, 의문을 갖다

2 (c)

해석 A: 제가 아직 방문하지 않은 학생이 있나요?
B: 아니요. 이 반 학생들 모두를 방문하셨어요.

해설 관계대명사가 와야 할 빈칸 앞의 선행사가 anybody로 사람이며, 동사 called on의 목적어 역할을 하는 관계대명사가 와야 하므로 목적격 관계대명사로도 쓰이는 that이 적절하다.

어구 call on 방문하다

3 (b)

해석 A: 급여 인상을 약속하는 새 CEO에 대해 어떻게 생각해?
B: 약속을 지킬 수 있을지 의문이야.

해설 선행사가 사람이고 3인칭 단수이므로 동사도 단수로 처리해
야 한다.

어구 pay hike 급여 인상　**keep one's word** 약속을 지키다

4 (a)

해석 마이클 김은 재능 있는 프로그래머로서, 그의 프로그래밍 기
술은 동료들 사이에서 존경의 대상이 되어 왔다.

해설 사람인 a talented programmer가 선행사로, 뒤에 나오는
programming skills를 소유하는 관계가 된다. 따라서 관계
대명사 whose가 적절하다.

어구 talented 재능 있는, 유능한　**subject** 대상　**veneration**
존경, 숭배, 추앙

5 (b)

해석 교수님께서 학생들에게 쿠르스크 전투에 관해 기술한 책을 몇
권 구입하라고 하셨다.

해설 관계대명사 which의 선행사인 some books가 복수 명사이
므로 관계대명사절의 동사는 복수가 되어야 하며 책이 특정
내용을 '설명하는' 것이므로 능동태가 적절하다.

어구 describe 서술하다, 묘사하다

6 (c)

해석 그 학교에서는 유학하고자 하는 학생들에게 온라인 학습 자료
를 제공할 예정이다.

해설 관계대명사 who의 선행사는 the students로 복수이다. 따
라서 관계대명사절 내의 동사 역시 복수가 되어야 한다. 문
맥상 과거에 일어난 일을 언급하는 게 아니므로 과거 동사
wanted는 적절하지 않다. 또한 주격 관계대명사 who를 생
략해서는 안 된다.

어구 study material(s) 학습 자료[교재]

7 (c)

해석 (a) A: 우리 형이 이번에 직업을 또 바꿨어.
(b) B: 또? 불과 한 달 전에 취업했다고 들었는데.
(c) A: 맞아. 그런데 자신한테 딱 맞는 다른 일이 있다지 뭐야.
(d) B: 아무래도 너희 형은 직장 생활을 유지할 수 없나 봐.

해설 (c)에서 which의 선행사 another job은 단수이므로 관계
대명사절 내의 동사 역시 단수 형태가 되어야 한다. 따라서
which suit을 which suits로 바꿔준다.

어구 suit ~에게 맞다, 어울리다　**hold down a job** 직장 생활을 유
지하다

8 (c)

해석 (a) A: 다음 주에 그 밴드가 콘서트 하는 거 알고 있었니?
(b) B: 응. 그 콘서트가 너무 기다려져. 난 이미 티켓을 예매
했어.
(c) A: 그 밴드의 보컬 목소리는 굉장한 것 같아.

(d) B: 맞는 말이야. 내 목소리도 그렇게 멋있었으면 좋겠다.

해설 소유격 관계대명사를 묻는 문제이다. (c)에서 목소리의 소
유자는 밴드 보컬이므로 that이 아니라 소유격 관계대명사
whose로 고쳐야 한다.

어구 vocalist 가수, 보컬

9 (d)

해석 (a) 오늘, 한 정부기관이 가난한 어린이들의 심리적인 행복에
관한 최근 연구 결과를 발표할 계획을 하고 있다. (b) 그 연구
는 궁핍한 환경에서 자란 아이들이 심리적으로 어떻게 영향을
받는지 알아보기 위해 시행되었다. (c) 연구는 3년의 기간 동
안 행해졌다. (d) 또한, 5세에서 17세까지 나이가 다른 천 명
이상의 아이들이 연구 대상이었다.

해설 (d)에서 '아이들의' 나이가 5세에서 17세까지 다양했다는
말이므로 관계대명사의 목적격 whom이 아니라 소유격
whose를 써야 맞다.

어구 government agency 정부기관　**well-being** 복지, 행복
underprivileged 궁핍한, 가난한　**if at all** 적어도 ~한다면
deprived 궁핍한　**vary** 다르다; 달리하다

10 (b)

해석 (a) 스팸 메일이란 요청하지도, 원하지도 않는 메시지를 무차
별적으로 전송하는 행태이다. (b) 때때로 웜 및 바이러스를 지
닌 스팸 메일은 1990년대 중반 인터넷이 대중화된 이후로 골
칫거리가 되었다. (c) 스팸 메일을 전송하는 데 사실상 비용이
들지 않기 때문에 스팸 메일을 보내는 사람은 많으며, 전 세계
이메일의 85퍼센트 가량이 스팸 메일인 것으로 추정된다. (d)
인터넷 서비스 제공업체들은 기하급수적으로 늘어나는 스팸
메일에 대처할 수 있도록 추가적인 보안기능을 갖춰야 한다.

해설 (b)에서 which의 선행사인 spam emails는 복수이므로 관
계대명사절 내의 동사 carries는 복수형태인 carry가 되어야
적절하다.

어구 practice 실천, 실행　**indiscriminately** 무차별적으로
unsolicited 청하지 않은　**problematic** 문제가 있는;
골칫거리의　**spammer** 스팸 메일 발송자　**numerous** 많은
be equipped with ~을 갖추다　**security** 보안
exponentially 기하급수적으로

Check-up TEST 30~32

1	(d)	2	(b)	3	(a)	4	(a)	5	(c)
6	(a)	7	(c)	8	(a)	9	(a)	10	(c)

1 (d)

해석 A: 서 씨가 지원한 자리가 여전히 공석인가요? 그렇다면 저
도 지원하려고요.
B: 죄송하지만 그를 고용하겠다고 그들이 어제 발표했어요.

해설 자동사 apply는 '~에 지원하다'라는 의미로서 항상 전치사
for를 수반한다. 사물인 the position을 선행사로 받으면서
전치사 for의 목적격 역할을 할 수 있는 관계대명사는 which
이다. 따라서 Is the position which Mr. Seo applied for
still available?이라고 쓸 수 있는데, 이런 경우 전치사 for는

관계대명사 앞으로 이동할 수 있다.

어구 **apply for** ~에 지원[신청]하다　**available** 이용할 수 있는

2 (b)

해석 A: 원샷!
B: 이봐, 네가 못하는 일을 남한테 강요하지 말라구.

해설 동사의 목적격 역할을 하며 선행사를 포함하고 있는 관계대명사는 '~하는 것'이라는 의미의 what뿐이다. 나머지 that, which 및 whom은 모두 앞에 선행사가 있어야 한다.

어구 **bottom up** 잔을 비우다, 원샷하다

3 (a)

해석 A: 스테파니는 정말 거만해. 넌 그 애에 대해 어떻게 생각하니?
B: 내가 생각하기에 그 애는 다른 사람에 대한 존중이 부족한 것 같아.

해설 관계대명사절의 동사 is lacking의 주격 역할을 하는 관계대명사가 필요하므로 who를 써야 한다. who와 is 사이에 I believe가 삽입되어 '내가 생각하기에'라는 의미가 추가된 형태이다.

어구 **arrogant** 거만한　**lack** ~이 없다, 부족하다

4 (a)

해석 마크는 근 일 년 간 매달려온 책의 집필을 끝내자 날아갈 듯이 기뻤다.

해설 동사 work는 자동사이므로 목적어를 취할 수 없다. 따라서 the book을 목적어로 취하기 위해선 전치사가 필요하다. 본래 문장은 he had been working on the book이므로 전치사 on이 which 앞에 온 (a)가 정답이다. 전치사를 동사 뒤에 붙여서 which he had been working on for almost a year~라고도 할 수 있다.

어구 **work on** ~에 공을 들이다, 애쓰다　**walk on air** (너무 좋아서) 하늘을 날 것만 같다, 기뻐 날뛰다

5 (c)

해석 오 씨는 급여에서 그가 간신히 생활할 정도를 제외한 나머지 대부분을 미국에 있는 아내와 딸에게 보낸다.

해설 except for 뒤에는 명사 또는 명사절이 와야 한다. '~하는 것'이라는 의미의 관계대명사 what은 명사절을 이끄므로 정답은 (c)이다. 그 외의 선택지인 that, which, who는 앞에 선행사를 수반해야 하므로 적절하지 않다.

어구 **salary** 봉급　**except for** ~을 제외하고는

6 (a)

해석 내가 훌륭한 스승으로 기억하는 스펜서 크리스탈 경께서 돌아가셨다.

해설 관계대명사절 내에 있는 I remember가 삽입구로 쓰인 것이 아니라는 점을 파악해야 한다. 선행사 Sir Spencer Crystal은 관계대명사절 내에서 동사 remember의 목적어가 되기 때문에 목적격 관계대명사인 whom을 써야 한다. 이 문장이 Sir Spencer Crystal has passed away. I remember him as an extraordinary teacher.라는 두 문장을 하나로 합친 문장이라는 것을 파악하면 목적격 관계대명사 whom이

와야 한다는 것을 더욱 쉽게 이해할 수 있다.

어구 **extraordinary** 놀라운, 비범한　**pass away** 돌아가시다

7 (c)

해석 (a) A: 너희 언니 아직도 비디오게임을 하고 있니?
(b) B: 응. 하루에 적어도 열 시간은 게임을 하는데 그만 좀 하라고 해도 들으려 하지 않아.
(c) A: 언니가 빠져 있는 게임 이름이 뭐니?
(d) B: 〈세계 전쟁〉이야! 언니는 걷잡을 수 없을 만큼 게임에 빠져 있고, 난 어떻게 해야 할지 모르겠어.

해설 addicted는 전치사 to와 함께 쓰이는 동사이다. (c) 후반부의 본래 문장은 she is addicted to the game인데, 관계대명사 which를 사용해서 the game which she is addicted to로 쓰거나 전치사 to를 관계대명사 앞으로 이동하여 the game to which she is addicted로 쓸 수 있다.

어구 **addicted** 중독된　**get out of hand** 과도해지다, 감당할 수 없게 되다

8 (a)

해석 (a) A: 내가 어제 한 말은 진심이 아니었어.
(b) B: 그래? 난 또 자네가 어제 마음을 바꾼 줄 알았지.
(c) A: 물론 그녀의 의견에 마음이 약간 흔들렸어. 하지만 그렇다고 해서 내가 그녀에게 동의했다는 건 아니야.
(d) B: 자넨 어제 그렇게 어리석은 말을 하지 말았어야 했어. 이제 그녀는 자네의 실수를 완전히 이용하고 있다고.

해설 선행사가 포함된 관계대명사 what은 '~하는 것'이라는 의미로 명사절을 이끌며 주어의 자리에 올 수 있다. (a)에서 which를 쓰려면 앞에 선행사가 와야 한다. 따라서 Which I said를 What I said로 바꿔야 한다.

어구 **sway** (마음을) 흔들다　**remark** 발언, 말　**take advantage of** ~을 이용하다

9 (a)

해석 (a) 조안나는 자신과 약혼한 약혼자가 돌아오면 목요일에 그와 결혼식을 올릴 계획이었다. (b) 장래의 남편인 브라이언은 월요일에 고국으로 돌아오는 비행기에 올랐다. (c) 하지만 그가 탄 비행기가 이륙한지 얼마되지 않아서 기체 결함으로 추락했고, 탑승자 전원이 사망했다. (d) 낙담스럽게도 조안나는 웨딩드레스 대신 장례식 예복을 입어야 했다.

해설 (a)의 the man to who she was engaged에서 who는 주격 관계대명사로, 바로 뒤에 또 다른 주어가 올 수 없다. 여기서는 선행사 the man을 수식해주면서 전치사 to의 목적격 역할을 하는 관계대명사가 오는 것이 적절하므로 whom이 쓰여야 한다. 따라서 the man to who를 the man to whom으로 바꿔 준다.

어구 **fiancé** 약혼자　**engaged to somebody** ~와 약혼한　**board** 탑승하다　**take off** (비행기 등이) 이륙하다, 날아오르다　**crash** 추락하다　**mechanical** 기계상의　**malfunction** (기계 등의) 기능 부전, 고장　**to one's dismay** 놀랍게도, 낙담스럽게도

10 (c)

해설 (a) 캐서린과 그녀의 남편 길버트는 수양아들을 학대한 혐의로 기소되었다. (b) 경찰은 이들의 두 살배기 아들인 제이슨이

심한 구타를 당한 사실을 밝혀냈으며 그 부부를 아동 학대 및 구타 혐의로 기소했다. (c) 그들은 서로에게 책임을 돌리고 있으며 경찰 측의 말은 사실이 아니라고 주장하고 있다. (d) 하지만 경찰은 그들이 유죄이며 처벌받아야 한다고 말한다.

해설 (c)의 which the police say는 주격 역할을 할 수 없고, which 앞에는 선행사가 필요하다. 따라서 '~하는 것'이라는 의미로, 명사절을 이끌고 주어 자리에 오며 자체 내에 선행사를 포함하는 관계대명사 what이 바람직하다. which the police say를 what the police say로 바꿔야 한다.

어구 accuse A of B A를 B 혐의로 기소하다   foster child 수양자녀   battery 구타   guilty 유죄의   punish 처벌하다

■Check-up TEST 33~34■

| 1 | (d) | 2 | (c) | 3 | (d) | 4 | (d) | 5 | (a) |
| 6 | (d) | 7 | (d) | 8 | (b) | 9 | (c) | 10 | (c) |

1 (d)
해석 A: 난 내가 사랑했던 그 누구로부터도 사랑받아본 적이 한 번도 없어.
B: 기운 내. 곧 네 진정한 짝을 만나게 될 거야.

해설 사랑해주는 대상은 사람이므로 whatever 또는 however는 올 수 없다. have loved의 목적어를 받는 목적격 역할을 하면서 동시에 전치사 by 뒤에서도 목적격의 역할을 해야 하므로 whomever가 오는 것이 적절하다.

어구 cheer up 기운을 내다   soul mate 영혼의 반려자, 마음이 통하는 사람

2 (c)
해석 A: 테이블 위에 과일이 한 아름이네!
B: 좋아하는 것 아무거나 가져가.

해설 빈칸 앞에 있는 Pick에 주목하자. '테이블 위에 있는 과일'이라는 한정된 범위 내에서 무언가를 선택하는 개념이므로 '어느 것을 ~하든 상관없이'라는 뜻의 복합관계대명사 whichever가 적절하다.

어구 bunch 더미, 많음

3 (d)
해석 그는 무슨 일이 있어도 항상 6시에 일어나 30분간 산책을 한다.

해설 동사 happen은 사람을 주어로 취하지 않으므로 whoever 또는 whomever는 쓰일 수 없다. happens의 주격 역할을 하며, 문맥상 '무슨 일이 일어나든'이라는 뜻이 되어야 적절하므로 '~하는 것은 무엇이든'의 의미를 지니는 복합관계대명사 whatever를 써야 한다.

4 (d)
해석 R&D 센터는 방문객들에게 신분증을 발급해주고 있으며, 방문객들은 이 신분증을 구내에서 항상 착용해야 합니다.

해설 선행사가 사물인 신분증(identification cards)이고 콤마(,)가 있기 때문에 which로 받아야 한다. 관계대명사 that과 what

앞에는 콤마를 사용할 수 없다.

어구 issue 발급[발부]하다   identification card 신분증   premises 구내

5 (a)
해석 나는 도로를 따라 차를 몰고 있었는데, 그 도로는 강과 나란히 뻗어 있었다.

해설 that은 계속적용법으로 사용할 수 없고, which나 who를 쓸 수 있다. 문장의 선행사가 the road로 사물이므로 which가 정답이다.

어구 run parallel to ~와 나란히 뻗어 있다

6 (d)
해석 (a) A: 검은 현수막이 걸려 있는 저 높은 건물은 뭐지?
(b) B: 우리 앞에 있는 30층짜리 건물 말이니?
(c) A: 응. 이 도시에 저렇게 높은 건물이 있는 줄은 몰랐어.
(d) B: 배럴 빌딩이라고 하는데, 네가 군 복무 중이던 1년 전에 세워졌어.

해설 (d)를 보면 사물 선행사인 the Barrel Building 뒤에 콤마(,)가 있고, 부가적인 설명이 나오고 있다. 관계대명사 that은 계속적 용법으로 쓰일 수 없으므로 that을 which로 고쳐야 한다.

어구 banner 현수막, 플래카드   military service 군 복무

7 (d)
해석 (a) A: 켄, 계속해서 나를 무시하는 이유가 뭐야?
(b) B: 난 그런 적 없어. 뭔가 오해가 있나 본데.
(c) A: 하지만 지난 2주 동안 내가 보낸 이메일에 답장을 하지 않았잖아.
(d) B: 말도 안 돼. 난 무슨 이메일이든 받은 이메일에는 항상 답장을 해.

해설 (d)의 두 번째 문장을 보면 문맥상 어떤 선택을 하는 경우가 아니므로 '어느 쪽이든, 어느 것을 ~하든'이라는 의미로 쓰이는 whichever는 부적절하다. 여기서는 '무슨 이메일에든 답장을 쓴다'라는 의미이므로 '~하는 것은 무엇이든'의 의미를 갖는 whatever를 써야 한다.

어구 tune out 무시하다, ~의 말을 듣지 않다   misunderstanding 오해   No way. 싫어, 안 돼, 천만에.

8 (b)
해석 (a) 쿠로시안은 그 나라 중앙에 위치한 마을이었다. (b) 그 마을은 요새로 세워졌으며, 200여 년 전에 3주에 걸쳐 건설되었다. (c) 요새가 세워지자마자 러시아군이 침공하여 마을은 파괴되었다. (d) 지금은 이 마을이 한때 존재했다는 것을 증명하는 문서만이 남아 있다.

해설 (b)에서 선행사 a fortress 다음에 콤마(,)가 나와 계속적 용법으로 쓰일 경우 that을 사용할 수 없다. 선행사가 사물이므로 which를 사용해야 한다. 또는 콤마를 없애고 that을 살려 한정적 용법으로 쓸 수도 있다.

어구 found 세우다, 만들다   fortress 요새   invade 침략하다, 침입하다

9 (c)

해석 (a) 콘베어는 미국의 항공기 제조사였다. (b) 이 회사는 델타윙 항공기를 포함한 여러 항공기의 개척자였다. (c) 그뿐 아니라 이 회사에서는 대형 진공관을 개발했는데, 이것이 CRT디스플레이의 전신이 되었다. (d) 1950년대에 콘베어는 자본과 노력을 미국 해군을 위한 미사일과 로켓 프로젝트로 옮기게 되었다.

해설 (c)에서 선행사 large vacuum tubes 뒤에 콤마(,)를 그대로 놔두는 경우 which를 사용해야만 계속적 용법이 되어 선행사에 대한 부연 설명을 제공할 수 있다. 또는 콤마 없이 that을 사용해서 한정적 용법으로 쓸 수도 있다는 것도 기억해두자.

어구 **aircraft** 항공기 **pioneer** 선구자 **vacuum** 진공의 **precursor** 선도자; 전신, 모체 **shift** 바꾸다, 변경하다

10 (c)

해석 (a) 사람들이 한 간통자를 예수에게 데리고 갔다. (b) 그들은 그녀를 돌로 쳐야 한다고 말하며 예수에게 어떻게 할 것인지를 물었다. (c) 예수는 군중에게 "누구든 죄 없는 사람이 먼저 저 여자를 돌로 쳐라"라고 말했다. (d) 자신들이 완벽하지 않음을 자각하고 사람들은 한 사람씩 자리를 떠났고 예수와 여인만 남게 되었다.

해설 (c)에서 목적격인 whomever가 답이 되려면 뒤에는 주어와 동사가 모두 와야 한다. 여기서는 동사 is만 나와 있고 is의 주격이 필요하므로 '~하는 사람은 누구든'이라는 의미의 whoever를 써야 한다.

어구 **adulterer** 간통하는 사람 **stone** 돌을 던지다 **crowd** 군중 **cast** 던지다 **one by one** 차례차례

▬ Check-up TEST ③⑤

1 (c)   2 (b)   3 (d)   4 (c)   5 (d)

1 (c)

해석 A: 우리가 처음 만난 날 아직도 기억해?
B: 당연하지. 내 인생이 완전히 바뀐 날인데.

해설 선행사로 시간을 나타내는 the day가 왔으므로 관계부사 when이 나와야 적절하다.

어구 **Definitely.** (구어) 그렇고 말고.

2 (b)

해석 그녀가 일주일 동안 갑자기 사라졌다가 아무 일도 없었다는 듯 다시 나타난 이유가 내게는 수수께끼였다.

해설 이유를 의미하는 the reason이 선행사로 올 경우 관계부사는 why가 적절하다.

어구 **disappear** 사라지다 **appear** 나타나다 **as if** 마치 ~인 것처럼

3 (d)

해석 유가가 치솟고 있는 시점에서 경제가 언제 다시 성장할지 예측하기란 어렵다.

해설 빈칸 앞에 나온 at a time을 통해 시간을 나타내는 관계부사가

와야 함을 알 수 있다. '~하는 시점에서'라는 뜻의 「at a time when + 주어 + 동사」를 한 덩어리로 외워두는 것이 좋다.

어구 **predict** 예측하다 **oil price** 유가 **soar** 치솟다

4 (c)

해석 (a) A: 괜찮으세요? 많이 피곤해 보여요.
(b) B: 회사에서 도입한 새로운 관리 프로그램이 익숙하지 않아서 그래요.
(c) A: 그 프로그램이 어떻게 작동하는지에 대한 전반적인 정보를 좀 드릴까요?
(d) B: 고마워요. 많은 도움이 될 거에요.

해설 (c)에 선행사를 포함하는 관계대명사 what이 왔다. 이때 what은 동사 works의 목적격이므로 어색한 문장이 된다. 내용상 '방법'에 관해서 설명을 하고 있기 때문에 how를 써야 한다.

어구 **be used to** ~에 익숙하다 **management** 경영, 관리, 운영 **adopt** 채택하다, 도입하다 **general** 전반적인, 일반적인

5 (d)

해석 (a) 16세 소년이 학교 앞에서 복면을 쓴 괴한들에게 유괴되었다. (b) 하지만 경찰이 본 사건에 대한 수사를 진행하자 온 나라를 충격에 빠뜨린 추한 진실이 드러났다. (c) 그 소년은 수업을 빼먹기 위해 친구들과 공모해 유괴극을 벌인 것이었다. (d) 결국 경찰은 그 소년과 친구들, 즉 공모자들이 모두의 눈을 피해 숨어 있던 곳을 밝혀냈다.

해설 (d)에서 which 앞에 the place라는 장소를 나타내는 선행사가 왔고, 그 뒤로 완전한 문장이 이어지므로 which가 아니라 관계부사 where를 써야 한다.

어구 **abduct** 유괴하다 **mask** 가면으로 가리다 **villain** 악한, 범죄자 **investigate** 수사하다, 조사하다 **conspire** 음모를 꾸미다, 공모하다 **stage** 계획하다, (계획을) 벌이다 **conspirator** 공모자

Unit 5 능동과 수동

▬ Check-up TEST ③⑥~③⑦

1 (c)   2 (b)   3 (c)   4 (d)   5 (d)
6 (a)   7 (d)   8 (d)   9 (c)   10 (d)

1 (c)

해석 A: 수석 졸업생으로 연설을 하게 되어 영광이야.
B: 너는 그럴 자격이 돼.

해설 '~해서 영광이다'라는 표현은 「be honored to + 동사원형」으로 쓴다.

어구 **deliver a speech** 연설하다 **valedictorian** 수석 졸업생 **You deserve it.** 너는 그럴 자격이 돼.

2 (b)

해석 A: 지금 브라운 씨와 통화 가능합니까?

B: 지금 바쁘신 것 같은데요.

해설 '지금 바쁘다'라는 의미는 be tied up at the moment로 표현한다.

3 (c)

해석 A: 제 딸이 온라인 쇼핑에 푹 빠져있어요. 어떻게 하면 좋을까요?

B: 따님의 관심을 컴퓨터에서 다른 곳으로 돌릴 뭔가를 찾으셔야 할 것 같네요.

해설 be absorbed in은 '~에 열중하다'라는 의미로 자주 사용되는 표현이다.

어구 divert (생각·관심을) 다른 데로 돌리다

4 (d)

해석 검찰 측은 자신들이 법정에 제출한 증거의 진위를 확신하고 있다.

해설 타동사 convince는 '~을 확신시키다'라는 의미이다. '~을 확신하는'이라는 의미의 수동태 '(be) convinced of'로도 자주 쓰이므로 기억해둬야 한다.

어구 prosecutor 검사   present 제출하다   truth 사실성, 진위

5 (d)

해석 경찰은 그 도시에 범죄 활동이 뿌리내리는 것을 막기 위해 혼신의 힘을 다해 왔다.

해설 복합형 문제이다. 우선 주어인 The police는 복수 취급하는 명사이다. 그래서 the police have~가 옳다. 동사 commit는 '혼신의 힘을 다하다'라는 뜻으로 사용되면 「be committed to + V-ing」 형태로 쓰여야 한다. 따라서 have been committed to preventing으로 써야 한다.

어구 prevent A from V-ing A가 ~하는 것을 막다   criminal 범죄의   activity 활동   take root 뿌리 내리다

6 (a)

해석 (a) A: 내 상사한테 질렸어. 정말 넌더리가 나.

(b) B: 무슨 일인데? 네가 상사랑 잘 지내는 줄 알았는데.

(c) A: 사실은 그렇지 않아. 그는 내가 프로젝트를 하고 있을 때마다 항상 날 들볶아대.

(d) B: 널 만만한 사람으로 생각하는 것 같다.

해설 be fed up with는 '~에 싫증이 나다, 질리다'의 의미로 자주 쓰이는 관용표현이므로 반드시 기억해둬야 한다. (a)에서 fed with를 fed up with로 고쳐야 한다.

어구 disgusting 역겨운, 넌더리나는   pushover 만만한 사람

7 (d)

해석 (a) A: 어젯밤 폭력배들 몇 명이 내 남동생한테 싸움을 걸었어.

(b) B: 어떻게 됐어? 동생은 괜찮아?

(c) A: 물론이지. 내 동생이 폭력배들을 심하게 때렸거든.

(d) B: 치료를 받기 위해 병원에 입원했겠구먼.

해설 hospitalize는 '입원시키다'라는 뜻의 타동사로 능동의 의미를 가진 동사이다. 주어가 They이므로 상대편이 맞아서 병원에 '입원된' 것이므로 수동태인 hospitalized로 쓰는 것이 바람직하다.

어구 thug 폭력배   knock the living daylights out of 심하게 때리다

8 (d)

해석 (a) 안와르 엘 사다트는 이집트의 3대 대통령이었다. (b) 그는 1973년 욤 키푸르 전쟁을 시작하여 승리를 거둔 후 아랍세계의 영웅이라는 찬사를 받았다. (c) 또한 그는 이스라엘 총리 메나헴 베긴과 함께 이집트–이스라엘 평화조약에 조인했으며 노벨 평화상을 수상했는데, 이로 인해 이슬람 과격주의자들로부터 신랄한 비난을 받았다. (d) 1981년 10월 6일, 사다트 대통령은 1973년 전쟁 중에 수에즈 운하를 건넌 것을 기념하는 연례 승리 퍼레이드 도중 암살범들에 의해 살해되었다.

해설 (d)를 보면, 수에즈 운하를 건넌 것을 '기념하는'의 의미이므로 현재분사를 사용한 능동태가 적절하다.

어구 launch (타격·공격을) 가하다; (기업·계획 따위에) 착수하다   hail 환호하다, 부르다, 소리치다   peace treaty 평화조약   Islamist extremists 이슬람 과격주의자   assassin 암살범, 자객   commemorate (중요 인물·사건을) 기념하다   crossing (강의) 도하, 횡단

9 (c)

해석 (a) 즉흥연주는 재즈가 다른 음악 장르와 구별되는 점이다. (b) 즉흥연주란 사전 준비나 연습 없이 공연을 하는 것을 말한다. (c) 재즈는 즉흥 작곡 기술이라 불리는 즉흥연주에 크게 의존한다. (d) 재즈 뮤지션들이 효과적인 즉흥연주를 하기 위해서는 일정 수준의 창의력에 도달해야 한다.

해설 (c)에서 즉흥연주가 '~라고 불려진다'란 뜻이므로 calling 대신 수동의 의미를 갖는 called가 알맞다. 참고로 called는 '~라 불리는'의 의미로서 사용 빈도가 매우 높다. 수식하고자 하는 명사 뒤에 위치하는데, which is called에서 which is가 생략된 형태라고 생각하면 된다.

어구 improvisation 즉흥연주; 즉석에서 하기   prior 사전의   composing 작곡   rise (~에서[~으로]) 향상하다

10 (d)

해석 (a) 전 미국 부통령 댄 퀘일은 지적으로 별볼일 없는 사람으로 악명이 높았다. (b) 그는 부통령 재임 당시 대중뿐 아니라 언론에 의해 공공연한 조롱의 대상이 되었다. (c) 그가 저지른 최악의 어이없는 실수는 한 초등학교의 영어 철자 맞추기 대회에서 한 참가자가 potatoes라고 맞게 얘기한 철자를 potatos로 정정한 것이었다. (d) 사실 그는 철자가 틀린 카드를 포함하고 있는 학교측에서 제공한 카드에 의존하고 있었으며, 후에 학교 측에서 제공한 자료를 신뢰했었노라고 말했다.

해설 (d)에서 the misspelled card가 cards provided by the school에 '포함되어 있다'라는 능동의 의미를 지닌다. 따라서 included가 아니라 '~을 포함한'이라는 의미를 가진 including으로 바꿔야 한다.

어구 notorious 악명 높은   intellectual 지적인   lightweight 가벼운, 경량의   vice presidency 부통령 임기   ridicule 조롱하다, 비웃다   infamous 악명 높은   blunder (어리석은) 실수   contestant 참가자   spelling bee (영어) 철자 맞추기 대회

Unit 6 가정법

Check-up TEST 38~39

1 (c)	2 (b)	3 (b)	4 (c)	5 (a)
6 (a)	7 (d)	8 (d)	9 (d)	10 (c)

---

1 (c)

해석 A: 잭이 계속해서 늦는 것에 이제 진절머리가 나.
B: 네가 잭의 처지라면 그렇게 말 못할걸.

해설 내용상 if절이 '네가 그의 처지에 처해 있다면'이라는 의미가 되어야 하는데, 이 말은 현재와 반대되는 상황을 가정하는 것이므로 가정법 과거로 써야 한다. 주절에 「would not + 동사원형」이 나온 것을 봐도 가정법 과거 구문이라는 것을 알 수 있다. 가정법 과거에서 if절의 be동사는 were로 처리한다.

어구 be fed up with ~에 진절머리 나다, 싫증나다
in one's shoes ~의 처지가 되어

2 (b)

해석 A: 혹시 내일 비가 온다면 그는 떠나지 않을 거야.
B: 내일 비가 올지 안 올지 난 모르겠어.

해설 가정법 미래 문제이다. 불확실하지만 미래에 발생할 여지가 있는 일일 때는 if절에 should를 쓴다. If it should rain으로 쓰거나 도치해서 Should it rain으로 쓸 수도 있다.

3 (b)

해석 A: 나는 사회 문제에 대해서 발표 준비가 안 되어 있어.
B: 혹시라도 뭐든 필요한 게 있으면 나한테 전화해.

해설 불확실하지만 미래에 발생할 수 있는 여지가 있는 일을 언급할 때 가정법 미래를 쓴다. if절에 should를 쓴다는 점에 유의하자. If you should need anything~ 혹은 Should you need anything~으로 쓸 수 있다.

어구 make a presentation 발표하다

4 (c)

해석 A: 계약 협상에서 내가 저지른 실수가 후회돼.
B: 나 역시 너랑 같은 상황에 있었더라면 똑같은 실수를 저질렀을 수도 있었을 거야.

해설 '내가 그 상황에 있었더라면'이라는 과거 사실과 반대되는 가정이 나오고 if절의 동사 시제가 had p.p.이므로 가정법 과거완료 문장임을 알 수 있다. 가정법 과거완료 문장의 주절은 「조동사 과거형 + have p.p.」로 써야 한다.

어구 regret 후회하다; 유감이다   contract negotiation 계약 협상

5 (a)

해석 회사 직원들은 그 신임 최고경영자가 2개월 전에 고용되지 않았더라면 오늘날 회사가 달라져 있을 거라고 생각한다.

해설 과거의 사건이 현재에 영향을 미치는 혼합 가정법 문장으로, 결정적인 힌트는 '현재, 오늘날'이라는 뜻의 시간을 나타내는 부사 today이다. 혼합 가정법 문장은 if절에 가정법 과거완료

시제가 오고 주절에는 가정법 과거 시제가 사용되므로 정답은 (a)이다.

어구 CEO 최고경영자   hire 고용하다

6 (a)

해석 내가 다시 젊어진다면 나는 그와 결혼하겠다.

해설 다시 젊어지는 것은 불가능한 일이다. 미래에 절대로 일어나지 않을 불가능한 일을 가정할 때는 가정법 미래를 사용해서 「if + 주어 + were to + 동사원형」을 쓴다. 따라서 If I were to be young again~ 으로 표현해야 한다.

7 (d)

해석 과거의 사람들이 오늘날 우리들이 가지고 있는 지식을 소유하고 있었다면 많은 과학적 발견들이 훨씬 더 일찍 이루어졌을 것이다.

해설 문장 끝에 today가 나온다고 덜컥 혼합 가정법 문장이라 결론지으면 안 되고 내용을 잘 살펴봐야 하는 문제이다. 여기서 that we have today는 선행사 knowledge를 수식하는 that 관계대명사절로, '오늘날 우리가 가지고 있는'이라는 뜻이지 '현재, 오늘날'이라는 시간 자체를 나타내지는 않으므로 이 문장의 시제에 영향을 미치지 않는다. if절의 내용이 과거 사실과 반대되는 가정이고, 주절도 could have p.p.인 것을 보아 가정법 과거완료 문장임을 알 수 있다. 따라서 if절을 「if + 주어 + had p.p.」로 쓰거나 if를 생략하고 주어와 had를 도치시켜 쓸 수 있다.

어구 discovery 발견   much earlier 훨씬 더 일찍이
possess 소유하다   knowledge 지식

8 (d)

해석 그녀가 교활한 사람이라는 사실을 생각해 볼 때, 네가 그녀의 요구를 들어준다면 멍청한 짓을 저지르는 것이다.

해설 가정법 문제이기는 하지만 접속사의 기본적 의미로만 접근해도 if가 가장 자연스럽다는 것을 알 수 있다.

어구 crafty 교활한   accept a request 요구를 받아들이다

9 (d)

해석 (a) A: 이제 내 나이도 서른 둘이네. 시간 참 빠르다!
(b) B: 그렇게 나이가 많은 게 아니니 너무 걱정 마.
(c) A: 20대로 돌아가게 된다면 넌 무엇을 하겠니?
(d) B: 더 많이 놀고 덜 안달복달하겠어.

해설 (c)에서 가정법 과거를 써서 묻고 있기 때문에 (d)에서도 가정법 과거를 써서 답변해야 한다. 따라서 I will이 아니라 I would로 답하는 것이 옳다.

어구 Time flies. 시간 참 빠르다.   in one's 20s 20대의
fret 초조해 하다, 안달하다

10 (c)

해석 (a) 지난 10년 동안 수십 명의 석탄 광부들이 호흡기 질환으로 병원에 입원했다. (b) 광부들은 더 나은 근로 환경을 강력히 요구했으나 이는 주로 높은 비용 때문에 경영진에게 거절당했다. (c) 노동조합에서는 탄광 회사가 근로자들의 건강에 대해 좀 더 관심을 가졌더라면 오늘날 노동력 부족 현상을 겪지는 않았을 것이라고 말하고 있다. (d) 지금이야말로 후속조치

를 마련하여 그 지역의 회사를 회생시켜야 할 때이다.

해설 (c)는 과거에 탄광 회사가 직원들의 건강에 좀 더 관심을 가졌더라면 오늘날 노동력이 부족하지 않았을 것이라는 내용이다. 그리고 문장의 주절에 today라는 힌트가 나와 있으므로 혼합 가정법이 확실하다. 따라서 if절을 가정법 과거완료로 처리하여 if the mining company had paid로 쓰는 것이 옳다.

어구 **dozens of** 수십의   **coal miner** 석탄 광부   **hospitalize** 입원시키다, 병원 치료하다   **respiratory illness** 호흡기 질환   **clamor** 강력히 요구하다; 외치다   **management** 경영진   **expense** 비용   **labor union** 노조   **labor shortage** 노동력 부족   **come up with** (아이디어 등을) 만들어내다, 내놓다, 마련하다   **follow-up measure** 후속 조치   **revive** 되살리다, 회생시키다

Check-up TEST ④

1	(a)	2	(a)	3	(d)	4	(c)	5	(c)
6	(c)	7	(d)	8	(c)	9	(c)	10	(d)

1 (a)

해석 A: 제대로 돌보지 않았더라면 그 아기는 그날밤을 넘기지 못했을 거야.
B: 그리고 그 때가 바로 역사가 바뀐 순간이라는 것은 우리 모두가 알고 있지.

해설 if는 없지만 Without을 보고 가정법 문제일 수 있음을 예측하고, 문맥을 통해 과거의 사건에 대해서 가정하고 있음을 파악해야 한다. '과거에 제대로 돌보지 못했다면 ～했을 것이다'라는 가정법 과거완료 문장이므로 빈칸에는 would not have survived가 적절하다.

어구 **survive** 생존하다   **history** 역사

2 (a)

해석 A: 네가 부러워. 나도 우리 집의 주택 담보 대출금을 지금 전부 갚을 수 있다면 좋겠어.
B: 걱정 마. 너도 분명히 주택 담보 대출금을 갚을 수 있을 거야. 하지만 시간은 걸리겠지.

해설 I wish～ 뒤에는 가정법 문장이 나온다. 문장 마지막에 now가 있으니 가정법 과거(=현재사실의 반대)임을 알 수 있다. 따라서 「과거 조동사 + 동사원형」으로 써야 하므로 could pay가 올바른 표현이다.

어구 **mortgage** 주택 담보 대출   **admit** 인정하다, 시인하다

3 (d)

해석 A: 어제 수와 점심을 같이 먹었어. 성격 정말 좋더라. 무엇보다도 점심값을 수가 냈어.
B: 어제 나도 너와 같이 있었더라면 좋았을 텐데.

해설 대화 내용 중에 yesterday가 나왔으므로 과거의 일에 관해 이야기하고 있고, B의 빈칸에 들어갈 구문은 가정법 과거완료임을 알 수 있다. 선택지 중에서 가정법 과거완료 형태의 어구는 I had been there뿐이다.

어구 **sweet** 성격이 좋은, 상냥한

4 (c)

해석 A: 괜찮아? 네가 많이 다쳤을 거라고 생각했어.
B: 방탄조끼가 없었더라면 나는 지금 여기에 없을 거야.

해설 '과거에 방탄조끼가 없었다면 현재 내가 여기 없을 것이다'라는 문맥으로 보아 과거가 현재에 영향을 미치는 혼합 가정법 문장임을 알 수 있다. 즉, if절에는 가정법 과거완료 시제가, 주절에는 가정법 과거 시제가 오면 된다. 이때, if절의 '～이 없었다면, ～이 아니었더라면'을 나타내는 표현은 if it had not been for이다. 여기서 if를 생략하면 주어와 동사가 도치되므로 Had it not been for가 정답이 된다.

어구 **seriously** 심각하게   **injured** 부상당한   **bulletproof vest** 방탄조끼

5 (c)

해석 매장에서 직원의 도움이 있었더라면 나의 80세 된 노모가 힘들지 않게 어머니의 첫 스마트폰을 살 수 있었을 텐데, 어머니는 그냥 빈손으로 오셨다.

해설 문장 앞에 나온 With는 '～이 있었다면'의 뜻을 갖는다. 문장 전체가 과거 시점에 대한 내용이므로 가정법 과거완료로 써야 한다. 문맥상으로도 '도움이 있었더라면 스마트폰을 무리 없이 살 수 있었을 텐데'가 되어야 하므로 「과거 조동사 + have p.p.」의 형태를 한 (c)가 정답이다.

어구 **have no trouble V-ing** 무리 없이 ～하다   **empty handed** 빈손인 채로

6 (c)

해석 그는 아이들과 아내가 없다면 직업을 그만두고 멘토의 권유를 따를 것이다.

해설 If it were not for～ 표현은 가정법 과거에서만 볼 수 있다. 따라서 주절에 「would + 동사원형」이 나와야 하므로 would quit이 올바른 표현이다.

어구 **quit** 그만두다   **follow** 따르다   **mentor** 삶의 조언자, 멘토   **recommendation** 추천, 조언

7 (d)

해석 (a) A: 쇼핑은 어땠니? 좋은 거라도 샀니?
(b) B: 아니요. 공교롭게도 백화점 앞에서 대규모 시위가 있더라고요.
(c) A: 왜 시위자들이 그곳에 모였는지 이유를 잘 모르겠네.
(d) B: 시위자들은 그 백화점이 없다면 소형 상점들이 그렇게 많이 부도가 나지 않을 거라고 주장해요.

해설 but for는 가정법 과거일 때는 '～이 없다면', 가정법 과거완료일 때는 '～이 없었더라면'으로 번역될 수 있다. (d)에서는 현재의 사실에 반대되는 가정을 하고 있으므로 가정법 과거를 사용해야 한다. 따라서 will을 would로 바꿔야 한다.

어구 **as luck would have it** 공교롭게도   **demonstration** 시위   **demonstrator** 시위자   **assemble** 집결하다   **go bankrupt** 파산하다   **in large numbers** 대규모로

8 (c)

해석 (a) A: 많이 안 먹네. 음식이 맛이 없니?
(b) B: 아니야. 내가 소식을 하잖니. 아무리 음식이 맛있어도 많이 먹지 않아.

(c) A: 그게 네 날씬한 몸매의 비결이구나. 네 식습관이 아니었다면 나처럼 살이 많이 쪘을 거야.

(d) B: 내 식습관과 체중과는 아무런 상관관계가 없는 것 같은데.

해설 '～이 아니었더라면, 없었더라면'을 나타내는 어구를 통째로 외워두자. had been it not for가 아니라 had it not been for이다.

어구 awful 끔찍한   eat like a bird 소식하다   tasty 맛있는   slim 날씬한   figure 몸매   eating habit 습관   gain weight 체중이 불다   correlation 상관관계

9 (c)

해석 (a) A: 지금 비가 엄청 오고 있는데 어떻게 할 거예요?
(b) B: 틀림없이 교통 정체에 걸리긴 하겠지만 집에 차를 몰고 가려고요. 차 안 가지고 왔어요?
(c) A: 안 가지고 왔어요. 시내 교통이 혼잡해서 회사 올 땐 차를 안 가지고 와요. 하지만 오늘 아침엔 차를 몰고 올 걸 그랬네요.
(d) B: 걱정 말아요. 내가 집까지 태워다 줄게요.

해설 주어 뒤에 과거분사가 바로 나올 수 없으므로 (c)에서 I driven은 문법적으로 틀렸다. 지금 시점에서 아침에 차를 가지고 올 걸 그랬다고 후회하는 것이므로 가정법 과거완료 시제를 써야 한다. 따라서 I driven it을 I had driven it으로 바꿔야 한다.

어구 rain cats and dogs 비가 억수로 오다   be certain to V 확실히 ～하다   heavy traffic 교통 정체   congested roads 교통이 정체된[차가 막히는] 도로

10 (d)

해석 (a) 최근에 발표된 보고서에 따르면 우리나라는 H1N1 플루 유행병의 잠재적 위험을 알리고 홍보하는 데만 4,000만 달러를 사용했다. (b) 이 액수는 백신, 긴급 대응, 위험 관리를 합하여 사용된 액수를 웃돌았다. (c) 그 결과 비판가들은 현재 정부가 무책임하고 무모하게 돈을 사용했다고 주장했다. (d) 독립적인 외부 기관이 적절히 개입을 했더라면 정부가 좀 더 책임감 있게 처신했을 거라고 비판가들은 덧붙였다.

해설 전반적인 내용을 꿰뚫어야 답을 맞힐 수 있는 다소 수준 높은 문제이다. H1N1의 위험을 알리기 위해 돈을 이미 사용해버린 상황임을 파악해야 한다. 즉, 과거 사건에 관해 되돌아보고 있다. 따라서 (d)는 '외부인이 사전에 개입했더라면 정부가 좀 더 현명하게 처신했었을 것'이라는 가정법 과거완료 문장이 되어야 한다. will act가 아니라 would have acted로 표현하는 것이 옳다.

어구 promote 촉진하다, 진흥하다   potential risk 잠재적인 위험   pandemic (국가적·세계적) 유행병   risk management 위기관리   combined 합하여   critic 비판가   irresponsible 무책임한   reckless 무모한; 부주의한   intervention 개입   independent outsider 독립적인 외부인, 독립 외부기관

Unit 7 조동사

Check-up TEST 41

| 1 (c) | 2 (b) | 3 (c) | 4 (a) | 5 (a) |
| 6 (a) | 7 (d) | 8 (d) | 9 (d) | 10 (c) |

1 (c)

해석 A: 난 아침에 일어나면 자주 속이 더부룩해.
B: 잠자기 전에 라면 먹는 것 좀 그만두는 게 좋을 거야.

해설 상대방에게 조언을 해주는 상황이므로 '～하는 편이 낫다'는 의미의 had better가 적절하다.

어구 have a heavy stomach 속이 더부룩하다   may well (～하는 것도) 당연하다   cannot help V-ing ～하지 않을 수 없다

2 (b)

해석 A: 네가 생각하는 것만큼 심각하진 않을지도 몰라.
B: 그랬으면 좋겠어. 하지만 난 아직도 그 상황에 대한 확신이 서질 않아.

해설 두 사람의 대화 내용을 보면 특정 상황에 대한 확신이 아닌 추측임을 알 수 있다. 따라서 '～일지도 모른다'는 의미의 may가 적절하다.

어구 serious 심각한   confidence 확신; 신뢰

3 (c)

해석 A: 우리 개는 확실히 야외 체질이야. 네 개들은 어떠니?
B: 어린 개는 공원을 여기저기 뛰어다니는 걸 좋아하지만, 나이 든 개는 집에 웅크리고 앉아 쉬는 걸 더 좋아해.

해설 나이 든 개는 뛰어다니기보다는 '쉬는 쪽을 선택할 것이다'라는 의지가 담겨있는 문장이다. 그러므로 would rather가 옳다. had better는 '～하는 편이 낫다'라는 뜻으로서 선택이나 의지보다는 당위성이 담겨있는 표현이다.

어구 outdoor 야외의   run around 뛰어다니다   curl up 몸을 둥글게 웅크리다

4 (a)

해석 우리 모두는 인간인지라, 나는 네가 불과 10초 후의 일도 예측할 수 없을 거라고 확신한다.

해설 문장의 의미를 정확히 파악해야만 정답을 고를 수 있다. '미래의 일을 예측할 수 없다'고 하는 것이 논리상 자연스럽다.

어구 predict 예측하다

5 (a)

해석 사진 속에 등장하는 군중의 어마어마한 규모를 고려해 볼 때 당시 대규모 시위가 있었음에 틀림없다.

해설 '～을 고려해 볼 때'라는 의미의 Given이 쓰인 것으로 보아 추측을 나타내는 조동사가 쓰일 가능성이 높다. 「must + have p.p」는 '～했었음에 틀림없다'는 의미의 강한 추측을 나타낸다.

어구 given ～을 고려해 볼 때   demonstration 시위, 데모

6 (a)

해석 효과적인 치료법으로 환자들을 치료하지 않았던 연구진들의 터스키지 매독 실험은 일부 음모론이 사실이라 해도 무리가 아닐 거라는 좋은 사례이다.

해설 터스키지 매독 실험이 음모론일 수도 있다는 것을 보여주는 사례라는 뜻이다. 따라서 문장의 의미상 가장 적절한 조동사는 '~하는 것도 당연한 일이다, ~하는 것도 무리가 아니다'라는 뜻의 might well이다.

어구 **syphilis** 매독   **cure** 치유법

7 (d)

해석 (a) A: 내 여자친구가 생일선물로 블루투스 스피커를 사줬어.
(b) B: 와, 대단하다. 한 번 봐도 되니?
(c) A: 물론. 여기 있어. 조작하기가 정말 쉬워.
(d) B: 정말이네. 두 살짜리 아이도 사용할 수 있겠다.

해설 might는 현재 또는 과거의 가능성을 나타낸다. (d)는 might를 써서 '두 살짜리 아이도 사용할지 모른다'는 어색한 문장이 되었으므로 '두 살짜리 아이도 사용할 수 있다'는 의미가 되도록 could로 바꾸는 것이 적절하다.

어구 **handle** 조작하다, 다루다

8 (d)

해석 (a) A: 어제 내 계정이 해킹당했어.
(b) B: 오, 저런. 해킹으로 입은 피해가 얼마나 되니?
(c) A: 우선, 해커가 비밀번호를 바꿔놨기 때문에 내 계정에 로그인할 수가 없어.
(d) B: 좀 더 주의했어야지. 어쨌든 내가 도울 일이 있거든 언제든 얘기하도록 해.

해설 (d)에서 「must + have p.p」는 '~했음에 틀림없다'는 강한 추측이므로 의미상 어색하다. 주의를 하지 않아서 해킹을 당한 것이므로 '~했어야 했는데'라는 의미로 과거에 일어난 일에 대한 유감을 나타내는 「should + have p.p」가 적절하다.

어구 **account** 계정, 계좌   **log in** 로그인하다, 접속하다

9 (d)

해석 (a) 미국 남북전쟁 당시 남부연방은 전투에서 적의 군함을 침몰시키고자 최초의 잠수함 헌리호를 가동했다. (b) 이 잠수함은 1863년 8월 12일 찰스턴 항구에서 북군의 호사토닉호를 공격, 침몰시켰다. (c) 그러나 공격 후 헌리호 역시 침몰하여 선원 전원이 사망했다. (d) 연구자들의 추측에 의하면 잠수함 내에 선원들이 오랜 시간 물속에서 생존하기에 충분한 산소가 있지는 않았을 것이라고 한다.

해설 (d)를 보면, 우선 과거의 일이므로 미래완료는 적절하지 않다. 또한 동사 speculate가 사용된 것을 볼 때 말하는 이의 추측 또는 가능성을 시사하는 것임을 알 수 있다. 따라서 '~했음에 틀림없다'는 의미의 「must + have p.p」가 적절하다.

어구 **the Confederates** 미 남부연방   **operate** 가동하다, 운용하다   **submarine** 잠수함   **vessel** 선박   **claim** (목숨을) 앗아가다   **speculate** 추측하다, 짐작하다

10 (c)

해석 (a) 지난 일 년 간 골드만삭스는 나쁜 평판에 고전했다. (b) 지난 주 증권거래위원회로부터 나온 사기 주장은 상황을 더욱

악화시켰을 뿐이다. (c) 우리들 대부분은 골드만삭스와 관련이 있다고 하기보다는 차라리 가게에서 물건을 훔쳤다고 인정할 것이다. (d) 그 회사는 세계에서 가장 미움 받는 은행이 되어가고 있다.

해설 (c)는 문맥상 '대부분의 우리들은 골드만삭스와 관련이 있다는 것 대신 가게에서 물건을 훔쳤다고 인정할 것이다'와 같이 선택의 의지가 담겨 있음을 알 수 있다. 그러므로 rather admit를 would rather admit로 바꿔야 한다.

어구 **publicity** 평판; 광고   **fraud** 사기   **allegation** (충분한 증거가 없는) 주장; (소송 당사자의) 진술   **Securities and Exchange Commission** 증권거래위원회   **admit to** ~을 인정하다   **shoplift** 가게에서 도둑질하다   **have something to do with** ~와 관계가 있다   **on one's way to** ~로 가는 길 도중에

Unit 8 접속사

=**Check-up TEST 42**=

1 (c)	2 (b)	3 (b)	4 (c)	5 (a)
6 (a)	7 (c)	8 (c)	9 (a)	10 (d)

1 (c)

해석 A: 난 아내를 만나기 전까진 컴맹이었어.
B: 뭐, 그녀는 뛰어난 컴퓨터 실력으로 유명하니까.

해설 문장에서 의미를 파악한 후 정답을 골라야 한다. 의미상 아내를 '만나기 전까지는(만나게 될 때까지는)' 컴맹이었다는 내용이 와야 하므로 until(~까지)이 정답이다.

어구 **computer illiterate** 컴맹, 컴퓨터에 익숙하지 않은 사람   **brilliant** 훌륭한, 멋진, 뛰어난

2 (b)

해석 A: 야당 정치인들은 여당 의원을 맹비난하고 있는 거 같아.
B: 맞아. 그 의원이 이번 시장 선거에서 승리하지 못하게 하려고 그러는 거야.

해설 야당과 여당이 싸우는 이유는 '그 의원이 이번 선거에 당선되지 않도록 견제하기 위해서'임을 파악할 수 있다. 따라서 '승리하지 않도록'의 뜻을 만드는 접속사 lest(~하지 않기 위해서)가 와야 한다.

어구 **opposition party** 야당   **bash** 맹비난 하다   **opponent** 적   **mayoral election** 시장 선거

3 (b)

해석 A: 어제 직장에서 톰 봤니?
B: 내가 잘못 알고 있지 않는 한 어제 회사에 나오지 않았는데.

해설 '내가 잘못 알고 있지 않는 한'이라는 의미가 되도록 Unless가 오는 것이 가장 알맞다. 참고로 I am mistaken.은 '내가 실수했다'는 뜻이 아니라 '내가 잘못 알고 있다'는 말이다. 논리상 빈칸에는 unless가 적절하다.

어구 **mistaken** 잘못 알고 있는   **at work** 회사[직장]에서

4 (c)
해석 그 지역에 주민 센터를 건립하자는 제안을 시에서 승인하자마자 ACE 팀은 그 프로젝트에 바로 착수했다.

해설 접속사 문제는 기본적으로 논리 문제이다. 접속사 자리 앞뒤의 논리 관계를 파악해야 한다. 시에서 승인하자마자 ACE 팀이 프로젝트에 착수했다는 문맥이 가장 자연스러우므로 as soon as(~하자마자)가 정답이다.

어구 **embark on** 착수하다, 시작하다   **approve** 승인하다   **proposal** 제안, 제안서   **community center** 주민 센터

5 (a)
해석 앞으로 며칠 동안 서해에 바람이 더 강해지고 비가 더 거세질 것이기 때문에 가라앉은 배를 인양하기는 어려울 것이다.

해설 의미를 파악한 후 답을 골라야 한다. 앞의 문장이 결과, 뒤의 문장이 원인이므로 '~때문에'의 의미를 나타내는 접속사가 적절하다.

어구 **salvage** (난파선 따위를) 인양하다; ~을 구조하다   **sunken ship** 침몰한 배   **heavy** 거센   **now and then** 이따금씩

6 (a)
해석 그에게 요구되었던 일을 해냈기 때문에 승진을 하긴 했지만, 그는 기분이 썩 좋지는 않았다.

해설 문장에서 의미를 파악한 후 앞뒤 문맥에 맞게 접속사를 골라야 한다. 뒤의 내용은 '승진을 했지만' 앞의 내용은 '기분이 좋지 않았다'로 서로 상반되는 내용이므로 빈칸에는 양보절 접속사가 와야 한다. (d) in spite of 뒤에는 명사(구)가 와야하기 때문에 답이 될 수 없다.

어구 **promote** 승진시키다   **expect** ~을 요구하다, 기대하다

7 (c)
해석 (a) A: 어디 있었던 거야? 20분 전에는 왔어야 하잖아.
(b) B: 정말 미안해. 일부러 늦은 게 아니야. 버스를 잘못 탔거든.
(c) A: 그러면 알아차리자마자 바로 그 버스에서 내렸어야지.
(d) B: 내렸어. 그런데 차가 막혔고 내가 타야 할 버스를 10분 더 기다려야 했다고.

해설 (c)에서 의미상 '알아차리기 전에 내렸어야 한다'는 말은 맞지 않으므로, '알아차리자마자'로 바꿔야 한다. 따라서 before를 as soon as로 고쳐야 한다.

어구 **mean to V** (의도적으로) ~을 하다   **get on** (버스 등을) 타다   **get off** ~에서 내리다   **realize** 깨닫다   **heavy** (교통이) 막히는, 정체되는

8 (c)
해석 (a) A: 대통령이 추진하는 프로젝트 때문에 최근 정치 싸움이 일어나고 있어.
(b) B: 무슨 이야기를 하는 거니?
(c) A: 부동표 투표자들을 만족시킬 수 있기 때문에 여당 의원들이 불필요한 건설 프로젝트를 밀어붙이고 있거든.
(d) B: 참 부끄러운 일이군!

해설 (c) 에서 if doing so는 의미상 전혀 맞지 않는다. 문장의 앞부분이 원인이고 뒷부분이 결과이므로 '~ 때문에'의 뜻이 있는 접속사가 와야 한다. 따라서 If doing so will please를 now that doing so will please로 바꿔야 한다.

어구 **bicker** 다투다, 싸우다   **pet project** 개인의 취향으로 밀어붙이는 프로젝트   **lawmaker** 의원, 입법가   **ruling party** 여당   **press ahead with** ~을 밀어붙이다   **construction** 건설   **swing voter** (선거의) 부동표 투표자

9 (a)
해석 (a) 자연과학을 전공하는 여성들이 부족함에도 불구하고, 우리는 더 많은 여학생들을 유치할 수 있다는 희망을 버리지 않았다. (b) 이러한 일의 일부는 학교에서 자체적으로 시작해야 하므로, 우리는 과학교사들이 여학생들의 학업을 칭찬하고, 여학생들이 과학자가 될 수 있게 북돋워 줄 것을 독려하고 있다. (c) 어떤 교사들은 마리 퀴리와 같은 유명한 여성 과학자에 초점을 맞추는 것을 중시한다. (d) 이런 식으로, 여학생들은 여성도 과학 분야에서 성공할 수 있음을 깨닫게 될 것이다.

해설 (a)를 보면 '여학생들이 부족하다'와 '여학생을 유치할 수 있는 희망을 포기하지 않았다'라는 상반된 내용이 나오므로 '~에도 불구하고'의 뜻을 가진 양보의 접속사가 와야 함을 알 수 있다. 따라서 While을 Although로 바꿔야 한다.

어구 **shortage** 부족, 결핍   **attract** 끌어들이다   **encourage** 장려하다   **make a point of V-ing** ~하는 것을 중시[강조]하다

10 (d)
해석 (a) 한국 최고의 대학 중 한 곳의 졸업식에 참석하게 되어 영광으로 생각합니다. (b) 저는 여러분이 미래에 성공하기 위해 어떤 포부를 가져야 하는지 말하고자 이 자리에 섰습니다. (c) 또한 어려움에 직면했을 때 무엇을 해야 하는지에 대해서도 이야기해 보겠습니다. (d) 오늘 제가 말씀드릴 내용은 실천하기는 어렵다 하더라도 매우 중대하다는 것을 알게 될 것입니다.

해설 어색한 접속사를 찾아내기 위해서는 내용 파악이 중요하다. (d)에서 '오늘 말하려는 것은 어렵다'와 '중대하다'가 상반되는 내용이어서 unless를 사용했지만 이 상태로는 '어렵지 않으면 중대하다'와 같은 이상한 문맥이 되어버린다. 따라서 '비록 ~일지라도'라는 의미의 접속사 albeit가 와야 한다. albeit 뒤에는 형용사가 바로 온다는 것에도 유의하자.

어구 **be honored** 영광이다   **graduation ceremony** 졸업식   **ambition** 야망, 포부   **face** 직면하다   **prove to be** (~임을) 증명[입증]하다   **vital** 없어서는 안 될, 중대한   **albeit** 비록 ~일지라도   **put into practice** 실천하다

Unit 9 전치사

══ **Check-up** TEST 43 ══

1	(c)	2	(d)	3	(d)	4	(b)	5	(b)
6	(b)	7	(a)	8	(a)	9	(a)	10	(d)

1 (c)

해석 A: 왜 저 검은색 옷을 입은 키 크고 아름다운 여자를 보고 있는 거니?
B: 저 검은 정장을 입고 있는 여자가 내 동생이기 때문이지.

해설 옷의 색깔을 나타낼 때 쓰는 전치사는 in이다.

어구 suit 정장

2 (d)

해석 A: 내가 부산행 KTX를 타고 있다는 사실을 깨달았을 때는 제정신이 아니었어.
B: 너 원래 부모님 뵈러 광주에 가기로 했었잖아.

해설 '~행'이라는 방향을 나타낼 때 쓰는 전치사는 for이다. to가 아니라는 점에 유의하자.

어구 frantic (걱정이나 두려움으로) 필사적인, 제정신이 아닌 find out 발견하다 be supposed to V ~하기로 되어 있다

3 (d)

해석 시위 참석자들은 교통 혼잡을 피하고 국회 의사당 앞에서 자신들의 주장을 표명하고자 새벽에 서울로 떠났다.

해설 시간을 나타낼 때 쓰는 전치사는 at이며, '새벽에'는 at daybreak로 쓴다. at night, at midnight, at noon 등으로 쓸 수 있다.

어구 demonstrator 시위자 beat the traffic 교통 혼잡을 피하다 National Assembly 국회 의사당 have[make] one's voice heard (의사, 주장 등을) 표명하다

4 (b)

해석 아시아 국가들에서 연구 프로젝트를 수행하는 아시아 재단은 아시아 대륙을 조명하고 그 유구한 역사 동안 아시아인들이 일구어낸 위대한 업적을 세상에 알리기 위해 설립되었다.

해설 문맥상 빈칸 이하는 '그 대륙의 유구한 역사 동안'이라는 뜻이 되어야 하는데 '~동안에'라는 뜻의 어구는 보기에서 during 뿐이다.

어구 foundation 재단 carry out 수행하다, 실행하다 found 설립하다 shed light on ~을 조명하다, 빛을 비추다 continent 대륙 great strides 위대한 업적

5 (b)

해석 뉴스 보도에 따르면, 오늘 아침 인도양 해저에서 지진이 발생했고 이로 인해 거대한 쓰나미가 해변을 휩쓸어 많은 나라에서 사망자가 나왔다.

해설 '아침에'라고 할 때 in the morning과 전치사 없이 쓴 this morning은 맞지만, in this morning이나 the morning은 잘못된 표현이다.

어구 news report 뉴스 보도 underwater 물속의, 수중의 earthquake 지진 the Indian Ocean 인도양 tsunami 쓰나미 sweep 휩쓸다 ashore 해안에, 물가에

6 (b)

해석 A: 요즘 뭐하고 지내니?
B: 1910년대 한국 역사를 연구하고 있어.
A: 할 일이 정말 많을 것 같구나.
B: 맞아. 하지만 난 이 연구가 정말 즐겁고, 일본의 한국 식민

지 통치에 대한 논문까지 냈어.

해설 연도를 나타낼 때 쓰는 전치사는 in이며, on은 어법상 맞지 않다. (b)에서 on을 in으로 고쳐야 한다.

어구 publish 출간하다, 출판하다 paper 논문, 보고서 colonial rule 식민지 지배

7 (a)

해석 (a) A: 국민의 신뢰를 얻기 위해 총리는 1월 초에 조기 선거를 발표할 거래.
(b) B: 그의 당이 선거에서 이길 것 같니?
(c) A: 확실히 말은 못하겠지만 그는 승리에 자신있어 보였어.
(d) B: 내 생각에 선거를 발표하는 것은 그에게나 당에게나 좋지 않은 생각인 것 같아. 패배할 확률이 높거든.

해설 달과 연도 앞에는 전치사 in을 쓰고 날짜가 나올 경우에는 on을 쓴다. (a)의 On을 In으로 바꿔야 한다.

어구 prime minister 총리 call an election 선거를 발표하다 confidence 신뢰 the public 국민 for sure 확실히 confident 자신감 있는 stand a chance of ~의 확률을 가지고 있다

8 (a)

해석 (a) 증가한 엔진 용량 덕분에 그 자동차의 성능은 비약적으로 증가했다. (b) 그 차는 V6 5.0 리터 엔진을 탑재하여 2.4초에 60마일의 속도를 낼 수 있다. (c) 기술상의 획기적 발전 덕분에 이처럼 놀라운 성능을 낼 수 있는 것이다. (d) 하지만 그 자동차보다 더 작은 4.0 리터 엔진의 동종 모델에 비하면 연비가 떨어진다.

해설 크기나 치수, 용량 등에는 전치사 in을 쓴다. (a)의 increase on을 increase in으로 바꿔야 한다.

어구 engine capacity 엔진 용량 performance 성능 significantly 상당히 reach 도달하다 amazingly 놀랍게도 technological 과학[공업] 기술의[에 관한]; (과학) 기술(상)의 breakthrough (과학·기술 따위의) 비약적[획기적] 발전; 눈부신 발견 fuel-efficient 연료 효율적인 brother (동종) 모델

9 (a)

해석 (a) 그 신문은 한국어로 쓰여져 있다. (b) 그 때문에 판매 부수가 3만부밖에 되지 않는 것이다. (c) 요즘 신문사 간부진들은 많은 독자를 확보하기 위해 여러 언어로 신문을 출간하는 것을 고려중이다. (d) 하지만 그 전에 해야 할 일은 번역가를 고용하는 일이다.

해설 (a)에서 언어 앞에는 on이 아닌 in이 온다.

어구 circulation (신문, 잡지) 판매부수 senior official 상급 직원, 간부진 secure 확보하다 reader 독자 translator 번역가

10 (d)

해석 (a) 라마단은 이슬람력의 아홉 번째 달이다. (b) 그 달은 이슬람인들이 일출에서 일몰까지 먹을것, 알코올 음료 및 담배를 삼가는 금식에 들어가는 달이다. (c) 금식의 핵심은 이슬람인들에게 인내, 겸손함, 영성을 가르치는 데 있다. (d) 아홉 번째 달이 끝나면 이슬람인들은 그동안 금했던 것들을 즐길 수 있다.

해설 (d)의 In the end of the ninth month는 '아홉 번째 달의 끝 동안에'라는 어색한 뜻이 되므로 라마단이 끝나는 특정한 시

점을 표현하려면 at을 써야 한다.

어구 **Islamic calender** 이슬람력 **fast** 단식하다 **refrain from** ~을 억제하다, 삼가다 **alcoholic** 알코올 성분의 **beverage** 음료 **point** 요지 **patience** 인내 **modesty** 겸손 **spirituality** 정신성, 영성

Check-up TEST 44

| 1 (a) | 2 (a) | 3 (d) | 4 (b) | 5 (b) |
| 6 (c) | 7 (c) | 8 (c) | 9 (c) | 10 (d) |

1 (a)
해석 A: 나와 결혼해 준다면 항상 당신 곁에서 이 세상이 끝날 때까지 사랑할게.
B: 당신을 정말 믿고 싶지만 당신의 행동을 보면 신뢰하기가 어려워.

해설 문맥상 '~때까지'를 나타내는 전치사가 필요하므로 until이 적절하다.

어구 **trust** 믿다, 신뢰하다

2 (a)
해석 A: 현재 공사 중인 주간 고속도로는 내 고향 집에서 라스베가스까지 가는 시간을 30분 이상 단축시켜 줄 거야.
B: 시민들이 떠안을 비용과 불편함을 감안하면 통행 시간이 그보다 30분은 더 단축돼야 마땅해.

해설 '~중인', '~하에'라는 뜻을 표현하는 전치사는 under이다.

어구 **interstate** 주간(州間) 고속도로(=interstate highway) **cut** 단축시키다 **travel time** 통행 시간 **expense** 비용 **inconvenience** 불편 **bear** (책임 등을) 떠맡다[감당하다]

3 (d)
해석 A: 경찰이 주지사의 저택에 침입한 범죄자를 잡았습니까?
B: 그 사건은 아직 수사 중입니다.

해설 '수사 중인'이라는 표현은 under investigation이다.

어구 **criminal** 범죄자 **break into** 침입하다 **governor** 주지사 **residence** 주택, 저택 **case** 사건 **investigation** 수사

4 (b)
해석 심혈관 질환은 40세 이상 한국 남성의 주요 사망 원인 중 일부가 되었다.

해설 '~사이에'를 나타낼 때 between은 두 명[개] 이하일 때 쓰고 세 명[개] 이상일 때는 among을 쓴다. some of 뒤에는 복수 명사가 와야 하고, 여기서의 death는 일반적인 사망, 죽음을 의미하지 특정하게 한정되는 죽음이 아니므로 관사 없이 쓰인다. 이러한 조건들을 모두 만족시키는 것이 선택지 (b)이다.

어구 **cardiovascular disease** 심장혈관관계 질병 **leading cause** 주요 원인

5 (b)
해석 콘서트홀에 인접한 최신 설비를 갖춘 그 영화관은 젊은 영화 팬들을 끌어 모으기 위해 2017년에 건립되었다.

해설 빈칸에는 문맥상 '~에 인접한'이라는 의미를 가지는 표현이 나와야 한다. 이 표현으로는 adjacent to, beside, next to 등이 있다.

어구 **equip (with)** 장비를 갖추다 **state-of-the-art** 최신의 **facilities** (pl.) 설비, 시설 **attract** 끌다, 유인하다

6 (c)
해석 새로 나온 그 책의 판매는 지난달 이후 급격히 증가했다.

해설 since는 '~한 이후, ~부터'의 뜻을 가진 전치사로, 동사의 현재완료 또는 과거완료형과 함께 쓰인다는 것을 알아두자.

어구 **sale** 판매, 매출 **rapidly** 급속히, 빨리

7 (c)
해석 중요한 협상에 앞서, 양측 임원들은 모두 심호흡을 하며 어떻게 하면 협상을 유리하게 이끌어갈 수 있을지 생각했다.

해설 문맥을 파악해야 답을 찾을 수 있는 문제이다. 양측 당사자들이 이 협상을 유리하게 할 방법을 생각하는 것은 '협상 전'이므로 '~하기 전에'라는 의미의 prior to가 정답으로 알맞다. since가 접속사로 사용되면 현재완료 시제가 나와야 하고 despite와 but for는 내용상 어울리지 않는다.

어구 **negotiation** 협상 **executive** 임원 **party** 당사자 **take a deep breath** 숨을 깊이 들이마시다 **stay ahead of the game** 상황에서 앞서 나가다

8 (c)
해석 (a) A: 너 정말 무지 바빠 보이는구나.
(b) B: 마감일이 코앞인데 시간은 없으니 말 걸지 말아줘.
(c) A: 그 일 자정까지 끝낼 수 있을 거 같은데.
(d) B: 그랬으면 좋겠다.

해설 until은 '계속'의 의미이고 by는 정해진 시간 내에 어떤 행위가 완료되는 '종결'의 의미이다. (c)에서는 작업이 자정까지 '완료'되는 것에 초점을 맞추고 있으므로 until이 아니라 by를 써야 한다.

어구 **super** (형용사·부사·명사에서) 엄청나게, 극도로, 대단히 **deadline** 마감 **approach** 다가오다 **run out of** ~을 다 써버리다, ~이 없어지다 **midnight** 자정

9 (c)
해석 (a) 그녀는 러시아에서 거의 30년 동안 주연 여배우였다. (b) 그녀는 대부분의 비평가들에게 대단한 "국민" 여배우라는 인정을 받았다. (c) 그러나 그녀는 최근에 자살했고, 그때부터 그녀는 매우 보수적인 사회에서 여성이 여전히 마주치게 되는 여러 문제의 상징이 되었다. (d) 안타깝게도, 그녀는 사생활에서도 문제가 있었을 뿐 아니라 인터넷에서 그녀에 관해 떠들어대는 사람들에게 시달리기도 했던 것 같다.

해설 (c)에서 '그때부터 (지금까지)'라는 의미의 시간 부사구 since then이 나왔기 때문에 과거시제인 became을 현재완료인 has become으로 바꿔야 한다.

어구 **leading actress** 주연 여배우 **something of a** 대단한, 상당한 **critic** 비평가 **commit suicide** 자살하다 **encounter** 마주치다 **conservative** 보수적인 **gossip** 남의 이야기를 지껄이다; 험담하다 **personal life** 사생활

10 (d)

해석 (a) 현재 태국 경제는 한국 경제와는 비교도 되지 않는다. (b) 한국의 일인당 국민소득은 2만 달러가 넘는 반면 태국은 겨우 천 달러 수준이다. (c) OECD 회원국인 한국은 현재 세계 15위의 경제 대국이다. (d) 하지만 1960년대에 태국은 경제 규모 면에서 한국보다 훨씬 앞서 있었다.

해설 문맥에 맞게 전치사를 넣어야 하는 문제이다. (d)는 문맥상 60년대에는 태국이 한국보다 더 잘 살았다는 내용이 와야 한다. '~보다 앞서 있는'이라는 뜻의 전치사는 ahead of이다.

어구 A pale in comparison with B A가 B 앞에서 무색해지다, B에 비해 못해 보이다[떨어지다] **per capita income** 일인당 소득 **whereas** 반면에 **OECD** 경제 협력 개발 기구 **in terms of** ~의 관점에서

▶ Check-up TEST 45

1	(c)	2	(a)	3	(c)	4	(a)	5	(c)
6	(a)	7	(c)	8	(b)	9	(c)	10	(a)

1 (c)

해석 A: 월요일 아침에 발생한 지진이 캘리포니아에 많은 문제를 일으켰어요.
B: 나도 들었어요. 주지사가 어제 자정 부로 비상사태를 선포했죠.

해설 전치사의 관용표현을 묻는 문제이다. 문맥상 '~ 부로'의 의미가 되어야 하므로 as of가 와야 한다.

어구 earthquake 지진 **numerous** 많은 **declare a state of emergency** 비상사태를 선포하다 **midnight** 자정

2 (a)

해석 A: 최근의 금융 위기로 인해 신용불량자 수가 놀라운 속도로 늘고 있어요. 정말 큰 문제예요.
B: 이 문제를 해결하지 않으면 국민들은 좌절하고 불만스러워할 거예요.

해설 비율, 속도 등을 나타낼 때는 앞에 전치사 at을 써야 한다.

어구 financial crisis 금융위기 **credit delinquency** 신용불량자 **frustrated** 좌절감을 느끼는 **disgruntled** 불만스러워 하는

3 (c)

해석 A: 자네, 미출간《해리포터》원고가 필요하다고 했었지? 그렇다면 내게 경의를 표하는 기념비를 세워야 할 거야.
B: 지금 농담하시는 거죠?

해설 A가 구하기 힘든《해리포터》원고를 구했다면서 생색을 내고 있으므로 '나를 기리기 위한 기념비를 세워야 할 것이다'라는 의미가 되어야 문맥에 어울린다. 따라서 in honor of(~에게 경의를 표하여; ~을 기념하여)가 가장 적절하다.

어구 unpublished 출간되지 않은 **manuscript** 원고; (필)사본 **monument** 기념비; 기념비적인 건조물 **erect** 건립하다, 세우다 **in lieu of** ~대신에 **by means of** ~에 의해

4 (a)

해석 A: 여보, 우리가 제시간에 공항에 도착할까요?

B: 뜻밖의 지연 사태만 없다면 9시 정각에 도착할 것 같아요.

해설 '~이 없다면, ~이 아니라면'을 나타내는 전치사로 barring이 있다는 것을 기억해 두자. 나머지 선택지는 논리적으로 어색하다.

어구 make it to ~에 제시간에 도착하다 **sharp** (하루 중 특정 시간을 나타내는 표현 뒤에 쓰여) 정각 **unexpected** 뜻밖의 **delay** 지연, 지체 **owing to** ~때문에

5 (c)

해석 일본 최대의 자동차 제조업체는 직원들에게 현금 대신 주식을 지급하는 것을 고려중이다. 그 이유는 차의 기계적 결함으로 인해 발생한 대규모 리콜 사태로 회사 유동성에 문제가 생겼기 때문이다.

해설 의미를 파악한 후 알맞은 전치사 관용표현을 고르는 문제이다. 유동성 문제로 인해 현금이 부족하므로 현금 '대신' 주식을 줄 것을 고려하고 있다는 내용이 되어야 한다.

어구 share 주식 **liquidity** (경제) 유동성, 환금성(換金性) **mechanical** 기계적인 **massive recall** 대량 리콜 **for the sake of** ~때문에, ~을 위해 **regardless of** ~에 상관없이 **in the interest of** ~을 위해서

6 (a)

해석 전 국민 의료보험 제도를 채택하려는 시도는 많았지만 그 같은 노력은 성과를 이루지 못했다.

해설 문맥상 '~임에도 불구하고'라는 의미가 들어가야 한다. 이에 해당하는 표현은 in spite of 혹은 despite이다.

어구 attempt 시도 **universal health care** 전 국민 의료 보험 제도

7 (c)

해석 경쟁이 치열해지면서 다른 사람들에 대한 존중이 높이 평가되고 있다.

해설 '~에 대한 존중'을 나타내는 표현은 respect for이다.

어구 respect 존중, 존경 **highly** 매우 **value** 평가하다; 소중하게 [가치 있게] 여기다 **competition** 경쟁 **escalate** 확대되다, 심화되다

8 (b)

해석 전 세계적인 경기 침체는 부동산 시장에 특히 큰 영향을 미칠 것이다.

해설 have an effect[influence] 뒤에 전치사 on이 와서 '~에 영향을 미치다'라는 의미의 표현이 된다.

어구 recession 침체 **real estate** 부동산

9 (c)

해석 (a) 제가 근무하는 회사의 최고위직에 임명된 후 한국을 처음으로 방문할 기회를 얻게 되어 매우 기쁩니다. (b) 저는 한국이 지난 50년 동안 급속도로 발전했다는 점을 언급하고 싶습니다. (c) 예를 들어, 한국의 일인당 소득은 한국인들의 근면성실에 힘입어 놀라운 속도로 증가했지요. (d) 뿐만 아니라, 한국인들은 기반시설을 발전시키기 위해 쉴 새 없이 일했고, 그 결과는 정말 믿기 어려울 정도입니다.

해설 속도, 비율 등을 나타낼 때는 「at a(n)＋형용사＋rate[speed

/pace]」등으로 표현한다. (c)에서 '매우 놀라운 속도로'라는 의미를 나타내고 있으므로 at astounding rate를 at an astounding rate로 바꿔야 한다.

어구 **extremely** 매우, 극단적으로 **appointment** 임명 **note** ~에 대해 언급하다 **by leaps and bounds** 급속히; 큰 폭으로 **per capita income** 일인당 소득 **at an astounding rate** 놀라운 속도로 **additionally** 추가적으로

10 (a)

해석 (a) 30년 전만 해도 인터넷 접속은 기껏해야 어설픈 수준이었다. (b) 그리고 당연히 인터넷을 휴대폰에서 이용할 수도 없었다. (c) 지금 당연하게 여겨지는 것이 그 당시에는 어려운 일이었다. (d) 하지만 현재에는 거의 모든 금융 거래가 사이버 상에서 이뤄지고 있다.

해설 명사와 맞는 전치사의 쓰임을 묻는 문제이다. (a)의 access 뒤에는 어디에 접속하는지 대상이 나와야 하는데, 이때 대상 앞에 전치사 to가 온다. 따라서 access the Internet을 access to the Internet으로 바꿔야 한다.

어구 **access** 접속, 접근 **spotty** 허점이 있는; 오점 투성이의 **at best** 기껏해야, 잘 해야 **take ~ for granted** ~을 당연하게 여기다 **virtually** 사실상, 거의 **financial transaction** 금융 거래 **cyberspace** 사이버 공간

═ Check-up TEST 46 ═

1	(c)	2	(a)	3	(d)	4	(d)	5	(d)
6	(b)	7	(b)	8	(b)	9	(a)	10	(d)

1 (c)

해석 A: 그냥 호기심에서 물어보는 건데 덴마크의 수도가 어디야?
　　B: 모르지.

해설 '호기심에서'라는 표현은 out of curiosity이다.

어구 **capital** 수도 **(It) beats me.** 전혀 모르겠다, 금시초문이다.

2 (a)

해석 A: 뭘 먹어야 할지 모르겠네. 먹어야 할 알약이 너무 많아.
　　B: 파란색 알약을 빨간색 알약과 같이 먹지 마.

해설 '~와 함께'라는 표현은 in conjunction with이다.

어구 **take** (약을) 복용하다 **pill** 알약, 정제

3 (d)

해석 인도네시아에 비해 한국은 천연자원이 거의 없는 작은 나라지만, 훌륭한 인적 자원 풀을 보유하고 있다.

해설 의미상 비교의 개념이 필요하다. '~와 비교해 봤을 때'라는 표현은 compared with이다.

어구 **natural resources** 천연자원 **pool** 이용가능 인력 **human resources** 인적 자원 **equivalent to** ~와 동일한 **consistent with** ~와 일치하는

4 (d)

해석 요즘 젊은 세대들은 교통비를 아끼고자 온라인 쇼핑을 선호한다.

해설 '~을 선호하다'라는 표현 중에 have a penchant for가 있다. penchant(선호, 애호) 대신에 preference를 써도 된다.

어구 **young adult** 청소년, 젊은이들 **transportation cost** 교통비, 운송비

5 (d)

해석 리더가 가져야 할 자질 중 하나는 책임감인데, 이 말은 뭔가 일이 잘못될 때 결국 리더가 책임을 져야 한다는 것을 의미한다.

해설 '책임을 지다, 책임이 있다'라는 표현은 be responsible for 이다.

어구 **quality** 자질; 질 **a sense of responsibility** 책임감 **at the end of the day** 결국

6 (b)

해석 그가 선거 공약을 어겼기 때문에, 그에게 찬성표를 던졌던 사람들은 한탄하고 있다.

해설 그가 선거 공약을 어겼기 때문에 투표자들이 자신들의 선택에 후회하고 있는 것이므로, 그에게 찬성표를 던진 것을 후회하고 있다고 볼 수 있다. 따라서 찬성의 의미를 나타내는 전치사 for가 알맞다.

어구 **renege** 어기다, 취소하다 **election pledge** 선거 공약

7 (b)

해석 (a) A: 남한으로 내려오는 탈북자들이 너무 많아.
　　(b) B: 상황이 더 나빠져서 걷잡을 수 없게 될까 두려워.
　　(c) A: 내 생각에는 지금이야말로 한국 정부가 뭔가 조치를 취해야 할 때야.
　　(d) B: 특히 걱정되는 것은 북한 정권이 내부에서 붕괴되는 거야.

해설 의미를 파악한 후 어색한 관용어구를 고쳐야 하는 문제이다. (b)의 get out of the problem은 '문제에서 벗어나다', 즉 '문제를 해결하다'라는 의미이므로 문맥상 틀린 내용이 된다. get out of problem을 get out of hand(감당할 수 없게 되다)로 바꿔야 한다.

어구 **defector** 망명자, 탈주자 **flood (into)** 쇄도하다, 물밀듯이 밀려들다 **internal collapse** 내부 붕괴 **regime** 정권, 체제

8 (b)

해석 (a) A: 몇 살이세요? 미성년자는 출입이 안 됩니다.
　　(b) B: 지난달에 성인이 됐어요. 제가 나이에 비해 어려 보인다는 소리를 들어요.
　　(c) A: 신분증을 꺼내 주시겠어요? 확인해 봐야겠습니다.
　　(d) B: 여기 있어요.

해설 (b)에는 '나이에 비해 어려 보인다'는 내용이 와야 한다. '나이에 비해, ~치곤'이라는 뜻이므로 to my age를 for my age로 바꿔야 한다.

어구 **minor** 미성년자 **come of age** 성년이 되다; 충분히 발달하다 **check out** 확인하다

9 (a)

해석 (a) A: 제게 보내주신 성원 너무 고마워요.
　　(b) B: 네가 금메달을 따기를 바랐는데. 그래도 잘했어.
　　(c) A: 모든 성원과 격려의 말씀에 만족해요.

(d) B: 다음번엔 더 잘할 수 있어.

해설 '～에게 …에 대해서 감사하다'라고 할 때 「thank＋사람＋for＋이유」로 쓴다. (a)에서 전치사 with가 아닌 for를 사용해야 한다.

어구 support 지지, 성원   words of encouragement 격려의 말

10 (d)

해석 (a) 화석 연료는 재생 불가능한 에너지원이다. (b) 이것은 생성되는 데 수백만 년이 걸린다. (c) 그리고 이 자원의 매장량은 새로운 화석 연료가 생성되는 속도보다 훨씬 더 빠르게 고갈되고 있다. (d) 이제 인류는 이 연료를 거의 소진해가고 있기 때문에 앞으로 화석 연료 없이 살아가야만 할지도 모른다.

해설 의미를 파악한 후 어색한 관용표현을 찾아내야 하는 문제이다. (d)에서 '～을 다 써버리다'라는 표현을 하려면 get out of 대신 run out of로 써야 한다.

어구 fossil fuel 화석 연료   nonrenewable 재생 불가능한   energy source 에너지원   form 형성하다   reserve 매장량; (후일을 위한) 비축, 예비품   deplete 고갈시키다   humanity 인간, 인류   run out of ～이 떨어져가다

Unit 10 관사

=== **Check-up TEST** (47~48) ===

1 (c)	2 (d)	3 (b)	4 (a)	5 (b)
6 (b)	7 (b)	8 (b)	9 (a)	10 (a)

1 (c)

해석 A: 네가 새빨간 거짓말을 하고 있는 거 다 알아. 네 대답은 알아들을 수가 없거든. 사실대로 말해.
B: 이미 말했잖아. 사실대로 말한 거야.

해설 honest의 h는 묵음이 되어 첫 발음이 모음인 [a]로 시작하므로 관사는 a가 아닌 an이 와야 한다. 또한 부정관사가 나오면 '(여러 개 중에서) 하나의'라는 의미가 내포되기 때문에 뒤에 복수 명사가 나올 수 없다.

어구 lie through one's teeth 속이 훤히 보이는 거짓말을 하다   as clear as mud (설명 등이) 알아들을 수 없는, 종잡을 수 없는

2 (d)

해석 A: 오늘 밤에 나랑 같이 저녁 먹는 게 어때?
B: 우선 스케줄부터 확인해볼게.

해설 '～하는 게 어때?'라는 의미의 「What do you say to + V-ing」 구문을 알아야 풀 수 있는 문제이다. What do you say to 뒤에는 동명사가 나와야 하고, dinner는 무관사 처리하기 때문에 (d) having dinner가 답이 된다.

3 (b)

해석 오늘날같이 먹고 먹히는 사회에서 대학 학위는 필수사항이며 고급 학위는 더 안정된 직장에 더 높은 직위로 인도할 것이다.

해설 university는 철자가 u로 시작하기 때문에 첫 소리가 모음으로 발음된다고 생각할 수 있으나 첫 음은 모음이 아닌 반자음 [j]로 시작하여 [ju] 소리가 난다. 그러므로 an이 아닌 a가 와야 한다.

어구 dog-eat-dog society 서로 먹고 먹히는 치열한 경쟁 사회   degree 학위   must 필수품, 필수사항   earn (학위 등을) 취득하다, 따다   advanced 고급의, 더 나아간   catapult ～으로 쏘다; 뛰어오르다; 급히 날다   position 직위   job security 직업 안정성, 고용 보장[안정]

4 (a)

해석 (a) A: 오늘 밤에 수와 근사한 레스토랑에서 맛있는 저녁을 먹을 거야.
(b) B: 멋진 계획 같네.
(c) A: 같이 갈래?
(d) B: 수가 싫어하지 않을 게 확실하다면 나도 갈게.

해설 breakfast, lunch, dinner는 일반적으로 관사 없이 쓰이나 앞에 수식하는 형용사가 나오면 관사가 붙는다. (a)에서는 형용사 nice가 dinner를 수식하고 있으므로 관사가 붙는다.

어구 fancy 멋진, 근사한   mind 신경 쓰다, 싫어하다

5 (b)

해석 (a) A: 비행기로 서울에서 부산까지 얼마나 걸려?
(b) B: 비행기를 타고 가본 적은 없지만 한 시간 정도 걸린다고 들었어.
(c) A: 정말? 진짜 금방 가는구나.
(d) B: 그렇지만 나 같으면 KTX를 타겠어. 김포공항으로 가서 비행기를 타고 김해공항에 도착한 후, 부산 시내까지 가는 것을 생각하면 KTX가 더 싸고 편리하거든.

해설 (b)에서 hour는 첫 글자가 h지만 묵음이 되기 때문에 사실상 발음은 모음인 [a]로 시작된다. 그러므로 a가 아닌 an이 와야 한다.

어구 or so ～쯤, ～가량   journey 여행; 여정   convenient 편리한   considering ～을 고려하면   downtown 시내, 도심지

6 (b)

해석 (a) 국립의료원은 성인 류머티스성 관절염 관리를 개선하기 위한 몇 가지 새로운 가이드라인을 발표할 것이다. (b) 류머티스성 관절염을 앓는 수천 명의 사람들이 이 새 가이드라인을 통해 혜택을 받을 것으로 예상된다. (c) 이번 가이드라인은 3월 1일부터 인터넷에서 받을 수 있을 것이다. (d) 하지만 일부 의료 전문가들은 이 가이드라인을 실행하는 것은 시기상조라고 지적하고 있다.

해설 (b)의 people은 앞에서 언급된 바 없으며, 문맥상 일반적인 사람들을 지칭한다. 따라서 people 앞에 있는 정관사 the를 빼야 한다.

어구 the National Institute of Health 국립의료원   rheumatoid 류머티즘성의   arthritis 관절염   benefit 혜택을 보다   available 이용할 수 있는, 입수 가능한   medical professional 전문 의료인   premature 시기상조의, 너무 이른   put A into practice A를 실행에 옮기다

7 (b)

해석 (a) 최근에 초등학생인 내 딸이 나에게 오더니 100억 원짜리 장난감 수표를 보여주며 나보다 자신이 더 부자라고 말했다. (b) 요즘 자기 학교 친구들 대부분이 점심시간 동안 장난감 수표책을 가지고 논다고 딸은 말했다. (c) 그런데 문제는 이런 수표들이 10억부터 1조 원에 이르기까지 천문학적인 단위로 표시되어 있기 때문에 실생활에서는 현실적이지 않다는 것이다. (d) 그 결과, 요즘 일부 청소년들은 수입이 없음에도 신용카드를 함부로 쓰고 부모에게 대신 돈을 지불하게 하는 일이 벌어지고 있다.

해설 일반적으로 식사명 앞에는 관사가 붙지 않으므로 (b)의 are having the lunch에서 the가 빠져야 한다.

어구 **come up to** ~에게 다가오다   **toy check** 장난감 수표   **checkbook** 수표책   **mark** 표시하다   **astronomical** 천문학적인, 방대한   **range from A to B** (범위가) A부터 B까지 걸치다   **trillion** (숫자 단위) 조   **unrealistic** 비현실적인   **youngster** 젊은이, 청소년   **recklessly** 무분별하게, 무계획적으로   **pay the bill** 계산서[청구서]를 지불하다

8 (b)

해석 (a) 정부청사 앞에 우물이 하나 있다. (b) 그 우물 안에 있는 물은 극심한 가뭄에도 결코 마르지 않는다. (c) 과거에는 많은 사람들이 그 우물에 의존해 물을 얻었다. (d) 현대적인 생활양식의 도래와 함께 그 우물의 지위는 삶의 원천에서 단순한 관광지로 격하되었다.

해설 (a)에서 우물에 대해 처음 언급했고, (b)는 (a)에서 말한 우물에 관해 계속 이야기하고 있다. 결국 (b)에서 언급된 물은 '그 우물 안에 있는 물'로 한정되므로 the를 써서 한정시켜야 한다.

어구 **government house** 정부청사   **well** 우물   **go dry** 말라붙다, 마르다   **severe** 극심한   **drought** 가뭄   **depend on** ~에 의존하다   **advent** 도래, 출현   **lifestyle** 생활양식   **status** 지위, 위치, 상태   **source of life** 생명의 근원[원천]   **mere** 단순한, 단지 ~에 불과한   **tourist spot** 관광지

9 (a)

해석 (a) 사형제도 폐지 요청에 대한 이론적 근거는 단순하다. (b) 어느 누구에게도 다른 사람의 생명을 빼앗을 권리는 없다는 것이다. (c) 더불어 인간의 판단이 완벽하지 않다는 것이다. (d) 일단 사형이 집행되면 나중에 사형당한 사람의 결백이 밝혀져도 되돌릴 방법이 없다.

해설 (a)에 나오는 rationale은 '이론적 근거'라는 뜻을 가진 단어로, 여기서는 '사형제도의 폐지를 위한 이론적 근거'라고 의미가 한정되고 있다. 따라서 정관사 the를 앞에 써서 The rationale이라고 써야 한다.

어구 **rationale** 이론적 근거, 근본적 이유   **behind** ~의 이면에   **call for** 요청하다   **abolition** 폐지   **capital punishment** 사형(제도)   **take one's life** 생명을 앗아가다   **execute** 사형에 처하다; (판결 등을) 집행하다   **undo** 원상태로 되돌리다, 본래대로 하다   **innocent** 결백한, 무죄의

10 (a)

해석 (a) 경기 침체로 인해 요즘 전 세계 청년 실업률이 역대 최고수준에 달하고 있습니다. (b) 구직자들이 원하는 일자리를 잡을 가능성을 높이려면 남들보다 더 경쟁력을 갖추기 위해 노력해

야 합니다. (c) 기업의 인사담당자들이 장래의 신입사원을 채용할 때 고려하는 몇 가지 중요한 자격조건이 있습니다. (d) 그 중에서도 특히 외국어 능력이 높게 평가됩니다.

해설 (a)의 youth unemployment rate(청년 실업률)는 '전 세계의 청년 실업률'이라고 구체적으로 한정되고 있으므로 앞에 정관사 the를 써서 the youth unemployment rate around the world라고 표현해야 한다.

어구 **youth unemployment rate** 청년 실업률   **at record high levels** (사상) 최고 수준인   **heighten one's prospect of** ~의 가능성을 높이다   **land** (노력의 결과로서) 획득하다   **applicant** 지원자   **competitive** 경쟁의, 경쟁할 수 있는   **crucial** 중요한, 핵심적인   **qualification** 자질, 자격; 조건   **personnel manager** 인사담당자   **prospective** 장래의, 잠재적인; 유망한   **value** 평가하다

■**Check-up TEST 49~50**■

1 (b)	2 (c)	3 (d)	4 (a)	5 (a)
6 (b)	7 (c)	8 (a)	9 (b)	10 (b)

1 (b)

해석 A: 왜 그리 풀죽어 보여? 무슨 심각한 일이라도 생겼어?
B: 의사가 나더러 5년 내에 머리카락 대부분이 빠질 거래.

해설 most of나 some of, any of, all of 등의 of 뒤에는 한정된 내용이 와야 하므로 most of my hair가 알맞다.

어구 **disheartened** 낙담한, 풀죽은   **completely** 완전히   **bald** 대머리의

2 (c)

해석 A: 다음 달 요가 수업에 등록하고 싶어요.
B: 수강할 수 있는 강좌가 몇 개 있습니다.

해설 several(몇 개)이라는 복수를 의미하는 형용사가 kind 앞에 나오므로 kinds가 되기 때문에 (d)는 답이 될 수 없다. kinds of[sorts of, types of] 뒤에는 관사 없이 단수 명사[불가산 명사] 또는 복수 명사가 나오는데, class는 셀 수 있는 명사이므로 (c) several kinds of yoga classes가 답이 된다.

어구 **sign up for** ~에 등록하다[가입하다], ~을 신청하다

3 (d)

해석 A: 웨이터! 최대한 빨리 물 한 잔 가득 따라서 갖다 줄래요?
B: 네, 알겠습니다. 잠시 기다리시면 가져다 드릴게요.

해설 '웨이터!'라고 부르는 것은 호격으로, 호격어 앞에는 관사를 쓰지 않는다.

어구 **ASAP** 가능한 빨리 (As Soon As Possible)   **hold on a second** 잠시 기다리다

4 (a)

해석 호세 리잘은 필리핀이 스페인의 식민지였을 때 필리핀의 개혁을 지지한 가장 탁월한 인사였다.

해설 나라 이름 앞에 붙는 관사의 쓰임을 묻는 문제이다. 필리핀은 여러 개의 섬으로 구성된 나라이기 때문에 복수형으로 써서

항상 뒤에 -s가 붙고 앞에는 정관사 the가 온다.

어구 **prominent** 뛰어난, 유명한　**advocate** 지지자, 대변자
reform 개혁　**colonize** 식민지화하다, 식민지로 만들다

5 (a)

해석 그 국회의원은 자신이 속한 선거구의 선거구민들을 만족시킬
만한 일을 거의 하지 않았기 때문에 최근의 총선에서 선거구의
유권자들이 그에게 표를 주지 않은 것이 놀라운 일은 아니다.

해설 most of 뒤에는 한정된 내용이 나오므로 the나 my 같은 한
정사를 써야 한다.

어구 **constituency** 선거구; 선거구민　**district** 지구, 지역
vote against ~에 반대투표를 하다　**general election** 총선

6 (b)

해석 (a) A: 귀사의 고객은 어떤 일을 하나요?
(b) B: 고객 중 일부는 최저 임금만 지불하는 잡일을 하는 비
정규직입니다.
(c) A: 고객들이 귀사의 서비스가 너무나 필요하지만 돈이 충
분치 않을 때도 그분들에게 요금을 청구하나요?
(d) B: 대개는 할인해 주고 낼 수 있는 만큼만 돈을 내게 합니
다. 그렇게 해서 그들에게 체면을 세울 수 있는 기회를
주는 거죠.

해설 some of는 '(어느 특정한 것의) 일부'이므로 most of와 마찬
가지로 뒤에 한정사가 와야 한다. (b)의 Some of clients를
Some of the clients로 바꿔 준다.

어구 **client** 고객　**irregular** 비정규의　**odd job** (임시적으로 하는)
잡일　**minimum wage** 최저 임금　**charge** (비용을) 청구하다
badly 대단히, 간절히　**discount** 할인　**save face** 체면을 세
우다[유지하다]

7 (c)

해석 (a) A: 인터뷰 어땠니?
(b) B: 꽤 괜찮았어. 회사에서 내게 마케팅팀 자리를 제안했고
내가 마케팅 학위를 따기로 결정하면 학비를 지불해 주
겠다고 했어.
(c) A: 잘됐다. 항상 그런 활동들을 하고 싶어했잖아.
(d) B: 응. 그래서 그쪽 제의를 수락하려고.

해설 (b)를 보면 회사가 화자 B에게 제안한 것은 마케팅팀의 자리
와 마케팅 학위를 따기 위한 학비 지원이었다. 화자 B는 전부
터 마케팅팀에서 일하는 것과 마케팅 공부를 하는 것, 두 가
지의 복수 활동을 하고 싶어했으므로, (c)의 do that kind of
activity를 do those kinds of activities로 고쳐야 한다.

어구 **offer** 제안[제의]하다; 제공하다　**tuition** 학비, 수업비
degree 학위　**accept** 받아들이다, 수락하다

8 (a)

해석 (a) 어젯밤 서울 정부청사에서 불이 났다. (b) 이번 화재는 한
달 전 다니던 회사에서 해고당한 것에 불만을 품은 한 남성의
소행이라고 한다. (c) 당연히 그 방화범은 공공 재산을 파괴한
죄로 경찰에 체포되었다. (d) 그는 최대 징역 5년형을 선고받
든가 5천만 원의 벌금을 부과받게 될 것이다.

해설 fire는 앞에 관사 a가 붙으면 가산 명사로 취급되며 '화재'라
는 뜻이 된다. (a)의 fire는 일반적인 불이라기보다 화재 사건

을 나타내므로 관사 a와 함께 써야 한다. (b)에서 the fire라
고 한 것을 봐도 (a)의 fire 앞에 부정관사 a가 와야 함을 알 수 있
다. 처음에 언급되는 단수 가산명사 앞에는 a를 쓰고 그 명사
를 다시 언급할 경우 the를 쓴다는 것을 명심하자.

어구 **government complex** 정부청사　**fire** 화재, 불　**set** (불을)
지피다, 지르다　**disgruntled** 불만이 쌓인　**let go** 해고하다
arsonist 방화범　**sabotage** (고의로) 파괴[파손]하다
public property 공공 재산　**face** 직면하다
incarceration 투옥, 감금　**fine** 벌금을 부과하다

9 (b)

해석 (a) 호격 표현은 불리는 대상 바로 그 사람이 직접 화법의 문장
내에서 특별히 언급될 때 사용된다. (b) 한 가지 예는 다음 문
장 "난 김 씨를 좋아하지 않아."이다. (c) Kim(김 씨)은 언급되
고 있는 대상을 가리키는 호격 표현이다. (d) 문법적으로, 관사
를 호격어 앞에 사용해서는 안 된다.

해설 본문에도 나와 있듯이 호격 앞에는 관사를 붙이지 않으므로
(b)의 Kim 앞에 있는 관사를 지워야 한다.

어구 **direct address** 직접 화법　**identity** 신원, 정체; 일치, 동일성
party 상대방, 당사자　**expressly** 특별히, 일부러　**point out**
가리키다; 지적하다　**article** 관사

10 (b)

해석 (a) 지도자가 자신의 휘하에 있는 사람들에게 확실한 우선 사
항들과 비전을 알리는 것은 매우 중요하다. (b) 이것은 다국적
기업의 CEO에서 4성 장군에 이르기까지 모든 종류의 지도자
에게 적용된다. (c) 가장 높은 지위에 있는 사람부터 가장 말단
에 이르기까지 모든 이에게 무슨 일이 일어나고 있는지를 알
림으로써 좀더 쉽게 이끌 수 있을 것이다. (d) 이는 당연해 보
일지도 모르겠지만, 지도자의 위치에 있는 많은 사람들은 놀
랍게도 이러한 비교적 단순한 과제를 해내지 못한다.

해설 type of 뒤에는 관사 없이 단수 명사가 온다. 따라서 (b)의
any type of a leader를 any type of leader로 바꿔야
한다.

어구 **crucial** 매우 중요한　**communicate** 알리다, 전달하다
priority 우선 사항　**multinational** 다국적기업의
obvious 명백한, 분명한　**relatively** 비교적

Check-up TEST 51

| 1 | (b) | 2 | (b) | 3 | (b) | 4 | (c) | 5 | (d) |

1 (b)

해석 A: 그녀를 처음 봤을 때 무슨 말을 해야 할지 갑자기 모르겠
더라고.
B: 무슨 말인지 알아. 그녀는 정말 멋진 여자지.

해설 '갑자기'라는 표현은 부정관사 a를 사용해 all of a sudden이
라고 한다는 것을 알아두자.

어구 **gorgeous** 멋진

2 (b)

해석 A: 패스트푸드 대신 슬로우푸드를 섭취하면 병도 낫고 장기

적으로 봤을 때 건강해질 겁니다.
B: 의사 선생님, 격려의 말씀 감사합니다. 충고대로 하겠습니다.

해설 슬로우푸드를 섭취하면 '장기적으로 봤을 때' 건강해지는 것이지 단기적으로 갑자기 건강이 좋아지는 것은 아니다. in the long run이 '장기적으로 (봐서)'라는 의미의 표현이므로 (b)가 답이 된다.

어구 consume 섭취하다   slow food 슬로우푸드[전통 음식]
recover 회복하다   words of encouragement 격려의 말

3 (b)

해석 존 그리샴의 소설 《더 펌》은 법률 용어를 익히고자 하는 사람들에게 필독서이다.

해설 must가 명사로 사용되면 '절대로 필요한 것, 꼭 보아야[들어야] 할 것'이라는 뜻을 가진다. 이 때 부정관사 a가 사용된다.

어구 must-read 필독서   legal jargon 법률 용어

4 (c)

해석 세계 최대의 자동차 제조업체에 고용된 근로자 중 2천 명 이상이 이달 초에 해고되었다. 하지만 그 해고는 빙산의 일각일 뿐이며 더더욱 많은 수의 직원들이 수개월 내에 일자리를 잃게 될 것이라고 업계 관계자들은 말하고 있다.

해설 빈칸 앞에는 '2천 명 이상이 해고되었다'는 내용이 나오고 뒤에는 '그보다 더 많은 직원들이 앞으로 해고당할 것'이라는 내용이 나오는 것으로 보아, 빈칸 앞의 사건은 이후에 발생할 사건에 비하면 작은 일이라는 것을 암시하는 표현이 나와야 한다. 따라서 '빙산의 일각'이라는 뜻의 the tip of the iceberg를 쓰는 게 맞다. 정관사 the를 쓴다는 사실에 주의하자.

어구 automaker 자동차 제조업체   lay off 해고하다   at the beginning of ~의 초에   industry insider 업계 관계자
significantly 상당히, 두드러지게   lose one's employment 직업을 잃다   in the months to come 장래에; 몇 개월 이내에

5 (d)

해석 (a) 신갈 나들목 근처 38번 고속도로에서 교통사고가 있었다. (b) 승용차와 소형 트럭이 서로 충돌했다. (c) 다행히 사망자는 없는 것으로 알려졌다. (d) 그러나 신갈부터 대전까지 남쪽으로 내려가는 차선은 전 구간 여전히 정체되고 있다.

해설 관용어구 안에 사용된 관사는 혼동되지 않게 반복해서 외우는 것이 중요하다. '정체 상태에 있다'라는 의미의 표현은 be at a standstill이므로 (d)의 at the standstill을 at a standstill로 바꿔야 한다.

어구 highway 고속도로   exit ramp 출구 연결 경사로, 나들목
passenger car 승용차   pickup truck 소형 (오픈) 트럭
collide with ~와 충돌하다   fatality 사망자(수), 죽음
southbound 남쪽으로 향하는   lane 차선

Unit 11 주어와 동사의 수 일치

Check-up TEST 52~53

1	(c)	2	(b)	3	(a)	4	(d)	5	(b)
6	(a)	7	(b)	8	(c)	9	(d)	10	(a)

1 (c)

해석 A: 존, 한국에 온 지 몇 년 됐어?
B: 지금이 2018년인데 2000년에 처음 한국 땅을 밟았으니 꽤 많은 세월이 지났네.

해설 현재는 2018년이고 B가 처음 한국에 온 게 2000년이므로 많은 시간이 흘렀음을 알 수 있다. 따라서 '많은 해가 지났다'라는 의미가 되도록 '꽤 많은, 상당수의'라는 뜻을 가진 quite a few를 쓴다. (a)는 '불과 몇 년', (d)는 '일 년도 채 지나지 않았다'는 의미가 되므로 문맥상 맞지 않다. (b)는 '햇수, 연수'라는 뜻이므로 고려 대상조차 되지 않는다.

어구 set foot on ~에 발을 딛다

2 (b)

해석 서울에 거주하는 인구 수는 남한 전체 인구의 5분의 1을 차지하는데, 한국에서 가장 인구가 많은 도시가 서울이다.

해설 account for는 '(부분, 비율을) 차지하다'라는 의미이고, 이 표현은 수동태로 쓰지 않는다. 그리고 '~의 수'라는 뜻의 the number of는 단수 취급하기 때문에 동사는 accounts for가 되어야 한다.

어구 reside (in) 거주하다   entire 전체의   population 인구

3 (a)

해석 90명이 넘는 승객들의 생명을 앗아간 비행기 추락사고의 생존자 중 추락 원인을 아는 사람은 거의 없다.

해설 few는 복수 개념이기 때문에 few 뒤에 나오는 명사는 무조건 복수 처리한다. 또한 few 뒤의 명사가 복수이니 동사도 복수 처리한다.

어구 survivor 생존자   plane crash 비행기 추락사고
passenger 승객

4 (d)

해석 스티브는 충분한 돈을 저축하지 않았기 때문에 살 수 있을 만한 차가 거의 없다.

해설 스티브는 충분한 돈이 없기 때문에 살 수 있을 만한 차가 '거의 없다'라고 해야 문맥에 맞는다. a few는 '약간 있는'의 뜻이고, few는 '거의 없는'의 뜻이다. 또한 few에는 복수의 의미가 포함되어 있으므로 there 뒤에 나오는 동사는 are가 되어야 한다. 따라서 (d)의 are few cars가 알맞다.

어구 afford to do ~할 여유가 되다

5 (b)

해석 (a) A: 당신이 남자 주인공으로 나온 TV 드라마의 성공 후에 뭔가 달라진 점이 있나요?

(b) B: 요즘은 거리를 걸으면 많은 사람들이 절 알아보고 사인을 요청해요.

(c) A: 정말 기쁘고 스스로가 자랑스러우시겠어요.

(d) B: 옛날에는 절 알아보시는 분들이 거의 없었는데, 지금은 제가 유명해진 것 같아요.

해설 드라마가 성공하면 주연을 맡은 배우 얼굴을 알아보는 사람이 많아진다. 또한 (d)를 봐도 '과거에는 날 알아보는 사람이 거의 없었는데 지금은 유명인이 된 것처럼 느껴진다'고 하니 (b)는 '많은 사람들이 나를 알아본다'가 되어야 맞다. 따라서 few가 아니라 '많은'이라는 뜻의 quite a few를 써야 한다.

어구 male 남자의 protagonist 주역, 주인공 autograph 서명, 사인 obscure 분명치 않은, 알아보지 못하는 figure 인물

6 (a)

해석 (a) 도시 생활의 매력적인 점 한 가지는 쇼핑몰부터 영화관 그리고 도심공원에 이르기까지 모든 것들에 대한 접근이 용이하다는 것이다. (b) 도시 생활의 한 가지 단점은 오염된 공기를 마시게 된다는 것이다. (c) 도시에 공기 오염을 유발시키는 주범은 자동차와 오토바이이다. (d) 공기 오염을 일으키는 데 있어 차량 배기가스가 50퍼센트 이상 책임이 있다.

해설 주어·동사 수의 일치 문제에서는 주어가 무엇인지를 잘 찾아야 한다. (a) 문장의 주어는 cities가 아닌 One appealing aspect이다. 주어가 단수이므로 뒤에 나오는 동사도 거기에 맞추어야 한다. 따라서 are가 아닌 is로 써야 한다.

어구 appealing 매력적인, 마음을 끄는 aspect 면; 관점 downside 불리한 면, 부정적인 면 culprit 범죄자, 범인 motorcycle 오토바이 vehicle 탈 것, 차 exhaust 배기가스; 배기 장치, 배기관 contamination 오염

7 (b)

해석 (a) 아주 오랫동안, 건강에 신경 쓰는 사람들은 초콜릿이 맛있음에도 불구하고 그것을 먹는 것을 피해왔다. (b) 그들의 견해에 따르면, 초콜릿은 여러 가지 이유로 건강에 좋지 못한 식품이다. (c) 그 이유에는 초콜릿의 지방, 정제 설탕 및 카페인 성분과의 관련성도 포함된다. (d) 흥미롭게도, 최근 연구는 초콜릿이 얻은 나쁜 평판 중 많은 부분이 사실상 부당함을 증명했다.

해설 (b)에서 '많은 여러 가지 이유들'을 'a number of ~'로 표현했다. a number of 뒤에는 복수 명사가 와야 하기 때문에 different reason을 different reasons로 바꿔야 한다.

어구 health-conscious 건강에 신경 쓰는 association 관련(성) refined sugar 정제 설탕 content 내용물 reputation 평판 acquire 획득하다 undeserved 받을 만하지 않은, 부당한

8 (c)

해석 (a) 미국인은 보통 매우 친절하고 우호적이다. (b) 내가 길을 물어본 한 미국인은 굳이 나를 우체국까지 직접 데려다 주었다. (c) 반면, 붐비는 버스에서 나를 친 노인을 포함해 일부 중국인은 매우 무례하다. (d) 나 같은 사람들은 자신들의 경험을 토대로 특정한 사실을 일반화하는 경향이 있다.

해설 (c)의 주어는 some Chinese people로, 복수 형태이다. including ~ on a crowded bus는 삽입절로, 삽입절은 주어의 수에 영향을 미치지 않는다. 따라서 동사를 is가 아닌

are로 고쳐야 한다.

어구 ask for directions 길을 묻다 go out of one's way 일부러 [굳이] ~하다 on the other hand 반면에 rude 무례한 tend (~하는) 경향이 있다 (to) generalize 일반화하다; 종합하다

9 (d)

해석 (a) 1980년대에 한국에서 민주화 운동이 일어났다. (b) 시위자 중 상당수가 군사독재정권을 무너뜨리기 위해 싸운 젊은 대학생들이었다. (c) 시위가 극에 달하자 계엄령이 선포되었다. (d) 학생을 포함한 많은 민간인이 중무장한 군인과 경찰에게 총격을 당해 목숨을 잃었다.

해설 (d)를 보면 문맥상 '많은 민간인이 죽임을 당했다'라는 의미가 되어야 한다. the number of는 '~의 수'라는 뜻이기에, '민간인의 수가 죽임을 당했다'가 되어 말이 되지 않는다. 따라서 The number of를 '많은'이라는 의미의 A number of로 고쳐야 한다.

어구 democracy 민주주의 take place 일어나다, 발생하다 protester 시위자 topple (권좌 등에서) 끌어내리다, 무너뜨리다 military dictatorship 군사독재정권 demonstration 시위, 데모 come to a head (사태가) 극도로 악화되다 martial law 계엄령 proclaim 선포[선언]하다, 공표하다 civilian 민간인, 일반 시민[국민] heavily armed 중무장한

10 (a)

해석 (a) 그 해양 사고로 여전히 행방불명인 군인들의 수는 100명이 넘는다. (b) 사고가 발생한 지 거의 3주나 됐기 때문에 실종자들은 죽었을 것으로 우려되고 있다. (c) 기온이 매우 낮고 바람이 많이 부는 날씨를 고려했을 때 그들의 생존 가능성은 매우 낮다. (d) 그러나 실종 군인들 가족들은 아직까지 그들이 무사귀환할 거라는 희망을 버리지 않고 있다.

해설 (a) 문장 뒷부분에 more than 100(백 명 이상), 즉 숫자가 나와 있다. 따라서 앞부분은 '실종된 군인들의 수'라는 의미가 되어야 한다. '~의 수'라는 표현은 the number of이며 a number of는 '많은'이라는 뜻이다.

어구 be unaccounted for 행방불명이다, 실종 상태이다 maritime 바다의 survival 생존 slim 아주 적은 given the fact that~ ~라는 사실을 고려해 보면 temperature 온도, 기온 safe return 무사귀환

■Check-up TEST 54~55■

1	(d)	2	(b)	3	(b)	4	(a)	5	(c)
6	(a)	7	(d)	8	(b)	9	(a)	10	(d)

1 (d)

해석 A: 누가 정답을 맞혔나요?

B: 수잔과 존 둘 다 못 맞혔어요. 둘 다 며칠 동안 아파서 대회 준비를 제대로 하지 못했어요.

해설 「neither A nor B」는 'A도 B도 둘 다 ~이 아니다'라는 의미의 표현이다. or가 아니라 nor가 온다는 것을 잊지 말자.

어구 get the answer right 답을 맞히다 ill-prepared 준비가 불충분한

2 (b)

해석 A: 그 두 국가대표 축구팀 중에 어떤 팀도 2년 전에 브라질 팀을 이길 수 없었어.
B: 브라질 팀이 양쪽 팀 둘 다 5 대 0으로 이겼지.

해설 neither of는 '(둘 중) 어느 쪽도 ~이 아니다'라는 의미로, neither of 뒤에 복수 명사가 나오지만 단수 취급하여 단수동사를 써야 한다는 사실을 꼭 기억하자. 또한 '2년 전'이라고 하니 동사는 과거 시제여야 한다. 여기에 모두 부합하는 것은 (b) was able to이다.

어구 **national football team** 국가대표 축구팀　　**beat** 이기다, 패배시키다

3 (b)

해석 직원들뿐 아니라 회사도 수출 3백억 달러 달성이라는 목표를 계속적으로 추구해 왔고 마침내 작년에 그 목표액을 달성했다.

해설 「B as well as A」는 'A뿐만 아니라 B도'라는 의미의 표현이다. 주의할 점은 동사를 B에 맞춰야 한다는 것이다. 이 문제에서 B에 해당하는 것은 The company로 단수이다. 따라서 동사도 단수 처리해야 하고, 문장 뒷부분의 finally attained that number last year를 통해 과거 시제로 써야 한다는 것을 알 수 있다.

어구 **billion** 10억　　**persistently** 계속적으로　　**pursue** 추구하다　　**attain** 달성하다, 이루다

4 (a)

해석 메이저급 외국 커피숍 체인점 두 곳 중 어느 쪽도 한국 시장에서 잘 안 되고 있다.

해설 neither of는 뒤에 복수 명사가 오지만 단수로 취급함을 명심하자. 따라서 동사도 거기에 맞춰야 한다. (c)와 (d)의 has/have는 목적어가 없기 때문에 올 수 없다. 따라서 (a) is doing well이 올바른 표현이다.

어구 **chain** 체인(점)　　**do well** 잘되다, 성공하다

5 (c)

해석 (a) A: 이번 아시안컵에서 호주가 우승할 거라고 생각해?
(b) B: 내 생각에는 일본이 호주를 이길 것 같아.
(c) A: 두 나라 다 우승할 가능성은 있지만 난 호주가 이겼으면 좋겠어.
(d) B: 난 그 반대를 바라는데.

해설 each of는 '각각의'라는 의미로 뒤에 복수 명사가 오지만, 단수 취급한다. 따라서 (c)에서 have가 아닌 has가 되어야 한다.

어구 **come in first** 우승하다, 1등이 되다　　**have a chance to V** ~할 가능성이 있다, ~할 기회가 있다　　**prevail** 이기다, 압도하다　　**otherwise** 다른 상태로, 다르게, 달리

6 (a)

해석 (a) A: 나뿐만 아니라 제인도 법관이 되기 위한 시험에 통과하기 위해 열심히 공부하고 있어.
(b) B: 얼마나 오랫동안 변호사 시험을 준비하고 있는 거야?
(c) A: 2016년에 법 공부를 시작했으니까 3년째네.
(d) B: 너하고 제인 둘 다 합격하길 바라.

해설 「not only A but also B」는 'A뿐만 아니라 B도'라는 의미를 가지는 표현이다. 이 표현이 쓰일 때 동사는 B에 맞춰야 한다. (a) 문장에서 B에 해당되는 것은 Jane이므로 동사는 work가 아니라 works나 is working이 되어야 한다.

어구 **bar exam** 변호사 시험

7 (d)

해석 (a) 현재 우리나라는 전례 없는 경제상황을 겪고 있다. (b) 지난 9월은 전국에서 사라진 일자리보다 더 많은 일자리가 49개월 연속으로 창출된 달이었다. (c) 이는 우리나라 역사상 최장기의 지속적인 경제성장이다. (d) 게다가 수출품의 달러 가치뿐만 아니라 수출물량도 지난 몇 개월간 지속적으로 상승했다.

해설 「A as well as B」는 'B뿐만 아니라 A도'의 뜻으로, A에 동사의 수를 일치시켜야 한다. A에 해당하는 'the number of ~'는 '~의 수'로 단수 취급하므로 동사도 have가 아닌 has로 바꿔야 한다.

어구 **unprecedented** 전례 없는　　**consecutive** 연속적인, 계속되는　　**uninterrupted** 중단되지 않은

8 (b)

해석 (a) 많은 경우 이란이 그렇듯이 북한도 벼랑 끝 정책과 허세에 능하다. (b) 두 불량국가 모두 자국민의 행복이나 복지에는 크게 신경 쓰지 않는 것처럼 보인다. (c) 가난에 찌든 북한은 화폐 개혁을 단행했지만 부작용도 겪었다. (d) 많은 북한 사람들이 그들의 나라를 버리고 남한으로 가고 있다.

해설 neither of 뒤에는 복수 명사가 오지만 단수 취급하므로 동사도 단수로 써야 한다. 따라서 (b)의 seem을 seems로 고쳐야 한다.

어구 **adept at** ~에 능숙한　　**brinkmanship** 벼랑 끝 정책　　**bluff** 허세, 엄포　　**as is often the case with** 흔히 있듯이, 흔히 있는 일이지만　　**rogue state** 불량국가, 깡패국가　　**wellbeing** 행복, 복리, 복지　　**welfare** 복지, 사회 복지　　**poverty-stricken** 가난에 찌든　　**carry out** 수행하다, 단행하다　　**currency reform** 화폐 개혁　　**adverse** 역의, 반대의　　**side effect** 부작용　　**desert** 버리다

9 (a)

해석 (a) 대통령과 그의 딸들이 탄 배가 금요일 밤에 태평양 한 가운데서 전복되었다. (b) 소문에 의하면 그 배는 테러 행위에 의해 전복되었다고 한다. (c) 몇몇 테러 단체들은 이번 사건이 자신들의 소행이라 주장했다. (d) 다행히도 대통령과 그의 딸들 중 그 사고로 다친 사람은 아무도 없었다.

해설 (a)의 The boat (that) the president and his daughters was on까지가 (a) 문장의 주어 부분으로, 이 주어부와 대응하는 문장의 본동사는 capsized이다. the president부터 was on까지는 The boat를 수식하는 관계대명사절로 that이 생략되어 있다. that절에서 주어는 the president and his daughters로 복수이다. 따라서 was가 아닌 were를 써야 한다.

어구 **capsize** 뒤집히다, 전복하다[시키다]　　**in the middle of** ~의 한 가운데서　　**rumor has it that ~** 들리는 바에 의하면, ~이라는 소문이다　　**overturn** 뒤집다, 전복시키다　　**act of terrorism** 테러 행위　　**organization** 단체　　**claim** 주장하다

responsibility 책임   incident 사건

10 (d)

해석 (a) 영국의 작곡가 앤드류 로이드 웨버가 작곡한 〈캣츠〉는 뮤지컬이다. (b) 이 뮤지컬은 웨스트엔드에서는 1981년에, 그리고 브로드웨이에서는 1982년에 각각 첫선을 보였다. (c) 웨스트엔드에서는 21년 동안 공연되었고 브로드웨이에서는 18년 동안 공연되었다. (d) 〈캣츠〉는 전 세계에서 여러 번 공연됐고 20개국 이상의 언어로 번역되었다.

해설 Cats는 뮤지컬 제목이다. 뮤지컬, 영화, 책 등의 작품 제목은 항상 단수 취급한다. 따라서 (d)는 Cats have been performed가 아니라 Cats has been performed가 되어야 한다.

어구 composer 작곡가   musical 뮤지컬   respectively 각각   run (연극·영화가) 계속 공연되다   perform 공연하다   translate 번역하다

Unit 12 기타 문법 포인트

Check-up TEST 56

1	(c)	2	(d)	3	(d)	4	(a)	5	(c)

1 (c)

해석 집수리 계획의 일환으로 그는 오래된 샹들리에를 매끈한 새 샹들리에로 바꾸기로 결정했다.

해설 우선, 단수의 의미를 갖는 부정관사 a가 앞에 나왔으므로 (a)는 답이 될 수 없다는 것을 알 수 있다. 오래된 샹들리에를 새 것으로 바꾸기로 했는데 이 새로운 샹들리에에는 특정한 것이 아니라 '일반적인' 불특정한 샹들리에이다. 불특정 명사를 대신하는 대명사는 one이므로 (c)가 답이 된다.

어구 renovation 수리, 수선   replace A with B A를 B로 바꾸다   chandelier 샹들리에   sleek 매끄러운; 산뜻한

2 (d)

해석 그 회사의 1분기 수익은 14퍼센트 올랐지만 북미 지역의 많은 고객들이 이 회사의 주력 상품을 멀리하면서 이 지역의 매출은 계속해서 감소했다.

해설 빈칸 뒤에 flagship products(주력 상품)가 나오는데 이것은 앞에서 언급한 '그 회사의' 주력 상품이므로 빈칸에는 특정 단수 사물인 the company를 받는 대명사 it이 와야 한다. 여기서는 '회사의'라는 의미를 가져야 하므로 소유격 its로 쓴다.

어구 first quarter 1분기   profit 이익, 수익   sales 매출   flagship product 주력 상품   stay away from ~을 멀리하다, ~에서 떨어져 있다

3 (d)

해석 (a) A: 머큐리 파이낸스가 파산 신청을 했다는 뉴스 들었어?
(b) B: 그 뉴스를 듣지는 않았지만 그런 일이 일어날 수 있다는 사실은 알고 있었어.

(c) A: 말도 안 돼. 그 회사는 작년에 상당한 수익을 벌어들였고 분석가들도 회사의 전망이 밝다고 했단 말이야.
(d) B: 진짜 가치 있는 정보는 내부자에게서 나오는 법이지. 원한다면 너에게 그런 정보를 알려줄 수도 있어.

해설 it은 앞에 나온 특정한 명사를 받고 one은 불특정 명사를 받는다. (d)의 두 번째 문장은 '내부자에게서 나온 정보를 하나 알려 주겠다'는 것인데 이는 특정한 정보가 아니므로 it 대신 one을 써야 한다.

어구 file for bankruptcy 파산 신청을 하다   considerable 상당한   revenue 수익, 수입; 세입   analyst 분석가   have a bright future 전도가 유망하다, 장래가 밝다   value 가치   insider 내부자, 업계 관련자; 소식통

4 (a)

해석 (a) 네트워크 상에서 허니팟은 잠재적 해커들이 서버를 붕괴하도록 내버려두는 대신 허니팟에 들어오도록 그들을 유인하는 덫을 일컫는다. (b) 허니팟은 방치된 독립된 시스템이지만 시스템 운영자들은 항상 허니팟을 감시한다. (c) 효과를 보기 위해서는 허니팟이 해커들에게 진짜처럼 보여야만 하지만 거기에 실질적인 가치를 지닌 자료가 들어 있어서는 안 된다. (d) 일단 침입자가 허니팟에 침입하면 네트워크 운영자는 침입자와 침입 방법을 조사할 수 있다.

해설 앞에 나온 특정 명사를 받을 경우 대명사 it을 쓰고 불특정 명사를 받을 때는 one을 쓴다. (a)에서는 앞에 나온 honeypot을 받기 때문에 one이 아닌 it으로 써야 한다.

어구 trap 덫, 함정; 음모, 계략   lure 불러들이다; 꾀내다, 유혹하다   would-be attacker 공격 가능성이 있는 자   disrupt 붕괴시키다; 분열시키다   isolated 독립된; 고립된   unguarded 보호되지 않는, 안전장치가 없는   monitor 감시[관리]하다; 모니터하다   administrator 운영자   intruder 침입자   break into 침입[난입]하다   intrusion 침입

5 (c)

해석 (a) 많은 한국인들은 단지 다른 나라 언어로 번역되고 출판된 책이 너무 적어서 한국문학을 아는 사람이 거의 없는 것이라고 주장한다. (b) 하지만 지난 10년간 70권이 넘는 책이 영어로 번역되었기 때문에 이 언급은 잘못된 것이다. (c) 그러나 어떤 이들은 이러한 많은 번역물들이 형편없는 영어로 되어 있어서 사람들이 완전히 이해할 수가 없다고 주장한다. (d) 이는 어느 정도 사실이지만, 많은 번역 작품의 품질은 최근 몇 년간 계속 향상되고 있다.

해설 (c)에서 복수 명사인 many of these translations를 대명사로 받으려면 it이 아니라 them을 써야 한다.

어구 literature 문학   translate 번역하다   translation 번역(물)   statement 말함, 언급   false 잘못된   poor English 형편없는 영어

Check-up TEST 57

1	(b)	2	(a)	3	(b)	4	(c)	5	(c)
6	(b)	7	(d)	8	(c)	9	(a)	10	(b)

1 (b)

해석 A: 어제 대통령이 한 취임사 어땠니?
B: 흠잡을 데가 없었어.

해설 leave nothing to be desired는 '흠잡을 데가 없다, 더 이상 바랄 것이 없다'라는 뜻이다.

어구 inaugural speech 취임사, 취임 연설

2 (a)

해석 A: 컴퓨터 활용능력이 과거 그 어느 때보다 현대 사회에 들어와 더 중요하다는 것은 말할 필요도 없어.
B: 맞아. 오늘날 컴맹은 살아남을 수 없다고 생각해.

해설 it is needless to say는 '~라고 말할 필요도 없다'라는 뜻이다.

어구 modern society 현대 사회   survive 살아남다
nowadays 요즘에는, 오늘날에는   computer illiterate 컴맹

3 (b)

해석 A: 너 요즘 우울해 보인다.
B: 응. 기말고사 준비하느라 힘든 시간을 보내고 있어.

해설 「have a hard time + V-ing」는 '~하느라 힘든 시간을 보내다, 힘들게 ~하다'라는 뜻이다.

어구 depressed 의기소침한   final exam 기말고사

4 (c)

해석 A: 나 차 좀 태워줄 수 있어?
B: 미안. 안 되겠다. 지금 방청소하느라 바쁘거든.

해설 be busy V-ing는 '~하느라 바쁘다'라는 뜻이다.

어구 give someone a lift ~을 차에 태워주다

5 (c)

해석 토마스가 쓴 책의 신판은 오타가 많아서 미진한 점이 많다.

해설 leave a lot to be desired는 '미진한 점이 많다'라는 표현이다.

어구 new edition 신판

6 (b)

해석 그들은 자기들의 분야에서 성공하려고 하루에 다섯 시간 이상 규칙적으로 연습한다.

해설 make it a rule to는 '규칙적으로 ~하다, 늘 ~하기로 하고 있다'라는 뜻의 숙어 표현이다.

7 (d)

해석 (a) A: 그 도시에 새로운 스트립 몰을 조성할 거라는 소식 들었니?
(b) B: 그래. 고급 백화점도 몇 개 들어서기로 되어 있대.
(c) A: 그러나 일각에서는 그 스트립 몰이 영세업체에 부정적인 영향을 끼칠 거라고 이야기하던데.
(d) B: 그러게. 규모가 작은 가게 몇 곳은 문을 닫게 되겠지.

해설 end up 뒤에는 V-ing형이나 명사형 또는 장소가 나와야 한다. (d)는 end up 뒤에 to부정사가 나왔기 때문에 잘못된 문장이다. to go를 going으로 고쳐 준다.

어구 put in (장비·가구 등을) 들여놓다[설치하다]   strip mall 스트립

몰 (번화가에 상점과 식당들이 일렬로 늘어서 있는 곳)
have a negative impact on ~에 나쁜 영향을 끼치다
go out of business 폐업하다

8 (c)

해석 (a) A: 이봐, 조시. 이제 가야 할 시간이야.
(b) B: 벌써? 이 영화 보느라 시간 가는 줄도 몰랐어.
(c) A: 좋은 시간 보냈어?
(d) B: 물론이지. 모든 게 완벽했어.

해설 '즐거운 시간을 보내다'라고 할 때는 have a good time을 쓴다.

어구 lose track of time 시간 가는 줄 모르다

9 (a)

해석 (a) 한때는 가난과 저개발에 시달렸으나, 오늘날 많은 아시아 사람들은 급증하는 비만에 대한 공포 속에서 살고 있다. (b) 대도시 지역에서부터 남태평양의 외딴 섬에 이르기까지, 지난 10년 사이에 비만은 건강을 위협하는 무서운 존재로 부상했다. (c) 비만이 급증하는 것은 더 높아진 생활수준, 패스트푸드의 소비 증가, 그리고 좌식 생활양식에서 기인한다고 할 수 있다. (d) 일본은 성인 인구의 절반 정도가 과체중이거나 비만이다.

해설 「end up + V-ing」는 '결국 ~하게 되다'라는 표현으로, end up 바로 뒤에 V-ing 형태가 와야 하는데 (a)에서는 living 앞에 to가 왔다. 따라서 to를 빼야 한다.

어구 in the grip of ~에 붙잡혀[사로잡혀]   poverty 가난, 궁핍
underdevelopment 저개발   in the fear of ~을 두려워하여
fast-growing 급증하는   obesity 비만   metropolitan
area (대)도시, 수도권   remote island 외딴 섬
the South Pacific 남태평양   emerge 나타나다, 나오다
formidable 무서운, 강력한   consumption 소비
epidemic 유행병, 전염병   A is attributed to B A는 B에서
기인한다   sedentary lifestyle 좌식 생활양식
living standard 생활수준   adult population 성인 인구

10 (b)

해석 (a) 유명 케이블채널 드라마인 〈소프라노〉가 드디어 마무리를 향해 가고 있으며 8년 만에 끝이 날 것이다. (b) 아직 마지막 편이 방영되지 않았지만, 그렇다고 해서 이에 대한 사람들의 추측을 막지는 못했다. (c) 많은 TV 방송 평론가들은 드라마가 어떻게 끝날 것인지, 또 가장 중요하게는, 마피아에서 영감을 얻은 이 드라마에서 누가 살고 누가 죽을 것인지 궁금해 한다. (d) 전 세계 시청자들은 마지막 화가 방영될 예정인 6월 10일에 결론을 알게 될 것이다.

해설 (b)는 '마지막 편이 방영되어야 하지만, 이에 대한 사람들의 추측을 막지 못했다'의 뜻이므로 앞뒤 문맥상 어색하다. '마지막 편이 아직 방영되지 않았지만'의 뜻이 되어야 자연스러워지므로 '아직 ~하지 못했다'의 뜻인 「have yet to + 동사원형」이 나와야 한다. 따라서 has to air를 has yet to air로 고쳐야 한다.

어구 run its course 자연히 끝이 나다   come to an end 끝나다
episode 에피소드, 일화   air 방송하다   speculate 추정하다
commentator (라디오, TV의) 시사 문제 해설자   as to ~에 관해
inspired 영감을 얻은   be scheduled to V ~할 것으로 예정
되다

1 (b)　　2 (a)　　3 (b)　　4 (d)　　5 (d)

1 (b)

해석 정부는 사회 보조금을 지급받는 아동에게는 무료 급식을 제공하여 끼니를 거르지 않고 학업에 전념할 수 있도록 하는 것이 중요하다.

해설 imperative 뒤에 나오는 that절의 내용이 당위성을 띠면 「should + 동사원형」 혹은 동사원형을 사용해야 한다. 따라서 give children이 맞는 표현이며 '사회 보조금을 받고 있는'이라는 표현은 on welfare로 쓴다.

어구 imperative 필수적인, 중요한　on welfare 생활[복지] 보조비를 받는　concentrate 집중하다

2 (a)

해석 국가보훈처는 1950년부터 1953년까지 한국전에 참전하여 사망한 이들을 국가유공자 목록에 올려야 한다고 권고했다.

해설 동사 recommend 뒤의 that절 내용이 당위성을 가지므로 should be put으로 쓰거나 should를 생략한 be put 중 하나를 선택해야 한다.

어구 the Ministry of Patriots and Veterans 국가보훈처　recommend 권유하다　national honoree 국가유공자

3 (b)

해석 (a) A: 왜 우리 클래스의 모든 남학생들은 군대에 갔지? 모두들 군인이 되는 걸 좋아하는 건가?
(b) B: 물론 아니지. 정답을 알려 줄게. 한국에선 신체적, 정신적으로 건강한 남자는 군대에 가는 게 의무야.
(c) A: 왜 그런 건데? 모든 남자에게 군복무를 시키는 건 시간 낭비 아닌가?
(d) B: 아니, 나는 그렇게 생각하지 않아. 우리는 엄밀히 말하면 북한과 전쟁 중인 셈이거든. 준비가 되어 있어야 해.

해설 (b)에서 형용사 mandatory 뒤의 that절의 동사는 「should + 동사원형」 혹은 동사원형으로 처리해야 한다. men in Korea (should) join ~으로 쓰는 것이 옳다.

어구 mandatory 의무적인　a waste of time 시간 낭비　force 강제하다　armed forces 군대　technically 엄밀히 말해서　be at war 전쟁 중인

4 (d)

해석 (a) 연방정부 윤리처는 미국 정부의 한 기관이다. (b) 이곳에서는 행정부의 수행 기준을 만든다. (c) 형사상의 이해 상충제한을 규정하는 규칙과 규제 사항을 발표한다. (d) 연방 정부 소속의 공무원들에게 윤리 강령을 지킬 것을 권고하기도 한다.

해설 (d)를 보면 '권유'의 뜻을 나타내는 동사 recommend가 사용되었고 that 이하의 내용이 윤리 강령을 지켜야 한다는 당위성을 띠고 있으므로 abides by가 아니라 (should) abide by로 써야 한다.

어구 the Office of Government Ethics 연방정부 윤리처　agency 기관　establish (기준을) 마련하다, 설립하다　conduct 수행　executive branch 행정부; 집행부서　issue 발표하다, 발행하다　regulation 규정　governing

관찰하는　criminal 형사상의, 범죄에 관한　conflict 갈등, 충돌　restriction 제한　recommend 권고하다　civil servant 공무원　federal government 연방 정부　abide by (규칙에) 따르다, 지키다　code of ethics 윤리 강령

5 (d)

해석 (a) 하이퍼텐션은 혈압이 상승하는 의학적 상태이다. (b) 이것은 또한 고혈압이라고도 알려져 있다. (c) 일반적으로 하이퍼텐션은 일차성 고혈압 혹은 이차성 고혈압으로 분류된다. (d) 어떤 종류의 고혈압이든지 간에 고혈압 환자는 소금이나 짠음식을 멀리 하라는 조언을 받는다.

해설 (d)에서 동사 advise 뒤의 that절 내용이 당위성의 의미를 지니므로 are advised that they will stay를 are advised that they (should) stay로 고쳐야 한다.

어구 hypertension 고혈압증　blood pressure 혈압　classify 분류하다　stay away from ~와 떨어져 있다

1 (c)　　2 (b)　　3 (a)　　4 (b)　　5 (d)

1 (c)

해석 A: 제가 여기서 담배를 피워도 되겠습니까?
B: 안 됩니다. 흡연은 지정된 장소에서만 가능합니다.

해설 mind는 동명사를 목적어로 취하는 동사이다. 담배를 피우는 주어는 나(I)이므로 동명사 smoking의 의미상 주어를 명시해야 한다. 동명사의 의미상 주어는 소유격이나 목적격으로 표현할 수 있으므로 my smoking here 혹은 me smoking here로 표현할 수 있다. 선택지 (a)가 답이 되려면 if I smoke here로 써야 한다.

어구 mind 꺼려하다　designated 지정된

2 (b)

해석 A: 그는 악수를 하기 위해 손을 내밀며 얼굴에 환영의 미소를 지었어요.
B: 그걸 보면 그가 당신을 거기 초대할 그 순간을 얼마나 기다렸는지 알 수 있었겠어요.

해설 분사구문 문제이다. Reaching은 분사로 사용되었고, Reaching out의 주어는 사람일 수밖에 없다. 따라서 선택지에서 주어가 사람으로 사용된 (b)가 정답이다.

어구 reach out 손을 내밀다　shake hands 악수하다　invite 초대하다

3 (a)

해석 이러한 이유로, 관리 감독이 없는 상황에서 일하는 사람들이 자기 통제라는 문제를 진지하게 생각하는 것은 절대적으로 중요하다.

해설 to take seriously the issue of self-regulation의 주어는 people이며, to부정사의 의미상 주어를 표시할 때는 앞에 전치사 for를 사용한다.

어구 absolutely 절대적으로　critical 중요한　supervision 관리, 감독　take seriously ~을 진지하게 받아들이다

self-regulation 자기규제, 자기 통제

4 (b)

해석 (a) A: 윌슨 초콜릿 공장을 물려받은 사람이 자기 저택과 백만 달러를 고아원에 기부했어.
(b) B: 정말 후한 사람이지. 그는 심지어 장기 제공자로 등록하기도 했어.
(c) A: 난 힘들게 번 돈을 다른 사람을 위해 쓰는 건 상상도 못 하겠는데.
(d) B: 나도 마찬가지야. 백만 달러는 정말 많은 돈이야.

해설 to부정사의 의미상 주어는 기본적으로 전치사 for를 사용하지만 의미상의 주어 앞에 사람의 성격을 나타내는 단어가 사용되면 of를 쓴다. (b)에서 generous(후한, 관대한)는 사람의 성격을 나타내는 단어이므로 전치사 for가 아니라 of를 써야 한다.

어구 **inherit** 재산을 물려받다　**donate** 기부하다　**mansion** 대저택　**orphanage** 고아원　**register** 등록하다　**organ donor** 장기 기증자　**hard-earned** 힘들게 번

5 (d)

해석 (a) 정상화를 반대하는 분위기에도 불구하고 많은 팔레스타인 언론인들은 계속해서 이스라엘과 화해에 도달하려는 노력을 해왔다. (b) 다양한 친목회와 만남이야말로 유태인과 아랍인을 가르는 벽 양면 사이에 있는 관용과 수용을 증진시키는 가장 빠른 방법이다. (c) 민간 부문은 이스라엘과 팔레스타인 간의 화해에 대한 바람을 수포로 돌아가게 하려 애쓰는 무리들을 제압할 필요성에 대해서 인정했다. (d) 이와 같은 조직에 제공되는 자금을 차단함으로써, 민간 부문은 극단주의자들이 테러 활동을 중단하도록 압박할 수 있을 것이다.

해설 매우 어려운 문제로 문법적 지식과 문장의 내용을 철저하게 따져야 한다. 극단주의자들이 이스라엘과 팔레스타인의 화해 무드를 방해하고 있는 입장이다. 이런 상황에서 cutting off의 주체는 극단주의자가 될 수 없고 민간 부문이 되어야 한다. 즉 (d)의 By cutting off funding to(~에 대한 자금을 차단함으로써)의 주어는 the private sector(민간 부문)이다. 따라서 extremists can be pressured를 the private sector can pressure extremists로 바꿔야 한다. 전치사 by가 있기는 하지만 분사구문의 개념이나 마찬가지이다.

어구 **normalization** 정상화　**atmosphere** 분위기　**reconciliation** 화해　**reunion** 재결합; 친목회　**encounter** 만남　**tolerance** 관용　**acceptance** 수용　**Jew** 유태인　**Arab** 아랍인　**acknowledge** 인정하다　**counter** 저지하다; (타격 따위에) 반격하다　**strive to V** ~하려고 노력하다, 애쓰다　**foil** 수포로 돌아가게 하다　**cut off** 차단하다　**extremist** 극단주의자　**pressure** 압력을 가하다　**cease** 중단시키다

═ Check-up TEST 60 ═

1 (c)　　2 (c)　　3 (b)　　4 (a)　　5 (d)

1 (c)

해석 A: 네가 45세가 될 때쯤이면 대출했던 학자금을 상환했을 만큼 충분한 돈을 벌었을 정도로 오래 일했을 거야.
B: 그건 내가 쉬지 않고 일했다고 가정했을 때 한해서지.

해설 문법상 이미 동사 will have worked가 나왔기 때문에 and / but / or 등의 접속사 연결 없이 또 다른 동사가 올 수 없으므로 (a), (d)는 틀렸다. 학자금을 상환하는 것이 오래 일하는 것보다 먼저 발생하므로 to have earned로 표현하는 것이 맞다.

어구 **pay back** 돈을 갚다, 상환하다　**take out the student loan** 학자금 대출을 하다　**assume** 가정하다　**take time off** 휴식을 취하다

2 (c)

해석 A: 나는 예전에 가난했던 것이 창피해.
B: 누구나 부자로 태어나는 건 아니잖아.

해설 동명사가 주절의 시제보다 한 시제 앞설 때는 having p.p로 표현한다. 가난했던 것은 과거 사실이고 부끄러워하는 것은 지금이므로 시제 차이가 난다. 따라서 having been poor로 표현하는 것이 맞다.

어구 **be born with a silver spoon in one's mouth** 태어날 때부터 부자인

3 (b)

해석 12세의 수영 선수가 결승선을 세계 신기록인 48.21초로 통과하면서 금메달을 따 전 세계를 놀라게 했다.

해설 분사구문의 동사가 주절보다 한 시제 앞설 때 분사구문의 형태를 묻는 문제이다. 금메달을 받아 전 세계를 놀라게 하기 전에 먼저 있었던 행동은 48.21초로 결승선을 통과한 것이다. 따라서 having passed the finish line으로 표현하는 것이 정확하다.

어구 **shock the world** 전 세계를 놀라게 하다　**win the gold medal** 금메달을 따다　**finish line** 결승선

4 (a)

해석 (a) A: 그는 어제 캐나다에서 비행기를 13시간 타고 와서는, 마감기한을 지키기 위해 끈기 있게 일하고 있어.
(b) B: 더욱 놀라운 건, 2주만 있으면 그는 70세가 될 거라는 거야.
(c) A: 육체만 50세처럼 보이는 게 아니라 정신도 그런 것 같아.
(d) B: 그는 인간 육체의 한계에 도전하는 것에 정말 열정적이야.

해설 (a)에서 '그 사람은 지금까지도 일을 하고 있다(has been working)'라고 하면서 어제는 13시간 비행기를 탔다고 말하고 있다. 비행기를 탄 행위가 일하고 있는 행위보다 먼저 발생했고, 두 행위의 주체는 모두 he로 같으며, 비행기를 탄 행위가 능동이므로 Flying in from을 Having flown in from으로 고쳐야 한다.

어구 **tirelessly** 지치지 않고; 끊임없이　**enthusiastic** 열정적인

5 (d)

해석 (a) '위기'라는 의미를 나타내는 한자가 나란히 놓인 각각의 한자 두 개에 의해 형성되었다는 것은 많은 사람들에게 잘 알려져 있습니다. (b) 첫 번째 글자는 '위험'을 뜻하고 두 번째 글자는 '기회'를 나타냅니다. (c) 오늘 저는 우리에게 위험과 기회를 둘 다 제공해 주는 현재 진행중인 위기에 관해 여러분에게 말하고자 합니다. (d) 물론, 저는 꽤 오랜 기간 동안 발생해오고 있는 듯한 지구의 기후 변화에 관해 말하려는 것입니다.

해설 (d)에서 화자가 '지구의 기후변화에 대해 말하려 하는 것'은 현재이고 '기후변화가 발생한 것'은 그 전에 이미 일어난 일이므로 본동사보다 시제가 앞선다. 따라서 완료형 to부정사를 써야 하므로 seem to be occurring을 seem to have been occurring으로 바꿔야 한다.

어구 **Chinese character** 한자 **represent** ∼을 나타내다, 표현하다 **next to** ∼의 옆에 **stand for** ∼을 상징하다, 나타내다 **ongoing** 현재 진행 중인 **quite** 꽤

Check-up TEST 61

1	(c)	2	(d)	3	(b)	4	(b)	5	(a)

1 (c)
해석 A: 담배에 불을 붙이려고 멈춰 섰어. 하지만 라이터를 찾을 수가 없더라고.
　　 B: 미안하지만 내가 네 라이터를 갖고 있어.
해설 문맥상 담뱃불을 붙이는 일을 멈춘 것이 아니라 담뱃불을 붙이기 위해서 멈추었던 것이다. 따라서 목적의 용법으로 사용되는 to부정사를 쓴 stopped to light가 올바른 표현이다.
어구 **light** 불을 붙이다 **cigarette** 담배

2 (d)
해석 A: 토마토랑 상추를 기를 수 있게 정원이 있는 집에서 살았으면 좋겠어.
　　 B: 정원을 위한 충분한 공간이 없으면 작은 판지 상자에 몇 가지 야채를 길러봐.
해설 try는 뒤에 to부정사가 오느냐, 동명사가 오느냐에 따라 의미가 완전히 달라진다. try to grow는 '채소를 기르기 위해 노력하다'라는 의미가 되므로 자연스럽지 못하다. 내용을 보면 '충분한 공간이 없다면 ∼을 시도해 보라'라는 의미가 되어야 한다. 따라서 상자에 채소를 기르는 것을 시도해 보라는 의미의 try growing이 정답이다.
어구 **so that** ∼하기 위하여, ∼이 되도록 **lettuce** 상추 **veggie** 채소 **carton** 판지 상자

3 (b)
해석 나는 계약서에 사인을 하기 전에 계약 조건을 꼼꼼히 읽어보지 않았던 것이 후회가 된다.
해설 regret 뒤에 to부정사가 오면 '∼하게 되어 유감이다'의 뜻이 되고 동명사가 오면 '∼했던 것을 후회하다'의 뜻이 된다. '계약서를 읽지 않게 되어 유감이다'라는 말은 어색하므로 '계약서를 읽지 않은 것을 후회한다'가 되어야 한다. 또한 동명사의 부정은 동명사 바로 앞에 not을 쓰므로 (b) regret not reading이 정답이다.
어구 **regret** 후회하다 **terms of the contract** 계약 조건 **agreement** 협정; 동의; 계약서

4 (b)
해석 그가 비서와 부적절한 관계를 맺었음을 실수로 인정한 사실을 왜 언론이 언급하는 것을 잊어버렸는지 모르겠다.
해설 forget은 뒤에 동명사가 오게 되면 '주어가 했던 행동을 잊어버렸다'는 뜻이 되고 to부정사가 오면 '주어가 ∼할 일을 잊어버려서 하지 않았다'는 의미가 된다. 여기서는 언론이 언급한 사실을 잊어버린 것이 아니라, 잊고 언급을 하지 않았다는 의미이므로 forgot to mention이 옳다.
어구 **the media** 언론, 매스컴 **mistakenly** 잘못하여, 실수로 **have a relationship with** ∼와 관계를 맺다.

5 (a)
해석 (a) A: 올해 그리스에서 실업률 상승이 멈출 거라고 생각하십니까?
　　 (b) B: 아닐 겁니다. 노동시장의 일자리 증가는 시간이 걸릴 거예요.
　　 (c) A: 그리스에서 경제가 일자리를 창출하는 것을 보려면 우리가 얼마나 기다려야 할까요?
　　 (d) B: 몇 달 후면 비정규직 노동시장에서 몇 가지 좋은 징조가 보이기 시작할 겁니다.
해설 stop 뒤에는 동사원형이 올 수 없고 동명사 rising이나 to부정사 to rise가 와야 한다. (a)의 stop 뒤에 to rise가 오면 '증가하기 위해 멈춘다'가 되므로 말이 되지 않는다. '실업률 상승이 멈춘다'는 의미이므로 stop rising이 되어야 한다.
어구 **unemployment rate** 실업률 **labor market** 노동시장 **temporary labor** 비정규직, 임시직

Check-up TEST 62

1	(b)	2	(a)	3	(b)	4	(b)	5	(c)

1 (b)
해석 A: 우리 여름 훈련에 3주 늦게 도착했군요. 무슨 일이라도 있었습니까?
　　 B: 이번에 미국 입국 비자를 받는 데 평소보다 더 오래 걸렸습니다.
해설 일단 a weeks 때문에 수가 일치하지 않는 (d)는 정답 후보에서 제외한다. 그리고 late과 lately 중 어느 것이 적절한지를 판단하면 된다. 문맥상 B가 '늦게 도착했다'라는 의미가 되어야 하므로 '최근에'란 의미의 lately가 아닌 '늦게'라는 의미의 late가 들어있는 (b)가 답이 된다.
어구 **obtain a visa** 비자를 취득하다

2 (a)
해석 이 지역에 사는 사람들은 특히 최근에 소방서 대원들이 직원 훈련을 받은 이후로 우리가 대부분의 산불에 대처할 능력이 있음을 알고 있습니다.
해설 소방서의 직원들이 받은 훈련이므로 '직원 훈련'이라는 의미가 되도록 personnel training이 되어야 한다. personal training이라고 하면 '개인적인 훈련'이 되므로 의미상 어색하다. 또한 personnel은 단수, 복수의 형태가 같으므로 뒤에 –s를 붙이지 않는다.
어구 **wildfire** 산불 **undergo training** 훈련을 받다

3 (b)
해석 오늘 인도팀 선수들이 제 실력을 발휘하지는 못했지만 4쿼터

에서 페이스를 되찾았는데, 그때가 너무 늦은 건 아니었죠.

해설 내용과 문법을 모두 생각해야 하는 문제이다. 실력을 발휘하지 못했다는 내용 뒤에 but이 있으므로 4쿼터에서 페이스를 되찾은 것이 '늦지 않았다'라는 의미가 되어야 한다. 따라서 부정문이 되어야 하며, '최근에'란 의미의 lately가 아닌 '늦게'라는 의미의 late가 들어가야 한다.

어구 **be oneself** ~답다 　**pick up the pace** 페이스를 되찾다 [회복하다]

4 (b)

해석 (a) A: 훌라후프를 하고 있는 여자분에게 다른 강습생들과 떨어져서 운동하라고 말씀해주시겠어요?
(b) B: 다른 사람들을 배려해주면 고맙겠다고 직접 말씀하시지 그러세요?
(c) A: 선생님은 이 체육관의 안전에 책임을 지고 계신 강사잖아요.
(d) B: 알았어요. 제가 얘기해 보죠. 그렇지만 다른 모든 사람들로부터 떨어지라고 말하지는 않을 거예요.

해설 '~해 주시면 감사하겠습니다'라는 표현을 나타내기 위해서는 「appreciate + it + if + 주어 + 동사」의 형태가 되어야 한다. appreciate 뒤에는 감사하는 것이 무엇인지를 나타내는 명사나 대명사가 오기 때문이다. 그런데 (b)에서는 it 없이 appreciate 뒤에 바로 if가 왔으므로 잘못된 문장이다. 따라서 appreciate if를 appreciate it if로 고쳐야 한다.

어구 **away from** ~에서 떨어져 　**be responsible for** ~에 대해 책임이 있다

5 (c)

해석 (a) 그 회사는 생산성을 높이기 위해 구조조정을 거칠 계획이다. (b) 그 회사는 경기 침체 때문에 큰 타격을 받았다. (c) 구조조정 계획에 따르면 인사부서는 인력의 절반을 줄여야 한다. (d) 다행히도 이번 구조조정 계획을 반대하는 직원들은 없었다.

해설 (c)에서 '인사과, 인사 부서'라는 의미가 되려면 personal department를 personnel department로 바꿔야 한다.

어구 **restructuring** 구조조정 　**boost** 향상시키다 　**productivity** 생산성 　**take a hit** 타격을 받다 　**economic recession** 경기 침체 　**workforce** 인력 　**say no** 반대하다

Check-up TEST 63~64

| 1 | (a) | 2 | (a) | 3 | (a) | 4 | (d) | 5 | (d) |

1 (a)

해석 A: 네가 다음 달에 해외 유학을 갈 거라고 들었어.
B: 맞아. 이제 내 꿈을 이루기 위해 좀 더 공부해야 할 때인 것 같아.

해설 '~해야 할 때이다'라는 뜻을 나타내는 「it is time that + 주어 + 과거동사/should + 동사원형」 구문을 묻는 문제이다. 과거 시제 studied가 쓰인 (a)가 정답이다.

어구 **study abroad** 해외로 유학 가다 　**come true** 이루어지다. 실현되다

2 (a)

해석 A: 나는 브래드 피트가 주연을 맡은 곧 개봉할 영화를 정말 보고 싶어.
B: 나도 그래.

해설 B가 '나도 마찬가지다'라고 A의 의견에 동의하는 것이므로 「so + 동사 + 주어」와 같이 도치된 문장을 쓴다. 그러므로 (b)와 (d)는 일단 답에서 제외된다. 다음으로는 대동사가 am인지 do인지를 따져봐야 한다. 두 번째 문장을 완전한 문장으로 바꿔보면 I want to see the movie, too.가 된다. 이때 일반동사 want를 받는 대동사는 do이므로 So do I가 정답이다.

어구 **upcoming** 곧 다가오는 　**star** 주역을 시키다

3 (a)

해석 핵 확산을 방지하기 위해 세계 각국이 끊임없는 노력을 해야 할 적기이다.

해설 '~해야 할 적기이다'라는 표현은 「it is high time that + 주어 + 과거동사/should 동사원형」이다. that절의 동사가 should make나 made가 되어야 하므로 정답은 (a)이다.

어구 **make efforts** 노력하다 　**ceaseless** 끊임없는 　**nuclear proliferation** 핵 확산

4 (d)

해석 (a) A: 여보세요. 캐슬 씨와 통화할 수 있을까요?
(b) B: 죄송합니다. 지금 통화 중이십니다.
(c) A: 음, 그럼 대신 마케팅 부서의 김 씨 좀 바꿔주시겠어요?
(d) B: 잠시만요. 김 씨도 통화 중이세요.

해설 (d)의 '김 씨도 통화 중입니다'를 완전한 문장으로 표현하면 Mr. Kim is on the phone, too.가 된다. 이를 So를 문두에 쓰고 대동사와 주어가 도치된 문장으로 표현하면 동사는 is를 받아 So is he가 되어야 한다. 그러므로 So did he를 So is he로 고쳐야 한다.

어구 **be on the phone** 통화 중이다 　**Hold on a second.** 잠깐 기다려주세요.

5 (d)

해석 (a) 전기는 우리가 편히 삶을 살 수 있도록 해준다. (b) 그러나 우리 수도에서 전력이 단절되면 지하철, 엘리베이터, 그리고 고속 통신망이 중단될 것이다. (c) 신뢰할 수 있는 전기 공급이 국가의 안녕에 핵심적인 요소라는 것을 염두에 두면서 관련된 관계자들은 합리적인 합의에 도달하기 위해 대화에 적극적으로 참여해야 한다. (d) 그리고 이제는 정부가 전기 생산에 발전된 기술을 도입하기 위해 광범위한 노력을 기울여야 할 때이다.

해설 '~해야 할 때이다'라는 뜻은 「it is time that + 주어 + 과거동사/should + 동사원형」으로 나타내야 한다. 그러므로 (d)의 the government will make에서 will을 should로 바꾸거나, will make 대신 과거 동사 made를 써야 옳은 표현이 된다.

어구 **live in ease** 편안하게 지내다 　**power** 전력 　**disruption** 파괴; 단절; 혼란 　**high-speed communication network** 고속 통신망 　**come to a halt** 중단되다 　**keep in mind** ~을 유의하다 　**reliable** 믿을 수 있는 　**dialogue** 대화; 토론 　**reach a consensus** 합의에 도달하다 　**rational** 합리적인 　**adopt** 도입하다, 채택하다 　**electricity generation** 전기

▄▄ Check-up TEST 65~66

| 1 | (d) | 2 | (b) | 3 | (b) | 4 | (b) | 5 | (c) |

1 (d)

해석 A: 선생님, 혹시 저희랑 자리를 좀 바꿔주실 수 있을까요?
B: 물론이죠. 하지만 이 메시지를 보내게 2분만 기다려 주실 수 있어요?

해설 '~와 자리를 바꾸다'라는 표현은 두 사람 사이에서 일어나는 행위이므로 복수 seats를 써서 exchange seats with로 표현한다.

2 (b)

해석 A: 데이브 메튜의 새 앨범 들어볼래?
B: 좋아. 언제 샀어?

해설 A가 물어본 내용을 그대로 반복해서 I'd love to hear Dave Mathew's new album.이라고 하거나, 대부정사를 사용해서 I'd love to까지만 쓸 수도 있다.

3 (b)

해석 (a) A: 마이크가 LA로 이사를 간지 벌써 몇 년이 지났어.
(b) B: 그래. 시간이 정말 빠르게 흘러. 여전히 그와 이메일을 주고받고는 있지만 그와 2년간 만나지 못했어.
(c) A: 그는 어떻게 지내? 특별한 일을 하고 있니?
(d) B: 언제나 그렇듯 여전해. 여자친구가 생겼다가, 헤어졌다가, 그러고 나서 또 다른 여자친구가 생겼지.

해설 (b)의 I am exchanging email with는 '~와 이메일을 교환하다'라는 뜻으로 쓰였다. 이때 두 사람이 서로 이메일을 교환하는 것이므로 email을 상호복수인 emails로 바꿔야 옳다.

어구 break up with ~와 헤어지다

4 (b)

해석 (a) A: 곰팡이가 피지 않는 실리콘으로 만든 마스크를 사.
(b) B: 나도 그러고 싶지만 20달러밖에 없어.
(c) A: 맞는 마스크를 고르는 데 쓰는 추가적인 돈이 차후에는 이익을 가져다줄걸.
(d) B: 좀 더 좋은 마스크를 살 수 있도록 돈 좀 빌려줄래?

해설 (b)를 보면 I'd like to 뒤에 앞에 나온 표현을 그대로 써서 I'd like to get a mask made of silicon that is mold-proof. 라고 하거나 대부정사를 써서 I'd like to.까지만 써야 한다. I'd like to be에서 be를 없애야 옳다.

어구 made of ~로 만들어진 silicon 실리콘 mold-proof 곰팡이가 피지 않는 spend money on (something) (어떤 것에) 돈을 쓰다 pay off 이익을 가져오다; 성과를 거두다

5 (c)

해석 (a) 에어로스미스의 리드싱어인 스티브 타일러는 거의 20년간 계속 약에 취하지 않고 맨 정신으로 지냈지만 그 후 진통제를 남용하기 시작했다. (b) 그 이후부터, 스티브가 그 밴드를 떠나 솔로 가수가 될지도 모른다는 소문이 떠돌았다. (c) 그리고 나머지 밴드 멤버들이 그와 거의 이야기를 나누지 않는 사이라는 것이 밝혀졌을 때, 그 소문은 현실이 되는 것 같았다. (d) 그러나, 그 가수는 자신은 결코 그 밴드를 떠나지 않을 것이라고 모두를 안심시켰고 동료 멤버들과의 문제를 해결했다.

해설 be on a speaking term with는 '~와 말을 건네는 사이이다'라는 뜻이다. 말을 건네는 것은 혼자서 할 수 없고 둘 이상이 서로 주고받아야 성립하는 행위이므로 상호복수를 써야 한다. a를 빼고 term 뒤에 -s를 붙여 be on speaking terms with로 고쳐야 한다.

어구 abuse ~을 남용하다 painkiller 진통제 sobriety 맨 정신, (술에) 취하지 않은 상태 pursue (일에) 종사하다; 추구하다 unveil (비밀을) 밝히다 barely 거의 ~하지 않는 assure 확신을 주다, 안심시키다

▄▄ Check-up TEST 67

| 1 | (a) | 2 | (b) | 3 | (d) | 4 | (d) | 5 | (b) |

1 (a)

해석 A: 신입직원을 위한 프로그램에 참석하기로 결정했니?
B: 물론이지. 내가 듣기로는 그 프로그램은 단연코 최고래.

해설 '단연코 가장 좋은 프로그램'의 의미를 지닌 최상급 표현의 어순을 묻는 문제이다. best와 명사, ever가 들어가는 최상급의 어순은 「the best+명사+ever」이다.

어구 attend 참석하다

2 (b)

해석 A: 싱가포르 여행은 어땠니?
B: 환상적이었어. 거기서 우리가 방문했던 박물관은 생각했던 것보다 훨씬 더 재미있었어.

해설 빈칸 뒤에 than we had imagined가 있기 때문에 빈칸에는 비교급 표현이 와야 함을 알 수 있다. 그러므로 정답은 (a)와 (b) 중 하나이다. 그런데 비교급을 강조하는 부사는 very가 아닌 a lot이므로 정답은 (b)이다.

3 (d)

해석 (a) A: 뉴스위크에 실린 그 기사를 정말 읽고 싶어.
(b) B: 아, 그거 엄청 재미있어. 난 그저께 한 부를 샀어.
(c) A: 10월호가 벌써 발행됐어?
(d) B: 지난주 목요일에 나왔어. 내 생각엔 10월호가 지금까지 중에 최고인 것 같아.

해설 (d)의 두 번째 문장은 10월호가 지금까지 발행되었던 것 중에 가장 좋다는 의미로, 최상급을 강조해주는 표현을 묻는 문제이다. best와 far를 사용하여 최상급을 나타내는 방법은 by far the best가 있다. 이때 위치를 바꿔 the best by far라고도 할 수 있다. 그러므로 too far에서 too를 by로 바꾼다.

어구 can't wait to V 정말 ~하고 싶다 hilarious 매우 재미있는 issue (정기 간행물) 호 hit the shelves 발매되다

4 (d)

해석 (a) A: 내 개가 전혀 나아지지 않는 것 같아 걱정이야.
(b) B: 약효가 나타나려면 며칠이 걸린다고 수의사가 말했

잖아.

(c) A: 그래. 하지만 약이 듣지 않으면 어떡하지?

(d) B: 며칠만 지나면 네 개는 분명히 훨씬 나아질 거야.

해설 (d)를 보면 비교급을 강조하기 위해 better앞에 very가 쓰였다. 그러나 '훨씬 나아진'이라는 의미로 비교급 better를 꾸며줄 수 있는 부사는 a lot / by far / much / even / still / far 이며 very는 비교급을 수식할 수 없다. 따라서 better 앞에 very 대신 위의 부사들 중 하나를 써야 한다.

어구 **get better** 나아지다, 회복하다　**veterinarian** 수의사　**kick in** 효과가 나타나기 시작하다

5 (b)

해설 (a) 남북회담에서 체결된 핵 협상을 이행하는 데는 앞으로 험난한 길이 놓여있지만 첫 번째 발자국은 내디뎠다. (b) 대부분의 한국인들이 안도의 한숨을 내쉬었겠지만, 가장 행복한 집단 중 하나는 경제관료들과 경제인들일 것이다. (c) 북한의 핵 프로그램을 끝내기 위한 협상은 장기적인 안보 위험을 완화시켜 줄 것이다. (d) 그것은 또한 국가신용도도 향상시킨다.

해설 최상급을 강조할 수 있는 단어로는 far, by far 등이 있다. 그러나 even은 비교급을 강조하는 단어이므로 (b)의 even을 far나 by far로 바꾸는 것이 옳다.

어구 **rocky road** 험난한 길, 어려움이 많은 길　**implement a deal** 협상을 이행하다　**heave sighs of relief** 안도의 한숨을 내쉬다　**ease risks** 위험을 완화시키다　**sovereign credit ratings** 국가 신용도

▬Check-up TEST 68

1	2	3	4	5
(d)	(c)	(d)	(c)	(b)

1 (d)

해석 A: 어떤 차를 살지 결정했니?

B: 저 두 대의 차 중에 나는 파란색을 사고 싶어. 그게 좀 더 멋지잖아.

해설 문두에 Of those two cars라는 어구가 있는 것으로 보아 두 가지를 비교하는 문장임을 알 수 있다. 그러므로 최상급 표현이 들어간 선택지 (b)와 (c)는 먼저 정답 후보에서 제외한다. 「of the two + 복수명사」 표현처럼 두 대상을 비교할 때는 비교급 앞에 the를 써야 하므로 the more stylish가 정답이다.

어구 **stylish** 멋진; 유행에 뒤쳐지지 않은

2 (c)

해석 피부가 태양에 더 오랫동안 노출될수록 햇볕에 화상을 입을 가능성이 높아진다.

해설 '~할수록 더 …해진다'의 내용으로 「the + 비교급, the + 비교급」 구문임을 알 수 있다. 비교급이 쓰이지 않은 (a)와 (b)는 답이 될 수 없으므로 제외시키고, (d)는 비교급 greater 앞에 the가 없으므로 정답이 될 수 없다.

어구 **expose A to** ~에 A를 노출시키다　**get a sunburn** 햇볕에 화상을 입다　**chance** 기회; 가능성

3 (d)

해석 (a) A: 자기야, 아직 프라이팬 안 바꿨지?

(b) B: 응, 다른 일을 하느라고 바빴거든.

(c) A: 인터넷에 있는 이 팬 좀 봐. 이 둘 중에, 어떤 것을 사고 싶어?

(d) B: 둘 중에서는 꽃무늬 팬이 더 예쁜 것 같아.

해설 '두 개 중 더 ~한 것'이란 뜻을 나타내는 표현은 「the + 비교급 + of the two」이다. 이때 비교급 앞에 반드시 the가 붙어야 한다. 따라서 (d)에서도 the prettier of the two (frying pans)라고 해야 옳다.

어구 **frying pan** 프라이팬　**be occupied V-ing** ~하느라고 바쁘다　**prefer** 선호하다　**floral** 꽃무늬의; 꽃의

4 (c)

해석 (a) 우리는 지난해 한국의 자살률이 OECD 국가 중 1위를 기록했다는 사실을 통해 우리의 삶과 사회를 심각하게 성찰해 보아야 한다. (b) 2018년 통계청의 사망 수치는 특히 당혹스러운데, 왜냐하면 자살이 모든 연령 집단에서 만연해 있기 때문이다. (c) 사회가 더욱 커질수록 자살이 더 많이 발생한다. (d) 40대 남성 자살자들의 대부분은 장기화된 경기침체 속에서 가족부양에 가중되는 부담을 느낀 사람들이다.

해설 「the + 비교급, the + 비교급」은 '~하면 할수록 더 …하다'라는 뜻이다. 그런데 문장 (c)를 잘 살펴보면, 앞쪽에는 the bigger가 나왔는데 뒤쪽의 more suicide에는 the가 빠진 것을 알 수 있다. 다시 말해 The bigger our society becomes, the more suicide occurs.로 바꿔야 옳은 문장이 된다.

어구 **suicide rate** 자살률　**be ranked first** 1위를 차지하다　**reflect on** ~에 대해 성찰[반성]하다　**the National Statistical Office** 통계청　**mortality figures** 사망률 수치　**rampant** 만연한　**age groups** 연령대, 연령집단　**commit suicide** 자살을 하다　**prolonged** 장기의　**recession** 불경기, 경기 후퇴

5 (b)

해석 (a) 나는 대학에서 경제학을 전공하는 학생이지만, 금융기관이 제공하는 많은 프로그램들을 완전히 이해하기 어렵다는 것을 깨달았다. (b) 최근에 나는 두 가지의 신용카드 제안을 받았고, 둘 중에 더 좋아 보이는 것을 선택했다. (c) 하지만 여전히 나를 비롯한 많은 사람들이 금융적인 문제에 대해 제대로 배울 기회가 없다고 생각한다. (d) 지식 부족은 신용 불량자들의 발생, 부유한 사람들에 대한 부정적 태도, 그리고 투기성 투자의 원인이 된다는 것이 나의 생각이다.

해설 (b)를 보면 of the two에서 보듯 비교 대상이 두 개인데, 두 개를 비교할 때는 비교급 앞에 the를 써야 한다. 따라서 the better of the two가 옳은 표현이다.

어구 **economics major** 경제학을 전공하는 학생　**financial institution** 금융기관　**a lack of knowledge** 지식 부족　**emergence** 발생　**delinquent** 채무 불이행자　**speculative investment** 투기성 투자

Actual Test 01

1 (c)	2 (c)	3 (a)	4 (c)	5 (d)
6 (a)	7 (b)	8 (b)	9 (c)	10 (a)
11 (c)	12 (b)	13 (c)	14 (d)	15 (c)
16 (b)	17 (c)	18 (d)	19 (d)	20 (b)
21 (a)	22 (b)	23 (a)	24 (b)	25 (d)
26 (d)	27 (d)	28 (c)	29 (c)	30 (b)

1 (c)

해석 A: 일 그만둔다고 들었어. 직장 상사는 뭐라고 해?
B: 내 결정에 무척 실망했다고 하더라.

해설 어순과 disappoint의 용법을 묻는 문제이다. disappoint 는 be disappointed with의 형태로 쓰이고, 부사는 일 반적으로 꾸며주는 말 바로 앞에 위치하므로 very는 be와 disappointed 사이에 와야 한다.

어구 **boss** (직장의) 상사, 상관　**be disappointed with** ~에 실망 하다

2 (c)

해석 A: 〈베놈〉 예고편을 봤는데, 보고 싶어 못 기다리겠어.
B: 그 영화는 올해 가장 기대되는 영화야.

해설 최상급의 어순 문제이다. 영화가 '사람들에 의해 기대되는' 것 이므로 –ing가 아닌 –ed가 와야 하며, 최상급 표현 순서상 the most ~의 어순을 취한다.

어구 **cannot wait to V** ~하고 싶어 안달 나다　**anticipate** 기대하 다; 예상하다, 예측하다

3 (a)

해석 A: 샘, 주저 말고 나에게 의견을 말해 줘요. 나는 항상 새로운 제안에 열려 있으니까요.
B: 그럴게요. 그렇게 말씀해 주셔서 고마워요.

해설 동사 hesitate는 to부정사를 목적어로 취하며, '~하는 것을 머뭇거리다, ~하기를 주저하다'로 해석하면 된다.

어구 **hesitate to V** ~하는 것을 망설이다　**view** 시각, 의견
open to ~에 열려 있다

4 (c)

해석 A: 그녀는 월급 5천 달러를 받는 조건이라면 일자리를 받아 들일 겁니다.
B: 알겠습니다. 동료들과 상의해 보겠습니다.

해설 on the condition that~ 이하는 미래의 내용이지만 조건절 이므로 현재형을 써야 한다.

어구 **be paid** 돈을 받다　**on the condition that** ~을 조건으로
colleague 직장 동료

5 (d)

해석 A: 금융 붕괴 사태가 너무 폭넓고 심각해서 많은 기업들이 도 산했어.
B: 맞아. 하지만 금융 회사들이 좀더 책임감이 있었다면 피할 수도 있었을 텐데.

해설 조동사 시제 문제이다. could have p.p.는 '~할 수도 있었다 (그런데 그렇게 못했다)'의 의미이고, 그 뒤로 이어지는 if절에 는 had p.p. 형태가 온다.

어구 **financial meltdown** 금융 붕괴　**severe** 극심한, 심각한
go bankrupt 파산하다, 도산하다　**accountable** 책임이 있는

6 (a)

해석 A: 나는 아주 멋진 일몰을 보며 선셋 대로를 걸었어.
B: 나도 그 길을 따라 걷는 것을 좋아해.

해설 while 뒤에는 「주어 + V-ing」가 오기도 하지만, 주어 없이 「while+V-ing」 형태로 쓸 수도 있다.

어구 **boulevard** 넓은 가로수길, 대로　**magnificent** 참으로 아름다운
walk down 길을 따라 걷다

7 (b)

해석 A: 난 폭력은 어떤 것이든 정당화될 수 없다고 생각해.
B: 나 또한 그렇게 믿고 있어.

해설 no matter what의 용법을 묻는 문제이다. 「no matter what + 주어 + 동사」 구문에서 주어와 동사가 생략되어 no matter what만 쓰였다.

어구 **justify** 정당화하다

8 (b)

해석 A: 대통령도 국민들도 국가가 분열되는 것을 원치 않아.
B: 다행이군. 난 요즘에 나라 상황에 대해 걱정했거든.

해설 「Neither A nor B」 구문에서 동사는 B의 수를 따른다.

어구 **divide** 분열시키다　**state** 상태, 상황　**lately** 최근

9 (c)

해석 A: 고고학자들은 공룡이 어떻게 멸종되었는지에 대해 논쟁 중이야.
B: 나 또한 그 이유를 알고 싶어.

해설 역사적 사실은 과거 시제로 표현한다.

어구 **archaeologist** 고고학자　**argue** 언쟁하다, 논쟁하다
extinct 멸종된, 사라진

10 (a)

해석 A: 이번 주에 그랜드 컨퍼런스 룸에서 회의가 열릴 예정이라 고 들었어.
B: 그 룸은 리모델링 때문에 아직 닫혀 있는 줄 알았는데.

해설 be scheduled to V는 '~할 예정이다'의 뜻이다. 회의가 '열리 는'의 수동의 뜻이므로 (a) is scheduled to be가 적절하다.

어구 **conference** 회의　**remodeling** 리모델링

11 (c)

해석 그는 참기 힘들 정도로 오만한 사람이라 거의 모든 사람들이 그를 싫어한다.

해설 형용사와 부사의 나열 순서를 묻는 문제이다. 「부사 + 형용사 + 명사」 순서로 쓴다.

어구 unbearably 참을 수 없게 arrogant 오만한

12 (b)
해석 일부 아프리카 국가들은 부패와 전쟁이라는 큰 이유 때문에 20년 동안 거의 변하지 않았다.

해설 부정부사 scarcely는 조동사 had와 본동사 changed 사이에 위치해야 한다. (d)의 경우 scarcely는 이미 부정어를 포함하고 있기 때문에 not이나 never와 같은 부정어는 필요가 없으므로 틀렸다.

어구 in no small part 적지 않은 corruption 부패

13 (c)
해석 하원의원들은 의료 보험 개혁안이 반드시 상원을 통과해야 한다고 주장했다.

해설 주절에 주장, 요구, 명령, 제안의 동사가 올 경우 종속절에는 조동사 should가 오거나 생략되므로 동사는 원형으로 써야 한다.

어구 House of Representative 하원의원 insist 주장하다 healthcare 의료 보험 reform 개혁 pass through 통과하다 the Senate 상원

14 (d)
해석 내가 대학 때 수학이나 경제학을 전공했다면 수치 데이터를 좀 더 잘 다룰 수 있었을 텐데.

해설 I wish 가정법 과거완료 문제이다. 과거에 ~했어야 했는데 하지 않았음을 뜻하는 문장이므로 had p.p.가 와야 한다.

어구 mathematics 수학 economics 경제학 handle 다루다 numerical 수의, 숫자상의

15 (c)
해석 전자 기기에 대한 아이들의 의존도가 낮아지지 않아 많은 부모들은 전자 기기에서 자녀들을 떼어놓으려 애쓰고 있다.

해설 문맥상 원인과 결과를 나타내는 문장이므로 because가 정답이다. for도 접속사로 사용되면 '~이기 때문에'의 뜻이지만 이 경우에는 「For + 주어 + 동사 ~, 주어 + 동사 ~」형태이거나 「주어 + 동사 ~, for + 주어 + 동사 ~」형태의 문장 구조를 이루어야 한다. 즉, 이 문제에서 for가 답이 되려면 for 앞에 ,(콤마)가 있어야 한다.

어구 desperate 필사적인 keep A away from B A를 B로부터 멀리 두다 electronic device 전자 기기 dependency 의존도 abate 감소하다

16 (b)
해석 몇몇 사람들은 사소한 문제들을 처리하느라 너무 많은 에너지를 소비해 지쳐버리지만, 시간이 많은 문제들을 해결해 주기 때문에 때로는 그 문제들을 그냥 내버려 둘 필요가 있다.

해설 사역동사 let의 어순은 「let + 목적어 + 동사원형」의 형태이다.

어구 be worn out 지치다 petty 사소한 take care of 처리하다, 신경 쓰다 let ~ be ~을 내버려 두다, 상관치 않다

17 (c)
해석 양측 협상팀은 어려운 문제에 동의했는데, 그래서 현재 협상을 마무리 짓기 위해 최선을 다하고 있다.

해설 문맥상 빈칸에 '~하기 위하여(목적)'를 나타내는 말이 와야 한다는 것을 알 수 있다. 또한 협상을 마무리 짓는 것이므로 수동태가 아니라 능동태로 써야 한다.

어구 negotiation 협상 thorny 곤란한, 어려운; 가시가 있는 conclude 결론짓다 deal 거래, 협상

18 (d)
해석 내 고장 난 컴퓨터를 서비스 센터에 가지고 갔더니 새 컴퓨터로 교체해 주었다.

해설 기존에 알고 있거나 지정된 컴퓨터가 아니기 때문에 부정관사 a와 대명사 one을 쓰면 된다.

어구 bring A to B A를 B에 가져가다 broken 고장 난 staff 직원 replace 교체하다

19 (d)
해석 미국 정부가 엄격한 조치를 취했음에도 불구하고 또 다른 금융 위기를 피할 수 없었다.

해설 「형용사[부사 / 명사 / 동사원형] + as + 주어 + 동사」는 양보구문을 이끄는 although, even though와 같이 '~라고 하더라도'의 의미를 나타낸다.

어구 tough 엄격한 financial meltdown 금융 위기

20 (b)
해석 교황은 지난 몇 달 동안 성 학대 문제에 대해 말을 아꼈다.

해설 for the past few months(지난 몇 달 동안)라는 어구가 있으므로 현재완료가 적절함을 알 수 있다.

어구 bishop 교황 abuse 학대 save one's words 말을 아끼다

21 (a)
해석 제이슨은 첫 데이트에 늦고 싶지 않기 때문에 집을 나선 뒤부터 계속 뛰었다.

해설 제이슨이 집을 나선 시점이 과거인데 그 이후 계속 뛰어오고 있었던 것이므로 과거완료 진행형이 알맞다.

어구 be late for ~에 늦다, 지각하다

22 (b)
해석 그가 무대에 등장하자마자 관객은 그를 우레와 같은 박수로 맞이해 주었다.

해설 「No sooner A than B」는 'A하자마자 B하다'라는 의미이다. 그가 무대에 나타난 것은 과거보다 앞선 시점이므로 had p.p.가 알맞다. No sooner가 문두에 오면 주어와 동사는 도치되어야 한다.

어구 greet 맞이하다 thundering applause 우레와 같은 박수

23 (a)
해석 그 팀은 연패에 종지부를 찍으려 전력을 다했기 때문에, 결국 지난 밤 첫 승을 거둘 수 있었다.

해설 표현의 정확성을 묻는 문제로, put an end to는 '~을 끝내다'

라는 의미의 숙어이므로 외워두자.

어구 **take pains** 수고하다, 애쓰다　**losing streak** 연패
manage to 간신히 ~하다

24 (b)

해석 그 회사는 요즘 개선된 유연성과 민첩성을 보여주고 있으므로 감원을 실시한 것이 틀림없다.

해설 조동사의 올바른 쓰임을 묻는 문제이다. 결과에 대한 원인을 추측하는 내용이므로 must have p.p.가 알맞다.

어구 **flexibility** 유연성　**agility** 민첩성

25 (d)

해석 연금 지급사에게 추가 비용을 지불할 수도 있다는 사실을 염두에 두셔야 합니다.

해설 동사와 목적어의 어순을 묻는 문제이다. 「pay + somebody +something」의 형식으로 써야 하므로 정답은 (d)가 된다.

어구 **keep in mind** 염두에 두다　**extra charge** 추가 비용
pension 연금　**provider** 지급하는 사람[단체]

26 (d)

해석 (a) A: 사무실에서 나 좀 도와줄 수 있어?
(b) B: 많이 바쁜가 보구나, 그렇지?
(c) A: 맞아. 어제 갑작스럽게 주문이 밀려들어서 일손이 필요해.
(d) B: 좋아. 시작하기 전에 내가 알아두어야 할 사항이 있으면 알려주겠어?

해설 (d)를 보면 사물인 the things가 선행사로서 관계대명사 앞에 있는데, 관계대명사 what은 선행사를 수반하지 않으므로 know의 목적격 역할을 하는 which를 쓰는 것이 적절하다. 이때 which 대신 that을 쓸 수도 있다.

어구 **help somebody out** 도와주다　**order** 주문

27 (d)

해석 (a) A: 자선 콘서트 티켓 예약했니?
(b) B: 아직 안 했는데. 오늘은 예약을 할 시간이 없어.
(c) A: 왜? 해야 할 일이 있니?
(d) B: 오늘 오후에 여동생이 고등학교를 졸업하거든. 졸업식장에 가야 해.

해설 '(학교를) 졸업하다'라는 표현을 할 때는 graduate 뒤에 전치사 from을 써야 한다.

어구 **reserve** 예약하다　**benefit concert** 자선 콘서트
be occupied with work 해야 할 일이 있다　**ceremony** 행사

28 (c)

해석 (a) 내가 알게 된 한 가지 사실은 액체가 리더십과 연결되는 몇 가지 특성을 공유한다는 것이다. (b) 그 특성 중 하나는, 어떤 액체는 굳어지지 않아도 견고한 결합을 구축할 수 있다는 것이다. (c) 이것은 많은 우리 지도자들이 매일 직면하는 과제이다. (d) 지도자들은 전략과 업무의 다른 측면을 실행하려 할 때 너무 경직되는 것을 피해야 한다.

해설 (c)의 each and every 뒤에는 단수 명사가 와야 한다. 따라서 days를 day로 바꿔야 한다.

어구 **notice** 의식하다, 알아보다　**rigid** 굳은, 경직된　**implement** 실행하다, 이행하다

29 (c)

해석 (a) 화학제품 회사 다우의 CEO인 앤드류 리버리스는 '물은 21세기의 석유이다'라고 주장했다. (b) 물은 석유처럼 세계경제에 필수적인 윤활유 역할을 한다. (c) 그리고 쉽게 구할 수 있는 깨끗한 물의 공급은 석유와 마찬가지로 커다란 압박을 받고 있다. (d) 그 이유는 세계 인구의 증가와 아시아 중산층의 대두 때문이다.

해설 (c)의 '압박[스트레스]을 받다'라는 표현은 be under strain 으로 표현한다. 따라서 전치사 in을 under로 바꿔야 한다.

어구 **chemical** 화학 약품의, 화학적인　**firm** 회사
chief executive 최고 경영자　**claim** 주장하다　**essential** 필수적인　**lubricant** 윤활유　**accessible** 접근 가능한
emerging 부상하는　**middle-class** 중산층

30 (b)

해석 (a) 항공사들은 연료 가격 인상에 대처하느라 진땀을 빼는 한편 '부수 수입'을 창출할 만한 새로운 방법을 모색해 왔다. (b) 이번 주 아메리칸 에어라인은 일부 항공편에서 베개와 담요에 7달러씩을 부과하기 시작하겠다고 밝혔다. (c) 다른 항공사들은 체크인 짐에 대해 추가 부담금을 청구하고 있다. (d) 게다가 전화 이용 시 분 당 2.5달러, 문자 한건 당 50센트를 부과할 방침을 계획 중이다.

해설 (b)에서 아메리칸 에어라인이 추가 부담금을 '부과당하는 것'이 아니라 '부과하는 것'이므로 수동형이 오면 안 된다.

어구 **airline** 항공사　**cope with** 대처하다　**fuel** 연료
generate 창출하다　**ancillary** 부수적인　**revenue** 수익
charge 부과하다　**pillow** 베개　**check in** 공항에서 짐을
맡기다　**text message** 문자 메시지

Actual Test 02

1	(d)	2	(b)	3	(a)	4	(d)	5	(b)
6	(a)	7	(d)	8	(c)	9	(a)	10	(b)
11	(c)	12	(d)	13	(b)	14	(a)	15	(b)
16	(d)	17	(a)	18	(c)	19	(b)	20	(c)
21	(a)	22	(c)	23	(d)	24	(a)	25	(d)
26	(c)	27	(b)	28	(c)	29	(b)	30	(c)

1 (d)

해석 A: 영화 〈어벤져스: 인피니티 워〉를 본 적 있니?
B: 응. 지난달에 두 번이나 봤어.

해설 현재완료 경험 용법과 함께 쓰이는 부사를 고르는 문제이다. once도 현재완료 경험 용법에 쓰이나 동사 앞보다는 문장 뒤에 붙는 것이 더 자연스럽다. never는 부정문에서 사용한다.

어구 **blockbuster** 블록버스터, 흥행작

2 (b)

해석 A: 난 안락사 법안이 의회에서 통과됐다는 소식에 놀라서 말

문이 막혀버렸어.

B: 나도 같은 심정이야.

해설 관사에 관한 문제이다. 특히 정관사는 앞서 언급한 내용을 다시 가리킬 때 사용한다. the same은 앞서 언급한 내용과 같다는 의미를 나타낸다.

어구 dumbstruck 놀라서 말도 못하는　　euthanasia 안락사
pass (법안을) 통과시키다　　Congress 의회

3 (a)

해석 A: 아시아 항공입니다. 무엇을 도와드릴까요?

B: 인천발 뉴욕 행 항공편 예약 확인을 하고 싶은데요.

해설 「would like to + 동사원형」은 '~하고 싶다'라는 의미로 상대방에게 자신의 바람이나 의도를 알릴 때 쓰인다. have to와 like to는 문법상으로는 문제가 없으나 대화의 문맥에는 맞지 않는다.

어구 confirm 확인하다

4 (d)

해석 A: 오늘밤 결혼식 피로연에 하객이 얼마나 올 것 같아?

B: 글쎄, 200명 정도 초대했는데. 아마 대부분 올 거야.

해설 간접 의문문에 '생각하다' 류의 동사가 쓰일 때에는 일반 간접 의문문처럼 'Do you think how many ~?'로 쓰면 틀린 표현이 된다. 의문사가 문두로 나와 'How many guests do you think ~?'가 되어야 한다.

어구 wedding reception 결혼식 피로연

5 (b)

해석 A: 어제 빌린 돈 갚는 거 잊지 않았지?

B: 그걸 잊었을 리가 있겠어? 벌써 다 갚았어.

해설 「remember + V-ing」는 '(과거에) ~했던 것을 기억하다'라는 의미이고 「remember + to부정사」는 '(미래에) ~할 것을 기억하다'라는 의미이다. 어제 '돈을 갚아야 할 것을' 잊지 않았는지 확인하는 내용이므로 to부정사가 바람직하다.

어구 pay back 빚을 갚다

6 (a)

해석 A: 어젯밤 무슨 일이 있었는지 기억나지 않아. 내가 말실수를 한건 아닌지 걱정돼.

B: 그러게 술 좀 작작 마셨어야지.

해설 어젯밤의 일이 기억나지 않는다고 했으므로 '술을 그렇게 많이 마시지 말았어야 해.'라고 응답하는 것이 적절하다. 「shouldn't have + p.p.」는 이미 과거에 한 일에 대해 '~하지 말았어야 했는데'라는 유감의 뜻을 표현할 때 쓴다.

7 (d)

해석 A: 왜 어제 우리랑 제이 지 콘서트 같이 안 갔어? 정말 대단했는데.

B: 나도 정말 가고 싶었어. 그런데 엄마가 급한 심부름을 부탁하셔서 말이지.

해설 과거에 콘서트에 가고 싶었다는 의미이므로 wanted to go to Jay Z's concert with you yesterday가 바람직한데, 상대방이 한 말을 그대로 반복할 필요 없이 to 뒤의 말은 생략하

여 대부정사로 쓸 수 있다.

어구 awesome 어마어마한　　run an errand 심부름을 하다

8 (c)

해석 A: 와, 저기 어마어마한 호텔 좀 봐.

B: 그러게, 한 번에 천 명 이상을 수용할 수 있을 정도로 크대.

해설 enough는 형용사와 부사를 뒤에서 수식하기 때문에 (c)의 large enough가 알맞다.

어구 enormous 거대한　　accommodate 수용하다. 공간을 제공하다

9 (a)

해석 A: 사람들이 그러는데 한국 국가대표팀이 이번 월드컵에서 8강에 들 수 있을 거래.

B: 나는 그럴 것 같지 않은데. 대표 팀을 보면 대부분 젊고 경험이 부족한 선수들이잖아.

해설 앞서 말한 내용에 공감하는 경우 I'm afraid so.(유감스럽게도 그럴 것 같다)를 사용하고, 공감하지 않는 경우 I'm afraid not.(유감스럽지만 그렇지 않을 것 같다)을 사용한다. 여기서는 문맥상 I'm afraid not.이 적절하다. 원래 문장은 I'm afraid the South Korean national soccer team could not make the quarterfinals in this World Cup.이다.

어구 make the quarterfinals 8강에 진출하다　　squad 선수단

10 (b)

해석 A: 이번 달 마스터스 대회에서 로저 페더러 경기 봤어?

B: 응, 그는 대회 내내 집중력을 잃지 않았어.

해설 전반적으로 과거에 국한된 내용이므로 과거 동사 stayed가 바람직하다.

어구 stay focused 집중력을 잃지 않다　　tournament 토너먼트, 선수권 대회

11 (c)

해석 그 유명 인사들은 무대 바로 옆에 위치한 좌석에서 그 공연을 지켜봤다.

해설 next to는 전치사구로 하나의 덩어리이기 때문에 이것을 쪼갤 수는 없다. 또한 부사 right은 전치사구 next to를 수식하므로 바로 앞에 두는 것이 가장 자연스럽다.

어구 celebrity 유명인사; 연예인　　situate ~을 (어느 장소에) 놓다. 설치하다.

12 (d)

해석 6.25 전쟁 당시 거의 완전히 파괴되었던 한국은 지난 수십 년간 눈부신 성장을 거두어왔다.

해설 over the past several decades와 같이 일정한 기간이 언급되면 현재완료의 계속적 용법일 가능성이 높다.

어구 dramatically 극적으로, 급격하게

13 (b)

해석 내가 비행공포증만 없었더라면 프랑스에 가서 요리사가 되었을 텐데.

해설 If it had not been for는 과거의 반대사실을 가정하는 가정

법 과거완료 구문이다. 따라서 주절도 「조동사 + had + p.p.」의 형태가 되어야 한다.

어구 **aerophobia** 비행공포증 **chef** 요리사, 주방장

14 (a)
해석 검찰은 그 살인사건과 관련하여 어떠한 결정적 증거도 발견하지 못했다.

해설 the prosecution은 집합명사로서 단수로 처리한다. 문장 마지막에 yet이 나온 것으로 보아 현재완료의 완료 용법임을 알 수 있으며 '아직 ~하지 못했다'는 의미이므로 부정문이 되어야 한다.

어구 **the prosecution** 검찰 **decisive** 결정적인 **homicide** 살인

15 (b)
해석 나는 살이 더 찌지 않도록 일주일에 5일은 체육관에 가는 습관을 들였다.

해설 to부정사를 부정하려면 부정어를 to부정사 바로 앞에 두면 된다. so as to는 '~하기 위해서'라는 의미이며, 문맥상 부정문이 되어야 하므로 so as not to라고 쓰면 된다.

어구 **make a habit of** ~하는 버릇[습관]을 들이다
put on weight 체중이 늘다, 살이 찌다

16 (d)
해석 숙제를 또 안 해서 선생님께 혼날까 두렵다.

해설 전치사 of 뒤에는 명사나 동명사가 와야 한다. 또한 논리상 선생님으로부터 꾸짖음을 받는 것이므로 수동태가 되어야 한다.

어구 **scold** 야단치다, 꾸짖다

17 (a)
해석 마크는 유능한 직원이었기에 올해 선임 관리자로 승진했다.

해설 such가 포함된 구문의 어순은 「such + a(n) + (형용사) + 명사」가 되어야 한다. 또한 이 문장은 원래 Because he was such a competent employee인데 분사구문으로 바꾼 것이다.

어구 **competent** 유능한, 능숙한 **promote** 진급[승진]시키다

18 (c)
해석 아이들뿐 아니라 그 역시 아내가 구운 초콜릿 쿠키를 정말 좋아한다.

해설 「A as well as B」는 'B뿐 아니라 A도'의 의미이므로 주어는 A이다. 따라서 동사의 인칭 및 태는 주어 A와 일치시킨다. 문장에서 주어는 He이므로 (c) loves가 알맞다.

어구 **bake** 굽다

19 (b)
해석 저의 프레젠테이션에 대해 궁금한 점이 있으시면 언제든지 연락 바랍니다.

해설 원래 문장은 If you should have any questions about ~인데 If가 생략되면서 주어와 should가 도치되었다. 빈칸에 You should를 쓸 경우 접속사가 없으므로 뒷문장과의 연결이 어색해진다.

어구 **at one's convenience** ~가 편리한 때에, 편한 시간에

20 (c)
해석 하버드 대학은 1636년 설립된 이후로 전 세계 최고의 영민한 인재들을 끌어 모았다.

해설 현재완료와 함께 오는 since절에는 특정 시점을 가리키는 과거 시제가 쓰인다. 또한 학교가 '설립된'의 수동의 뜻이 되어야 하므로 (c) was established가 알맞다.

어구 **the best and brightest** 가장 뛰어난[총명한]

21 (a)
해석 그 공상 과학 영화는 너무 인상적이었기 때문에 나중에 꼭 다시 보고 싶다.

해설 such를 써서 '매우 인상적인 영화'를 표현하려면 「such + a(n) + (형용사) + 명사」 어순으로 써야 하므로 (a) such an impressive가 알맞다.

어구 **impressive** 인상적인 **science fiction movie** 공상 과학 영화

22 (c)
해석 석유, 석탄과 같은 화석연료는 무한한 자원이 아닐 뿐더러 재생 가능하지도 않다.

해설 nor나 neither 뒤에는 「동사 + 주어」의 어순이 온다. nor 대신에 and neither가 올 수 있다.

어구 **fossil fuel** 화석연료 **petroleum** 석유 **inexhaustible** 고갈되지 않는, 무한한 **renewable** 재생 가능한

23 (d)
해석 마이크는 그들의 손실에 대해 유감스러워 하면서도, 그 일은 그들 스스로 초래했다고 생각한다.

해설 두 개의 문장을 연결해주는 접속사가 필요하다. Since와 Because는 이유를 뜻하며 이 문장에서는 논리적이지 않다. 문맥상 '~하는 한편'이라는 의미의 While이 적절하다.

어구 **bring something on** ~을 초래[야기]하다

24 (a)
해석 해외 임무를 수행할 병사들은 어떠한 상황에서도 싸울 수 있도록 준비태세를 갖춰 파병되어야 한다.

해설 병사들이 '준비된' 상태가 되어야 하는 것이므로 수동의 의미를 가진 과거분사 prepared가 적절하다. prepare 뒤에는 「to + 동사원형」 또는 「for + 명사」가 올 수 있으므로 prepared to fight 또는 prepared for fighting이 가능하다.

어구 **overseas mission** 해외 임무 **dispatch** 파견하다, 보내다
circumstance 환경, 상황

25 (d)
해석 뇌물 스캔들에 연루된 회장은 자신이 진퇴양난에 빠졌음을 깨달았다.

해설 find oneself 뒤에는 현재분사 또는 과거분사가 올 수 있으나 문맥상 '어떠한 상황에 처하게 되는'의 수동의 의미이므로 과거분사 caught가 적절하다.

어구 **bribery** 뇌물   **catch-22** 곤경, 진퇴양난

26 (c)

해석 (a) A: 이번 여름에 어디 갔었니?
(b) B: 영국 맨체스터로 여행갔었어.
(c) A: 그럼 맨유 구장인 올드 트래포드에도 가봤겠구나, 그렇지?
(d) B: 당연하지. 어떻게 거길 그냥 지나치겠어?

해설 부가의문문을 만들 때는 앞 문장에 쓰인 동사와 시제, 수를 일치시켜야 한다. (c)에서 주어는 you이고 동사는 visited이므로 이에 대한 부가의문문으로는 didn't you?가 적절하다.

어구 **take a trip to** ~로 여행가다   **stadium** 축구장, 육상 경기장

27 (d)

해석 (a) A: 어디 가니?
(b) B: 옷 좀 사러 롤리 백화점에 가는 길이야.
(c) A: 네 옷장 속에 들어있는 옷에 싫증이 난 모양이구나.
(d) B: 무슨 소리야? 난 단지 이번 봄에 입을 옷이 없을 뿐이라고.

해설 something은 긍정문, anything은 부정문과 의문문에 쓰인다. (d)의 두 번째 문장은 부정문이므로 anything이 적절하다.

어구 **head** (특정 방향으로) 가다, 향하다   **on one's way to** ~로 가는 길[도중]에   **fed up with** ~에 물린, 싫증난

28 (c)

해석 (a) 냉장고에는 습기가 없는 것이 아니라, 실제로는 약 11퍼센트 정도의 습기가 있다. (b) 하지만, 사람이 냉장고 문을 열 때마다 일정한 양의 습기가 빠져 나간다. (c) 그 결과 과일, 야채 및 다른 식품이 문이 열리지 않았을 경우보다 신선도를 더 빨리 잃을 수 있다. (d) 다행히도, 식품을 넣어둘 수 있는 플라스틱 용기의 발달로 식품 안에 든 습기를 보존할 수 있어서 식품이 신선도를 빠르게 잃는 것을 방지할 수 있다.

해설 (c)문장의 후반부에 than이 있으므로 원급이 아닌 비교급 부사가 와야 한다. 따라서 more가 부사 앞에 붙어야 하므로 rapidly than을 more rapidly than으로 바꿔야 한다.

어구 **refrigerator** 냉장고   **be devoid of** ~이 없다   **moisture** 습기, 습도   **freshness** 신선도   **rapidly** 빠르게   **preserve** 보존하다

29 (b)

해석 (a) 1990년대 북한의 기근이 절정에 달한 이후로 많은 북한주민들이 국경을 넘어 중국으로 갔다. (b) 미 국무부에 따르면 약 3만~5만 명의 탈북자들이 현재 중국에 머물고 있다고 한다. (c) 그들은 북한으로 송환될 경우 수개월 간 노동 교화와 심지어 처형과 같은 무거운 처벌을 받게 될 것이라고 믿는다. (d) 일반적으로 북한은 세계에서 인권 탄압이 가장 심한 곳으로 알려져 있다.

해설 (b)에서 주어 North Korean refugees는 복수이므로 뒤에 오는 동사 역시 복수여야 한다. 따라서 stay가 적절하다.

어구 **reach one's peak** 절정에 이르다   **refugee** 난민, 망명자   **repatriation** 본국 송환   **execution** 처형, 사형   **violator** 위반자, 침해자

30 (c)

해석 (a) 인권은 '모든 인간에게 부여되는 기본권 및 자유'를 가리킨다. (b) 하지만 아직까지도 인권이 경시되고 심지어 남용되는 곳들이 존재한다. (c) 이에 대하여 다양한 비 정부기구(NGO)와 국제기구에서는 인권 보호를 위해 각국 정부와 긴밀히 공조하고 있다. (d) 1948년 UN 총회에서 인권 보호 및 증진을 위해 세계 인권선언이 채택되었다.

해설 (c)에서 close가 앞에 나오는 동사 work를 수식해주기 위해서는 부사인 closely가 되어야 한다. close가 부사로 쓰일 경우 '가까이'라는 의미가 된다.

어구 **entitle** 자격[권리]을 주다   **neglect** 등한시하다, 방치하다   **abuse** 남용하다; 학대하다   **adopt** 채택하다   **facilitate** 가능하게 하다, 용이하게 하다

Actual Test 03

1 (c)	2 (a)	3 (a)	4 (c)	5 (c)
6 (c)	7 (a)	8 (c)	9 (d)	10 (a)
11 (d)	12 (b)	13 (c)	14 (a)	15 (d)
16 (b)	17 (b)	18 (a)	19 (c)	20 (b)
21 (d)	22 (c)	23 (b)	24 (c)	25 (b)
26 (a)	27 (a)	28 (c)	29 (c)	30 (d)

1 (c)

해석 A: 안녕 새러. 뭐 들고 있니? 내가 도와 줄 수 있을 거 같은데.
B: 그렇게 말해 주다니 참 친절하구나.

해설 to부정사의 의미상 주어 앞에 쓰는 전치사는 보통 for이지만 사람의 성격 및 성품을 나타내는 형용사가 올 경우 of를 쓴다.

어구 **carry** 들다, 운반하다

2 (a)

해석 A: 이번 학기에 새로운 선생님을 뵙게 되어 너무 좋아. 너희 선생님은 어때?
B: 내가 듣기론 우리 선생님은 학교에서 가장 엄격하신 선생님 중 한 분이시래.

해설 strict는 1음절이므로 최상급으로 쓸 때, 앞에 most를 붙이지 않고 -est 형태로 쓰면 된다.

어구 **excited** 흥분된, 들뜬   **semester** 학기   **strict** 엄격한

3 (a)

해석 A: 내일 럭셔리 레스토랑에서의 저녁 식사가 매우 기대된다. 거기 예약했니?
B: 물론이지. 우리 좌석 예약할 것을 기억했었다고. 걱정 마.

해설 「remember + to동사원형」은 '(앞으로) 해야 하는 것을 기억하다'이고 「remember + V-ing」는 '(과거에) 한 일을 기억하다'라는 의미이다. B가 Of course.라고 답한 것으로 보아 예약할 것을 잊지 않고 예약했다는 것을 알 수 있다.

어구 **anticipate** 기대하다   **make a reservation** 예약하다

4 (c)

해석 A: 너도 알다시피, 우린 운전 면허증을 따기 전에는 차를 몰 수 없잖아, 안 그래?
B: 그래, 네 말이 맞아. 내가 잘못 생각했어. 우리 다음 달에 같이 운전 학원 다니자.

해설 부사절 until 뒤에는 내용이 미래라 하더라도 현재 시제가 온다.

어구 driver's license 운전 면허증 driving lesson 운전 교육

5 (c)

해석 A: 대통령이 고개를 숙이며 해병들을 애도하는 모습을 봤니?
B: 봤어. 정말 가슴 아픈 순간이었어.

해설 to부정사의 용법을 묻는 문제이다. (b)와 (d)는 문법적으로 틀리고 (a)는 어색한 표현이다.

어구 lower one's head 고개를 숙이다 sailor 선원, 해병 pay condolences to ~에 애도를 표하다 touching 가슴 아픈; 감동적인

6 (c)

해석 A: 그거 알아? 사이먼은 어제 저녁 경기에서 3점 숏 대부분을 막을 수도 있었어.
B: 맞아. 하지만 컨디션이 좋지 않았던 것을 우린 알잖아.

해설 A의 말 마지막 부분에 last night's game이 있으므로 과거의 사실을 가정하고 있다는 것을 알 수 있다. '3점 숏을 막을 수 있었다. (그런데 막지 못했다)'의 뜻이 되어야 하므로 (c) could have blocked가 적절하다.

어구 3-point shot 3점 숏 condition 상태, 컨디션 block 막다

7 (a)

해석 A: 난 그녀를 10년 동안 알아 왔지만 절대 살이 안 찌는 것 같아.
B: 맞아. 아무리 많이 먹어도 살이 절대 찌지 않아. 신진대사가 매우 활발해.

해설 no matter how(아무리 ~해도)구문의 용법을 묻는 문제이다. 「no matter how + 형용사 / 부사 + 주어 + 동사」의 어순이 됨을 기억해 두자.

어구 put on pounds 살찌다, 몸무게가 늘다 metabolism 신진대사

8 (c)

해석 A: 어제 눈이 기록적으로 많이 와서 너무 많은 운전자가 꼼짝 못 했어.
B: 그래서 지금 다른 학교나 우리학교나 모두 휴교잖아.

해설 「neither A nor B」 구문에서 동사는 B에 맞춘다. B의 mine은 my school을 뜻하며 단수이므로 동사도 단수로 맞춰야 한다. (d)의 opening 뒤에는 목적어가 와야 하므로 답이 될 수 없다.

어구 snowfall 강설 record 기록적인, 최고의 get stranded 갇히다, 움직이지 못하다, 꼼짝 못하다

9 (d)

해석 A: 1950년 6월 25일에 한국전쟁을 시작한 쪽은 북한이었어.
B: 그래. 일어나지 말았어야 하는 일이지. 그 전쟁은 지금까지도 우리나라를 갈라놓고 있어.

해설 역사적 사실은 과거 시제로 쓴다.

어구 divide 갈라놓다 up to this day 지금까지

10 (a)

해석 A: 대통령은 요즘 경기를 개선하고자 큰 노력을 기울이고 있어.
B: 내 생각엔, 금융 업계가 스스로 앞장서서 우리가 더 나은 시스템으로 바뀌도록 이끌지 않으면 또 다른 금융 위기를 피할 수 없을 거야.

해설 조건을 나타내는 unless 뒤에는 미래의 내용이 오더라도 현재 시제로 미래를 표현한다.

어구 make an effort 노력하다 improve 개선하다 avoid 피하다 financial meltdown 금융 위기 lead 이끌다, 앞장서다

11 (d)

해석 엄마가 나에게 햄버거를 만들어 주셨는데, 내 평생 그렇게 크고 맛있게 생긴 버거는 본 적이 없다.

해설 여러 개의 형용사가 나열될 때에는 「대소 형용사 + 상태 형용사」 순으로 쓴다.

어구 giant 거대한, 매우 큰 delicious-looking 맛있게 생긴

12 (b)

해석 어제 저녁 짐의 성과는 내 기대를 뛰어 넘었지만 제임스와 어깨를 나란히 하기에는 아직 부족하다.

해설 enough는 형용사나 부사를 뒤에서 수식하므로 fast 뒤에서 꾸며 주는 형태가 맞다.

어구 performance 성과, 실적 beyond one's expectation ~의 기대 이상인 stand shoulder to shoulder with ~와 어깨를 나란히 하다, 견주다

13 (c)

해석 재무부 장관은 은행 임원들에게 그들이 하는 일에 대해 더 책임감을 가질 것을 요구했다.

해설 요구, 주장, 명령, 권유를 나타내는 동사가 당위성을 띠는 that절을 목적어로 취할 경우, that절에는 「(should) + 동사원형」이 온다.

어구 treasury secretary 재무부 장관 demand 요구하다 responsible 책임감 있는 respond 대응하다, 응답하다 responsive 즉각 반응하는, 관심을 보이는

14 (a)

해석 나는 회의하는 동안 좀 더 중립을 지켰어야 했는데, 미팅 참가자들은 내가 감정을 표출한 것으로 생각했다.

해설 일어나지 않은 과거의 일을 소망하고 있으므로 가정법 과거완료인 had p.p.로 쓰는 것이 적절하다.

어구 neutral 중립의 participant 참석자 give away one's feelings ~의 감정을 표출하다

15 (d)

해석 타운홀 미팅 동안 그 상원 의원은 주민들의 의견에 열심히 귀 기울였는데, 그의 새로운 법안에 대한 관심이 증가하고 있었기 때문이다.

해설 문맥을 따져보면 뒷문장이 앞의 문장에 대한 이유를 나타내므로 (d) for가 알맞다.

어구 senator 상원 의원 town hall meeting 타운홀 미팅 (지역 주민들을 모아놓고 의견을 듣고 표출하는 모임) bill 법안

16 (b)

해석 그는 식당에서 고함을 치며 소란을 일으켰기 때문에 두 명의 경찰관이 그를 데리고 나와 근처 경찰서로 연행했다.

해설 구동사의 목적어로 대명사가 올 경우, 동사와 부사 사이, 또는 동사와 전치사 사이에 들어가야 한다.

어구 cause a disturbance 소란을 피우다 get ~ out ~를 데리고 나오다 take ~ to… ~을 …로 데리고 가다 nearby 근처의 police station 경찰서

17 (a)

해석 샘이 내게 준 잡지에서 실시한 설문에 답한 대부분의 사람들은 동성 간의 결혼에 찬성했다.

해설 선행사는 the magazine으로 사물이고 gave의 목적어 역할을 하므로 관계대명사 which가 적절하다.

어구 majority 대다수 survey 설문하다; 설문 magazine 잡지 same-sex marriage 동성 결혼

18 (a)

해석 그 회장은 자신의 최근 사기 사건에 대해 언급할 만큼 뻔뻔했다.

해설 '~할 만큼 충분히 …하다'라는 표현은 「형용사/부사+ enough +to+동사원형」으로 쓴다. 또한 회장이 '발언을 한' 능동의 의미이므로 to make가 알맞다.

어구 chairman 회장 presumptuous 뻔뻔한 comment 발언 fraud 사기 case 사례, 사건

19 (c)

해석 내게 맞는 짝을 찾으려 하니까, 재스민이 바로 나의 짝이라는 사실을 알겠다.

해설 one은 앞에서 언급한 a good match for myself를 받는 대명사이고, 정해지지 않은 짝이 아니라 앞에서 말한 '바로 그' 짝이므로 정관사 the가 앞에 붙어야 한다.

어구 match 짝 realize 깨닫다

20 (b)

해석 바람과 파도가 거칠었음에도 불구하고, 피해자들이 아직 살아 있음을 알았기에 구조대는 결코 수색 및 구조 노력을 중단하지 않았다.

해설 문맥상 빈칸에는 '~에도 불구하고'라는 양보의 의미를 나타내는 어구가 필요하다. 양보절은 보통 「형용사+ as + 주어+동사」의 어순으로 쓰인다.

어구 wild 거친 wave 파도 rescue team 구조대 victim 피해자, 희생자 alive 생존해 있는, 살아있는

21 (d)

해석 그는 지난 2년 동안 대통령 선거에 출마해 지치지 않는 노력을 기울인 끝에 결국 경쟁이 심했던 선거에서 박빙의 차이로 승리했다.

해설 over the past two years로 보아 2년 전부터 지금까지 있었던 일, 즉 현재완료 시제임을 알 수 있다.

어구 tireless 지칠 줄 모르는 run for the presidency 대통령 선거에 출마하다 competitive 경쟁이 심한 by a narrow margin 좁은 투표 차로, 가까스로

22 (c)

해석 하수 처리의 중요성은 도시 설계자들에게 도시 건설의 중요한 부분으로 거의 고려되지 않는다.

해설 원래 문장은 The importance of sewage treatment is seldom considered by ~이다. 부정부사 seldom이 문두에 나오면 주어와 동사는 도치되므로 Seldom is the importance of sewage treatment ~로 써야 한다.

어구 sewage treatment 하수 처리 urban designer 도시 설계자 critical 매우 중요한, 결정적인 city construction 도시 건설

23 (b)

해석 어젯밤 대형 자동차 사고를 당했을 때 조는 기적적으로 살아남았고 그가 다친 곳이라고는 얼굴의 살짝 긁힌 상처뿐이었다.

해설 관용어의 의미를 묻는 문제이다. 문맥상 '~보다 더 큰 상처는 아니었다'라는 어구가 필요하므로 nothing more than(~에 지나지 않는)'이 적절하다.

어구 by some miracle 기적적으로 escape 피하다, 도망치다 get in a car accident 자동차 사고를 당하다 injury 부상 scratch 긁힌 자국, 찰과상 none other than 다름 아닌

24 (c)

해석 나의 상사는 늦어도 이 프로젝트가 다음 금요일까지 끝나길 원한다.

해설 5형식 동사로 쓰인 want의 목적격 보어가 와야 하는데, this project가 '끝나는'의 수동의 의미가 되어야 하므로 과거분사인 done이 와야 한다.

어구 at the latest (아무리) 늦어도

25 (b)

해석 그녀의 동료들은 그녀가 며칠 동안 출근하지 않았기 때문에 분명 해고당했을 것이라고 생각했다.

해설 의미상 '~했음이 틀림없다'라고 추측하는 어구가 필요하므로 must have p.p.가 적절하다.

어구 colleague 동료 let ~ go ~을 해고하다 show up 나타나다

26 (a)

해석 (a) A: 캘리포니아 연구소는 거의 15년 만에 최초의 새로운 에이즈 약을 만들 수 있는 중요한 발견을 했다고 발표할 거야.
(b) B: 현재 사용되고 있는 항바이러스 약은 AIDS 퇴치에 더 이상 효과가 없기 때문에 아주 시기적절한 발견이야.
(c) A: 그 연구소 과학자들은 지구상에 존재하는 가장 치명적인 질병 중 하나인 에이즈의 영향을 줄일 비결을 밝히려고 AIDS 유전학을 연구 중이야.
(d) B: 잘 하면 너무 오랫동안 지지부진했던 AIDS와의 전쟁에서 획기적인 발명이 되겠네.

해설 (a)에서 서수가 먼저 와야 하므로 the new first가 아니라 the

first new가 올바른 표현이다.

어구 **significant** 중요한 **finding** 연구 결과 **pave the path** 길을 열다 **antiviral** 항바이러스의 **genetics** 유전학 **fatal** 치명적인 **breakthrough** 획기적인 일, 발명 **drag on** 질질 끌다

27 (a)

해석 (a) A: 그 영화가 엄청난 기대감을 불러일으키면서 마침내 개봉했어. 너무 기대된다.
(b) B: 그 후속작 영화는 업그레이드 된 화력의 무기를 보여준대.
(c) A: 맞아. 그 로봇은 걸리적거리는 적들을 다 날려버릴 거야.
(d) B: 너무 늦기 전에 인터넷으로 영화 티켓을 사야겠어.

해설 (a)에서 큰 기대를 불러일으킨 것은 영화가 개봉된 지금보다 더 전의 일이므로 완료 분사구문인 having p.p. 형태로 시작해야 한다.

어구 **incredible** 믿기 힘든 **release** 개봉하다, 출시하다 **sequel** 후속작 **upgraded** 업그레이드된, 개선된 **firepower** 화력 **blow up** ~을 폭파하다, 날려 버리다 **in one's way** ~을 방해하는

28 (c)

해석 (a) 그 은행의 부은행장은 청문회 위원회 앞에서 눈덩이처럼 불어나는 부채 조절의 실패에 대해 증언했다. (b) 그곳에서 그는 몇몇 상원의원이 퍼붓는 신랄한 공격 세례를 받았다. (c) 그 의원들은 그의 회사가 좀 더 책임감 있게 행동했었다면 파급 효과는 좀 더 경미했을 것이라고 주장했다. (d) 공청회 후, 그 심문 과정을 지켜본 사람들은 그 은행가가 사임할 만하다고 생각했다.

해설 (c)의 that절을 살펴보면 회사가 '과거에 책임감 있게 행동했다면~'이라며 과거의 반대 사실에 대해 가정하고 있음을 알 수 있다. 그 뒤에 이어지는 주절에서도 would have p.p. 형태가 나오므로 if절은 가정법 과거완료인 had acted가 되어야 한다.

어구 **vice president** 부회장, 부통령 **stand before** ~앞에 서다 **hearing committee** 청문회 위원회 **testify** 증언하다 **snowball** 눈덩이처럼 불어나다 **debt** 부채 **bombard** 폭격하다 **a series of** 일련의 **ripple effect** 파급 효과 **questioning** 심문 **retire** 퇴직하다, 은퇴하다

29 (c)

해석 (a) 레오나르도 다 빈치는 르네상스 시대에 살았던 유명한 발명가였다. (b) 그는 최초의 비행기가 하늘을 날기 전인 약 400년 전에 비행기 모양을 그렸다. (c) 다빈치는 발명품들외에도 〈모나리자〉를 포함한 다수의 예술 작품을 창작하기도 했다. (d) 다빈치의 발명품들은 시대를 훨씬 앞서나갔고, 그의 그림은 오늘도 전세계의 사랑을 받고 있다.

해설 (c)문장의 콤마 이하는 '~을 포함하여'라는 능동의 의미이므로 included가 아니라 including으로 써야 한다.

어구 **renowned** 유명한 **draw sketches** 그림을 그리다 **approximately** 대략 **take flight** 비행하다

30 (d)

해석 (a) 영국은 풍부한 천연자원을 보유하고 있기 때문에 영국 정당의 지도자들은 에너지 정책에는 별로 손을 대지 않았다. (b)

북해의 석유와 가스 덕분에 영국은 삼십 년 간의 풍요를 얻어, 운 좋게도 에너지 문제에 신경쓰지 않고 지낼 수 있었다. (c) 하지만 에너지 문제는 개발도상국가들 뿐 아니라 다른 많은 선진국의 지도자들을 수년 간 괴롭혔다. (d) 그러나 최근 예상치 못했던 변화가 영국 여론에 일어나, 영국은 이제 확실히 에너지 문제에서 자유롭지 못하게 되었다.

해설 (d)에서 occur는 능동으로만 쓰이는 자동사로서, 수동형으로 쓸 수 없다. 또한 변화가 최근 일어나 지금까지 영향을 미치므로 현재완료형이 되어야 한다.

어구 **political party** 정당 **touch on** 다루다 **abundant** 풍부한, 풍요로운 **plenty** 풍요 **thorny** 까다로운 **issue** 이슈, 문제 **haunt** (생각 따위가) ~에게 끊임없이 붙어 다니다, ~을 괴롭히다 **advanced country** 선진국 **developing country** 개발도상국

Actual Test 04

1	(d)	2	(c)	3	(c)	4	(d)	5	(d)
6	(d)	7	(c)	8	(a)	9	(a)	10	(c)
11	(b)	12	(c)	13	(d)	14	(a)	15	(d)
16	(b)	17	(c)	18	(a)	19	(b)	20	(a)
21	(b)	22	(c)	23	(c)	24	(b)	25	(c)
26	(a)	27	(c)	28	(c)	29	(c)	30	(d)

1 (d)

해석 A: 어떡해! 노트북을 버스에다 놓고 내렸어.
B: 정말? 너무 어처구니없는 일을 저질렀구나.

해설 감탄문의 어순을 잘 익혀 두어야 한다. What으로 시작할 경우 「what a + 형용사 + 명사 + (주어 + 동사)」의 형태를 띠고 How의 경우 「how + 형용사 + (주어 + 동사)」이다. 따라서 선택지 중에 위 형태에 맞는 것을 찾아야 한다.

2 (c)

해석 A: 자네 아들이 마침내 직장을 구해서 정말 기쁘네.
B: 너무 고마워. 말로 표현할 수 없을 정도로 기쁘다네.

해설 간접 의문문의 경우 「의문사 + 주어 + 동사」의 순으로 와야 한다. 그리고 이 문장의 경우 how는 happy를 꾸며주므로 두 단어는 같이 붙어 있어야 한다.

어구 **get a job** 일자리를 구하다

3 (c)

해석 A: 지난밤에 뭐했니? 너무 피곤해 보인다.
B: 지붕 위로 떨어지는 빗소리를 들으며 저녁 내내 자지 않고 있었어.

해설 잠을 자지 않은 사람과 빗소리를 들은 사람이 같고 시제도 과거로 동일하므로 분사구문은 listening으로 시작해야 한다. having listened는 한 시제 앞설 때 쓴다.

어구 **sit up late** 늦게까지 자지 않고 있다

4 (d)

해석 A: 존은 좋은 사람인 거 같아. 열심히 일하잖아.
　　 B: 하지만 종종 화를 내. 인내심이 부족한 젊은 남자들에게 흔히 있는 경우지.

해설 As is often the case with는 '흔히 있는 일이지만, 흔히 있듯이'라는 의미의 관용구이므로 통째로 외워두자.

어구 **diligently** 성실하게, 부지런히　**lose one's temper** 화를 내다
as is often the case with 흔히 있는 일이지만, 흔히 있듯이

5 (d)

해석 A: 많은 사람들이 2차 세계대전 때 목숨을 잃었어.
　　 B: 아마도 다음 전쟁은 우리가 상상할 수 있는 것보다 더 잔인할 거야.

해설 cruel의 비교급은 crueler than이다.

어구 **cruel** 잔혹한

6 (d)

해석 A: 케빈의 삶에는 참 우여곡절이 많아.
　　 B: 최근에는 근심 걱정할 일 없나?

해설 현재완료의 의문문은 「Have / Has + 주어 + p.p.」 형태를 취한다.

어구 **ups and downs** 오르내림, 기복　**free of** ~로부터 자유로운, ~가 없는

7 (c)

해석 A: 너희 회사 언제 텐진으로 이전했어?
　　 B: 그곳으로 이전한 지 15년이 지났어.

해설 since는 '~한 이래로'라는 의미로 「현재완료 + since + 과거」의 형태를 띤다. 즉 since 뒤에는 과거 시제, 앞에는 현재완료 시제를 쓴다.

어구 **relocate** 이전하다, 다시 배치하다

8 (a)

해석 A: 한국이 올림픽을 개최했다는 것 아니?
　　 B: 물론이지! 1988년 서울에서 올림픽이 열렸잖아.

해설 The Olympic Games는 복수로 받아야 하고, 1988년도라는 과거의 특정 시점이 나왔으므로 과거 시제를 써야한다. 따라서 be동사의 복수이면서 과거 시제인 were가 적절하다.

어구 **host** 개최하다

9 (a)

해석 A: 이번 주 토요일에 나랑 점심 같이 할래요?
　　 B: 미안해요. 그러고 싶은데 선약이 있어요.

해설 앞에 나온 have lunch의 중복을 피하기 위해 would like to까지만 쓴다.

어구 **previous engagement** 선약

10 (c)

해석 A: 나 내일 HP 인사부장이랑 면접 있어.
　　 B: 왜! 놓치기엔 너무 좋은 기회다.

해설 B문장의 뒤에 나온 to be lost를 보고 too ~ to 구문임을 파

악할 수 있어야 한다. 'too ~ to…'는 '너무 ~해서 …할 수 없다'라는 의미이며 「too + 형용사 + 관사 + 명사」의 어순으로 써야 한다.

어구 **personnel director** 인사부장　**lose** 잃다, 놓치다

11 (b)

해석 대학에 들어가려는 사람들에게 오늘날만큼 선택의 기회가 많았던 적은 없었다.

해설 Hardly ever와 같은 부사구가 앞에 나오면 주어와 동사의 위치가 도치된다. 원래 문장의 there have been이 have there been으로 도치된 것이다.

어구 **hardly ever** 좀처럼 ~않다, 거의 ~않다

12 (c)

해석 언덕 넘어 숲을 지나면 그의 부모님이 살고 있는 집이다.

해설 Over the hill and through the woods라는 부사구가 앞에 나왔으므로 주어와 동사의 위치가 도치된다. 원래 문장의 the house is where가 is the house where로 도치된 것이다.

13 (d)

해석 외국인은 은행에 갈 때 여권을 가지고 가면 수표를 현금으로 바꾸기가 쉬워질 것이다.

해설 앞에 나와 있는 명사와의 관계를 잘 보아야 한다. 수표가 '현금화되는' 것이므로 수동의 의미이다. 따라서 과거분사 형태를 써야 한다.

어구 **passport** 여권　**check** 수표　**cash** 현금으로 바꾸다

14 (a)

해석 그들 자체는 완벽하지 않지만, 그들이 완벽한 기관을 설립할 수는 있다.

해설 문맥을 살펴보고 알맞은 말을 찾아야 한다. 앞, 뒤 문장을 보면 상반 관계이다. '~이지만'의 상반 관계를 나타내는 접속사를 넣어야 한다.

어구 **institution** 학회, 시설

15 (d)

해석 지난 수년간의 전체적인 지구 온난화 현상이 한 해 동안의 어떤 현상보다 더 중요하다.

해설 주어인 single year's trend가 뒤에 나왔으므로 도치구문이다. 따라서 「than + 대동사 + any single year's trend」 형태가 되어야 한다. 또한 single year's trend가 단수이므로 대동사 do는 does로 바뀌어야 한다.

어구 **overall** 전반적인　**warming trend** 온난화 현상
significance 중요, 의미

16 (b)

해석 나는 별나기로 유명한 다른 한 소년과 교실에 같이 있어야 했다.

해설 who 뒤에 was, 즉 3인칭 단수 be동사가 나왔다. 이를 통해 who 앞의 선행사가 단수임을 알 수 있다. 또한 '또 다른 한 명'의 소년을 나타낼 때는 another를 써야 한다.

어구 **notorious** 악명 높은　**eccentricity** 남다름, 기행

17 (c)

해석 이 학교는 1954년에 설립됐는데, 오랫동안 이 나라에서 손꼽히는 학교 중 하나로 여겨졌다.

해설 '~ 중 하나'라고 할 때는 「one of the + (형용사) + 복수 명사」 형태로 쓴다. 그리고 '손꼽히는, 으뜸인'이라는 표현으로는 leading을 써야 맞다.

어구 **found** 설립하다, 세우다   **leading** 손꼽히는, 일류의, 뛰어난

18 (a)

해석 그는 직장을 구하기 전에는 학교를 그만 두지 않는 편이 낫다.

해설 had better는 '~하는 것이 낫다'는 뜻의 조동사로 부정문은 had better not으로 쓴다.

어구 **quit** 그만두다, 떠나다   **find a job** 직장을 구하다

19 (b)

해석 그녀의 남자친구의 배신이나 양부모의 비난은 그녀에게 엄청난 스트레스를 주었다.

해설 「either A or B」 뒤에 나오는 동사는 B에 맞춰야 한다. (a)와 (d)를 쓰면 주어와 수가 일치하지 않고 (c)를 쓰면 본동사가 없는 문장이 된다.

어구 **betrayal** 배반   **foster** 길러주는, 수양~   **criticism** 비평, 혹평

20 (a)

해석 그 시는 시민들을 위해 더 많은 기반 시설을 마련해야 한다.

해설 It is imperative that은 당위성을 띠므로 「(should) + 동사원형」이 나와야 한다.

어구 **imperative** 피할 수 없는, 긴급한   **infrastructure** 기반 시설   **citizen** 시민

21 (b)

해석 그들은 원하는 결과를 얻기 위해서는 가능한 한 빨리 일할 필요가 있다.

해설 '가능한 ~하게'라는 표현은 as ~ as possible이고 as 사이에는 fast의 부사형이 와야 한다. fast의 형용사형, 부사형은 모두 fast이다. fastly라는 단어는 없다.

어구 **in order to V** ~하기 위해서   **desired** 희망하는

22 (c)

해석 3세 아이는 약 5,000 단어의 기초 어휘를 가지고 있다.

해설 「some + 숫자 + 명사」의 순서가 되어야 한다. 또한 thousand는 앞에 숫자가 올 때는 복수로 쓸 수 없다.

어구 **basic** 기초의   **vocabulary** 어휘

23 (c)

해석 변호사는 그의 고객에게 손해를 보상할 필요가 없다며 안심시켰다.

해설 동사 assure의 성질을 잘 알아야 한다. assure는 '확신시키다'라는 의미의 동사로 뒤에 바로 「목적어 + that절」을 취한다.

어구 **attorney** 대리인, 변호사   **client** 고객, 의뢰인   **assure** 확신시키다, (확신시켜) 안심하게 하다   **damage** 손해

24 (b)

해석 가죽 소파를 깨끗이 유지할 수 있는 유일한 방법은 적합한 세정제를 쓰는 것으로, 이는 소파를 오래 쓸 수 있도록 도와준다.

해설 '~함으로써'의 의미, 즉 '방법'을 나타낼 때는 전치사 by를 쓴다.

어구 **leather** 가죽   **cleanser** 세정제   **prolong** 늘이다, 연장하다

25 (c)

해석 이 기관은 음식의 소화와 체내의 당 수치 조절과 관련된 기관이다.

해설 앞에 나와 있는 organ을 꾸며주는 형태의 어구가 와야 한다. organ이 '~와 관련되는'의 뜻이므로 과거분사가 오는 것이 맞다.

어구 **organ** 기관   **digestion** 소화   **regulation** 규제, 조절

26 (a)

해석 (a) A: 창설 이후 저희 연구소는 많은 다양한 기술에 초점을 맞춰왔습니다.
(b) B: 다양한 기술의 결합으로부터 무엇을 기대할 수 있을까요?
(c) A: 저희 상상 이상입니다. 가능성은 무궁무진하니까요.
(d) B: 지금 불가능한 일이 결국은 가능해질 것이라는 말씀인가요?

해설 (a)에 쓰인 since로 보아 '창설 이후부터 현재까지' 초점을 맞춰왔다는 의미이므로 현재완료 시제가 적절하다.

어구 **creation** 창설   **research lab** 연구소   **focus on** ~에 집중하다   **diverse** 다양한   **marriage** 결합   **various** 다양한   **beyond one's imagination** 상상 이상인   **possibility** 가능성   **endless** 무한한   **ultimately** 궁극적으로

27 (c)

해석 (a) A: 괜찮니? 너 당황한 것 같다.
(b) B: 글쎄, 강좌를 등록하려는데 문제가 좀 있어서.
(c) A: 지도 교수님 뵙고 이 문제 상의해 봤어?
(d) B: 아직. 그런데 빠른 시일 내로 만나 뵈어야 할 것 같아.

해설 (c)에서 주어가 you이므로 동사는 has가 아닌 have를 써야 한다.

어구 **perturb** 당황스럽게 하다   **obstacle** 장애   **register for** 등록하다   **course** 과정   **advisor** 지도 교수

28 (c)

해석 (a) 나는 최근 노란 신호등에 교차로를 지나다가 가까스로 구급차와 충돌을 면했다. (b) 내가 교차로를 반쯤 지나고 있을 때 내 쪽으로 돌진해 오고 있는 구급차가 빨간 불을 무시하는 것을 보았다. (c) 난 급정거를 할 수 없었기 때문에 속력을 유지한 채 구급차가 나를 향해 직진하는 것을 지켜볼 수밖에 없었다. (d) 양쪽 다 즉시 멈췄지만 거의 충돌할 뻔했었다.

해설 (c)에서 주절의 시제와 종속절의 시제가 일치하지 않는다. 주절의 시제가 과거이므로 since 안에 있는 종속절의 시제도 can이 아니라 could로 써야 옳은 표현이다.

어구 **narrowly** 가까스로   **intersection** 교차로   **disregard** 무시하다   **maintain** 유지하다   **head toward** ~으로 향하다   **extremely** 매우   **collide with** 충돌하다

29 (d)

해석 (a) 미국 대부분의 도시들은 자전거족이 쉽게 자전거를 타고 다닐 수 있는 곳들이 아니다. (b) 그 주된 이유 중 하나는 미국에는 잘 발달된 자동차 문화가 있다는 것이다. (c) 차가 널리 보급되어 있기 때문에 많은 사람들은 자전거로 출근하기를 주저하게 된다. (d) 그래서 미국의 많은 시의회들은 자기네 도시에 자전거 전용 도로를 만들어 자전거 애용자들에게 더욱 더 자전거에 적합한 환경을 만들어 주려고 노력하고 있다.

해설 (d)에 나오는 cyclist(자전거 타는 사람)는 셀 수 있는 보통명사이다. 셀 수 있는 명사는 관사 처리를 해야 하므로 a cyclist로 쓰거나 관사 없이 복수형 cyclists로 써야 한다.

어구 **bicyclist** 자전거를 타는 사람 **navigate** 이리저리 돌아다니다; 운행하다 **well-developed** 선진화된, 잘 발전된 **prevalence** 유행, 보급 **bicycle-friendly** 자전거 타기에 안성맞춤인

30 (d)

해석 (a) 많은 한국인들은 중국과 러시아가 자국 영역에서 대규모 합동 군사 훈련을 실시하는 것을 지켜보면서 불안감을 느끼고 있다. (b) 이런 그들의 우려는 미국·일본·타이완이 대응군사 훈련을 한다는 소식을 들을 때 더욱 더 가중된다. (c) 그것은 마치 주요 군사 강대국들이 동북아시아에서 21세기에 전세계 패권을 장악하기 위해 냉전 시대를 되살리고 있는 것처럼 보인다. (d) 이러한 군비 경쟁은 이곳을 일촉즉발의 위기 지역으로 만들고 있다.

해설 arms race는 '군비 경쟁'이라는 뜻을 지닌 복합 명사로 단수이므로 동사도 그에 맞게 단수 동사로 써야 한다.

어구 **uneasy** 불안한 **massive** 크고 묵직한, 대량의 **joint** 합동의, 연합의 **military drill** 군사 훈련 **territory** 영토, 영역 **apprehension** 걱정, 근심 **push for** 추진하다 **counter-drill** 대응 군사 훈련 **revive** 소생시키다, 회복시키다 **hegemony** 주도권, 지배권, 패권 **arms race** 군비 경쟁 **volatile** 불안한; 변덕스러운

Actual Test 05

1 (d)	2 (d)	3 (c)	4 (c)	5 (d)
6 (a)	7 (c)	8 (b)	9 (d)	10 (b)
11 (b)	12 (d)	13 (a)	14 (a)	15 (a)
16 (d)	17 (c)	18 (b)	19 (a)	20 (b)
21 (a)	22 (a)	23 (d)	24 (b)	25 (c)
26 (c)	27 (c)	28 (b)	29 (c)	30 (a)

1 (d)

해석 A: 안녕, 제임스. 너무 오랜만이야. 그동안 어디서 지냈니?
　　 B: 차 사고가 나서 병원에 입원해 있었어. 지난 한달 동안 밖에도 못 나갔지 뭐야.

해설 sometimes, ever, seldom 모두 현재완료와 함께 쓰일 수는 있으나 문맥에 어울리지 않는다. 입원하는 바람에 한 달간 외출을 하지 못했다는 논리가 적절하다.

어구 **hospitalize** 입원시키다 **seldom** 좀처럼 ~않는; 드물게

2 (d)

해석 A: 내가 술집에서 만난 남자는 키도 크고 잘 생겼는데 멍청했어.
　　 B: 지적인 사람치고 신체적으로 매력적인 경우는 별로 없지.

해설 부정 부사 rarely가 문두에 쓰이면 주어와 동사는 도치된다. 본래 문장은 An intelligent individual is rarely physically attractive.인데 rarely가 문두에 오면서 Rarely is an intelligent individual physically attractive.로 도치된 것이다.

어구 **dull** 우둔한, 멍청한 **rarely** 거의 ~ 아닌, 좀처럼 ~하지 않는 **intelligent** 지적인 **attractive** 매력적인

3 (c)

해석 A: 너 최근에 살이 많이 쪘구나, 그렇지?
　　 B: 응. 그래서 신경이 많이 쓰여. 곧 여름이니 다시 운동을 시작해야겠어.

해설 should를 제외한 need, have, would like는 to와 함께 써야 한다.

어구 **put on weight** 체중이 늘다, 살찌다 **bother** 신경 쓰이게 하다, 괴롭히다 **work out** 운동하다

4 (c)

해석 A: 저기, 이 버스가 어디로 가는지 알아?
　　 B: 나도 잘 모르는데. 운전기사한테 물어보는 게 좋겠다.

해설 Do you think가 다른 의문문과 합쳐져 간접 의문문이 되면 do you think는 의문사 뒤에 위치한다. 따라서 Where do you think this bus is headed?의 어순이 되어야 한다.

어구 **head** (특정 방향으로) 향하다

5 (d)

해석 A: 미국 여행 때 가장 인상적이었던 경험은 뭐였니?
　　 B: 애리조나주의 그랜드 캐년에 갔던 일을 절대 잊을 수 없을 거야.

해설 「forget + V-ing(~했던 것을 잊다)」와 「forget + to부정사(~해야 할 것을 잊다)」를 구분하는 문제이다. 문맥상 과거 경험에 대해 말하고 있으므로 V-ing 형태가 오는 것이 적절하다.

어구 **impressive** 인상적인, 감명 깊은

6 (a)

해석 A: 집에 오는 길에 소나기를 만났어. 비에 쫄딱 젖고 말았네.
　　 B: 일기예보 확인 안 했니? 나가기 전에 우산을 챙겼어야지.

해설 이미 소나기를 만나 비에 젖은 상황에서 우산을 가져갔어야 했는데 가져가지 않았다고 유감스러워하는 내용이므로 should have p.p.를 쓰는 것이 적절하다.

어구 **be caught in a shower** 소나기를 만나다 **soak** 흠뻑 적시다, (액체 속에) 담그다

7 (c)

해석 A: 군대에 있는 내 남자친구는 매주 편지를 보내.
　　 B: 정말? 편지에 뭐라고 적어 보내니?

해설 특정한 과거의 한 순간이 아니라 일상적인 행동을 나타내므로

현재 시제가 적절하다.

8 (b)

해석 A: 그렇게 비싼 스포츠카를 살 돈이 충분하니?
　　B: 아니. 하지만 할부로 사려고 해.

해설 '~을 할 만큼 충분한'이라는 의미는 「enough + 명사 + to + 동사원형」으로 나타낸다.

어구 **installment** 분할 불입금, 할부금

9 (d)

해석 A: 왜 이렇게 일찍 가니? 이제 겨우 9시인데.
　　B: 지금 가봐야 할 것 같아. 놓치고 싶지 않은 TV 프로그램이 있거든.

해설 I'm afraid~는 유감스러운 내용을 말할 때 앞에 덧붙여 '유감이지만 ~하다'라는 의미로 사용하는 표현이다. 또한 afraid는 형용사이므로 be동사와 함께 쓰여야 한다.

어구 **miss** (못 보고) 놓치다

10 (b)

해석 A: 너희 회사에 무슨 일이 일어나고 있는지 아니?
　　B: 최근 공개 공모에 대해 심각한 말들이 많았어.

해설 a lot of serious talk로 보아 동사는 단수 형태가 적절하다. 부사 recently는 과거의 특정한 시점을 가리키지 않으므로 현재완료가 더 어울린다.

어구 **initial public offering** (증권) 공개 공모

11 (b)

해석 '빅애플'이라고 불리는 뉴욕은 미국에서 가장 매력적인 관광 명소 중 하나이다.

해설 뉴욕시가 어떠한 별명으로 '불리는' 것이므로 수동의 의미를 나타내는 과거분사형태가 적절하다. New York, which is called the "Big Apple,"~에서 「주격 관계대명사 + be동사」, 즉 which is가 생략된 형태이다.

어구 **attractive** 매력적인　**tourist destination** 관광지

12 (d)

해석 한국은 1980년대 군사독재 종식 이후 민주주의를 향한 눈부신 발전을 거뒀다.

해설 뒤에 since와 함께 특정 시점이 언급되므로, 그 시점부터 현재까지 계속됨을 나타내는 현재완료의 계속적 용법이 쓰였음을 알 수 있다. 따라서 has made가 적절하다.

어구 **make strides** 큰 발전을 거두다　**military dictatorship** 군사독재

13 (a)

해석 혼잡한 시간대였기 때문에 미셸은 지하철을 탔다. 그러지 않았다면 제 시간에 공항에 도착하지 못했을 것이다.

해설 otherwise는 '그러지 않았다면'이라는 의미로 가정법과 함께 자주 쓰인다. 문맥상 과거 사실에 대한 가정이므로 가정법 과거완료 「would not have + 과거완료」가 와야 한다. 여기서 otherwise는 If she hadn't taken the subway라는 의미이다.

어구 **rush hour** 혼잡한 시간대, 러시아워　**otherwise** 그렇지 않았다면, 그러지 않으면　**make it to** (장소에) 도착하다

14 (a)

해석 내 약혼자가 이혼남이라는 이유로 우리 가족 모두 나의 결혼을 반대하고 있다.

해설 family는 집합명사로서 단수 및 복수 모두 가능하다. 이 문장에선 가족 구성원 하나하나를 언급하는 것이 아니라 모두를 통틀어서 가리키므로 단수 동사가 오는 것이 적절하다. 여기서 opposed는 과거분사로 오해할 수 있으나 형용사로 쓰였다.

어구 **be opposed to** ~에 반대하다　**divorce** 이혼하다

15 (a)

해석 그녀는 보통 점심식사 후 직장에서 졸지 않으려고 진한 커피를 마신다.

해설 to부정사를 부정하려면 to부정사 바로 앞에 not을 쓰면 된다. 마찬가지로 so as to의 부정형은 so as not to가 된다.

어구 **doze** 졸다, 깜빡 잠이 들다

16 (d)

해석 잠자리에 들기 전에 양치질하는 습관을 들여야 한다.

해설 잠자리에 드는 행위는 주어가 하는 것이므로 능동태가 적절하다. 원래 문장은 before you go to bed인데 앞의 주어와 동일하므로 주어를 생략하고 동명사 going을 쓸 수 있다.

어구 **make it a habit to** ~하는 습관을 들이다

17 (c)

해석 그 야구 감독은 팀이 경기에서 지자 당황하여 팀 포메이션을 재조직했다.

해설 동사 fluster는 '당황하게 만들다, 허둥지둥하게 만들다'라는 뜻이므로 감독의 입장에서는 '당황하다'라는 수동 개념으로 쓰여야 한다. 따라서 과거분사 Flustered가 정답이다. (d)는 '당황하게 만들기 위하여'라는 의미가 되므로 문맥상 어울리지 않는다.

어구 **fluster** 어리둥절하게 하다　**reorganize** 재조직하다, 재편성하다　**formation** 포메이션, 구성

18 (b)

해석 유니세프에 의하면 현재 사하라 사막 이남 지역의 5세 미만 아동의 경우, 여섯 명 중 한 명은 예방 가능한 질환으로 사망한다고 한다.

해설 부사 currently로 보아 현재 시제가 적절하며, 문장의 주어는 여섯 명 중 '한 명'이므로 단수이다.

어구 **sub-Saharan** 사하라 사막 이남의　**preventable** 예방 가능한, 막을 수 있는

19 (a)

해석 오늘밤 〈보헤미안 랩소디〉보러 갈 거면 볼 만한지 알려줘.

해설 원래 문장은 If you should see *Bohemian Rhapsody* tonight ~인데 여기서 If를 생략하게 되면 주어와 동사가 도치되어 Should you ~의 어순이 된다.

어구 **worth** ~할 가치가 있는

20 (b)

해석 그는 명문대 공학 석사학위를 가지고 있음에도 불구하고 벌써 1년 넘도록 구직활동 중에 있다.

해설 주절에 현재완료 계속적 용법이 쓰였다고 해서 빈칸에 과거 시제를 고르지 않도록 주의하자. 학위를 가지고 있는 것은 예나 지금이나 사실이다. 반복적인 습관 또는 일반적 사실을 나타낼 때는 현재 시제를 써야 한다.

어구 **search for** 물색하다, 찾아 나서다   **master's degree** 석사학위   **prestigious** 명망 있는, 일류의

21 (a)

해석 나는 출근길에 지하철에서 읽으려고 신문을 사곤 했다.

해설 일반적으로 paper(종이)는 불가산 명사로서 a piece of나 a sheet of 등과 함께 쓰인다. 하지만 '신문'을 나타낼 경우에는 a paper로 쓸 수 있다.

어구 **a paper** 신문   **on one's way to** ~로 가는 길에

22 (a)

해석 나는 가까운 미래의 경제에 관한 한 낙관론자도 비관론자도 아니다.

해설 nor나 neither 뒤에는 「동사 + 주어」의 어순이 적절하다. 단, 이 문장에서 neither를 쓰려면 and neither am I로 써야 한다.

어구 **When it comes to** ~에 관한 한   **optimist** 낙관론자, 낙천주의자   **pessimist** 비관론자, 비관주의자

23 (d)

해석 밥은 상사의 결정에 반대했지만 그 말에 따를 수밖에 달리 도리가 없었다.

해설 빈칸 뒤에 완전한 문장이 이어지므로 전치사인 Despite는 사용할 수 없다. 논리적으로 앞 문장이 뒷문장의 이유가 될 수 없으므로 Since나 Because 역시 어색하다. 문맥상 '~하는 반면에, ~에도 불구하고'라는 의미의 While이 가장 적절하다.

어구 **have no choice but to** ~하지 않을 수 없다   **abide by** (규칙·절차 등에) 따르다, (약속 따위를) 지키다

24 (b)

해석 노동시장의 치열한 경쟁으로 인해 대졸자들은 업무 현장에 대한 준비를 더 잘 갖추고 대학을 떠나야만 했다.

해설 prepare 뒤에는 「to + 동사원형」이나 「for + 명사」가 와야 한다. 여기선 대졸자들이 보다 잘 '준비된' 상태로 졸업을 해야 한다는 의미이므로 완료와 수동의 의미를 가진 과거분사 prepared가 적절하다.

어구 **cutthroat competition** 치열한 경쟁   **workplace** 업무 현장

25 (c)

해석 북한은 핵 도발을 목적을 위한 수단으로 생각하지 목적 그 자체로 생각하지는 않는다고 한 외교 문제 전문가가 말했다.

해설 means는 '방법, 수단'이라는 뜻이며 복수처럼 보이지만 단수 취급한다. 따라서 부정관사 a가 와야 한다.

어구 **foreign relations** 국제[외교] 문제   **nuclear** 핵무기의; 핵무기   **provocation** 도발   **means** 수단, 방법   **end** 목적, 목표

26 (c)

해석 (a) A: 이번 주말에 뭐할 거니?
　　(b) B: 딱히 별 일 없어. 무슨 일 있어?
　　(c) A: 영화 보러 가자. 어때?
　　(d) B: 좋은 생각이야.

해설 Let's로 시작하는 권유문의 경우 부가의문문으로 shall we?를 쓴다.

어구 **up to** ~을 하려고 하여; ~에 종사하여

27 (a)

해석 (a) A: 마이크가 카지노에서 큰 돈을 번 거 알아?
　　(b) B: 우왜! 마이크가 그 돈으로 뭘 할 것 같니?
　　(c) A: 고급 승용차를 살 거라고 장담해.
　　(d) B: 나도 그래. 그나저나 우리도 라스베이거스에 가보지 않을래?

해설 money와 같이 셀 수 없는 명사는 a large amount of나 a great deal of 또는 much 등으로 수식할 수 있다.

어구 **luxury** 사치스러운

28 (b)

해석 (a) 전 세계 국가들은 날로 커지는 에너지 수요를 충족하는 동시에 환경상의 우려를 줄일 수 있는 최선책으로서 원자력에 의지하고 있다. (b) 원자력 발전소를 더 많이 건설하면서도 원자력의 평화로운 이용을 증진하고자 우리는 원자력 관련 문제 해결을 위한 관련 인프라를 구축하고 유지해야 한다. (c) 뿐만 아니라 핵연료를 안정적으로 공급하고 핵폐기물을 좀 더 친환경적으로 처리할 수 있는 능력을 강화해야 할 필요가 있다. (d) 국제원자력기구의 역할이 그 어느 때보다 중요해진 것도 바로 그런 이유에서이다.

해설 (b)에서 more를 보면 두 곳 이상의 원자력 발전소를 건설한다는 의미임을 알 수 있으므로 복수 형태로 써야 적절하다.

어구 **turn to** ~에게 도움을 청하다, ~에 의지하다   **alleviate** 완화하다   **promote** 촉진하다, 홍보하다   **infrastructure** 인프라   **dispose of** 처리하다   **environment-friendly** 친환경적인

29 (c)

해석 (a) 수력 발전은 전 세계 전력 생산의 15퍼센트 이상을 차지한다. (b) 게다가 전 세계 청정 재생에너지의 약 90퍼센트가 수력 발전에서 나온다. (c) 하지만 풍력이나 태양열과 같은 기타 재생에너지가 머지않아 수력 발전량을 넘어서게 될 것이다. (d) 온실가스가 우리에게 위협이 되고 있는 가운데 재생에너지는 이 시대의 환경적·사회적·경제적 요구를 충족할 잠재력을 지니고 있다.

해설 short는 보통 형용사로 쓰이며 드물게 '짧게'라는 의미의 부사로도 쓰인다. (c)에서는 문맥상 '곧'이라는 의미의 부사인 shortly로 쓰는 것이 적절하다.

어구 **hydropower** 수력   **renewable energy** 재생에너지   **surpass** 능가하다, 뛰어넘다   **generation** 발생   **greenhouse gas** 온실가스

30 (a)

해석 (a) 정보 네트워크의 확산은 전 세계의 새로운 신경계가 되었다. (b) 한 지역에서 어떤 일이 발생하면 다른 지역의 우리들도 실시간으로 그 소식을 접하게 된다. (c) 그러므로 우리 역시 마찬가지로 실시간 대응을 할 수 있다. (d) 이는 불과 수십 년 전만 하더라도 상상조차 못했던 일이다.

해설 (a)에서 information networks 때문에 주어가 복수라고 판단할 수 있으나 사실 주어는 The spread이다. 따라서 동사 역시 단수가 되어야 한다. 또한 문맥상 현재 시제 수동태보다는 현재완료 능동태로 바꾸는 것이 자연스럽다.

어구 **nervous system** 신경계 **keep up with something**
(뉴스, 유행 등에 대해) 알게 되다 **in real time** 실시간으로, 즉시

Actual Test 06

1	(b)	2	(b)	3	(c)	4	(d)	5	(a)
6	(b)	7	(a)	8	(c)	9	(c)	10	(a)
11	(c)	12	(b)	13	(b)	14	(d)	15	(d)
16	(b)	17	(c)	18	(c)	19	(b)	20	(a)
21	(a)	22	(c)	23	(b)	24	(a)	25	(a)
26	(c)	27	(b)	28	(d)	29	(c)	30	(b)

1 (b)

해석 A: 우리나라는 표현의 자유가 있다는 것에 자부심을 가지고 있어. 우리나라의 장점이지.
B: 맞아. 또, 분리나 차별도 없어야 해.

해설 pride oneself on은 '~을 자랑스럽게 여기다'라는 표현이다. A문장의 주어는 Our country로, 3인칭 단수이므로 빈칸에는 prides itself on이 와야 한다. 여기서 itself는 앞에 나온 country를 받는다.

어구 **freedom of speech** 표현의 자유 **beauty** 장점, 묘미
pride oneself on ~을 자랑스럽게 여기다
segregation (인종, 종교, 성별 등) 분리 (정책)
discrimination 차별

2 (b)

해석 A: 요즘 내가 문제가 많은 것 같아. 네게서 충고를 좀 듣고 싶어.
B: 걱정 마. 곧 모든 게 다 잘 될 거야. 포기하지만 마.

해설 advice는 불가산 명사이므로 앞에 부정관사 an이 올 수 없고, -s를 붙여 복수형을 만들 수 없다. 대신 some이나 a piece of를 써서 수량을 표시해준다.

3 (c)

해석 A: 제시카에 대해서 어떻게 생각하니?
B: 제시카가 예쁘다는 사실은 인정하지만 그래도 그 아일 좋아하지는 않아.

해설 인정하는 행위의 주체가 I이고, 제시카가 예쁘다는 것을 내가 '인정한다'는 능동의 의미이므로 현재분사 admitting을 써야 한다.

---

4 (d)

해석 A: 그 온라인 쇼핑 사이트에 가입하는 데 왜 아직도 망설이는 거니?
B: 난 그 사이트가 고객 보호를 위해 보안을 더욱 강화하지 않는 한 가입하지 않을 거야.

해설 시간이나 조건의 부사절에서는 미래에 관한 내용이라도 현재 시제를 쓴다.

어구 **hesitate** 망설이다 **security** 안보, 보안 **protect** 보호하다

5 (a)

해석 A: 남한과 북한이 분단된 지 거의 70년이 되어가.
B: 그로 인해 손해만 입으면서 많은 시간과 에너지, 돈, 그리고 생명을 희생시켰지.

해설 B문장에서 주절의 주어는 this이고 while절의 주어도 this이기 때문에 while절의 주어는 생략되어 있는 상태이다. 또 this가 '해를 끼친 것'이므로 수동이 아니라 능동으로 봐야 한다. 따라서 빈칸에 맞는 어구는 doing이다.

어구 **divide** 분열하다, 나누다 **cost** ~을 희생시키다, 잃게 하다
do more harm than good 백해무익하다

6 (b)

해석 A: 미국에서 대규모 기름 유출 사태가 있었는데, 그 일이 환경에 끼칠 영향은 막심할 거야.
B: 슬픈 일이지. 그 정유 회사는 안전 문제에 대해 더 신경을 썼어야 했어.

해설 내용상 '~했어야 했다'는 과거에 대한 아쉬움이나 유감의 뜻이 되어야 하므로 빈칸에는 should have p.p.가 적절하다.

어구 **oil spill** 기름[석유] 유출 **impact** 영향 **devastating** 대단히 파괴적인, 엄청난 손상을 가하는

7 (a)

해석 A: 우리 아빠는 언젠가 담배를 끊으려고 엄청나게 노력했지만 실패하셨어.
B: 가족을 위해서 아무리 힘들어도 끊으셨어야 했는데.

해설 '~가 아무리 …하더라도'의 뜻인 「no matter how + 형용사 + 주어 + 동사」의 어순을 묻는 문제이다.

어구 **quit + V-ing** ~을 그만두다[끊다]

8 (c)

해석 A: 학교에 불이 나서 대피하는 동안 학생들이나 선생님 모두 다치지 않았어요.
B: 정말 다행이다. 다들 무사하다니.

해설 「neither A nor B」 구문에서 동사는 B의 수에 일치시킨다.

어구 **evacuate** 대피시키다

9 (c)

해석 A: 오늘 강의의 요지가 뭐었어?
B: 북한이 1950년에 한국을 공격했고, 그 이후부터 양국은 엄밀히 말해 서로 전쟁 중이라는 거였어.

해설 역사적인 사실에 대해서 이야기하고 있으므로 과거 시제를 써야 한다.

어구 **main point** 요지 **attack** 공격하다 **technically** 엄밀히 말

해석　**at war** 전쟁 중인

10 (a)

해석　A: 내가 복권에 당첨되리라고는 생각도 못했었지. 하지만 오늘부턴 아니야.
　　B: 대박을 터뜨렸구나, 짐! 그 돈으로 다 뭐 할 거니?

해설　문두에 only나 never 같은 부사가 올 경우, 주어와 동사가 도치된다. that절의 내용보다 밑줄에 들어갈 내용이 먼저 일어난 일이므로 과거완료 시제를 사용한 Never had I thought가 적절하다.

어구　**win the lottery** 복권에 당첨되다　**hit the jackpot** 대박을 터뜨리다

11 (c)

해석　그 회사는 은빛의 큰 금속성 건물의 건설을 드디어 마쳤다.

해설　형용사 나열의 순서를 묻는 문제이다. 「크기＋성질＋색깔」의 어순으로 쓴다.

어구　**construction** 건설　**metallic** 금속성의

12 (b)

해석　대부분의 여성과 비흡연자들은 길거리에서 담배를 피우고 침을 뱉는 사람들을 싫어한다.

해설　빈칸 뒤의 smoke가 동사이므로 빈칸에는 주격 관계대명사가 필요하다. those who 자체를 '~하는 사람들'이라는 하나의 관용표현으로 알아두면 편리하다.

어구　**majority** 대부분　**nonsmoker** 비흡연자　**dislike** 싫어하다　**spit** (침을) 뱉다

13 (b)

해석　대규모 기름 유출 사건 이래로, 대통령은 환경 피해가 최소화되어야 한다고 주장해 왔다.

해설　주장, 명령, 제안 등의 동사 뒤에 이어져 당위성을 띠는 that절에는 「should＋동사원형」이 쓰이며, 이 때 should는 생략 가능하다.

어구　**oil spill** 기름 유출　**insist** 주장하다　**environmental** 환경의　**minimize** 최소화하다

14 (d)

해석　지난 밤 콘서트장의 청중을 완전히 매료시켰던 그 보컬처럼 나도 그렇게 노래를 부를 수 있다면 좋겠다.

해설　그 보컬처럼 노래할 수 있으면 좋겠다는 의미이므로 현재사실의 반대이다. 따라서 가정법 과거로 써야 한다.

어구　**vocalist** 보컬, 가수　**mesmerize** 마음을 사로잡다

15 (d)

해석　그의 개가 도움을 구하기 위해 짖은 덕분에 수색구조대가 마침내 그를 찾을 수 있었다.

해설　의미를 바탕으로 알맞은 접속사를 찾아야 한다. 문맥상 수색구조대가 그를 찾을 수 있었던 '이유'가 필요하다.

어구　**bark** 짖다　**summon** 소환하다, 부르다　**search** 수색　**rescue** 구조　**spot** 찾아내다

16 (b)

해석　매니저는 향후 문제 예방을 위해 예기치 않은 일이 일어나면 무엇이든 자신에게 통보해 줄 것을 근로자들에게 지시했다.

해설　「notify＋A(사람)＋of＋B(목적어)」의 형태로 'A에게 B를 통보하다'라는 뜻으로 쓰인다.

어구　**incident** 사건　**manager** 매니저　**instruct** 지시하다　**notify** 통보하다　**unexpected** 예기치 않은　**event** 사건

17 (c)

해석　한 연구는 여성 흡연자의 수가 하락하고 있음을 보여주었지만 가장 최근의 연구는 그 수치가 다시 오르고 있음을 발견했다.

해설　the figure는 앞에 나온 the number of(~의 수)를 받는 것이므로 단수 동사가 와야 한다. the most recent study(가장 최근의 연구)로 보아 현재 시제가 적당함을 알 수 있다.

어구　**figure** 수치　**rise** 증거하다

18 (c)

해석　내 친구 중 다수는 내가 원하는 종류인 그 스마트폰을 샀다.

해설　대명사 one의 쓰임을 묻는 문제이다. 친구들이 구입한 것과 같은 종류의 전화 중 하나를 가지고 싶다는 의미이므로 one을 쓴다.

19 (c)

해석　비록 어리석어 보일지라도 그는 굉장히 계산적이고 신중하기 때문에 네가 그를 과소평가했다가는 그 대가를 치를 수도 있다.

해설　「형용사＋as＋주어＋동사」의 형태로 쓰면 양보절이 되어 '비록 ~일지라도'라는 의미를 나타낸다.

어구　**calculating** 계산적인　**underestimate** 과소평가하다　**pay the price** 대가를 치르다

20 (a)

해석　상원과 하원의원들은 지난 한 해 동안 대마불사의 금융 기업들에 관한 사안을 열띠게 토론했다.

해설　뒤에 나온 over the last year를 보면 '지난 한 해 동안'의 의미이므로 현재완료 형태가 와야 한다는 것을 알 수 있다.

어구　**House of Representatives** 하원　**Senate** 상원　**fiercely** 맹렬히, 열렬히　**issue** 사안　**too-big-to-fail** 대마불사의 (너무 규모가 커서 파산시킬 수 없다는 의미)

21 (a)

해석　내가 호텔 로비에 도착했을 때 그녀는 나를 30분이나 기다리고 있었다.

해설　내가 호텔 로비에 도착하기 전부터 그녀는 이미 기다리고 있었던 것이므로 동사 arrived보다 앞선 시점부터 계속되고 있는 행위를 나타낸다. 따라서 과거완료진행, 즉 had been V-ing가 적절하다.

어구　**lobby** (호텔·극장 따위의) 로비; (대기실·휴게실로 쓰이는) 큰 복도

22 (c)

해석　머도프는 법정에서 나오자마자 기자들에게 수많은 질문 공세를 받았다.

해설　no sooner가 문장 앞에 나오면 주어와 동사가 도치된다.

「no sooner A than B」는 'A하자마자 B하다'라는 의미로 쓰인다.

어구 court 법정, 법원   be asked 질문을 받다   numerous 많은   reporter 기자

23 (b)
해석 클라우드 컴퓨팅의 신뢰성에 관한 한, IT기업들 간에는 의견 불일치가 있다.

해설 when it comes to는 '~에 관한 한'이라는 뜻의 관용표현이다.

어구 disagreement (의견) 불일치   reliability 신뢰성

24 (a)
해석 소비자들의 반응이 그다지 긍정적이지 않았기 때문에 애플의 신 모델 판매가 저조했을 것이라고 경쟁사들은 생각했다.

해설 문맥상 빈칸에는 '분명 ~이었을 것이다'라는 의미의 어구가 와야 한다.

어구 competitor 경쟁자[사]   product 상품   sluggish 부진한   consumer 소비자   reaction 반응   positive 긍정적인

25 (a)
해석 오래 기다려온 상품을 출시한 두 회사는 두 제품의 디자인이 너무 비슷했기에 충격에 빠졌다.

해설 alike의 올바른 사용을 묻는 문제이다. look alike는 '비슷하게 생기다'라는 뜻의 관용표현이다.

어구 long-awaited 오래 기다려 온   shock 충격을 주다   look alike 비슷하게 생기다   strikingly 눈에 띄게, 두드러지게

26 (c)
해석 (a) A: 우리나라 관광 산업은 좀 더 개선돼야 해.
     (b) B: 맞아. 우리나라엔 멋진 장소와 먹을거리가 많지만 외국인 관광객에게 충분히 소개되지 않았지.
     (c) A: 또 다른 문제는 한국 숙박 시설에서 관광객에게 숙식비용을 높이 부과한다는 거야.
     (d) B: 내 말이 그 말이야. 하지만 다른 나머진 거의 완벽해!

해설 accommodation은 단수일 때 '적응, 순응; 편의; 융통' 등의 뜻을 지니며 복수일 때는 '숙박 시설'이라는 의미가 된다. 따라서 Korean accommodation charges를 Korean accommodations charge로 바꿔야 한다.

어구 tourism industry 관광 산업   introduce 소개하다   accommodations 숙박 시설

27 (b)
해석 (a) A: 사람과 동물의 차이가 뭐라고 생각하니?
     (b) B: 우리가 다른 사람을 위해 좋은 일을 할 때 따뜻한 감정을 가지게 된다는 것이지.
     (c) A: 일부 사람들이 참여하는 자원봉사나 박애주의를 의미하는 거니?
     (d) B: 그래. 대부분의 사람들이 타인을 위해 일하는 것에 높은 가치를 두지.

해설 -thing으로 끝나는 명사는 형용사가 뒤에서 수식한다. 따라서 (b)의 good something은 something good이라고 써야

한다.

어구 volunteering 자원봉사   philanthropy 박애주의   engage 관여하다   attach 부여하다; 첨부하다

28 (d)
해석 (a) 과거에 몇몇 미디어 전문가들은 TV가 서서히 사라져갈 것이라고 예견했다. (b) 1990년대에 한 저명한 미국 작가는 기존의 TV는 20세기 말에 다 없어질 것이라고 주장했다. (c) 그 주장 이면의 이유는 웹 기반 미디어가 주문형 비디오를 제공해 TV를 대체할 것이기 때문이었다. (d) 하지만 만약 그가 웹과 TV 간의 쌍방향 통신의 가능성을 알았다면 그런 주장을 하지 않았을 것이다.

해설 전체적으로 과거에 대한 이야기를 하고 있다. (d)에는 '만일 ~했더라면 …했을 것이다'라고 과거에 대해 가정하는 가정법 과거완료 구문인 If he had known이 와야 한다.

어구 pundit 전문가   predict 예측하다   head to ~을 향해 가다   demise 종말, 소멸; 사망   renowned 유명한   conventional 전통적인   extinct 절멸한, 멸종된   web-based 웹 기반의   displace 대신하다   content 내용   on-demand 주문형의   two-way communication 쌍방향 통신

29 (c)
해석 (a) 특정 지역의 기후는 종종 그 지역에서 어떤 질병이 발견될지를 결정한다. (b) 예를 들어, 많은 심각한 질병은 아주 더운 지역에서만 발견된다. (c) 따라서 아프리카와 아시아와 같은 지역은 때때로 인류에게 알려진 가장 치명적인 질병의 본거지이다. (d) 그래서 날씨가 더운 일부 지역에 사는 사람들의 사망률은 좀더 추운 지역에 거주하는 사람들의 사망률보다 더 높은 경우가 많다.

해설 known as는 '~로 알려진(자격)'의 뜻이므로 문맥상 어울리지 않는다. '~에게 알려진'이라는 뜻의 known to로 바꿔야 한다.

어구 home to ~의 본거지   mortality rate 사망률   frigid 몹시 추운

30 (b)
해석 (a) 경제학자들은 최근 미국 경제가 역사상 가장 큰 변화를 겪게 될 것이라고 예측했다. (b) 경제 지표와 패턴을 기반으로 한 몇 년간의 연구 결과, 부채와 소비의 경제에서 저축과 수출의 경제로 향하고 있다는 결론에 도달했다. (c) 이 거시경제적 변화는 생활 스타일과 직업 환경 또한 변화시킬 것이다. (d) 문제는 미국 경제가 현재의 혼란 속에 그런 거대한 변화를 받아들일 준비가 되었느냐이다.

해설 (b)에서 they는 경제학자들이고 그들이 '결론을 내린 것'이므로 수동이 아닌 능동태 동사가 와야 한다. 따라서 are concluded를 concluded로 고쳐야 한다.

어구 economist 경제학자   forecast 예측하다   undergo 겪다   transformation 변형   indices (index의 복수) 지표   consumption 소비   macroeconomic 거시경제적인   bring about ~을 일으키다   embrace ~을 받아들이다; 포용하다   shift 변화, 전환, 이동   gigantic 거대한   chaos 혼동, 혼돈

어휘
Vocabulary

파트별
Voca Point

Part I

VP 01 │ 구어체

Check-up TEST

1	(c)	2	(a)	3	(d)	4	(a)	5	(b)
6	(b)	7	(c)	8	(d)	9	(a)	10	(b)
11	(c)	12	(a)	13	(d)	14	(d)	15	(b)
16	(c)	17	(d)	18	(b)	19	(a)	20	(d)

1 (c)

해석 A: 네이튼, 7시 45분이야! 알람시계가 울렸는데 또 잤구나.
B: 이럴 수가! 학교에 한 번이라도 더 지각하면 방과 후에 남아야 될 거예요.

해설 '학교에 지각하다'라는 뜻의 통상적인 표현은 be late for school인데, 이보다 조금 어려운 표현으로 be tardy for school을 쓸 수 있다. tardy는 late와 마찬가지로 '지각한, 늦은'이란 의미를 갖는다.

어구 sleep through the alarm 알람 소리를 듣지 못하고 자다
detention (학교에서 처벌 수단으로) 방과 후 남기

오답 살펴보기 (a) absent 결석한 (b) punctual 시간을 잘 지키는
(d) delayed 연기된

2 (a)

해석 A: 난 스페인어를 정말 열심히 공부하고 있어. 그래서 나는 스페인어를 어느 정도 잘한다고 할 수 있을 것 같아.
B: 너무 겸손해하지 마, 제니스. 네 스페인어 실력은 탁월한 수준이야.

해설 somewhat이 힌트가 될 수 있는데 스페인어를 '조금' 잘한다고 말했으므로 다소 겸손해하는 제니스에게 할 수 있는 말은 Don't be so modest.(너무 겸손할 필요 없어)이다.

어구 diligently 열심히, 부지런히   somewhat 다소, 조금

오답 살펴보기 (b) modern 현대의 (c) moderate 보통의, 중간의
(d) meek 온순한, 온화한

3 (d)

해석 A: 총액이 40달러 나왔어. 어떻게 지불했으면 좋겠니?
B: 반반씩 낼까? 각자 20달러씩 내면 되겠다.

해설 '비용을 각자 부담하다'라고 할 때는 '(비용) 나누다'라는 뜻의 split을 써서 split the bill이라고 한다. 유사 표현으로 go Dutch, 혹은 go fifty-fifty가 있다.

어구 the total 총액   comes to (총액이) ~에 달하다

오답 살펴보기 (a) cut 삭감하다 (b) partition (공간을) 분할하다

(c) divide (일반적으로) 나누다

4 (a)

해석 A: 선물이 마음에 들었으면 좋겠다. 특별히 널 위해 선물을 선택했어.
B: 걱정 마. 마음이 중요한 것 아니겠어, 안 그래?

해설 대화의 흐름상 선물 그 자체보다 선물을 준 마음 씀씀이가 중요하다는 내용이 오는 것이 옳다. 동사 count는 '개수를 세다'라는 뜻 외에도 '중요하다'라는 뜻이 있다.

오답 살펴보기 (b) mean 의미하다 (c) register 등록하다
(d) happen 발생하다

5 (b)

해석 A: 남편이 어젯밤 내내 비디오 게임을 하면서 밤을 샜어.
B: 남편이 나잇값 좀 하고 철 좀 들어야겠군.

해설 grow up과 act one's age는 같은 뜻의 표현으로 '철이 들다, 나잇값을 하다'라는 뜻이다.

오답 살펴보기 (a) resemble 닮다

6 (b)

해석 A: 브라이언, 오늘은 모험심을 가지고 새로운 것을 주문할 거니?
B: 정말 그러고 싶지만 그냥 내가 원래 먹던 것으로 주문하겠어.

해설 usual은 '보통의'라는 형용사로 쓰일 뿐만 아니라 '원래 먹던 것'이라는 명사의 뜻도 함께 가진다. '원래 먹던 것으로 먹겠다'라는 표현은 have the usual이다.

어구 adventurous 모험적인

오답 살펴보기 (a) typical 전형적인 (c) common 일상적인 (d) meal 식사

7 (c)

해석 A: 안녕하세요. 닉 발렌시아에게 연결해 주실 수 있을까요?
B: 죄송하지만 그런 이름을 가지신 분은 여기에 없는데요.

해설 '여기에 그런 이름을 가지신 분이 없습니다'라는 표현은 There is no one here by that name이다. 전치사 by를 쓴다는 점에 유의하자.

8 (d)

해석 A: 새로운 살사 클럽이 시내에 이제 막 개장했다더라. 같이 갈래?
B: 오늘 밤은 안 되겠어. 정말이지 춤출 기분이 아니야.

해설 '~할 기분이다'라는 뜻의 표현은 「be in the mood for + (동)명사」의 형태로 쓴다.

오답 살펴보기 (a) state 상태 (b) attitude 태도 (c) condition 조건

9 (a)

해석 A: 오늘 자네가 강의한 수학 원리를 학생들이 이해한다고 생각하나?
B: 그렇다고 생각하네. 모든 내용을 학생들에게 분석해 주었지.

해설 break down에는 '고장 나다'라는 뜻 말고도 '분석하다'의 뜻이 있다.

어구 **theorem** (수학의) 정리, 원리   **lecture** 강의하다; 강의

오답 살펴보기 (b) **tear** 찢다 (d) **dismantle** 분해하다, 해체하다

10 (b)

해석 A: 어디에 가십니까?
　　B: 공항에 내려 주세요.

해설 '(차가) 사람을 장소에 내려 주다'라고 할 때 「drop + 사람 + off + at 장소」의 형태로 쓴다.

어구 **head** 향하다

11 (c)

해석 A: 어느 야구팀을 응원하니?
　　B: 개인적으로 난 항상 홈 팀을 응원해.

해설 A가 한 말 중 support(응원하다)와 같은 뜻의 표현을 찾으면 되는 문제다. root for(~을 응원하다)가 정답이다.

어구 **home team** 홈 팀(본거지 구장에서 경기를 치르는 팀)

오답 살펴보기 (a) **catch up** 따라 잡다 (b) **muscle in** 끼어들다 (d) **pass out** 기절하다

12 (a)

해석 A: 조지, 내 생각에는 네가 애나에게 가서 네가 정말로 어떻게 느끼는지 이야기해야 할 것 같아.
　　B: 나는 그저 그렇게 할 용기가 없는걸.

해설 '용기, 배짱'이라는 단어를 찾아야 한다. guts는 '동물의 내장'이라는 뜻도 있지만 '용기, 배짱'이라는 뜻이 있음을 기억하자. '~할 배짱이 있다'라는 뜻의 표현은 「have the guts to + 동사원형」의 형태로 사용된다.

오답 살펴보기 (b) **incentive** 장려책, 우대책 (c) **ambition** 야망 (d) **heart** 심장; 열정

13 (d)

해석 A: 얘들아, 늦었어. 이제 집에 가야 할 것 같아.
　　B: 무슨 소리야? 아직 초저녁이야!

해설 선택지에 의미가 비슷한 어휘가 나와 있는데, '아직 초저녁이다'라고 할 때는 형용사 young을 써서 표현한다.

오답 살펴보기 (a) **immature** 성숙하지 않은, 미숙한 (b) **early** 이른 (c) **fresh** 신선한

14 (d)

해석 A: 게리, 나는 정말 이 일을 해야 해. 네가 나를 도와 줄 수 있겠니?
　　B: 내가 힘을 써 볼 테니 내가 뭘 할 수 있는지 두고 보라고.

해설 어떤 일자리를 얻게 힘 좀 써달라고 A가 부탁하는 상황이다. '힘을 쓰다, 영향력을 쓰다'라는 뜻의 표현은 pull some strings이다.

오답 살펴보기 (a) **tug** 잡아당기다 (b) **yank** 홱 잡아당기다 (c) **sever** 절단하다, 자르다

15 (b)

해석 A: 마틴 교수님의 수업은 정말 어려워.
　　B: 나도 그렇게 생각해. 교수님이 너무 어려운 단어를 사용해서 강의를 전혀 이해할 수 없어.

해설 '따라가다'라는 뜻의 동사 follow에는 '이해하다'라는 뜻도 있음을 알아두자.

어구 **unbelievably** 믿을 수 없이   **advanced** 고급의

오답 살펴보기 (a) **announce** 발표하다 (c) **presume** 추정하다 (d) **track** 추적(하다)

16 (c)

해석 A: 이 경주에 내기를 해야 할지 잘 모르겠어.
　　B: 아니, 왜? 잃는다고 해도 단지 몇 달러뿐이잖아.

해설 '손해 볼 것 없다'라는 뜻의 표현은 have nothing to lose이다.

어구 **bet** 내기를 걸다   **except for** ~을 제외하고는

17 (d)

해석 A: 여보, 테이블 세팅 좀 해 줄래요? 저녁식사가 거의 준비됐어요.
　　B: 식사를 못 기다릴 정도예요. 벌써부터 군침이 도는군요.

해설 '군침이 돈다'라는 표현은 My mouth is watering이다. 선택지에 있는 단어 중에도 비슷한 어휘가 많지만 이 상황에서는 watering을 쓴다는 점을 기억하자.

어구 **set the table** (테이블, 상을) 차리다   **can't wait to V** 빨리 ~하고 싶다

오답 살펴보기 (a) **harken** 귀를 기울이다 (b) **moisturize** 습기를 공급하다 (c) **salivate** 침을 흘리다

18 (b)

해석 A: 은행 강도를 잡은 것을 축하드립니다.
　　B: 고맙습니다. 우리가 빨리 행동하지 않았다면 강도들이 처벌을 받지 않고 도망쳤을 겁니다.

해설 강도들이 잡히지 않았을 경우의 상황을 가정하면 (나쁜 일을 하고) 잡히지 않다, 처벌 받지 않다'라는 뜻의 get away with를 생각해 볼 수 있다.

오답 살펴보기 (a) **run up** (액수, 부채가) 쌓이다 (c) **sneak off** 몰래 빠져나가다 (d) **hide out** 숨다, 잠복하다

19 (a)

해석 A: 콘서트 예약을 해야 할까?
　　B: 아니. 선착순 입장이야.

해설 예약을 해도 되지 않는다면 선착순일 것이다. '선착순'이라는 표현은 First come, first served이다.

20 (d)

해석 A: 회사 프로젝트는 어떻게 되어가고 있어?
　　B: 엉망이야. 나는 그 일에 별로 안 맞나 봐.

해설 '어떤 일에 적성이 있다'라는 뜻을 나타낼 때는 be cut out for라는 표현을 쓴다.

오답 살펴보기 (a) **bring out** 끌어내다, 발휘하게 하다 (b) **make out** 이해하다 (c) **work out** 운동하다; 계산하다, 산출하다

VP 02 | 구동사

Check-up TEST

1	(a)	2	(c)	3	(d)	4	(a)	5	(a)
6	(c)	7	(b)	8	(c)	9	(d)	10	(b)
11	(c)	12	(a)	13	(a)	14	(c)	15	(d)
16	(b)	17	(a)	18	(b)	19	(b)	20	(b)

1 (a)
해석 A: 요즘 어떻게 지내세요?
　　 B: 해고된 이후로 실직 상태에 있어요.

해설 실직(unemployment)이란 말이 언급되어 있기 때문에 해고를 당했다고 추측해볼 수 있다. '해고하다'라는 뜻의 구동사는 lay off이며 fire도 '해고하다, 파면하다'라는 의미가 있다.

오답 살펴보기 (b) **ease up** (자동차 속도를) 줄이다 (c) **strike together** 충돌하다 (d) **work out** (문제를) 해결하다

2 (c)
해석 A: 나는 레베카에게 장문의 사과 편지를 쓰고 있어.
　　 B: 좋은 마음가짐이지만 그런다고 해서 그녀의 생일을 잊어 버린 사실을 만회할 수는 없을 거야.

해설 생일을 잊어버린 것을 '만회하기' 위해 편지를 쓰는 것이므로 make up for(~을 만회하다)가 정답이다.

어구 **sentiment** 감정

오답 살펴보기 (a) **do away with** ~을 없애다 (b) **reach out to** ~와 접촉하려고 하다 (d) **get down to** ~에 착수하다

3 (d)
해석 A: 제 회사 이메일 주소 알려드릴게요.
　　 B: 잠시만 기다려 주세요. 제 공책에 그 정보를 적어야 겠어요.

해설 '적다, 필기하다'라는 뜻을 가진 표현은 write down인데, 이보다 좀 더 어려운 표현으로 jot down을 쓸 수도 있다.

어구 **notebook** 공책; 노트북 컴퓨터

오답 살펴보기 (a) **wait about** 서성이며 기다리다 (b) **fall through** 일이 성사되지 못하다 (c) **screw up** 일을 망치다

4 (a)
해석 A: 헬렌이 대학을 그만뒀다는 이야기 들었니?
　　 B: 아니, 못 들었어. 헬렌은 재능이 뛰어난 학생이라 학교를 그만 둘 이유가 없는데.

해설 대화 중에 나온 quit(그만두다)와 같은 의미의 단어를 찾으면 되는 문제다. '학교를 중퇴하다'라는 뜻의 drop out이 정답이다.

어구 **talented** 재능이 있는, 유능한

오답 살펴보기 (b) **end up** 결국 ~하게 되다 (c) **reason with** 논리적으로 설명하다 (d) **jump in** 대화 중에 불쑥 끼어들다

5 (a)
해석 A: 우유가 남은 게 없어.
　　 B: 내가 식료품점에 물건 사러 갔을 때 우유가 다 떨어졌다고 알려주지 그랬니.

해설 우유가 남아있지 않다고 했으니 '~가 다 떨어지다, 바닥나다'라는 뜻의 run out of가 정답이다.

오답 살펴보기 (b) **fed up with** ~에 싫증나다 (c) **come over to** ~로 넘어가다 (d) **put down for** 등록하다

6 (c)
해석 A: 일은 어떻게 되어가고 있습니까?
　　 B: 별로예요. 두 가지 과제를 받아들이면서 내가 처리할 수 있는 것 이상으로 일을 맡게 된 것 같아요.

해설 뒤에 by accepting이란 말이 있으므로 같은 의미의 표현을 찾으면 된다. '일을 떠맡다'라는 뜻의 구동사는 take on이다.

어구 **assignment** 과제, 일

오답 살펴보기 (a) **jump at** 이야기 도중에 끼어들다 (b) **empty out** 텅 비우다 (d) **pull apart** 뜯어내다

7 (b)
해석 A: 최근 들어 대통령의 인기가 급락했어.
　　 B: 그래. 일부 사람들은 그의 퇴임까지 요구했지.

해설 B가 Yes라고 하면서 A의 의견에 맞장구를 치고 있으므로 앞 내용과 같은 맥락의 말이 와야 한다. 인기가 급락했다고 했으니 '퇴임을 요구하다'라는 뜻으로 구동사 call for(~을 요구하다)를 쓸 수 있다.

어구 **popularity** 인기, 지지도　　**plummet** 급락하다, 추락하다 **resignation** 사임, 퇴임

오답 살펴보기 (a) **brush up** 복습하다, 연습하다 (c) **take over** 넘겨받다 (d) **ring up** (금전 등록기에) 가격을 입력하다

8 (c)
해석 A: 해고당한 이후 재정 상황이 어떤가?
　　 B: 힘들었지만 그럭저럭 지내고 있네.

해설 힘들었다는 내용 뒤에 but이 있으므로 문맥상 가장 어울리는 것은 '그럭저럭 살아가다'라는 의미의 get by이다.

어구 **lay off** 해고하다

오답 살펴보기 (a) **hang out** ~에서 시간을 보내다 (b) **stay put** 그대로 있다 (d) **lay down** ~을 내려놓다, 그만두다

9 (d)
해석 A: 컴퓨터 제조업체와의 합병이 언제 마무리될 예정입니까?
　　 B: 이번 달에 마무리될 예정이었는데 아쉽게도 협상이 결렬되었습니다.

해설 but, unfortunately를 통해 부정적인 결과를 예상할 수 있다. '(계획이나 프로젝트가) 실패하다, 수포로 돌아가다'라고 할 때 fall through를 쓴다.

어구 **merger** 합병　　**negotiation** 협상

오답 살펴보기 (a) **get together** 모이다, 회합하다 (b) **move ahead** 순조롭게 진행되다 (c) **drop off** (차를 태우고 특정 장소에) 내려주다

10 (b)
해석 A: 걱정하지 마세요. 오늘 저녁은 우리가 식사를 계산할게요.

B: 내가 20달러는 부담하게 해주세요. 이 정도라도 하고 싶어요.

해설 B가 돈을 조금이라도 보태고 싶어 하는 상황이므로 '제 몫을 내다'라는 뜻을 가진 chip in이 정답이다.

어구 It's the least I can do. 내가 할 수 있는 것은 이게 다입니다.

오답 살펴보기 (a) bend over 구부리다 (c) give up 포기하다 (d) turn in 제출하다, 반납하다

11 (c)
해석 A: 지난주에 파티에서 그를 본 것이 확실해.
　　 B: 네 주장을 뒷받침하는 확실한 증거를 대지 않으면 널 믿을 수 없어.

해설 '뒷받침하다, 지지하다'라는 의미를 갖는 back up이 정답이다. 참고로 같은 의미의 단어 buttress(지지하다)도 출제된 적이 있으니 함께 기억해 두자.

어구 I am positive that ~이 확실하다　claim 주장　evidence 증거

오답 살펴보기 (a) hand down 반환하다 (b) give off (광선이나 열을) 발산하다 (d) call off 취소하다

12 (a)
해석 A: 네가 그 불량배에 맞서 싸웠다니 믿을 수가 없어. 정말 대단했어!
　　 B: 나는 한 번도 대치 상황에서 물러난 적이 없어.

해설 동사 back의 쓰임새를 잘 알아야 한다. 앞 문제에서 언급된 back up은 '뒷받침하다'라는 뜻이지만 back down은 '물러나다'라는 뜻이다. 서로 혼동하지 않도록 주의하자.

어구 stand up 대항하다　bully 약자를 괴롭히는 사람; 불량배 confrontation 대치, 갈등

오답 살펴보기 (b) buckle down 본격적으로 착수하다 (c) bang out 단숨에 일을 해치우다 (d) block off 차단하다

13 (a)
해석 A: 소셜 웹사이트에 우리 제품을 마케팅해 보는 것은 어떨까요?
　　 B: 좋은 생각입니다. 당신이 방금 우리 회사의 재정 문제를 해결할 수 있는 방법을 생각해낸 것 같군요.

해설 '생각이나 아이디어를 떠올리다'라고 할 때 쓰는 hit upon이 적절하다.

어구 financial 재정의, 금융의

오답 살펴보기 (b) dig into 파헤치다 (c) tear down 무너뜨리다, 허물다 (d) put towards 보태 주다

14 (c)
해석 A: 왜 여름 내내 에어컨을 계속 가동하지 않는 거야?
　　 B: 예전에는 그렇게 했는데 회사 측에서 에어컨 사용이 너무 많은 비용을 차지한다고 판단했어.

해설 에어컨을 많이 사용해서 전기세가 많이 들었다는 뜻이므로 '차지하다, 소요되다'라는 뜻의 take up이 정답이다.

어구 resources 재원, 자금; 자원

오답 살펴보기 (a) stand up 대항하다 (b) free up 해방하다, 풀어주다 (d) work up 북돋우다

15 (d)
해석 A: 내일 여행 일정이 어떻게 되죠?
　　 B: 오전 8시에 호텔에서 출발하여 컨벤션 센터로 갈 예정입니다.

해설 여행 일정(itinerary)에 관한 대화로, 빈칸 뒤에 장소와 시간이 나왔기 때문에 '출발하다'라는 의미의 set off가 들어가는 것이 가장 적절하다.

어구 itinerary 여행 일정　head 향하다

오답 살펴보기 (a) tap out 리듬에 맞춰서 두드리다 (b) run through 퍼지다, 번지다 (c) fasten down (뚜껑을) 덮다

16 (b)
해석 A: 이제는 전달해야 할 공지가 더 이상 없는 것 같군요.
　　 B: 그렇다면 각자가 해야 할 일을 하죠.

해설 get down to(일에 착수하다)가 정답이다. get down to business(해야 할 일을 하다)가 하나의 표현이므로 한 덩어리로 외워두도록 하자.

오답 살펴보기 (a) end up with 결국 ~하다 (c) hold back from 참다, 자제하다 (d) shut out ~ of ~를 …로부터 제외시키다

17 (a)
해석 A: 조, 셀린이야말로 정말 내가 기다려 왔던 사람인 것 같아.
　　 B: 만나는 모든 여자들에게 사랑에 빠져버리면 안 돼, 앤디.

해설 '~을 사랑하다, ~에게 푹 빠지다'라는 뜻의 fall for가 정답이다.

오답 살펴보기 (b) kick back 쉬다 (c) open up 개봉하다 (d) break away 분리하다, 탈퇴하다

18 (b)
해석 A: 엄마, 학교 가고 싶지 않아요. 여자애들이 너무 심술궂어요.
　　 B: 다음에 그 아이들이 널 괴롭히거든 선생님께 말씀드리렴.

해설 여자 아이들이 mean(심술궂은)이라고 했으므로 심술궂은 아이들이 취할 만한 행동인 pick on(괴롭히다, 못살게 굴다)이 정답이다.

어구 mean 야비한; 심술궂은

오답 살펴보기 (a) get around 돌아다니다 (c) grow upon (습관 등이) 더 심해지다 (d) come across 이해되다; ~라는 인상을 주다

19 (b)
해석 A: 경찰에게 강도 사건을 신고한 것이 후회돼.
　　 B: 넌 올바른 일을 했어. 뭔가 잘못된 일이 일어날 때 용기를 내서 말하는 것이 중요해.

해설 강도 사건을 신고한 것을 후회하는 A의 말에 B가 그렇지 않다고 답하고 있다. B가 A의 행동에 대해 두둔할 수 있는 표현을 고르면 된다. speak out은 '용기를 내어 말하다' 혹은 '거리낌 없이 말하다'라는 의미이다.

오답 살펴보기 (a) speak up 더 크게 말하다 (c) move ahead 전진하다 (d) move on 앞으로 나아가다; 행동하다

20 (b)
해석 A: 자넨 내 강의가 그렇게 재미없나?
　　 B: 수업시간에 졸아서 죄송합니다, 교수님. 사실 어젯밤에 잠

을 제대로 못 잤습니다.

해설 강의가 재미없는지 물어보는 교수의 질문과, 잠을 제대로 자지 못했다는 학생의 변명으로 미루어 볼 때 빈칸에 들어갈 말은 졸았다는 의미의 dozing off가 가장 적절하다.

어구 uninteresting 재미없는

오답 살펴보기 (a) get about 걸어 다니다 (c) fall back 물러나다 (d) wake up 깨우다

VP 03 | 고난도 어휘

Check-up TEST

1	(c)	2	(a)	3	(d)	4	(b)	5	(a)
6	(d)	7	(a)	8	(a)	9	(b)	10	(b)
11	(c)	12	(b)	13	(b)	14	(c)	15	(a)
16	(c)	17	(b)	18	(d)	19	(a)	20	(b)

1 (c)

해석 A: 우리 내일 오페라 보러 가야겠어.
　　B: 그렇다면 호텔 안내원에게 티켓을 예약해 달라고 부탁해야겠어요.

해설 선택지 중 오페라 티켓을 예약해 줄 적임자를 찾아보면 '호텔 안내원'이라는 뜻의 concierge가 가장 적절하다.

어구 reserve 예약하다

오답 살펴보기 (a) housekeeper 가정부 (b) attendant 종업원 (d) bellhop 보이, 사환

2 (a)

해석 A: 내가 재키에게 달은 치즈로 만들어진 것이라고 말했더니 그걸 믿더라고. 정말 어이가 없었어.
　　B: 재키는 아주 잘 속아서 네가 말하는 건 뭐든지 다 믿을 거야.

해설 남의 말을 쉽게 믿거나 잘 속아 넘어가는 사람을 일컬을 때 '잘 속는'이란 뜻의 형용사 gullible을 쓸 수 있다.

오답 살펴보기 (b) guarded 신중한 (c) garrulous 말이 많은 (d) gabby 수다스러운

3 (d)

해석 A: 왜 그렇게 많은 야구 수집품을 갖고 있니?
　　B: 몰랐니? 나는 수년 동안 열렬한 야구팬이었어.

해설 야구 수집품이 많다고 했으므로 야구를 좋아한다고 추측할 수 있다. 따라서 '열렬한, 열정적인'이란 뜻의 avid가 정답이다.

어구 memorabilia 기념품, 수집품

오답 살펴보기 (a) drab 칙칙한, 생기 없는 (b) bare 벌거숭이의 (c) puny 허약한

4 (b)

해석 A: 프랭크 브라운과 넌 친구 아니니?
　　B: 그를 알기는 하지만 단순히 얼굴만 아는 사이일 뿐이야.

해설 정식으로 인사를 나눈 사이는 아니지만 지나가면서 얼굴을 본 적이 있는 사람을 일컬어 a casual acquaintance라고 한다.

오답 살펴보기 (a) trusted mentor 믿을만한 멘토, 스승 (c) family member 가족 구성원 (d) personal trainer 개인 트레이너

5 (a)

해석 A: 배우 그레이스 콜린스가 사망했다는 소식 들었니?
　　B: 그래, 들었어. 실은 방금 신문에서 그녀의 부고를 읽었어.

해설 '죽었다'의 완곡한 표현인 passed away가 나와 있고 신문(paper)이 있으므로 '부고'라는 뜻의 obituary가 정답이다.

오답 살펴보기 (b) testimonial 추천서 (c) biography 전기 (d) inscription 새겨진 글

6 (d)

해석 A: 스티븐 킹이 얼마나 많은 책을 썼는지 믿을 수 없을 정도야.
　　B: 그는 수십 권의 소설과 단편 소설을 집필한 다작 작가야.

해설 many books와 dozens of(수십의)에서 보듯 많은 책을 저술했기 때문에 prolific(다작의)이 정답이다. 참고로 이 단어에는 '다산의'라는 뜻도 있다.

오답 살펴보기 (a) popular 인기 있는 (b) competent 능력이 있는 (c) reluctant 마지못해 하는

7 (a)

해석 A: 열대 우림에는 수 천여 종의 동물이 서식하고 있어.
　　B: 맞아. 그곳의 우거진 잎들 속에서 동물들이 잘 자랄 수 있어.

해설 be home to는 '~의 서식지, 본거지'라는 뜻이다. 수천 종의 동물들의 서식지라고 했으므로 그곳은 나뭇잎이 '우거진(lush)' 곳일 거라고 유추할 수 있다.

어구 rainforest 열대 우림　thrive (동물, 식물이) 잘 자라다; 번창하다 foliage 나뭇잎

오답 살펴보기 (b) barren 땅이 척박한 (c) stark 냉혹한, 엄연한 (d) iconic 상징의, 우상의

8 (a)

해석 A: 이 상자는 몇 백 파운드는 나가겠어.
　　B: 그래, 하지만 네가 지렛대를 사용하면 들어 올릴 수 있을 거야.

해설 지렛대로 상자를 '들어 올리다'라고 하는 것이 자연스럽다. 이때 raise보다 조금 더 어려운 단어로 hoist를 쓸 수 있다.

어구 weigh 무게가 나가다　lever 지렛대

오답 살펴보기 (b) appraise 평가하다 (c) plunge 폭락하다 (d) guzzle 마구 마셔대다

9 (b)

해석 A: 내일 날씨가 어떨지 아니?
　　B: 비가 왔다가 햇빛이 쬐다가 할 거야.

해설 전혀 반대되는 단어인 rain and sunshine이 함께 왔으므로 '간간이 일어나는'이라는 뜻의 intermittent가 정답이다. 동사 call for 뒤에 날씨가 와서 '예측하다'라는 의미로 쓰인다는 점도 같이 기억해 두자.

오답 살펴보기 (a) rhythmic 리듬감이 있는 (c) arbitrary 임의적인 (d) interminable 끝없이 계속되는

10 (b)

해석 A: 해롤드가 집안 청소해야 한다고 오늘 밤에 못 온다네.

B: 그건 해롤드가 맨날 하는 구차한 변명 중에 하나야. 난 그가 전혀 바쁘지 않을 거라고 확신해.

해설 빈칸 뒤의 he's not busy at all에서 보듯 바쁘지 않은데 바쁘다고 핑계를 대고 있다고 생각하는 상황이다. 따라서 '구차한 변명'이란 뜻의 lame excuses가 들어가는 것이 가장 적절하다.

오답 살펴보기 (a) valid reason 합당한 이유 (c) weak argument 설득력이 약한 주장 (d) timid remark 소심한 언급

11 (c)

해석 A: 그 문제를 어떻게 해결했니?

B: 실은 다른 방법을 사용해서 문제를 회피했어.

해설 연결어 actually는 앞의 내용을 반대로 뒤집는 역할을 한다. 따라서 문제를 정석으로 푼 것이 아니라 다른 방법을 써서 회피했다는 내용이 와야 알맞다. '(곤란, 어려움을) 피해가다, 회피하다'라고 할 때 쓰는 단어는 circumvent이다.

오답 살펴보기 (a) disregard 무시하다, 경시하다 (b) acquiesce 묵인하다 (d) abjure (신념, 신앙을) 포기하다

12 (b)

해석 A: 혹시 이 약은 부작용이 있습니까?

B: 네. 이 약을 복용하시면 나른해질 수 있습니다. 그러니 중장비를 작동시켜야 하는 경우에는 이 약을 복용하지 마십시오.

해설 A가 언급한 부작용과 관계있는 단어를 선택해야 한다. lethargic(나른한)이 들어가는 것이 가장 적절하다.

어구 side effect 부작용 heavy machinery 중장비

오답 살펴보기 (a) apathetic 무관심한 (c) energetic 기운이 넘치는 (d) invigorated 활기 넘치는

13 (b)

해석 A: 겨울 방학 때 뭐할 예정이야?

B: 우리 가족은 스키 타러 2주간 산에서 체류할 계획이야.

해설 2주간 산에서 머문다는 내용이므로 sojourn(체류)이 정답이다.

오답 살펴보기 (c) layover 경유 (d) sabbatical 안식일

14 (c)

해석 A: 나는 레이디 가가의 음악이 정말 좋아.

B: 나도 좋아해. 그런데 그녀의 이상한 패션 감각도 좋더라. 아주 독특해.

해설 unique(독특한)가 있으므로 sense of fashion을 수식할 수 있는 가장 적절한 형용사를 고르면 '기괴한, 이상한'이라는 뜻의 quirky가 들어가는 것이 가장 자연스럽다.

오답 살펴보기 (a) tepid 미지근한 (b) adept 능숙한 (d) routine 일상적인

15 (a)

해석 A: 대부분의 억만장자들이 돈으로 무엇을 한다고 생각하니?

B: 그들 중 다수는 못사는 사람들과 그들의 재산을 공유하기 위해 자선가가 돼.

해설 share their fortunes라는 말이 힌트로, 가난한 사람들에게 돈을 기부하는 사람은 philanthropist(자선가)이다.

어구 fortune 부; 재산 less fortunate 못사는 사람들

오답 살펴보기 (b) sympathizer 동조자 (c) antagonist 적대자 (d) evolutionist 진화론자

16 (c)

해석 A: 이 일을 하면 휴가는 얼마나 제공되나요?

B: 첫 해에는 10일의 휴가가 주어지고 그 후에 매년마다 추가적으로 5일씩 늘어납니다.

해설 빈칸 뒤의 '추가적인'이라는 뜻의 extra가 있으므로 '축적되다'라는 뜻의 accrue가 들어가는 것이 가장 적절하다.

오답 살펴보기 (a) dissipate 소멸되다 (b) berate 질책하다 (d) yield 양보하다; 산출하다

17 (b)

해석 A: 어제는 결국 어떻게 지냈어?

B: 정말 후회스럽게도 아무것도 하지 않고 빈둥거리다 끝났어.

해설 doing nothing과 동일한 의미의 선택지를 찾아야 한다. end up 뒤에는 동명사가 오므로 '빈둥거리다'라는 의미인 dawdle의 동명사 형태가 정답이다.

어구 end up V-ing 결국 ~로 끝나다

오답 살펴보기 (a) dwindle 감소하다 (c) dwarf 왜소해 보이게 하다 (d) dazzle 현란하게 하다, 눈부시게 하다

18 (d)

해석 A: 우리는 대피 계획을 짤 때 모든 가능한 결과를 고려해야 해.

B: 맞아. 혹시나 발생할 수 있는 어떤 돌발 상황에도 대비해야 해.

해설 내용상 '돌발 상황, 긴급 상황'이라는 의미의 contingency가 가장 적절하다.

어구 evacuation 대피, 피난 outcome 결과 befall 닥치다

오답 살펴보기 (a) expectancy 기대 (b) prerequisite 전제조건 (c) undertaking 일, 프로젝트

19 (a)

해석 A: 삼촌의 재산으로부터 받은 상속이 얼마나 되니?

B: 아쉽게도 없어. 삼촌의 모든 자산이 그가 진 막대한 빚을 갚는 데 쓰였거든.

해설 A가 말한 estate(재산)와 같은 맥락의 단어를 선택지에서 찾아야 한다. '자산, 재산'이라는 뜻의 assets가 정답이다.

어구 inheritance 상속 estate 토지; 재산 substantial 실질적인, 많은

오답 살펴보기 (b) liability 부채, 책임 (c) virtue 미덕 (d) statute 법령, 법규

20 (b)

해석 A: 학교로부터 자금 지원을 더 이상 못 받으니 연구를 계속할 수 있을지 모르겠어.

B: 네가 현재 직면한 문제에도 불구하고 끝까지 해내려고 노력해야 한다고 생각해.

해설 힘들겠지만 계속 연구하라고 격려하고 있는 상황이다. '인내심

을 가지고 끝까지 해내다'라는 뜻의 persevere가 정답이다.

어구 hardship 역경　face 직면하다

오답 살펴보기 (a) vacillate 흔들리다 (c) succumb 굴복하다
(d) preserve 보존하다

Part II

VP 04 | 동사

■ Check-up TEST ■

1	(c)	2	(b)	3	(c)	4	(b)	5	(b)
6	(a)	7	(d)	8	(d)	9	(c)	10	(b)
11	(c)	12	(a)	13	(b)	14	(d)	15	(b)
16	(b)	17	(a)	18	(a)	19	(c)	20	(a)

1 (c)

해석 나는 현금이 없어서 현금 인출기에 들러서 돈을 약간 인출해
야 한다.

해설 ATM이라는 단어가 나왔고 목적어가 some money이므로,
'(돈을) 인출하다'라는 뜻의 동사 withdraw가 들어가는 것이
가장 자연스럽다. 참고로 '(돈을) 입금하다'라고 할 때는 동사
deposit을 쓴다.

어구 out of cash 현금이 없는　stop by 잠깐 들르다

오답 살펴보기 (a) deposit 입금하다 (b) select 선택하다 (d) invest
투자하다

2 (b)

해석 정부는 공공장소에서 흡연을 금지하는 법을 최근에 통과시
켰다.

해설 공공장소 흡연을 불법화한다는 내용이 되도록 '금지하다'라는
뜻의 ban을 쓰는 것이 내용상 가장 적절하다.

어구 pass a law 법을 통과시키다

오답 살펴보기 (a) enforce 집행하다 (d) situate 위치시키다

3 (c)

해석 인간은 사실상 어떤 환경에서도 적응할 수 있는 능력이 있기
때문에 지구 어디에서나 거주하고 있다.

해설 모든 환경에서 적응할 수 있으니 모든 장소에서 살 수 있다는
내용이 되어야 자연스럽다. adapt(적응하다)가 정답으로, 전
치사 to와 함께 쓰인다는 것을 기억해 두자.

어구 populate 살다, 거주하다　virtually 사실상

오답 살펴보기 (a) adopt 채택하다 (b) invoke (어떠한 감정을) 불러일
으키다 (d) revoke 취소하다

4 (b)

해석 물건을 구입할 때 최상의 거래를 하고 싶다면 반드시 가격 흥
정을 해야 한다.

해설 빈칸 뒤에 전치사 over가 있고 목적어로 가격(prices)이 나왔

으므로 '흥정하다'라는 뜻의 haggle이 정답이다.

오답 살펴보기 (a) argue 주장하다 (c) quarrel 말다툼하다
(d) contest (시합에서) 경쟁하다

5 (b)

해석 그 자동차 회사는 소비자로부터 수많은 불평건수를 받은 후에
자사 제품의 품질을 향상시키기 위해 최선을 다하고 있다.

해설 '～하는 데 최선을 다하다'를 뜻하는 표현 「strive to + 동사원
형」을 물어보는 문제이다.

어구 numerous 수많은

오답 살펴보기 (a) meditate 명상하다 (d) ignore 무시하다

6 (a)

해석 곰은 일반적으로 유순한 동물이지만 화나게 했을 때는 위험해
질 수 있다.

해설 become dangerous라는 말로 미루어볼 때 곰을 화나게 했
을 때 위험해질 거라고 추측할 수 있다. '상대방을 도발하다,
화나게 하다'라는 뜻의 동사는 provoke를 쓴다.

어구 docile 유순한　creature 생명체

오답 살펴보기 (b) revoke 철회하다 (c) invoke (느낌, 상상을) 불러일
으키다 (d) prohibit 금지하다

7 (d)

해석 내가 어렸을 때 우리 어머니께서는 세 자녀를 키우며 두 개의
직장 일까지 병행하셔야 했다.

해설 세 아이를 키우며 직업도 두 개나 가졌다고 했으므로 '여러 가
지 일을 처리하다, 병행하다'라는 뜻의 juggle이 정답이다. 여
러 개의 공을 가지고 juggling하는 모습을 생각하면 그 의미
가 쉽게 이해될 수 있을 것이다.

오답 살펴보기 (b) decipher 해독하다 (c) fortify 강화하다

8 (d)

해석 저녁을 어디에서 먹을지 결정하지 못해 아내와 나는 서로 타
협하여 테이크아웃 음식을 주문하기로 했다.

해설 앞에 Unable to decide가 있는데 뒤에는 음식을 주문했다
는 말이 있다. 따라서 '타협하다'라는 뜻의 compromise를
쓰는 것이 가장 적절하다. 참고로 compromise는 '(명예를)
더럽히다'라는 뜻도 있으니 같이 외워두자.

어구 take-out 포장해서 가지고 가는 음식

오답 살펴보기 (a) confuse 혼란스럽게 하다 (b) conserve 보존하다
(c) collapse 붕괴하다

9 (c)

해석 회사는 고객들이 자사의 제품을 구매하도록 유혹하기 위해 현
란한 광고를 사용한다.

해설 광고(advertisements)와 관련이 있고 목적어 customers
와 어울리는 동사를 생각해 보면 '유혹하다'라는 뜻의 entice
가 정답이다. 「entice + 목적어 + into + 동명사」 형태로 쓴다.

어구 flashy 현란한

오답 살펴보기 (a) deceive 속이다 (b) repel 쫓아내다 (d) tumble
굴러떨어지게 하다

10 (b)

해석 방목형 가축은 울타리에 가두어서 키우는 것이 아니라 목초지를 자유롭게 떠돌아다니도록 하는 것이다.

해설 「A rather than B」에서 A와 B의 내용은 상반되어야 한다. 즉, 여기서는 confined와 반대되는 내용의 단어를 찾으면 된다. 빈칸 뒤에 freely(자유롭게)라는 부사도 있으므로 '떠돌아다니다'라는 뜻의 roam이 정답이다.

어구 free-range 방목형의   pasture 목초지   confine 가두다   pen (가축의) 우리

오답 살펴보기 (a) strut (뽐내는 자세로) 걷다 (c) plunge 폭락하다 (d) assemble 조립하다

11 (c)

해석 필기를 빨리 하려면 일반적인 용어와 구를 약어로 표기하는 것이 중요하다.

해설 빠른 필기와 관계있고 목적어인 common terms and phrases와 가장 잘 어울리는 동사는 '축약하다, 간략화하다'라는 뜻의 abbreviate이다.

어구 take notes 적다, 필기하다   term 용어   phrase 구

오답 살펴보기 (a) promote 홍보하다 (b) implement 실행하다 (d) recite 암송하다

12 (a)

해석 며칠 동안 먹지 못한 난파선의 생존자들은 식사를 단번에 뚝딱 해치웠다.

해설 며칠 동안 먹지 못했다고 했으므로 식사를 '걸신들린 듯 먹어치우다'라는 뜻의 동사 devour가 적절하다.

어구 shipwreck 난파선

오답 살펴보기 (b) digest 소화하다 (c) consume 소비하다 (d) swallow 삼키다

13 (b)

해석 지금은 날씨가 화창하지만 폭풍 구름이 지평선상에 서서히 생겨나고 있다.

해설 현재 날씨는 화창하다고 했는데 but 뒤에 storm clouds가 주어로 주어졌으므로 '서서히 나타나다'라는 뜻의 loom을 쓰는 것이 내용상 적절하다.

어구 horizon 지평선

오답 살펴보기 (a) wander 떠돌아다니다 (c) recede 후퇴하다 (d) implement 실행하다

14 (d)

해석 정부는 모든 학생들이 제대로 된 식사를 하게 하려고 학급 점심 급식 보조금을 지원한다.

해설 모든 학생들이 점심을 먹도록 하려면 정부가 돈을 대야 할 것이다. '보조금을 지원하다'라는 뜻의 동사는 subsidize이다.

오답 살펴보기 (a) loan 대출하다; 대출 (b) constitute 구성하다 (c) regulate 규제를 가하다

15 (b)

해석 선생님은 시험에서 부정행위를 한 학생들을 꾸짖었다.

해설 부정행위를 한 학생들에게 가해질 가장 적절한 행동은 혼을 내는 것이다. '꾸짖다, 질책하다'라는 뜻의 동사는 reprimand이다.

오답 살펴보기 (a) congratulate 축하하다 (c) laud 칭찬하다 (d) elevate 상승시키다

16 (b)

해석 몇 년 동안 법을 기각한 후, 시는 다시 한 번 더 미성년자를 대상으로 통금을 실시하기로 했다.

해설 목적어인 curfew(통금)와 가장 잘 어울리는 동사는 '실행하다, 실시하다'라는 뜻의 enforce이다.

어구 ignore 무시하다; 기각하다   curfew 통금   minor 미성년자

오답 살펴보기 (a) repeal (법을) 폐지하다 (c) detain 감금하다 (d) obstruct 방해하다

17 (a)

해석 그 정당 후보는 지역구민들에게 간곡히 지지를 요청했다.

해설 정치 후보가 지지를 호소한다는 의미이다. '간곡히 요청하다'라는 뜻의 동사는 implore이다.

어구 constituent 지역구민, 선거권자

오답 살펴보기 (b) regale 마음껏 즐기다 (c) condemn 비난하다

18 (a)

해석 의사 선생님이 나에게 오래 살고 싶으면 술을 자제해야 한다고 했다.

해설 전치사 from과 뒤에 나온 alcohol이 힌트가 될 수 있다. '(술이나 담배를) 자제하다'라는 뜻의 abstain이 정답이다.

오답 살펴보기 (b) indulge (도덕적으로 바람직하지 않은 것을) 즐기다 (c) decline 하락하다; 거절하다 (d) suspect 의심하다

19 (c)

해석 사회적인 성격의 게임을 하는 것은 어색한 분위기를 해소하고 서로 모르는 사람들 사이에서 대화를 더 잘 이어가게 하는 훌륭한 방법이다.

해설 어색한 분위기를 해소한다고 했는데 빈칸 뒤 목적어가 conversation(대화)이므로 '촉진하다'라는 뜻의 동사 facilitate가 정답이다.

오답 살펴보기 (a) prohibit 금지하다 (b) mediate 중재하다 (d) discourage 낙담시키다

20 (a)

해석 소수의 종교 지도자들 사이에서 성추행이 있었다는 주장이 교회 전체에 낙인을 찍어 버리게 되었다.

해설 비도덕적인 일이 있었던 것이므로 부정적인 의미를 갖는 동사를 찾는다. '낙인을 찍다'라는 뜻의 stigmatize를 쓰는 것이 가장 적절하다.

어구 allegation 주장   sexual misconduct 성추행   a handful of 소수의

오답 살펴보기 (b) emancipate 해방시키다 (c) personify 의인화하다 (d) invigorate 활기차게 하다

Check-up TEST

1	(d)	2	(c)	3	(a)	4	(b)	5	(a)
6	(c)	7	(c)	8	(b)	9	(a)	10	(b)
11	(b)	12	(d)	13	(c)	14	(d)	15	(a)
16	(b)	17	(a)	18	(c)	19	(b)	20	(a)

1 (d)

해석 항공사는 항공편이 취소된 승객들을 대상으로 하룻밤 숙박을 제공했다.

해설 항공편이 취소되었을 때 항공사가 제공할 수 있을 만한 것으로 가장 적절한 것은 '숙박시설'을 의미하는 accommodations이다.

어구 airline 항공사   overnight 일박의; 단기 숙박용의

오답 살펴보기 (a) submission 제출 (b) consequence 결과 (c) legislation 입법

2 (c)

해석 내 아버지는 내 고향의 유명한 변호사이며 거의 모든 사람들에게 알려져 있다.

해설 뒤에 나온 is known by nearly everybody가 힌트로, 같은 맥락의 단어인 prominent(유명한)가 정답이다.

오답 살펴보기 (a) distracting 방해하는 (b) stubborn 고집이 센 (d) temporary 일시적인

3 (a)

해석 수소 자동차가 미래에는 일반화될지도 모르겠지만 지금은 신기한 물건에 머물러 있다.

해설 맨 앞에 Although가 나왔기 때문에 주절의 내용은 앞과 반대되는 내용이 나와야 한다. 즉 common과 반대되는 단어가 나오면 되므로 '신기한 것, 새로운 것'을 의미하는 novelty가 정답이다.

어구 hydrogen 수소

오답 살펴보기 (b) portion 한 부분, 1인분 (c) grief 슬픔 (d) designation 지명, 지정

4 (b)

해석 다수의 기성세대 구성원들은 오늘날의 젊은이들을 지나치게 피상적이고 물질주의적이라 비난한다.

해설 and가 힌트가 될 수 있다. materialistic(물질적인)과 가장 의미가 유사한 단어는 '피상적인, 천박한'이라는 의미의 superficial이다.

어구 generation 세대   overly 지나치게, 몹시   materialistic 물질주의의

오답 살펴보기 (a) contradictory 상충되는 (c) infectious 전염성이 강한 (d) inept 부적절한, 무능한

5 (a)

해석 과학자들은 그 병에 대한 치료법을 발견하여 의학 분야에서 엄청난 성과를 거두었다.

해설 치료법을 발견했다고 했으므로 긍정적인 영향을 미쳤음을 알 수 있다. 따라서 '획기적인 성과'를 의미하는 breakthrough가 정답이다.

어구 tremendous 대단한   cure 치료법

오답 살펴보기 (b) vaccination 예방 접종 (c) assignment 과제, 숙제 (d) privilege 특권

6 (c)

해석 '게으른'이라는 단어는 대부분의 사람들에게 부정적인 함축적 의미를 지니고 있다.

해설 lazy라는 단어에 부정적인 뭔가가 있다고 했으므로 '함축적 의미'를 뜻하는 connotations가 들어가는 것이 적절하다. (d) denotations는 '지시적 의미'라는 반대되는 뜻이므로 혼동하지 않도록 주의하자.

오답 살펴보기 (a) suggestion 제안 (b) transmission 변환 (d) denotation 지시적 의미

7 (c)

해석 그 그림은 사실 램브란트의 제자들 중 한 명이 그렸는데 수년간 램브란트의 작품이라고 잘못 생각되었다.

해설 실제로는 램브란트가 그림을 그린 게 아니라 다른 사람이 그렸다고 했으므로 '잘못 생각되어, 오류로 인해'라는 뜻의 erroneously가 정답이다.

어구 be attributed to (작품을) ~의 저작으로 간주하다

오답 살펴보기 (a) absurdly 어리석게 (b) implicitly 암시적으로; 절대적으로 (d) methodically 방법적으로

8 (b)

해석 뉴욕에서 교사의 최고 연봉 상한선은 연봉 86,000달러이다.

해설 이 문제는 선택지를 빈칸에 일일이 대입해 틀린 것을 걸러나가는 것이 효과적인 풀이 방법이다. 돈 액수와 per year라는 말이 나왔으므로 '연봉 상한선'이라는 뜻의 salary cap이 정답이다. 교사의 '순소득'이라고 하면 어색하므로 (c)는 답이 될 수 없다.

오답 살펴보기 (a) growth rate 성장률 (c) net income 순소득 (d) market share 시장 점유율

9 (a)

해석 최근의 경제 위기는 은행 분야가 가진 주요한 결함을 노출시켰다.

해설 형용사 economic(경제적인)과 가장 잘 어울리는 명사는 '위기'라는 뜻의 crisis이다.

어구 deficiency 결핍; 결함

오답 살펴보기 (b) agreement 동의 (c) tariff 관세 (d) coalition 연합

10 (b)

해석 티파니는 사람들을 다루는 수완으로 긴장된 상황을 해소할 수 있었다.

해설 사람을 다루는 데 수완이 있다는 의미인데 '수완, 솜씨'를 finesse라고 한다.

어구 diffuse 해소시키다   tense 긴장된

오답 살펴보기 (a) canniness 약삭빠름 (c) deficiency 결핍, 결점
(d) aggressiveness 공격적인 성향

11 (b)

해석 11월에 소비재 가격이 전달 대비 불과 0.1% 소폭 하락했다.

해설 just 0.1 percent를 보고 가격이 아주 조금만 변했음을 알 수 있다. 따라서 '소폭으로, 적게'라는 뜻의 marginally가 정답이다.

어구 consumer goods 소비재

오답 살펴보기 (a) undoubtedly 의심의 여지없이
(c) incrementally 점진적으로 (d) sufficiently 충분하게

12 (d)

해석 우리 회사는 회사 제품에 넣은 꼼꼼한 세부사항으로 널리 호평을 받았다.

해설 빈칸 뒤의 detail과 잘 어울리는 형용사를 고르면 되는 문제이다. '세부적인, 꼼꼼한'이라는 뜻의 meticulous가 정답이다.

어구 be praised for ~로 호평 받다   incorporate ~into ~을 첨가하다

오답 살펴보기 (a) noxious 유독한, 유해한 (b) inordinate 과도한, 지나친 (c) predictable 예측 가능한

13 (c)

해석 소셜 네트워킹 웹 사이트는 하버드 대학 중퇴생의 발명품이다.

해설 dropout(중퇴생)이 사람명사라는 것을 안다면 쉽게 풀 수 있는 문제로 '발명품, 소산물'이라는 의미의 brainchild가 정답이다.

어구 dropout 중퇴생

오답 살펴보기 (a) conception 구상, 계획 (b) hierarchy 계급, 계층
(d) facsimile 복제, 복사

14 (d)

해석 새로 지은 시청의 현대적인 디자인은 원래 시청 건물의 고딕 건축 스타일과 확연한 차이를 보인다.

해설 contrast to(~와 반대로)가 나왔으니 앞뒤 내용이 반대가 되어야 한다. 이때 반대 내용을 좀 더 강조할 때 사용할 수 있는 단어는 '확연한, 두드러진'의 뜻을 갖는 stark이다.

어구 contemporary 현대의; 동시대의   architectural 건축의
original 본래의; 독창적인

오답 살펴보기 (a) outlandish 이상한, 기이한 (b) enchanting 매력적인 (c) bleak 암울한

15 (a)

해석 계획을 좀 더 꼼꼼하게 세웠더라면 이 불운한 곤경은 피할 수 있었을 것이다.

해설 계획을 세우지 않아서 곤란을 겪게 되었다는 내용의 문장이다. '곤란, 곤경'이라는 뜻의 predicament가 정답이다.

오답 살펴보기 (b) pastime 취미, 오락 (c) wreckage 잔해; 파멸
(d) premonition 불길한 예감, 경고

16 (b)

해석 정부는 시민들의 식자율을 높이기 위한 목적으로 읽기 프로그램에 자금 지원을 늘리기로 결정했다.

해설 읽기 프로그램에 자금을 지원한다고 했으므로 문맹률을 낮추고 식자율을 높이려는 시도임을 알 수 있다. 빈칸 앞에 improving이 있으므로 '글을 읽고 쓸 수 있는 능력, 식자'를 의미하는 literacy가 정답이다.

어구 funding 자금   aim 목적

오답 살펴보기 (a) discourse 담화 (c) acumen 명민함
(d) hyperbole 과장(법)

17 (a)

해석 지원 과정의 주 요소는 대면 면접이다.

해설 어느 과정 중의 한 요소라는 의미에서 component(구성 요소, 성분)가 알맞다.

어구 face-to-face 대면의, 얼굴을 직접 맞대는

오답 살펴보기 (b) partition 칸막이; 분할 (c) division 분할, 분배
(d) segment 부분

18 (c)

해석 소년은 들키고 싶지 않아서 방 건너편에 있는 아름다운 소녀를 은밀히 응시했다.

해설 Not wanting to be noticed라는 말이 있으므로 furtively (은밀한, 비밀스럽게)가 정답이다. 같은 의미의 단어 clandestinely(비밀리에)도 함께 외워두자.

어구 glance 응시하다

오답 살펴보기 (a) effusively 넘쳐흐르게 (b) vapidly 흥미 없이, 재미 없이 (d) willingly 적극적으로

19 (b)

해석 그 이론은 생명체는 진화할 수 있다는 주장을 거부한다.

해설 that 이하에 나오는 문장을 한 단어로 표현할 수 있는 어휘를 찾으면 '진술, 주장'이라는 뜻의 proposition이 정답이다.

어구 reject 거절하다, 거부하다   be capable of ~할 수 있다
evolve 진화하다

오답 살펴보기 (a) paradigm 패러다임 (c) propagation 번식, 증식
(d) pervasion 침투, 퍼짐

20 (a)

해석 한국에서 자격이 되는 모든 젊은 남성은 2년간의 의무적인 군 복무를 마쳐야 한다.

해설 조동사 must가 있으니 강제성, 의무성과 관련된 표현이 와야 함을 생각할 수 있다. compulsory(의무적인)가 정답으로, 같은 의미의 단어인 mandatory, obligatory도 함께 외워두자.

어구 eligible 자격이 되는   enlistment (병역) 복무 기간; 입대

오답 살펴보기 (b) tactile 촉각의 (c) persistent 지속적인
(d) elective 선별적인

VP 06 | 고난도 어휘

Check-up TEST

1	(b)	2	(a)	3	(a)	4	(c)	5	(b)
6	(d)	7	(b)	8	(a)	9	(b)	10	(c)
11	(d)	12	(c)	13	(a)	14	(c)	15	(d)
16	(b)	17	(a)	18	(c)	19	(b)	20	(b)

1 (b)
해석 미 검찰총장이 불법 내부 거래에 대해서 불길한 경고를 했다.

해설 빈칸 뒤에 나온 명사 warnings과 가장 잘 어울리는 형용사는 ominous(불길한)이다.

어구 **Attorney General** (미국의) 검찰총장　**insider trading** 내부 거래

오답 살펴보기 (a) **refractory** 다루기 힘든, (행실이) 불량한 (c) **convulsive** 발작하는 (d) **ebullient** 패기만만한, 사기가 높은

2 (a)
해석 교사는 학습을 저해한다는 이유로 전통적인 교수법을 피했다.

해설 학습을 저해한다는 부정적인 이유가 제시되었으므로 '피하다, 회피하다'라는 뜻의 eschew를 쓰는 것이 내용상 가장 적절하다.

어구 **on the grounds that** ~을 근거로

오답 살펴보기 (b) **flatter** 아첨하다, 아부하다 (c) **plagiarize** 표절하다 (d) **admonish** 훈계하다, 혼내다

3 (a)
해석 1830년에 벨기에 왕국은 네덜란드에서 분리하여 독립 국가가 되었다.

해설 별개의 국가(separate nation)가 되려면 일단 다른 나라로부터 분리되어 나와야 할 것이다. '분리하다, 탈퇴하다'라는 뜻의 동사는 secede로 전치사 from과 같이 쓴다.

오답 살펴보기 (b) **oust** 축출하다 (c) **beleaguer** 둘러싸다, 포위하다 (d) **perpetuate** 영구화하다

4 (c)
해석 수 년 간의 쓰라린 내분을 겪고 난 후, 두 단체는 정치적 견해에 대한 차이점을 좁혀나갈 수 있었다.

해설 다툼 후에 화해한 상황으로 '(생각을) 조화시키다, (분쟁이나 차이점을) 조정하다'라고 할 때 동사 reconcile을 쓴다.

어구 **bitter** 쓴; 쓰라린　**discord** 내분

오답 살펴보기 (a) **abduct** 납치하다 (b) **epitomize** 전형적으로 보여주다 (d) **vindicate** 입증하다

5 (b)
해석 미 육군은 사실상 어떠한 전투 상황에서도 자연스럽게 스며들어갈 수 있는 새로운 위장복을 배급했다.

해설 blend into가 힌트이다. 환경에 잘 조화된다는 뜻이므로 '위장, 위장복'을 의미하는 camouflage가 적절하다.

어구 **issue** 배급하다, 지급하다　**blend** 어울리다, 조화되다 **virtually** 사실상　**combat** 전투

오답 살펴보기 (a) **aberration** 일탈 (c) **disguise** 변장 (d) **specimen** 표본

6 (d)
해석 10대인 나는 부모님이 나에게는 일찍 자라고 하면서 본인들은 늦게까지 주무시지 않았을 때 부모님의 위선을 알아챘다.

해설 부모님의 언행이 일치하지 않으므로 이는 자녀의 입장에서 보면 위선(hypocrisy)이 될 수 있다.

어구 **become aware of** ~을 알아채다, 깨닫다

오답 살펴보기 (a) **pretentiousness** 허세 (b) **deception** 속임 (c) **forthrightness** 솔직함

7 (b)
해석 디지 길레스피의 음악이 비밥과 모던 재즈에 대한 나의 관심을 불러 일으켰다.

해설 동사 pique는 '감정을 상하게 하다'라는 뜻이 있지만 목적어로 interest(흥미, 관심)가 나오면 '(흥미를) 돋우다'라는 의미를 갖는다.

어구 **bebop** 비밥(재즈의 일종)

오답 살펴보기 (a) **sustain** 유지하다 (c) **ferment** (감정을) 자극하다; 흥분하다 (d) **placate** 달래다, 진정시키다

8 (a)
해석 가르치는 일과 글 쓰는 일을 시도한 후에 토니는 마침내 요리사로서 일하면서 자신에게 딱 맞는 일을 찾아냈다.

해설 여러 직업을 시도한 후에 결국 자신에게 어울리는 직업을 찾았다는 의미이다. 따라서 '꼭 맞는 자리[일], 적소'를 의미하는 niche가 정답이다.

오답 살펴보기 (b) **acme** 절정 (c) **hiatus** 중단 (d) **coalition** 연합

9 (b)
해석 오늘날 많은 부모들은 그들의 자녀들이 그들이 시키는 것과 고의적으로 반대되는 일을 하기 때문에 그들을 다루기가 매우 힘들다는 사실을 깨닫고 있다.

해설 부모가 시키는 것과 반대되는 일을 한다고 했으므로 '말을 잘 듣지 않는, 다루기 힘든'이라는 뜻의 intractable이 정답이다.

어구 **deliberately** 고의적으로

오답 살펴보기 (a) **retractable** 집어넣을 수 있는 (c) **disagreeable** 유쾌하지 못한 (d) **apprehensible** 이해할 수 있는

10 (c)
해석 학부모들은 현지 초등학교를 폐교시키지 말라고 학교 위원회에 간청했다.

해설 학부모들이 폐교를 막기 위해 학교 위원회에게 할 수 있는 행동을 생각해 보면 된다. '간청하다'라는 뜻의 동사는 beseech이다.

오답 살펴보기 (a) **divulge** 누설하다, 폭로하다 (b) **assuage** 누그러뜨리다 (d) **extenuate** (죄 등을) 경감하다, 정상 참작하다

11 (d)

해석 교황청만이 신임 주교를 카톨릭 교회에 임명할 수 있다.

해설 목적어인 new bishops와 어울리는 단어를 찾아보면 '(성직을) 부여하다, 임명하다'라는 뜻의 ordain이 정답이다.

어구 the Vatican 바티칸, 교황청 bishop 주교

오답 살펴보기 (a) consecrate 신성하게 하다 (b) admonish 훈계하다 (c) encounter 마주치다

12 (c)

해석 나는 세금이 계획성 없는 방법으로 부과되어서는 안 되며 대신 체계적으로 부과되어야 한다고 주장하는 바이다.

해설 but이 있으므로 systemically(체계적으로)와 반대되는 단어를 찾으면 된다. '주먹구구식의, 계획성 없는'의 뜻을 갖는 haphazard가 정답이다.

어구 contend 주장하다 levy 부과하다 systemically 체계적으로

오답 살펴보기 (a) foreboding 예감하는, 전조의 (b) meticulous 꼼꼼한 (d) deliberate 고의적인

13 (a)

해석 의료 개업자들 사이에서 중요한 규칙은 해를 끼치지 않는 것이다.

해설 명사 rule(규칙)과 잘 어울리는 형용사는 cardinal(주요한, 중요한)이다.

어구 practitioner 개업의, 개업자

오답 살펴보기 (b) pious 신앙심이 깊은 (c) staunch 신념이 매우 깊은 (d) antithetical 정반대의

14 (c)

해석 그 회사는 빚을 상환할 수 없게 되자 회사가 가진 대부분의 자산을 매각할 수밖에 없었다.

해설 부채를 갚을 수 없는 상황에서 회사가 할 수 있는 일은 자산을 매각하는 것이다. liquidate(청산하다, 매각하다)가 정답이다.

어구 be forced to V ~할 수밖에 없다 asset 자산 debt 빚

오답 살펴보기 (a) expedite 신속히 처리하다 (b) vie 경쟁하다 (d) taper 줄이다; 가늘어지다

15 (d)

해석 매 문장마다 '~와 같이'라는 말로 끝맺는 그녀의 독특한 경향 때문에 그녀의 동료들은 그녀를 지적이라고 생각지 않았다.

해설 특유의 말버릇에 관한 내용이므로 선택지 중에서 '독특한, 이상한'이라는 뜻의 idiosyncratic이 내용상 가장 적절하다.

어구 tendency to V ~하는 경향 punctuate 구두점을 찍다 peer 동료, 또래

오답 살펴보기 (a) blatant 주제 넘는, 뻔뻔한 (b) repellent 혐오감을 주는, 불쾌한 (c) ornate (문체가) 화려한, 잘 꾸민

16 (b)

해석 대통령은 일 년 내내 여러 교육 개혁에 대해서 거부권을 행사했기 때문에 교육에 대한 대통령의 열정은 거짓이라고 비판자들은 주장한다.

해설 대통령이 교육 개혁안에 대해 계속 반대했기 때문에 그의 교

육 열정이 '허위의, 거짓된(spurious)' 것이라고 판단할 수 있다.

어구 detractor 비판자, 비난자 enthusiasm 열정 veto 거부권을 행사하다; 거부권 reform 개혁

오답 살펴보기 (a) disaffected 불만을 품은 (c) veracious 진실한; 정직한 (d) premeditated 미리 계획된

17 (a)

해석 영국 정부는 아편 전쟁 종결 시에 중국과 체결했던 불평등한 조약을 폐지했다.

해설 목적어로 treaties(조약)가 나왔기 때문에 어울리는 동사를 찾아보면 '폐지하다'라는 뜻의 abrogate가 내용상 가장 적절하다.

어구 treaty 조약 conclusion 종결 the Opium Wars 아편 전쟁

오답 살펴보기 (b) abridge 요약하다, 축소하다 (c) admonish 훈계하다, 충고하다 (d) administer 관리하다, 지배하다

18 (c)

해석 대중의 원성 때문에 주지사는 재임기간에 저질렀던 부정행위로 인해 탄핵되었다.

해설 문장 전반이 부정적인 내용으로, 탄핵될 만한 행위를 생각해 보면 된다. 따라서 '(공직자의) 부정행위'를 의미하는 malfeasance가 정답이다.

어구 outcry 원성 governor 주지사 impeach 탄핵시키다 commit (범죄를) 저지르다

오답 살펴보기 (a) multifariousness 다양함; 다방면에 걸침 (b) impropriety 점잖지 못함 (d) delinquency 비행

19 (b)

해석 그 영화는 가족이 보기 좋은 영화라고 홍보되었지만 사실 너무나도 많은 인종차별적 언어들이 나와서 아이들이 보기에는 부적절했다.

해설 '빗대어 하는 말, 암시하는 말'이라는 뜻의 innuendo가 들어가는 것이 적절하다.

오답 살펴보기 (a) exculpation 무죄의 증명 (c) aberration 탈선, 궤도에서 벗어남 (d) referendum 국민 투표

20 (b)

해석 소심한 그 교사는 의무적으로 정해져 있는 교과과정을 따르지 않고 게임을 하면서 학생들을 달래주려 했다.

해설 정해져 있는 교과과정이 있는데 교사가 그것을 따르지 않고 아이들의 마음을 달래주려 했다면 소심한(pusillanimous) 성격이라고 할 수 있다.

어구 appease (사람을) 달래다 mandated 법에 규정된; 위임을 받은

오답 살펴보기 (a) rabid 과격한 (c) gregarious 사교적인 (d) obsequious 아첨하는

5 (b)

해석 A: 재판을 위해서 그날 밤 당신이 목격한 것을 설명해 주시겠
　　　습니까?
　　 B: 네. 저는 한 여성이 남자에게 소리를 지르고 결국에는 방아
　　　쇠를 당기는 것을 봤습니다.

해설 명사 trigger와 함께 쓸 수 있는 동사는 pull이다. pull the
　　 trigger(방아쇠를 당기다)라는 표현을 물어보는 문제이다.

어구 **describe** 기술하다　　**trigger** 방아쇠

오답 살펴보기 (c) **grab** 잡다 (d) **press** 압력을 가하다

6 (c)

해석 A: 우리가 자동차로 여행을 갈 때마다 항상 너는 약을 먹더라.
　　 B: 맞아. 멀미를 예방하는 걸 도와주거든.

해설 자동차로 여행 가기 전에 약을 먹는 것과 관련된 표현은 멀미
　　 (motion sickness)이다.

어구 **road trip** 차로 하는 여행　　**prevent** 막다, 예방하다

7 (a)

해석 A: 앨런은 그 많은 옷을 어떻게 다 살 수 있는 거지? 같은 옷
　　　을 두 번 입는 것을 본 적이 없어.
　　 B: 남편이 돈이 많거든. 그래서 매달마다 백지수표를 받아서
　　　원하는 건 뭐든지 다 하는 거야.

해설 '백지 수표'라는 뜻의 blank check를 물어보는 문제이다. 백
　　 지에 금액을 마음대로 기입할 수 있다는 의미가 확장되어 '마
　　 음대로 할 수 있는 권리'를 뜻하기도 한다.

어구 **afford** (금전적으로) 감당하다　　**outfit** 복장

오답 살펴보기 (d) **vacant** 방이 빈

8 (c)

해석 A: 소셜 네트워킹 사이트에 가입하는 게 어때? 모든 사람들
　　　이 쓰고 있잖아.
　　 B: 미안하지만 난 그런 기술이 개인 사생활에 위협이 된다고
　　　생각해.

해설 B는 소셜 네트워킹 사이트에 부정적인 입장이므로 '위협을 가
　　 하다'라는 뜻의 pose a threat가 와야 적절하다.

어구 **personal** 개인적인　　**privacy** 사생활

오답 살펴보기 (b) **ritual** 종교적인 의식 (d) **grudge** 원한

9 (d)

해석 A: 오늘 신문을 보니 미국과 북한이 회담을 다시 시작한다고
　　　하네.
　　 B: 부디 이번에는 양국이 서로 긴밀한 관계를 구축할 수 있으
　　　면 좋겠어.

해설 '관계를 구축하다'라고 할 때 동사 forge를 써서 forge ties라
　　 고 한다.

어구 **resume** 다시 시작하다

오답 살펴보기 (a) **bolster** 강화하다 (b) **forage** (먹을 것을) 찾아 돌아

Part I, II

VP 07 | collocation

▬ Check-up TEST ▬

1	(a)	2	(c)	3	(b)	4	(d)	5	(b)
6	(c)	7	(a)	8	(c)	9	(d)	10	(a)
11	(c)	12	(a)	13	(b)	14	(c)	15	(b)
16	(c)	17	(a)	18	(b)	19	(b)	20	(d)

1 (a)

해석 A: 이건 무슨 종류의 나무지?
　　 B: 사과나무야. 봄마다 열매를 맺지.

해설 '열매를 맺다'라고 할 때 bear fruit라고 한다. 말 그대로 '열매
　　 를 맺다'라는 뜻도 있지만 상징적으로 '결실을 거두다'라는 의
　　 미도 되므로 함께 기억해 두자.

오답 살펴보기 (c) **possess** 소유하다 (d) **invade** 침략하다

2 (c)

해석 A: 레이첼. 간단하게 물어볼 게 있어. 이 자판기가 지폐도 받
　　　니?
　　 B: 아니. 확실하게 동전만 받아.

해설 A가 간단히 대답할 수 있는 질문을 던진 상황으로, '간단한 질
　　 문'은 quick question이라고 한다.

어구 **vending machine** 자동판매기

오답 살펴보기 (a) **brief** 간단한, 짧은 (d) **drab** 생기 없는, 칙칙한

3 (b)

해석 A: 내 고양이가 이번 달에 20살이 될 거야.
　　 B: 우와, 상당히 인상적인데. 고양이의 평균 수명은 12년에서
　　　15년이잖아.

해설 고양이의 나이에 대한 대화이므로 '수명'이란 뜻의 life span
　　 이 오는 것이 알맞다.

어구 **impressive** 인상적인

오답 살펴보기 (a) **gap** 차이, 격차 (c) **period** 기간 (d) **distance** 거리

4 (d)

해석 A: 좀 들어 봐요, 여보. 나는 당신이 집 안에 총을 소지하고 있
　　　는 게 불편해요.
　　 B: 무슨 소리예요? 나는 단지 무기를 소지할 수 있는 권리를
　　　행사하는 것뿐이에요.

해설 빈칸 뒤의 my right에 주목하자. '권리를 행사하다'라는 뜻의
　　 표현 exercise one's right를 물어보는 문제이다.

다니다 (c) furnish (가구를) 갖추다

10 (a)

해석 A: 재판 결과가 어떻게 나왔는지 알아?
B: 불일치 배심 때문에 미결정 심리가 되었어.

해설 mistrial이 힌트로, 배심원이 유죄, 무죄 판단을 내리지 못한 것을 hung jury(배심원 불일치)라고 한다.

어구 outcome 결과　trial 재판　mistrial (배심원의 의견 불일치로 인한) 미결정 심리; 오심

오답 살펴보기 (b) deliberate 고의적인　(c) taut 엄격한, 간결한
(d) brazen 뻔뻔한

11 (c)

해석 아버지께서 집에 오시면 너 큰일 날 거야.

해설 trouble(곤란)을 강조할 때 쓸 수 있는 형용사는 big으로, be in big trouble은 '큰 곤란에 처하다'라는 뜻이다.

어구 get home 집에 오다

12 (a)

해석 수천 명에 달하는 군중들이 고인이 된 배우에게 작별을 고하기 위해 모여들었다.

해설 '작별을 고하다'라는 뜻의 표현은 bid farewell이다.

어구 turn out 모여들다　farewell 작별　the late 고인이 된

오답 살펴보기 (b) mourn 애도하다

13 (b)

해석 급속히 발전하는 국가에서 세대 차이는 선진국보다 더 크다.

해설 '세대 차이'는 generation gap이라고 한다.

어구 developing nation 개발도상국　developed country 선진국

14 (c)

해석 백악관은 이번 공격을 테러행위라고 규탄하는 성명서를 발표했다.

해설 '성명서를 발표하다'라고 할 때 issue a statement라고 한다.

어구 condemn 규탄하다, 비난하다

오답 살펴보기 (b) testimonial 증명서, 감사장

15 (b)

해석 필리핀의 수도인 마닐라는 전 세계에서 가장 인구 밀도가 높은 도시이다.

해설 '인구 밀도가 높은'은 densely populated라고 한다. 반대로 '인구 밀도가 희박한'은 sparsely populated이다.

어구 populate 거주하다

오답 살펴보기 (a) tightly 단단히　(c) rigidly 엄격하게　(d) closely 밀접하게

16 (c)

해석 피고에게 불리한 결정적인 증거에도 불구하고 판사는 유죄가 아니라는 평결을 내렸다.

해설 법정과 관련된 표현이 와야 하는데 '평결을 내리다'라는 뜻의

표현은 deliver a verdict이다.

어구 convince 확신시키다　defendant 피고　verdict 평결

오답 살펴보기 (a) dispatch 파견하다　(b) forward 전송하다

17 (a)

해석 외교관은 연설 후에 뉴스 기자들의 질문에 흔쾌히 응했다.

해설 '질문에 흔쾌히 응하다'라고 할 때 questions 앞에 '환대하다'라는 의미의 entertain을 써서 표현한다.

어구 diplomat 외교관

오답 살펴보기 (c) appreciate 감사해하다　(d) intimidate 위협하다

18 (b)

해석 나는 런던에서 상하이까지 비행기를 타고 난 뒤 심한 시차로 고생했다.

해설 jet lag은 비행기를 이용한 장거리 여행 시 '시차로 인한 피로감'을 의미한다.

오답 살펴보기 (a) fatigue 피로　(c) weariness 피로

19 (b)

해석 과학자들은 아밀로이드 베타라고 불리는 단백질 상부 구조에서 알츠하이머 질병의 원인을 파악했다.

해설 '(문제의) 원인을 파악하다'라고 할 때 동사 identify(밝혀내다)를 쓴다.

어구 protein 단백질　superstructure 상부 구조

오답 살펴보기 (a) categorize 분류하다　(c) exacerbate 악화시키다
(d) recuperate 회복하다

20 (d)

해석 열등감으로 고통받고 있는 이들은 본인의 자존감을 높이기 위해 타인을 비난한다고 심리학자들은 확인했다.

해설 '열등감'이라고 할 때 inferiority complex라고 한다. 여기서 complex는 '강박 관념'을 뜻한다.

어구 ascertain (실험, 검사를 통해) 확인하다　inferiority 열등, 하위
lash out at ~을 비난하다　self-esteem 자존감

오답 살펴보기 (b) complication 복잡함　(c) cognition 인지, 인식

VP 08 | 형태가 비슷한 어휘

═ Check-up TEST ═

1 (b)	2 (d)	3 (b)	4 (c)	5 (a)
6 (c)	7 (a)	8 (d)	9 (a)	10 (c)
11 (d)	12 (b)	13 (a)	14 (d)	15 (b)
16 (a)	17 (b)	18 (c)	19 (c)	20 (d)

1 (b)

해석 A: 다니엘, 상태가 안 좋아 보이는구나. 감기에 걸렸니?
B: 아니, 그냥 어제 저녁에 술을 많이 마셔서 지금 숙취가 심해서 그래.

해설 B의 말 중 had too much to drink를 통해 술을 많이 마셔서 숙취(hangover)로 고생한다는 것을 알 수 있다.

어구 catch the flu 감기에 걸리다　drink (술을) 마시다

오답 살펴보기 (a) hangout 집합소, 소굴 (c) hanger-on 주위를 어슬렁거리는 사람 (d) hang-up 장애, 콤플렉스

2 (d)

해석 A: 그 회사의 일자리 제의에 대해 결정을 내렸니?
　　B: 아직이야. 그 일자리를 수락해야 할지 말아야 할지 아직 모르겠어.

해설 Not yet에서 보듯 아직 결정을 내리지 못한 상황이다. 이럴 때 쓸 수 있는 형용사는 '상반되는 감정을 가진'이란 뜻의 ambivalent이다. '애매모호한'이라는 뜻의 (c) ambiguous는 주어가 사람일 때는 쓸 수 없으므로 주의하자.

어구 job offer 일자리 제의

오답 살펴보기 (a) ambulant 걸어 다닐 수 있는 (b) ambience 분위기 (c) ambiguous 애매모호한

3 (b)

해석 A: 그 도시는 차량 탈취 문제를 억제하기 위해 정말이지 무언가를 할 필요가 있어.
　　B: 맞아, 그래서 이번에 CCTV 카메라 수백 대를 도시 곳곳에 설치하기로 했지.

해설 목적어로 CCTV cameras가 나왔는데 차량 탈취를 막기 위해서는 이것을 '설치'하면 될 것이다. '설치하다'의 뜻을 갖는 install이 정답이다.

어구 curb 제한하다, 억제하다　carjacking 차량 탈취

오답 살펴보기 (a) instill 스며들게 하다, 서서히 주입시키다 (c) instigate 실시[착수]하다; 선동하다 (d) instruct 지시하다

4 (c)

해석 A: 회사 정치 자금 사건에 대한 대법원 판결은 뭐였니?
　　B: 법원은 보기 드물게 만장일치로 불법이라고 결정했어.

해설 법원의 판결에 대한 내용이므로 '만장일치의'라는 뜻을 가진 unanimous가 정답이다.

어구 Supreme Court 대법원　ruling 판결　outlaw (법적으로) 무효화하다; 비합법화하다

오답 살펴보기 (a) unannounced 예고 없는 (b) anonymous 익명의 (d) anomie 사회적 무질서

5 (a)

해석 A: 지금 일자리를 잃은 상황에서 어떻게 학자금 대출을 갚아 나갈 거니?
　　B: 다행히 내 금전적 상황이 나아질 때까지 상환을 늦출 수 있어.

해설 빈칸 뒤를 보면 until이라는 기간을 나타내는 접속사가 쓰였다. 따라서 그때까지 상환을 미룬다는 의미로 defer(미루다, 연기하다)가 들어가는 것이 가장 적절하다.

어구 payment 상환; 지불　student loan 학자금 대출

오답 살펴보기 (b) deter 단념시키다, 그만두게 하다 (c) detach 떼어내다 (d) detract (주의를) 딴 데로 돌리다

6 (c)

해석 A: 정부가 모든 공공장소에서 흡연을 불법으로 해놓았어. 그리 좋은 생각 같지는 않아.
　　B: 나도 그렇게 생각해. 완전히 금지하는 대신 사례별로 불법화해야 해.

해설 A의 말 중 in all public places가 힌트이다. B도 A의 의견에 동의하고 있으므로, '완전한, 전체의'라는 뜻을 가진 형용사 outright가 정답이다.

어구 illegal 불법의　on a case-by-case basis 사례별로

오답 살펴보기 (a) outward 겉보기의, 외형의 (b) outworn 낡은 (d) outburst (감정의) 폭발

7 (a)

해석 A: 시 의회에서 오늘 도시 주변에 그린벨트 구역을 설정할 건지 결정할 거야.
　　B: 음, 통과되었으면 좋겠어. 도시 지역이 계속해서 퍼져 나가는 것을 막기 위해 조치가 취해져야 해.

해설 도시가 계속해서 퍼지는 것을 막는다는 의미가 되도록 답을 골라야 한다. '도시의'라는 뜻의 단어 urban이 정답이다. 참고로 반대 단어는 rural(시골의)이다.

어구 in favor of ~을 찬성하여　sprawl (보기 흉하게) 퍼져 나가다

오답 살펴보기 (b) urgent 시급한 (c) urbane 세련된, 점잖은 (d) urging 재촉하는, 성가신

8 (d)

해석 A: 우리 회사가 도산해서 내 마지막 월급을 주지 않았어. 어쩌지?
　　B: 안타깝게도 회사가 파산하면 상환을 청구할 수 있는 선택권이 거의 없어.

해설 has gone out of business(파산했다)라고 했으므로 마찬가지로 insolvent(파산한)가 들어가는 것이 적절하다.

어구 go out of business 파산하다　paycheck 급료　option 선택권　recourse 상환 청구

오답 살펴보기 (a) indolent 게으른, 나태한 (b) inadvertent 고의가 아닌; 게으르지 않은 (c) insolent 버릇없는, 무례한

9 (a)

해석 A: 정부가 새로운 천체 망원경을 만드는 데 얼마나 많은 돈을 낭비했는지 터무니가 없을 정도야.
　　B: 글쎄, 나는 그 망원경으로 관측을 하면 우리 행성에 대해 더 잘 이해할 수 있을 거라고 생각해.

해설 망원경으로 무엇을 할 수 있을지 생각해 보면 '관찰, 관측'이라는 뜻의 observations가 정답임을 알 수 있다.

어구 ridiculous 터무니없는; 우스꽝스러운　space telescope 천체 망원경

오답 살펴보기 (b) observance 준수 (c) obsession 집착 (d) obscenity 외설, 음란

10 (c)

해석 A: 그 눈부신 형광등을 없애 버리고 백열등을 다니 좋구나.
　　B: 고마워. 등을 바꿨더니 전체적인 방 분위기가 더 좋아진 것 같아.

해설 등의 교체로 인해 방의 분위기(ambience)가 좋아졌다는 의미가 적절하므로 정답은 (c)이다.

어구 **harsh** (색이) 현란한, 눈에 거슬리는 **fluorescent** 형광성의; 형광등 **in favor of** ~에 찬성하여 **incandescent** 백열성의

오답 살펴보기 (a) **ambivalence** 반대 감정의 병존; 모순, 대치 (b) **ambiguous** 애매모호한 (d) **ambition** 야망, 포부

11 (d)

해석 모든 외향적인 면에서 켄과 헤더는 행복한 결혼 생활을 했다.

해설 appearances(겉모습)를 수식할 만한 적절한 형용사를 골라 보면 '외형의, 표면상의'라는 뜻을 가진 outward가 적절하다.

오답 살펴보기 (a) **outworn** 낡은 (b) **outburst** (감정의) 폭발 (c) **outright** 완전한; 전면적인

12 (b)

해석 군인들은 의도적인 명령 불이행으로 큰 징계를 받았다.

해설 명령 불이행으로 인해 군인들에게 벌어질 수 있는 일을 찾아 보면 '징계'라는 의미의 rebuke가 적절하다.

어구 **intentionally** 의도적으로 **disobey** 불복종하다, 거역하다

오답 살펴보기 (a) **rebut** 반박하다 (c) **revoke** 취소; 취소하다 (d) **revolt** 반란, 봉기

13 (a)

해석 그 프로젝트는 심각한 재정 부족이라는 한 가지 문제만 빼고 다른 모든 면에서 튼실하다.

해설 save는 except와 마찬가지로 '~을 제외하고'라는 뜻으로도 쓰인다. 한 가지 문제만 빼고 모든 면에서 완벽하다는 의미가 되도록 hang-up(장애, 문제)이 정답이다.

어구 **solid** 굳건한, 튼실한 **save** ~을 제외하고 **severe** 심각한

오답 살펴보기 (b) **hanger-on** 주위를 어슬렁거리는 사람 (c) **hangout** 거처, 집합소 (d) **hangover** 숙취

14 (d)

해석 무례한 행동은 용인되지 않으니 삼가 주십시오.

해설 용인되지 않는 행동이 어떠한 행동일지 생각해 보면 '버릇없는, 무례한'이라는 뜻의 insolent가 정답이다.

어구 **refrain from** ~을 자제하다, 삼가다 **tolerate** 묵인하다; 참다

오답 살펴보기 (a) **indocile** 교육하기 힘든, 순종하지 않은 (b) **insolvent** 파산의 (c) **indolent** 게으른, 나태한

15 (b)

해석 크리스마스 휴일을 맞아 12월 25일에 우리 가게 문을 닫을 예정입니다.

해설 빈칸 앞뒤에 있는 in과 of에 주목해야 한다. in observance of 뒤에 기념일이 나오면 '(기념일을) 기념하여, 축하하여'라는 뜻이 된다. observance에 '준수'라는 의미 외에 '(기념일에 대한) 축하'라는 뜻도 있음을 알아두자.

오답 살펴보기 (a) **obsession** 집착, 강박 (c) **observation** 관찰, 관측 (d) **obscenity** 외설, 음란

16 (a)

해석 마틴의 정중하고 세련된 성격은 그의 저녁 만찬 손님들을 대

단히 즐겁게 해주었다.

해설 초대 손님들이 즐거워했으니 마틴의 성격은 긍정적으로 묘사되어야 한다. '세련된, 점잖은'이라는 뜻의 urbane이 정답이다.

어구 **suave** 정중한, 상냥한 **immensely** 대단히

오답 살펴보기 (b) **urban** 도시의 (c) **urgent** 시급한 (d) **urging** 재촉하는, 성가신

17 (b)

해석 오늘날 많은 교육자들은 부모들이 자녀들에게 교육에 대한 사랑을 가르치지 못한다고 꼬집고 있다.

해설 교육에 대한 사랑을 아이들에게 가르치지 못했다는 내용의 문장이다. instill은 in과 함께 쓰여 '~에게 …을 가르치다'라는 뜻으로 쓰인다.

오답 살펴보기 (a) **instate** 임명하다 (c) **instigate** 선동하다, 부추기다 (d) **install** 설치하다

18 (c)

해석 보건부는 몇 가지 보건법을 위반한 데 대해 해당 식당의 식품 면허를 취소했다.

해설 보건법을 위반했다면 처벌을 받을 것이므로 식품 면허(food license)를 취소한다는 내용이 가장 잘 어울린다. '취소하다, 철회하다'라는 뜻의 단어는 revoke이다.

어구 **violate** 위반하다, 어기다 **code** 법규, 규정

오답 살펴보기 (a) **rebuke** 꾸짖다 (b) **rebut** 논박하다, 반박하다 (d) **revolt** 반란을 일으키다

19 (c)

해석 가시철조망은 기물 파손자들의 공장부지 침입을 억제하지만 전부 막지는 못한다.

해설 주어인 The barbed wire fence(가시철조망)는 사람을 못 들어오게 하는 역할을 하므로 '단념시키다, 저지하다'라는 뜻의 deter가 동사로 오는 것이 알맞다.

어구 **barbed** 가시가 있는 **wire fence** 철조망 **vandal** 기물 파손자

오답 살펴보기 (a) **detach** 떼어내다 (b) **defer** 미루다, 연기하다 (d) **detract** (주의를) 딴 데로 돌리다

20 (d)

해석 나는 영화 엔딩을 애매모호하게 만들어서 사람들이 스스로 해석해 보도록 했다.

해설 빈칸 뒤의 내용을 보면 앞의 내용을 유추할 수 있다. 엔딩이 명확하지 않고 애매하게 끝나야 관객이 스스로 의미를 해석해 볼 수 있을 것이므로 ambiguous(애매모호한)가 정답이다.

어구 **interpret** 해석하다

오답 살펴보기 (a) **ambitious** 야심 있는 (b) **ambience** 분위기 (c) **ambivalent** 반대 감정이 병존하는

VP 09 | 의미가 비슷한 어휘

Check-up TEST

1 (b)	2 (a)	3 (a)	4 (b)	5 (d)
6 (d)	7 (a)	8 (d)	9 (b)	10 (c)
11 (b)	12 (a)	13 (a)	14 (a)	15 (b)
16 (d)	17 (b)	18 (b)	19 (d)	20 (c)

1 (b)

해석 A: 저 불쌍한 새끼 고양이는 한동안 굶주렸음에 틀림없어.
　　B: 맞아. 우리가 준 음식을 뚝딱 해치워 버렸잖아.

해설 starving(굶주린)이 힌트로, '(배가 몹시 고파서) 음식을 게걸스럽게 먹다'라는 뜻의 devour를 쓸 수 있다. 참고로 실제 시험에서 '책을 닥치는 대로 읽다'라는 뜻으로 devour books라는 표현이 출제되었으므로 함께 기억해 두자.

어구 **kitten** 새끼 고양이　**starving** 굶주린　**in mere moments** 순식간에

오답 살펴보기 (a) **swallow** 삼키다 (c) **munch** 우적우적 소리내어 먹다 (d) **ingest** 소화하다

2 (a)

해석 A: 공직에 출마하기 위한 절차를 알고 계세요?
　　B: 알고 있어요. 우선 만 달러의 기금을 조성하고 당신이 살고 있는 지역에서 천 명의 사람들로부터 서명을 받아야 해요.

해설 빈칸 뒤에 나온 signatures와 함께 쓸 수 있는 동사를 찾아야 한다. '서명을 받다'라고 할 때 동사는 collect를 쓴다.

어구 **procedure** 절차　**run for** 출마하다　**public office** 공직　**raise** 기금을 조성하다　**signature** 서명　**community** 지역사회

오답 살펴보기 (b) **stockpile** 비축하다 (c) **assemble** 조립하다 (d) **compile** 수집하다; 편집하다

3 (a)

해석 A: 네가 자원봉사 활동을 하려고 하는 건 좋은 일이지만, 매일 생활하면서 필요로 하는 것은 어떻게 충당하려고 그러니?
　　B: 걱정 마세요, 엄마. 이번 프로그램은 매달 소액의 음식과 기타 비용을 지원해줘요.

해설 단체나 기관에서 지원해주는 정기적인 수당이나 보조금을 stipend라고 한다.

어구 **volunteer** 자원봉사; 자원 봉사 일을 하다　**cover** 충당하다

오답 살펴보기 (b) **grant** (학교나 대학에 지원하는) 보조금 (c) **subsidy** (기업에 지원하는) 보조금 (d) **fund** 기금

4 (b)

해석 A: 이 공항은 정말 멋져. 모든 것이 아주 깨끗하고 완벽하게 제대로 작동하고 있어.
　　B: 맞아. 대규모의 청소 직원과 기술자들이 모든 것이 완벽하도록 최선을 다하고 있어.

해설 Yes라고 A의 의견에 동의하고 있으므로 A가 한 말 중에 perfect와 비슷한 의미의 단어를 찾으면 되는 문제다. '흠이

없는, 완벽한'이라는 뜻의 immaculate이 정답이다.

어구 **in perfect working order** 완벽하게 작동 중인

오답 살펴보기 (a) **meticulous** 꼼꼼한, 세심한 (c) **specific** 상세한 (d) **detailed** 세부적인

5 (d)

해석 A: 오늘 해변가에 있을 때 수영하러 갈 수 있었니?
　　B: 실은 파도가 위험할 정도로 높아서 수영을 할 수 없었어.

해설 수영을 할 수 없었다고 했고 빈칸 뒤에 large가 있으므로 waves(파도)가 들어가는 것이 가장 적절하다.

오답 살펴보기 (a) **plume** 깃털 (b) **billow** 연기의 기둥 (c) **ripple** 잔잔한 물결

6 (d)

해석 A: 몇 번 연기가 된 후에 두 국가 간의 평화 회담이 결국 재개되었어.
　　B: 그거 좋은 소식이구나. 마침내 양국 간에 관계가 개선될 수 있겠군.

해설 평화 회담으로 인해 개선될 수 있는 것은 양국 간의 관계 (relationship)이다.

어구 **peace talks** 평화회담　**resume** 다시 시작하다

오답 살펴보기 (a) **correlation** 상관관계 (b) **affiliation** 제휴 (c) **connection** 연결

7 (a)

해석 A: 그래, 결국 네가 꿈에 그리던 회사에서 일할 수 있게 되었구나.
　　B: 꼭 그런 것만은 아니야. 3개월 간 수습 기간을 거치고 난 다음에 언제든지 통지 없이 회사에서 쫓겨날 수도 있거든.

해설 회사에 입사했다고 했는데 해고될 수도 있다고 했으므로 '수습 기간'을 의미하는 probation이 정답이다.

어구 **secure a position** 직책을 차지하다　**let go** (직원을) 내보내다

오답 살펴보기 (b) **perjury** 위증 (c) **parole** 가석방 (d) **patrol** 순찰

8 (d)

해석 A: 당신 아내는 외출하기 전에 준비하느라 많은 시간을 보내는 것 같아요.
　　B: 나도 잘 알고 있지요. 아내는 자기 외모에 대해서는 항상 세심하다니까요.

해설 외출 전에 준비 시간이 길다고 했으므로 외모에 많이 신경 쓰는 성격임을 알 수 있다. 따라서 '꼼꼼한, 세심한'이라는 뜻의 meticulous가 정답이다.

어구 **Don't I know it.** 나도 알고 있다.

오답 살펴보기 (a) **selective** 선별적인, 우수한 (b) **immaculate** 완벽한 (c) **detailed** 세부적인

9 (b)

해석 A: 지구 온난화의 가장 큰 원인은 자동차 산업이야.
　　B: 너 아직 못 들었어? 가장 큰 자동차 업체 세 군데가 지구 온난화를 막는 연합을 구성했어.

해설 어떤 목적을 위해 조직하는 '연합, 연합회'를 coalition이라고 한다.

어구 **global warming** 지구 온난화 **form** 구성하다 **campaign** 운동을 벌이다

오답 살펴보기 (a) **merger** 합병 (c) **union** 조합 (d) **fusion** 융합, 결합

10 (c)

해석 A: 밖에 경찰차와 소방차가 왜 이렇게 많은 거지?
B: 오늘 아침에 조이스 빌딩에서 폭탄이 터졌거든. 건물에서 나오는 큰 연기 기둥을 쉽게 볼 수 있어.

해설 화재가 발생하여 생기는 '연기의 기둥'을 billow라고 한다.

어구 **fire truck** 소방차 **go off** 폭발하다

오답 살펴보기 (a) **wave** 파도 (b) **ripple** 물결 (d) **swell** 부어오름

11 (b)

해석 소화 불량을 막기 위해서는 음식을 삼키기 전에 적어도 20번은 씹도록 해야 한다.

해설 chew(씹다) 뒤에 올 수 있는 행동으로 가장 적절한 것은 swallow(삼키다)이다.

어구 **indigestion** 소화불량

오답 살펴보기 (a) **devour** 게걸스럽게 먹다 (d) **taste** 맛보다

12 (a)

해석 합병 후에 두 회사는 세계에서 가장 큰 통신 회사가 될 것이다.

해설 두 회사가 가장 큰 업체가 된다고 했으므로 '합병'이라는 뜻의 merger가 정답이다.

어구 **following** ~한 후에 **telecom** 전기 통신

오답 살펴보기 (b) **union** 조합 (c) **fusion** 융합 (d) **coalition** 연합

13 (a)

해석 수 년 간의 연구 결과에 따르면 교육적 성취와 성인으로서 전반적인 소득 사이에 상관관계가 있다.

해설 어떤 원인과 결과에 관련된 내용이므로 단순히 관계(relationship)보다는 상관관계(correlation)라고 표현하는 것이 더 적절하다.

어구 **attainment** 성취

오답 살펴보기 (b) **relationship** 관계 (c) **causation** 야기, 인과관계 (d) **affiliation** 제휴

14 (a)

해석 몇몇 극악무도한 범죄를 저지르고 난 후 그 연쇄살인범은 여러 차례의 종신형을 받았다.

해설 범죄에 대한 대가를 받은 것이므로 sentence(형벌, 선고)가 들어가는 것이 내용상 가장 적절하다.

어구 **commit** (범죄를) 저지르다 **heinous** 극악무도한

오답 살펴보기 (b) **ruling** 판결 (c) **verdict** 평결 (d) **judgment** 판단

15 (b)

해석 위원회는 정 씨를 근소한 표 차이로 이사회 의장으로 선출했다.

해설 by a narrow margin을 통해 투표를 통해 선출한 상황임을 알 수 있다. 이때 쓸 수 있는 동사는 '선출하다'라는 의미의 elect이다.

오답 살펴보기 (a) **appoint** 임명하다 (c) **select** 선택하다 (d) **designate** 지명하다

16 (d)

해석 올해 그 대학은 거의 절반에 해당하는 가난한 학생들에게 장학금을 지원했다.

해설 대학에서 학생들에게 주는 장학금이나 보조금을 grant라고 한다. 특히 need-based grant는 형편이 어려운 학생들에게 지급하는 장학금을 말한다.

오답 살펴보기 (a) **fund** 자금 (b) **capital** 자본 (c) **subsidy** (정부의) 보조금

17 (b)

해석 대학 측은 와그너 박사를 화학과 학장으로 임명했다.

해설 사람을 어떤 직책에 임명했다는 의미가 되어야 한다. '임명하다'는 동사 appoint를 쓴다.

오답 살펴보기 (a) **select** 선택하다 (c) **elect** 선출하다 (d) **opt** 선택하다

18 (b)

해석 대규모 시위자들은 유명한 운동선수의 살인 재판에서 유죄 평결이 난 것에 대해 불만을 토로했다.

해설 배심원단이 내리는 유죄, 무죄 여부를 '평결(verdict)'이라고 한다.

어구 **mass** 무리 **demonstrator** 시위자 **turn out** 나타나다, 등장하다 **protest** 시위하다 **murder trial** 살인 재판

오답 살펴보기 (a) **decision** 결정 (c) **judgment** 판결 (d) **sentence** 선고

19 (d)

해석 내 변호사는 우리 사건을 더 확실히 하기 위해서 나보고 위증을 저지르라고 요청했지만 나는 그것을 거부했다.

해설 재판에서 거짓말하는 행위를 위증(perjury)이라고 한다.

어구 **commit** 범죄를 저지르다 **solid** 견고한

오답 살펴보기 (a) **patrol** 순찰하다 (b) **probation** 집행유예, 수습기간 (c) **parole** 가석방

20 (c)

해석 이 잡지는 수년 동안 펴낸 단편 소설을 묶어서 양장본 책으로 출간했다.

해설 여러 이야기를 묶어서 하나의 책으로 펴내는 것을 compile(편집하다)이라고 한다.

어구 **publish** 출판하다 **hardcover book** 양장본 책

오답 살펴보기 (a) **collect** 수집하다 (b) **assemble** 조립하다; 집결하다 (d) **gather** 집결하다

Check-up TEST

1	(b)	2	(b)	3	(c)	4	(b)	5	(d)
6	(b)	7	(d)	8	(c)	9	(b)	10	(a)
11	(b)	12	(d)	13	(b)	14	(d)	15	(b)
16	(b)	17	(a)	18	(a)	19	(c)	20	(b)

1 (b)
해석 A: 내일이 중요한 날인 네게 행운을 빌게!
B: 고마워. 무대에서 주눅들지나 않았으면 좋겠어.

해설 '~하지 않길 바란다'라고 했으므로 문맥상 부정적인 어감의 표현이 들어가야 적절하다. 선택지 중에서 '주눅들다'라는 의미의 get cold feet이 정답이다.

어구 big day 중요한 날

오답 살펴보기 (a) turn a blind eye 못 본 척하다 (c) have a leg up (on) 선행하다, ~보다 먼저 시작하다 (d) play it by ear 그때그때 상황을 봐서 처리하다

2 (b)
해석 A: 죄송합니다, 경찰관님. 제가 규정 속도를 위반한 줄 몰랐네요.
B: 좋습니다. 이번에는 봐드리죠. 다음부턴 과속하지 마세요.

해설 과속을 적발한 경찰관이 운전자에게 All right이라고 했고, 뒤에는 don't do it again이라고 충고하고 있으므로 '처벌을 면한'이라는 의미의 off the hook이 정답이다.

오답 살펴보기 (a) around the clock 밤낮으로 (c) down the tubes 못 쓰게 된, 파괴된 (d) on the rocks 파탄 직전인

3 (c)
해석 A: 이제 제품 광고 제작으로 넘어가야 하지 않을까?
B: 기다려 봐. 섣불리 행동하지 말자. 제품설계를 마저 마무리해야 하거든.

해설 아직 끝내지 못한 작업이 있으므로 성급하게 행동하지 말자는 논리가 적합하다. 따라서 '섣불리 행동하다'라는 의미의 jump the gun이 정답이다.

오답 살펴보기 (a) call it quits 비긴 것으로 하다 (b) ring a bell 낯이 익다, 들어본 적이 있다 (d) get the picture 이해하다

4 (b)
해석 A: 제리는 항상 불평만 해서 날 정말 짜증나게 해.
B: 동감이야. 사무실의 모든 사람들에게 골칫거리지.

해설 다른 사람들을 짜증나게 하는 점으로 보아 부정적인 의미의 표현이 적절하다. '골칫거리'라는 의미의 pain in the neck이 정답이다.

어구 get on one's nerves 신경을 건드리다, 짜증나게 하다

오답 살펴보기 (a) shot in the arm 활력소, 기운을 회복시켜 주는 것 (c) bundle of nerves 신경과민인 사람 (d) skeleton in the closet 남에게 알리기 싫은 비밀

5 (d)
해석 A: 이 도시는 내가 지난번에 왔을 때보다 훨씬 좋아진 것 같아.
B: 맞아. 지난 몇 년 동안 정말 눈부신 발전을 했거든.

해설 도시가 훨씬 좋아졌다고 언급한 점을 보아 '크게 발전하다'라는 의미의 come a long way가 정답이다.

오답 살펴보기 (a) bridge the gap 격차를 좁히다 (b) turn a blind eye 못 본 척하다 (c) make out like a bandit 손쉽게 큰돈을 벌다, 쉽게 성공하다

6 (b)
해석 A: 이제는 혼자서 금전등록기를 맡아도 무리가 없나요?
B: 아직 배워가는 중이지만 곧 잘 할 수 있을 것 같아요.

해설 곧 잘 할 수 있을 것 같다는 말 앞에 올 수 있는 표현을 유추해 보면 '~에 대해 배우다, 요령을 터득하다'라는 의미의 learn the ropes가 적절하다.

어구 get the hang of ~을 할 줄 알게 되다, 이해하다

오답 살펴보기 (a) make ends meet 겨우 먹고 살만큼 벌다 (c) come to a head (종기가) 곪아서 터질 듯하다 (d) gather stream 속도가 붙다

7 (d)
해석 A: 정부가 불법노동자들을 단속할 거라고 들었어.
B: 맞아. 불법으로 노동자를 고용하는 고용주에게는 무거운 벌금을 부과할 거래.

해설 illegal이라는 단어가 사용된 것으로 보아 '불법으로'라는 의미의 under the table이 들어가는 것이 적절하다.

어구 crack down on 엄히 단속하다, 탄압하다

오답 살펴보기 (a) under the radar 알려지지 않은 (b) across the board 전반에 걸쳐 (c) around the clock 밤낮으로

8 (c)
해석 A: 많이 피곤해 보이는데 집에 가서 좀 쉬지 그래요.
B: 많이 지쳤지만 제 교대 근무를 끝마쳐야 해요.

해설 exhausted와 마찬가지로 '기진맥진한'이라는 의미의 dead on one's feet이 들어가는 것이 적절하다.

어구 exhausted 지친 shift 교대 근무

오답 살펴보기 (a) bring home the bacon 밥벌이를 하다, ~에 성공하다 (b) look on the bright side 긍정적으로 생각하다 (d) run off one's mouth 시끄럽게 떠벌리다

9 (b)
해석 A: 이 그림은 그림 속 여자의 입 모양이 이상한 것 빼고는 자연스러워요.
B: 그러게요. 입 모양이 옥의 티네요. 다시 가서 고쳐야겠어요.

해설 여자의 입 모양만 유일하게 이상하다는 점을 미뤄볼 때 '옥의 티' 또는 '허점'이라는 의미의 fly in the ointment가 적절한 정답이다.

오답 살펴보기 (a) thorn in one's side 눈엣가시, 고민거리 (c) house of cards 엉성한 계획 (d) drop in the bucket 새 발의 피

10 (a)
해석 A: 정확히 30분 내에 제안서를 제출해야 해요.

B: 걱정하지 말아요. 저는 막판에 일을 가장 잘 하거든요.

해설 시간이 얼마 남지 않은 상황을 미뤄볼 때 '막판에' 또는 '마지막 기회에'라는 의미의 at the eleventh hour가 가장 적절한 정답이다.

오답 살펴보기 (b) at the drop of a hat 즉각, 주저하지 않고
(c) in the hot seat 매우 곤란한 처지에 놓인
(d) in the nick of time 아슬아슬하게 때를 맞추어

11 (b)
해석 올스타 팀은 NBA 선수들 중에서도 최고들로 구성되어 있다.

해설 올스타 팀은 최고들만 뽑아서 구성한 팀인 만큼 '최고' 또는 '정선된 것'을 의미하는 the cream of the crop이 정답이다.

오답 살펴보기 (a) a close call 위기의 순간, 아슬아슬한 상황
(c) an open secret 공공연한 비밀
(d) the bottom of the barrel 밑바닥, 최악의 상황

12 (d)
해석 그린 상원의원은 언론에서 그의 은밀한 비밀을 폭로하자 사퇴하라는 압력을 받았다.

해설 동사 expose의 목적어로 가장 적합하며 문맥상 가장 논리적인 표현은 '남에게 말할 수 없는 비밀'을 의미하는 a skeleton in one's closet이다.

어구 step down from office 사퇴하다, 물러나다

오답 살펴보기 (a) an ace in the hole 비장의 무기
(b) a nail in the coffin 결정타, 심각한 타격
(c) water under the bridge 지나간 일, 과거지사

13 (b)
해석 우리는 부장님이 버럭 화를 낼까 봐 나쁜 소식을 보고하기가 꺼려진다.

해설 나쁜 소식을 보고할 수 없는 이유를 유추해볼 때 '버럭 화를 내다'라는 의미의 fly off the handle이 정답이다.

오답 살펴보기 (a) keep one's cool 침착하다, 냉정을 유지하다
(c) beat a dead horse 헛수고하다, 이미 끝난 일을 다시 문제 삼다 (d) hit the floor 춤을 추다

14 (d)
해석 그 철학자의 강의는 아무리 이해하려고 애를 써봐도 도저히 이해할 수 없었다.

해설 강의 내용을 따라가기 위해 최선의 노력을 다했음에도 불구하고 이해할 수 없었다는 논리가 적합하다. 따라서 '이해하기 힘든'이라는 의미의 over one's head를 쓸 수 있다.

오답 살펴보기 (a) across the board 전반적으로 (b) down and out 빈털터리인 (c) under the table 불법으로, 비밀리에

15 (b)
해석 순진해 보일지 몰라도 그녀에겐 눈에 보이는 것 이상의 것이 있다.

해설 '눈에 보이는 것 이상의 것'이라고 할 때 more than meets the eye라는 표현을 쓴다. 여기서는 more 뒤에 to her가 삽입된 형태이다.

오답 살펴보기 (a) have more than one string to one's bow 차선책이 있다 (c) There's more than one way to skin a

cat. 문제를 해결하는 데는 여러 가지 방법이 있다.
(d) shake a stick at ~을 알아차리다

16 (b)
해석 나는 모든 시민들에게 누구든 도움이 필요한 사람이 있으면 적극적으로 나서서 도와줄 것을 당부한다.

해설 적극적으로 나서서 도움이 필요한 사람을 돕는다는 의미가 적합하므로 come to the fore(중요한 역할을 하다)가 정답이다.

오답 살펴보기 (a) play it by ear 그때그때 상황을 봐서 처리하다
(c) kick the bucket 죽다
(d) come to a head (종기가) 곪아서 터질듯하다

17 (a)
해석 말투가 거친 그 DJ는 방송에 실릴 수 있는 내용의 한계를 초월함으로써 유명세를 탔다.

해설 내용상 선택지 중에서 가장 적절한 표현은 '한계를 초월하다'는 의미의 push the envelope이다.

어구 potty-mouthed 말투가 거친　rise to fame 유명해지다, 명성을 날리다

오답 살펴보기 (b) face the music (자신의 행동에 대해) 비난[벌]을 받다 (c) put one's foot in one's mouth (본의 아니게) 실언을 하다 (d) fight an uphill battle 힘겨운 싸움을 하다

18 (a)
해석 그 가수가 토크쇼에서 자신의 음반 회사에 대해 비난을 한 것은 정말로 실언이었다.

해설 가수가 자신의 음반 회사에 대해 비난했다면 '실언'이었다고 할 수 있다. '본의 아니게 실언을 하다'라는 뜻을 가진 숙어는 put one's foot in one's mouth이다.

어구 record label 레코드 레이블, 음반 회사

오답 살펴보기 (b) show one's hand 손에 든 패를 보이다, 속셈을 보여주다 (c) open the floodgates 오랫동안 금지되어 온 것을 해금하다 (d) put the cart before the horse 일의 순서를 뒤바꾸다

19 (c)
해석 남들에게 뒤지지 않으려고 애를 쓰면 물질적으로는 부유해질지 몰라도 재정 건전성 개선에는 별 도움이 되지 않는다.

해설 '남에게 뒤지지 않으려 애쓰다'라는 의미의 keep up with the Joneses가 가장 적합한 표현이다.

오답 살펴보기 (a) bring home the bacon 밥벌이를 하다, ~에 성공하다 (b) have an ax to grind 불평불만이 있다
(d) think outside the box 고정관념에서 벗어나다

20 (b)
해석 그 전자회사는 훌륭한 신형 휴대폰 디자인이라는 비장의 카드를 가지고 있다.

해설 brilliant(훌륭한, 멋진)라는 긍정적인 단어가 나왔으므로 '비장의 카드'라는 의미의 an ace in the hole이 문맥상 가장 적합한 표현이다.

오답 살펴보기 (a) a carrot on a stick 목표 달성을 위한 유인책
(c) the best of both worlds 두 가지 상이한 것 각각의 장점
(d) have nothing to show 보여줄 만한 성과가 없다

오답 살펴보기 (a) **duty-free** 면세의 (c) **frugality** 절약, 검소
(d) **tax-exempt** 비과세의

5 (b)

해석 A: 차 구입에 가격을 얼마나 보고 있니?
B: 2만 5천 달러에서 3만 달러 가격 범위 내에서 생각 중이야.

해설 twenty-five to thirty thousand dollars라는 가격 범위 (price range)가 언급되었으므로 '범위'라는 뜻의 range가 정답이다.

어구 **look to V** ~하는 것을 고려해보다, 생각해보다

오답 살펴보기 (a) **variety** 여러 가지, 각양각색
(c) **assortment** 모음, 조합 (d) **gathering** 모임

6 (d)

해석 A: 이 셔츠 좀 헐렁해 보여. 이것보다 한 치수 적은 걸 사야 할 것 같아.
B: 세탁하면 옷이 줄어들 수도 있다는 걸 명심해서, 보다 큰 치수를 사는 편이 좋을 거야.

해설 세탁하면 옷이 변형될 수도 있다는 점 때문에 치수가 큰 걸 사는 편이 좋겠다고 B가 말하는 것으로 보면, 빈칸에 들어갈 말은 '(옷이) 줄어들다'라는 의미의 shrink이다.

어구 **keep in mind** 명심하다

오답 살펴보기 (a) **stretch** 늘어나다, 펴지다 (b) **skid** 미끄러지다
(c) **stink** 냄새가 나다

7 (b)

해석 A: 미치가 제시간에 출근한 적이 있니?
B: 전혀. 내가 아는 한 그는 항상 늦어.

해설 제시간에 온 적이 없다는 B의 대답으로 미루어 보면, 빈칸에 들어갈 말은 '꾸준하게' 혹은 '지속적으로'라는 의미의 consistently이다.

어구 **on time** 정시에, 늦지 않은　**as far as I know** 내가 아는 한

오답 살펴보기 (a) **delightfully** 기쁘게 (c) **infrequently** 드물게, 어쩌다 (d) **remorsefully** 뉘우치면서

8 (a)

해석 A: 아야! 칼에 손을 베었어.
B: 반창고를 붙이기 전에 항균 비누로 상처를 소독해야 한다는 점을 명심해.

해설 항균 비누를 이용해서 상처에 해야 할 일은 소독이므로 빈칸에는 '소독하다'라는 의미의 disinfect가 들어가야 한다.

어구 **antibacterial** 항균의　**bandaid** 반창고

오답 살펴보기 (b) **vaccinate** 예방 접종하다
(c) **hospitalize** 입원시키다 (d) **recuperate** 건강을 회복하다

9 (c)

해석 A: 자동차 정비사들이 차에 무슨 문제가 있는지 알아냈어?
B: 어, 엔진 내부에 뭔가 문제가 있어서, 정비사들이 수리를 하기 위해서는 엔진을 분해해야 할 거야.

해설 엔진 내부 문제이므로 이를 해결하기 위해서는 엔진을 분해해

Section 3
Actual Test 01-06

Actual Test 01

1	(c)	2	(d)	3	(d)	4	(b)	5	(b)
6	(d)	7	(b)	8	(a)	9	(c)	10	(c)
11	(a)	12	(c)	13	(b)	14	(a)	15	(c)
16	(c)	17	(b)	18	(a)	19	(c)	20	(d)
21	(b)	22	(c)	23	(a)	24	(d)	25	(b)
26	(b)	27	(d)	28	(c)	29	(d)	30	(c)

1 (c)

해석 A: 죄송합니다만, 박물관 가는 길 좀 알려 주시겠습니까?
B: 네, 전쟁 기념관에서 우측으로 가신 다음에 직진하세요.

해설 war memorial은 '전쟁 기념관'을 뜻한다. 따라서 문맥상 빈칸에 들어갈 말로는 memorial이 가장 적합하다.

어구 **war memorial** 전쟁 기념관

오답 살펴보기 (a) **souvenir** 기념품 (b) **artifact** 인공물, 공예품
(d) **remembrance** 기념품, 유물

2 (d)

해석 A: 이 롤렉스시계는 모조품 같은데요.
B: 고객님, 제가 이것은 진품임을 보증해 드리겠습니다.

해설 물건이 가짜인지 의심하는 고객에게 진품이라고 주장하는 내용이므로 '진품의'를 의미하는 genuine이 들어가야 한다.

어구 **imitation** 모조품

오답 살펴보기 (a) **resistant** 저항력 있는 (b) **dominant** 우세한
(c) **cozy** 아늑한

3 (d)

해석 A: 마침내 시에서 공공장소에 쓰레기통을 설치하기 시작했다는 것을 알았어.
B: 쓰레기를 줄이려는 그들의 노력에는 찬사를 보내지만, 그보다는 더 노력해야 해.

해설 시에서 공공장소에 쓰레기통을 설치한 사실은 B가 말하는 쓰레기를 줄이기 위한 노력으로 볼 수 있기 때문에 '갈채를 보내다, 칭찬하다'라는 의미의 applaud가 들어가야 한다.

어구 **litter** 쓰레기

오답 살펴보기 (a) **deify** 신격화하다 (b) **retaliate** 보복하다
(c) **manifest** 드러내다, 나타나다

4 (b)

해석 A: 저가로 가정용품을 사기에 좋은 곳을 알고 있니?
B: 할인 판매점을 알아보는 편이 좋을 거야.

해설 저가 판매점을 묻고 있으므로 '저가의 물건'을 의미하는 bargain이 가장 적절하다.

야 할 것이다. 따라서 빈칸에 들어가야 할 단어는 '분해하다'라는 의미를 지닌 disassemble이다.

어구 **mechanic** 자동차 정비사 **figure out** 파악하다, 알아내다

오답 살펴보기 (a) **dissuade** ~를 하지 않도록 설득하다, 만류하다 (b) **disparage** 폄하하다 (d) **discriminate** 차별하다

10 (c)

해석 A: 법원이 그 제조업체에게 강을 오염시켰다는 이유로 3천만 달러의 벌금을 부과했어.
B: 금액이 큰 것 같이 들리지만, 그처럼 큰 회사한텐 사소한 액수야.

해설 such a large company(그처럼 큰 회사)란 표현을 통해 B는 벌금의 액수가 그 회사에게 그다지 크지 않은 것으로 보고 있음을 알 수 있다. 따라서 빈칸에 들어갈 말로는 '사소한'이라는 의미의 trivial이 가장 적절하다.

어구 **sum** 액수

오답 살펴보기 (a) **lucrative** 수익성이 좋은 (b) **consequential** 중대한 (d) **provocative** 도발적인

11 (a)

해석 막차는 오늘밤 11시에 역에서 출발할 것입니다.

해설 막차가 밤 11시에 출발한다는 의미에서 '출발하다'는 의미를 지닌 동사 depart를 쓰는 것이 가장 적절하다.

오답 살펴보기 (c) **meander** 두서없이 거닐다 (d) **fleet** 도망치다

12 (c)

해석 그녀는 자신의 혐의를 인정하지 않았는데, 그럴 만한 이유가 있었던 게 혐의는 사실이었다.

해설 for good 뒤에 reason이 사용되면 '그럴 만한[충분한] 이유가 있는'이라는 의미가 된다. 참고로 for no reason은 '아무런 이유 없이'란 뜻이다.

어구 **admit to** ~을 인정하다 **charge** 혐의

오답 살펴보기 (a) **rationale** 근거; 이론적 설명 (d) **basis** 기초, 토대

13 (b)

해석 1969년 7월, 닐 암스트롱이 달 표면을 걸었을 때 인류 역사상 중요한 이정표가 세워졌다.

해설 milestone은 역사적 중요성이 있는 '획기적인 사건'을 의미한다. landmark는 주로 특정 지역을 상징적으로 나타내는 자연물이나 건물 등을 의미하기 때문에 정답으로 보기 힘들다.

오답 살펴보기 (a) **benchmark** 기준점 (d) **breakthrough** 돌파구

14 (a)

해석 수십 년간, 미국 정부는 불법적인 마약에 대한 전쟁을 벌여왔다.

해설 wage a war는 '전쟁을 벌이다'라는 표현이다. 참고로 engage를 사용해서 '전투하다'라는 뜻을 나타내려면 engage in battle이 되어야 한다.

오답 살펴보기 (b) **battle** 전투하다 (c) **engage** 약속하다; (적군과) 교전하다

15 (c)

해석 모든 인간이 언젠가는 육류의 섭취를 멈출 것이라는 이 단체의 믿음은 단지 희망사항일 뿐이다.

해설 wishful thinking은 '희망사항' 또는 '희망사항에 불과한 일'을 나타낸다.

오답 살펴보기 (a) **ignorant** 무식한 (d) **optimistic** 긍정적인

16 (c)

해석 근로자의 점심시간을 45분에서 30분으로 단축한 것이 현재 노조의 파업을 초래한 화근이었다.

해설 lead to의 의미를 고려해 보면 빈칸에는 어떤 사건의 원인을 가리키는 표현이 들어가야 한다. 따라서 '한계', '화근'을 의미하는 straw that broke the camel's back이 정답이다.

오답 살펴보기 (a) **storm in a teacup** (별것도 아닌) 괜한 소동 (b) **square peg in a round hole** 부적임자, 부적격한 것 (d) **shot heard around the world** 전 세계에 울려퍼진 역사적 사건

17 (b)

해석 해외에서의 한국 TV 프로그램 및 음악에 대한 인기는 한국문화의 또 다른 측면에 관한 국제적인 관심을 불러 일으켰다.

해설 '관심을 불러일으키다'라는 의미로 동사 kindle을 사용한다. kindle은 본래 '불을 붙이다'의 뜻인데, 주로 '(흥미 등을) 불러 일으키다'라는 의미로 사용된다.

어구 **aspect** 측면, 양상

오답 살펴보기 (a) **illuminate** 비추다, 밝히다 (c) **suffocate** 질식시키다 (d) **quench** (갈증을) 풀다; (불을) 끄다

18 (a)

해석 G20 회원국들은 점차 증가하는 기후 변화 문제에 대응하기 위해 정상회담을 개최할 예정이다.

해설 문맥상 현안을 풀기 위해 G20 회원국들이 개최할 수 있는 것을 찾아야 한다. 이와 가장 밀접한 관계가 있는 것은 '정상회담'을 의미하는 summit talks이다.

오답 살펴보기 (c) **conference** 회의 (d) **forum** 공개 토론, 포럼

19 (c)

해석 출근 시간이 다가오는데도 그는 여전히 출근길에 꾸물거리고 있다.

해설 in spite of가 있으므로 출근 시간이 다가오는데도 빨리 가는 것이 아닌 그 반대 행동을 한다는 내용이 들어가야 자연스럽게 연결된다. '꾸물거리다'라는 뜻의 dawdle이 정답이다.

어구 **running late for work** 출근에 늦어지다 **on the way to** ~에 가는 길에

오답 살펴보기 (a) **meddle** (남의 일에) 간섭하다 (b) **waddle** 뒤뚱뒤뚱 걷다 (d) **twiddle** 만지작거리다

20 (d)

해석 만약 기분이 울적하거나 자신감이 없다고 느껴지면, 우리의 생활 지도 카운슬러들이 여러분을 돕기 위해 여기에 있다는 점을 기억해 주세요.

해설 guidance counselor는 '(학생들을 위한) 생활 지도 카운슬

러'를 의미한다.

어구 **feel down** 기분이 울적하다

오답 살펴보기 (a) **council** 의회, 자문 위원회 (b) **councilor** 고문관; 평의원, 의원 (c) **counsel** 조언, 충고

21 (b)

해석 손톱을 깨무는 습관을 치료하기 위한 가장 손쉬운 방법은 손톱에 쓴 맛이 나는 물질을 바르는 것이다.

해설 손톱에 쓴 맛이 나는 물질을 바르면 손톱을 깨물 때 쓴맛을 느낄 것이므로, 손톱을 깨무는 습관을 치료할 수 있을 것이다. 습관을 '치료하다'라는 의미에서 treat를 써야 한다.

어구 **nail-biting** 손톱을 깨무는   **bad-tasting** 쓴 맛이 나는

오답 살펴보기 (a) **approach** 접근하다 (c) **recover** 회복하다 (d) **inhibit** 억제하다, 제지하다

22 (c)

해석 한 지역 주민이 최근 급류 타기에서 구사일생으로 살아남았다.

해설 narrowly survived라는 말이 있으므로 '위기일발, 구사일생'이라는 뜻의 close call을 생각해 볼 수 있다.

어구 **narrowly** 가까스로   **white-water rafting** 급류 타기

오답 살펴보기 (d) **tight** 단단한, 꽉 죄인

23 (a)

해석 그 소규모 제조업체는 적대적 인수 합병을 성공적으로 물리칠 수 있었다.

해설 적대적 인수 합병에 성공적으로 대처했다는 의미에서 '물리치다'라는 뜻을 지닌 repel이 가장 적절하다.

어구 **hostile takeover** 적대적 인수 합병

오답 살펴보기 (b) **repeal** 폐지하다 (c) **rectify** 바로잡다 (d) **remit** 송금하다; 처벌을 면제해 주다

24 (d)

해석 로켓 기술의 발전은 우주 탐험이라는 새로운 시대의 도래를 알렸다.

해설 '알리다, 포고하다'라는 뜻의 herald는 age나 era등과 결합하여 '새로운 시대의 도래를 알리다'라는 의미를 갖는다.

어구 **exploration** 탐험

오답 살펴보기 (a) **marshal** (사람, 생각 등을) 결집시키다 (b) **punctuate** 간간이 끼어들다; 구두점을 찍다 (c) **tolerate** 참다

25 (b)

해석 내가 여직원에게 그녀가 원치 않는 접근을 했다는 혐의는 내 명성을 깎아 내리려는 의도로 만들어진 새빨간 거짓말이다.

해설 내용상 자신의 혐의가 명예를 훼손하려고 만들어진 거짓말이라고 주장하고 있기 때문에 downright가 적절하다. downright lie는 '새빨간 거짓말'을 의미한다.

어구 **accusation** 혐의   **unwanted** 원치 않는   **advances** (성관계 등을 노린) 접근   **reputation** 평판, 명성

오답 살펴보기 (a) **discourteous** 예의 없는 (c) **hospitable** 친절한 (d) **probable** 있을 법한

26 (b)

해석 협상을 체결하기 위해서는 객관적인 중재자의 도움이 필요하다.

해설 협상을 완결하기 위해서는 사심 없이 객관적으로 중재하는 사람이 필요할 것이다. disinterested는 '객관적인'이란 의미를 갖는다.

어구 **mediator** 중재자

오답 살펴보기 (a) **interested** 타산적인, 이해관계가 있는 (c) **uninterested** 무관심한, 냉담한 (d) **uninteresting** 재미없는, 시시한

27 (d)

해석 포도주를 마시면 건강에 이롭다고 주장하는 연구가 나올 때마다, 이를 반박하는 다른 연구가 나오는 것처럼 보인다.

해설 포도주가 건강에 이롭다는 주장에 대해 또 다른(another) 연구가 나왔다는 것은 문맥상 이를 반박하는 연구가 나오고 있다는 점을 의미한다. '반박하다'라는 의미를 지닌 단어는 refute이다.

어구 **bring about** ~을 초래하다, 야기하다

오답 살펴보기 (a) **espouse** 지지하다, 신봉하다 (b) **groom** 다듬다 (c) **bolster** 지지하다, 받치다

28 (c)

해석 이번 연구는 자부심과 우울함이 장차 서로 연관되어 있다는 점을 나타내 준다.

해설 가까운 장래에 서로 연관이 있을 거라는 의미가 알맞으므로 '가망성 있게'라는 뜻으로 미래의 어떤 가능성을 나타내는 부사인 prospectively가 정답이다.

어구 **self-esteem** 자부심

오답 살펴보기 (a) **lucratively** 유리하게, 이익이 되게 (b) **introspectively** 내성적으로, 자기 반성적으로 (d) **deceptively** 기만적으로, 남을 현혹하게

29 (d)

해석 죄송합니다만, 홀링스 교수님께서 안식 기간 중이셔서 다음 학기까지는 돌아오지 않으실 것입니다.

해설 교수가 일상 업무에서 벗어나 연구나 여행 등을 하는 기간을 sabbatical(안식 기간)이라고 부른다.

오답 살펴보기 (a) **colloquium** 학회, 세미나 (b) **edification** 교화, 의식 고양 (c) **tenure** 재임 기간; 종신 재직원

30 (c)

해석 마약 단속반들은 국내로 들어오는 극소량의 마약도 금지시킬 수 있다.

해설 마약 단속원들이 하는 일은 마약의 국내 반입을 금지시키는 것이다. 선택지에서 '금지하다'라는 의미를 갖는 단어는 interdict이다.

어구 **drug enforcement agent** 마약 단속원   **narcotics** 마약

오답 살펴보기 (a) **denigrate** 모욕하다 (b) **wrangle** 언쟁을 벌이다 (d) **flank** 측면에 위치하다

Actual Test 02

1 (c)	2 (d)	3 (a)	4 (a)	5 (c)
6 (a)	7 (a)	8 (c)	9 (a)	10 (d)
11 (b)	12 (a)	13 (b)	14 (a)	15 (c)
16 (c)	17 (b)	18 (a)	19 (b)	20 (a)
21 (b)	22 (b)	23 (c)	24 (a)	25 (d)
26 (c)	27 (c)	28 (b)	29 (c)	30 (d)

1 (c)

해석 A: 파리들이 내 머리 주변에서 계속 윙윙거리고 있어.
B: 그래, 정말 성가신 놈들이야. 파리채로 몇 놈들을 잡아볼게.

해설 파리가 윙윙거리고 있는 것은 꽤나 성가신 일임을 쉽게 유추할 수 있다. '성가신 것'이라는 표현은 nuisance로 나타낸다.

어구 buzz 윙윙거리다   fly swatter 파리채

오답 살펴보기 (a) fusion 융합 (b) retreat 후퇴
(d) diploma 졸업 증서

2 (d)

해석 A: 여기 이번에 태어난 내 아들 사진이야.
B: 확실히 자네 아들임을 알 수 있겠군. 아이가 자네랑 꼭 닮았어.

해설 B가 사진을 보고 A의 아들임을 분명히 알 수 있겠다고 말하는 점으로 보아, A의 아들이 A와 꼭 닮았다고 유추해 볼 수 있다. the spitting image는 '꼭 빼닮은 것', 혹은 '꼭 빼닮은 사람'을 의미한다.

어구 definitely 분명히   tell 구별하다, 식별하다

오답 살펴보기 (a) a broken record 같은 말을 계속 되풀이하는 사람
(b) the whole kit and caboodle 이것저것 모두, 전부
(c) moral fiber 도덕심

3 (a)

해석 A: 공주님의 서거 소식을 들었을 때 어떤 기분이 들었니?
B: 난 엄청난 충격을 받고 곧바로 울어 버렸어.

해설 공주의 사망 소식에 바로 울어버렸다는 점에서 B가 받은 충격이 컸음을 쉽게 알 수 있다. devastated가 '충격을 받은'이라는 의미이다.

어구 break down into tears 울음을 터뜨리다

오답 살펴보기 (b) elated 마냥 행복한 (c) procrastinated 질질 끄는
(d) intrigued 매우 흥미로워 하는

4 (a)

해석 A: 새로 온 매니저가 상점을 완전히 성공적인 곳으로 바꾸어 놓았어.
B: 정말 그렇다니까. 우리 가게가 망해가던 곳에서 순식간에 수익성이 좋은 곳으로 변했어.

해설 turned this store around란 표현을 통해서 사업이 잘 되지 않던 곳이 높은 수익성을 거두는 곳으로 전환되었음을 유추해 볼 수 있다. 따라서 정답은 '수익성이 높은'이라는 의미를 지닌 lucrative가 된다.

어구 turn around 상황을 호전시키다   I'll say. 그러니까 말이야.

오답 살펴보기 (b) pricey 값비싼 (c) compelling (너무 흥미로워서) 눈을 뗄 수 없는 (d) fabulous 기막히게 좋은

5 (c)

해석 A: 왜 그 커피숍이 이름을 바꿨을까?
B: 내가 알기로는, 다른 커피숍에서 예전 이름이 자신들의 저작권을 침해했다고 주장했대.

해설 목적어 copyright와 어울리는 동사를 찾으면 되는 문제로, infringe는 '(권리 등을) 침해하다'라는 의미로 쓰이는 동사이다.

어구 as far as ~하는 한   copyright 저작권

오답 살펴보기 (a) obstruct 막다, 방해하다 (b) certify 증명하다
(d) aggravate 악화시키다

6 (a)

해석 A: 항상 겨울 난방 요금이 너무 비싸게 나와.
B: 나한테는 네 집에 단열 처리가 더 필요하다는 소리로 들려. 단열 처리를 하면 난방비를 줄이는 데 도움이 될 거야.

해설 겨울의 난방비를 줄이기 위해 필요한 것은 단열 처리이다. 따라서 정답으로는 '단열', 혹은 '절연'의 뜻을 지닌 insulation이 적합하다.

어구 bill 청구서

오답 살펴보기 (b) insurance 보험 (c) compliance 준수, 명령에 따름
(d) complication 복잡(함); 합병증

7 (a)

해석 A: 나는 아직도 히트팀이 결승전에서 우승했다는 것을 믿을 수가 없어.
B: 나도 마찬가지야. 상대방이 확실히 더 나은 팀이었지만, 결국 히트팀이 운이 더 좋았어.

해설 마지막에 히트팀이 운이 더 좋았다는 B의 말로 미루어 보면, 실상 상대방이 더 나은 팀이었음을 유추해 볼 수 있다. 따라서 '확실히, 의심의 여지없이'라는 의미를 지닌 undoubtedly가 정답이 된다.

어구 luck out 운이 좋다

오답 살펴보기 (b) undeservingly 받을 자격 없이
(c) understandably 당연하게도 (d) unabashedly 염치없이

8 (c)

해석 A: 사령관님, 제 생각에는 이번 전투에서 우리가 이길 확률이 없습니다.
B: 왜 그렇게 생각하나? 우리는 3대 1로 적군보다 수가 우세하네.

해설 3대 1이라는 수치가 나온 것으로 보아, 문맥상 아군의 수가 적보다 많다는 의미가 되어야 한다. 따라서 '수적으로 우세하다'라는 의미를 지닌 outnumber가 정답이 된다.

오답 살펴보기 (a) simulate 흉내 내다, 가장하다 (b) fortify 강화하다
(d) suppress 진압하다

9 (a)

해석 A: 클라라의 아기가 곧 태어날 예정이지, 그렇지?
B: 이런, 소식을 듣지 못한 모양이구나. 그녀는 유산하는 바람

에 아이를 잃고 말았어.

해설 아이를 잃었다는 표현을 통해서 아기가 유산되었음을 알 수 있다. '유산'이란 표현은 miscarriage로 나타낼 수 있다.

어구 due ~하기로 예정된

오답 살펴보기 (b) mishap 작은 사고 (c) miracle 기적
(d) mitigation 완화, 경감

10 (d)

해석 A: 본인의 성격 중 어떤 측면이 자신이 이 일에 적합하다고 생각하게끔 만들었나요?
　　 B: 저는 자신감이 있는 사람이기 때문에, 다른 사람들에게 제 의견을 제시하는 데 전혀 문제가 없을 것입니다.

해설 다른 이에게 자신의 의견을 제시하는 일에 아무런 문제가 없을 것이라는 점은 본인에게 자신감이 넘친다는 말이다. 따라서 정답은 '자신이 있는'이라는 의미를 가진 assertive가 된다.

어구 fit 적합한, 맞는　individual 사람, 개인

오답 살펴보기 (a) taciturn 과묵한 (b) slothful 게으른
(c) resentful 억울해 하는

11 (b)

해석 그녀는 논쟁에서 타협을 거부하고 원칙을 고수했다.

해설 원칙을 고수했다는 것으로 보아 의미상 타협하지 않았다라는 뜻이 들어가야 자연스럽다. compromise(타협하다)가 정답이다.

어구 hold to 고수하다

오답 살펴보기 (a) concede 인정하다, 수긍하다 (c) condone 용납하다 (d) constitute ~을 이루다, 구성하다

12 (a)

해석 의회는 방금 동성 결혼을 합법화하는 연방법을 제정했다.

해설 '(법을) 제정하다'라는 의미를 나타내기 위해서는 동사 enact를 사용해야 한다.

어구 federal 연방 정부의　legalize 합법화하다

오답 살펴보기 (b) verify 확인하다; 입증하다 (c) pacify 진정시키다, 달래다 (d) enshrine 소중히 간직하다; 모시다

13 (b)

해석 세계의 주요 대도시들은 배출 기준을 강화하고 버스의 동력을 수소로 전환시킴으로써 오염을 감소시켜 왔다.

해설 배출 기준 강화 및 버스의 수소 연료 채택 등은 오염 감소를 위한 조치로 볼 수 있다. 따라서 정답은 '오염'이란 뜻을 지닌 pollution이 된다.

어구 tighten 더 엄격하게 강화하다　emission 배출　convert 전환시키다　hydrogen 수소　power 동력, 에너지

오답 살펴보기 (a) preservation 보존 (c) recycling 재활용
(d) anomaly 변칙, 이례

14 (a)

해석 양면 거울은 한 쪽 면이 투명하고, 다른 한 쪽 면은 불투명하다.

해설 양면 거울 혹은 양방향 거울(two-way mirror)의 속성을 생각해 보면, 한 면은 불투명하고 다른 한 면은 투명하다는 점을

유추해 볼 수 있다. 따라서 정답은 '투명한'이라는 의미를 지닌 transparent가 된다.

어구 two-way mirror 한 쪽이 유리창인 거울, 양면 거울　opaque 불투명한

오답 살펴보기 (b) lucid 명쾌한, 명료한 (c) fractured 탈골된, 골절된
(d) dire 대단히 심각한

15 (c)

해석 시는 공사 기간 동안 교통 차량들을 메인 스트리트에서 세컨드 애비뉴로 우회시킬 것이다.

해설 시에서 공사를 하기 때문에 우회로가 생길 것이라는 내용이다. divert는 '방향을 바꾸게 하다'라는 의미이며 divert traffic은 '교통량을 우회시키다'라는 의미가 된다.

오답 살펴보기 (a) fulfill 성취하다, 완료하다 (b) initiate 개시하다, 착수하다 (d) harness 활용하다

16 (c)

해석 이 음식점은 선착순제이기 때문에 예약을 할 필요가 없습니다.

해설 문맥상 선착순으로 손님을 받는 곳이기 때문에 예약을 할 필요가 없다는 의미이다. 따라서 정답은 '선착순'을 나타내는 first come, first served가 된다.

어구 make reservations 예약하다

오답 살펴보기 (a) better late than never 늦더라도 안 하는 것보다는 나은 (b) not my cup of tea 내가 좋아하는 일이 아닌
(d) no strings attached 아무 조건이 없는

17 (b)

해석 법의학적 증거는 목격자가 그날 밤의 사건에 대해 설명해 준 것을 입증해 준다.

해설 선택지 중에서 증거와 사건에 대한 진술을 연결해 줄 수 있는 단어는 '입증하다'라는 뜻을 가진 corroborates뿐이다.

어구 forensic 법의학적인, 과학 수사의　account 설명

오답 살펴보기 (a) intimidate 위협하다 (c) digress 주제에서 벗어나다
(d) ascend 상승하다

18 (b)

해석 일반적으로 한 국가의 재무부는 국가의 금리를 결정할 책임을 맡고 있다.

해설 금리를 결정하는 일은 재무부의 소관이다. '재무부'는 treasury department로 나타낸다.

어구 interest rate 금리

오답 살펴보기 (a) budget 예산 (d) allocation 할당액, 할당량

19 (b)

해석 군은 천문학적 비용에도 불구하고 국방 계획을 실시하기로 결정했다.

해설 군과 국방 계획 간의 관계를 고려해 보면, '실시하다, 이행하다'라는 뜻을 가진 implement가 가장 적절하다.

어구 defense plan 국방 계획　astronomical 천문학적인

오답 살펴보기 (a) implore 한탄하다 (c) intercept 가로채다
(d) interchange 교환하다

20 (a)

해석 저희의 상설 전시물들은 1층에 위치하고 있으며 특별 전시물들은 2층에 위치해 있습니다.

해설 특별 전시물품에 대응이 될 수 있는 표현은 상설 전시물품이다. 따라서 정답은 '영구적인'이라는 뜻을 지닌 permanent가된다.

어구 collection 수집품, 소장품   exhibition 전시회, 전시물품

오답 살펴보기 (b) preliminary 예비의, 사전의 (c) peripheral 주변적인, 지엽적인 (d) prominent 저명한, 유명한

21 (b)

해석 보건 검사원들은 불량한 위생 상태를 이유로 그 식당을 폐쇄시켰다.

해설 보건 검사원들이 식당의 문을 닫게 하는 조치를 취했다면 식당의 위생 상태가 좋지 않음을 유추해 볼 수 있다. 따라서 정답은 '위생의'라는 의미를 지닌 sanitary가 되어야 한다.

어구 health inspector 보건 검사원, 보건 감독관

오답 살펴보기 (a) prosaic 평범한, 단조로운 (c) lenient 관대한 (d) evocative (좋은 생각을) 연상시키는

22 (b)

해석 야간 TV 프로그램들은 야구 경기 중계방송으로 대체되었다.

해설 TV 프로그램과 야구 경기 방송은 어느 한 쪽이 방송되면 다른 쪽이 방송될 수 없다. 따라서 어느 한 쪽이 다른 한 쪽을 '대신하다'라는 의미를 나타내야 하기 때문에 preempted가 정답이 된다.

오답 살펴보기 (a) pervade 만연하다 (c) confiscate 압수하다 (d) resume 재개하다

23 (c)

해석 나는 결혼 직전에 내 약혼자를 개종시키기로 결심했다.

해설 '(종교 등을) 바꾸다, 개종시키다'라는 표현은 convert로 나타낸다.

오답 살펴보기 (d) transfer 옮기다

24 (a)

해석 구급차의 사이렌 소리가 도시 전역에 울렸다.

해설 '소리가 울리다' 또는 '공명하다'라는 의미의 동사는 resonate이다.

오답 살펴보기 (b) obliterate 지우다, 말살하다 (c) thrive 번창하다 (d) resurrect 부활시키다

25 (d)

해석 경찰은 배포 목적으로 마약을 소지했던 마약상을 체포했다.

해설 peddler는 '밀매인' 또는 '마약 판매상'을 지칭한다.

어구 arrest 체포하다   possession 소유   narcotics 마약 distribute 배포하다

오답 살펴보기 (c) hawker 행상인

26 (c)

해석 종종 권력층에 있는 사람들은 좋은 소식만 전해 주고 격려의 말만 해주는 아첨꾼들에게 둘러싸여 있다.

해설 좋은 소식만을 말하고 격려의 말만 해주는 사람은 아첨꾼이라 할 수 있다. 따라서 정답은 '아첨하는'이라는 뜻을 지닌 obsequious가 되어야 한다.

어구 underling 아랫사람   encouragement 격려

오답 살펴보기 (a) legitimate 합법적인 (b) resilient 회복력 있는, 탄력 있는 (d) proficient 능숙한

27 (c)

해석 그 나라의 경제는 경기 침체로 인해 심한 충격을 받았으며 아직도 회복되지 못하고 있다.

해설 일국의 경제에 아직까지 회복되지 않는 타격을 줄 수 있는 것을 찾아보면 '경기 침체'를 나타내는 recession이 정답이다.

어구 be hit hard 큰 타격을 입다

오답 살펴보기 (a) recruitment 고용 (b) recuperation 회복 (d) reception 환영(회)

28 (b)

해석 나는 몇 가지 간단한 변화를 줌으로써 이 단조로운 아파트를 세련된 장식이 있는 주거 공간으로 탈바꿈시킬 수 있었다.

해설 단조로운 아파트를 어떻게 변화시켰는지에 주목한다. decorated를 가장 잘 수식할 수 있는 단어를 찾으면 되므로 정답은 '세련되게'란 의미를 지닌 urbanely이다.

어구 decorated 꾸며진, 장식된

오답 살펴보기 (a) tantalizingly 감질나게 (c) prudently 사려 깊게, 신중하게 (d) sordidly 탐욕스럽게

29 (c)

해석 폭풍을 피해 대피했을 때 우리는 우리 물건 대부분을 버리고 왔어야했다.

해설 '버리다, 포기하다'라는 뜻을 가진 forsake가 목적어 most of our possessions와 가장 어울리는 단어이다.

어구 possession 소유(물)   evacuate from ~로부터 대피하다

오답 살펴보기 (a) hospitalize 입원시키다 (b) render 만들다; 주다, 제출하다 (d) augment 늘리다, 증가시키다

30 (d)

해석 그 나라의 상류 계층과 하류 계층 간의 소득 격차는 지속적으로 확대되고 있다.

해설 disparity는 '차이, 불일치'라는 의미로, '소득 격차'라는 표현은 income disparity로 나타낸다.

오답 살펴보기 (a) enmity 원한 (b) plight 곤경 (c) influx 유입, 쇄도

1	(a)	2	(d)	3	(b)	4	(a)	5	(b)
6	(c)	7	(a)	8	(b)	9	(b)	10	(c)
11	(c)	12	(a)	13	(c)	14	(a)	15	(b)
16	(b)	17	(c)	18	(c)	19	(d)	20	(d)
21	(a)	22	(d)	23	(a)	24	(a)	25	(d)
26	(d)	27	(c)	28	(b)	29	(a)	30	(a)

1 (a)

해석 A: 블랙 씨가 우리가 무엇을 하기를 원하는지 알고 있나요?
B: 사실 그렇지 않아요. 그는 제게 자신의 계획을 제대로 전달하지 못했어요.

해설 A의 질문에 B가 부정적인 대답을 했으므로, B도 블랙 씨가 자신에게 무엇을 시키려고 했는지에 대해 제대로 이해하지 못하고 있음을 알 수 있다. 따라서 빈칸에 가장 알맞은 표현은 get across(의미 등을 전달하다, 이해시키다)이다.

오답 살펴보기 (b) enter into (논의 등에) 들어가다 (c) knuckle under ~의 권위를 받아들이다 (d) open up 마음을 터놓다

2 (d)

해석 A: 이 기념비는 정말 인상적이군요.
B: 네, 이 기념비는 베트남전 참전 용사들을 기리기 위해 세워졌어요.

해설 참전 용사들을 기리기 위해 무엇이 세워졌는지를 생각해 보면 쉽게 정답을 찾을 수 있다. '기념비'는 monument로 나타낸다.

어구 veteran 참전용사

오답 살펴보기 (a) courtesy 공손함 (b) editorial 사설 (c) reconciliation 화해; 조화

3 (b)

해석 A: 여권을 제시해 주시겠습니까?
B: 죄송하지만, 가지고 있지 않은데요. 가지고 와야 하는지 몰랐어요.

해설 B는 여권을 가져 와야 한다는 점을 몰랐기 때문에 여권을 제시해 달라는 A의 요청을 받아들일 수 없다. 따라서 정답은 '깨닫다' 혹은 '알다'라는 의미의 realize가 된다.

오답 살펴보기 (a) organize 준비하다 (c) recognize 알아보다 (d) appear 등장하다

4 (a)

해석 A: 당신이 누군가를 고용해서 당신 방을 칠하게 했을 것이라고 생각했어요.
B: 그랬지만, 그가 일을 대충해서 제가 다시 직접 칠하고 있어요.

해설 B가 직접 다시 페인트칠을 해야 했다고 했으므로 B가 고용한 사람이 일을 잘 하지 못했음을 알 수 있다. 따라서 정답은 '엉성한'이라는 뜻을 지닌 sloppy이다.

어구 do over 다시 단장하다, 청소하다

오답 살펴보기 (b) pristine 완전 새 것 같은, 오염되지 않은 (c) weighty 중대한, 무거운 (d) divine 신의, 신성한

5 (b)

해석 A: 그래서 차의 시동을 걸려면 점화 장치에 열쇠를 꽂고 엔진을 가동시켜야 한다는 거죠?
B: 바로 그거에요. 정확히 맞는 말씀을 하셨네요.

해설 B의 반응을 통해 A가 정확히 맞는 말을 했음을 알 수 있다. '정확히 맞는 말을 하다'라는 표현은 hit the nail on the head로 나타낸다.

어구 ignition 차량 점화 장치 crank 엔진을 작동시키다 motor 엔진

오답 살펴보기 (a) speak with a silver tongue 유창하게 말하다 (c) get in on the act 행동에 가담하다 (d) put the final nail in the coffin 결정타를 먹이다

6 (c)

해석 A: 인근에서 차량 절도 사건의 수가 최근 급격히 늘어났어.
B: 맞아. 경찰에서 조치를 취해야 해.

해설 increased를 수식할 수 있는 부사를 묻는 문제이다. '급격히 증가하다'라고 할 때 부사 sharply(급격하게)를 쓸 수 있다.

어구 carjack 차량 탈취

오답 살펴보기 (a) dully 둔하게 (d) readily 쾌히

7 (a)

해석 A: 부장님께서 당신의 제안에 대해 어떻게 생각하셨나요?
B: 제게 직설적으로 쓸모가 없다고 말씀해 주셨어요.

해설 B의 제안에 대한 부장의 의견을 묻는 A의 질문에 B는 부장이 자신의 제안에 대해 쓸모없다고 말했다고 대답했다. 이는 일종의 직설적인 반응으로 볼 수 있으며, 따라서 정답은 '직설적인'이라는 의미를 지닌 bluntly가 된다.

어구 stink 쓸모없다, 질이 나쁘다

오답 살펴보기 (b) redundantly 장황하게 (c) crudely 조잡하게 (d) vocally 구두로

8 (b)

해석 A: 우왜! 머릿결에 윤기가 넘치고 빛이 나는데. 비법이 뭐니?
B: 매일 잊지 않고 유기농 샴푸만 써서 머리를 감고 있어.

해설 샴푸 이야기를 하고 있으므로 머리 스타일이 아닌 머릿결에 관한 이야기임을 알 수 있다. '(머리카락이) 윤기가 있는'이라고 할 때 쓸 수 있는 단어는 sleek이며, polished는 문질러서 윤이 나는 상태를 말하므로 여기서는 쓸 수 없다.

어구 organic 유기농의

오답 살펴보기 (a) polished 광이 나는 (c) elegant 우아한 (d) graceful 우아한

9 (b)

해석 A: 대통령의 새로운 사회 보장 계획은 지금까지 그다지 성공적이지 못했어.
B: 그래, 그 때문에 정부가 기존 시스템을 되살리려고 하고 있지.

해설 새로운 계획이 성공하지 못함으로써 정부가 취할 수 있는 조치를 생각해 보면 된다. resurrect는 '부활시키다' 혹은 '되살

리다'라는 의미이다.

어구 social security 사회 보장

오답 살펴보기 (a) establish 설립하다 (c) invigorate 기운 나게 하다
(d) stabilize 안정화시키다

10 (c)

해석 A: 그 판사는 살인자에게 겨우 5년간의 징역형을 선고했어.
B: 그러한 처벌은 살인자가 저지른 범죄의 심각성에 비해 너무 관대해.

해설 A는 범죄자에게 주어진 형벌이 겨우 5년밖에 되지 않는다고 말하고 있다. 따라서 이러한 조치는 범죄의 심각성에 비추어 볼 때 너무 관대하다고 볼 수 있다. 정답은 lenient(관대한)이다.

어구 sentence 형을 선고하다

오답 살펴보기 (a) critical 비판적인 (b) complicit 연루된
(d) licentious 음란한

11 (c)

해석 이 쿠키 제조법에 따르면, 칼로리 함량을 줄이기 위해 달걀 대용으로 사과 소스를 사용해도 좋다.

해설 전치사 for를 통해, 빈칸에 들어갈 동사로 가장 적절한 것이 substitute임을 알 수 있다. substitute는 for와 함께 쓰이면 '~를 ...로 대용하다'라는 뜻을 갖는다.

오답 살펴보기 (a) alternate 번갈아 일어나게 하다 (b) nourish 영양분을 공급하다 (d) invent 발명하다

12 (a)

해석 건강한 체중을 유지하기 위해, 의사들은 매일 2,000에서 3,000사이의 칼로리를 섭취할 것을 권하고 있다.

해설 칼로리라는 단어와 어울리는 동사는 '(음식 등을) 섭취하다'는 의미의 consume이다.

오답 살펴보기 (b) prescribe 처방하다 (c) swallow 삼키다
(d) breathe 숨 쉬다

13 (c)

해석 그 한국 음식점은 2010년 베이징에서 최초의 해외 지점을 개설했다.

해설 음식점, 상점, 혹은 기업 등이 해외에 여는 '지점'이나 '지사'를 의미하는 단어는 branch이다. chain은 우리가 말하는 '체인점의 집합'을 의미하지, 개별 상점을 의미하지는 않는다.

오답 살펴보기 (a) division 분할, 분배 (b) chain 상점, 호텔 등의 체인
(d) limb 일부, 일원; 분과

14 (a)

해석 수년 간 적절하지 않은 영농 관행으로 토양의 질이 저하되었기 때문에, 작물은 더 이상 그 곳에서 재배될 수 없었다.

해설 작물이 재배될 수 없게 된 이유를 생각해 보면 정답을 찾을 수 있다. impoverish는 '가난하게 하다, 메마르게 하다'란 의미이다.

오답 살펴보기 (b) generate 발생시키다 (c) enrich 부유하게 하다
(d) evaporate 증발시키다

15 (b)

해석 그 백만장자에게는 수많은 정부들과 함께 사생아들도 여럿 있었다.

해설 수많은 정부들을 거느렸다면, 사생아들도 있었을 것이라고 추측해 볼 수 있다. illegitimate는 주로 '불법의'이란 뜻으로 사용되며, '사생아'는 illegitimate child로 나타낼 수 있다.

어구 mistress (보통 기혼 남자의) 정부

오답 살펴보기 (a) scandalous 수치스러운 (c) culpable 과실이 있는 (d) imperative 반드시 해야 하는

16 (b)

해석 어떤 경찰관들은 때때로 규정을 어길지도 모르지만, 존스 경관은 언제나 원칙대로 행동한다.

해설 규정을 어기는 다른 경관들과 존스 경관을 대조시키고 있다. 따라서 존스 경관은 원리원칙대로 행동하는 사람임을 알 수 있다. '원칙대로 행동하다'라는 표현은 go by the book으로 나타낸다.

오답 살펴보기 (a) play it by ear 사정을 봐 가면서 처리하다
(c) keep one's eye on the ball 경계하다
(d) have one's hands full 매우 바쁘다

17 (c)

해석 최고 경영자께서는 오늘 회의에서 직원들의 보건에 관한 문제들을 다루실 것입니다.

해설 문맥상 최고 경영자가 회의에서 직원들의 문제를 다룰 것이라는 점을 생각해 볼 수 있다. 따라서 정답은 address(~에 대해 다루다)가 된다.

어구 surrounding ~에 관한

오답 살펴보기 (a) tackle (힘든 상황과) 씨름하다
(d) lecture ~에 관해 강의하다

18 (c)

해석 옷에 대한 귀하의 흠 잡을 데 없는 취향에 찬사를 보내야 하겠군요.

해설 상대방의 옷에 대한 취향을 칭찬하고 있는 내용으로 미루어 볼 때, 칭찬받는 사람의 취향이 뛰어나다는 점을 알 수 있다. impeccable은 '결점이 없는' 또는 '흠 잡을 데 없는'이라는 뜻이다.

어구 commend 칭찬하다

오답 살펴보기 (a) full 가득 찬 (b) pliable 유연한 (d) whole 전체의

19 (d)

해석 한 개인의 성격 발달과 관련하여 유명한 한 심리학자는 선천적인 성격이 환경적 요소에 종속되어 있다고 최근 발표했다.

해설 선택지에 있는 단어를 대입해서 푸는 것이 효과적이다. 환경적 요소가 성격 발달에 결정적임을 나타내는 문장이므로 subordinate(종속되는)가 정답이다.

어구 renowned 유명한   proclaim 선언하다   innate 타고난, 선천적인   in regard to ~와 관련하여   personality 성격

오답 살펴보기 (a) obstinate 고집이 센 (b) residual 남은, 잔여의
(c) apathetic 무관심한

20 (d)

해석 복권에 당첨된다는 내 예감은 올바른 것으로 드러났다.

해설 복권에 당첨된다는 생각이 맞았다는 것이 본문의 내용이다. 따라서 premonition(예감)이 정답이다.

오답 살펴보기 (a) promotion 승진 (b) proposition 제안 (c) premeditation 계획

21 (a)

해석 대부분의 다른 농장 동물들과는 달리, 소에게는 풀을 뜯어먹을 수 있는 넓은 땅이 필요하다.

해설 소가 넓은 땅에서 할 수 있는 것으로 의미가 가장 자연스럽게 통하는 것은 graze(풀을 뜯어먹다)이다.

오답 살펴보기 (b) slaughter 도축하다 (c) burrow 굴을 파다 (d) lurk 숨어 있다

22 (d)

해석 우리 팀이 21점을 앞서 나가자, 승리는 피할 수 없는 결과라는 점이 분명해 졌다.

해설 '피할 수 없는 분명한 결과'는 foregone conclusion으로 나타낸다.

어구 lead 앞서감, 리드함

오답 살펴보기 (a) predetermined 예정된 (b) rudimentary 기초적인 (c) surmountable 극복할 수 있는

23 (a)

해석 직장을 잃는 것이 처음에는 재앙인 것처럼 보였지만, 전화위복임이 드러났다.

해설 문맥상 but이 있으므로 실직이 재앙이 아닌 그 반대의 결과가 되었음을 알 수 있다. 따라서 '뜻밖의 좋은 결과'를 의미하는 blessing in disguise가 정답으로 가장 적절하다.

어구 turn out to be 결국 ~로 판명되다

오답 살펴보기 (b) bolt from the blue 마른하늘에 날벼락 (c) diamond in the rough 흙 속의 진주 (d) labor of love 사랑의 수고(사랑을 위해 기꺼이 하는 수고)

24 (a)

해석 일련의 경제, 군사, 그리고 정치적 관계가 여전히 과거 식민지와 본국을 묶어 놓고 있다.

해설 두 나라가 경제, 군사, 정치적 문제로 서로 연관되어 있음을 추측해 볼 수 있다. bind는 with와 함께 쓰여, '묶다, 매다'의 의미를 갖는다.

오답 살펴보기 (b) unite 통합하다 (c) resolve 해결하다 (d) contemplate 숙고하다, 고려하다

25 (d)

해석 엄청난 슬픔이 소설 구석구석에 스며들어 있다.

해설 소설에 어떠한 분위기가 만연해 있다고 할 때 pervade(만연해 있다, 스며들다)를 사용한다.

오답 살펴보기 (a) invade 침입하다 (b) outstrip 능가하다, 앞지르다 (c) convey 전달하다

26 (d)

해석 그 단체는 오늘날 많은 TV 프로그램이 음란하며 도덕적으로 타락했다고 비판한다.

해설 보기 중에서 moral corrupt(도덕적으로 타락한)에 상응하는 의미를 가질 수 있는 것은 licentious(음란한) 뿐이다.

오답 살펴보기 (a) staunch 견고한, 튼튼한 (b) ethereal 지극히 가볍고 어린; 천상의 (c) vacuous 멍청한

27 (c)

해석 인근 공장으로 인한 오염 때문에, 강물은 더 이상 마실 수 없게 되었다.

해설 강이 오염되었으면 강물을 마시기가 불가능할 것이다. potable은 '마셔도 되는'이라는 의미이며 철자가 비슷한 portable(휴대할 수 있는)과 착각하면 안 된다.

어구 contamination 오염

오답 살펴보기 (a) pious 신앙심이 깊은 (b) prolific 다작의, 다산의 (d) portable 들고 다닐 수 있는

28 (b)

해석 게임 회사들은 비디오 게임을 여성에게 적합한 취미로 정당화시킬 목적으로 광고에 수백만 달러를 썼다.

해설 빈칸에 들어갈 단어는 게임 회사들이 수백만 달러를 광고에 쓴 이유와, 여성도 취미로 삼을 수 있는 비디오 게임이라는 개념을 서로 연결시켜 줄 수 있어야 한다. 비디오 게임을 취미로 받아들이는 분위기를 만든다는 의미에서 legitimize(정당화하다)가 가장 적절하다.

어구 acceptable 수용 가능한, 용인 가능한

오답 살펴보기 (a) induce 유도하다 (c) obliterate 없애다 (d) demean 품위를 떨어뜨리다

29 (a)

해석 두바이는 주택 시장을 괴롭히는 걷잡을 수 없는 부동산 투기를 억제하고자 노력해왔다.

해설 real estate(부동산)이란 단어와 주택 시장을 괴롭히고 있는 것에 대한 개념을 연결시켜 줄 수 있는 단어를 찾아야 한다. 따라서 정답으로 '투기'를 의미하는 speculation이 가장 적절하다.

어구 rampant 걷잡을 수 없는 plague 괴롭히다, 성가시게 하다

오답 살펴보기 (b) anticipation 전망 (c) increment 증가 (d) misappropriation 남용; 횡령

30 (a)

해석 매년 겨울, 우리 가족은 크리스마스에 대비하여 다채로운 색의 전구와 장식품으로 집을 꾸민다.

해설 크리스마스에 대비하여 장식품과 전구를 가지고 집에서 할 수 있는 일을 생각해 보면 정답을 찾을 수 있다. 정답은 bedeck(장식하다)이다.

어구 ornament 장신구

오답 살펴보기 (b) herald 예고하다, 알리다 (c) appease 달래다; 요구를 들어주다 (d) rattle 덜거덕거리다

Actual Test 04

1	(a)	2	(b)	3	(c)	4	(d)	5	(b)
6	(c)	7	(a)	8	(b)	9	(d)	10	(a)
11	(c)	12	(b)	13	(d)	14	(c)	15	(b)
16	(c)	17	(d)	18	(c)	19	(c)	20	(a)
21	(c)	22	(d)	23	(b)	24	(c)	25	(d)
26	(b)	27	(b)	28	(b)	29	(c)	30	(b)

1 (a)

해석 A: 난 그 감독관이 널 그렇게 심하게 대했다는 것을 믿을 수가 없어.
B: 걱정 마. 그녀는 언젠가 내게 한 일에 대한 대가를 받게 될 거야.

해설 B에게 심하게 대한 감독관을 B가 어떻게 생각하고 있을지 유추해 보면 정답을 찾을 수 있다. pay for는 '~에 대한 대가를 치르다'라는 의미이다.

오답 살펴보기 (b) insist on 주장하다 (c) come by ~을 얻다, 획득하다 (d) hear of ~에 대해 듣다

2 (b)

해석 A: 조지는 직장을 그만 둔 후 카리브해의 저택을 한 채 샀어. 어떻게 그럴 여력이 있었을까?
B: 듣자 하니 그는 부동산 시장에서 큰돈을 벌었다고 해.

해설 카리브해에 저택을 구입할 정도라면 돈을 많이 벌었을 것으로 추측해 볼 수 있다. '큰돈을 벌다'라는 의미는 make a fortune으로 나타낸다.

어구 can afford to V ~할 경제적 여유가 되다
apparently 듣자 하니   real estate 부동산

오답 살펴보기 (a) shelter 피신처 (c) venture 벤처, 사업적 모험 (d) portion 부분

3 (c)

해석 A: 최근 일과 아이 육아 때문에 정말 스트레스가 심해.
B: 온천에서 하루 정도 행복을 누려야 할 필요가 있을 것으로 들리는군.

해설 spoil oneself with는 '~로 행복하게 지내다'라는 의미이다.

어구 stressed out 스트레스가 쌓인

오답 살펴보기 (a) torture 고문 (b) embody 상징하다, 구현하다 (d) caution 주의

4 (d)

해석 A: 이렇게 늦게 말해서 미안하지만, 또 다른 친구가 저녁 식사를 하기 위해 이리로 오고 있어요.
B: 문제없어요. 다른 한 사람이 먹을 수 있는 음식은 충분히 있어요.

해설 A는 친구가 한 명 더 오게 되어 걱정하고 있지만, B가 문제가 없다고 말하는 것으로 보아 음식의 양이 충분하다는 점을 유추해 볼 수 있다. 따라서 정답은 sufficient(충분한)이다.

오답 살펴보기 (a) mobile 이동하는 (b) pathetic 애처로운 (c) serene 고요한

5 (b)

해석 A: TV 소리 좀 줄여 줄래? 지금 전화통화를 하고 있거든.
B: 이런, 미안해. 그렇게 할게.

해설 A는 전화통화를 하기 때문에 TV를 보는 B에게 TV 소리를 줄여 달라고 요청했을 것임을 추측해 볼 수 있다. 따라서 정답은 mute(소리를 줄이다)이다.

오답 살펴보기 (a) distract 주의를 산만하게 만들다 (c) fade 서서히 사라지다 (d) eliminate 없애다, 제거하다

6 (c)

해석 A: 나 지쳤어. 우리가 정상에 도착하기까지 얼마나 걸릴까?
B: 걱정하지 마. 바로 저 위에 정상이 있어.

해설 정상이 멀었는가에 대한 A의 질문에 B가 걱정하지 말라고 대답한 것으로 보아, 빈칸에는 '정상'을 나타내는 단어가 들어가야 한다. 따라서 정답은 peak(정상)이다.

오답 살펴보기 (a) peek 훔쳐보다 (b) peel 껍질을 벗기다 (d) pear 배

7 (a)

해석 A: 휴가 여행 일정은 다 짰나요?
B: 물론이에요. 남극처럼 사람의 발길이 닿지 않는 곳을 골랐어요.

해설 off the beaten path는 '사람의 발길이 닿지 않은'이라는 의미를 갖는다. 따라서 B가 고른 곳이 남극과 같은 곳임을 감안하면 빈칸에는 path가 들어가야 한다.

어구 itinerary 여행 일정표   Antarctica 남극 대륙

오답 살펴보기 (d) trek 트레킹, 오래 걷기

8 (b)

해석 A: 차량 정비사들이 차에 무슨 문제가 있는지 알고 있나요?
B: 아니요, 문제의 원인을 알아내지 못하더군요.

해설 정비사들이 차량의 문제를 알고 있는지 물었는데 B가 아니라고 대답했으므로, 정비사들이 문제의 근원을 파악하지 못하고 있음을 알 수 있다. 따라서 정답은 identify(확인하다, 식별하다)가 된다.

어구 mechanic 차량 정비사

오답 살펴보기 (a) overwhelm 압도하다 (c) suppress 진압하다 (d) recruit 고용하다, 채용하다

9 (d)

해석 A: 오늘 저녁에 볼링을 하러 가고 싶어. 관심 있어?
B: 그다지. 집에 있으면서 TV나 보고 싶어.

해설 A의 제안에 B가 거절의 뜻을 비치고 있다. 따라서 집에서 TV나 보고 싶다는 의미가 이어져야 하며 정답은 feel like(~을 하고 싶다)가 된다.

오답 살펴보기 (a) leave behind 남겨 두고 가다 (b) come by ~을 얻다, 획득하다 (d) dispense with 없애다, 생략하다

10 (a)

해석 A: 난 네가 짐 싸는 것을 도와주려고 시내를 가로질러 계속 운전해 왔어.
B: 정말 고마운데, 하지만 날 위해서 그렇게까지 노력할 필요는 없어.

해설 B의 대답에 but이 쓰이고 있다는 점을 주목한다면 정답은 '엄청난 노력을 하다'라는 의미의 bend over backward가 되어야 한다.

어구 packing 짐 싸기

오답 살펴보기 (b) lose one's temper 화를 내다
(c) test the waters 미리 상황을 살피다
(d) go through the motions ~을 하는 시늉을 하다

11 (c)

해석 피부를 더 아름답고 환하게 보이도록 하기 위해, 잊지 말고 매일 밤 주무시기 전에 저희 박피크림을 바르십시오.

해설 apply는 '지원하다'라는 뜻도 가지고 있지만, '(크림 등을) 바르다'라는 의미도 가지고 있다.

어구 radiant 빛나는, 환한   exfoliating 박피의

오답 살펴보기 (d) rub 문지르다

12 (b)

해석 조울증 장애를 가진 사람들은 종종 완전한 행복과 완전한 불행을 한순간에 겪는다.

해설 happiness와 어울리는 단어를 찾으면 되는데, 뒤에 and가 있으므로 빈칸에는 complete와 같은 맥락의 형용사가 와야 한다는 것을 알 수 있다. 따라서 sheer happiness(완전한 행복)라고 하는 것이 가장 알맞다.

어구 bipolar 조울증 disorder 장애 misery 불행

오답 살펴보기 (a) pitiful 동정적인 (c) inferior (d) assiduous 근면한

13 (d)

해석 오늘은 귀하의 물품을 배달해 드릴 수 없었으나, 내일 다시 한 번 시도해 보겠습니다.

해설 second란 말이 있으므로, 내일 또 다시 배송을 해보겠다는 내용이 이어져야 할 것이다. make a second attempt는 '다시 한 번 시도해 보다'라는 의미이다.

어구 deliver 배달하다

오답 살펴보기 (a) endurance 인내 (c) allocation 할당

14 (c)

해석 인터뷰 필기록이 곧 웹사이트에 게시될 것이다.

해설 동사 post는 자료를 인터넷상에 올릴 때 사용하는 동사이다. 글로 기록된 인터뷰 내용이 인터넷에 게시된다는 의미로 transcript(글로 옮긴 기록)가 정답이다.

어구 post 게시하다

오답 살펴보기 (a) verse 운문, 시 (b) conversion 대화
(d) transaction 거래

15 (b)

해석 나의 부모님은 매우 엄격하셨는데, 심지어는 내가 대학에 들어갈 때까지도 남자 친구를 사귀지 못하게 하셨다.

해설 대학 때까지 남자 친구를 사귀지 못하게 했다는 점에서 부모가 매우 엄격했음을 알 수 있다. 따라서 정답은 stern(엄격한, 근엄한)이 된다.

오답 살펴보기 (a) frugal 절약하는 (c) tolerant 관대한
(d) reclusive 은둔한

16 (c)

해석 원치 않는 선물을 받을 때는 사려 깊은 태도를 보이며 상대방의 호의에 트집을 잡지 않는 것이 중요하다.

해설 considerate(사려 깊은)과 상응할 수 있는 표현은 not to look a gift horse in the mouth인데, look a gift horse in the mouth는 '남의 호의에 트집을 잡다'라는 뜻이다.

어구 considerate 사려 깊은

오답 살펴보기 (a) stick out like a sore thumb 눈에 띄다, 두드러지다 (b) fly by the seat of your pants 직감으로 조종하다
(d) make out like a bandit 엄청난 수익을 얻다

17 (d)

해석 승객 수의 감소로 인해, 시는 대중교통에 제공해 주는 보조금을 늘릴 수밖에 없었다.

해설 문맥상 대중교통 이용자 수가 감소했기 때문에 시에서 대중교통에 제공하는 보조금을 증액시켜 줄 것이라고 생각해볼 수 있다. 따라서 정답은 '보조금'을 뜻하는 subsidy가 되는데, grant는 주로 교육이나 연구 목적으로 제공되는 보조금을 뜻하기 때문에 여기서는 정답이 될 수 없다.

어구 ridership 승객 수   be forced to V ~해야 한다
public transportation 대중교통

오답 살펴보기 (a) donation 기부금 (b) grant (교육 및 연구 등에 제공되는) 보조금, 지원금 (c) stipend 봉급, 급료

18 (c)

해석 국제 사회로부터의 반발에도 불구하고, 그 불량국가는 자국 핵무기 프로그램의 폐기를 거부했다.

해설 문맥상 불량국가가 국제 사회의 항의에도 불구하고 핵무기를 존속시키고 있다는 내용이다. 따라서 정답은 abandon(포기하다, 폐지하다)이 된다.

어구 rogue nation 불량국가

오답 살펴보기 (a) betray 배반하다 (b) merit 칭찬을 들을 만하다
(d) enhance 강화하다

19 (c)

해석 결혼을 한 적이 없었기 때문에, 왕은 왕위를 이를 후사를 남기지 못했다.

해설 왕이 결혼을 하지 않았다면 자녀를 갖지 못했을 것이고, 따라서 왕위를 이를 후사가 없었음을 추측해 볼 수 있다. 따라서 답은 heir(후사, 계승자)가 된다.

어구 throne 왕좌

오답 살펴보기 (a) representative 대표 (b) beneficiary 수혜자
(d) protege 피보호자; 제자

20 (a)

해석 현직 시장은 재선 선거에서 정치 신인에게 패배했다.

해설 reelection campaign(재선)이란 단어와 시장이 upstart politician(정치 신인)에게 졌다는 표현을 통해 정답을 유추해 볼 수 있다. 따라서 정답은 incumbent(현직의)이다.

어구 upstart 신흥의　　reelection 재선

오답 살펴보기 (b) elective 선거로 선출된; 선거권이 있는
　　　　(c) urgent 급박한 (d) condescending 거들먹거리는

21 (c)
해석 이 지역의 많은 폭력 사건들은 경쟁 관계에 있는 갱단들에 의해 선동된 것이다.

해설 문맥상 '폭력을 선동하다'는 의미의 instigate를 쓰는 것이 가장 적절하다.

오답 살펴보기 (a) install 설치하다 (b) instill 스며들게 하다
　　　　(d) instruct 지시하다

22 (d)
해석 그 남자는 피고가 범죄 현장으로부터 도망치는 것을 보았다고 법정에서 증언했다.

해설 '(법정에서) 증언하다'라는 의미는 testify로 나타낸다.

어구 defendant 피고　　flee from ~에서 도망치다

오답 살펴보기 (a) verify 입증하다 (b) vouch 보장하다, 단언하다
　　　　(c) depose 폐위시키다

23 (b)
해석 어느 편도 들기 싫었기 때문에, 나는 그들의 논쟁에서 중립을 유지하기로 결정했다.

해설 편을 들지 않는다는 것은 논쟁에서 중립을 지킨다는 것과 의미가 상통한다. 따라서 neutral(중립의)이 정답으로 가장 적절하다.

어구 take sides 편을 들다

오답 살펴보기 (a) serene 고요한 (c) upright 똑바른 (d) deficient 부족한

24 (c)
해석 이 식당에서는 식사보다 인테리어가 더 우선시된다.

해설 take a backseat to는 '~에게 양보하다'라는 의미로, 문맥상 식당은 음식보다 인테리어에 더 신경을 쓴다는 점을 알 수 있다.

어구 decor 장식, 인테리어

오답 살펴보기 (d) blue moon 매우 드문 기간

25 (d)
해석 에세이에서 인용문 없이 출처의 정보를 그대로 가져오는 것은 용인되지 않는다.

해설 에세이에서 정보를 인용할 때 주의해야 할 점을 나타내고 있다. 따라서, 문맥상 출처에서 정보를 '글자 그대로' 가져 오면 안 된다는 의미가 되도록 빈칸에는 verbatim이 들어가야 한다.

어구 cite 인용하다

오답 살펴보기 (a) inadvertently 우연히, 무심코 (b) literally 말 그대로
　　　　(c) offhand 무뚝뚝한

26 (b)
해석 양국 간 증대되고 있는 적대감으로 인하여 그 지역 내에서는 또 다른 전쟁이 촉발될 수 있을 것이다.

해설 적대감, 전쟁 등의 단어를 고려해 보면 빈칸에 들어가기에 가장 적절한 단어는 '(전쟁 등을) 촉발하다'는 의미의 trigger가 된다.

오답 살펴보기 (a) mediate 중재하다 (c) embark 승선하다; 착수하다
　　　　(d) torture 고문하다

27 (b)
해석 카멜레온은 주변 환경에 색을 맞추기 위해 몸의 색깔을 변화시킬 수 있는 특이한 적응력을 갖추고 있다.

해설 문맥상 빈칸에는 주변 환경에 색을 맞추기 위하여 몸의 색깔을 변화시킬 수 있는 카멜레온의 능력을 한 마디로 표현한 단어가 들어가야 한다. 따라서 정답은 adaptation(적응)이다.

어구 surroundings 주변

오답 살펴보기 (a) instinct 본능 (c) motive 동기
　　　　(d) phenomenon 현상

28 (b)
해석 새로운 게임기에 대한 수요가 그에 대한 공급을 계속해서 넘어서고 있으며, 전국적으로 수백만 대가 날개 돋친 듯 팔려 나가고 있다.

해설 날개 돋친 듯 팔려 나간다는 점에서 공급량보다 수요량이 더욱 많다는 점을 유추해 볼 수 있다. 따라서 정답은 '~을 넘어서다, 앞지르다'의 의미를 지닌 outstrip이 된다.

어구 video game console 게임기　　fly off store shelves 날개 돋친 듯 팔리다

오답 살펴보기 (a) overarch 지배하다 (c) overturn 뒤집히다, 전복되다
　　　　(d) outreach 원조 활동

29 (c)
해석 이 산은 금속을 녹일 수 있기 때문에, 매우 조심해서 다루어야 한다.

해설 산의 속성을 생각하면 산이 금속을 녹일 수 있다는 점을 쉽게 알 수 있다. 따라서 정답은 dissolve(용해하다, 녹이다)이다.

어구 with caution 조심해서

오답 살펴보기 (a) resolve 결심하다 (b) absolve 죄를 용서하다

30 (b)
해석 어렸을 때부터, 나는 할아버지께서 자신의 어린 시절에 대해 두서없이 하시는 말씀을 좋아했다.

해설 우선 listen to란 표현이 있으므로 듣는 것과 관련된 것이 빈칸에 들어가야 한다. grumble(투덜거리다)과 ramble(두서없이 말하다)이 정답 후보에 오를 수 있는데, '~하는 것을 듣기를 좋아한다'라고 했으므로 rumble이 오는 것이 더 자연스럽다.

오답 살펴보기 (a) grumble 투덜거리다 (c) scribble 갈겨쓰다
　　　　(d) embellish 장식하다

1	(c)	2	(a)	3	(b)	4	(c)	5	(d)
6	(b)	7	(d)	8	(b)	9	(a)	10	(d)
11	(d)	12	(b)	13	(d)	14	(d)	15	(a)
16	(c)	17	(a)	18	(a)	19	(c)	20	(d)
21	(a)	22	(a)	23	(b)	24	(a)	25	(a)
26	(b)	27	(b)	28	(a)	29	(d)	30	(a)

1 (c)

해석 A: 앤디는 자기가 나를 위해서 도움을 주고 있다고 주장해.
　　 B: 난 믿을 수 없어. 분명히 다른 동기가 있을 거야.

해설 B는 앤디가 도움을 주는 의도를 의심하고 있다. 따라서 '동기'의 의미를 지닌 motive가 정답이다.

어구 for one's sake ~를 위해

오답 살펴보기 (a) union 결합 (b) suggestion 제안
　　 (d) adaptation 적응

2 (a)

해석 A: 이번 학기의 모든 강의가 마침내 끝난다니 기쁘군.
　　 B: 확실히 그래. 이제 마음대로 놀면서 즐겨 보자고.

해설 kick up one's heels는 '마음껏 뛰어 놀다'라는 뜻이다.

오답 살펴보기 (b) socks 양말

3 (b)

해석 A: 실례합니다. 룸에 있는 세면도구를 사용하려면 추가 금액을 지불해야 하나요?
　　 B: 아닙니다, 고객님. 그것은 무료입니다.

해설 추가 금액을 지불해야 하나고 묻는 A의 질문에 B가 아니라고 답하고 있다. 따라서 정답은 '무료의'란 의미를 가지고 있는 complimentary가 된다.

어구 toiletries 세면도구

오답 살펴보기 (a) extraordinary 보기 드문, 비범한
　　 (d) unrestrained 억제되지 않은

4 (c)

해석 A: 여보, 여기 와서 이 식료품을 제자리에 넣는 것 좀 도와줘요.
　　 B: 문제없어요.

해설 문맥상 시장에서 구입한 물건들을 냉장고에 넣거나 선반에 두고 있는 상황이다. '(물건 등을) 보관 장소에 넣다, 다른 곳으로 치우다'라는 표현은 put away로 나타낸다.

오답 살펴보기 (a) make up 구성하다; 화장하다 (b) empty out 비우다
　　 (d) look around 주위를 둘러보다

5 (d)

해석 A: 이 오래된 잡지들은 어디에 두어야 하죠?
　　 B: 그냥 저쪽 구석에 쌓아 주세요.

해설 잡지를 어디에 두어야 하는지 묻는 질문에 답하고 있는 상황이다. 물건을 놓아두는 행동을 나타내는 단어로 적절한 것은 pile(쌓아 올리다)이다.

오답 살펴보기 (a) stock 비축하다, 갖추다 (b) alter 변경하다
　　 (c) neglect 방치하다

6 (b)

해석 A: 재키, 이리 와서 이 기사 좀 봐. 정말 웃겨.
　　 B: 제발 산만하게 만들지 마. 공부하려고 애를 쓰고 있잖아.

해설 A가 이리 와서 기사를 보라고 하자 B가 공부를 하고 있는 중이라고 답하고 있는 상황이다. 따라서 정답은 distract(산만하게 하다, 주의를 딴 데로 돌리다)가 된다.

오답 살펴보기 (a) scorn 꾸짖다 (c) mourn 애도하다
　　 (d) testify 증언하다

7 (d)

해석 A: 혜성을 보기 위해서는, 망원경과 같은 특별한 장비가 필요한가요?
　　 B: 그렇지는 않을 거예요. 육안으로도 보일 거예요.

해설 망원경 없이도 혜성을 볼 수 있다는 의미이므로 정답은 '눈에 보이는'이란 뜻의 visible이 된다.

어구 naked eye 육안

오답 살펴보기 (a) fluid 유동적인 (b) prominent 저명한
　　 (c) obscured 흐릿한

8 (b)

해석 A: 올해 작황이 매우 좋지 않군요.
　　 B: 그 말이 맞지만, 강수량이 너무 적었던 해여서 어쩔 수 없는 결과예요.

해설 비가 거의 오지 않아서 흉작이 든 것은 어찌할 수 없는 불가피한 결과로 볼 수 있다. 따라서 inevitable(불가피한)이 정답이 된다.

어구 outcome 결과

오답 살펴보기 (a) enviable 부러움을 살 만한 (c) intangible 무형의
　　 (d) ineligible 부적합의

9 (a)

해석 A: 다음 주유소까지는 얼마나 더 남았나요?
　　 B: 표지판에는 30마일이라고 되어 있지만, 그 전에 기름이 떨어질 것 같아 우려가 되는군요.

해설 다음 주유소까지 30마일이 남은 상황에서 우려가 될 수 있는 일은 휘발유가 다 떨어지는 것이다. 따라서 '다 쓰다, 소진시키다'라는 의미의 run out of가 정답이 된다.

오답 살펴보기 (b) break out of 탈출하다 (c) put up with 참다, 견디다 (d) face up to 정면으로 맞서다

10 (d)

해석 A: 어, 조심해. 금을 밟으면 엄마의 허리가 부러질 거야.
　　 B: 바보 같은 소리 마. 그건 그냥 미신일 뿐이야.

해설 금을 밟으면 엄마의 허리가 부러진다는 A의 말에 대해 B가 바보 같은 소리라고 답하고 있다. 따라서 정답은 superstition(미신)이다.

오답 살펴보기 (a) curiosity 호기심 (b) fallacy 오류
　　 (c) tongue twister 발음하기 힘든 어구

11 (d)

해석 문제의 복잡한 성격 때문에 다각적인 해결책이 필요하다.

해설 복잡한 문제를 풀기 위해서는 해결책이 다양해야 한다는 맥락을 파악해야 한다. 따라서 multifaceted(다각적인)가 정답이다.

오답 살펴보기 (a) ludicrous 터무니없는 (b) flagitious 극악무도한 (c) haphazard 무계획적인

12 (b)

해석 무서움을 느끼게 되면, 스컹크는 천적을 물리치는 데 사용되는 강력한 악취를 내뿜는다.

해설 적을 쫓기 위해 스컹크가 하는 행동을 생각해 보면 쉽게 답을 찾을 수 있다. 따라서 정답은 '(냄새 등을) 발산하다, 내뿜다'라는 의미를 지닌 emit가 된다.

어구 ward off 피하다, 막다

오답 살펴보기 (a) permit 허가하다 (c) dispose 폐기하다, 처분하다 (d) contaminate 오염시키다

13 (d)

해석 탐욕스러운 그 슈퍼모델은 언젠가 어마어마한 부동산을 물려받고자 하는 바람을 갖고 늙은 억만장자와 결혼했다.

해설 부동산을 물려받으려는 의도로 늙은 억만장자와 결혼했다고 했으므로 슈퍼모델이 탐욕스러운 사람인 것을 쉽게 알 수 있다. avaricious(탐욕스러운, 욕심 많은)가 정답이다.

어구 billionaire 억만장자 inherit 물려받다 vast 광대한 estate 부동산

오답 살펴보기 (a) felicitous (행동, 말이) 적절한 (b) convivial 명랑한, 유쾌한 (c) morose 시무룩한

14 (d)

해석 우리 환경 단체는 산업 폐기물에 의해 오염된 지역을 개간하는 일을 한다.

해설 환경 단체가 할 만한 일을 찾는다. 정답은 '개선하다' 혹은 '개간하다'라는 뜻을 갖는 reclaim이다.

어구 contaminate 오염시키다

오답 살펴보기 (a) ban 금지하다 (b) navigate 항해하다 (c) disinfect 소독하다

15 (a)

해석 싱가포르는 화려한 스카이라인과 건실한 경제를 가지고 있는 동남아시아의 자랑이다.

해설 동남아의 자랑이 될 수 있는 싱가포르라면 그곳의 경제가 건실할 것임을 알 수 있다. 따라서 정답으로는 robust(건강한, 건장한)가 가장 적절하다.

어구 glittering 반짝이는, 화려한 skyline (산, 고층 건물 등의) 하늘을 배경으로 한 윤곽

오답 살펴보기 (b) faultless 흠잡을 데 없는 (c) misleading 호도하는 (d) stark 삭막한

16 (c)

해석 전쟁이 발발함으로써 수년 동안 지속되었던 두 집단 간의 적대 관계는 오늘 아침에 극도로 악화되었다.

해설 전쟁이 시작되면 당사국들의 관계가 나빠질 것이다. '위기에 빠지다' 혹은 '극도로 악화되다'라는 표현은 come to a head로 나타낸다.

어구 hostility 적의, 적개심 break out (전쟁 등이) 발발하다, 발생하다

오답 살펴보기 (a) turn a deaf ear 무시하다 (b) jump on the bandwagon (다수 또는 유행에) 편승하다 (d) bite the bullet 이를 악물고 버티다

17 (a)

해석 과학자들의 줄기 세포 연구로 인해 에이즈 치료의 돌파구가 생겼다.

해설 어떠한 문제를 타개할 해결책을 찾게 되었다는 의미가 되어야 하므로, 정답은 breakthrough(돌파구)가 된다.

어구 stem cell 줄기 세포

오답 살펴보기 (b) landmark 획기적인 사건 (c) milestone 이정표; 중요한 단계 (d) signpost 표지판

18 (a)

해석 허리케인 이사벨은 오늘 새벽 상륙한 이후 열대 폭풍으로 약화되었다.

해설 허리케인이 열대 폭풍우가 되었으므로 그 세력이 약화된 것이다. 허리케인과 열대 폭풍우 간의 관계를 모르더라도, 선택지 중에서 변화의 의미를 갖고 있는 것은 downgraded뿐이다. downgrade는 '(강등시키다, 격하시키다)'라는 의미이다.

어구 tropical storm 열대 폭풍우 make landfall 상륙하다, 착륙하다

오답 살펴보기 (b) update 최신의 것으로 갱신하다 (c) overturn (판결 등을) 뒤집다 (d) renounce 포기하다

19 (c)

해석 저희 제품에서 결함을 발견하시면, 아래의 주소로 반송해 주셔서 전액 환불 받으시기 바랍니다.

해설 상품을 반송하고 환불을 받는 이유는 상품에 문제가 있기 때문일 것이다. 따라서 정답으로 가장 적합한 것은 defect(불량, 결함)이다.

오답 살펴보기 (a) compliance 준수, 순응 (b) component 부품, 구성 성분 (d) display 화면

20 (d)

해석 농장을 개발해 내기 이전에, 우리 조상들은 식량을 찾아다니는 수렵 채집 생활을 했다.

해설 hunter-gatherer는 수렵 채집을 하는 사람을 의미하며 이들은 식량을 찾아다니는 사람들이다. forage는 for와 함께 쓰여 '(음식 등을) 찾아다니다'라는 의미를 갖는다.

오답 살펴보기 (a) abandon 버리다 (b) graze 풀을 뜯어 먹다 (c) scrape 긁어모으다

21 (a)

해석 휴대 전화로 문자 메시지를 보내는 동안, 제니는 주변을 의식하지 못했다.

해설 어떤 일을 하느라 주변 상황을 파악하지 못하는 상태를 가장 잘 묘사해 주는 단어를 찾으면 된다. 정답은 '의식하지 못하는,

염두에 없는'이라는 뜻을 가진 oblivious가 된다.

오답 살펴보기 (b) obsequious 아부하는 (c) obsessive 집착하는
(d) obvious 명백한

22 (a)

해석 수년 동안, 담배 산업은 흡연이 해롭지 않은 행동이라고 믿게
함으로써 소비자들을 호도했다.

해설 기업들이 소비자들로 하여금 잘못된 정보를 믿게 하였다는 점
에서 정답의 단서를 찾을 수 있다. '호도하다'라는 뜻의 단어는
mislead이다.

오답 살펴보기 (b) facilitate 용이하게 하다 (c) prosecute 기소하다
(d) insult 모욕하다

23 (b)

해석 내 남동생은 장난감 차보다는 인형을 갖고 놀기를 좋아하는
특이한 아이였다.

해설 남자 아이가 인형을 가지고 놀았다는 것은 그가 평범하지 않
았음을 의미한다. 따라서 정답은 odd(특이한)가 된다.

오답 살펴보기 (a) bitter 혹독한; 억울한 (c) hyper 들뜬 (d) ripe 익은

24 (a)

해석 방문객들은 전시실 내에서 사진을 찍는 것이 금지되어 있다.

해설 전시실 내부라는 상황과 사진을 찍는 행동 간의 관계를 생각해
보면 답을 찾을 수 있다. 정답은 prohibit(금지하다)이다.

오답 살펴보기 (b) implore 한탄하다 (c) compel 강요하다
(d) torture 고문하다

25 (a)

해석 수년 동안, 의사들은 무분별한 항생제 처방에 대해 경고해 왔
는데, 그 이유는 바이러스가 그에 대한 내성을 가지게 될 것이
기 때문이었다.

해설 의사들이 무분별한 항생제 처방의 위험성에 대해 경고하고 있
다. 정답은 '경솔하게, 무분별하게'라는 뜻의 rashly이다.

어구 prescribe 처방하다 antibiotic 항생제 resistant 저항하
는, 저항력이 있는

오답 살펴보기 (b) belatedly 뒤늦게 (c) prudently 신중하게
(d) frivolously 경박하게

26 (b)

해석 은행 계좌를 개설하기 위해서는 운전 면허증, 출생증명서, 또
는 여권으로 귀하의 신분을 증명할 수 있어야 합니다.

해설 운전 면허증, 출생증명서, 여권 등은 신분을 증명하는 데 사용
되는 것들이다. 정답은 verify(입증하다, 증명하다)이다.

어구 identity 신원

오답 살펴보기 (a) testify 증언하다 (c) nullify 무효화하다
(d) quantify 양을 나타내다

27 (b)

해석 가장 최근의 인구 통계 조사에 따르면, 도시 인구가 거의 10퍼
센트 정도 감소했다.

해설 인구를 조사하는 '인구 통계 조사'는 census로 나타낸다.

오답 살펴보기 (a) censure 견책, 불신임 (c) consent 동의

(d) consensus 합의

28 (a)

해석 이번 학기에 7개의 강의를 신청했을 때 내가 감당할 수 있는
것 이상의 욕심을 냈던 것 같다.

해설 관용적인 표현인 bite off more than one can chew는 '분
에 넘치는 일을 하려고 하다'라는 의미이다.

어구 enroll 등록하다

오답 살펴보기 (b) swallow 삼키다 (d) handle 다루다

29 (d)

해석 오늘은 새로운 토론 주제에 대해 논의해 보고자 합니다. 바로
대현장입니다.

해설 전치사 into 와 함께 쓰여 '주제에 대해 깊이 연구하다, 논의하
다'를 뜻할 수 있는 단어는 delve이다.

오답 살펴보기 (a) relinquish 포기하다 (b) instigate 실시하다, 착수
하다 (c) scour 샅샅이 뒤지다

30 (a)

해석 그 보건 검사원은 너무나 꼼꼼해서 오염의 징후를 찾기 위해
가능한 모든 구석과 갈라진 틈을 검사했다.

해설 모든 구석과 틈을 검사하는 것으로 볼 때 검사원이 매우 철
저했음을 알 수 있다. 정답은 '꼼꼼한, 세심한'이란 뜻을 갖는
meticulous이다.

어구 health inspector 보건 검사원 nook 구석, 후미진 곳
cranny 갈라진 틈

오답 살펴보기 (b) repugnant 불쾌한 (c) hedonistic 쾌락주의적인
(d) blunt 무딘

Actual Test 06

1	(d)	2	(c)	3	(b)	4	(d)	5	(c)
6	(a)	7	(a)	8	(d)	9	(c)	10	(a)
11	(d)	12	(b)	13	(c)	14	(d)	15	(b)
16	(a)	17	(d)	18	(b)	19	(a)	20	(c)
21	(c)	22	(b)	23	(c)	24	(a)	25	(c)
26	(c)	27	(a)	28	(d)	29	(b)	30	(b)

1 (d)

해석 A: 더블 베이컨 치즈버거를 계속 판매하나요? 메뉴에서 보이
질 않네요.
B: 손님, 죄송합니다만, 그 메뉴는 더 이상 판매하지 않습니다.

해설 특정 메뉴를 찾는 손님에게 점원이 사과를 하는 것으로 보
아 정답을 유추해 볼 수 있다. '~을 그만두다'라는 의미는 do
away with로 나타낸다.

오답 살펴보기 (a) keep up with (최신 뉴스나 유행 등에 대해) 알게 되다
(b) come over to ~로 가다; (경쟁사 등에 가기 위해) ~를 떠나다
(c) give up on 포기하다

2 (c)

해석 A: 굉장한 독립 기념일 행사였어, 그렇지 않았니?
　　 B: 정말 그랬어. 특히 마지막에 있었던 불꽃놀이가 굉장했어.

해설 firework display는 '불꽃놀이'라는 의미로 쓰인다.

오답 살펴보기 (a) stain 얼룩, 오점 (b) assault 공격, 폭행
　　 (d) chaos 혼란, 혼돈

3 (b)

해석 A: 최근 조사에 따르면, 우리 고객 중 절반 이상이 남성이에요.
　　 B: 정말이요? 시장이 크게 변했군요.

해설 고객의 절반 이상이 남성이라는 사실에 B가 놀라워하고 있다. 따라서 시장에 큰 변화가 있었다는 내용이 이어져야 가장 자연스럽다. 정답은 '~을 나타내다'라는 의미의 represent이다.

오답 살펴보기 (a) maximize 극대화하다 (c) incorporate (일부로서) 포함하다 (d) downsize 축소하다

4 (d)

해석 A: 의사 선생님, 저는 만성적인 허리 통증을 앓고 있어요. 통증을 좀 줄일 수 있는 방법이 있을까요?
　　 B: 혹시 허리 보조기를 착용해 보신 적이 있나요? 착용하시면 허리 아래쪽의 압박이 줄어들 거예요.

해설 질병이나 통증 앞에 자주 쓰이는 표현으로서 '만성적인'을 의미하는 chronic이 정답이 된다.

어구 back brace 허리 보조기, 복대

오답 살펴보기 (a) extensive 광대한, 대규모의 (b) habitual 습관적인 (c) routine 일상적인

5 (c)

해석 A: 실례합니다. 식당 안에서 흡연을 삼가 주시겠습니까?
　　 B: 죄송합니다. 금연이라는 걸 몰랐네요.

해설 식당 안이 금연이라는 점으로 미루어 볼 때, 실내에서 흡연을 삼가라는 요청이 이루어지고 있음을 알 수 있다. 따라서 from과 함께 쓰여 '삼가다'라는 의미를 갖는 refrain이 정답이다.

오답 살펴보기 (a) compel 강요하다 (b) disassemble 분해하다, 해체하다 (d) hesitate 주저하다

6 (a)

해석 A: 팀, 네가 가지고 온 보드 게임을 하는 게 어때?
　　 B: 여기에는 사람이 충분하지 않은 것 같아. 게임을 하려면 적어도 4명이 필요하거든.

해설 게임을 하기에 사람의 숫자가 충분하지 않은 상황이다. 따라서 '최소한도'를 의미하는 minimum이 가장 적합한 표현이 된다.

오답 살펴보기 (b) possession 소유 (c) riot 폭동 (d) novelty 새로움

7 (a)

해석 A: 프로젝트에 관해 드레이크의 도움을 얻는 것은 정말 어려웠을 거예요.
　　 B: 천만에요. 그는 우리를 기꺼이 도와주겠다고 했어요.

해설 not at all이 쓰인 것으로 미뤄볼 때, B는 A의 말과 정반대의 내용을 말하고 있음을 알 수 있다. 따라서 '기꺼이'라는 의미의

---

readily가 정답이다.

오답 살펴보기 (b) painstakingly 공들여 (c) begrudgingly 마지못해 (d) pointedly 날카롭게; 비난하듯이

8 (d)

해석 A: 피고측은 새로운 혐의에 대하여 어떻게 대처하시겠습니까?
　　 B: 판사님, 답변을 드리기에 앞서 제 의뢰인과 먼저 상의를 할 수 있게 해주십시오.

해설 판사에게 답변을 하기에 앞서 할 수 있는 행동을 생각해 보면 된다. confer는 with와 함께 쓰여 '~와 상의하다'는 의미를 나타낸다.

어구 allegation 혐의, 주장

오답 살펴보기 (a) retaliate 보복하다 (b) unearth 파내다, 밝혀내다 (c) enlist 요청하다

9 (c)

해석 A: 당신의 제안이 매력적이기는 하지만, 너무 좋은 조건이라 믿기가 어렵네요.
　　 B: 손님, 장담하건대 저의 제안에는 정말로 어떠한 추가 조건도 없습니다.

해설 with no strings attached는 계약이나 거래에서 부대 조건이 없는 경우에 쓰일 수 있는 표현으로, '아무런 조건이 없이'라는 의미를 갖는다. 따라서 strings가 정답이 된다.

어구 too good to be true 너무 좋아서 믿어지지 않는

오답 살펴보기 (b) knot 매듭

10 (a)

해석 A: 아내와 저는 개를 키울까 생각하고 있어요.
　　 B: 그럼 콜리를 키워보시는 건 어때요? 정말 순하고 충성스러운 반려 동물이죠.

해설 friendly에 상응하는 의미를 갖는 단어가 들어가야 자연스러운 문장이 될 수 있다. 따라서 '충성스러운'이라는 의미의 loyal이 정답이다.

어구 companion 동료, 반려

오답 살펴보기 (b) predictable 예측할 수 있는 (c) aggressive 공격적인 (d) lenient 관대한

11 (d)

해석 대학을 졸업하려면 모든 학생들이 일반 교육 자격 과정을 완료해야 한다.

해설 requirements를 목적어로 취하는 동사로서 선택지 중에서 가장 적합한 어휘는 '이행하다' 또는 '완료하다'의 의미의 지닌 fulfill이다.

어구 general education requirement 일반 교육 자격

오답 살펴보기 (a) unveil 공개하다, 발표하다 (b) uphold 유지시키다, 지키다 (c) kindle 불을 붙이다

12 (b)

해석 나는 외국을 방문할 때마다 그 나라의 문화를 온몸으로 체험하기를 좋아한다.

해설 문맥상 '외국 문화에 빠져들다' 등의 표현이 되어야 가장 자

연스럽다. '~에 열중하다' 또는 '~에 몰두하다'라는 표현은 immerse oneself in으로 나타낸다.

오답 살펴보기 (a) detain 구금하다, 억류하다 (c) encourage 격려하다 (d) recall 생각해 내다; (제품 등을) 회수하다

13 (c)
해석 페미니스트들은 언론이 여성들을 무력하고 남성에게 복종하는 존재로 묘사하는 것에 반대한다.
해설 여성에 대한 고정관념을 심어주는 언론의 특성을 생각해 보면, '묘사'라는 의미의 portrayal이 정답임을 알 수 있다.
어구 subservient to ~에 복종하는, ~보다 부차적인
오답 살펴보기 (b) confirmation 확인 (d) skepticism 회의론

14 (d)
해석 세계 역도 연맹은 착용자에게 부당한 이점을 준다는 이유로 벤치 셔츠의 착용을 금지하고 있다.
해설 부당한 이익을 준다는 점을 근거로 취할 수 있는 조치를 생각해 보면 답을 찾을 수 있다. '금지하다'의 의미를 갖는 동사는 ban이다.
오답 살펴보기 (a) exclude 제외하다, 배제하다 (b) omit 누락하다 (c) preclude ~하지 못하게 하다

15 (b)
해석 켈리의 열정에는 전염성이 있어서, 모든 사람들이 그녀의 열정을 공유하게 되었다.
해설 모든 사람들이 특정한 것을 공유하게 되었다는 점으로 보아, '전염성이 있는'이라는 의미의 contagious가 정답으로 가장 적절하다.
어구 enthusiasm 열정
오답 살펴보기 (a) overwhelming 압도적인 (c) sentimental 감정적인 (d) impeccable 흠 잡을 데 없는

16 (a)
해석 짐이 저녁을 먹으러 오면 결코 남는 음식이 없는데, 그 이유는 그가 대식가이기 때문이다.
해설 남는 음식이 없는 이유로 적합한 표현은 '매우 많이 먹다'의 의미인 eat like a horse이다.
오답 살펴보기 (b) have one's cake and eat it too 독차지하다 (c) bite the dust 패배하다; 전사하다 (d) clear the table 식탁을 치우다

17 (d)
해석 외국에서 살아보는 것은 세계의 더 많은 부분을 보고 자신의 시야를 넓힐 수 있는 좋은 방법이다.
해설 외국 생활을 통해 가질 수 있는 이점에 대해 생각해 보면 된다. '시야를 넓히다'라는 의미는 broaden one's horizons로 표현할 수 있다. 따라서 broaden이 정답이 된다.
오답 살펴보기 (a) restrict 제한하다 (b) naturalize 귀화시키다 (c) uphold 유지시키다

18 (b)
해석 기혼 남녀의 역할이 최근 몇 년간 변화해 왔는데, 집에 머물면

서 자녀를 양육하는 남편의 수가 점점 증가하고 있다.
해설 갈수록 많은 남편들이 집에 머물며 자녀를 양육한다는 점으로 보아, '역할'을 의미하는 role이 정답임을 알 수 있다.
오답 살펴보기 (a) section 부분 (c) task 일, 과업 (d) rank 지위

19 (a)
해석 한 달 후에는 운전 면허증이 만료되기 때문에, 교통국에 가서 갱신시켜야 한다.
해설 운전 면허증을 갱신해야 한다는 것으로 보아 면허증이 곧 '만료될' 것임을 추측해 볼 수 있다. 따라서 정답은 expire(소멸하다, 만료되다)이다.
어구 DMV 면허 시험장, 교통국(Department of Motor Vehicles) renew 갱신하다
오답 살펴보기 (c) perish 멸망하다, 사멸하다 (d) die off (하나도 안 남을 때까지) 하나하나씩 죽어 가다, 멸망하다

20 (c)
해석 우리는 이 컴퓨터 모델을 사용해서 그 약이 인체에 미치는 영향을 시뮬레이션할 것이다.
해설 컴퓨터 모델을 사용해야 하는 상황을 고려해 보면 '시뮬레이션을 하다, 모의실험을 하다'라는 의미의 simulate가 정답이다.
오답 살펴보기 (a) relish ~을 즐기다 (b) restore 회복시키다, 복원하다 (d) expel 추방하다

21 (c)
해석 하이브리드 자동차는 경제적인 운송 수단으로서, 기존의 자동차에 비해 최대 70퍼센트나 적은 연료를 사용한다.
해설 하이브리드 차량이 기존 자동차와 대비하여 연료 절감률이 높다는 점으로 보아, '경제적인'을 의미하는 economical이 정답으로 가장 적절하다. economic은 '경제의' 또는 '(사업, 활동 등이) 경제성이 있는'이라는 의미이다.
오답 살펴보기 (a) economic 경제의, 경제성이 있는 (b) absolute 완전한, 확실한 (d) obsolete 더 이상 쓸모가 없는, 구식의

22 (b)
해석 오전 8시 이후에는 정문을 잠그기 때문에, 수업 시작 시간을 엄수해야 한다는 점을 명심해 주시기 바랍니다.
해설 8시에는 문을 잠그므로 그 전에 등교를 해야 한다는 내용이다. 따라서 '시간을 엄수하는'이라는 의미의 punctual이 정답이다.
오답 살펴보기 (a) immediate 즉각적인 (c) delinquent 비행의; 채무를 이행하지 않은 (d) seasonable 계절에 맞는

23 (c)
해석 그 회사는 모든 직원들이 업계의 최근 동향을 잘 파악할 수 있도록 새로운 직원 교육 프로그램을 실시하기로 결정했다.
해설 자칫 혼동될 수 있는 동사들의 정확한 의미를 묻는 문제이다. '(정책 등을) 시행하다'는 의미의 implement가 목적어 program과 가장 잘 어울린다.
어구 keep abreast of 최근 정황을 잘 파악하다
오답 살펴보기 (a) activate 활성화시키다 (b) enforce 집행하다, (법률을) 시행하다 (d) operate (기계를) 가동하다, (시스템을) 운용하다

24 (d)

해석 오늘 아침 교통 혼잡 시간대에 베이브리지의 한 구간이 무너져 물속으로 가라앉는 사고로 수십 명의 통근자들이 중상을 입었다.

해설 다리가 가라앉은 상황이다. '붕괴하다'라는 의미의 동사는 collapse이다.

오답 살펴보기 (a) ascend 오르다 (b) disturb 방해하다 (c) subside 진정되다, 내려앉다

25 (c)

해석 정부는 민간 기업이 선거 운동에 기부할 수 있는 금액을 제한하고 있다.

해설 주로 어떠한 것에 대한 제한을 둘 경우, '부과하다'라는 의미의 impose가 restriction(제한)과 함께 쓰인다.

어구 political campaign 정치 캠페인, 선거 운동

오답 살펴보기 (a) threaten 위협하다 (b) penalize 처벌하다, 불이익을 주다 (d) gouge 찌르다; 바가지를 씌우다

26 (c)

해석 불과 수세기 전만 해도, 젊은 연인들이 공공장소에서 손을 잡는다는 것은 적절하지 않다고 생각되었다.

해설 공공장소에서 손을 잡는 행위에 대한 예전의 생각이 지금과는 달랐음을 나타내고 있다. 따라서 '올바른, 적절한'을 의미하는 proper가 정답이 된다.

어구 scant 거의 없는, 부족한

오답 살펴보기 (a) lucid 명쾌한, 명료한 (b) typical 전형적인 (d) habitual 습관적인

27 (a)

해석 보건 당국은 독감이 재발하는 것을 막기 위해 시민들을 대상으로 예방 접종을 해야 했다.

해설 비슷한 형태의 단어들에 대한 정확한 의미를 묻는 문제이다. 여기서는 '예방 접종을 하다'라는 의미의 inoculate가 정답이다.

어구 outbreak (질병 등의) 발생, 창궐

오답 살펴보기 (b) innovate 혁신하다 (c) innocuous 악의 없는, 무해한 (d) inculpate 죄를 씌우다

28 (d)

해석 아이의 잘못된 행동을 바로잡으려면, 잘못을 저지른 직후에 벌을 줘야 한다.

해설 목적어 punishment와 함께 쓰일 수 있는 동사로 '(벌을) 주다'라는 의미의 administer가 가장 적합하다.

오답 살펴보기 (a) diagnose 진단하다 (b) prescribe 처방하다 (c) sanction 제재를 가하다

29 (b)

해석 우리 글로벌 다이내믹스사는 남들과 다르고 창의적인 사고력을 가진 직원들을 높게 평가합니다.

해설 '틀을 벗어나 생각하다', 즉 '창의적으로 생각하다'라는 의미는 think outside the box로 나타낸다.

어구 follow the herd 다른 사람과 똑같이 하다

오답 살펴보기 (a) go by the book 규칙을 따르다 (c) step out of line 규칙을 어기다 (d) take a shot in the dark 막연하게 일을 추진하다

30 (b)

해석 여러분 가족이 환경 보호에 일조할 수 있는 몇 가지 간단한 방법에는 대중교통 이용, 수도 및 전기에 대한 현명한 사용 등이 포함됩니다.

해설 환경 보호를 위해서는 물과 전기를 '현명하게' 사용해야 한다. 따라서 '사려 깊게, 현명하게'를 의미하는 judiciously가 정답이 된다.

오답 살펴보기 (a) nocturnally 야간에, 밤마다 (c) vicariously 대리로, 대신에 (d) heedlessly 부주의하게

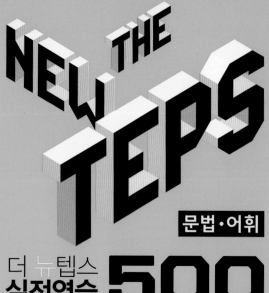

NEW THE TEPS

문법·어휘

더 뉴텝스
실전연습 **500**

시험에 나오는 문법·어휘 최다 빈출 출제 포인트만 담았다!

문법

철저한 출제 경향 분석으로 NEW TEPS 문법 완전 정복

★ 최다 빈출 68개 문법 포인트 완벽 핵심 정리

★ Check-up Test로 학습 내용 점검 및 기본 실력 증진

★ 최신 출제 경향을 철저히 반영한 Actual Test 6회분

어휘

기출 어휘, 기출 가능 어휘를 엄선 선별하여 풍부한 양의 어휘 제시

★ 문제를 풀며 익히는 Mini Test

★ 학습한 어휘를 점검하는 Check-up Test와 Voca Review

★ 최신 출제 경향을 철저히 반영한 Actual Test 6회분